In the Village Hidden in the Leaves, a fire ignites

The fire, angered, becomes a spirit
The fire's spirit then turns into a blaze
And that blaze repels any who would harm
the village

The fire spreads and becomes light
The light of the fire nurtures the heart
The fire spreads throughout the village

The fire gathers and attains a will
The fire's will is strong and spirited
And thus the Leaf Village is protected

The fire expands to become Kage
The Kage illuminates the village
The Village Hidden in the Leaves is reborn
And again the fire becomes Kage

TOTAL NINJA

A vivid recap of how Naruto and his companions raced along the path of the

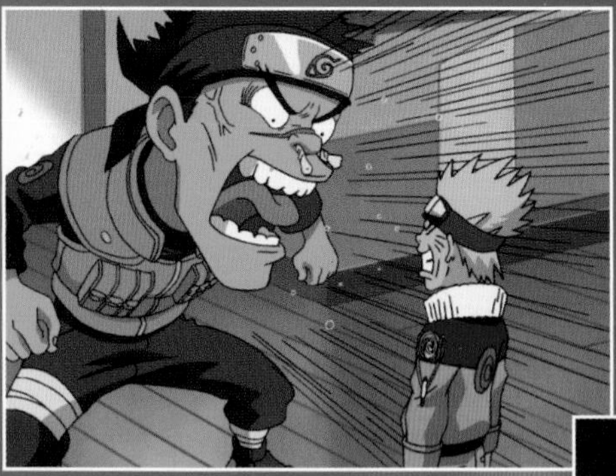

Enter Naruto Uzumaki—Leaf Village Ninja!

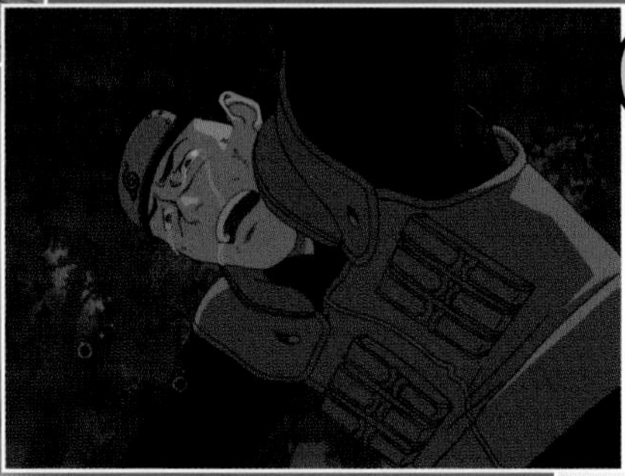

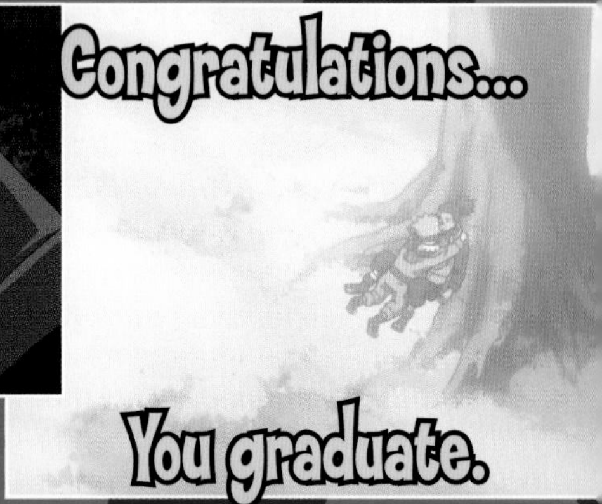
Congratulations...
You graduate.

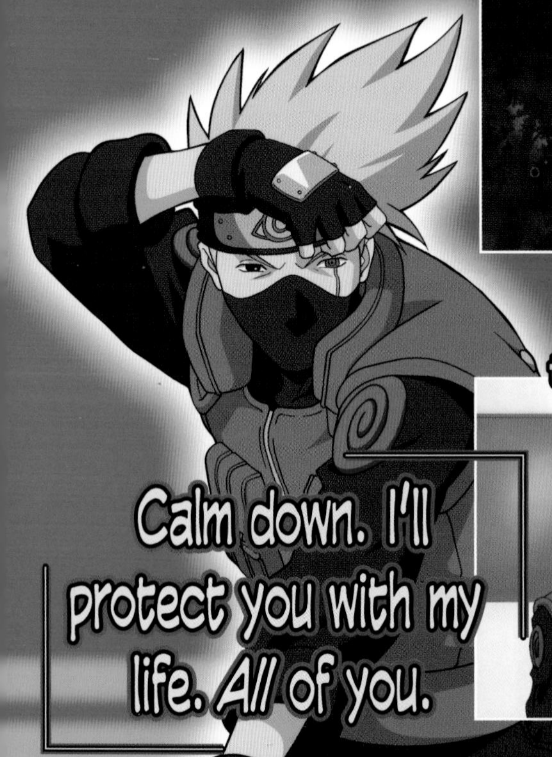
Calm down. I'll protect you with my life. *All* of you.

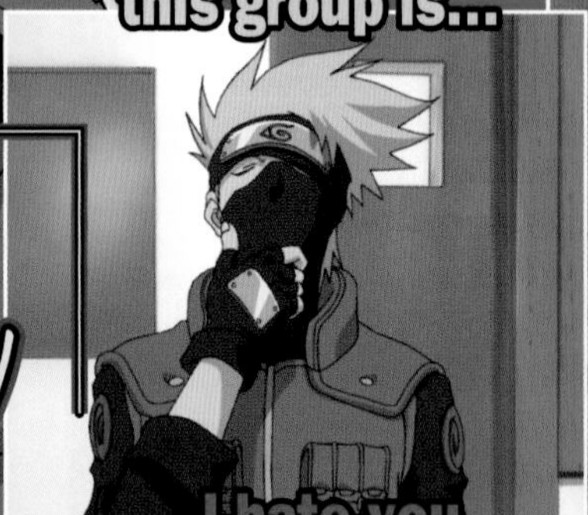
My first impression of this group is...
I hate you.

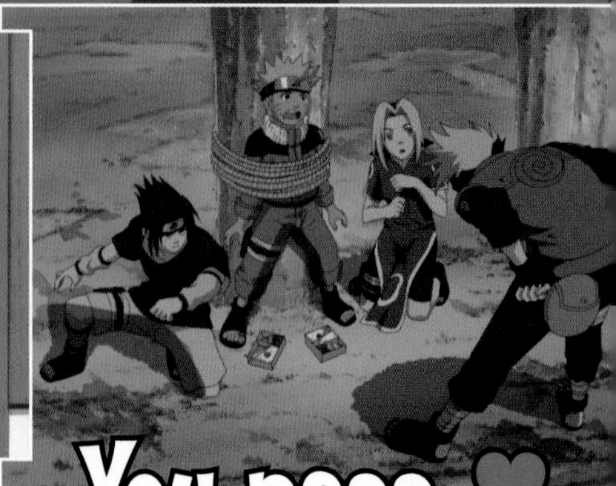
You pass. ♥

The Story So Far...

In the Leaf Village, a new genin has arisen!

Troublemaker Naruto Uzumaki, from the Village Hidden in the Leaves, was the Ninja Academy's biggest underachiever. Still, he trained hard in the hope of one day becoming the village's best ninja and even someday earning the title of Hokage.

Naruto graduated from the academy by perfecting the Shadow Clone Jutsu he learned from the Sacred Sealed Scroll, which Mizuki was plotting to steal. With the Shadow Clone Jutsu, and help from his teammates Sasuke and Sakura, Naruto was also able to pass Kakashi's survival training. All this means that Naruto is on his way to fulfilling his dream of becoming the greatest ninja ever.

RECALL!

ninja from their time at the Ninja Academy to the first rounds of the Chunin Exam.

Your Favorite Shinobi Embark on a Dangerous Journey!

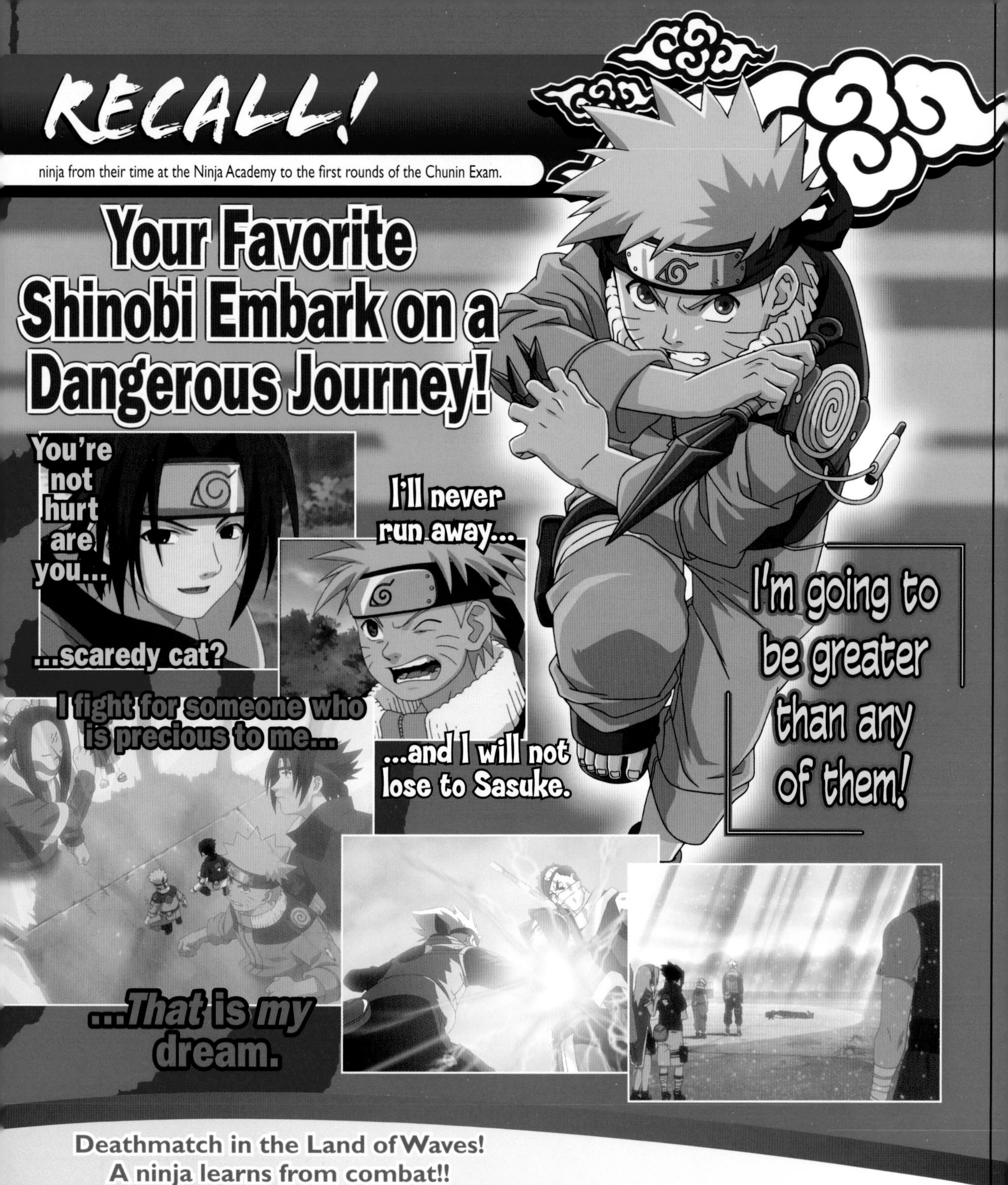
I'm going to be greater than any of them!
I'll never run away...
...and I will not lose to Sasuke.
You're not hurt are you...
...scaredy cat?
I fight for someone who is precious to me...
...That is my dream.

Deathmatch in the Land of Waves! A ninja learns from combat!!

Naruto and his companions were assigned a protective security mission. What was supposed to have been an easy bodyguard job turned into a potential death trap after the appearance of Zabuza, the Demon of the Hidden Mist. Zabuza was hired by Gato, who controlled the Land of Waves – and wanted to keep it that way.

Things got even more complicated when Zabuza's consort, Haku, was thrown into the equation. Haku, like Sasuke, was a powerful and deadly ninja with a Kekkei Genkai, an ability inherited through his bloodline. The resulting battle with Haku and Zabuza was a difficult one. But when Naruto and the citizens of the Land of Waves came out the winners, Naruto matured as both a ninja and a human being.

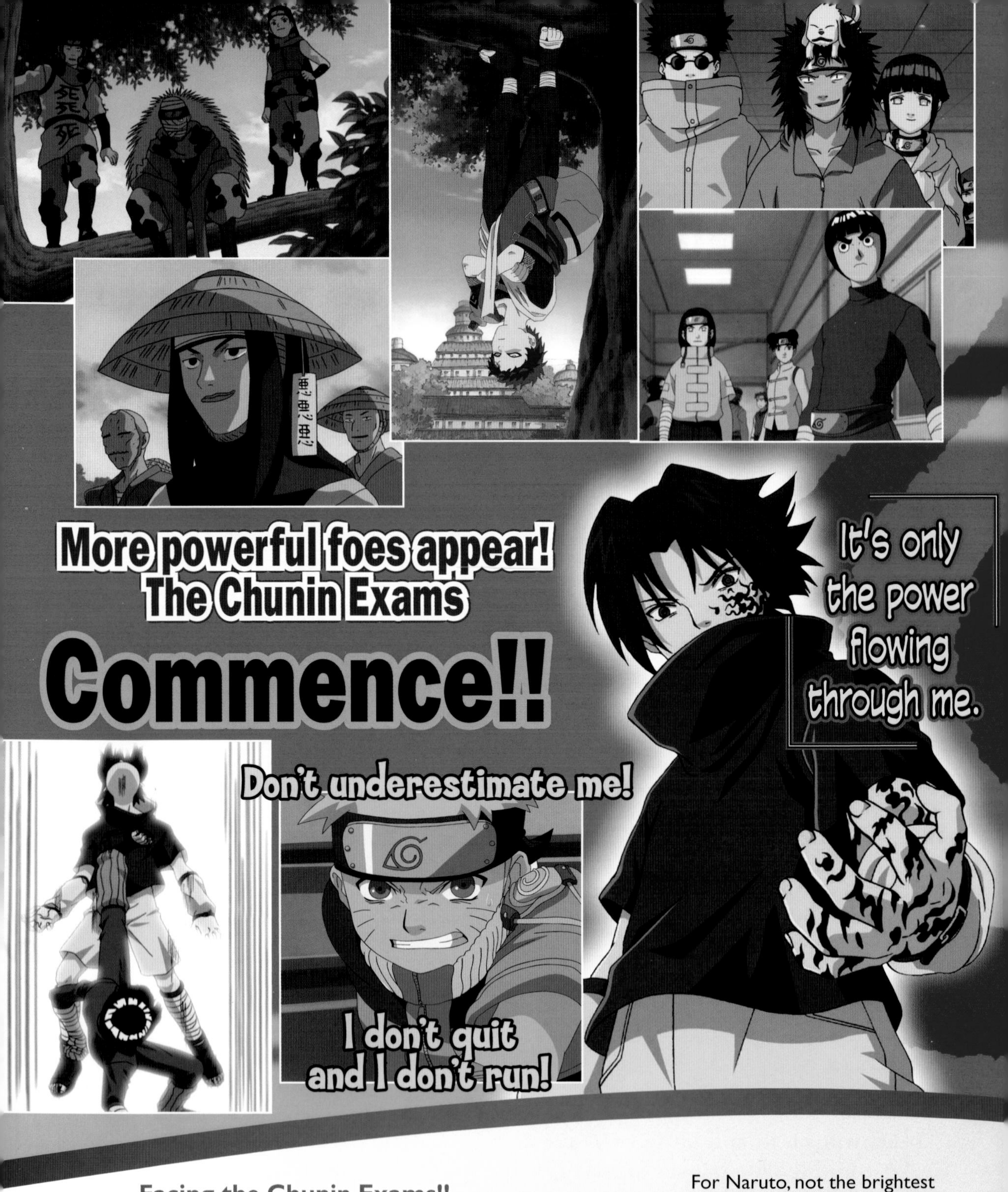
More powerful foes appear!
The Chunin Exams
Commence!!
It's only the power flowing through me.
Don't underestimate me!
I don't quit and I don't run!

Facing the Chunin Exams!!

Of course, there were more trials just around the corner for the new genin, Naruto and his friends. They were now competitors in the Chunin Exams. Ninja from other villages, such as Sand, Grass and Sound, with new and strange powers, gathered in the Village Hidden in the Leaves. The tension only got worse when the participants realized that their first Chunin Exam challenge was not a fight, but a written test with a near-impossible difficulty rating.

For Naruto, not the brightest student, things already looked bleak. But teetering on the brink of failure, Naruto pulled through and passed! Finally, he was able to proceed to stage two, where the ninja put their courage, pride and honor on full display.

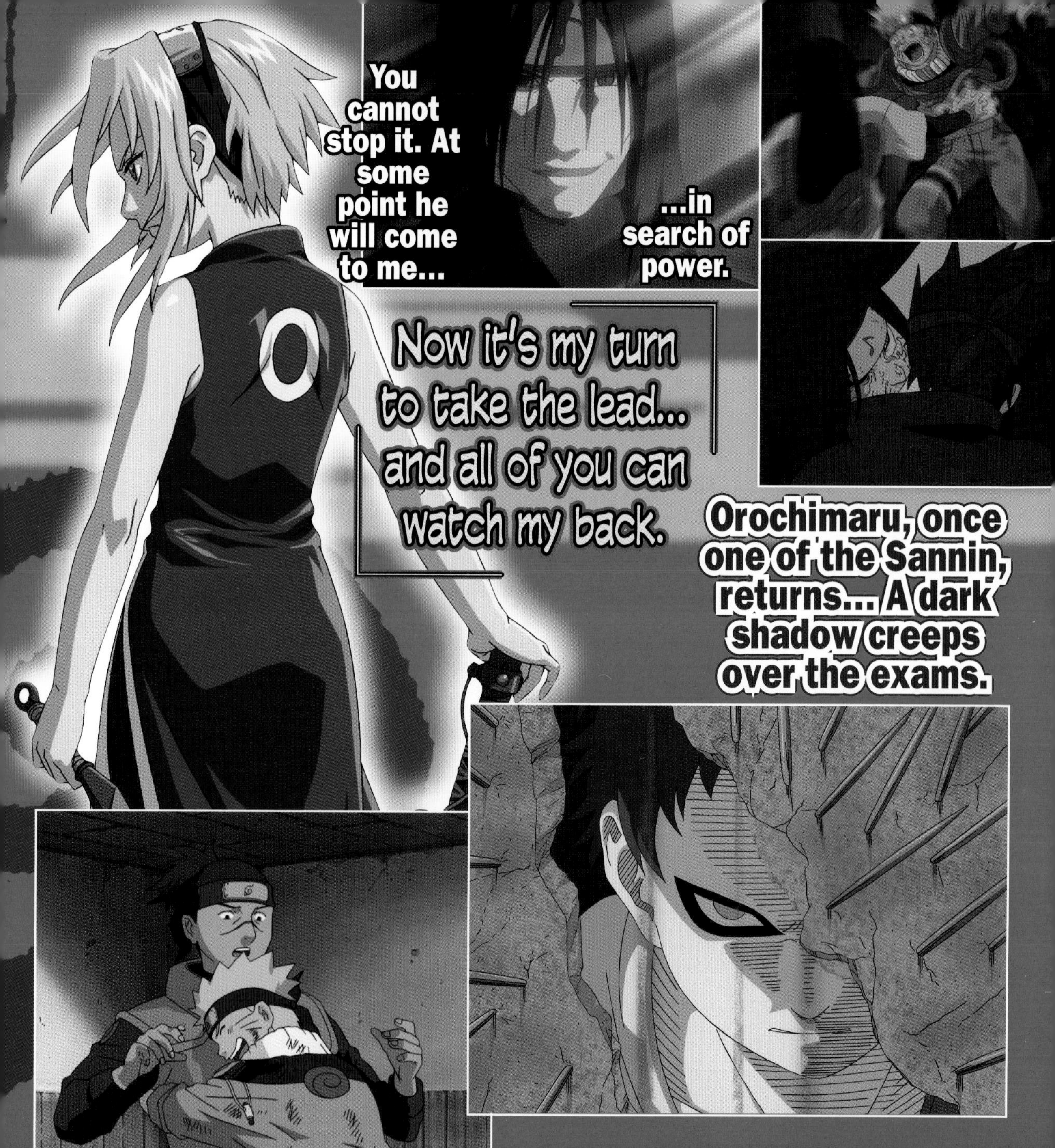
You cannot stop it. At some point he will come to me...
...in search of power.
Now it's my turn to take the lead... and all of you can watch my back.
Orochimaru, once one of the Sannin, returns... A dark shadow creeps over the exams.

Orochimaru brings a chill to the Leaf Village...!!

Stage two of the Chunin Exams was an anything-goes survival battle to collect scrolls. Orochimaru, a legendary shinobi of incredible power, appeared to block Naruto and his squadmates from capturing the scrolls. Orochimaru disappeared after planting a mysterious curse mark on Sasuke, who might be permanently scarred by the encounter.

Overcoming a fierce battle with the Sound ninja and enduring an exhausting fight with the Rain ninja, Naruto's squad—battered and worn out—finally made it through and passed the exam. Now, under the shadow of Orochimaru's evil plot, the Chunin Exams proceed to the third stage.

NARUTO ANIME PROFILES

Contents

Nine shinobi are revealed in never-before seen secret profiles! And their mystically summoned animal partners get the same special treatment!

Be sure to check out *Naruto Anime Profiles* Episodes 1-37 for even more Profiles and Inside Secrets.

Secret Shinobi Picture Album

Explore the world of Naruto with these incredible design sketches! This time, check out the Village Hidden in the Leaves both inside and out!

Anbu Special Report

Top secret information obtained by Hidden Leaf Village Anbu Black Ops investigations is revealed!

Basic knowledge for those who are lost. Unrivaled shinobi technique introduced via a secret scroll.

More detail than you've ever seen! A dazzling collection of special edition illustrations.

Tons of fun in Naruto's world! A whirling swirling cyclone of bonus pages that will blow you away! Believe it!

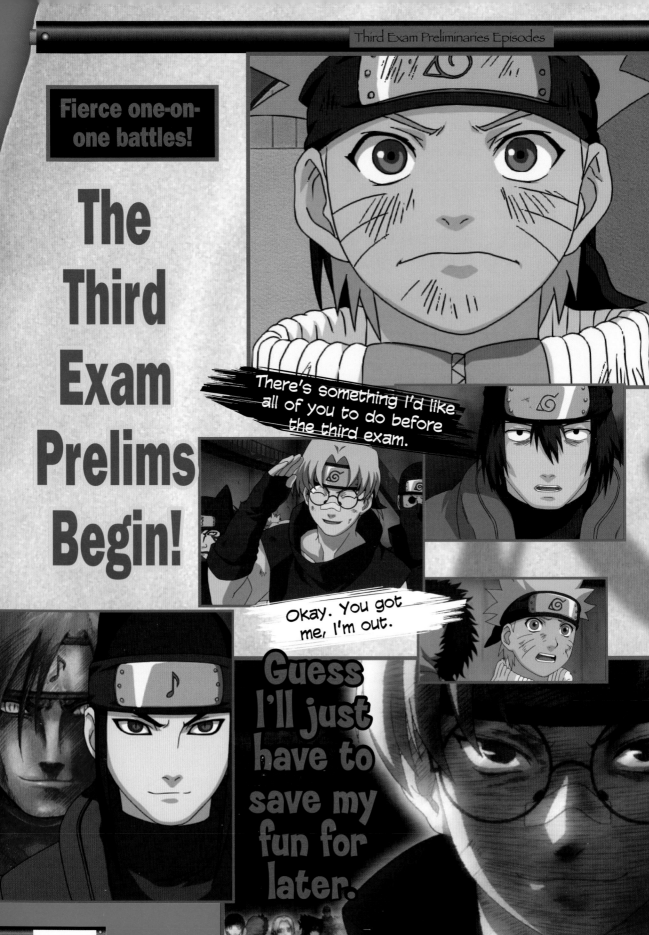

Fierce one-on-one battles!

The Third Exam Prelims Begin!

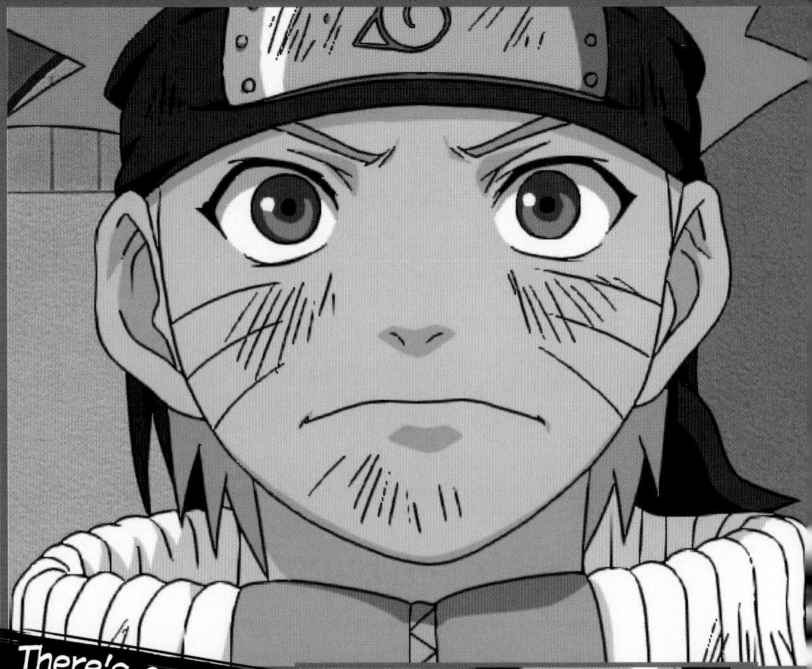

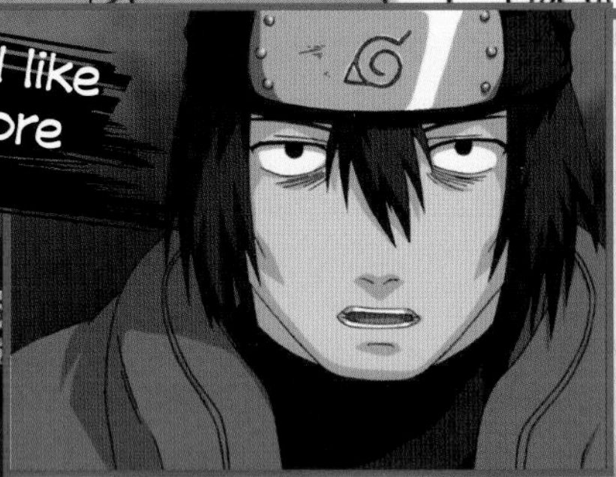
There's something I'd like all of you to do before the third exam.

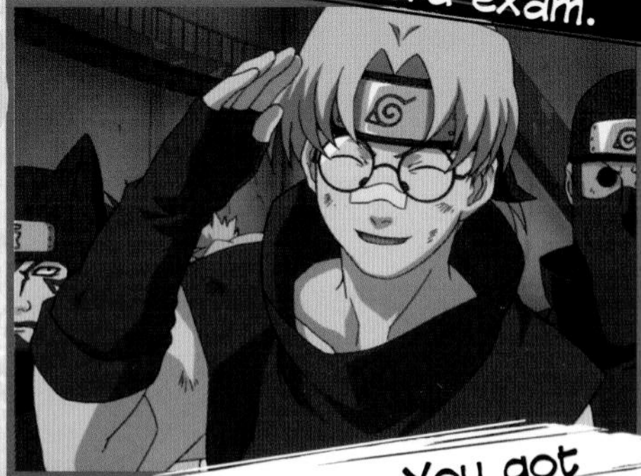
Okay. You got me, I'm out.

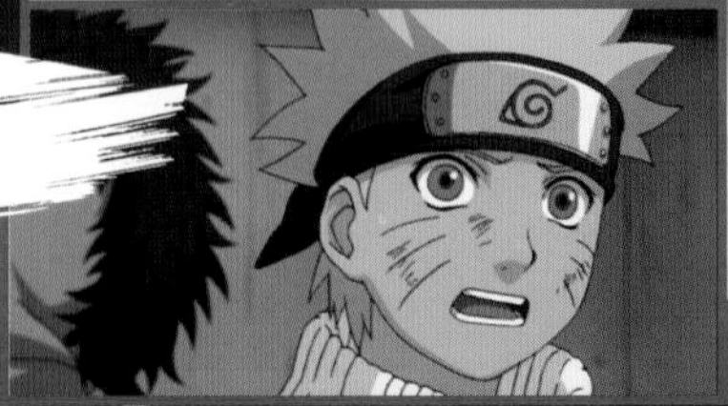

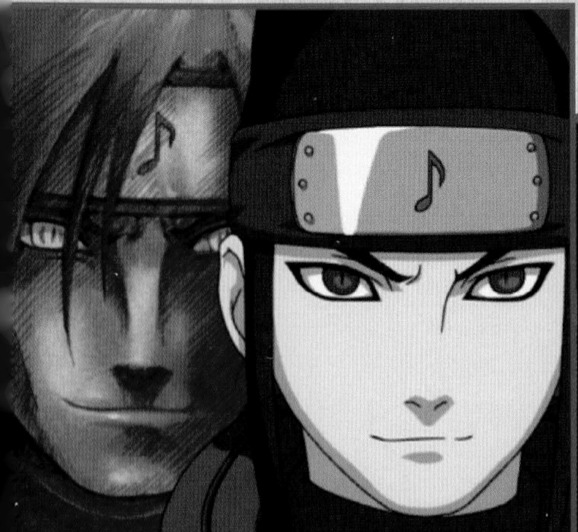

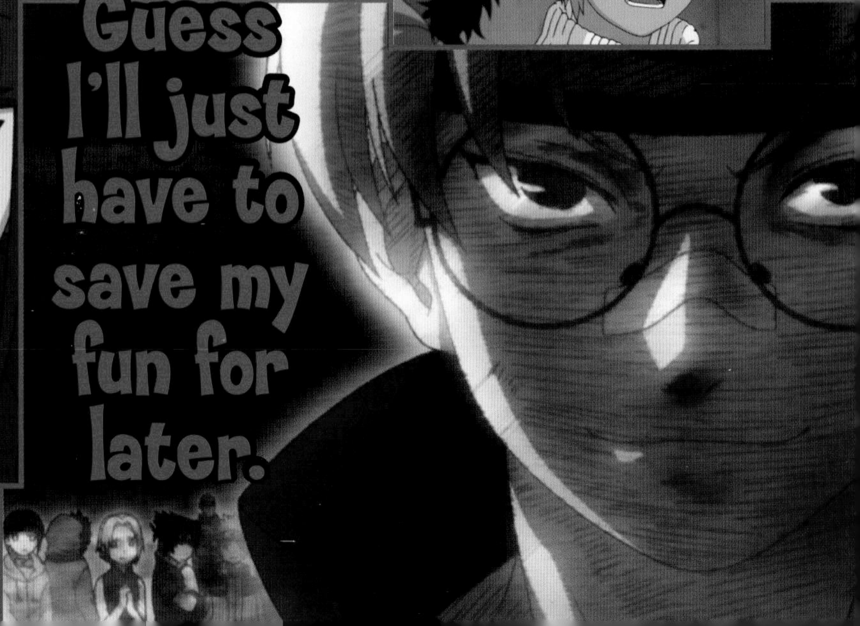
Guess I'll just have to save my fun for later.

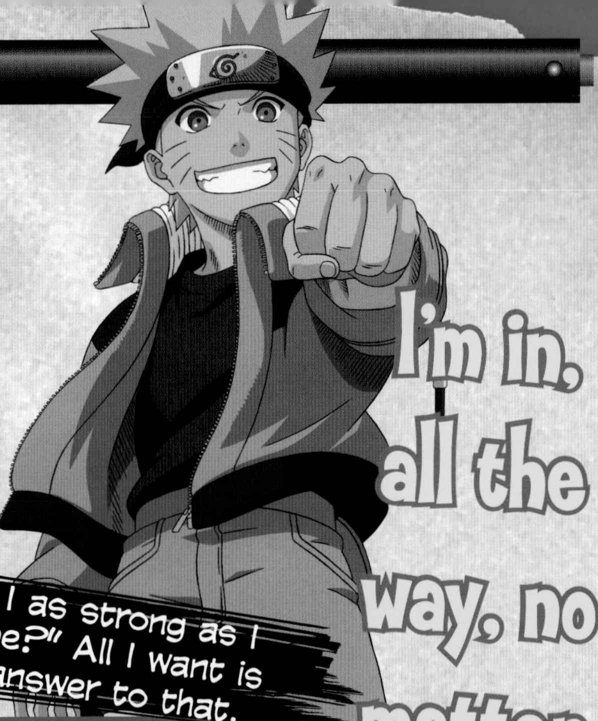
I'm in, all the way, no matter what...

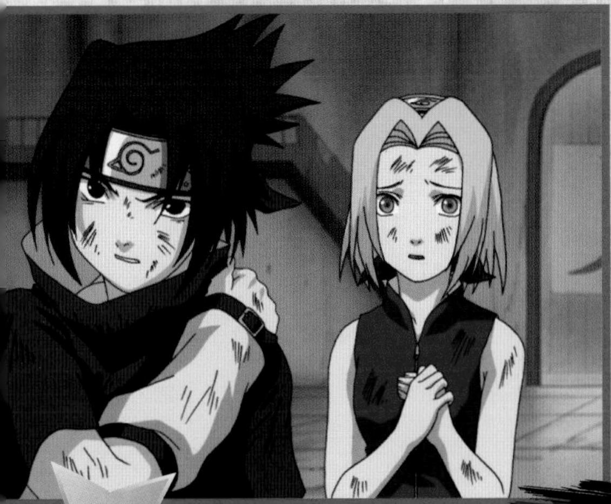

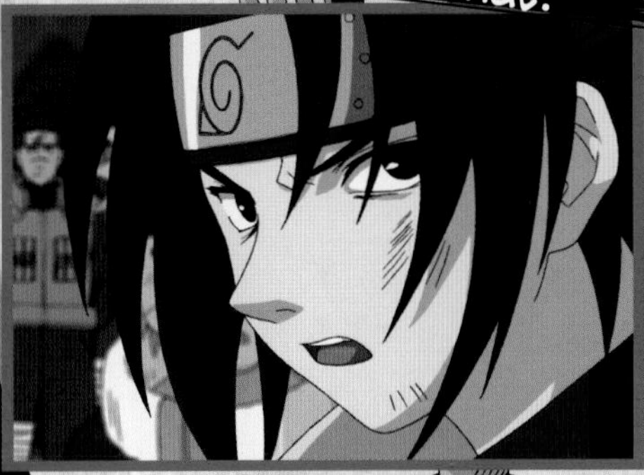
"Am I as strong as I can be?" All I want is the answer to that.

The beginning of the preliminaries is announced and Kabuto unexpectedly bows out. Amidst all this confusion, a dark plot begins... This is a stage of one-on-one matches, and the battles are already underway!

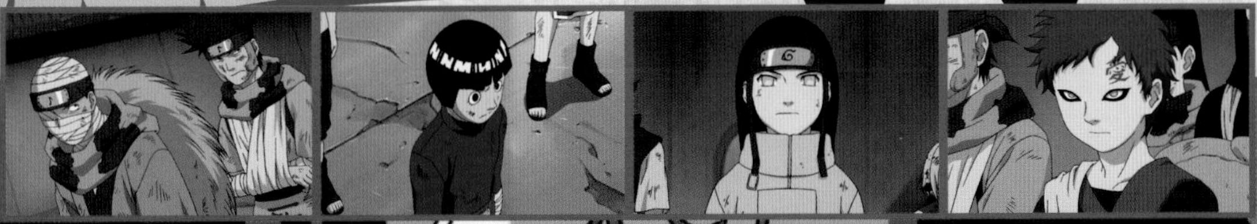

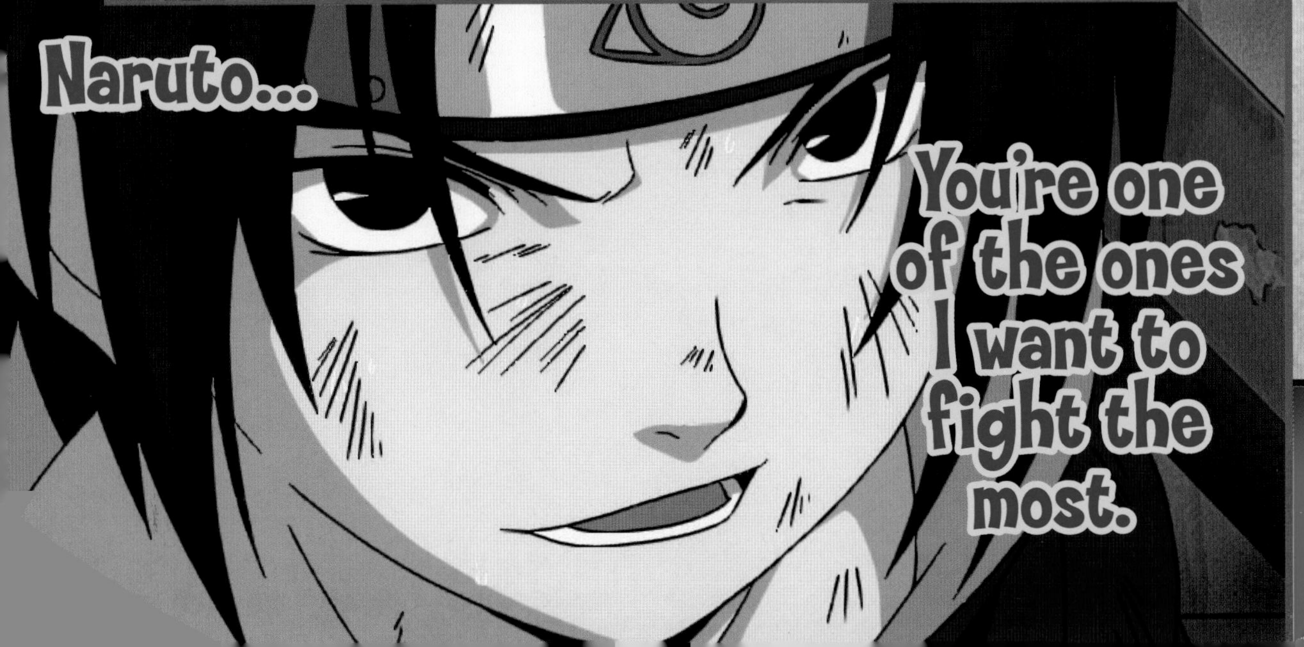
Naruto...
You're one of the ones I want to fight the most.

Sasuke struggles!

The Curse Mark!

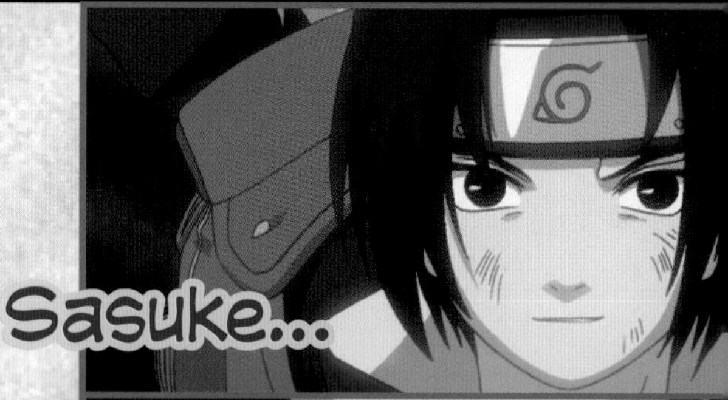
Sasuke...

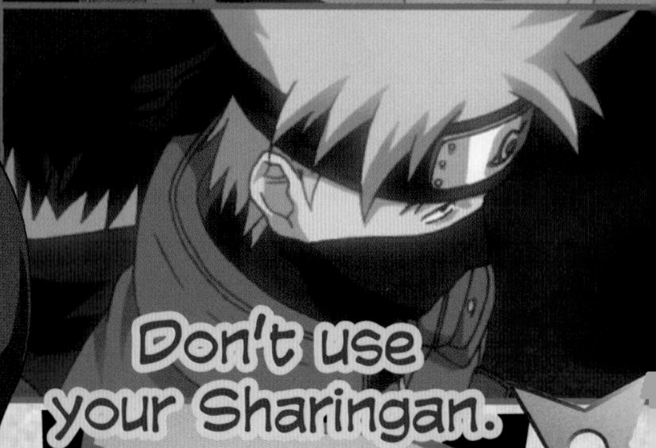
Don't use your Sharingan.

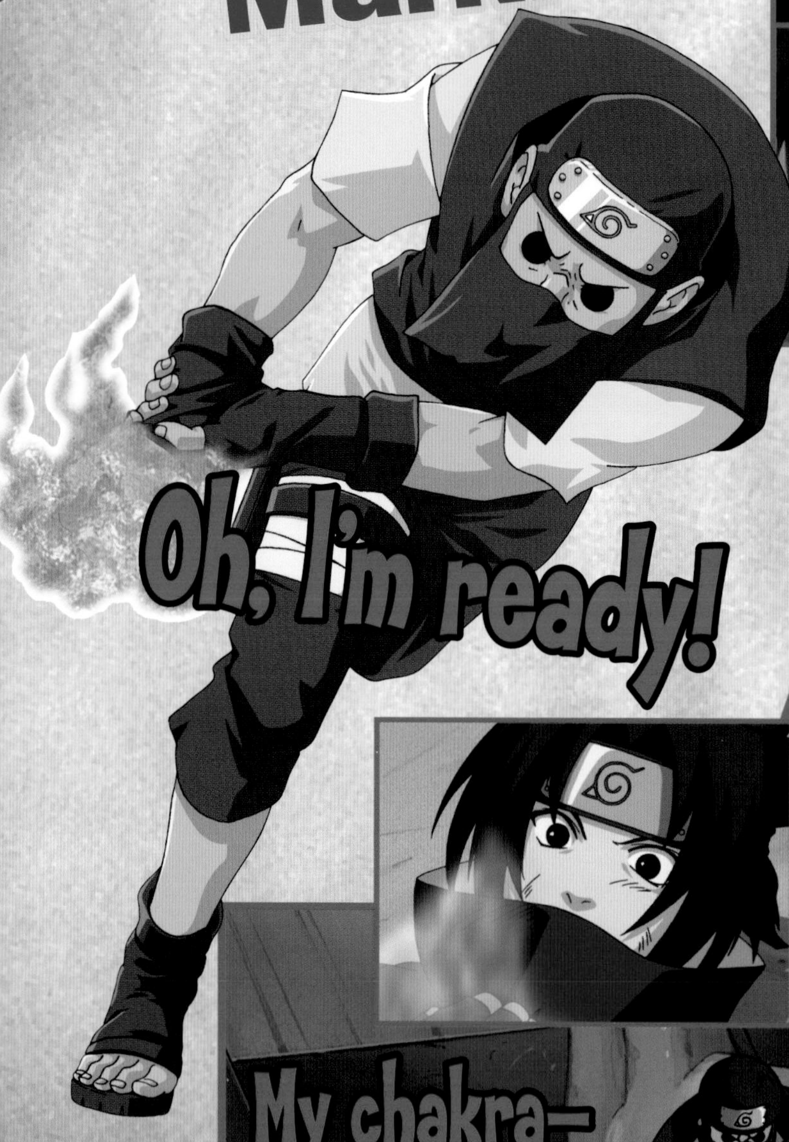
Oh, I'm ready!

The piercing pain of the curse mark, the result of a furious attack, leaves Sasuke partially crippled and apparently helpless... Infuriated at the sight, Naruto cries out. Does Sasuke even have a chance?

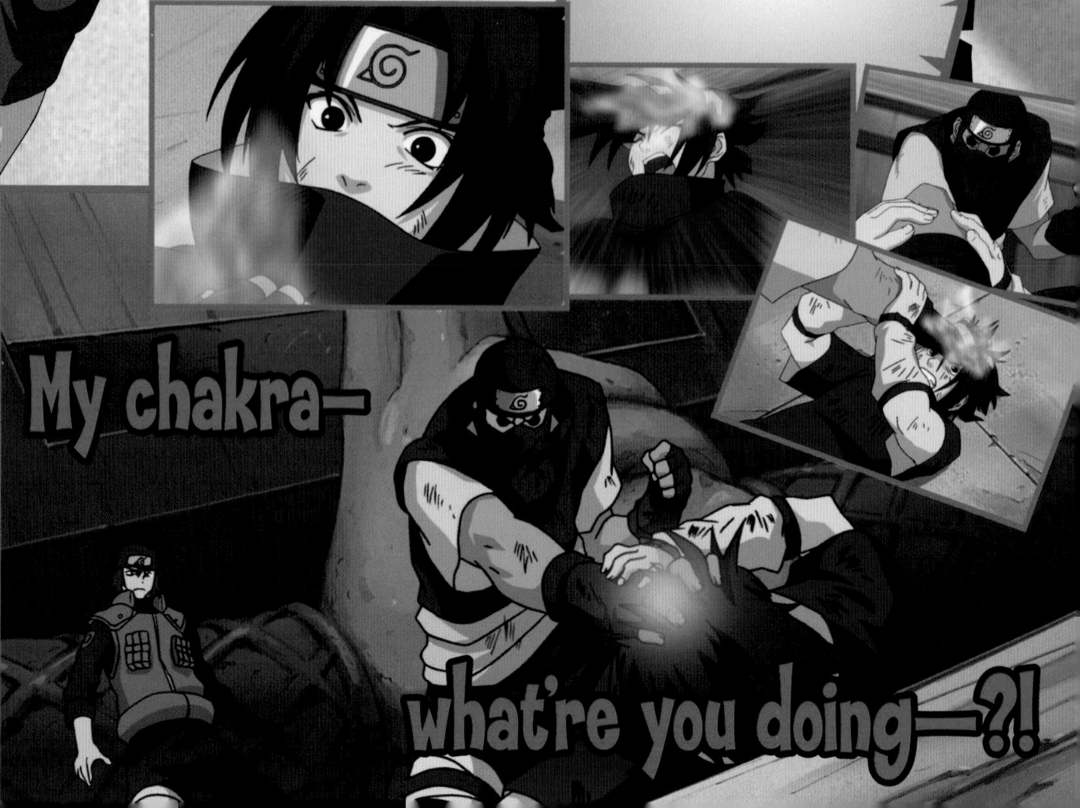
My chakra—
what're you doing—?!

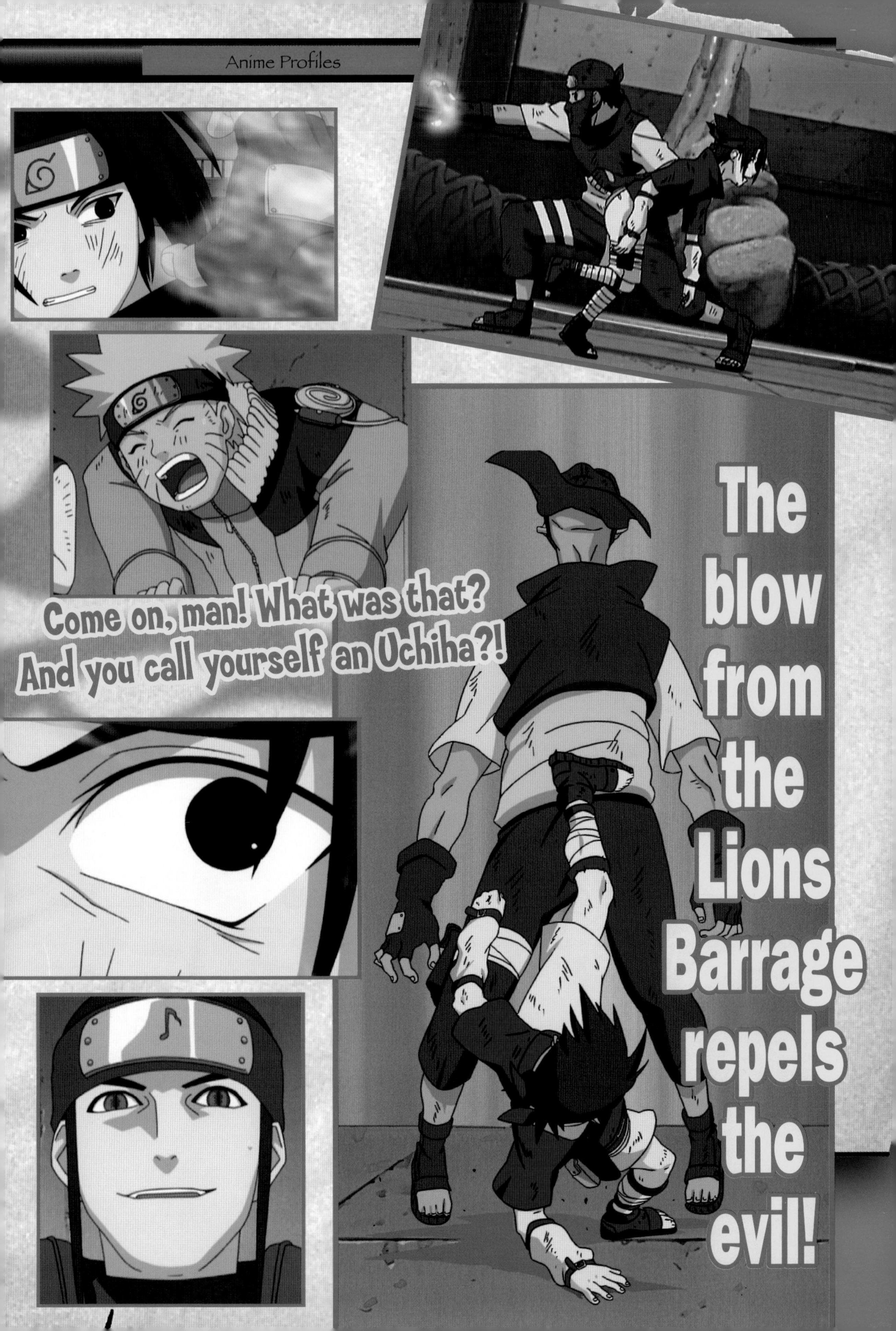
The blow from the Lions Barrage repels the evil!
Come on, man! What was that? And you call yourself an Uchiha?!

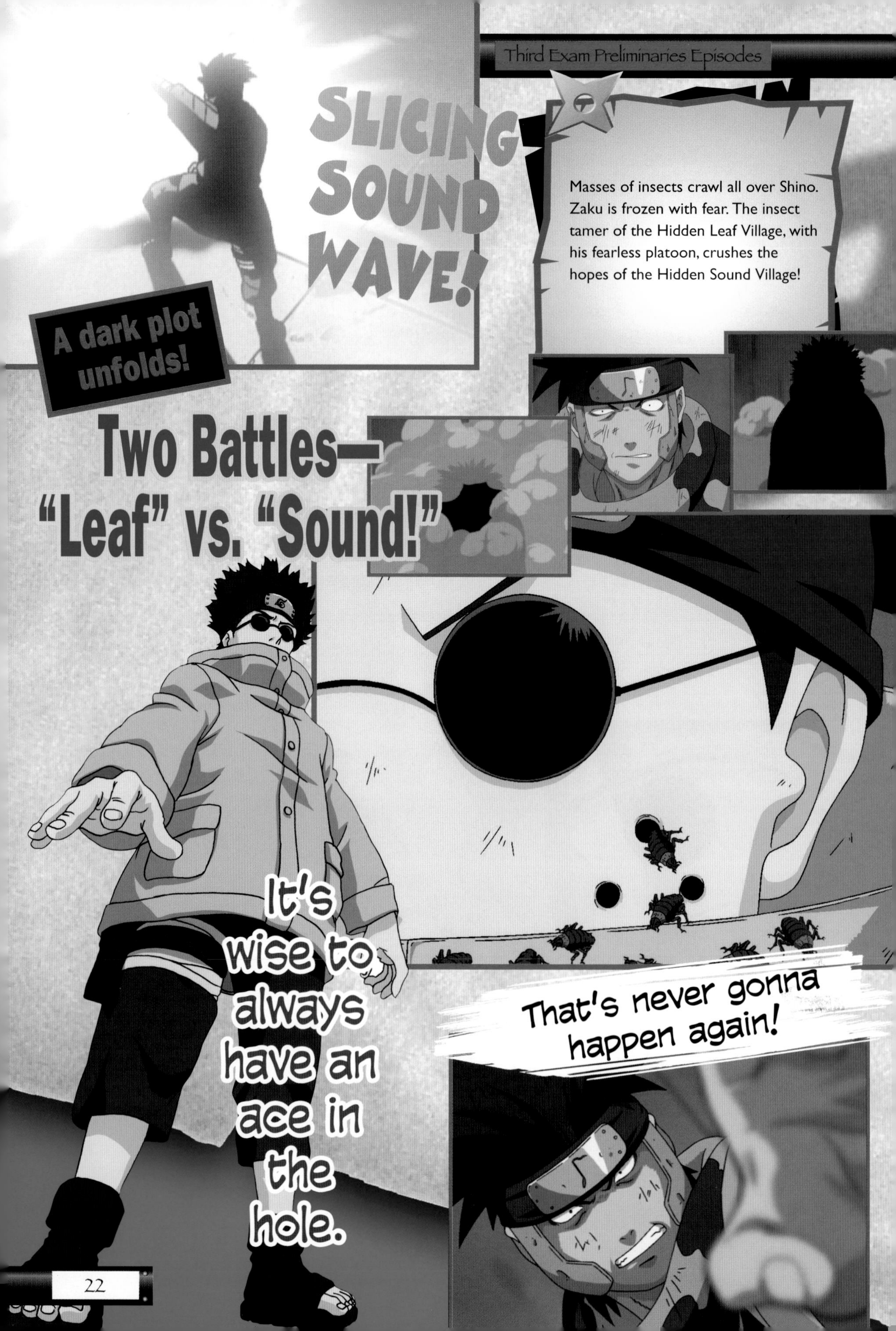
SLICING SOUND WAVE!
Masses of insects crawl all over Shino. Zaku is frozen with fear. The insect tamer of the Hidden Leaf Village, with his fearless platoon, crushes the hopes of the Hidden Sound Village!
A dark plot unfolds!
Two Battles—“Leaf” vs. “Sound!”
It's wise to always have an ace in the hole.
That's never gonna happen again!

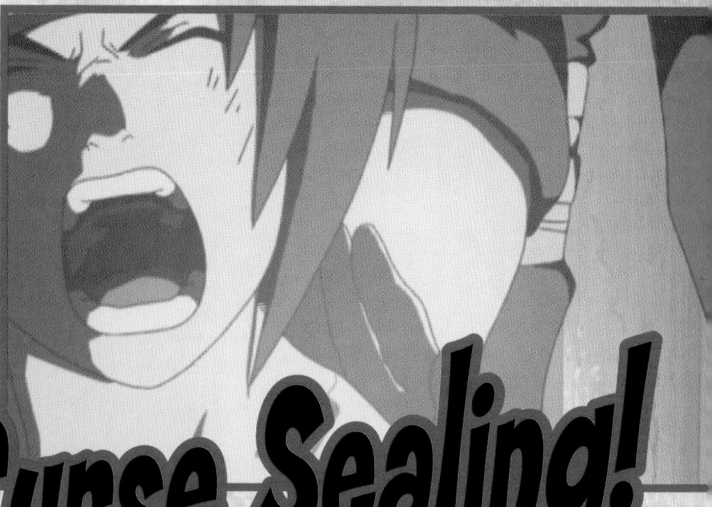

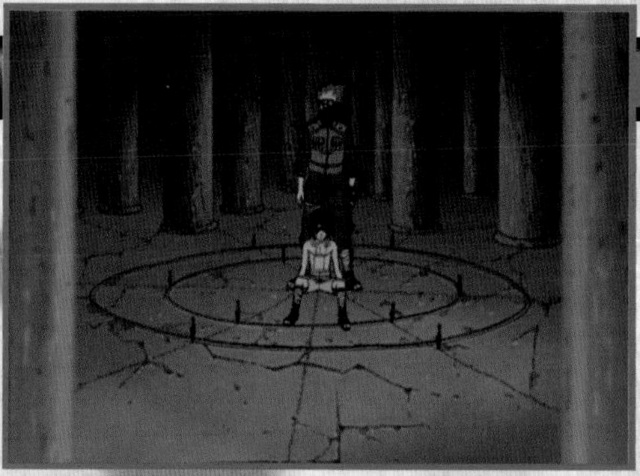

Curse Sealing!

Orochimaru's ambitious plot includes conquering the Hidden Leaf Village and finding the missing Sasuke. With sinister intentions, he appears before Kakashi… What is reflected in his sinister eyes…?!

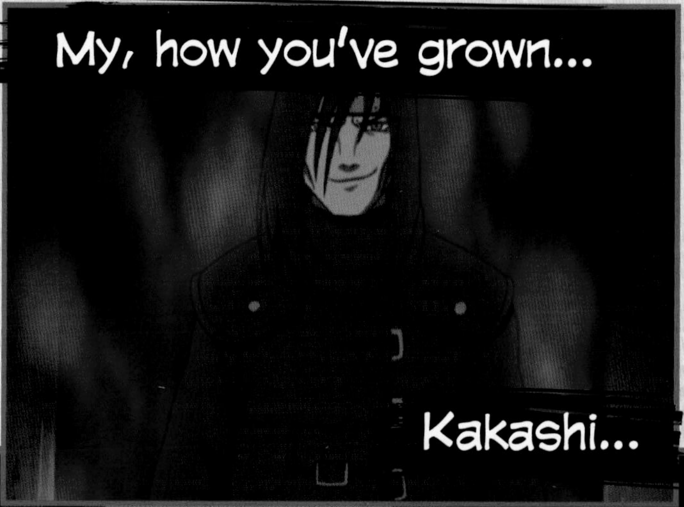
My, how you've grown...
Kakashi...

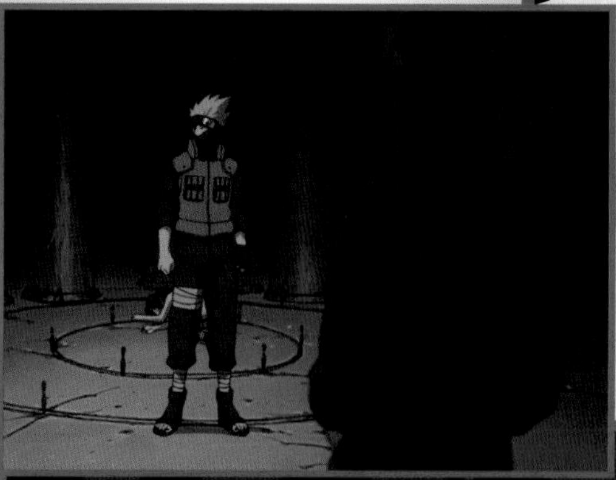

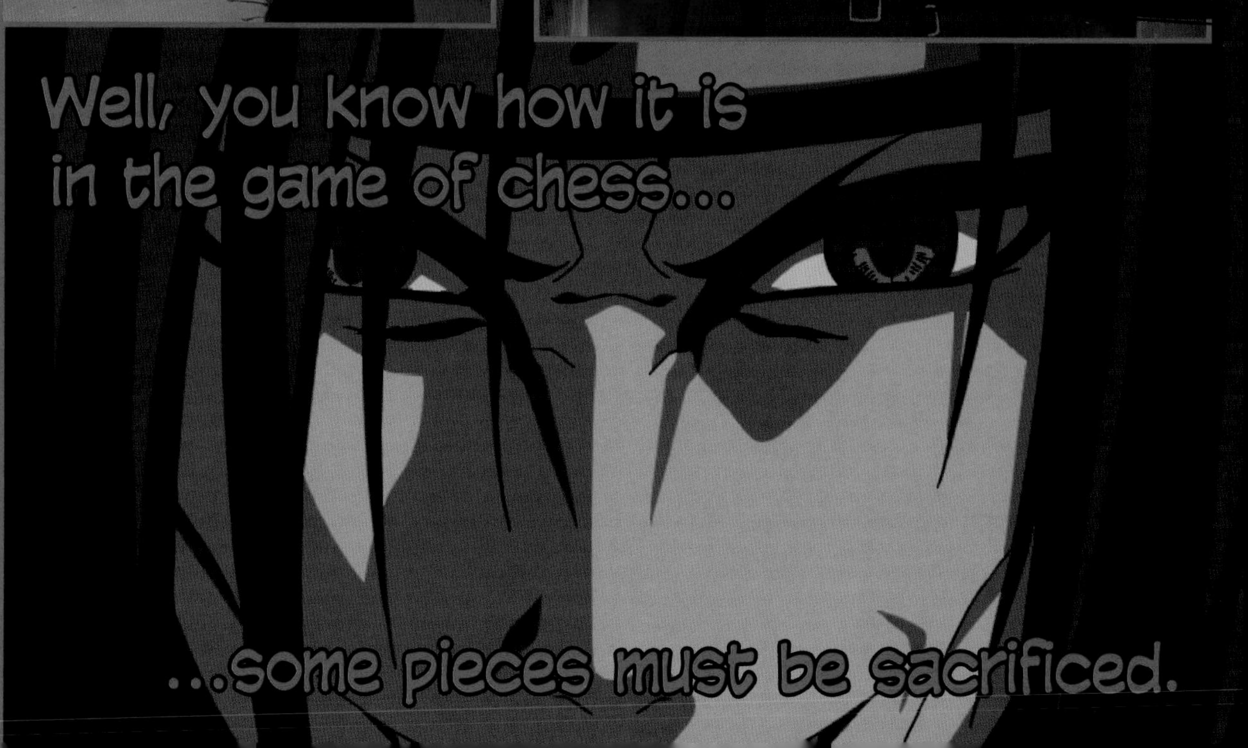
Well, you know how it is in the game of chess...
...some pieces must be sacrificed.

A Startling Twist! A Sand Village Puppet!

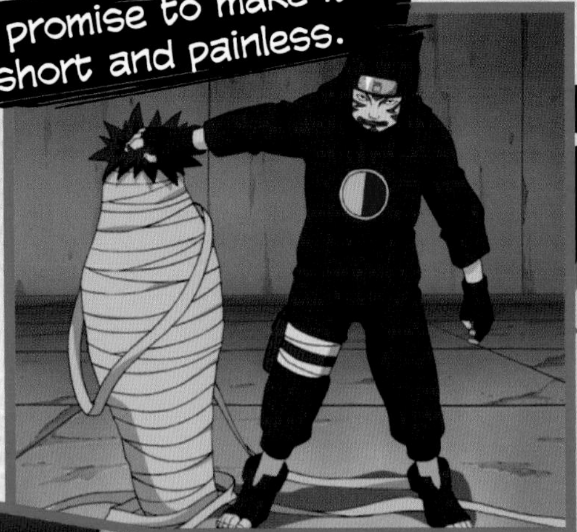
I promise to make it short and painless.

Enveloping Kankuro with his arms and crushing him with his legs, Misumi attacks with his elastic body. But can the match really be over just like that…? What horrible scene will be revealed next…?!

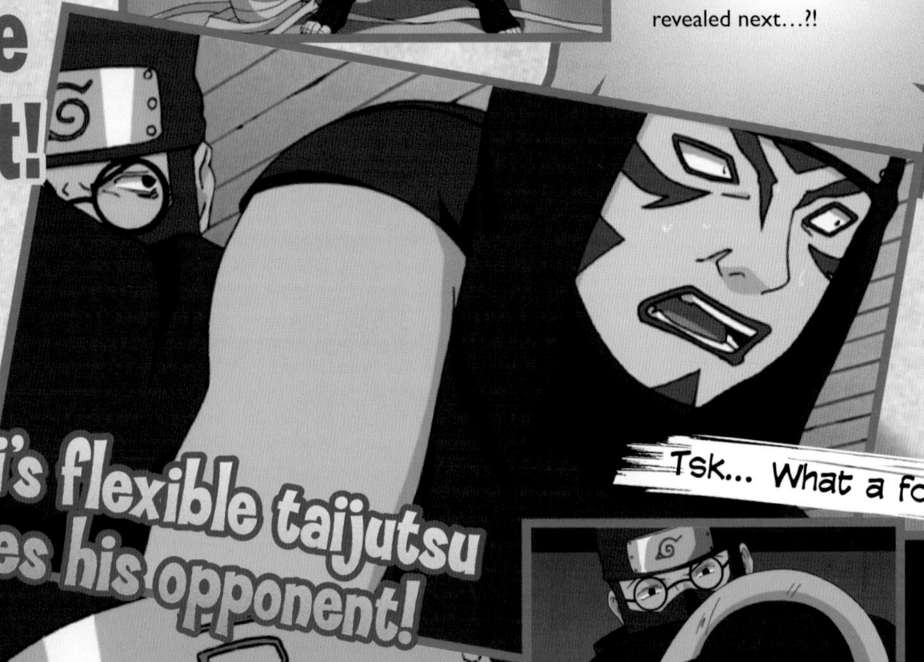
Misumi's flexible taijutsu crushes his opponent!

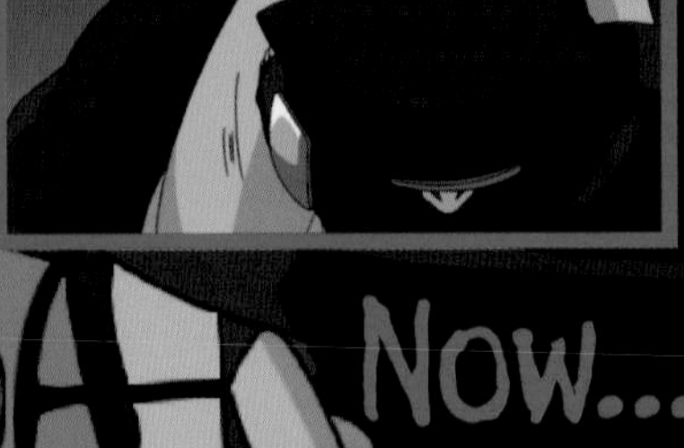
Tsk… What a fool.

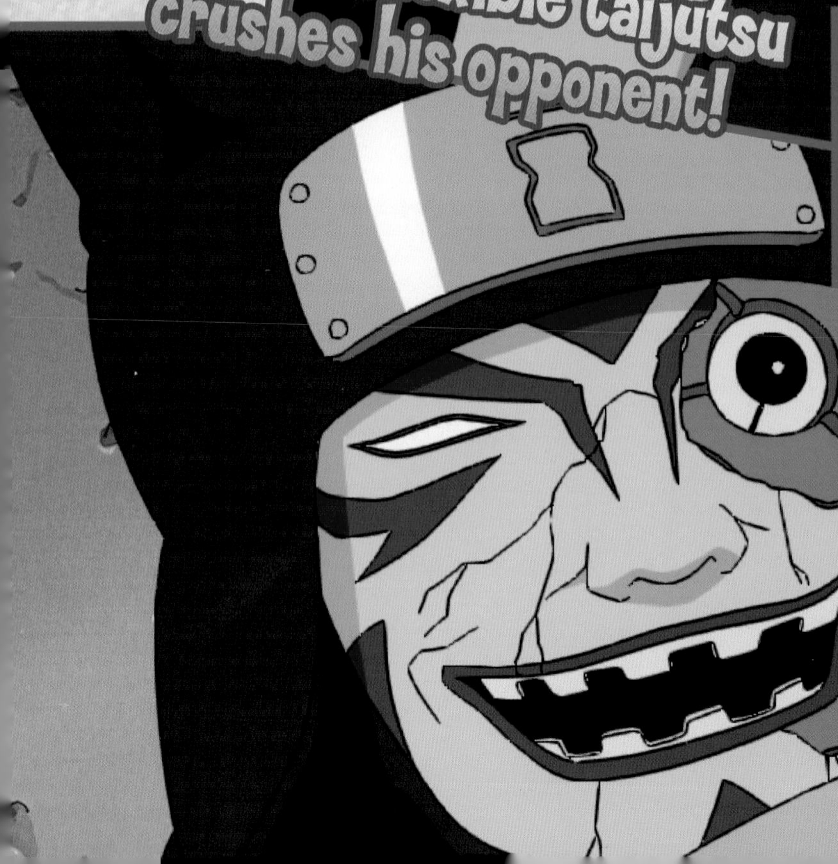
Now… It's my turn, so say good-bye.♥

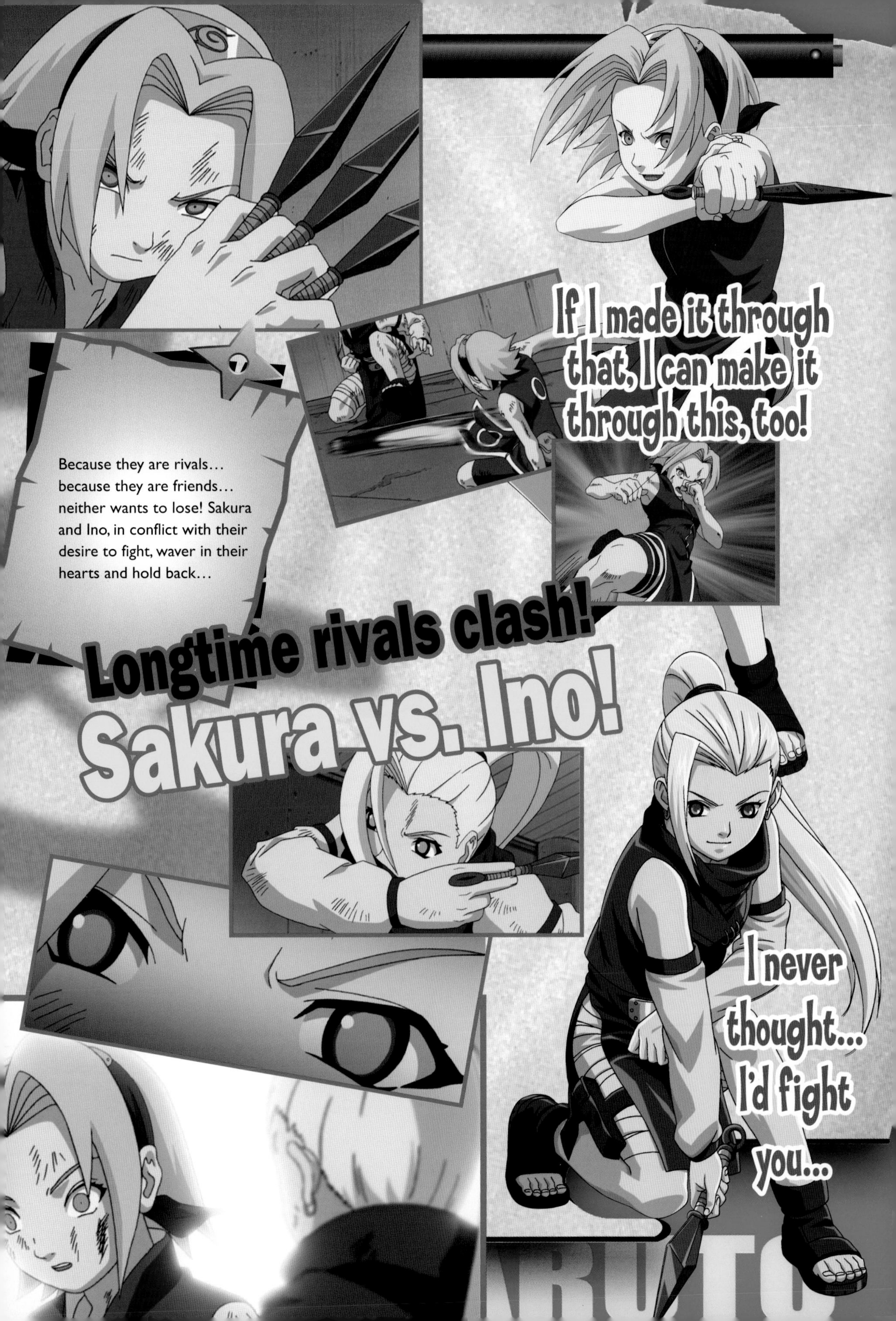

If I made it through that, I can make it through this, too!
Because they are rivals… because they are friends… neither wants to lose! Sakura and Ino, in conflict with their desire to fight, waver in their hearts and hold back…
Longtime rivals clash!
Sakura vs. Ino!
I never thought… I'd fight you…
NARUTO

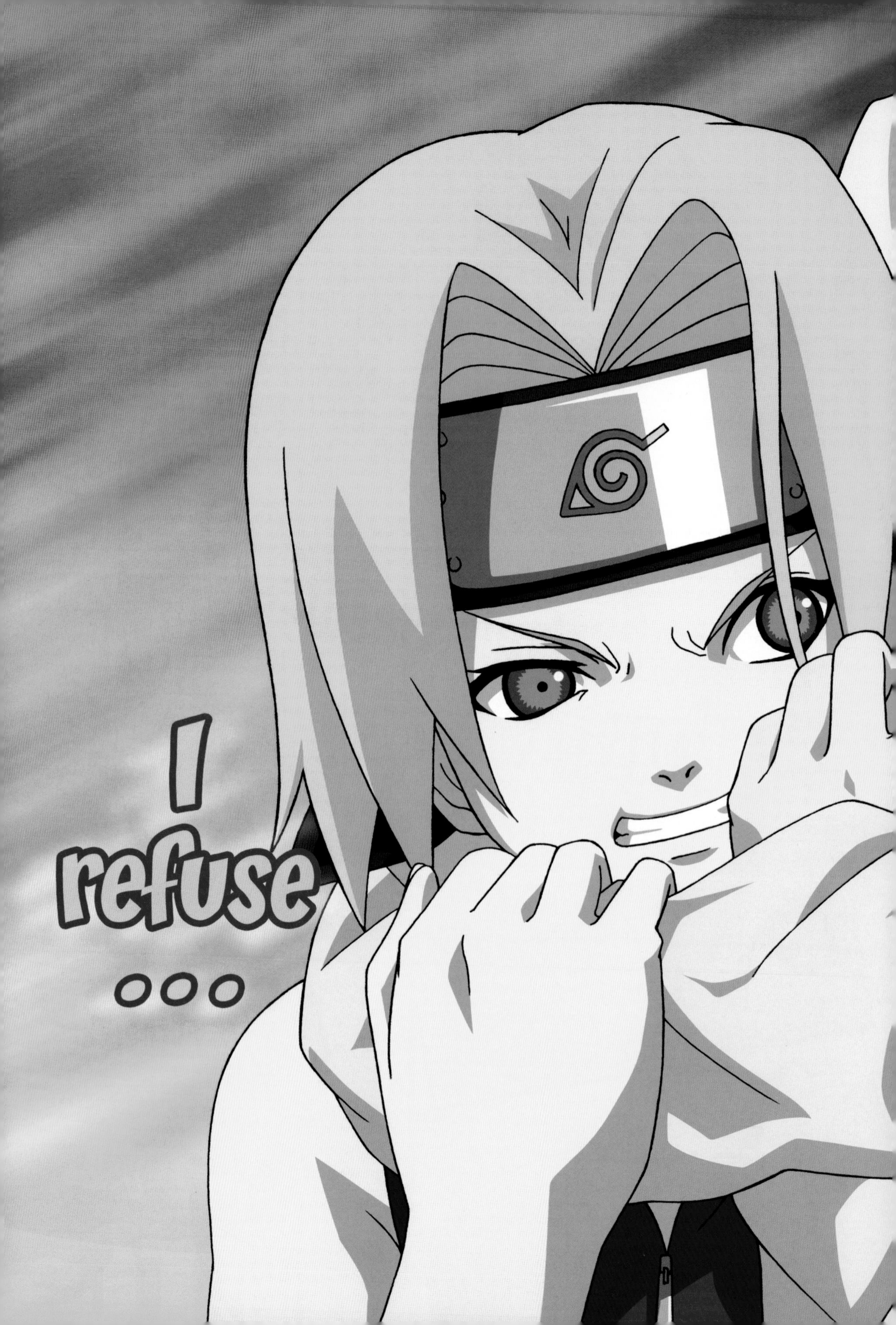
I refuse ...

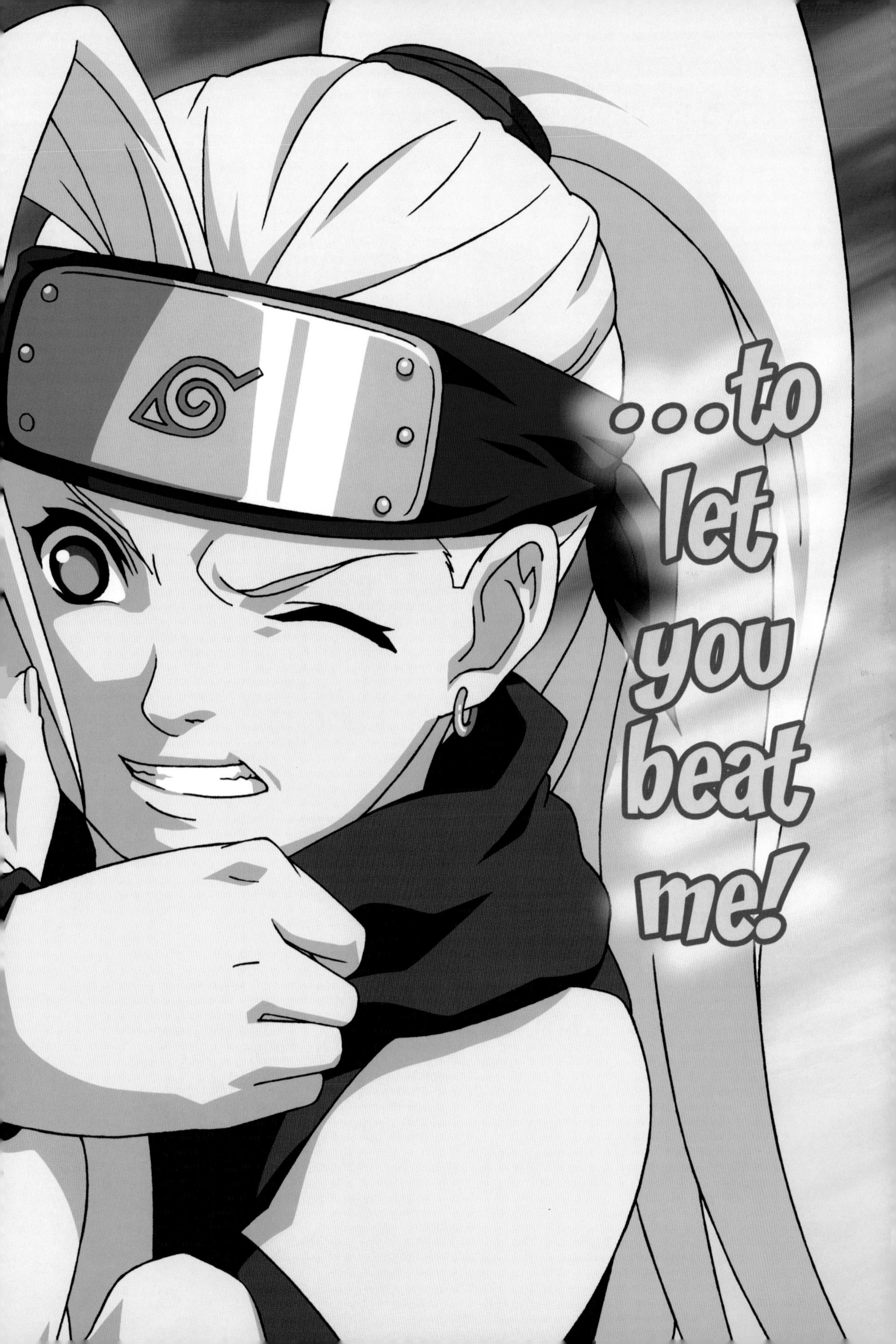
...to let you beat me!

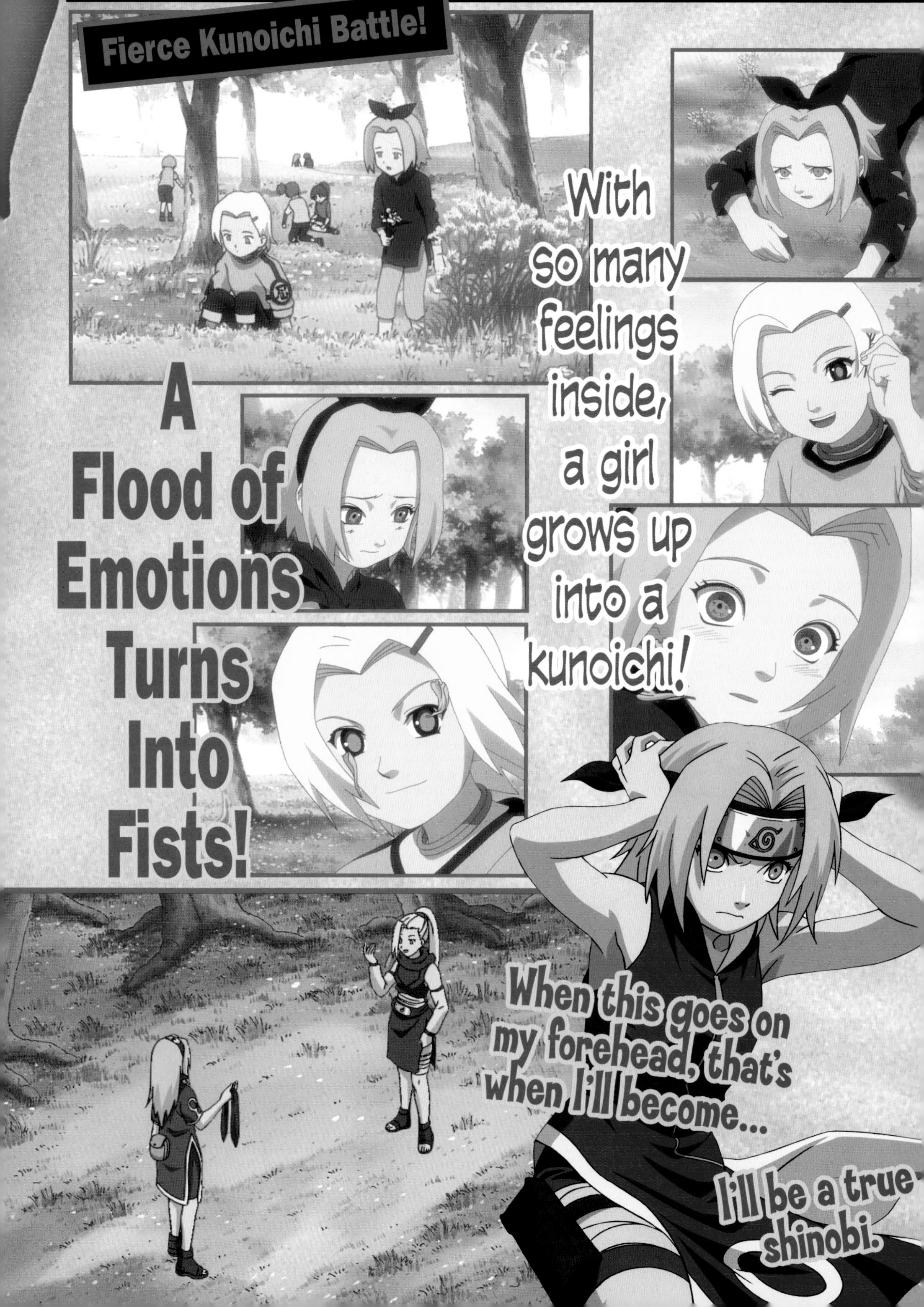
Fierce Kunoichi Battle!
A Flood of Emotions Turns Into Fists!
With so many feelings inside, a girl grows up into a kunoichi!
When this goes on my forehead, that's when I'll become...
I'll be a true shinobi.

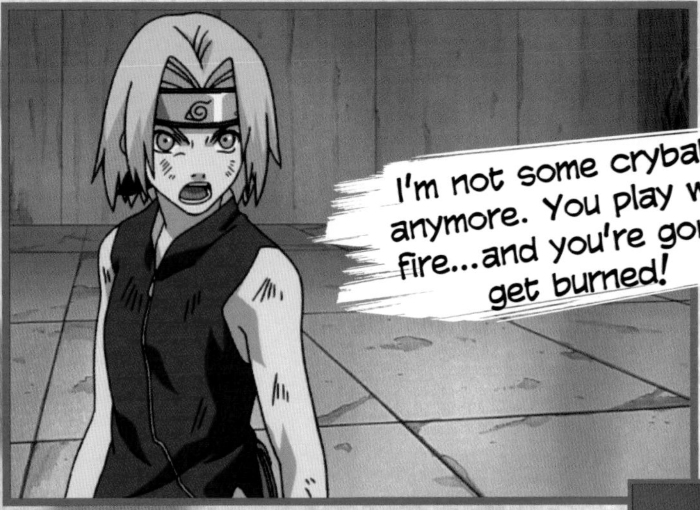
I'm not some crybaby anymore. You play with fire...and you're gonna get burned!

Their deep past is the very reason they stand and fight each other! Sakura's and Ino's memories hark back to the day they made an oath over Sakura's headband… all that emotion ends with fists… Now!

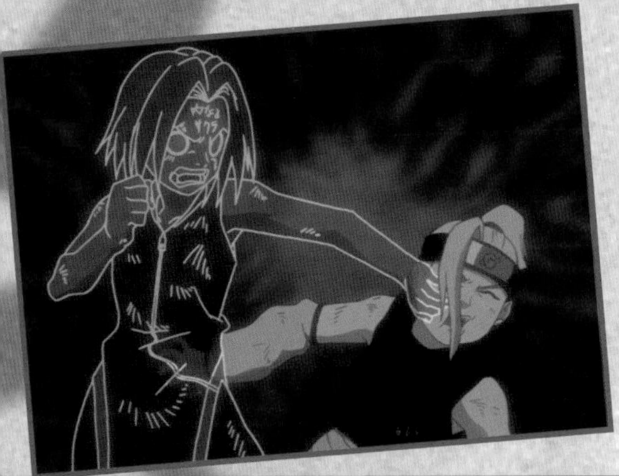

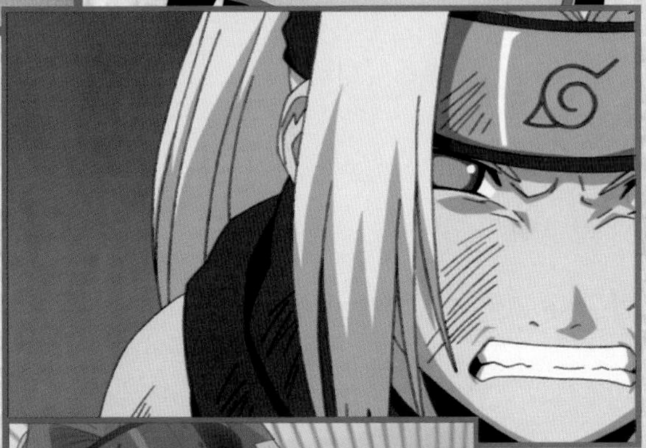

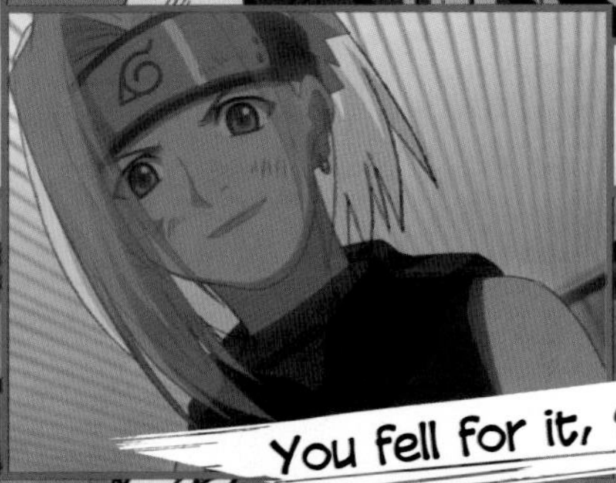
You fell for it, Sakura!

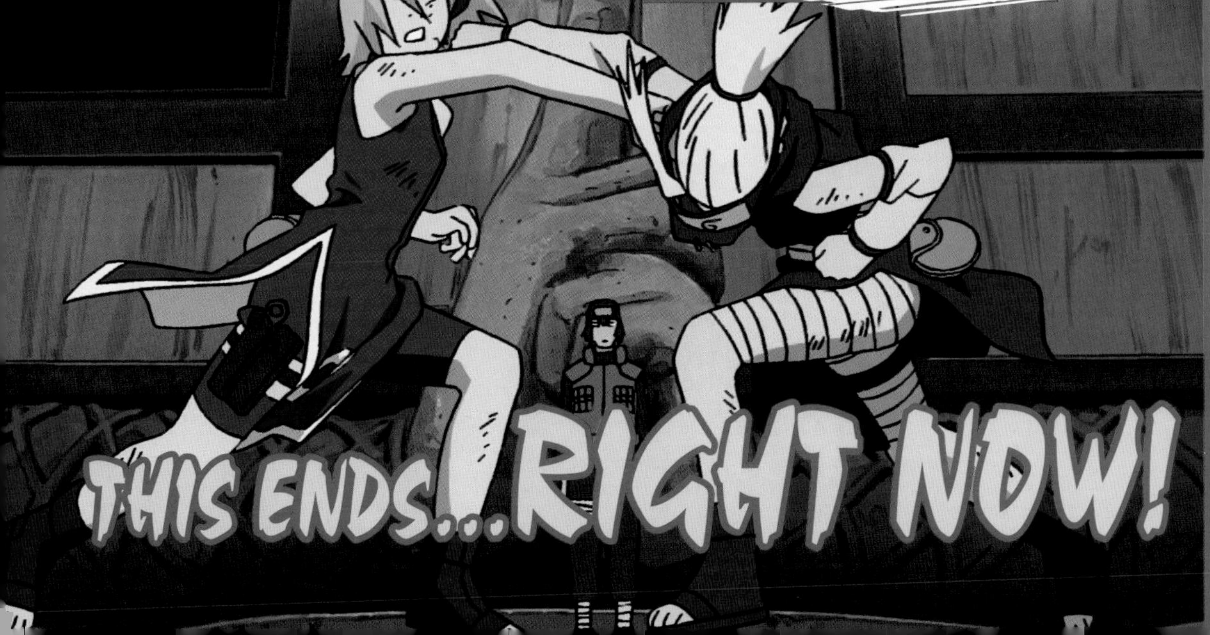
THIS ENDS...RIGHT NOW!

Big trouble for the Leaf ninja?!

Sand's Wind Turbine! Sound's hallucination technique!

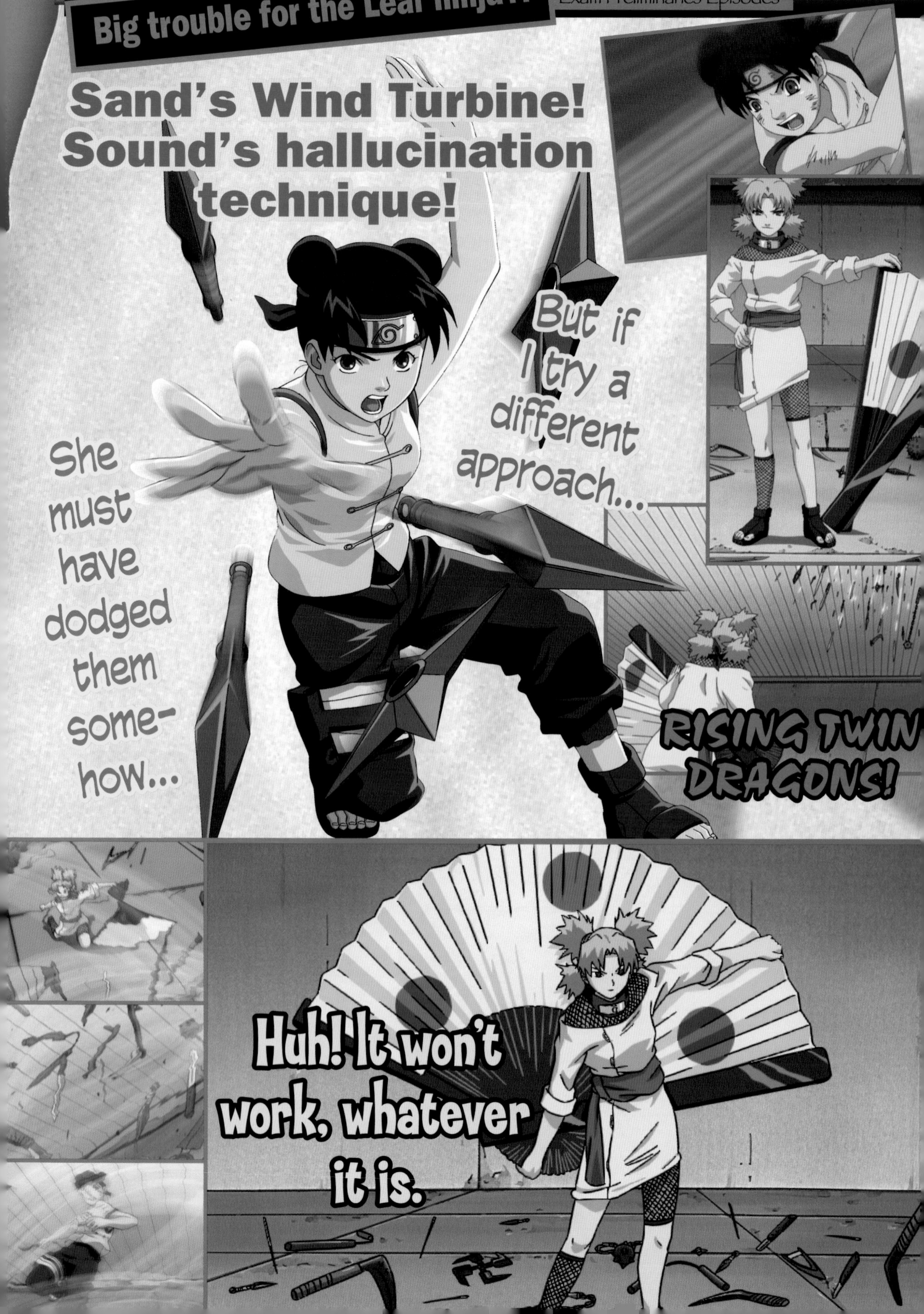
But if I try a different approach...
She must have dodged them somehow...
RISING TWIN DRAGONS!
Huh! It won't work, whatever it is.

Shikamaru fell for the hallucination-bell sound trap and took numerous hits from the senbon needles. With his ace technique, Shadow Possession Jutsu, held in check, is Shikamaru already beaten…?

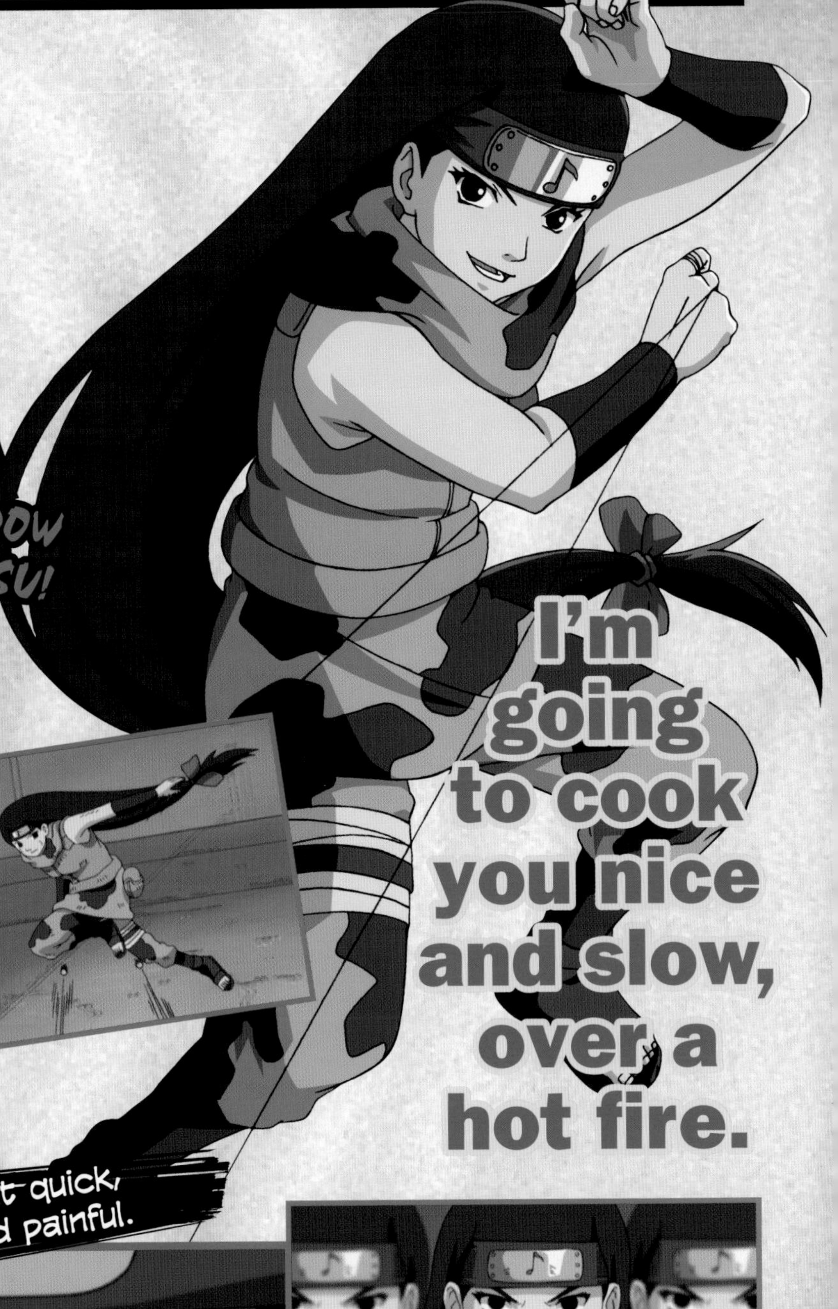
I'm going to cook you nice and slow, over a hot fire.

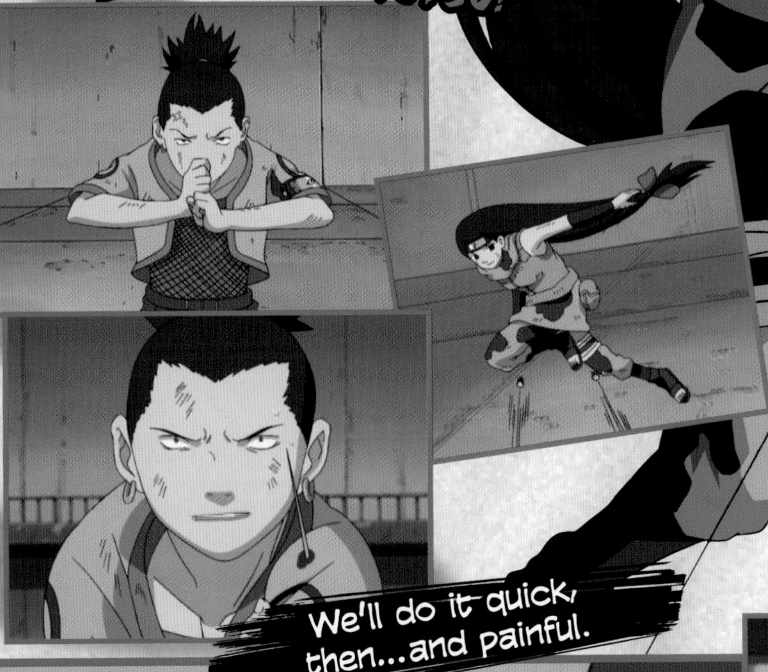
NINJA ART! SHADOW POSSESSION JUTSU!
We'll do it quick, then...and painful.

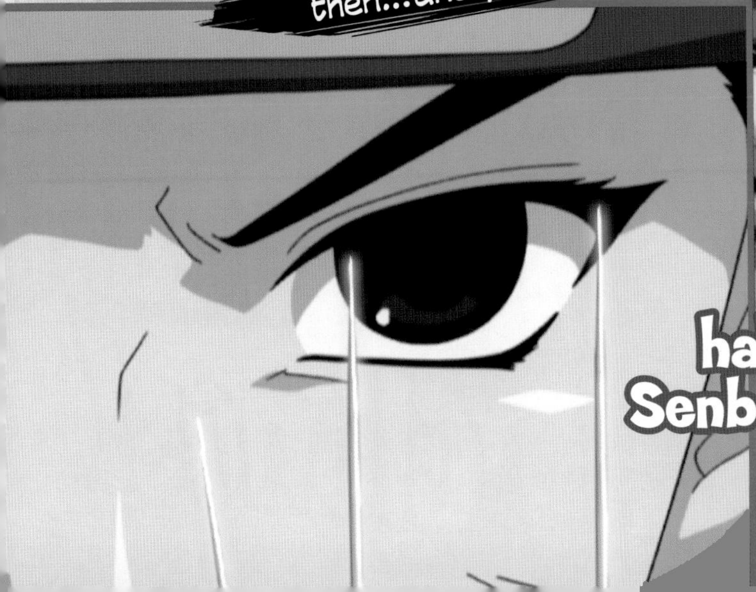

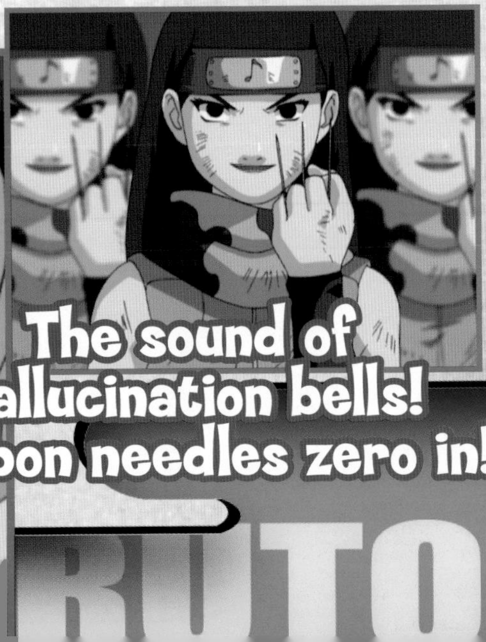
The sound of hallucination bells! Senbon needles zero in!

Enter Naruto!

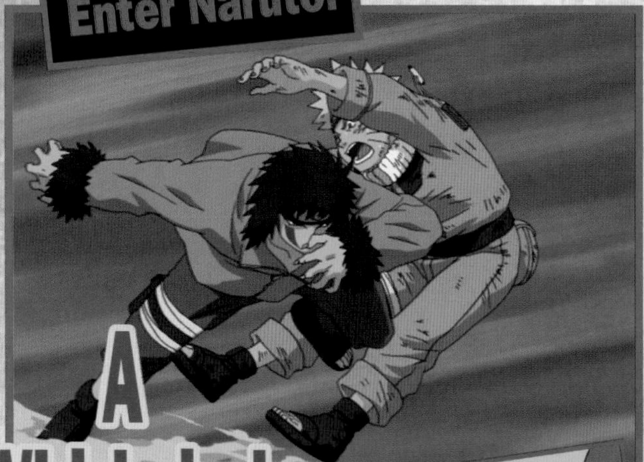

A Whirlwind of Power Explodes!

Like wild beasts, Kiba and Akamaru attack ferociously. Naruto fights back with his powers of improvisation and his strong desire to win. What move did Naruto—definitely the number one ninja in unpredictability—unleash to break through this seesaw battle?!

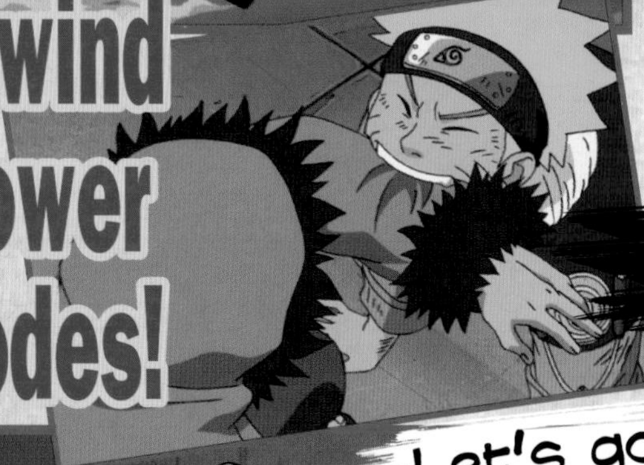
Surprise! Gotcha!

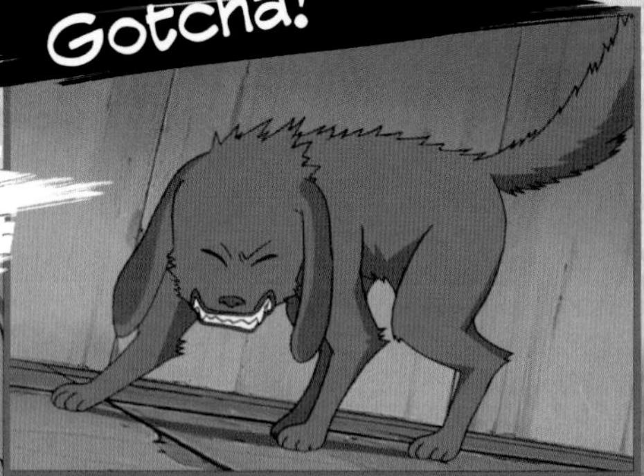

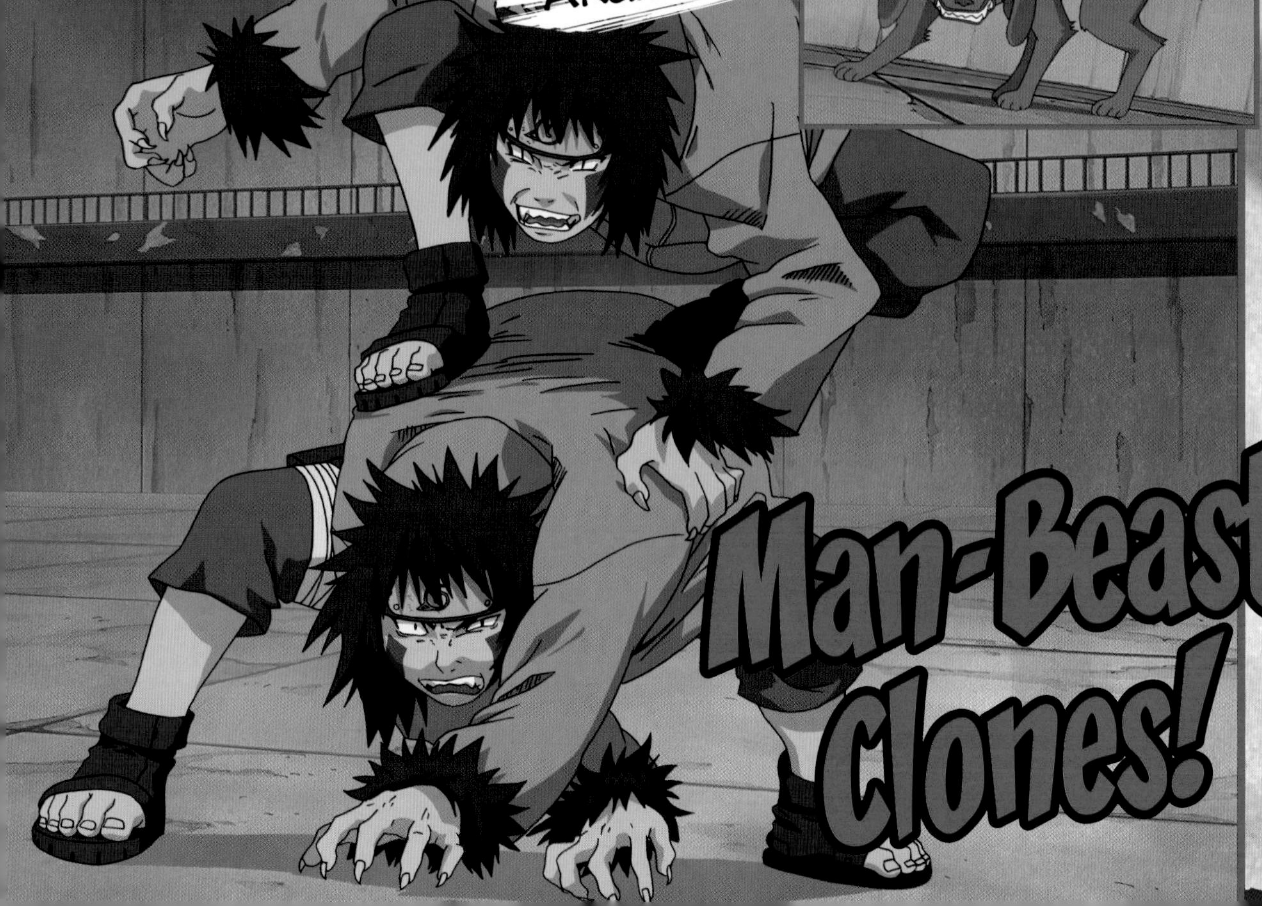
Let's go, Akamaru!

Man-Beast Clones!

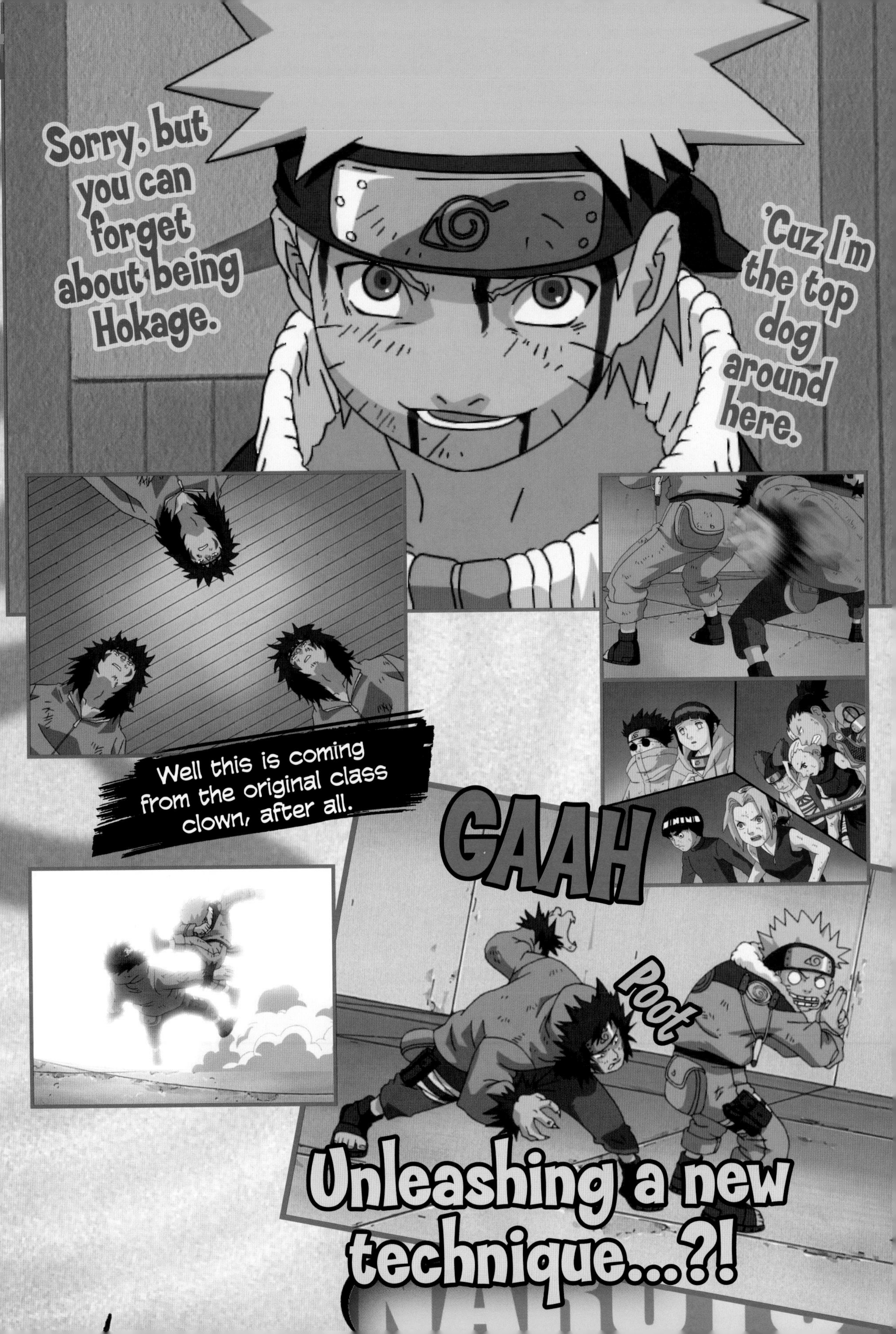
Sorry, but you can forget about being Hokage.
'Cuz I'm the top dog around here.
Well this is coming from the original class clown, after all.
GAAH
Poot
Unleashing a new technique...?!

Merciless Showdown!

A Determined Hinata Stands Tall!

Even though she shares the Hyuga bloodline with Neji, Hinata has always suffered from an inferiority complex. Hinata pours all her resolve into this battle…to break away from what she used to be!

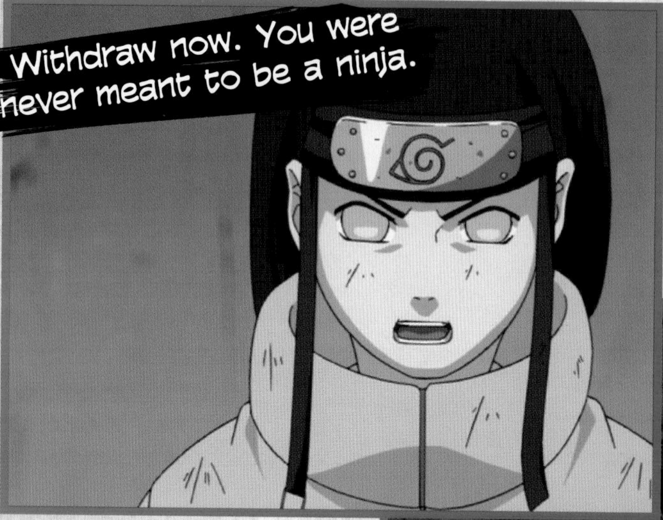

Withdraw now. You were never meant to be a ninja.

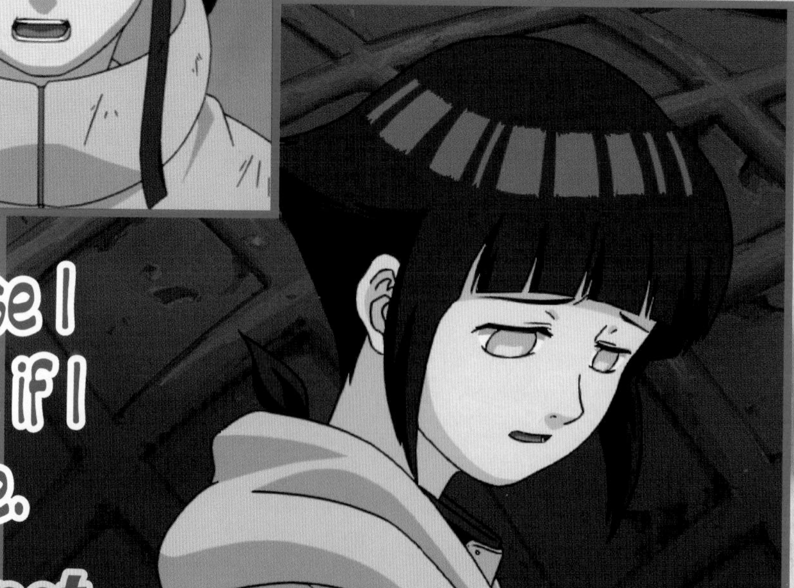

I did it because I wanted to see if I could change.

My eyes cannot be deceived.

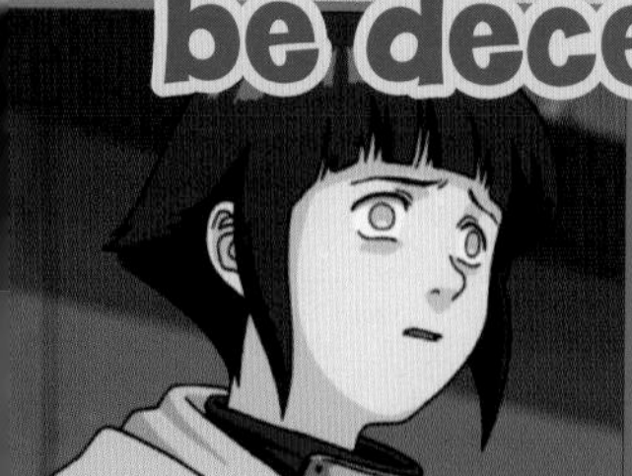

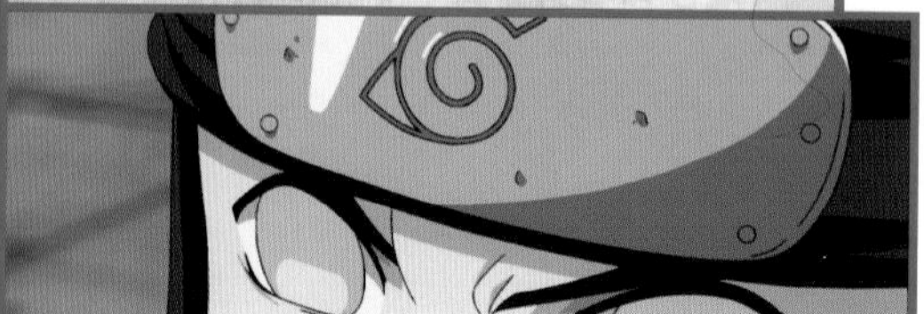

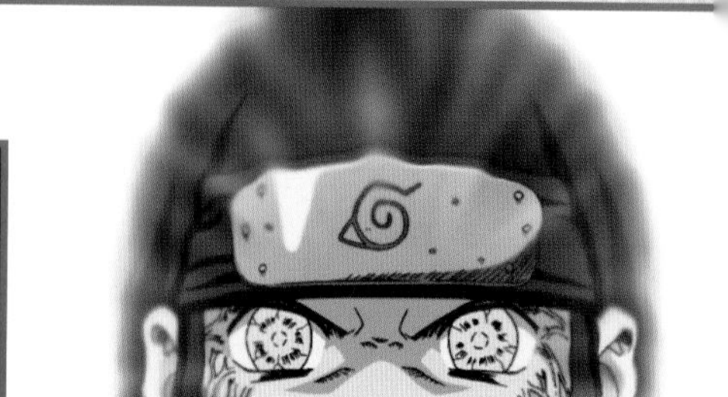

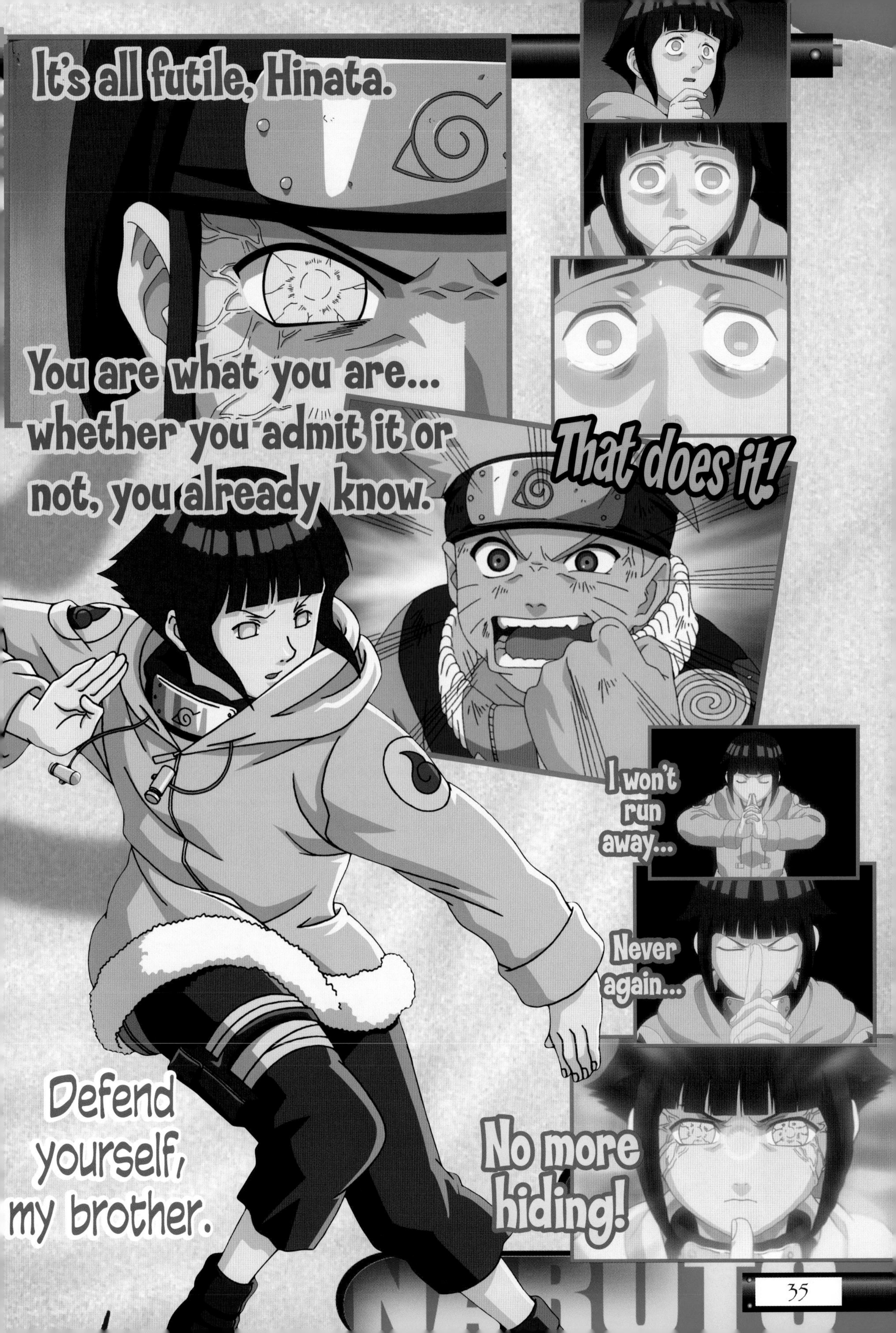
It's all futile, Hinata.
You are what you are... whether you admit it or not, you already know.
That does it!
I won't run away...
Never again...
No more hiding!
Defend yourself, my brother.

In front of the person I admire most...

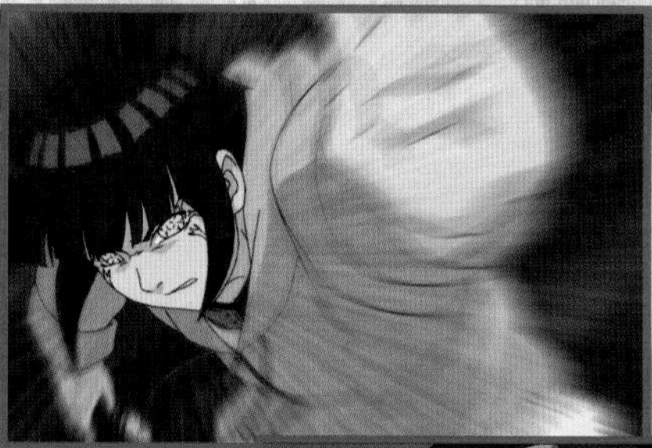

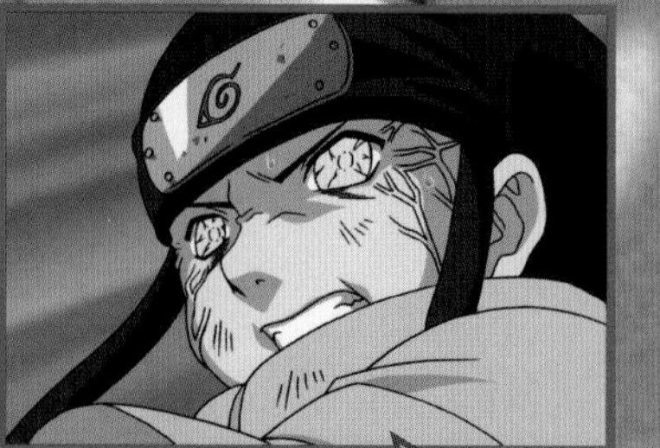

To achieve her nindo, she must defy her fate.

Hinata is beaten down by the genius Neji. She faces an opponent far out of her league and is burdened with the heavy load of the Hyuga Clan's fate… Even so, Hinata gets back on her feet. And as long as Naruto is watching her, she'll keep getting up…

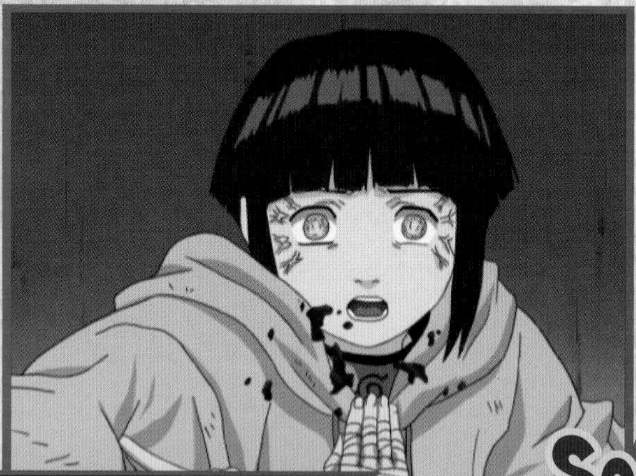

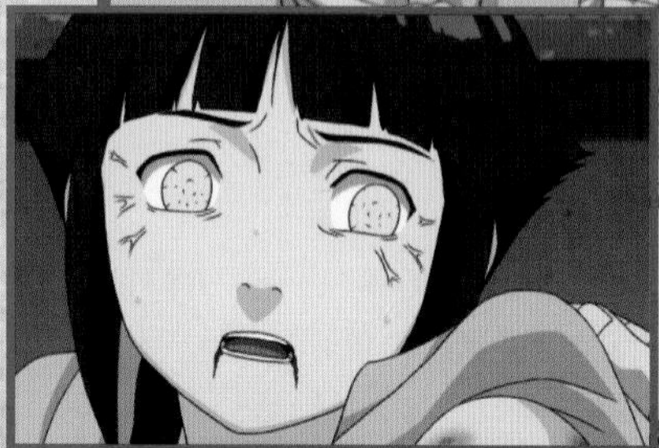

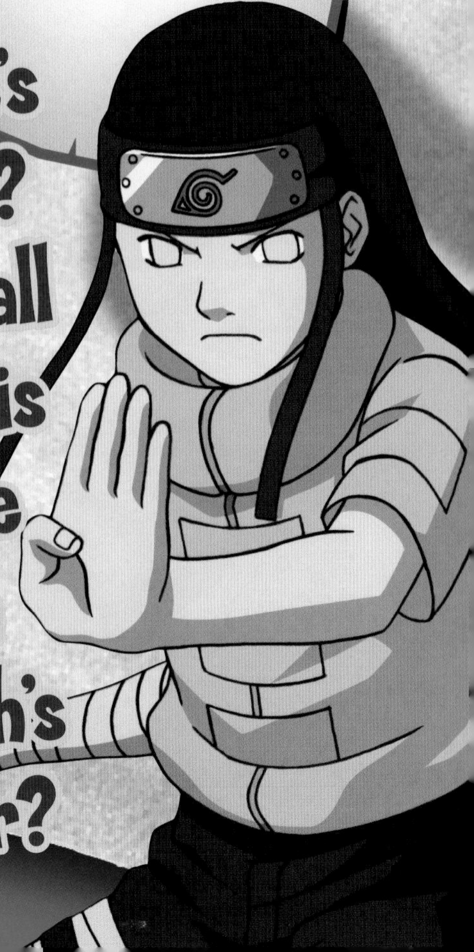
So that's it, huh? That's all there is to the Main Branch's power?

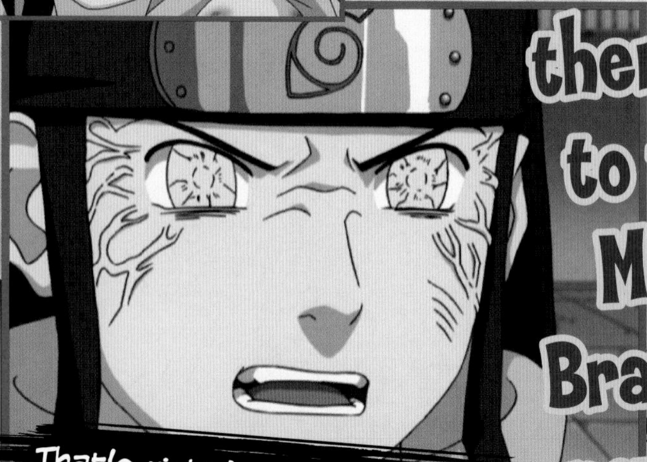
That's right! I could see your chakra points this whole time.

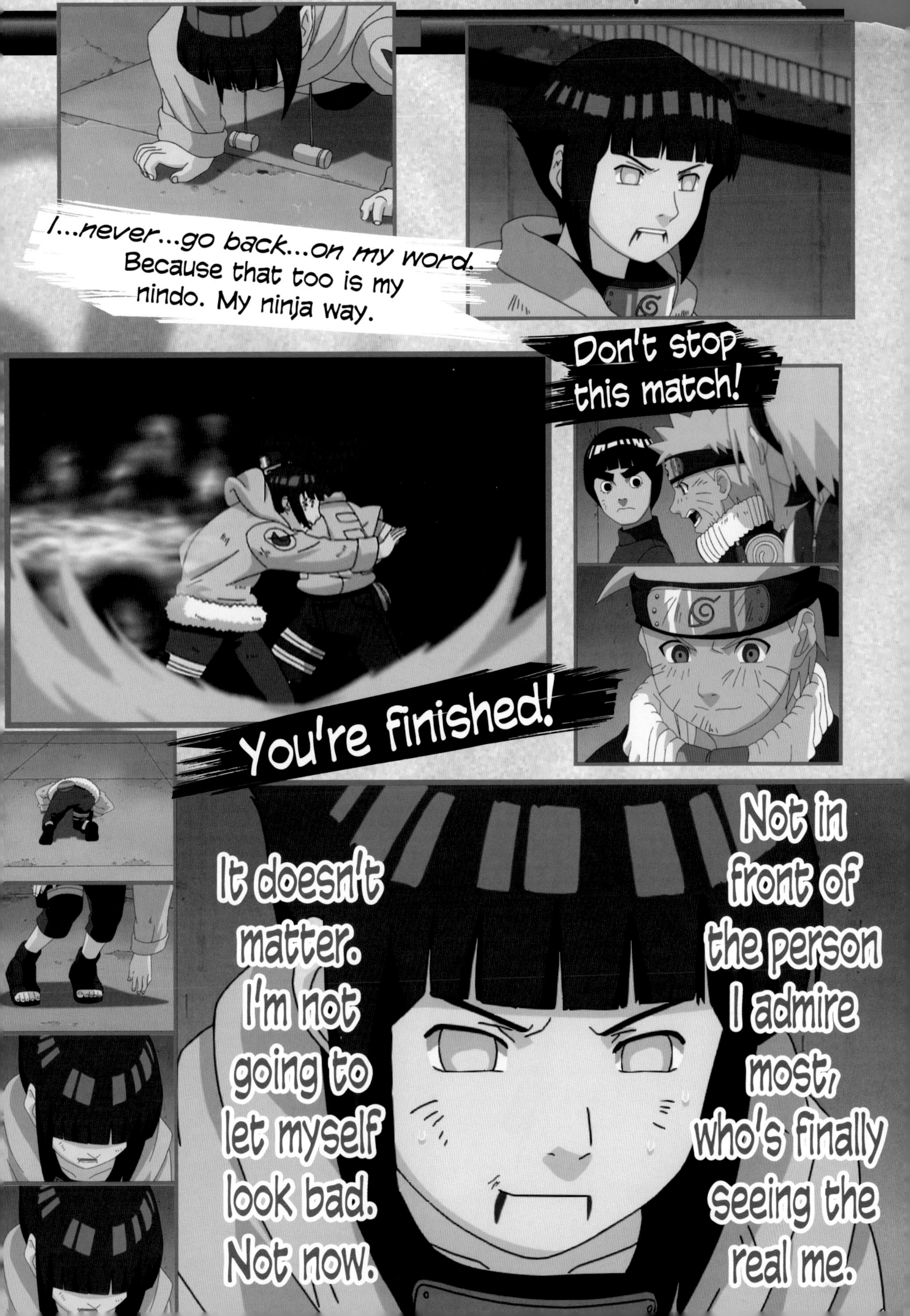
I...never...go back...on my word. Because that too is my nindo. My ninja way.
Don't stop this match!
You're finished!
It doesn't matter. I'm not going to let myself look bad. Not now.
Not in front of the person I admire most, who's finally seeing the real me.

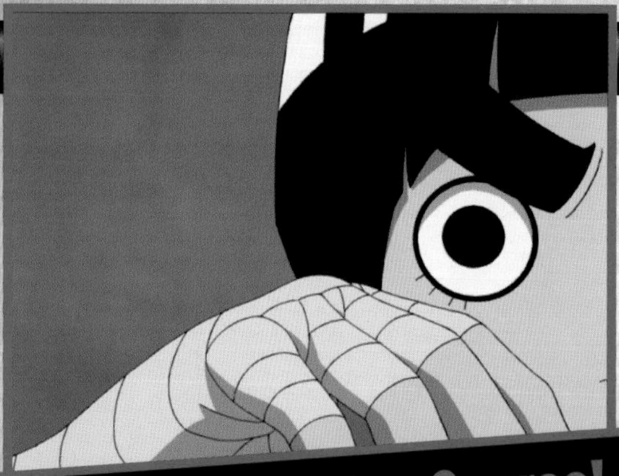

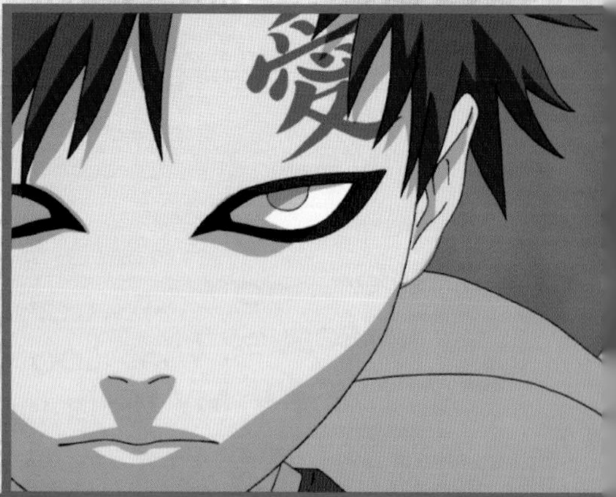

Match #9: Collision Course!

Heated! Intense! Rock Lee takes on Gaara!

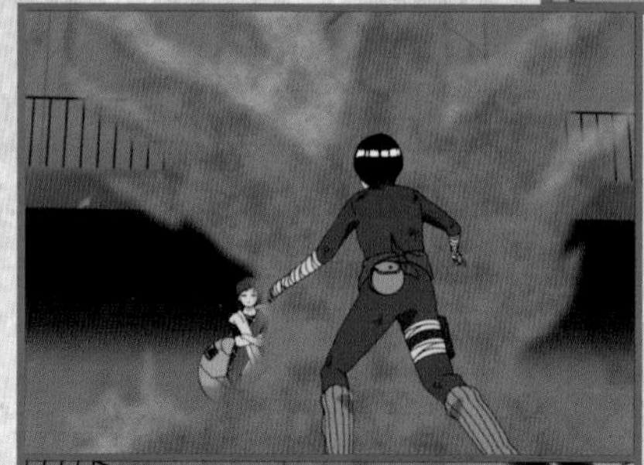

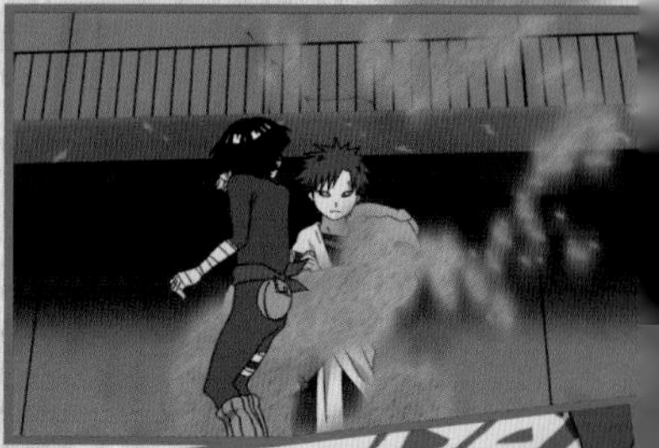

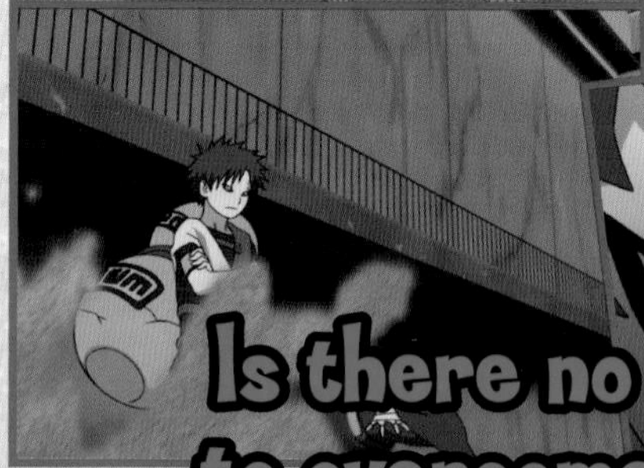

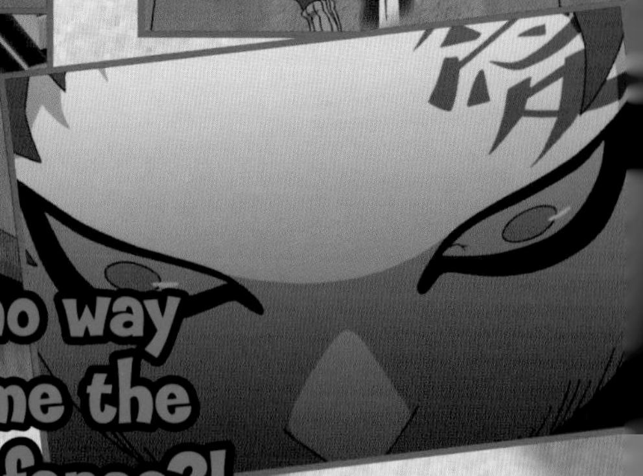

Is there no way to overcome the ultimate defense?!

Gaara's sand armor completely shuts down Lee's taijutsu, forcing Lee to remove his leg weights and seek permission from his mentor, Guy, to use the forbidden technique of opening his chakra gates and using the Hidden Lotus.

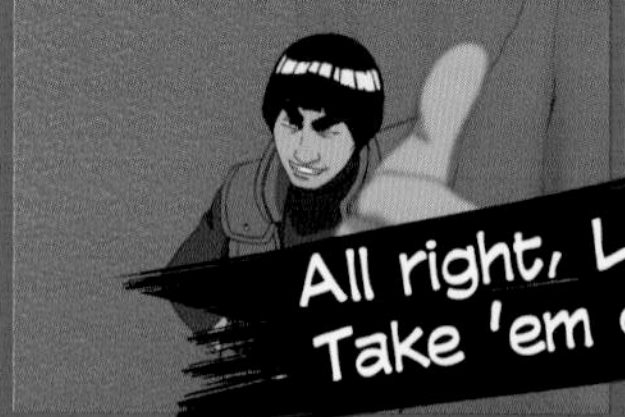
All right, Lee!
Take 'em off!

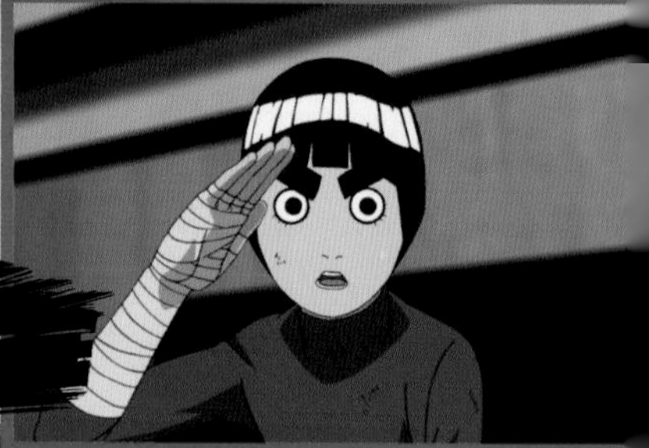

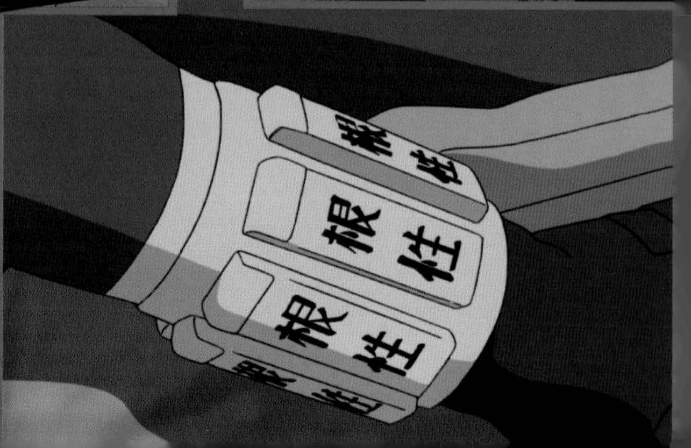

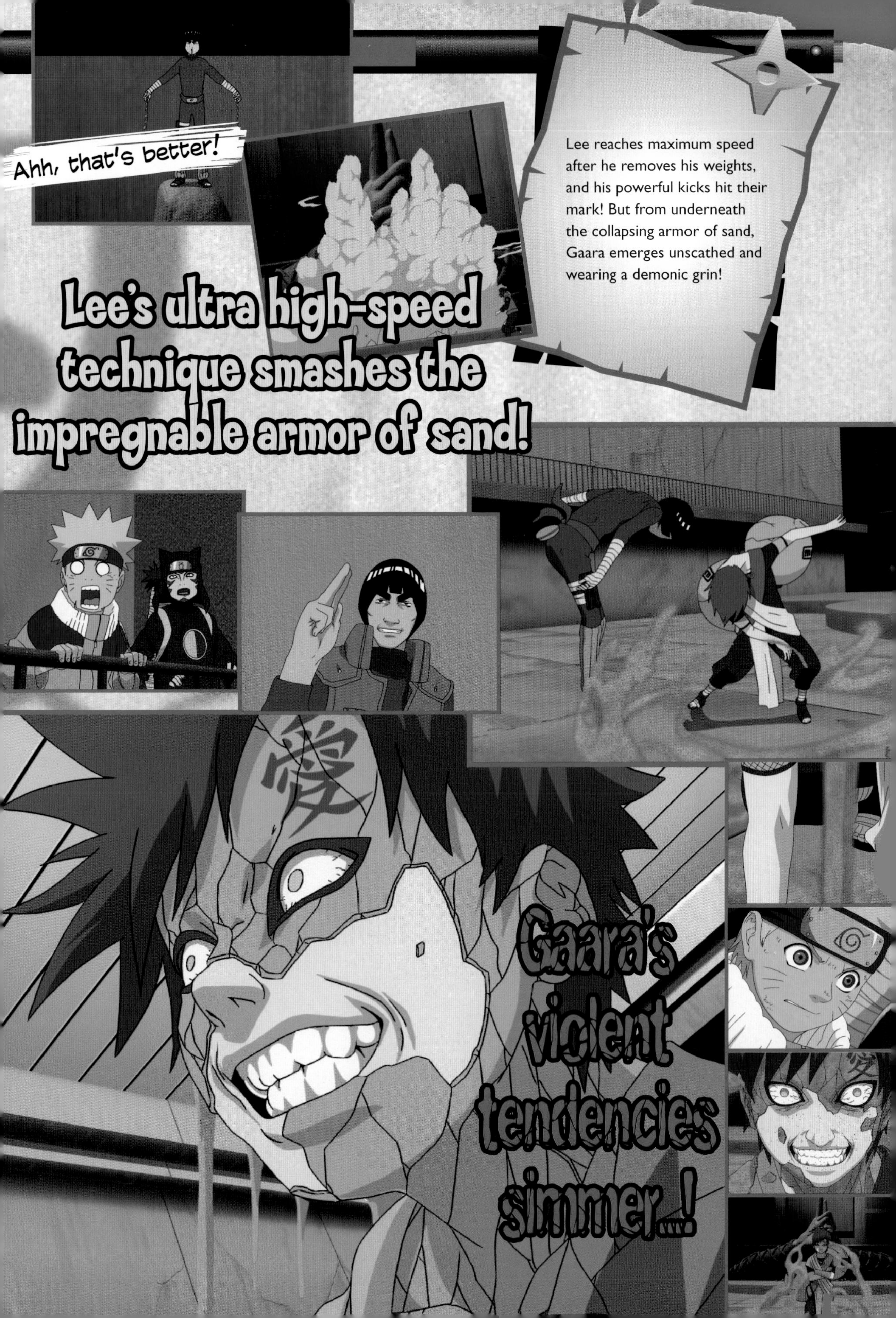

Ahh, that's better!
Lee reaches maximum speed after he removes his weights, and his powerful kicks hit their mark! But from underneath the collapsing armor of sand, Gaara emerges unscathed and wearing a demonic grin!
Lee's ultra high-speed technique smashes the impregnable armor of sand!
Gaara's violent tendencies simmer...!

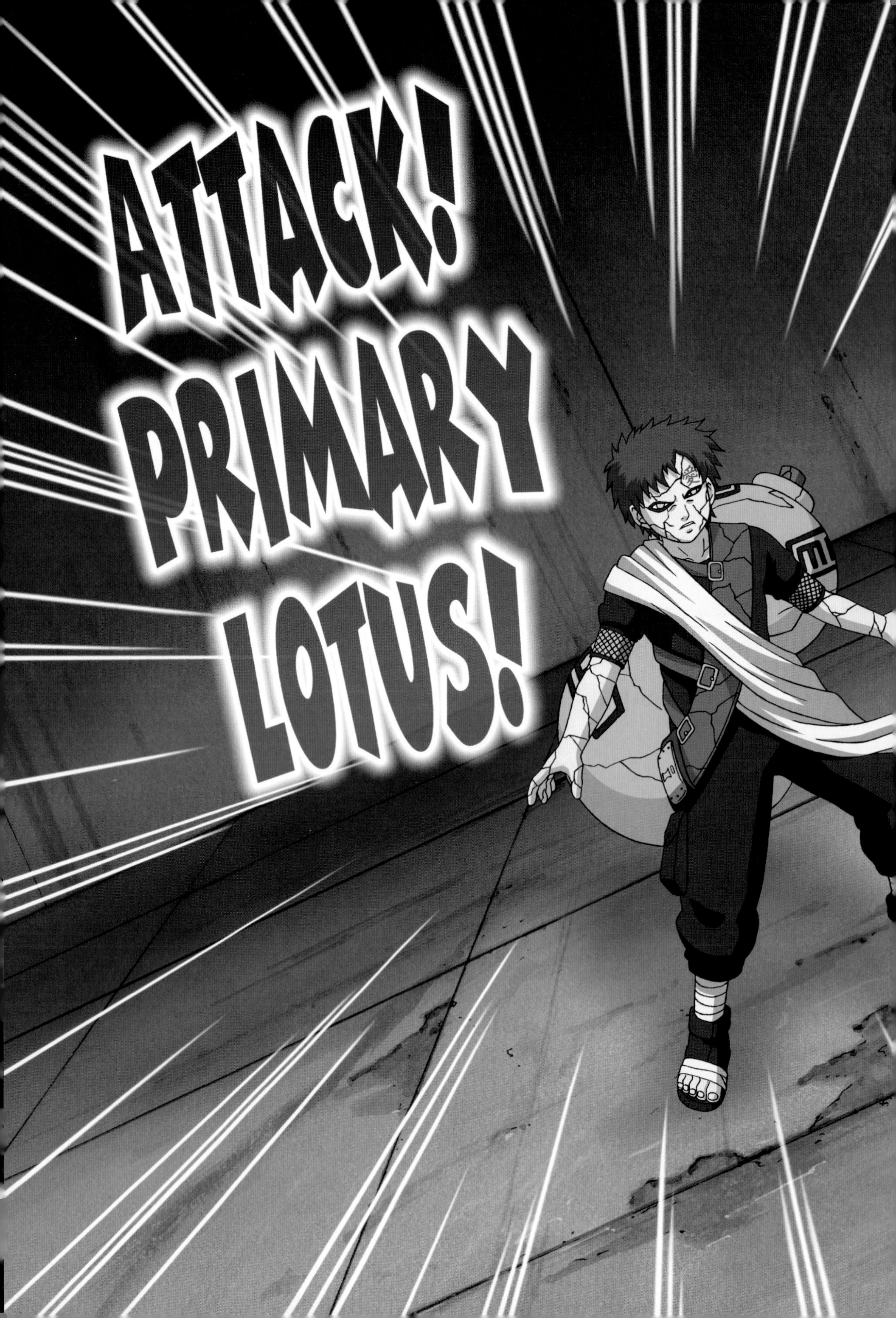
ATTACK! PRIMARY LOTUS!

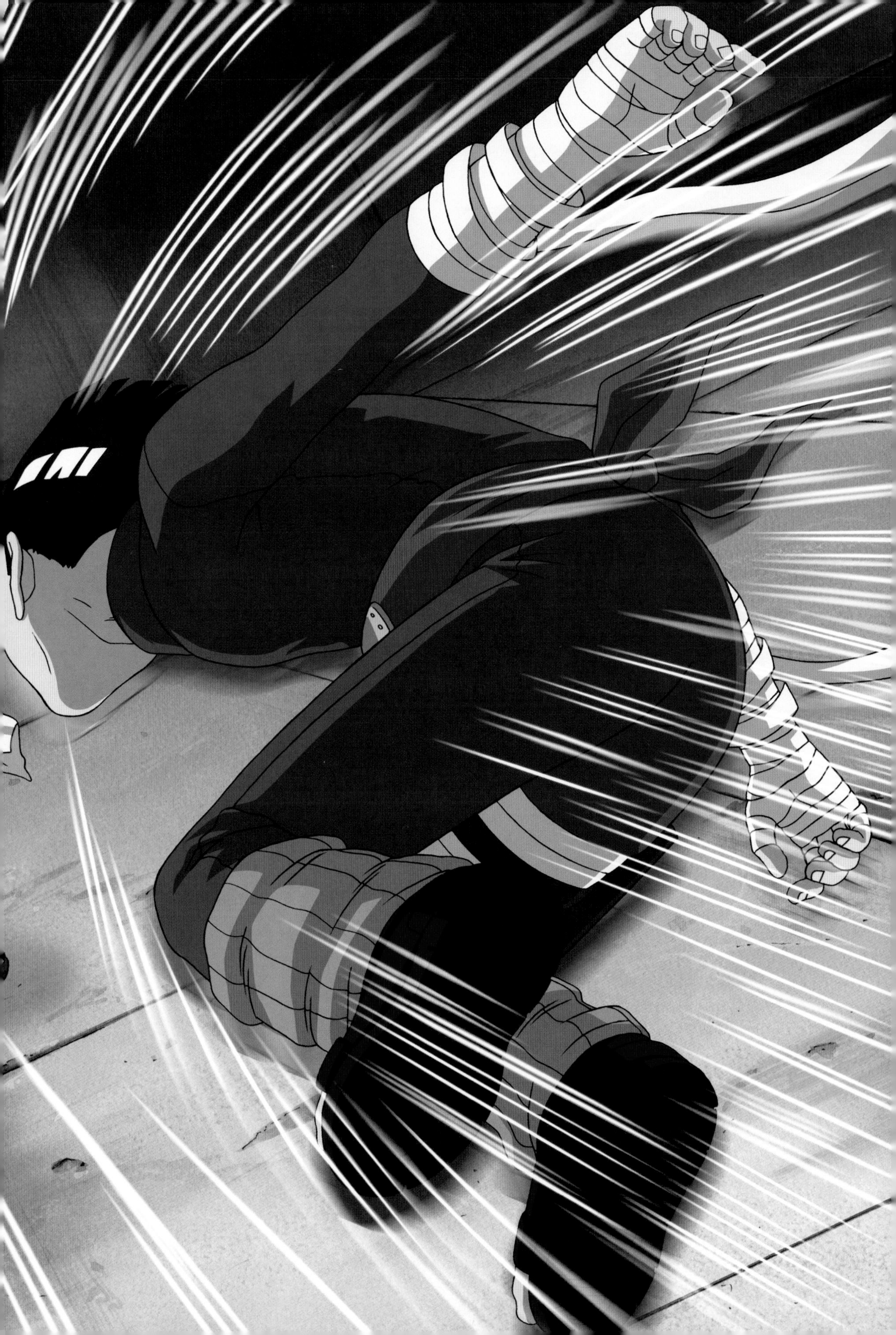

Gaara strikes!

Violent sand unleashed!

Defeating Lee's Primary Lotus, Gaara strikes back and exposes his true nature! With murderous glee, he blasts Lee with sand!

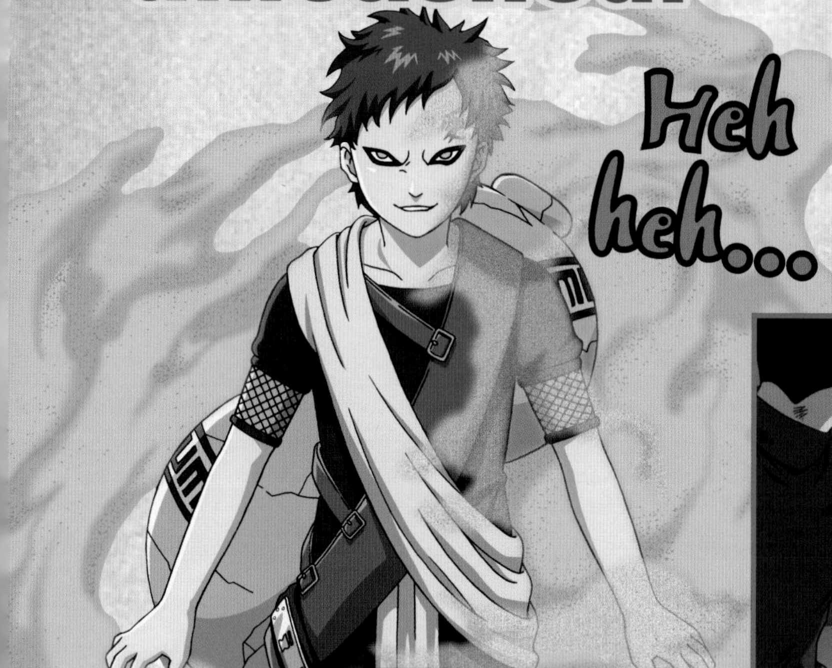
Heh heh...

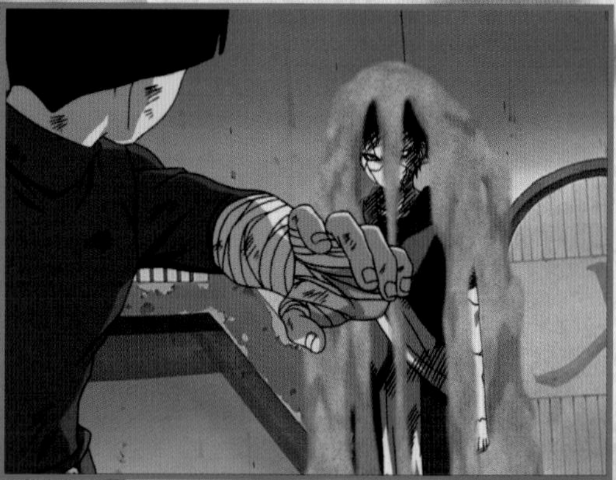

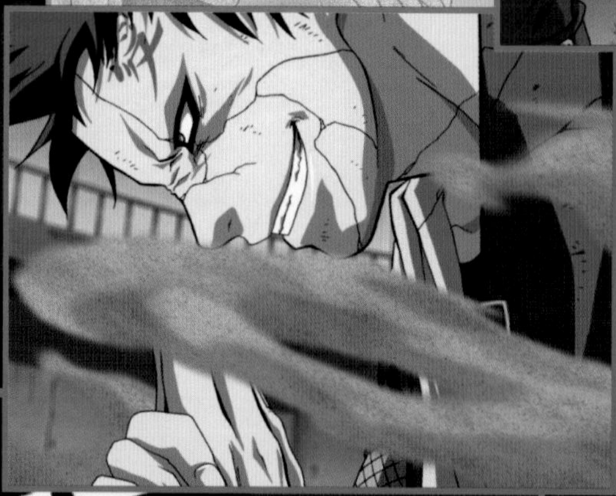

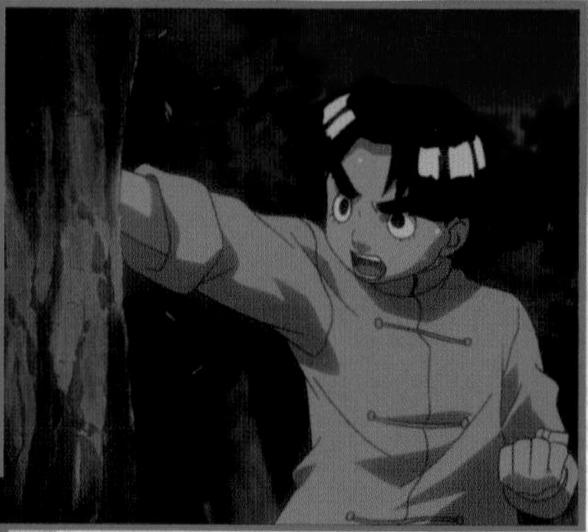

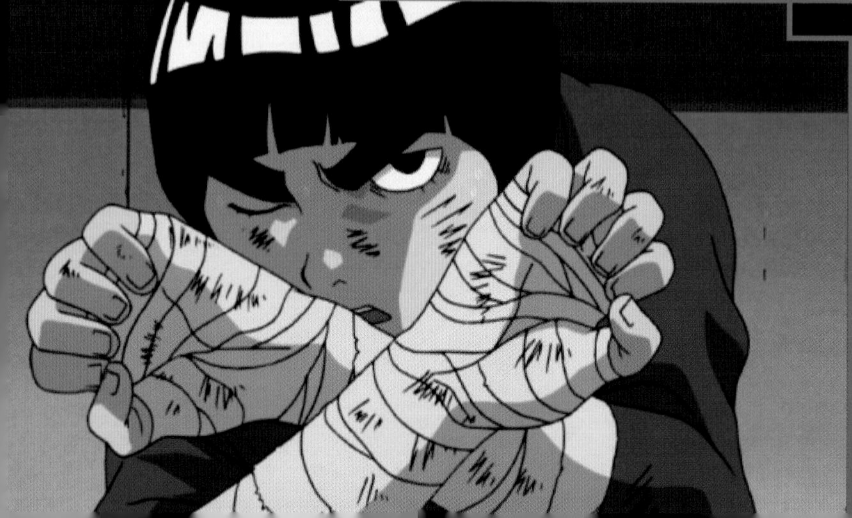

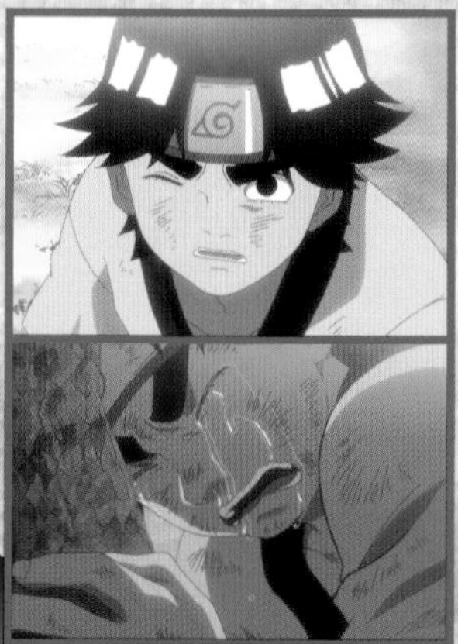

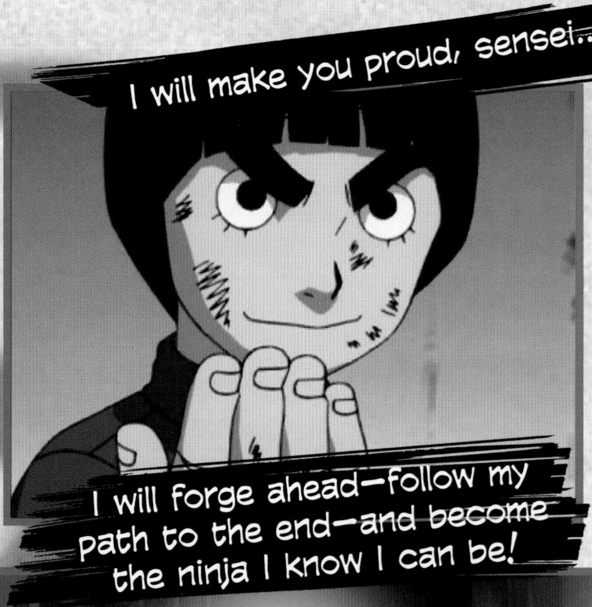
I will make you proud, sensei...
I will forge ahead—follow my path to the end—and become the ninja I know I can be!

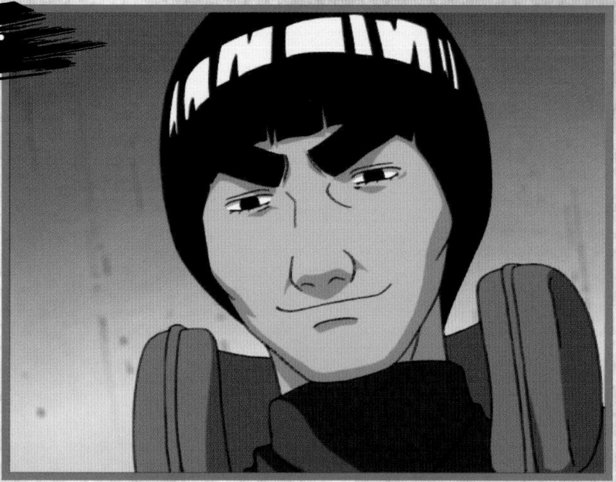

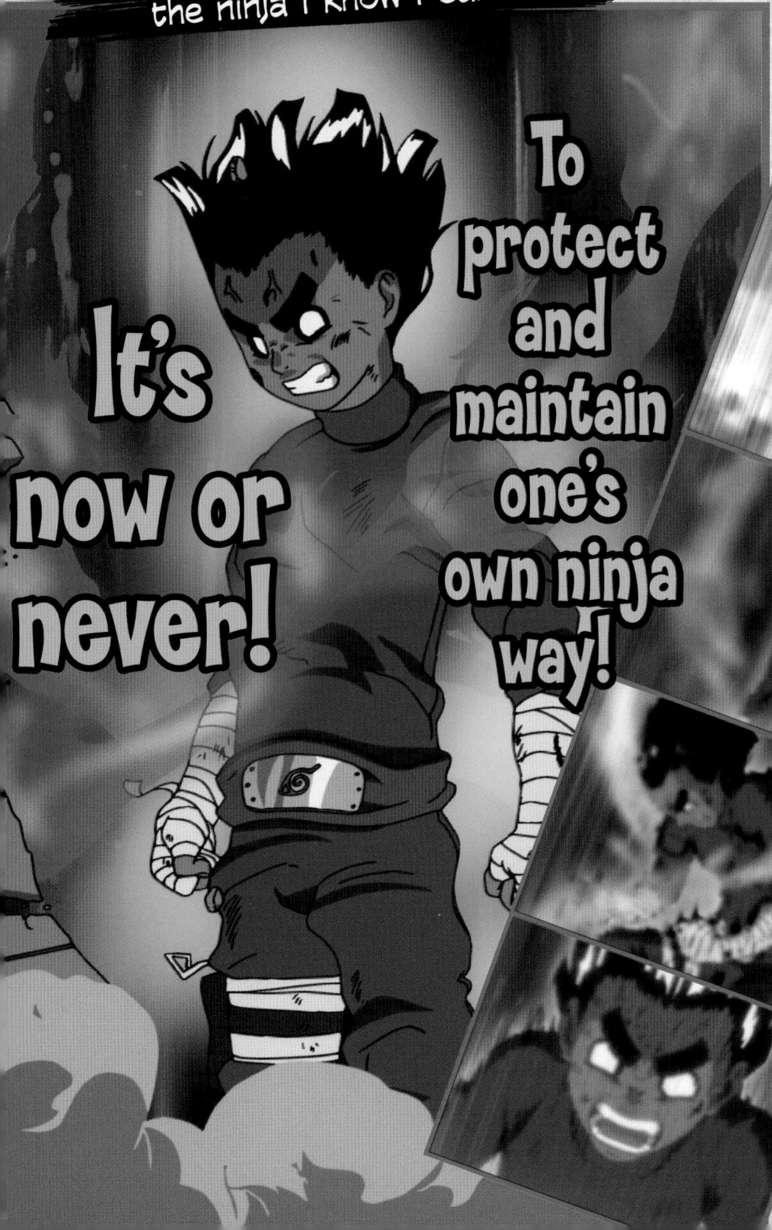
It's now or never!
To protect and maintain one's own ninja way!

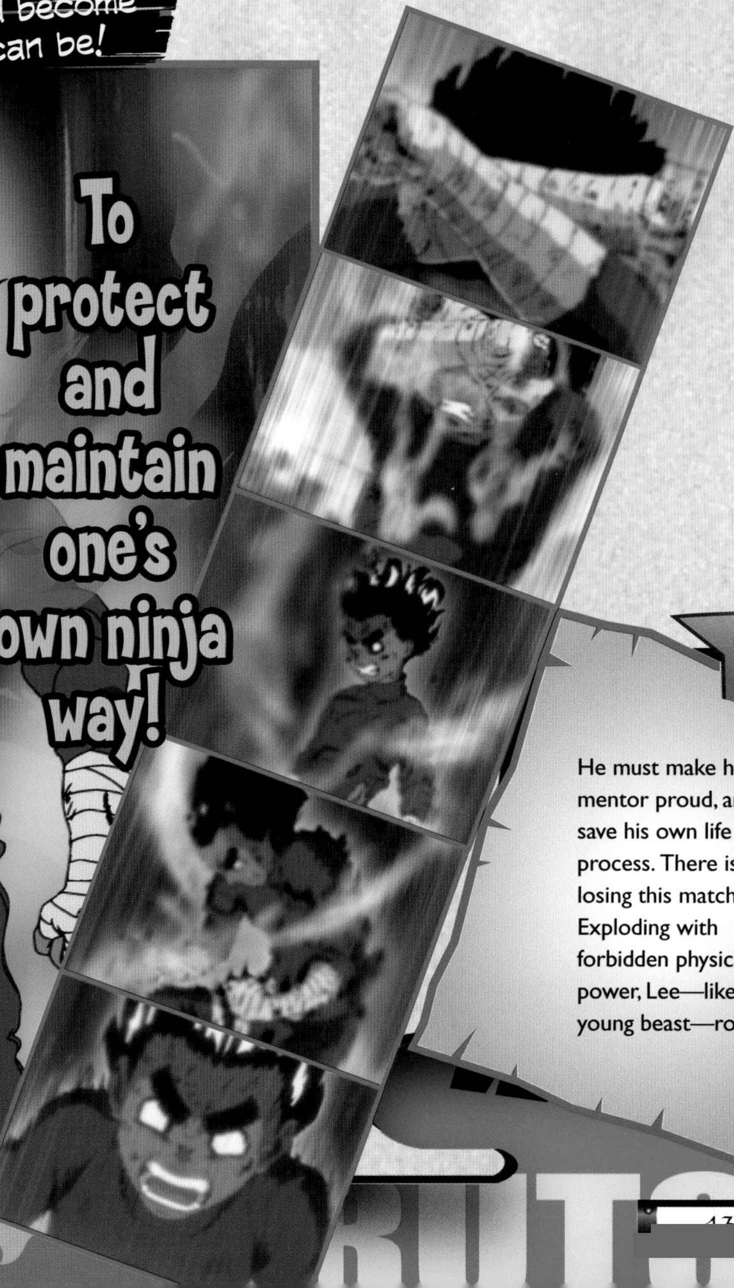

He must make his mentor proud, and save his own life in the process. There is no losing this match! Exploding with forbidden physical power, Lee—like a young beast—roars!

The finale!

The last battle of the prelims! And behind the scenes— a dark plot!

Match # 10.

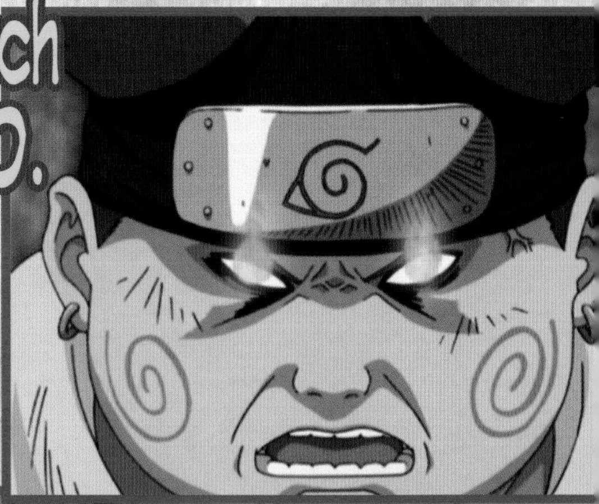

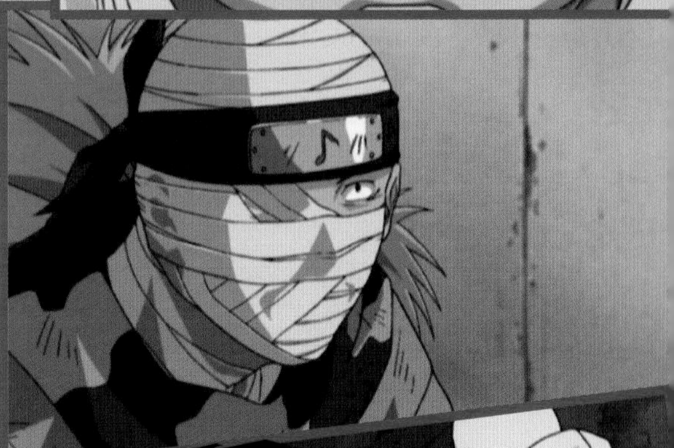

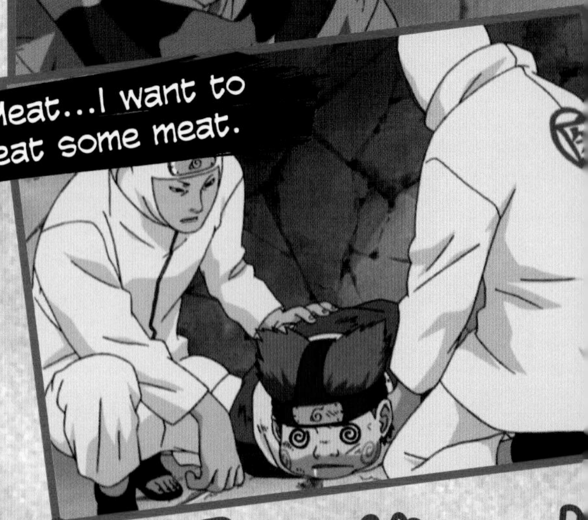
Meat...I want to eat some meat.

The young ninja arrive at the final match! The Sound ninja Dosu wants to battle Sasuke, and Choji wants some barbequed meat! Neither will back down! However...

The winner is... Dosu Kinuta!

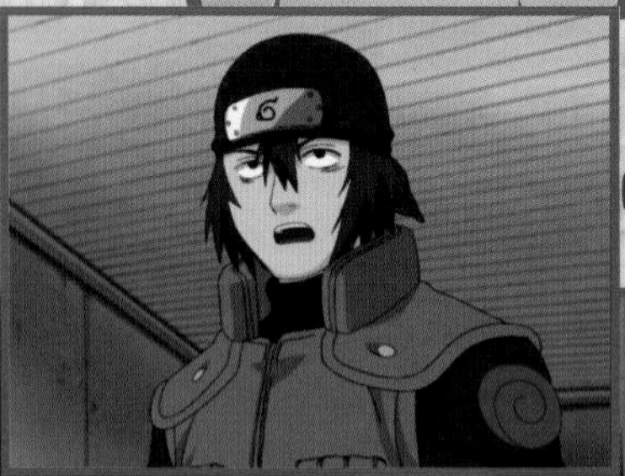

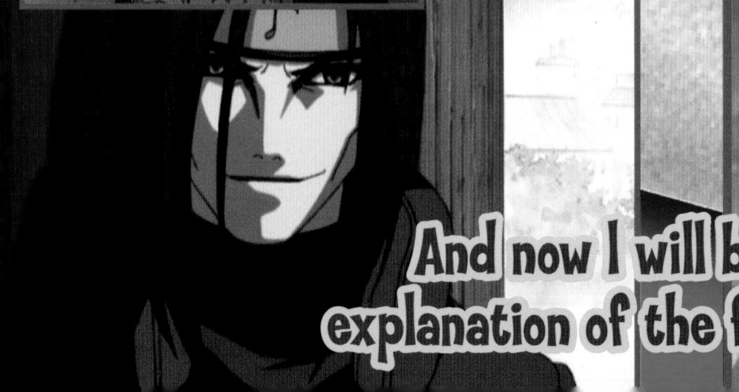

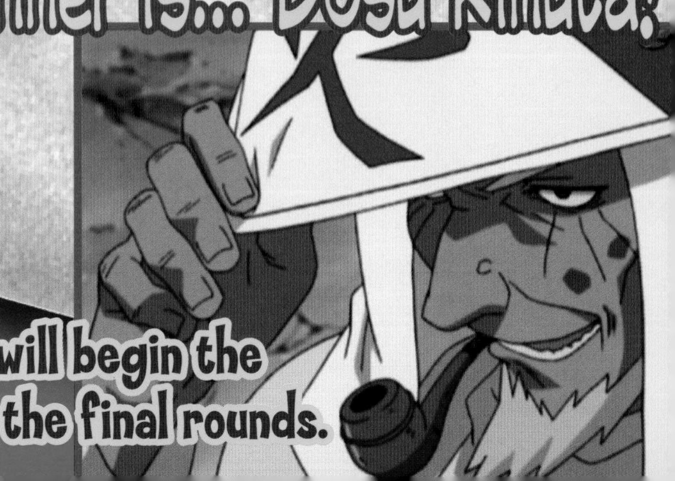
And now I will begin the explanation of the final rounds.

Orochimaru's assassin creeps up!

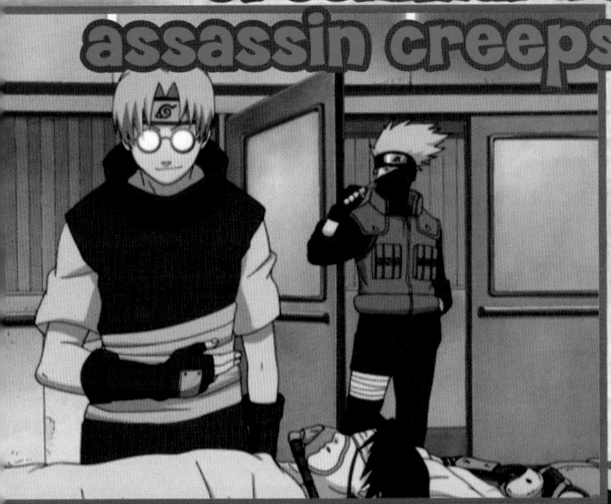

During the preliminary rounds, Orochimaru resumes his schemes. On orders from Orochimaru, Kabuto sneaks into Sasuke's hospital room. Kakashi arrives on the scene in the nick of time and an explosive conflict erupts!

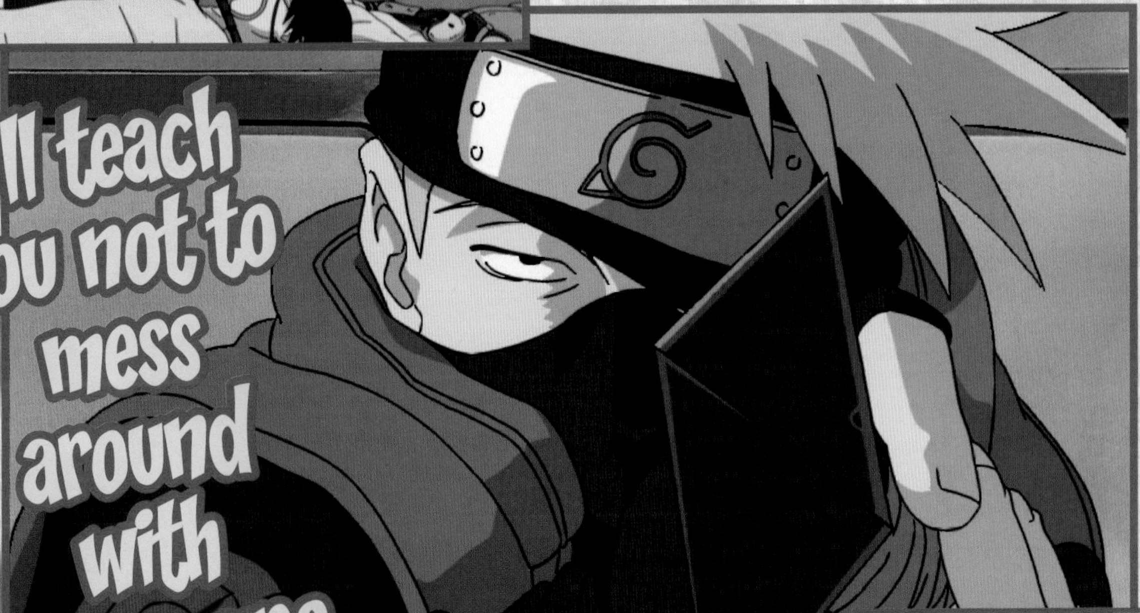
I'll teach you not to mess around with grown-ups.

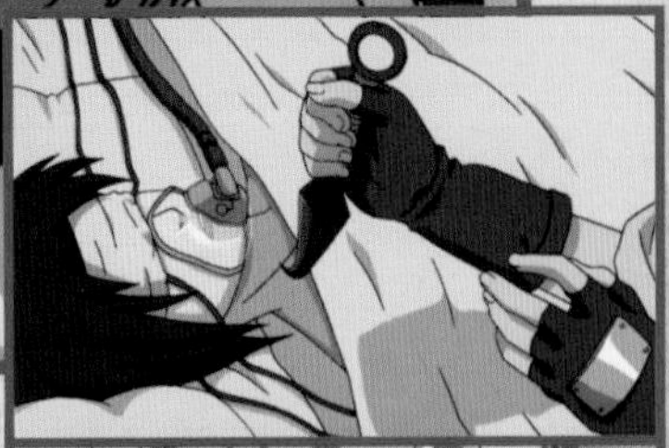

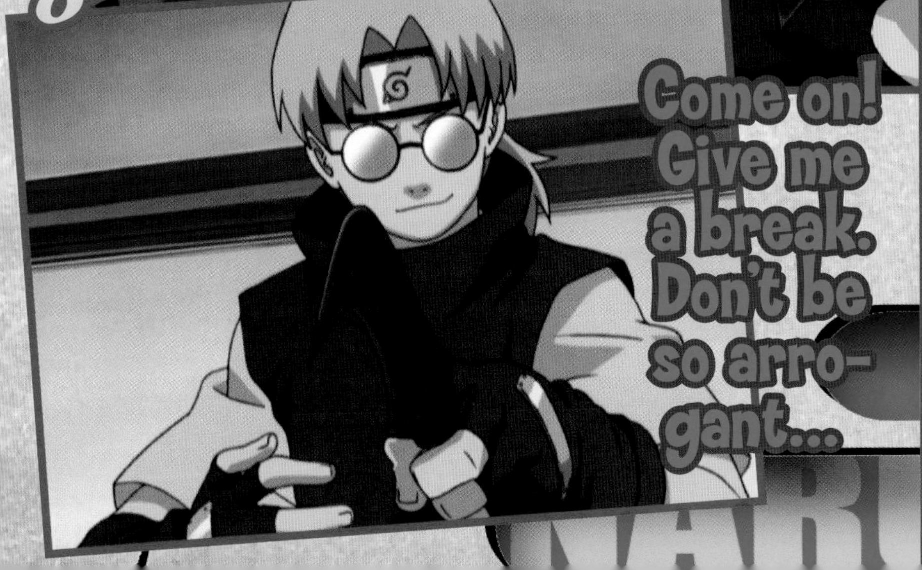
Come on! Give me a break. Don't be so arro-gant...

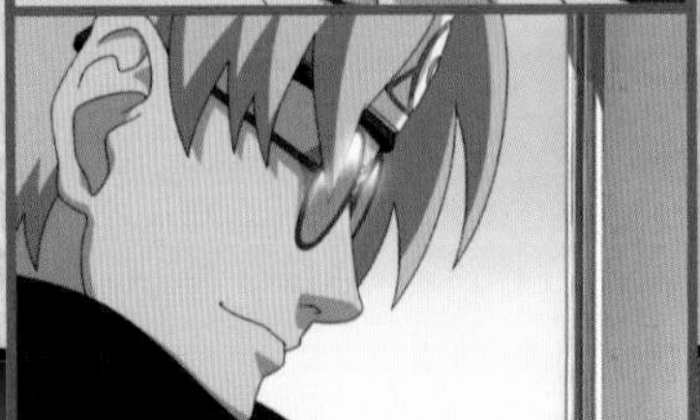

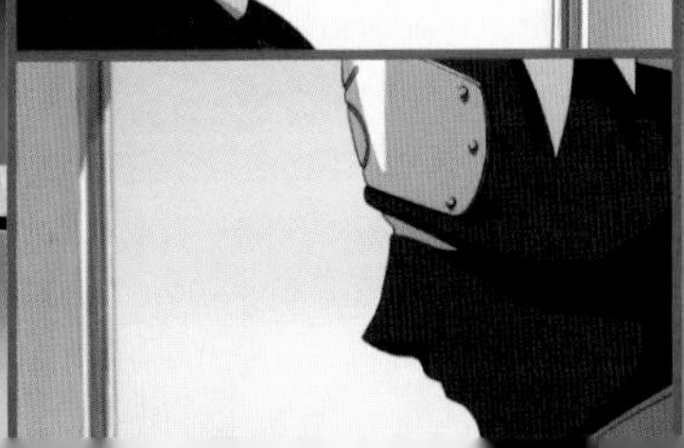

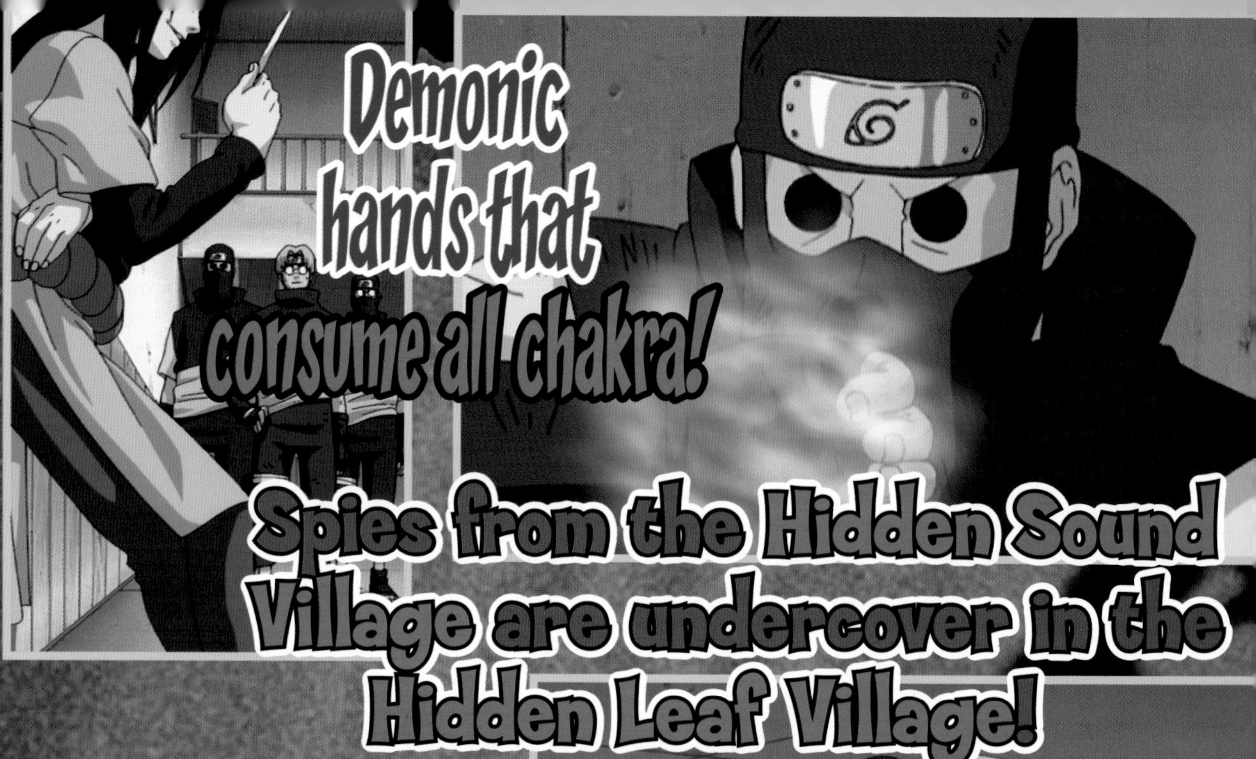
Demonic hands that consume all chakra!
Spies from the Hidden Sound Village are undercover in the Hidden Leaf Village!

Orochimaru's Squad!
Masquerading as Leaf shinobi, a highly skilled three-man squad engages in espionage under Orochimaru's command. Yoroi absorbs his opponent's chakra with his palm. Misumi has complete control over all the joints in his body and can dislocate or manipulate them at will. Kabuto works underground while concealing his true abilities. They work together for their assignments but they share no camaraderie.

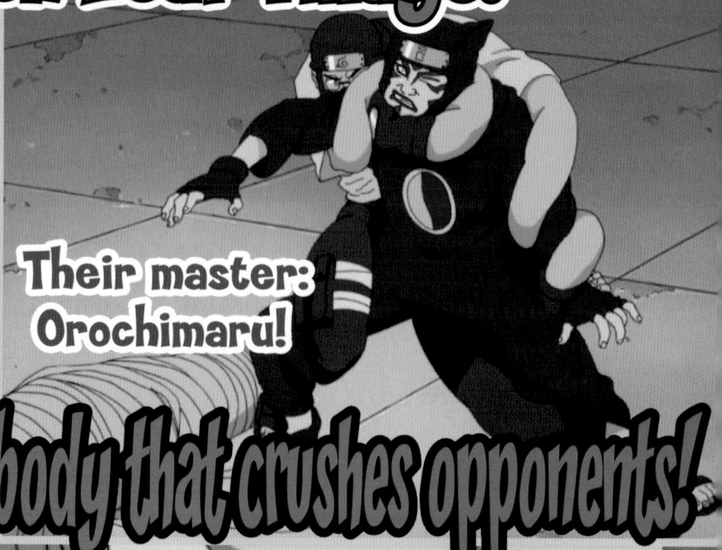
Their master: Orochimaru!
A flexible body that crushes opponents!

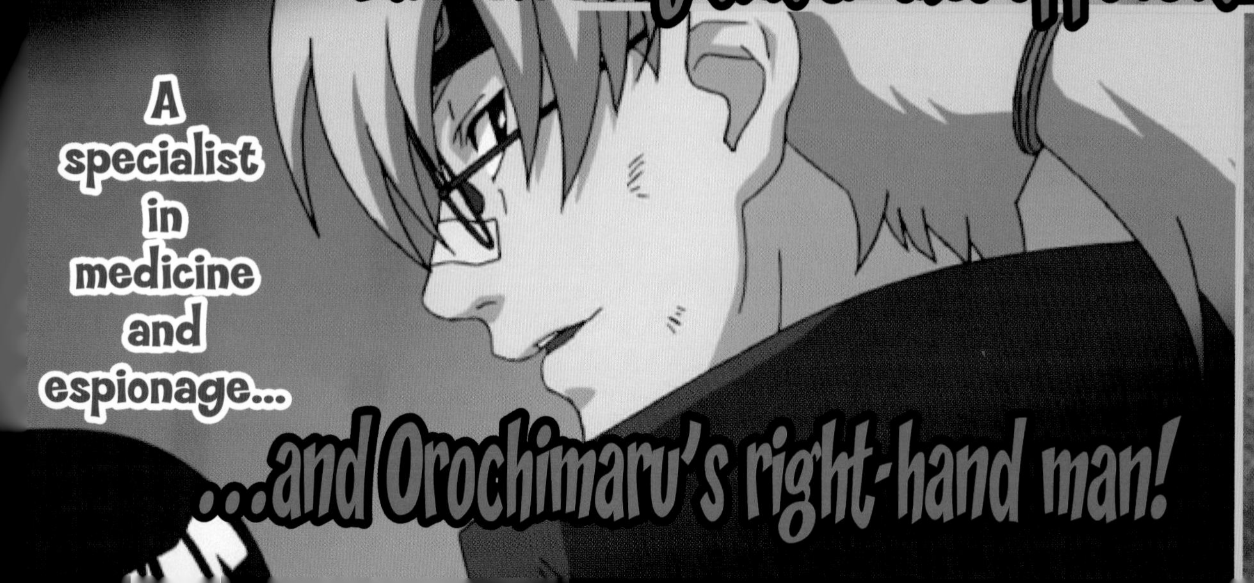
A specialist in medicine and espionage...
...and Orochimaru's right-hand man!

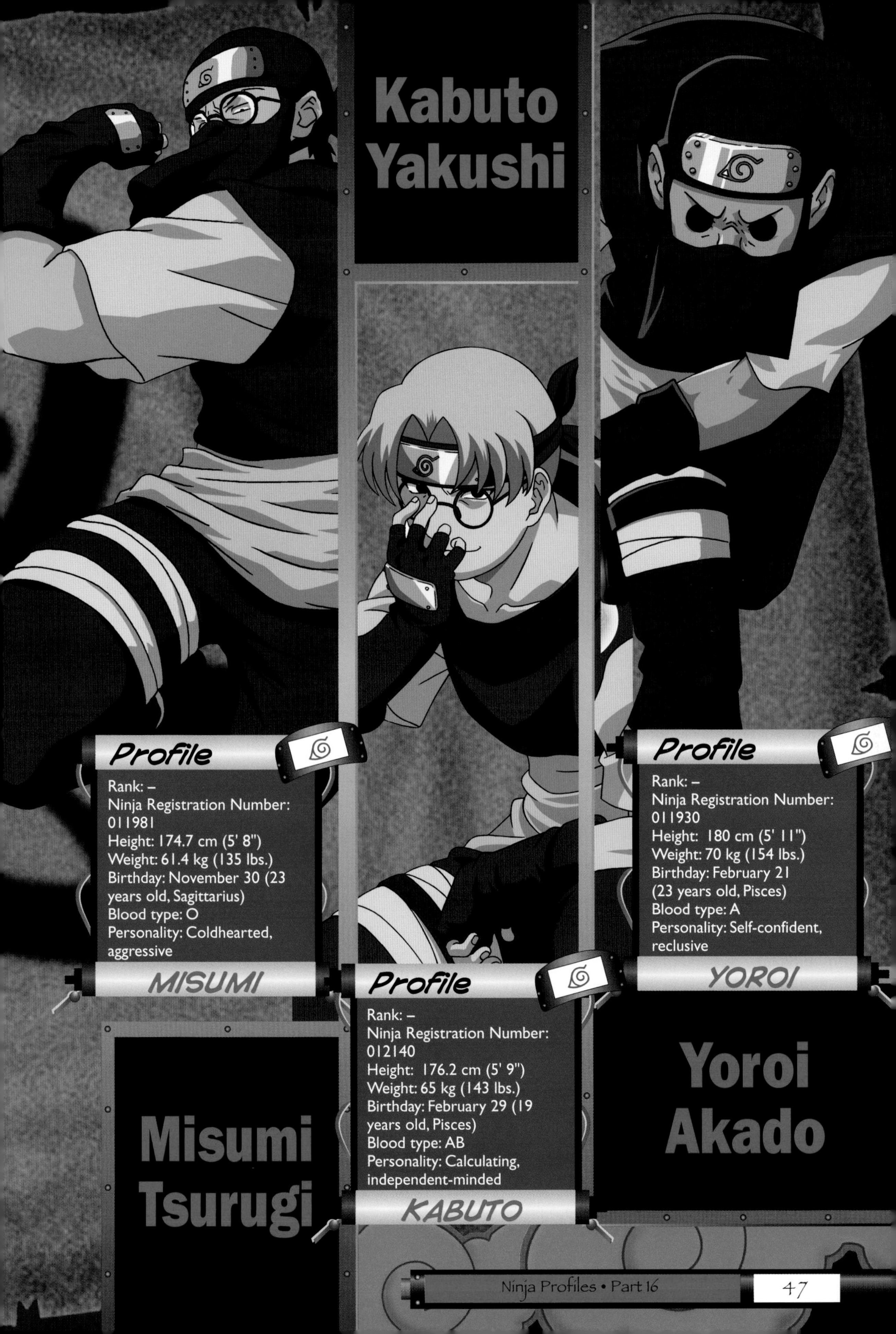

Kabuto Yakushi

Profile

Rank: –
Ninja Registration Number: 012140
Height: 176.2 cm (5' 9")
Weight: 65 kg (143 lbs.)
Birthday: February 29 (19 years old, Pisces)
Blood type: AB
Personality: Calculating, independent-minded

KABUTO

Misumi Tsurugi

Profile

Rank: –
Ninja Registration Number: 011981
Height: 174.7 cm (5' 8")
Weight: 61.4 kg (135 lbs.)
Birthday: November 30 (23 years old, Sagittarius)
Blood type: O
Personality: Coldhearted, aggressive

MISUMI

Yoroi Akado

Profile

Rank: –
Ninja Registration Number: 011930
Height: 180 cm (5' 11")
Weight: 70 kg (154 lbs.)
Birthday: February 21 (23 years old, Pisces)
Blood type: A
Personality: Self-confident, reclusive

YOROI

Haruka Kanata

You may have noticed that *Naruto* had a new theme song beginning with Episode 53. The first hard-driving *Naruto* opening number for Episodes 1-52, by Jeremy Sweet and Ian Nickus, was in English and was called *Rise, Tsuyosa!* But things changed when *Haruka Kanata (Far and Away)* by Asian Kung-Fu Generation became the new ninja anthem. In Japan, this awesome song started way back at Episode 26. America took a while to catch up. But it was worth the wait!

So if you've ever wondered what the new theme was all about, here are all the high-octane lyrics from *Haruka Kanata!*

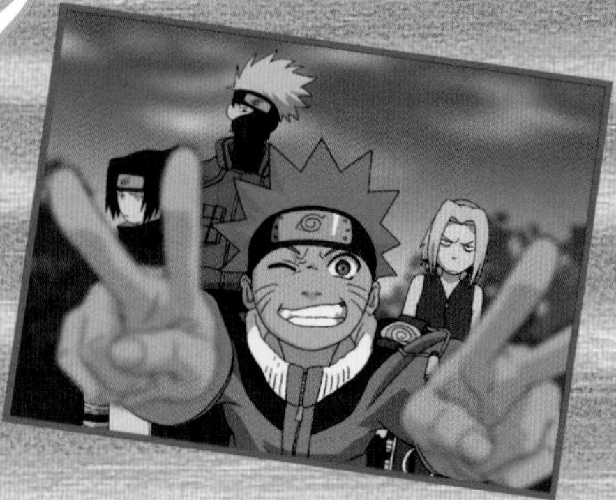

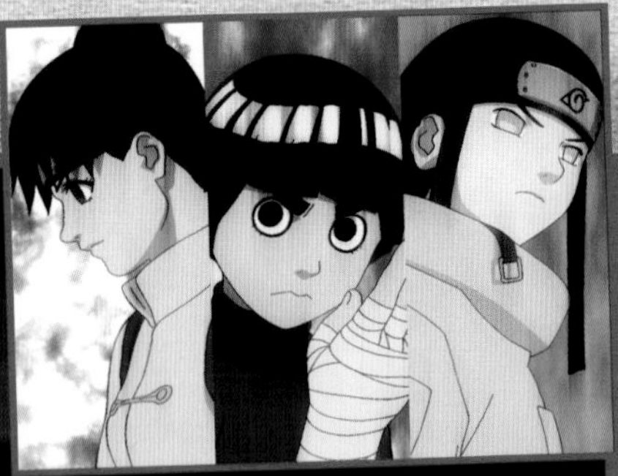

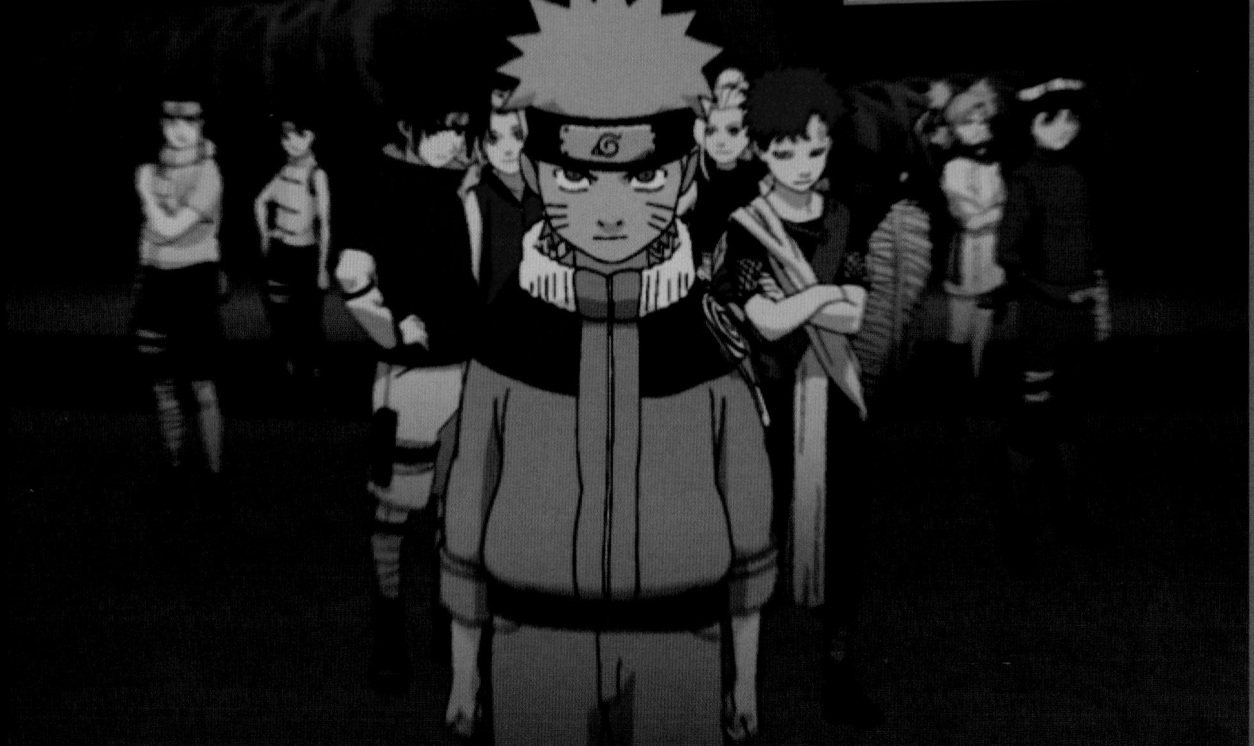

♪ (Far and Away) ♪

遥か彼方
Haruka Kanata (Far and Away)

踏み込むぜ　アクセル
Press down hard on the gas
駆け引きは無いさ、そうだよ
That's right, there's no compromise
夜をぬける
We'll slip through the night
ねじ込むさ　最後に
At the final moment push hard
差し引きゼロさ、そうだよ
That's right, all the way to zero
日々を削る
Until we wipe away the days

心をそっと開いて
Gently open your heart
ギュッと引き寄せたら
If you pull it close to you
届くよ　きっと
It will reach you, without a doubt
伝うよ　もっと
It will come closer

生き急いで　搾り取って
We're speeding through life,
squeezing it for all it's worth
縺れる足　だけど前より
Our feet are tied
ずっとそう、遠くへ
But we still keep going farther

奪い取って　掴んだって
Even if I take it back, and grasp it
君じゃないなら
If you're not the one
意味は無いのさ
There will be no meaning
だからもっと遥か彼方
And so we'll go far and away.

CREDITS:
Song: *Haruka Kanata (Far and Away)*
Music & Lyrics: Masafumi Gotoh
Artist: Asian Kung-Fu Generation
U.S. Episodes: 53-77

It's all about fashion sense! Who's more stylin'?!

ALL-OUT FASHION FACE-OFF! Sakura vs Ino

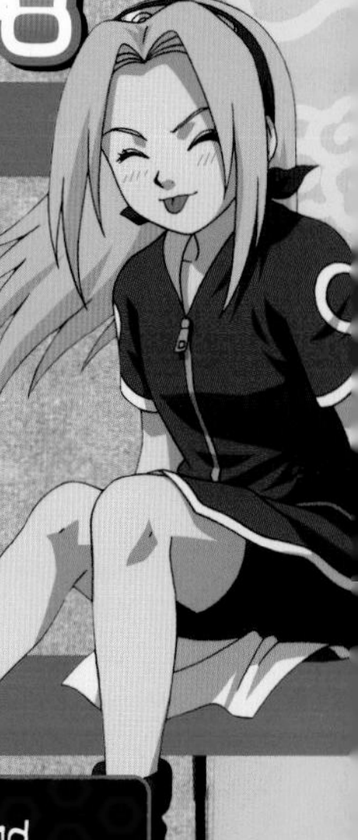

Battle No. 1: Accessories Showdown

Ino's choice!

Shikamaru's earrings

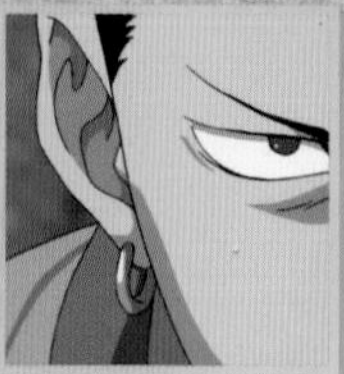

It's not just Shikamaru. Me and Choji wear earrings, too. 'Cause my team's got style!

Sakura's choice!

Lee's "guts" weights

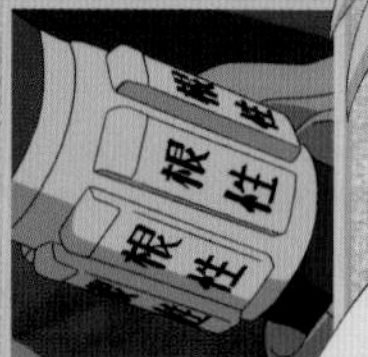

根性
根性

The word "guts" really fits Lee. I'm not into his annoying personality, but I will say these are pretty cool.

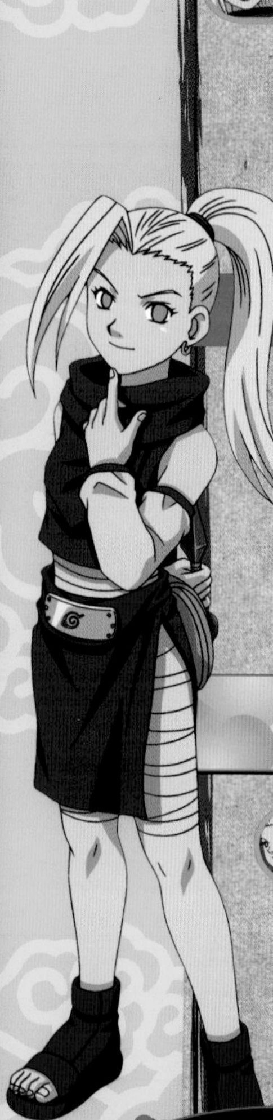

Battle No. 2: Headbands

Ino's choice!

Choji's headband

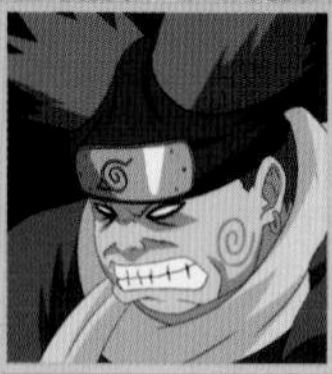

It looks like he's wearing under-wear on his head. It's probably custom-made to fit his hairstyle!

Sakura's choice!

Neiji's headband

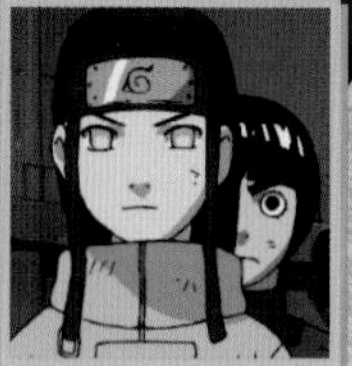

Neji's headband has straps that adjust behind his head. It's probably custom-made to fit his hairstyle!

Battle No. 3: Sasuke Square-Off

Ino's choice!

Sasuke's wristbands ♥

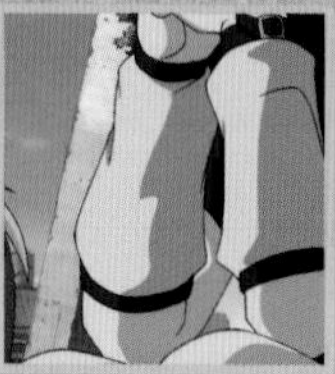

Hey, look! Mine are just like Sasuke's! It must be destiny!

Sakura's choice!

Sasuke's hairstyle ♥

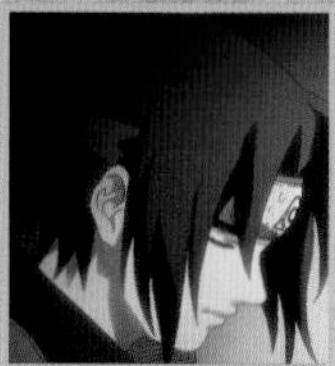

So manly and sexy…it's sinful—pure sin! I dream of the day I can style his gorgeous hair…

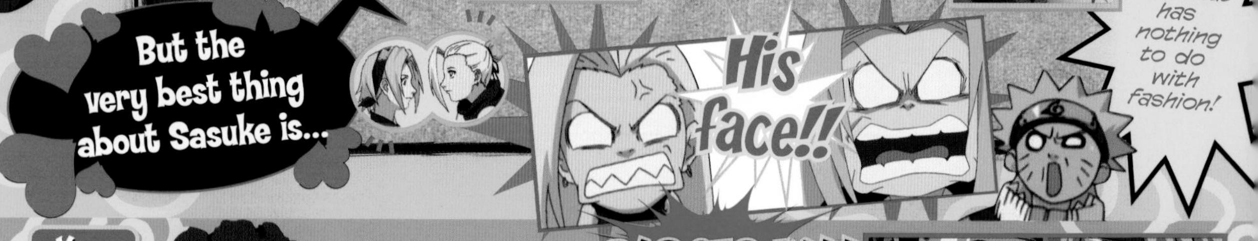

But the very best thing about Sasuke is...
His face!!
But that has nothing to do with fashion!

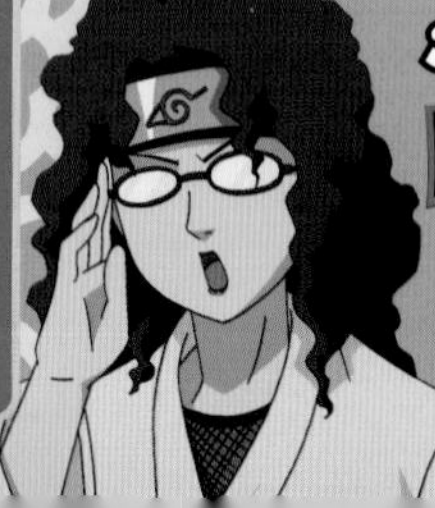

You just don't get it yet!

SUZUME-SENSEI BARGES IN!! Eyewear Collection 2007

Glasses make a man so attractive. Yeah, these guys are so cool…

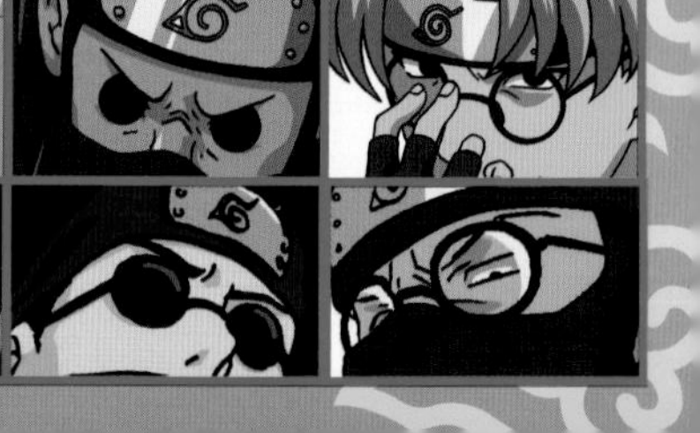

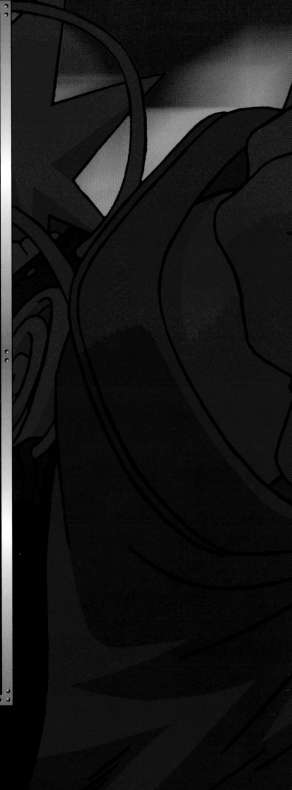

The Ninja Way: Tales of Bravery

Third Exam Preliminaries Episodes

Episodes 38 to 51: After passing the second exam, Naruto and the others proceed to the next challenge. The third exam begins!

Everyone's chakra is ablaze for the prelims!

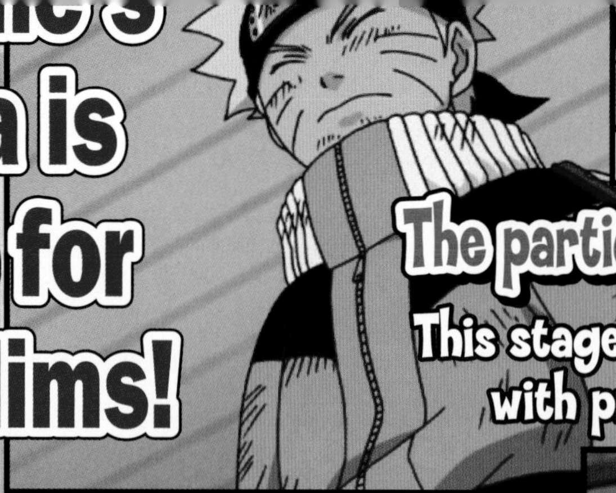

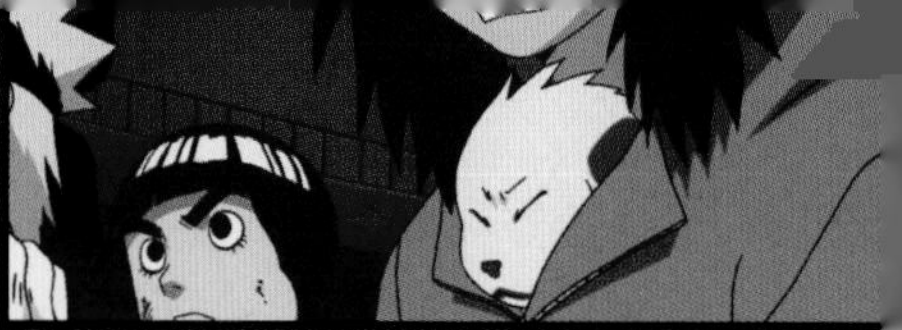

The participants are stunned!!

This stage of the exam will begin with preliminary rounds?!

How do Naruto and the others react to the unexpected situation?

The announcement of prelims for the third exam causes mass confusion. Sakura is further distracted by her concern over the curse mark on Sasuke. She desperately tries to convince Sasuke to bow out, but even she can't compete with Sasuke's will to follow his nindo…

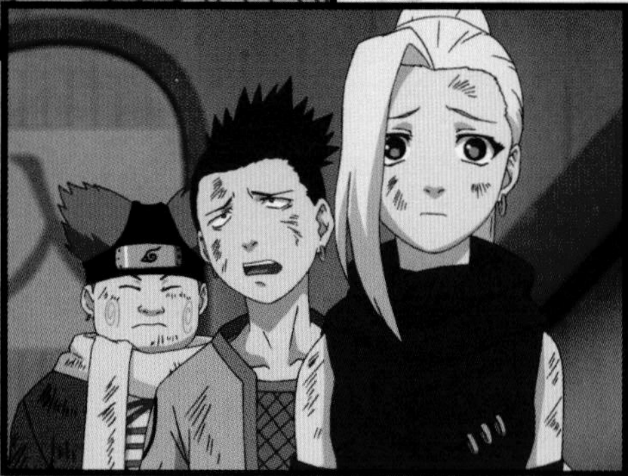

⬆ Everyone is mentally and physically exhausted after risking life and limb in the second exam…

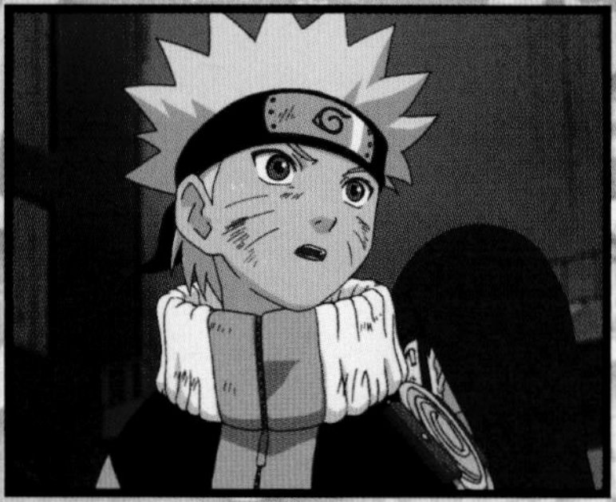

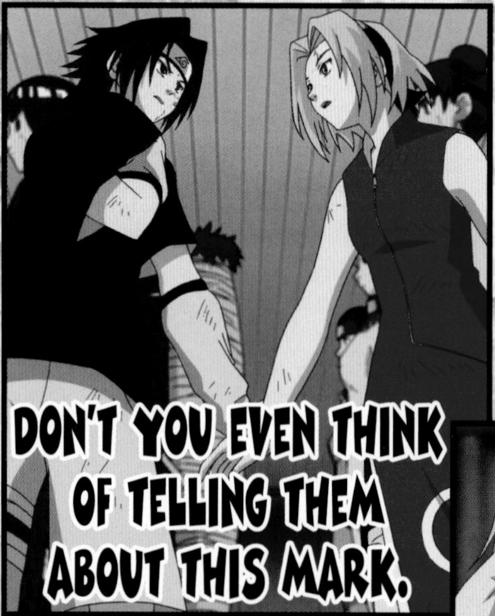
DON'T YOU EVEN THINK OF TELLING THEM ABOUT THIS MARK.

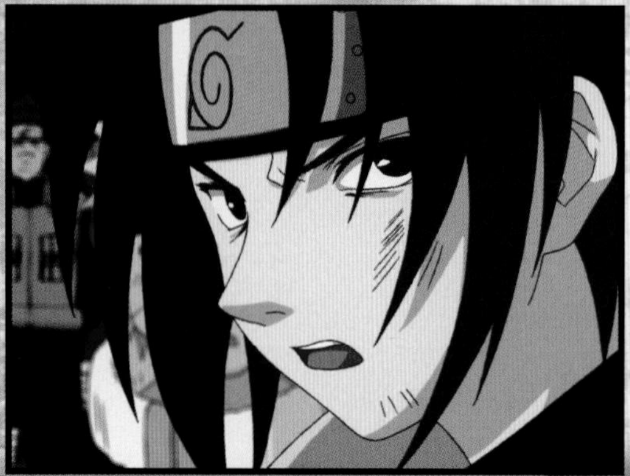

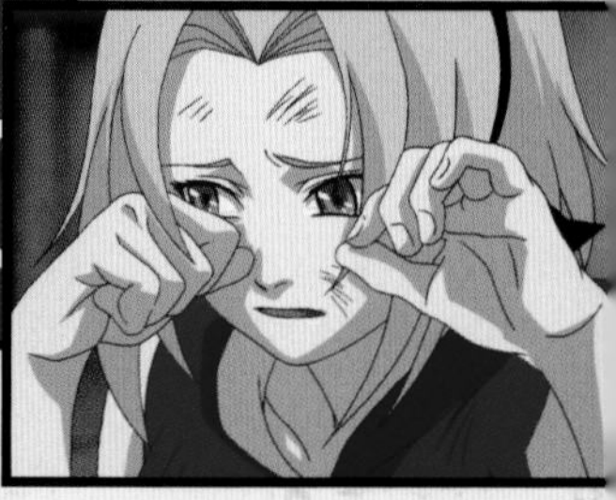

➡⬆ Sakura witnessed something she never wants to see again: Sasuke's transformation during the battle with the Sound ninja.

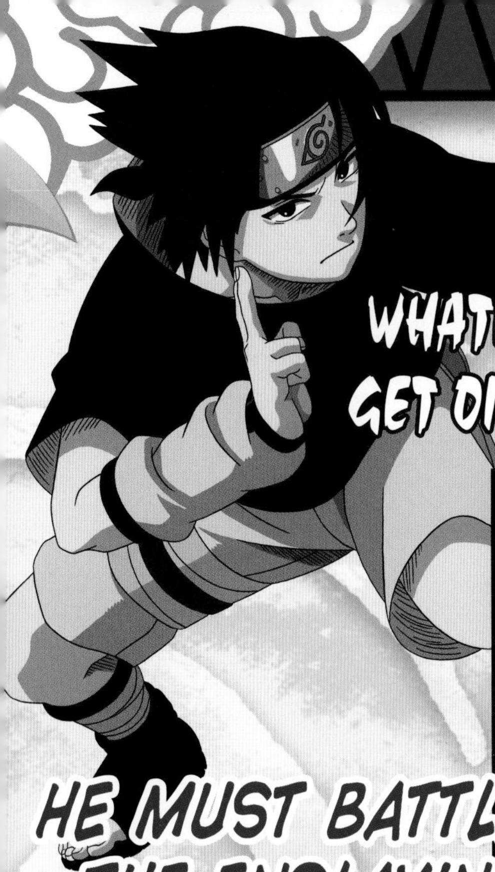

WHATEVER. LET'S GET ON WITH THIS.

The enemy within...! Orochimaru's mark possesses Sasuke!

In the heat of battle, the curse mark on Sasuke's neck takes over. As a shinobi, a member of the Uchiha clan and an avenger, Sasuke uses his fighter's instinct to shake off Orochimaru's hold.

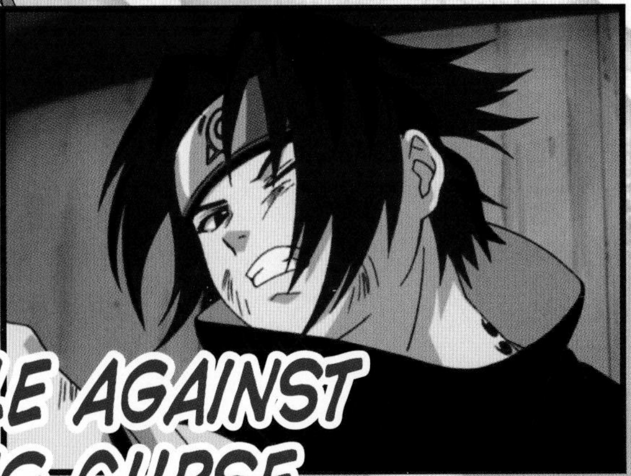

⬅ The curse mark has a terrifying power. Sasuke struggles to use his chakra properly.

HE MUST BATTLE AGAINST THE ENSLAVING CURSE.

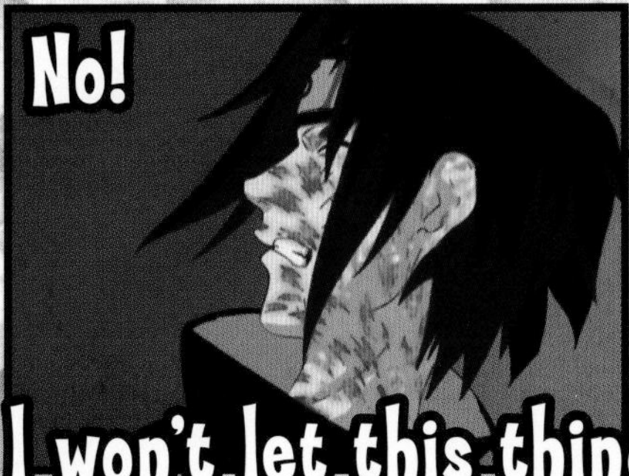

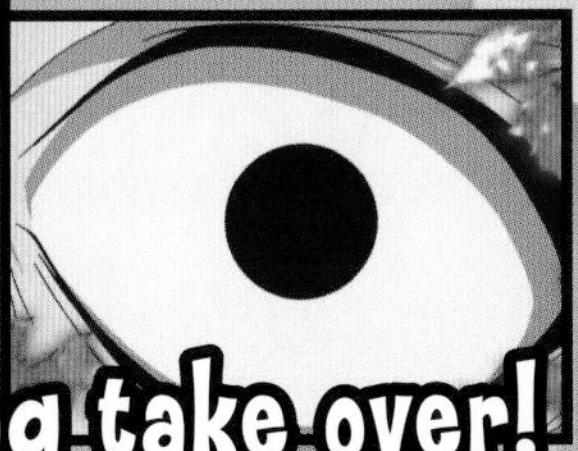

No!

I won't let this thing take over!

⬆ A nightmare revisited?! Through sheer willpower, Sasuke overcomes Orochimaru's jutsu!!

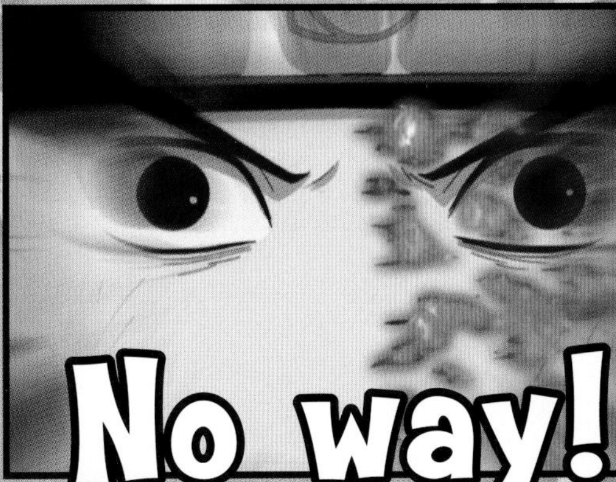

No way!

Rules for the prelims:

1. Matches are one-on-one individual combat.
2. In combat, no moves are disallowed.
3. A winner is determined when one combatant concedes defeat, is rendered physically incapable of continuing, or dies.
4. Proctors may occasionally intervene and stop the match at their own discretion when the outcome is clear.
5. Only winners proceed to the third and final exam.

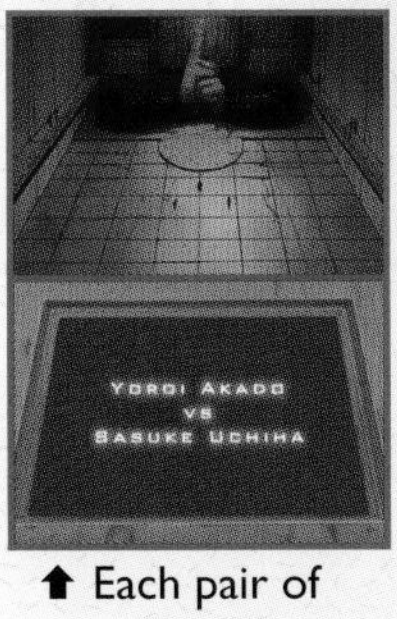
YOROI AKADO
VS
SASUKE UCHIHA

⬆ Each pair of opponents appears on the arena's display board.

Winners are determined by one-on-one combat.

According to the rules of the Chunin Exams, preliminary rounds may be held in order to reduce the number of candidates remaining for the third exam. However, this is rare, and it's the first time in five years that prelims have been held.

LOSING IS NOT AN OPTION!

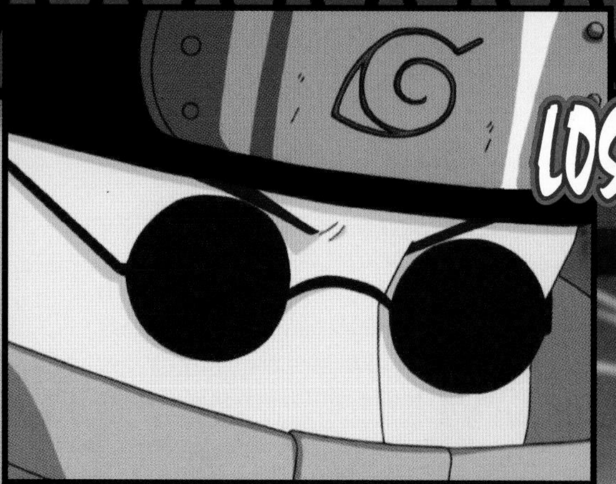

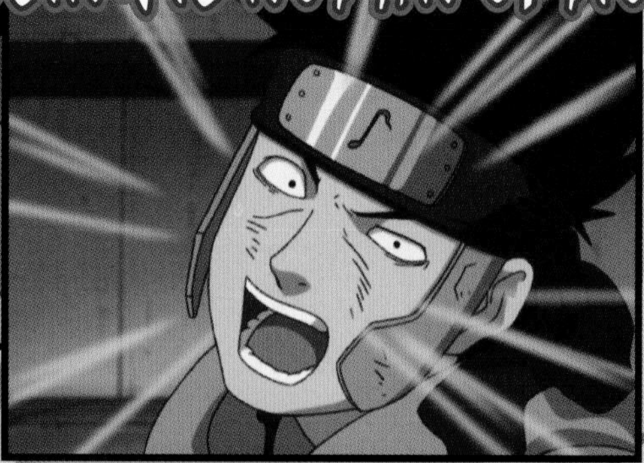

⬆➡ "Your defeat will be certain." Shino's words stir up Zaku's pride. He can't afford to lose!

There is a reason...

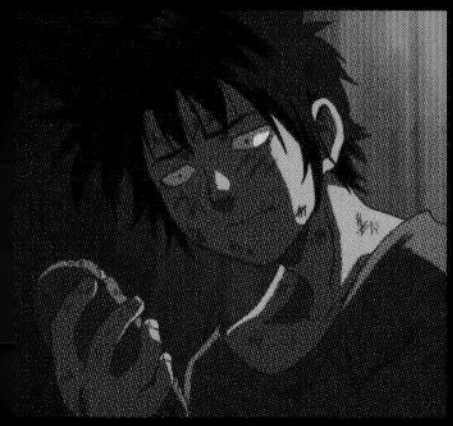

⬅⬇ Childhood days tainted with disgrace, when even a daily meal was uncertain...

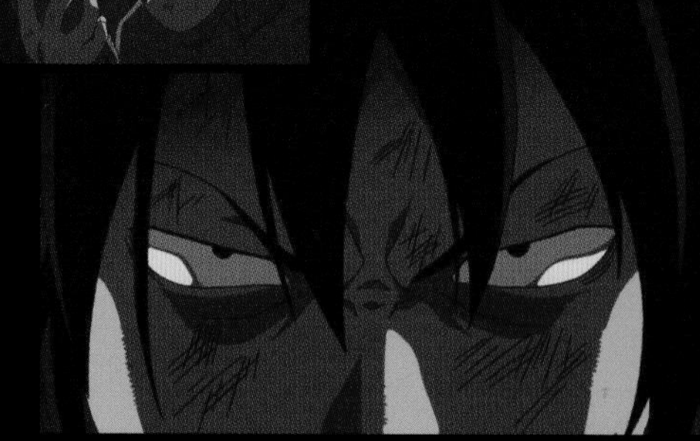

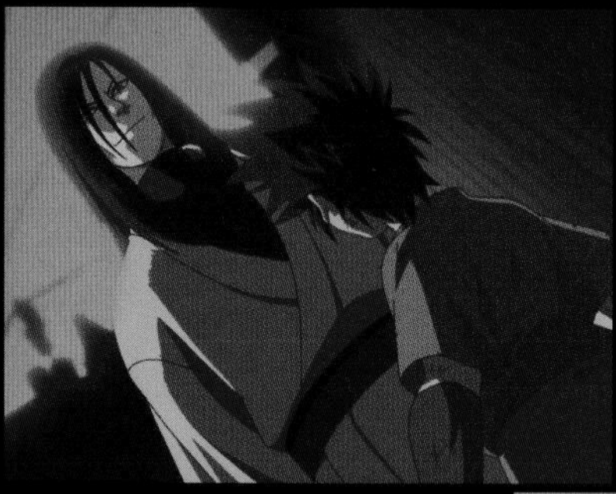

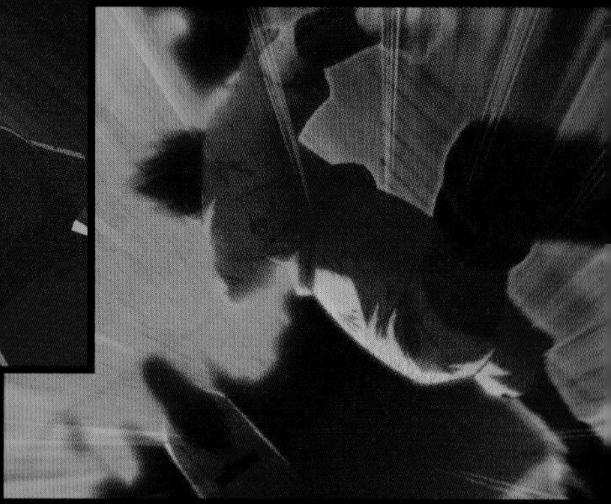

⬆➡ "I will make you strong, boy." Those words alone are Zaku's bond to Orochimaru.

...that losing is unacceptable

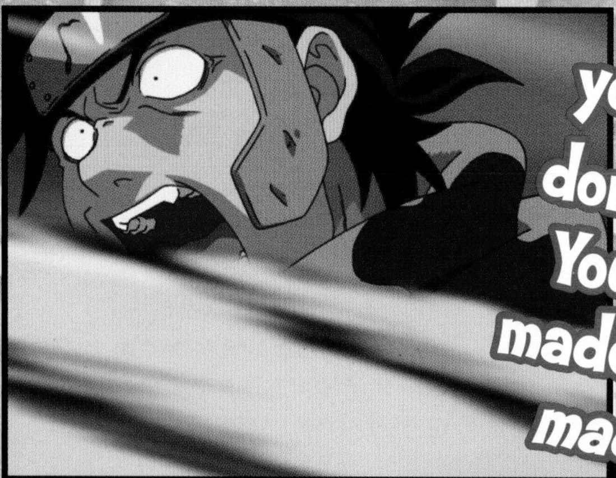

Now you've done it. You've made me mad!!

Pride and ego are Zaku's drive!

Now cornered, memories flash through Zaku's mind—of his miserable childhood and the time he first met Orochimaru. Zaku has always relentlessly pursued unmatchable power. Defeat is not an option and Zaku throws down his ace in the hole. But...?!

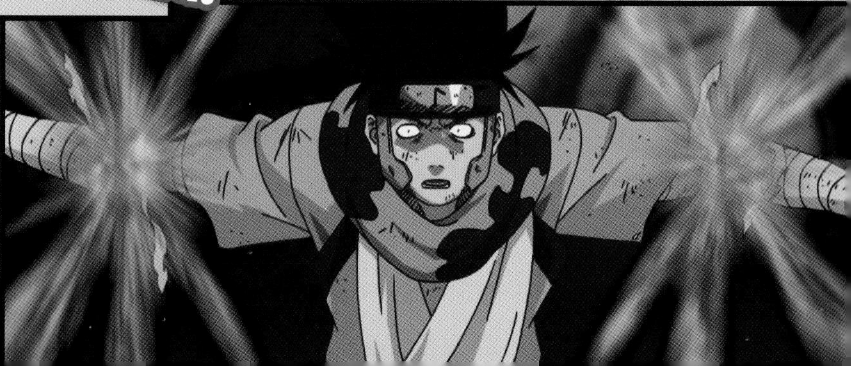

➡⬆ Zaku puts it all on the line and attempts to unleash the Slicing Sound Wave with both arms... But the moment Zaku tries, his arms are rendered useless...!

To protect Sasuke and the village, Kakashi faces down Orochimaru!

As Kakashi places a seal sign on Sasuke to suppress the curse mark, a dark shadow looms, and Orochimaru reveals his threat against the Hidden Leaf Village.

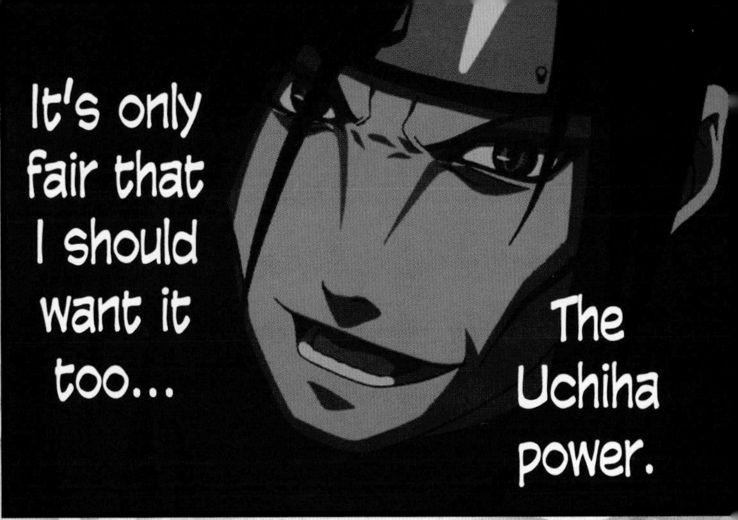
It's only fair that I should want it too...
The Uchiha power.

⬆ Orochimaru wants Sasuke in order to steal the bloodline trait of the Hidden Leaf Village's preeminent Uchiha clan. For this dark ambition, his giant snake fangs close in...

Orochimaru's terrifying ambition!

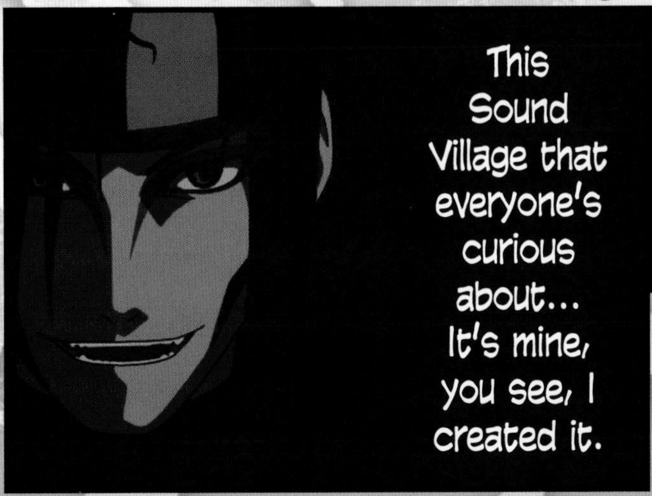
This Sound Village that everyone's curious about... It's mine, you see, I created it.

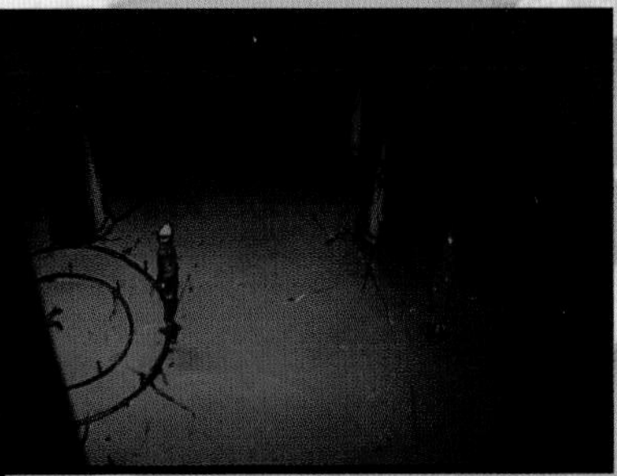

⬆ An ambition so great he created his own village to achieve it... What is his true objective...?

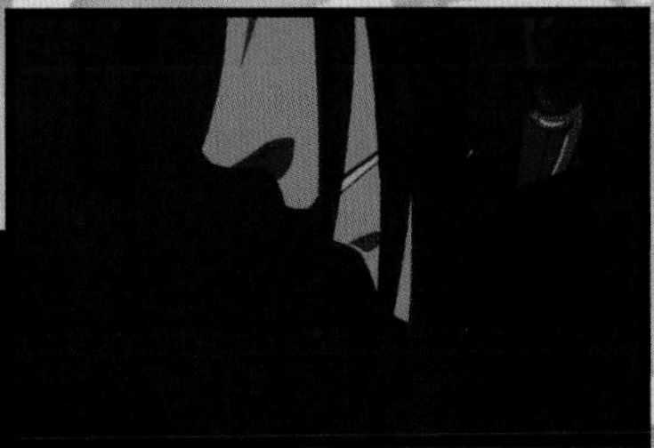

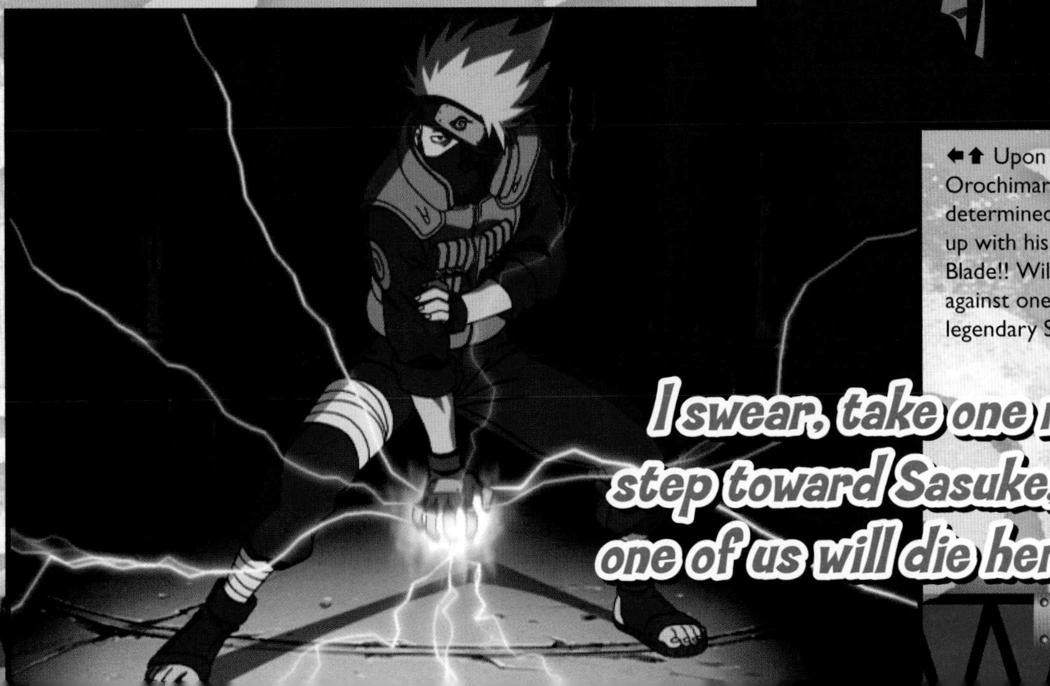
I swear, take one more step toward Sasuke, and one of us will die here.

⬅⬆ Upon hearing what Orochimaru is up to, a determined Kakashi steps up with his Lightning Blade!! Will it be enough against one of the legendary Sannin?!

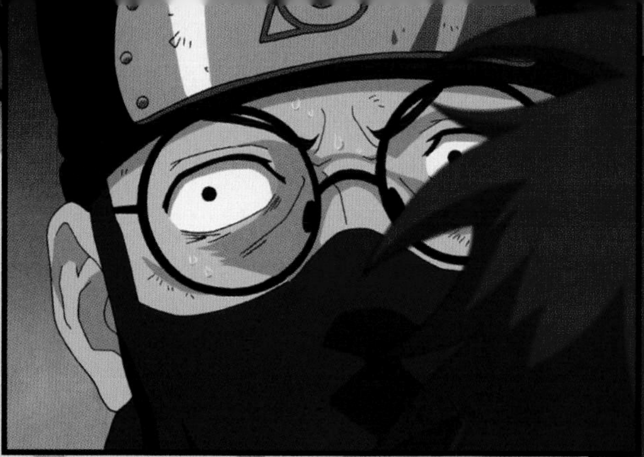

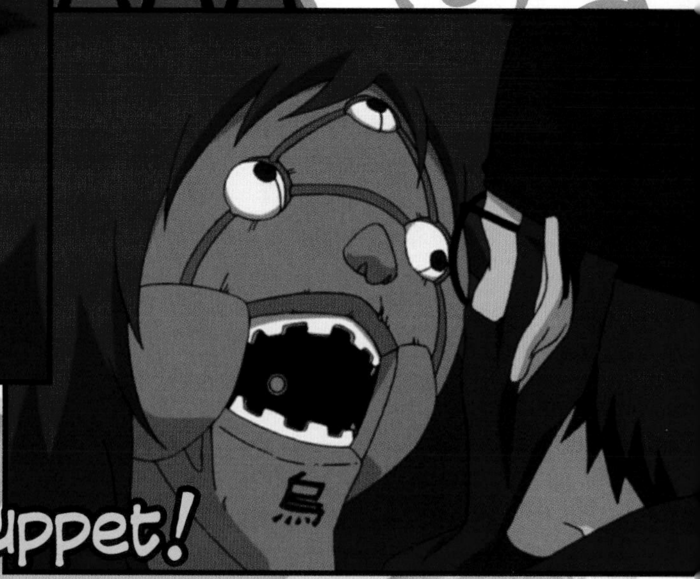

⬆➡ The whole time it was a ruse! As realization hits, Misumi's expression changes to dread…!

This is just a puppet!

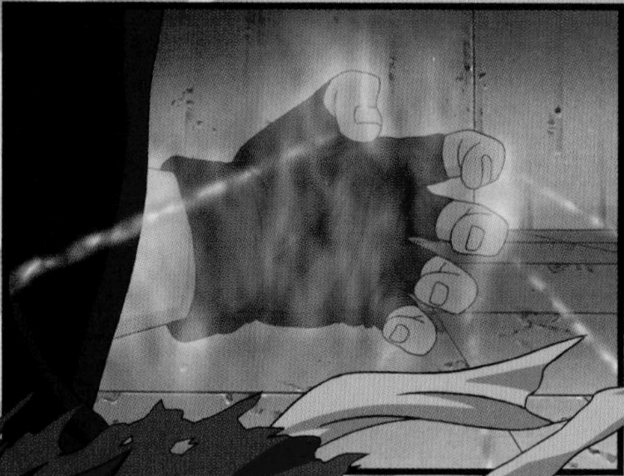

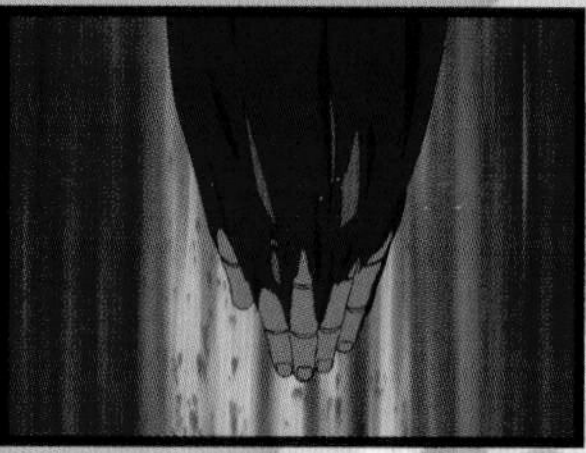

ENTANGLED BY THE DREADED DUMMY!

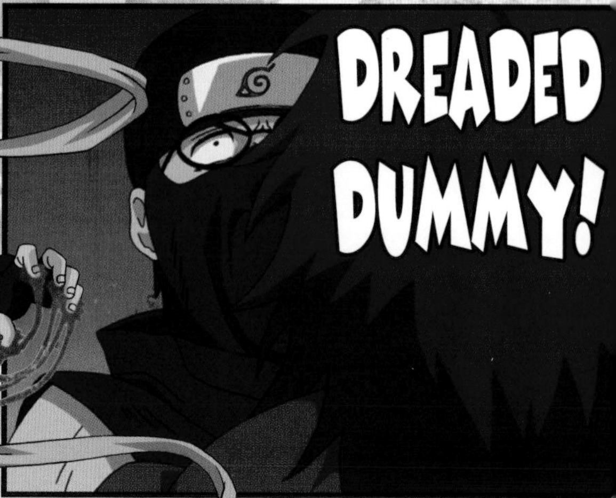

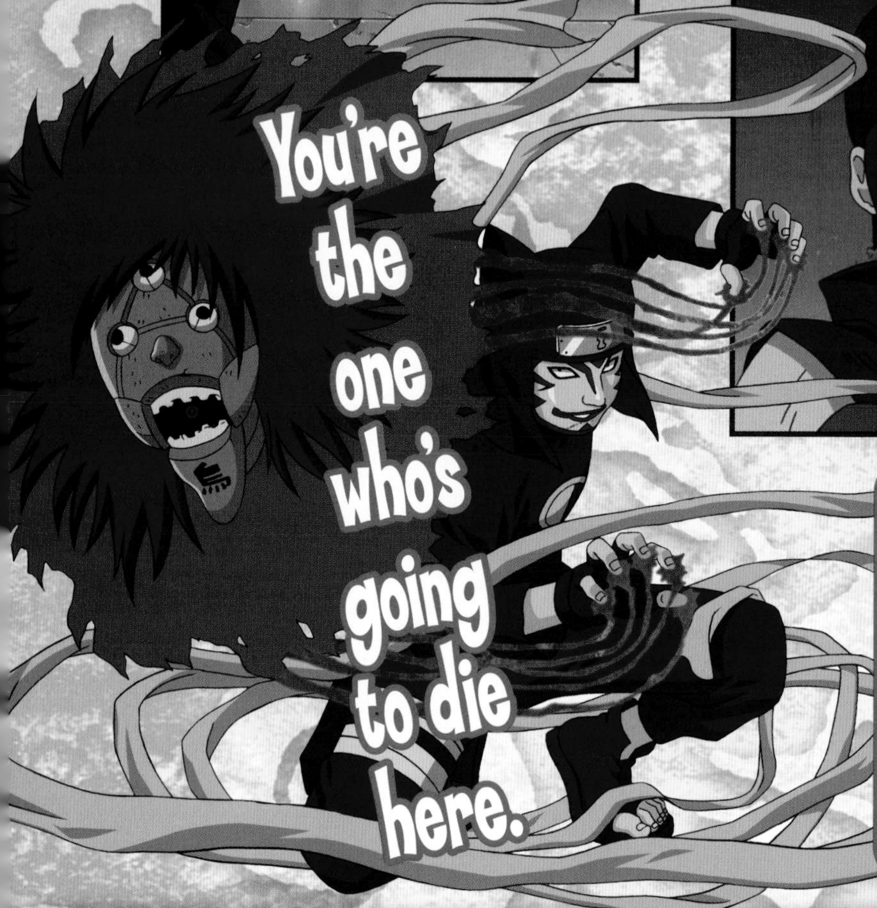

You're the one who's going to die here.

The puppet master, Kankuro, shows his true ability and crushes Misumi!

Kankuro's marionette, The Crow, wraps around Misumi and squeezes! Misumi is immobilized and concedes defeat, but Kankuro ruthlessly finishes him off!

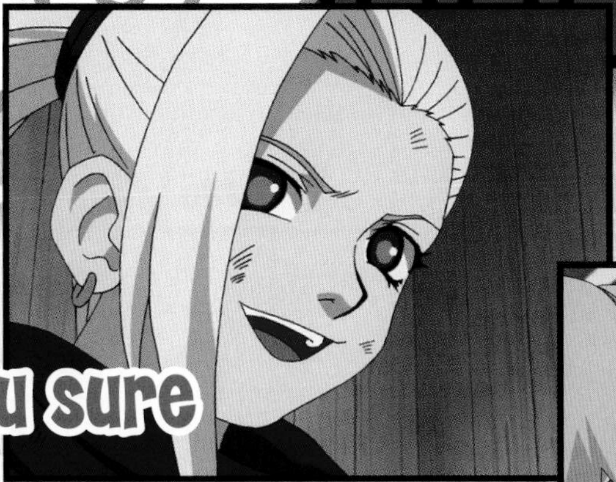

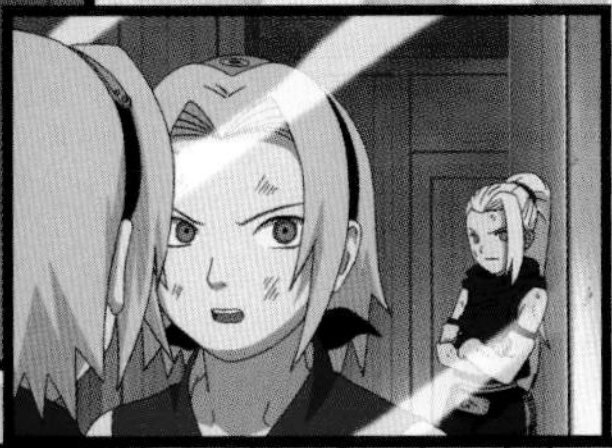

⬅⬇ Earlier, Sakura and Ino had a meeting in the ladies' room and exchanged some harsh words. They had no idea that immediately after they'd be poised for actual combat.

A match prelude?!

You sure are jumpy, Sakura.

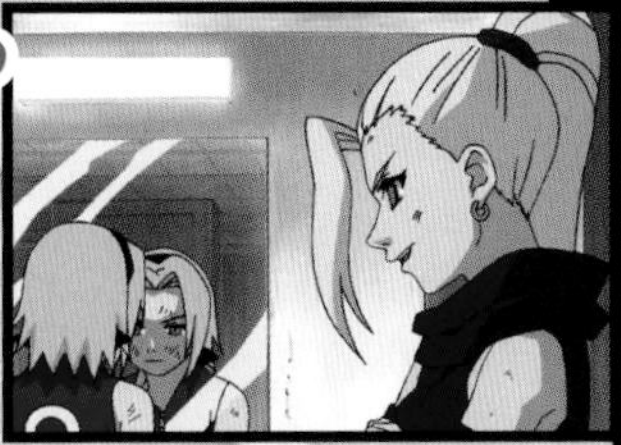

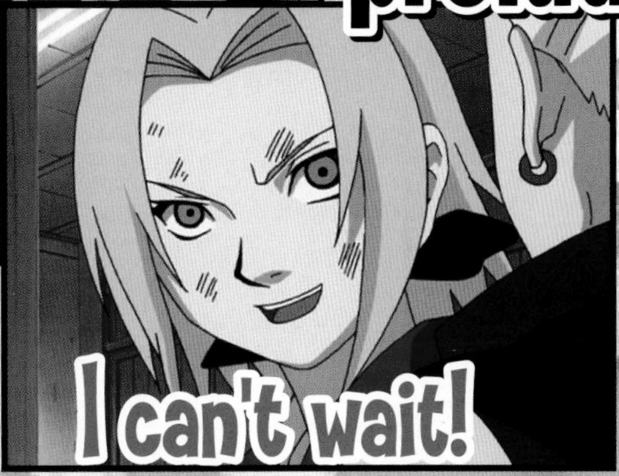

I can't wait!

Kunoichi Rumble! Sakura vs. Ino!

The next match flashes on the display board: Sakura vs. Ino! There should have been an intense battle between these longtime rivals, but they were both holding back. Why…?

SPARKS FLY! FEMALE FIGHTING SPIRIT!

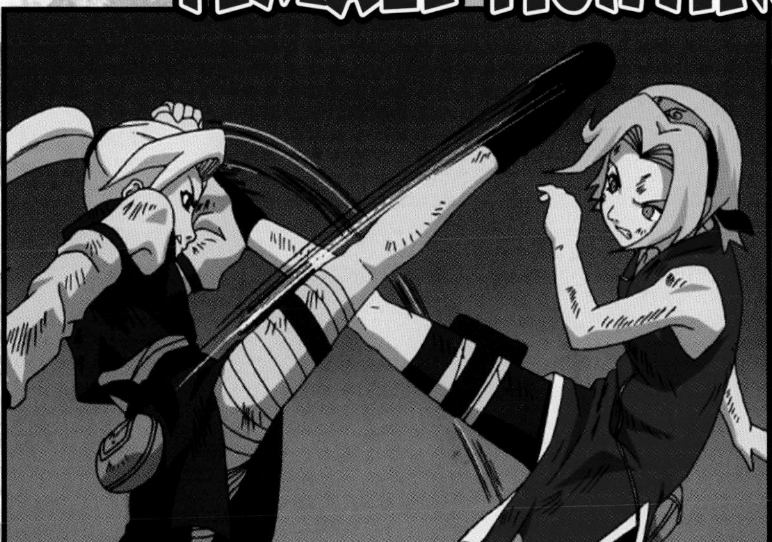

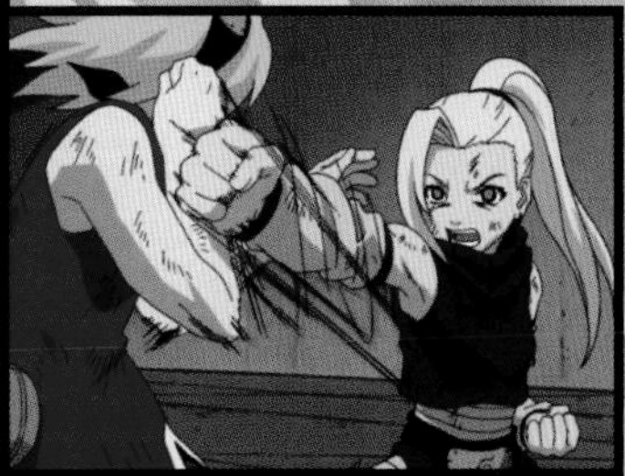

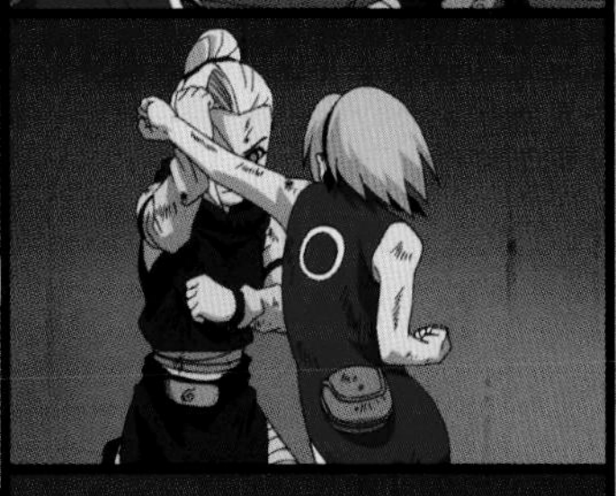

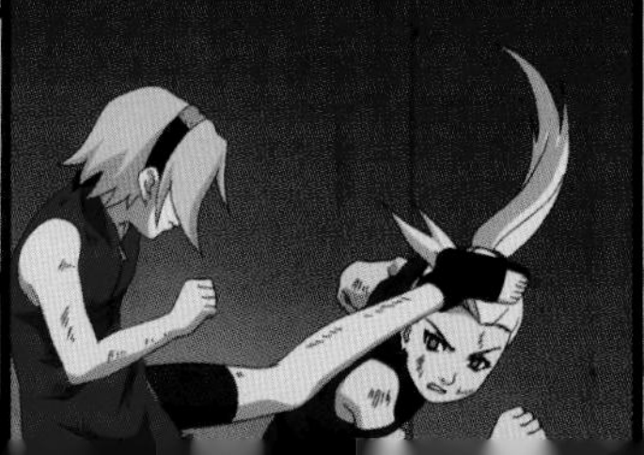

⬆➡ Are the two combatants the only ones who don't realize that they're both holding back? Everyone was expecting so much more!

I WANT TO FIGHT HER WITH ALL I'VE GOT BECAUSE I ADMIRE HER...

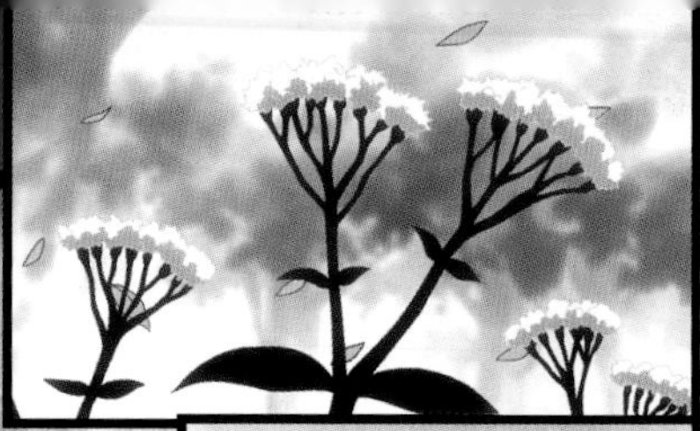

➡ "Ino, if you're a cosmos flower…then am I just a thoroughwort?" Sakura's feelings for Ino, who came to Sakura's rescue when she was teased, are complicated.

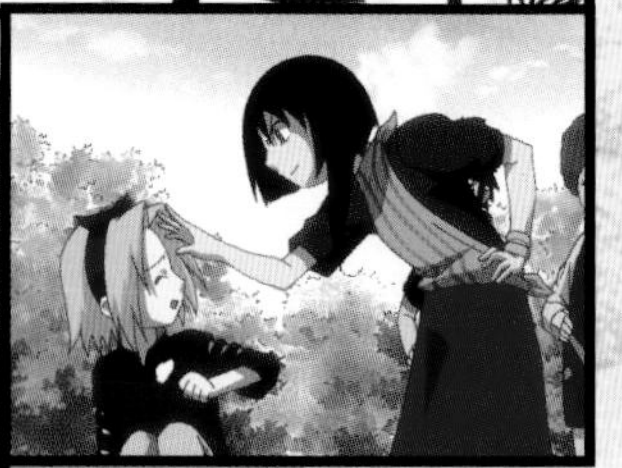

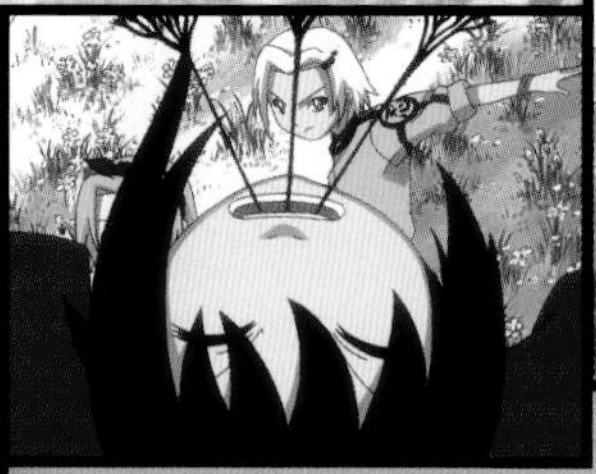

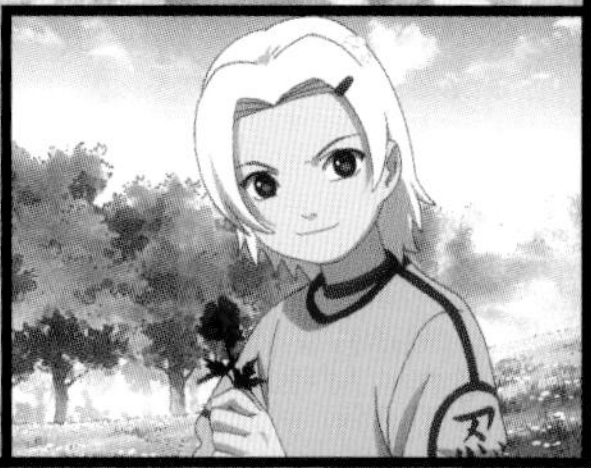

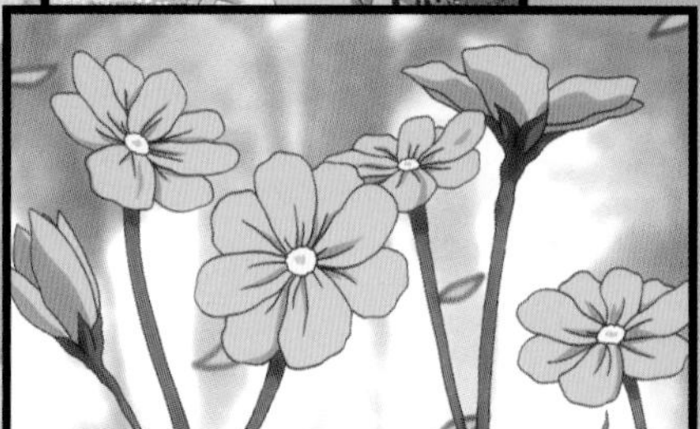

Sakura is momentarily overcome by fond memories of Ino.

Ino was always cute, cheerful and looked out for Sakura. She wants to go all out to show her dear friend that the girl she once protected is now strong—and a fierce rival!

⬇ Ino's words echo through Sakura's mind… Even now they lend Sakura emotional support.

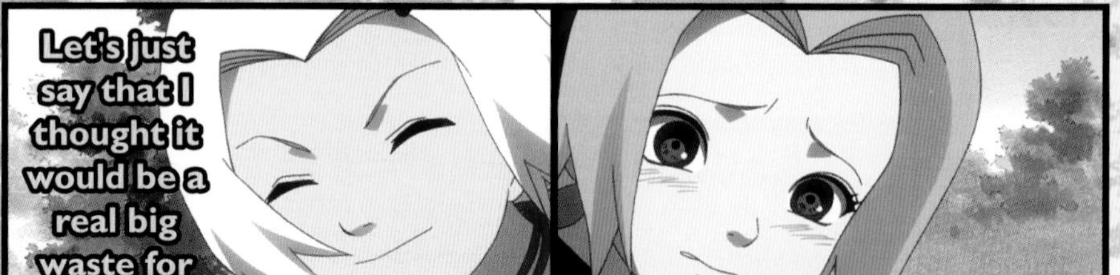
Let's just say that I thought it would be a real big waste for you to wilt away as nothing but a bud.
Thank you, Ino... Thank you.

A flower that blooms on the battlefield

Kunoichi

For a ninja, there are many tasks and roles that require a feminine touch. The Academy teaches not only ninjutsu but also conducts kunoichi classes to instill in its students the knowledge and refinement required by female ninja.

Renowned kunoichi of the Leaf Village

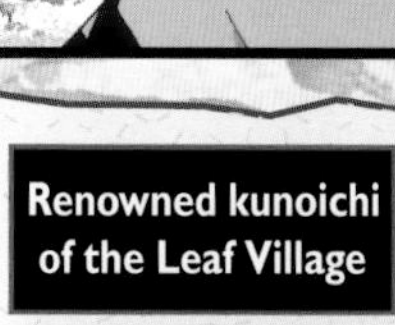

Anko Mitarashi

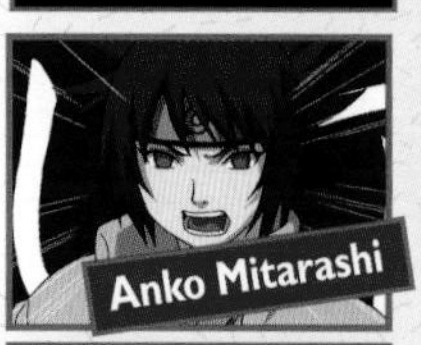

Kurenai Yuhi

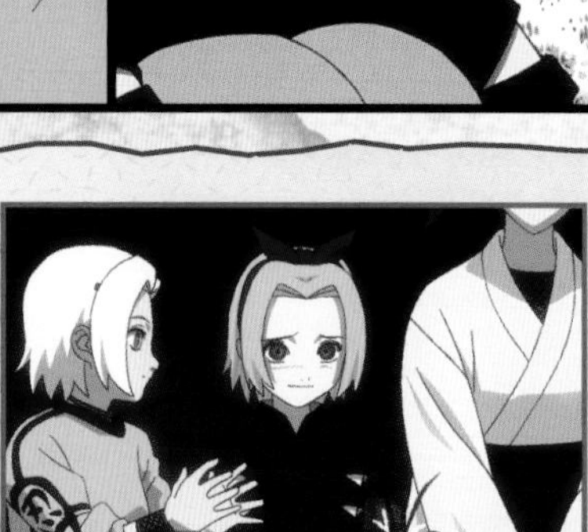

⬆ Flower arranging lessons are a part of refinement.

This is the way of the kuno-ichi!

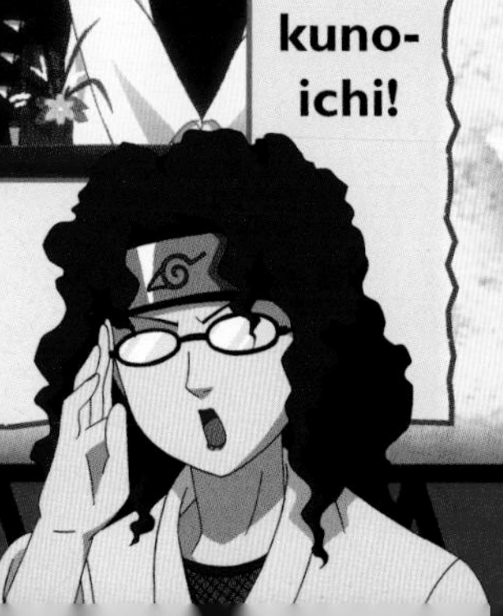

➡ Sakura wraps her headband around her forehead. She's as determined as Ino to fight as a real shinobi. Both get ready to unleash their full power, and then they clash!

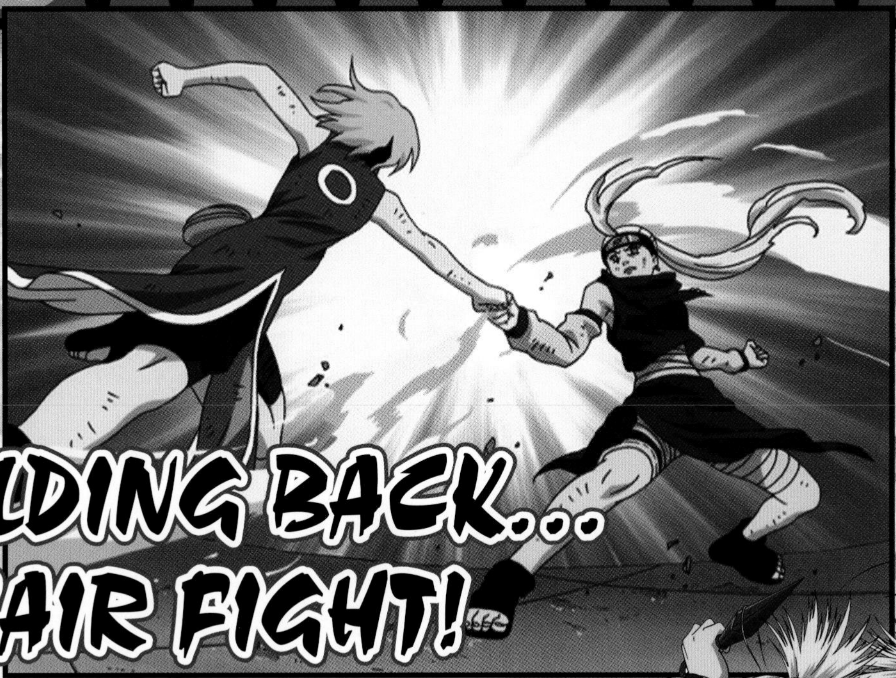

NO HOLDING BACK... A FAIR FIGHT!

⬇➡ Ino releases her Mind Transfer Jutsu, but Sakura quickly dodges. The time for holding back is over!

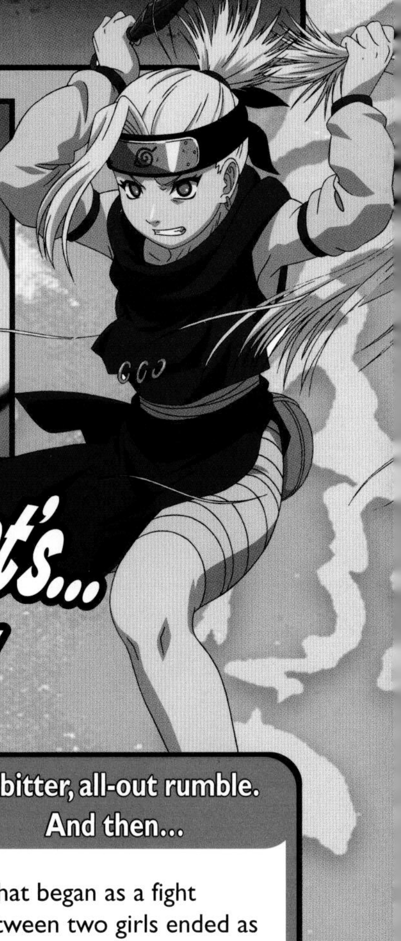
That's... it!

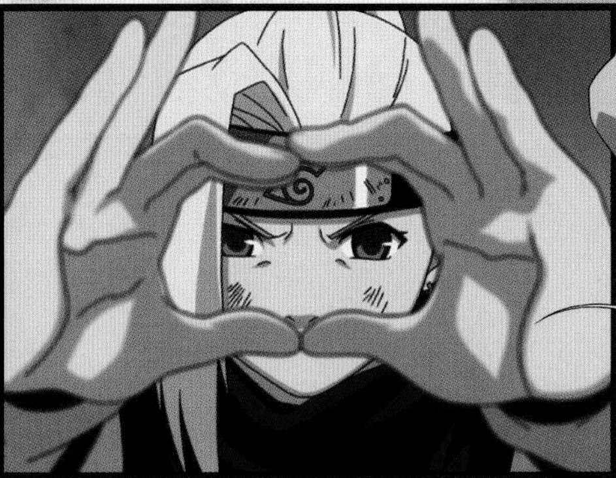

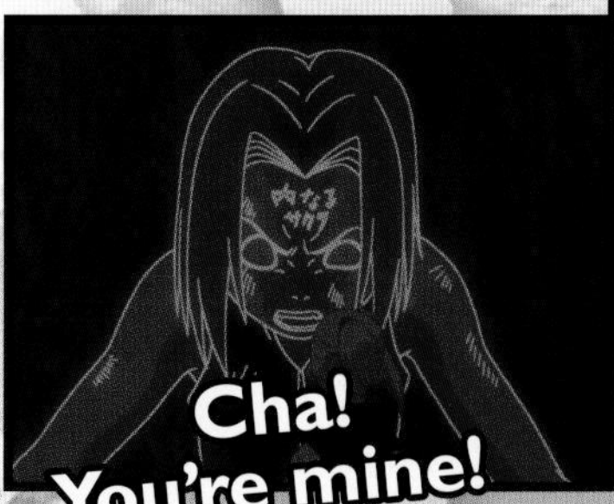
Cha!
You're mine!

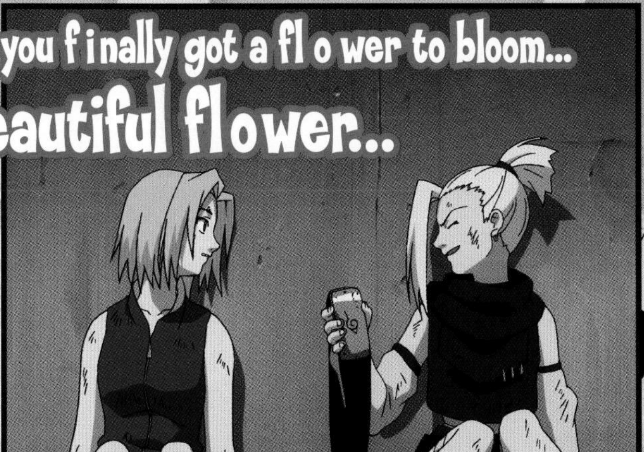
Guess you finally got a flower to bloom...
A beautiful flower...

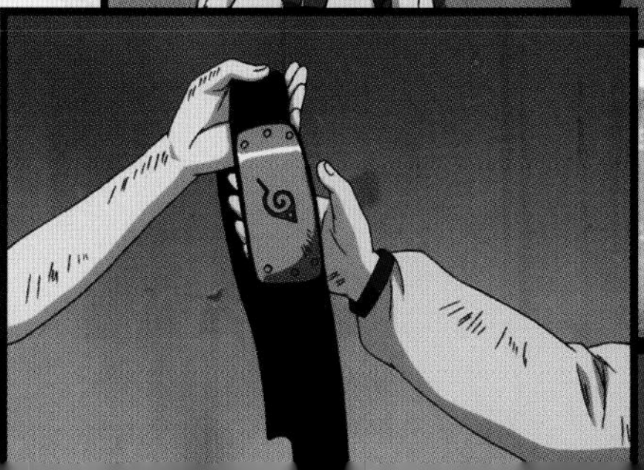

⬅⬆ Up to this point Sakura was merely a bud. But now, through her battle with Ino, Sakura has burst vibrantly into bloom...

A bitter, all-out rumble. And then...

What began as a fight between two girls ended as a battle between two kunoichi!

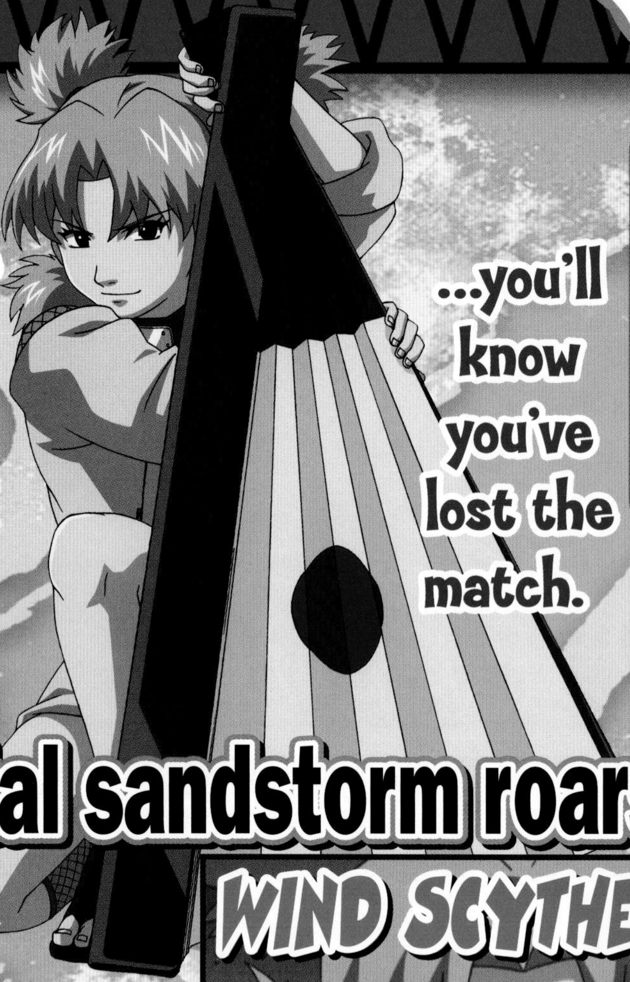
When you see all three moons...
...you'll know you've lost the match.

Temari's overwhelming victory! Temari shows Tenten no mercy!!

With one sweep of her giant fan, Temari shuts down Tenten's weapon attacks and then unleashes her Wind Scythe Jutsu! The piercing wind blades hit their marks.

A brutal sandstorm roars through!

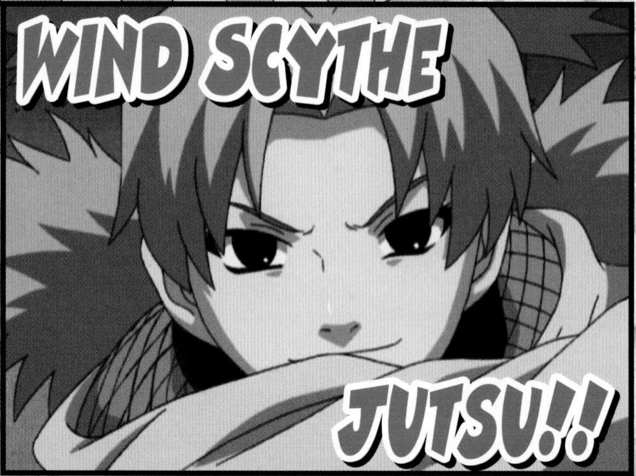
WIND SCYTHE
JUTSU!!

⬇➡ Temari enjoys ultimate victory, driving her opponents to the point of despair. She gives no quarter, even though Tenten is utterly beaten.

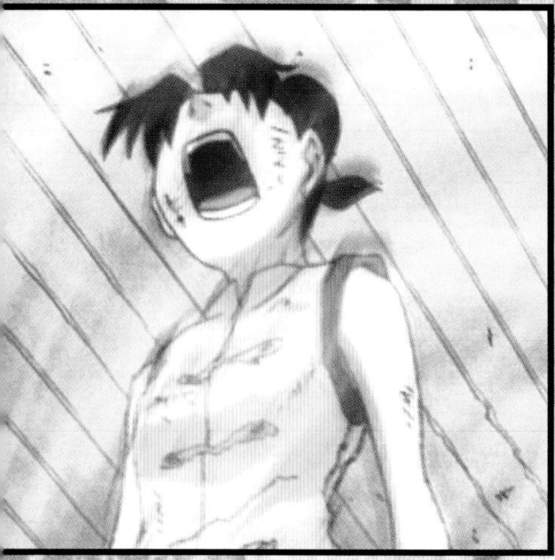

➡ Savage, ruthless beatings. So this is the custom of the Sand?

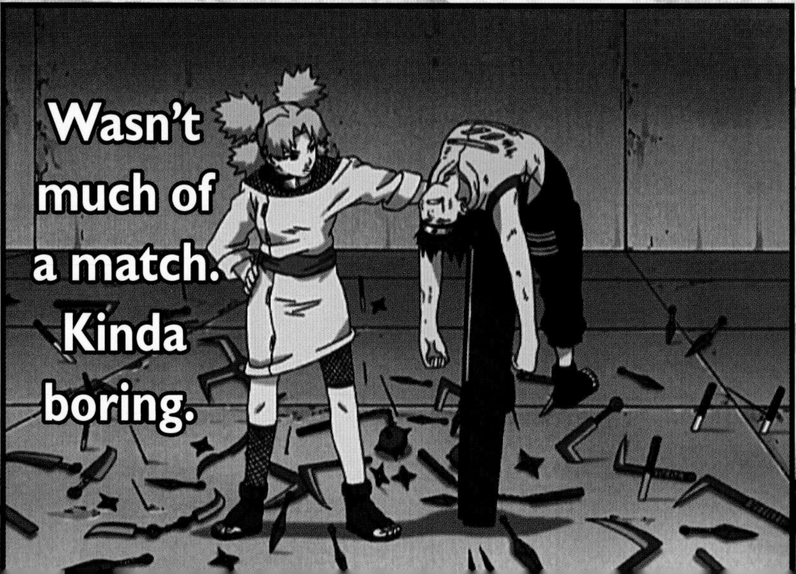
Wasn't much of a match. Kinda boring.

A whirling seesaw battle of wits!

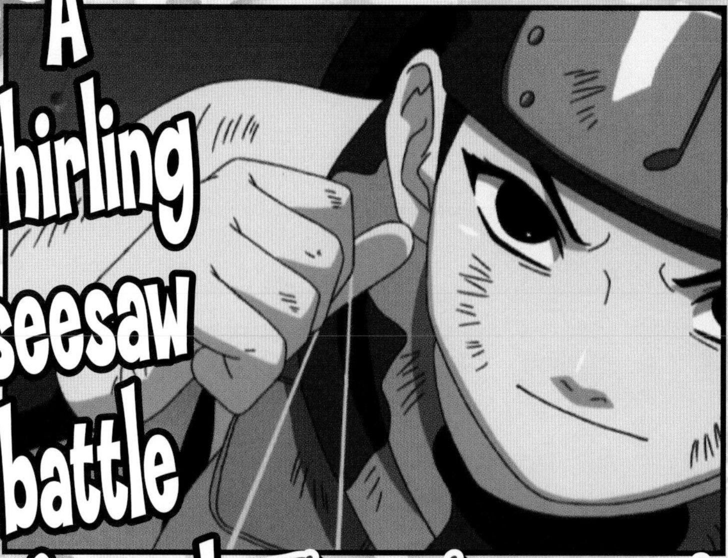

⬅⬇ A genjutsu combination assault using the sound of bells and senbon needles. Unable to dodge, Shikamaru gets perforated.

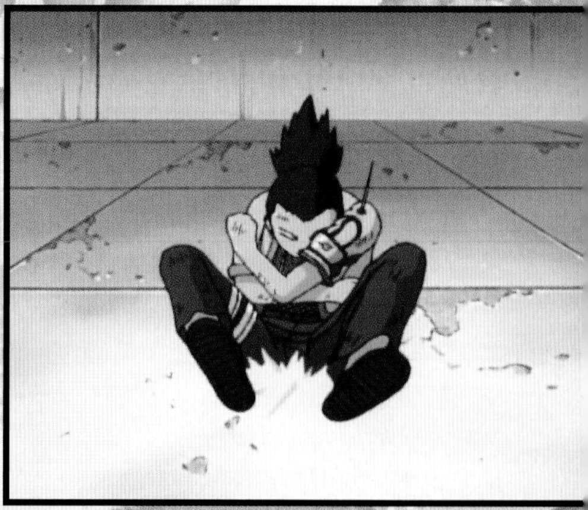

The sharp advance of the sound trap!

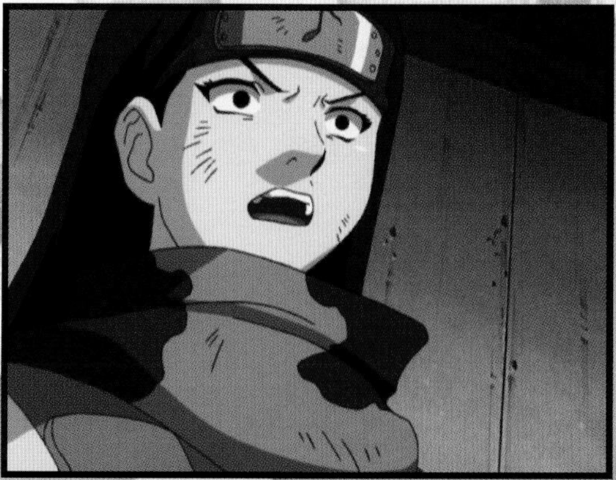

⬆ "Huh? What do you mean?" Kin, who thought she had everything under control, starts to worry.

An unprecedented mental battle! Which side will prevail?

Shikamaru seems defenseless against Kin's relentless senbon needle attack. Kin, sure of victory, closes in for the kill. But then, catastrophe for Kin! Shikamaru's ever-reliable Shadow Possession Jutsu strategy takes hold!

The Hidden Leaf Village's master tactician calmly waits for the perfect moment to strike!

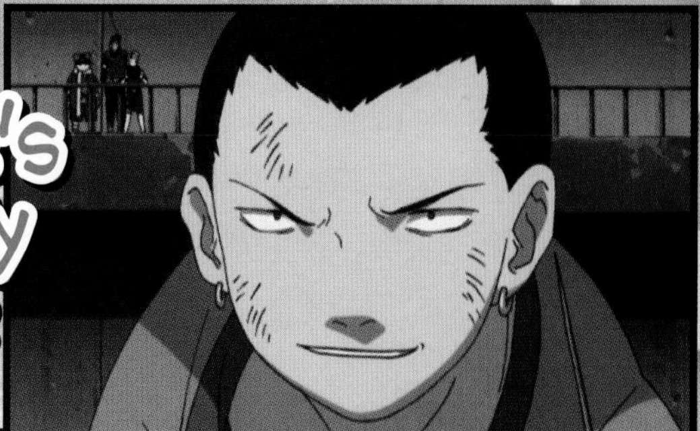

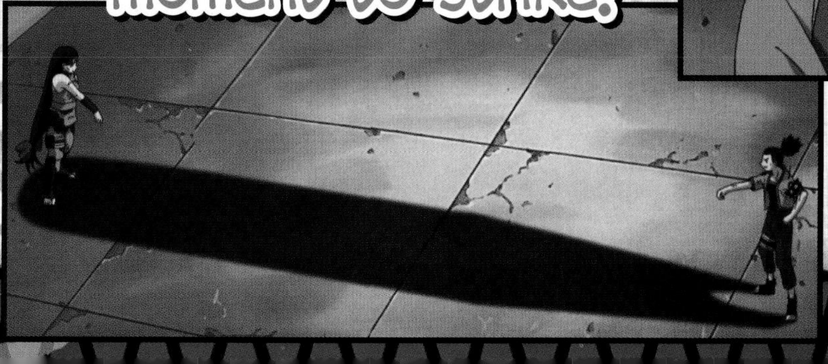

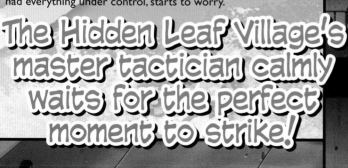

⬅⬆ Taking the punishment was all part of Shikamaru's strategy! This is the true ability of the Hidden Leaf Village's best strategist.

Finally, I get a chance to show what I've got!

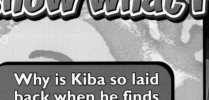

The wait is over! Naruto takes center stage!

← ↑ Naruto and Kiba are both rookie genin, but they've known each other for a long time and already have a strong rivalry.

Why is Kiba so laid back when he finds out his opponent is Naruto?

Even before the match begins Kiba is relaxed and confident because he already knows Naruto from their school days.

Look at that, it's us against the kid! Hey Akamaru, I think you and I just won the lottery!

Kiba remembers their time together at the Academy...

➡ ⬇ Naruto was hopeless. He couldn't even perform a decent Transformation Jutsu. Kiba took Naruto for a total fool.

➡ ↑ Food pills not only increase chakra, they also change how you look.

⬆ Only the size of your fingertip, but they pack a massive punch.

Shinobi Supplements

Food Pills

A pill containing various active ingredients that enables sustained activity for three days and nights without a break. Also, using a different blend, chakra strength can be temporarily doubled. This is why these pills are often used during battle.

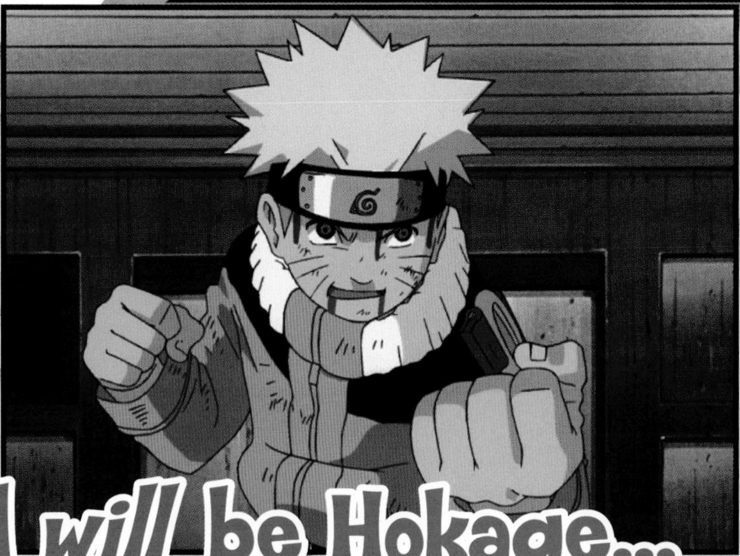

←↓ Naruto gradually corners Kiba with his innate tenacity. The fight is so intense, there is no sign of the old slacker Naruto!

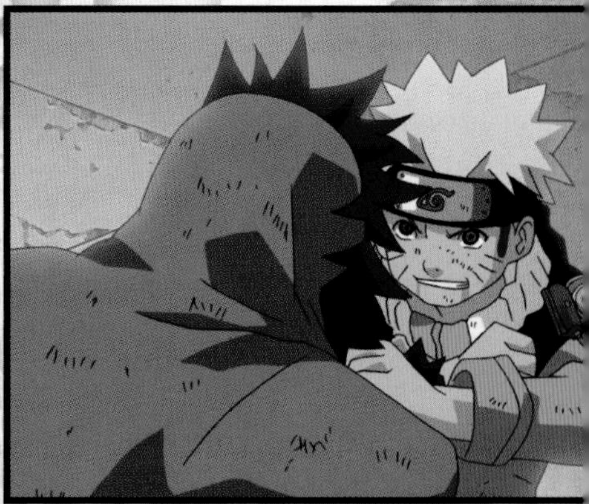

I will be Hokage...

I will never lose to you, or anyone here!

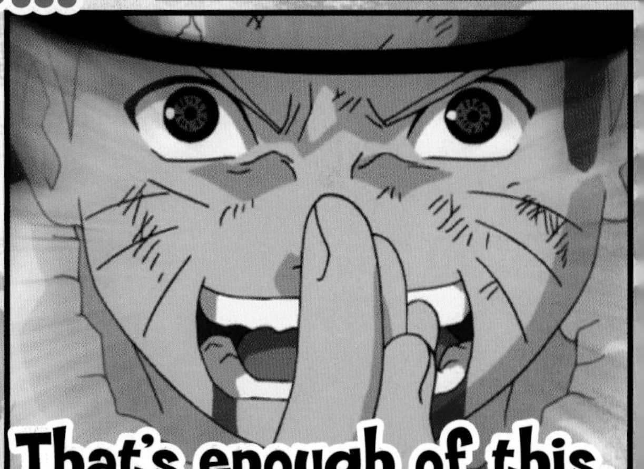

Explosion! Naruto Uzumaki Barrage!

Naruto hangs on during Kiba and Akamaru's intense, continuous attacks. Kiba starts to get frustrated and lose his cool seeing Naruto get back on his feet again and again. Meanwhile, Naruto doesn't miss his chance to counter when Kiba lets his guard down, exploding with a new deadly technique!

That's enough of this. It's time to unveil my new technique!

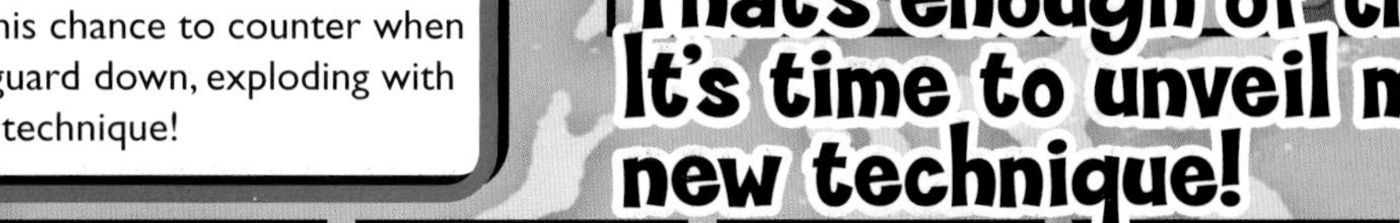

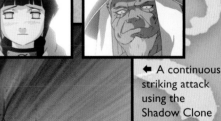

UZUMAKI BARRAGE!!

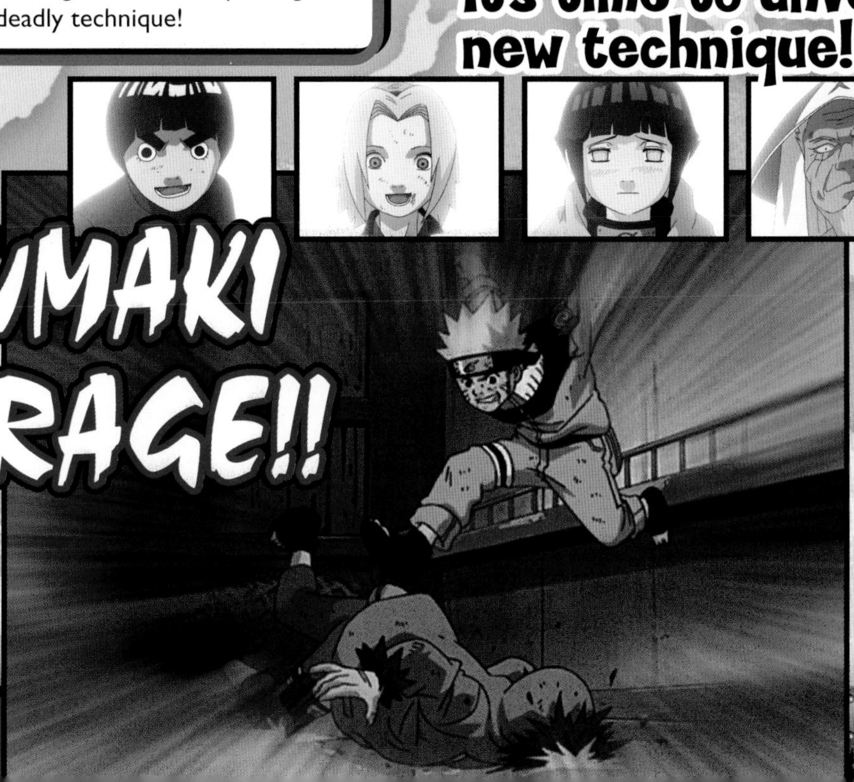

← A continuous striking attack using the Shadow Clone Jutsu, Naruto's Uzumaki Barrage explodes!

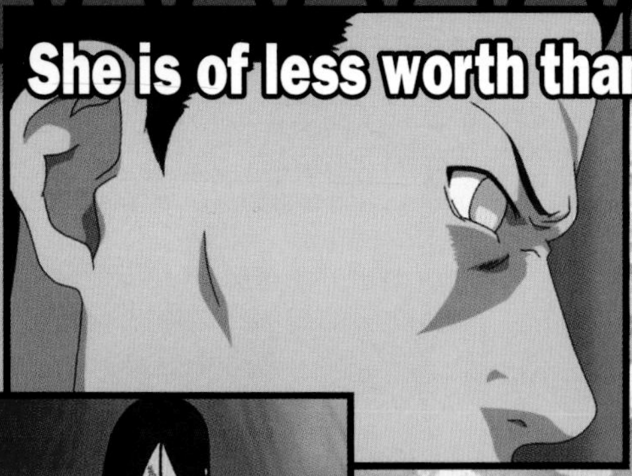

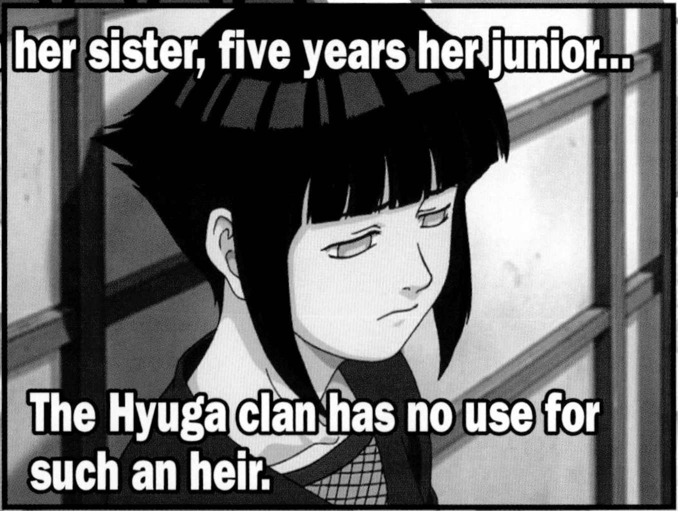

She is of less worth than her sister, five years her junior...

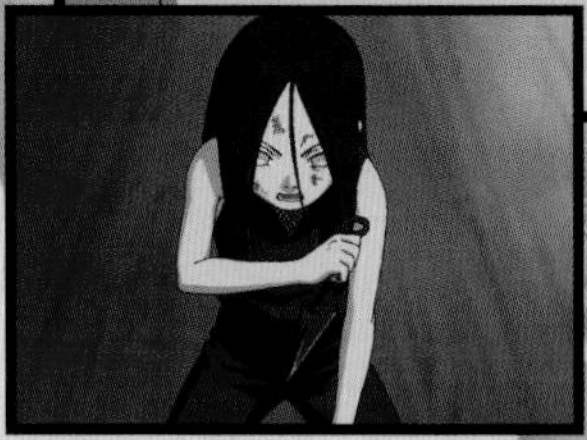

⬅⬆➡ Surpassed by her younger sister, forsaken by her father. Where does she fit in?

The Hyuga clan has no use for such an heir.

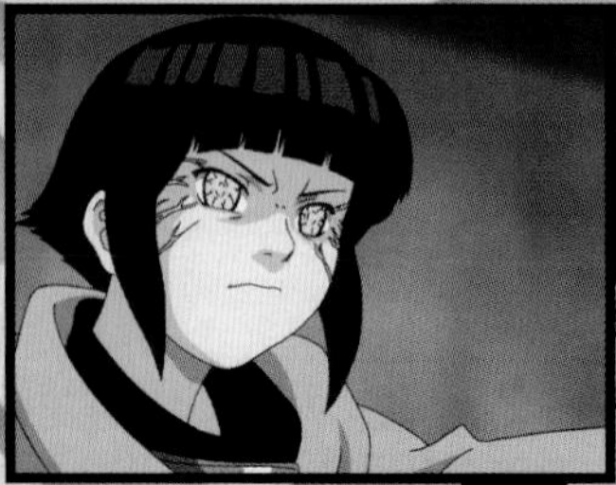

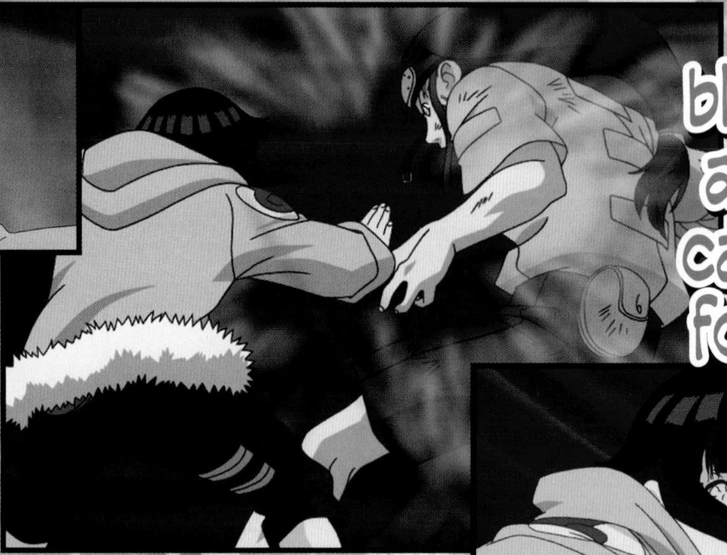

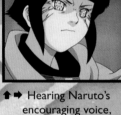

⬆➡ Hearing Naruto's encouraging voice, Hinata fights for herself for the first time in her life. The raw power she displays, that shocks even Neji, is the power of determination!

Clan bloodlines and fate cannot be forsaken.

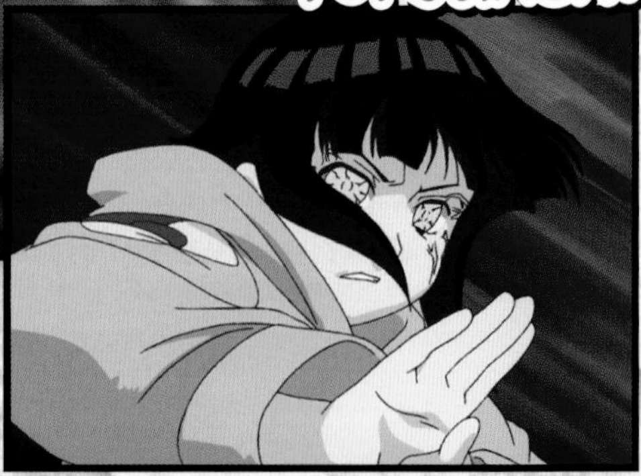

Now is the time to overcome!

Hinata Hyuga in a battle to change herself!

A member of the Main Branch, she has been denied a sense of self-confidence. However, that will end today. Now she simply battles for her own sake.

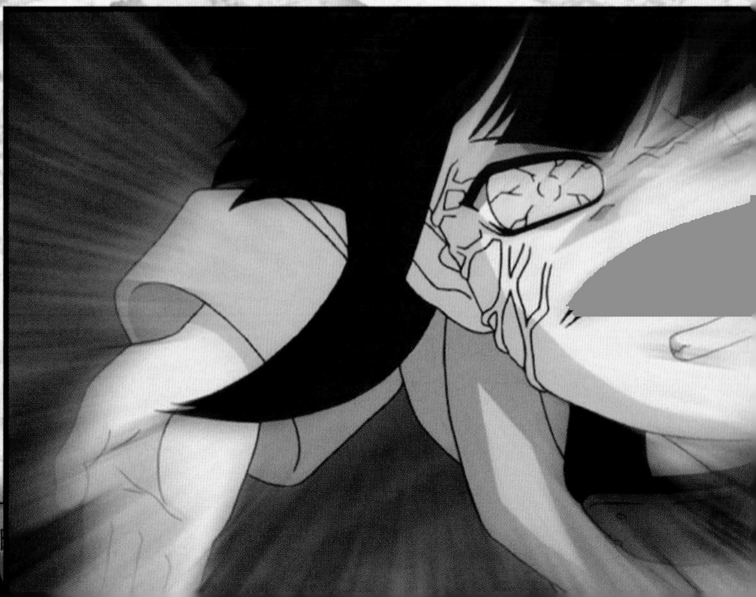

The fate of the Hyuga Clan sways them both.

Hinata continues to fight a losing battle, angering Neji. Is his irritation directed at Hinata or the Hyuga Clan's fate…?!

The fight against fate.

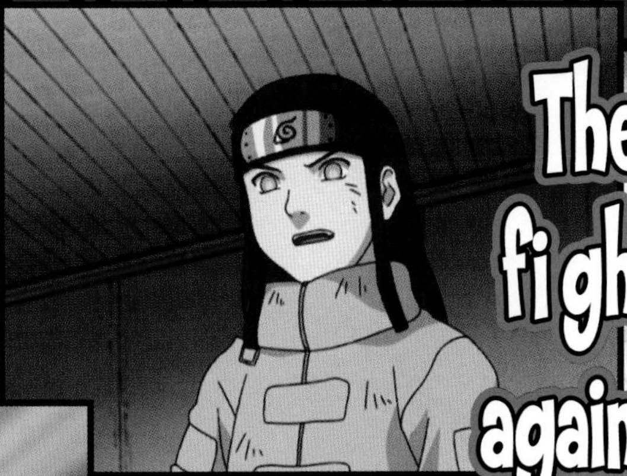

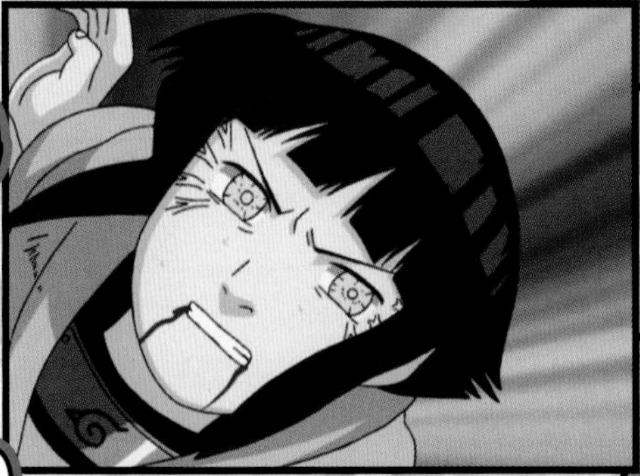

⬅⬆ "You may not like it, but it's a fact." Hinata battles, desperately hoping to prove Neji wrong. She's determined to change her destiny.

People can't change the way they are. That's just how it is.

Main Branch vs. Side Branch
The brutal conclusion!

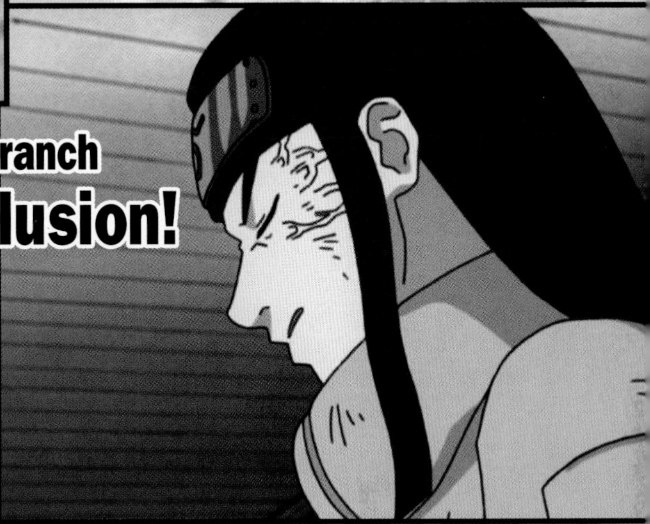

⬅⬆ Hinata speaks out to Neji, who seems as though he merely lives life bowing to fate. She understands his agony because she too has wounds from being manipulated by destiny.

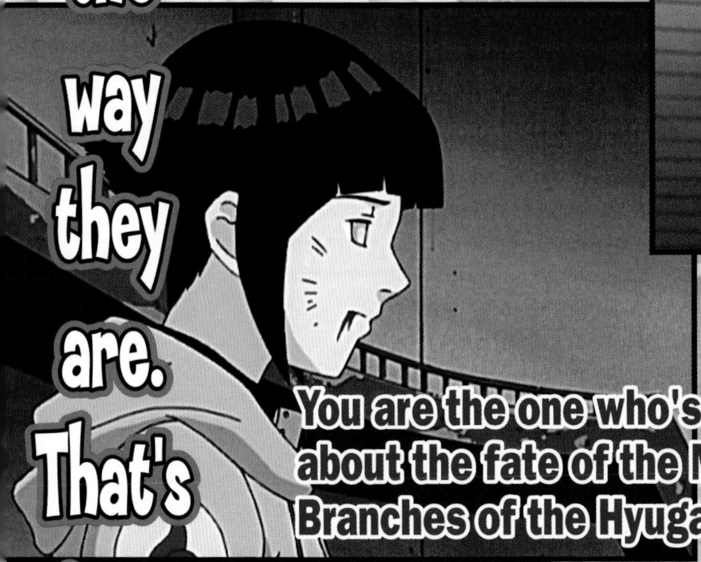

You are the one who's all torn up about the fate of the Main and Side Branches of the Hyuga Clan.

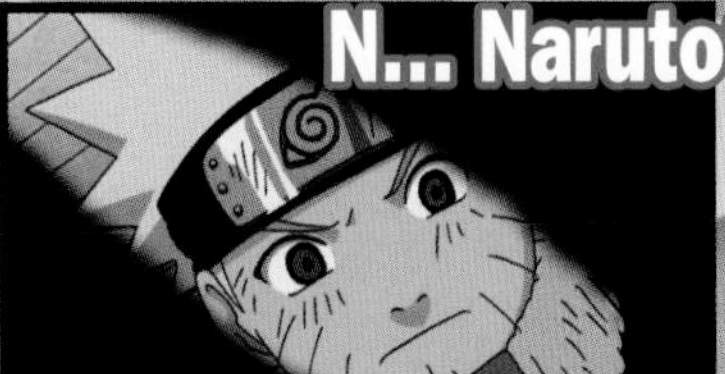

N… Naruto?

⬅⬆ Hinata risked her life to gain the courage to change…

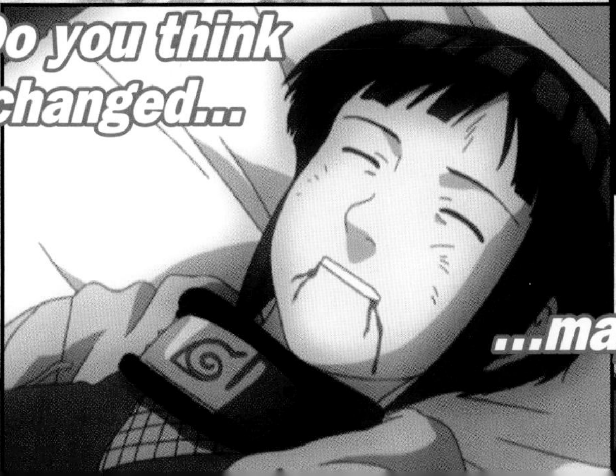

Do you think I changed…

…maybe a little bit?

Eagerly antici-pated! Rock Lee is ready to roll!

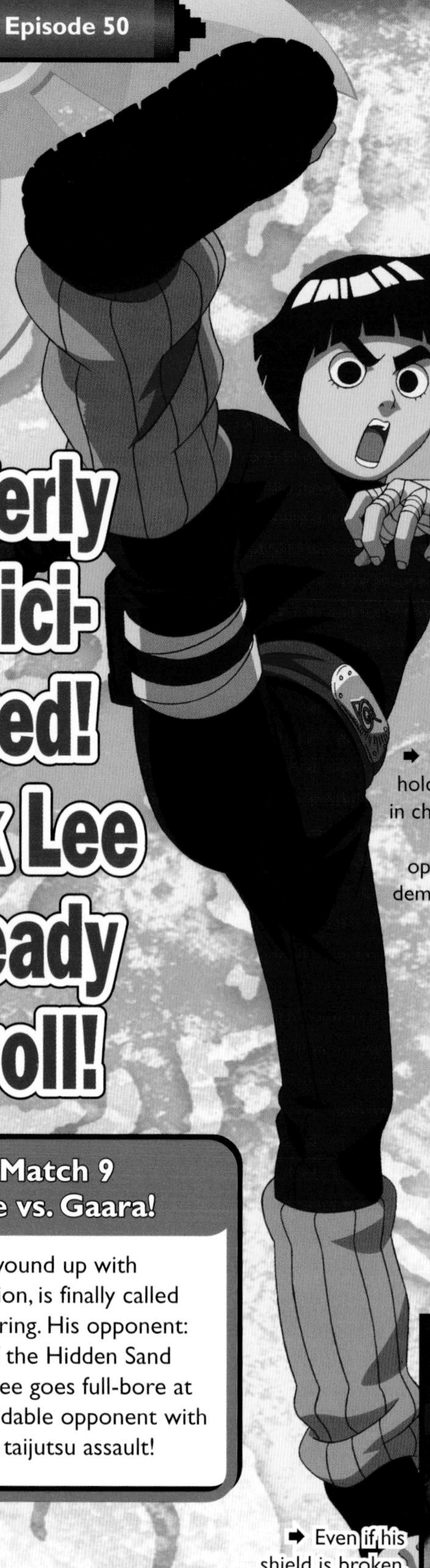

Match 9
Lee vs. Gaara!

Lee, all wound up with anticipation, is finally called into the ring. His opponent: Gaara of the Hidden Sand Village. Lee goes full-bore at his formidable opponent with a blazing taijutsu assault!

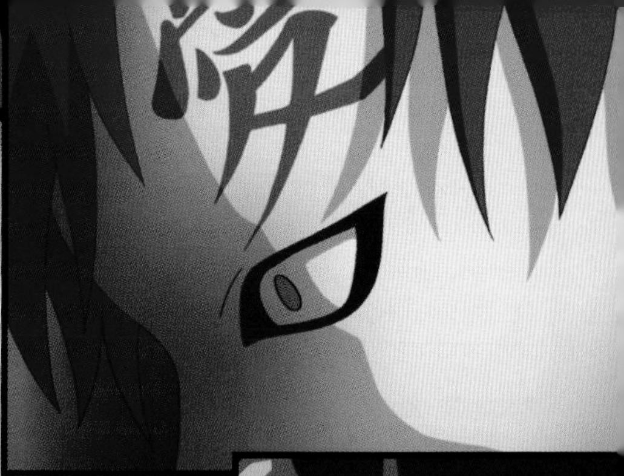

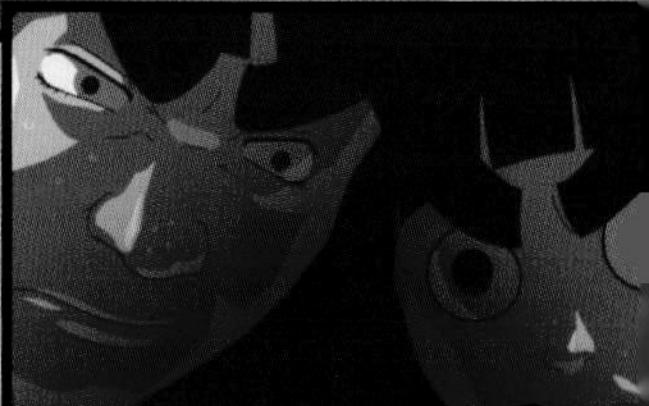
You see that gourd that Gaara is wearing? Watch out. There's something *weird* about it.

➡⬆ A stone-cold Gaara stands expressionless. Will Guy's hot-blooded advice work for Lee?

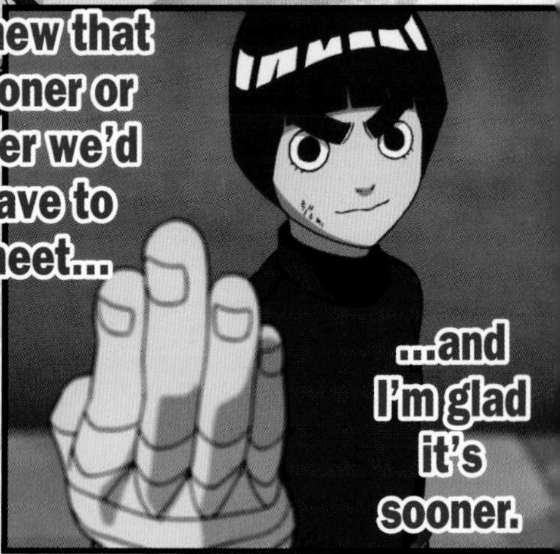
I knew that sooner or later we'd have to meet...
...and I'm glad it's sooner.

➡ Lee can barely hold his emotions in check. Defeating a truly strong opponent means demonstrating the brilliance of taijutsu!

Lee is a surging wave of offense! However...

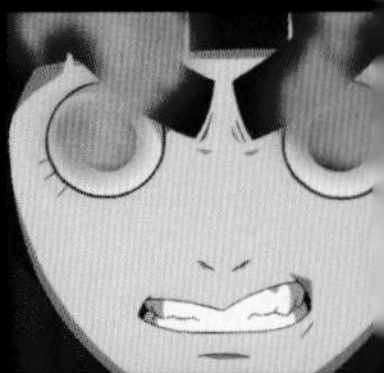

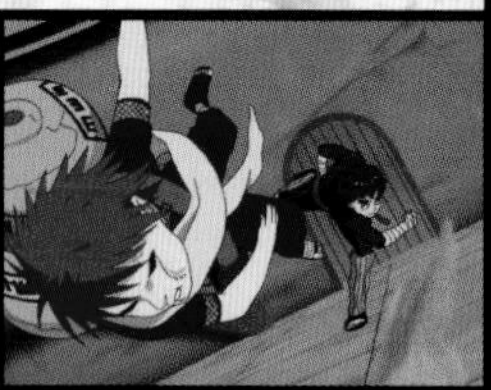

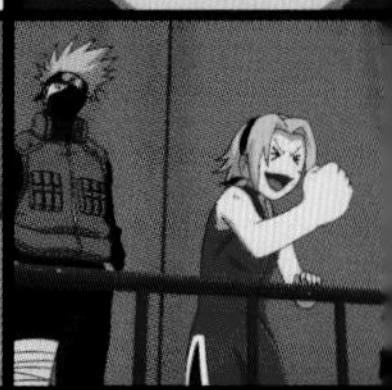

➡ Lee removes his weights and overpowers Gaara...?!

A berserker armored in impregnable sand!

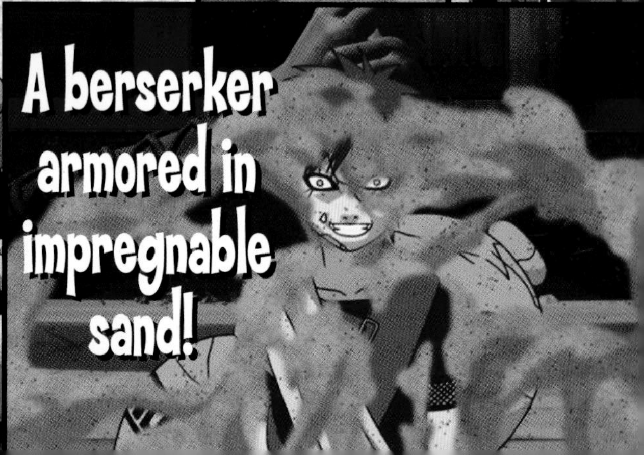

➡ Even if his shield is broken, his armor provides complete defense!

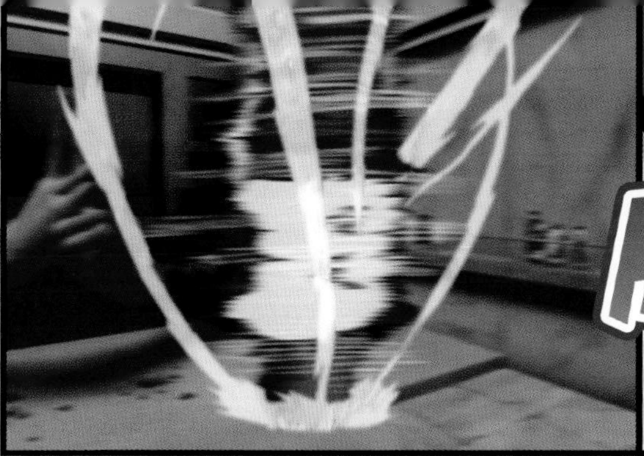

HIDDEN LOTUS FAILS TO BLOOM!

⬇ He takes hold of Gaara. There's an enormous crash! Game over?!

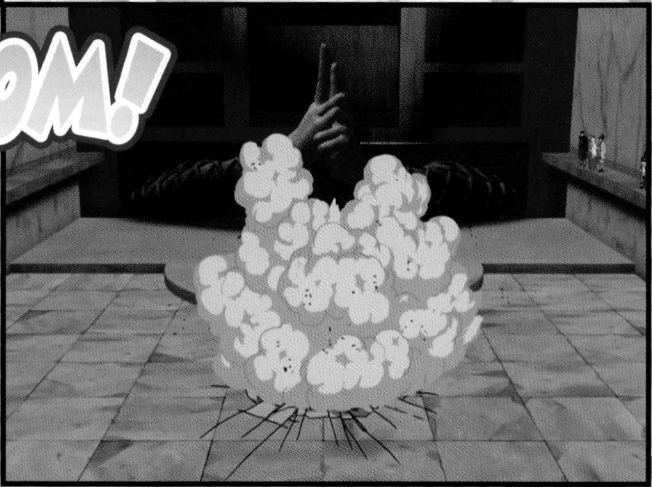

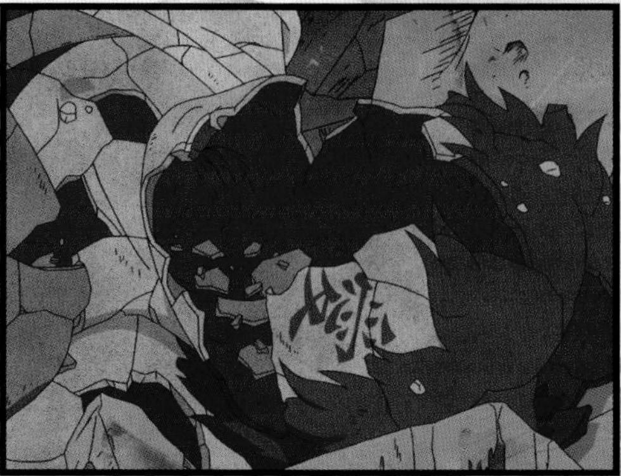

⬆ The collapsed sand armor is empty. Gaara escaped in the nick of time!

The Hidden Lotus, the Ferocious Fist secret technique, is defeated!

The Lotus is the only major technique to inflict heavy damage and take down the sand defense! It seemed Lee's furious blow would end the match. But Gaara didn't miss his split-second opportunity!

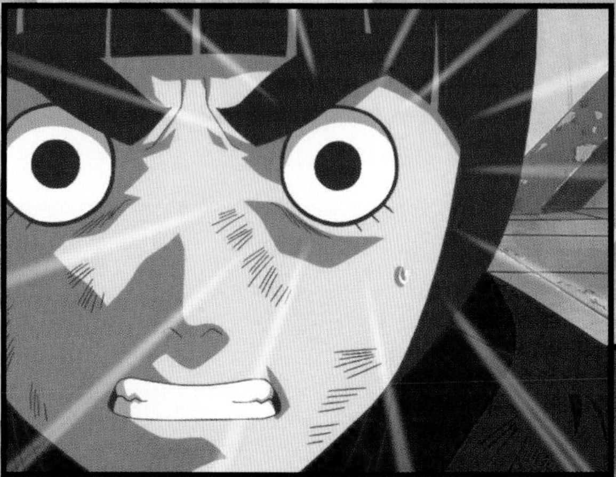

⬆ The shock is great when this technique, the ultimate knockout blow forged of extreme physical effort, is defeated.

The demon awakens!

➡ The real Gaara emerges! His cold-blooded, expressionless face now wears an eerie grin…!

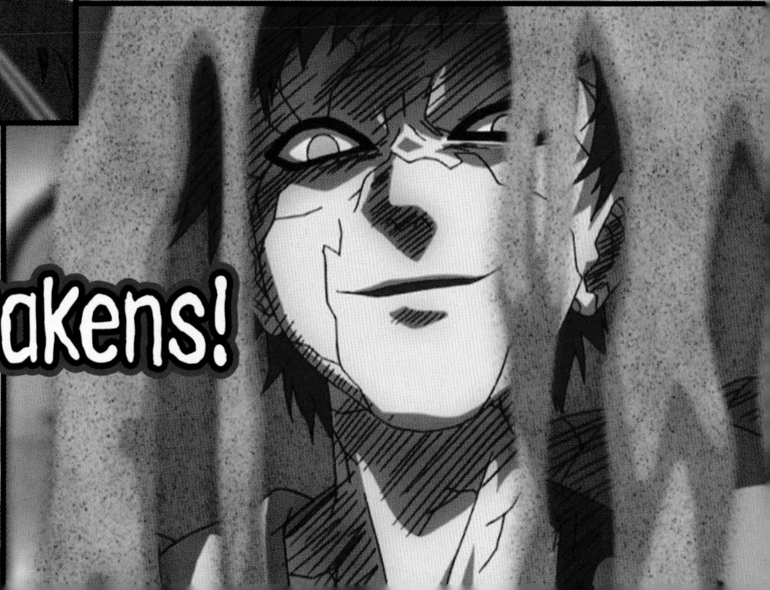

Single-mindedly following the way of effort!

Lee is barely able to maintain his defense at Gaara's onslaught. But still, his eyes don't lose their spark. They are the same brilliant, clear eyes as when he made a promise to his mentor. As long as there is hope, he will never give up. That vow constitutes the bond between him and Guy.

➡ When he first entered the Academy he was dubbed "Loser Lee."

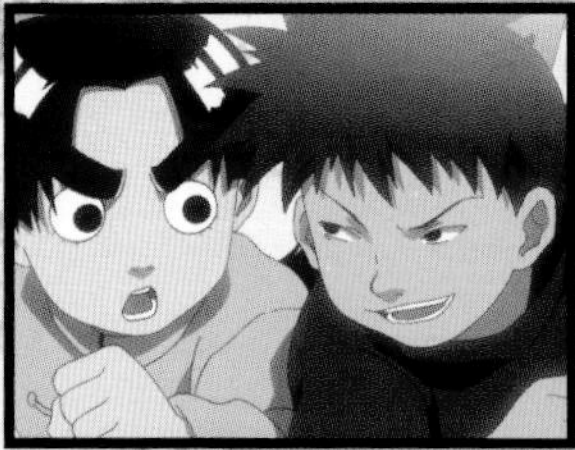

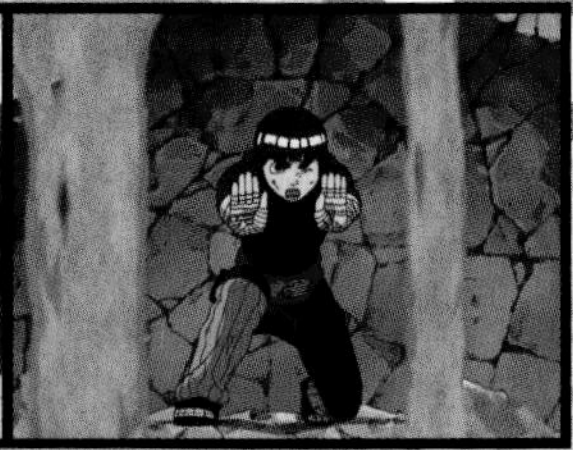

Even if you can't use ninjutsu or genjutsu...

Stick with it... "Effort"!

➡⬇ Becoming a great ninja is all about effort! And in times when he felt he might lose heart his mentor was there.

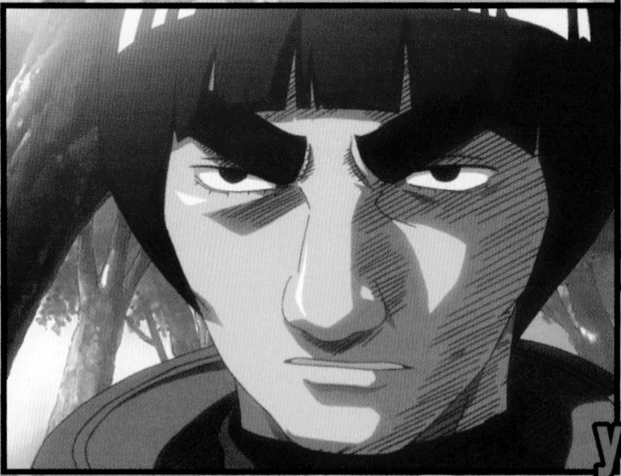

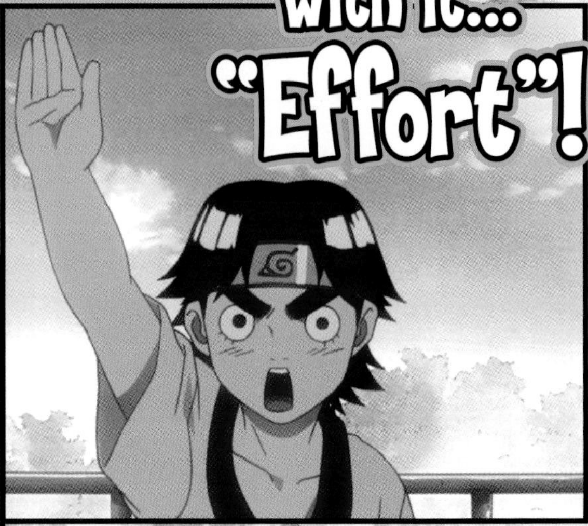

All the effort is pointless if you don't believe in yourself.

➡ There is someone who has faith in you, even if you are a loser, and to live up to that faith a man makes himself stronger!

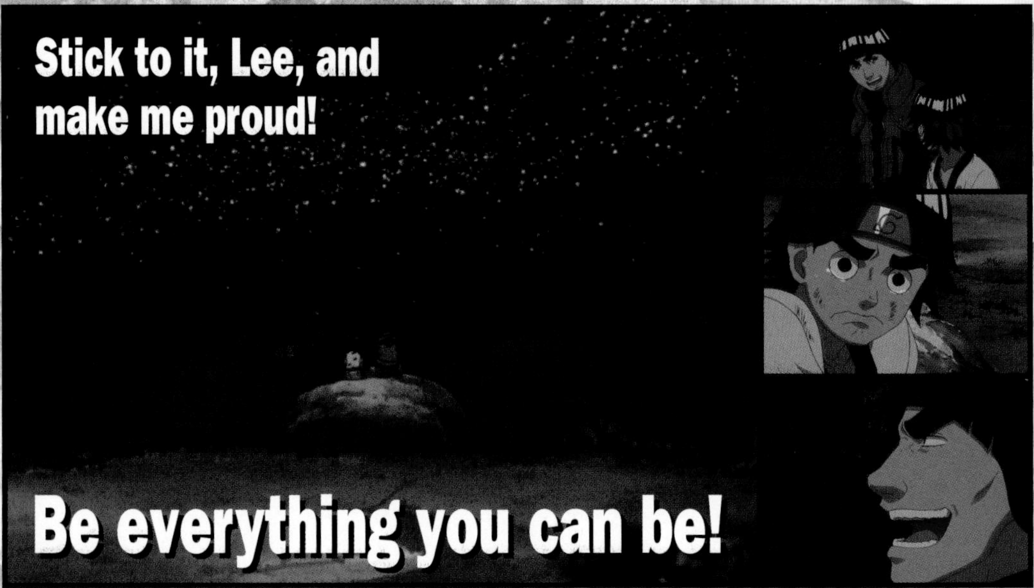
Stick to it, Lee, and make me proud!
Be everything you can be!

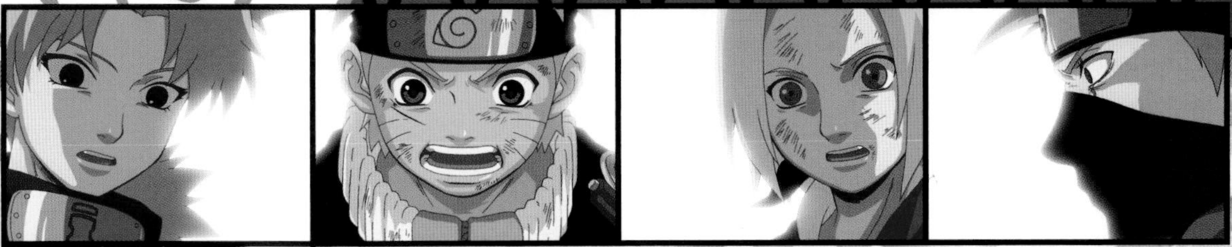

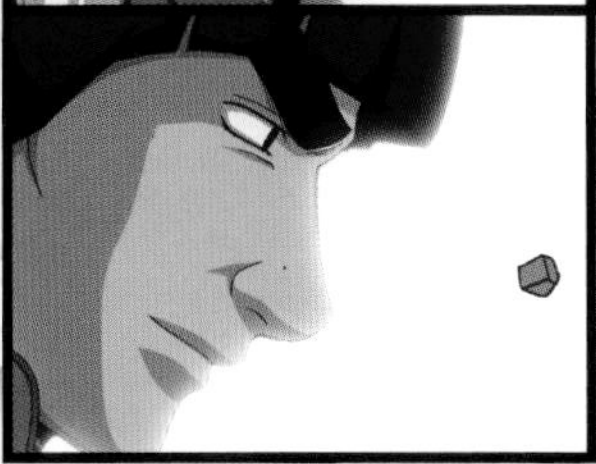

↑ While everyone is astonished by Lee's drastic transformation, Guy calmly keeps his eyes on Lee.

The Lotus of the Leaf Village blooms twice!

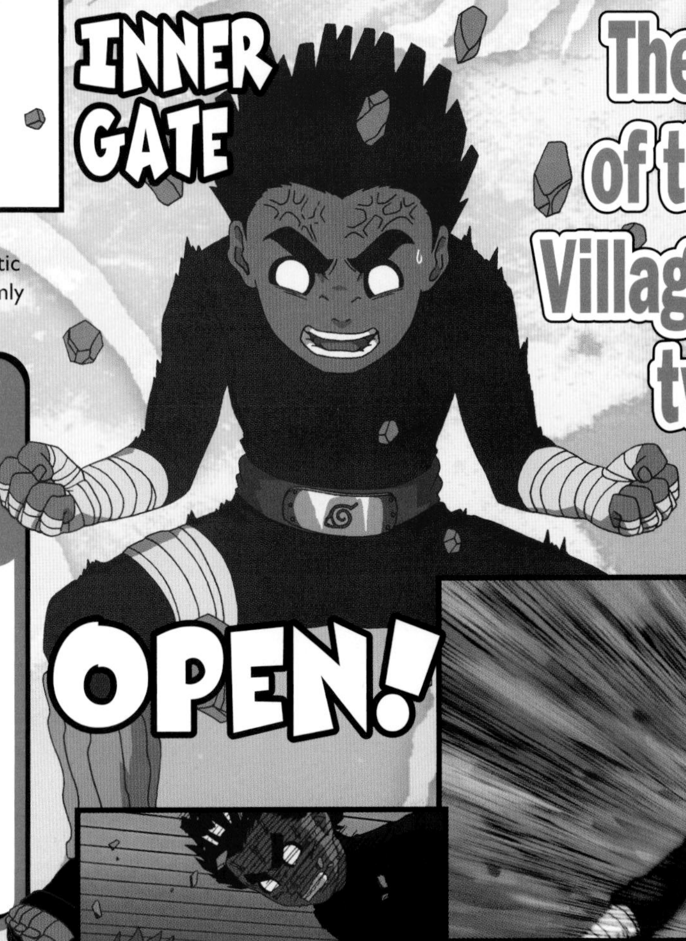
INNER GATE
OPEN!

The ult-imate secret technique unleashed at last!

Lee opens the forbidden inner gates for the final confrontation! He must fight to protect and maintain his own ninja way and to bloom along with the Lotus!

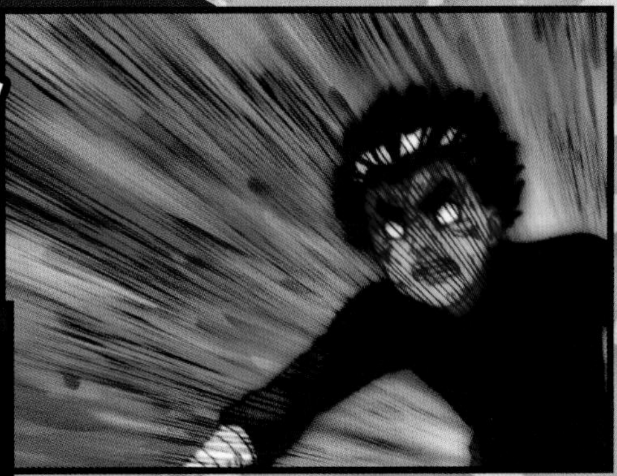

↑ An ultra high-speed combo that even Gaara can't keep up with!

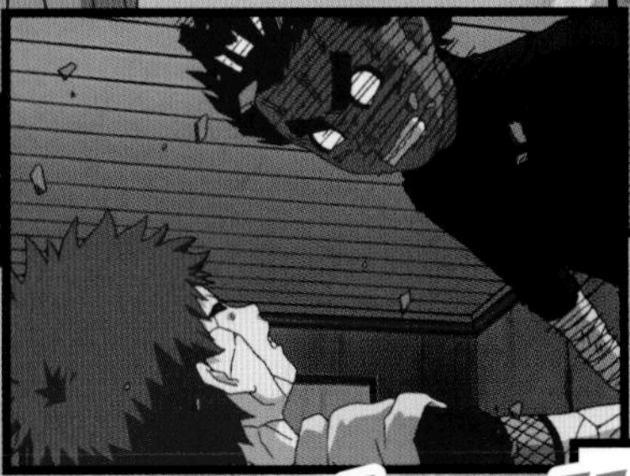

➡ Lee releases his power limiter and furiously moves in on Gaara!

Now, to finish it!!

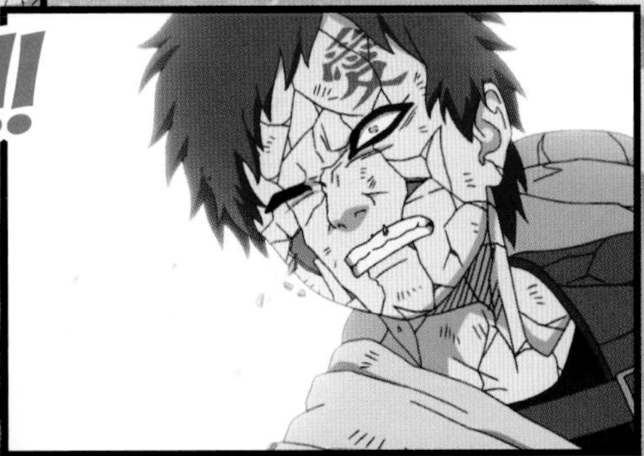

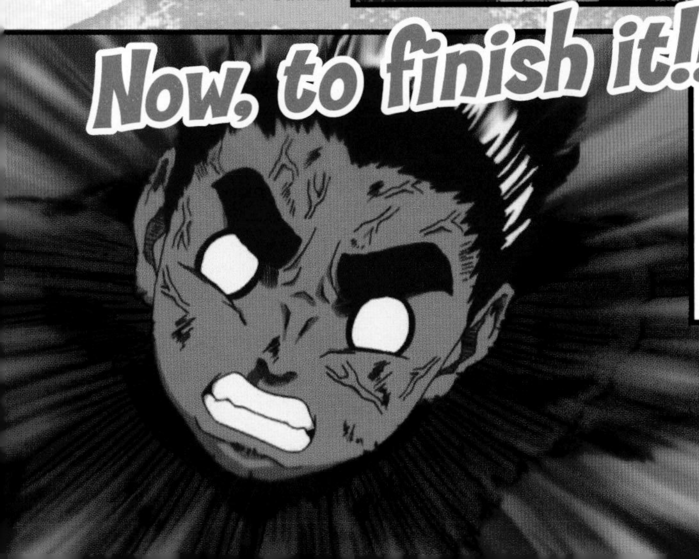

↑← The sand defense starts to come apart, but Lee's body is almost at its limit. Needing to end it quickly, Lee launches his final strike!

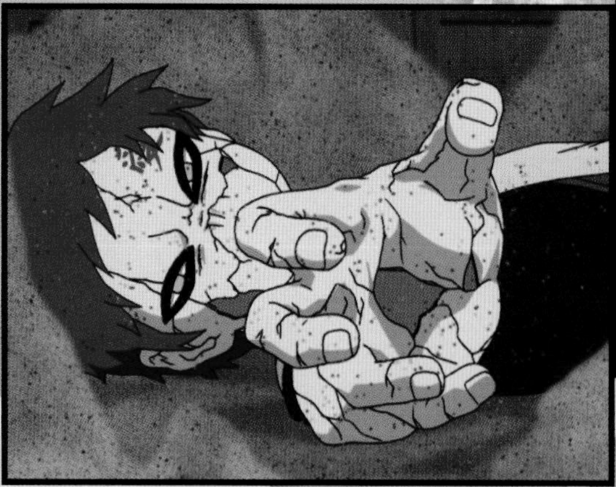

⬆ Gaara lands on the sand gourd, absorbing the impact of Lee's Lotus and saving him. With his remaining strength Gaara unleashes Sand Coffin!

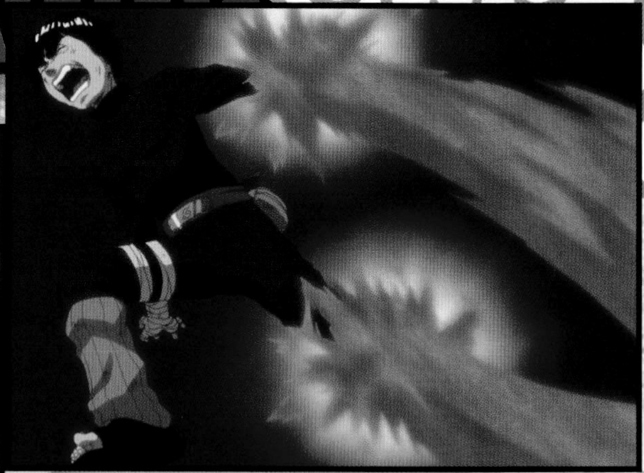

⬆ Gaara's sand attacks. The sound of bones being crushed and screams of pain echo through the arena…

The sand ruthlessly crushes Lee!

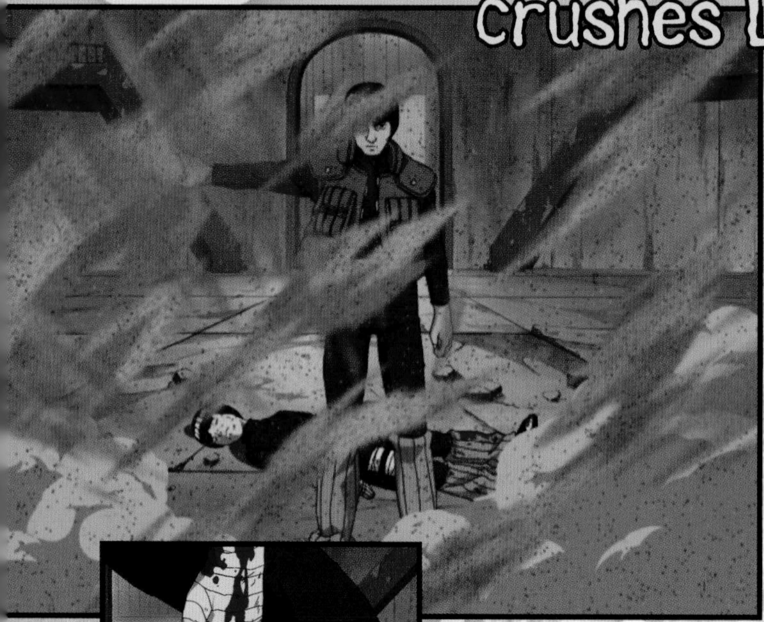

⬅ The demonic hand of Gaara could not halt its own attack, and, to protect the student that is precious to him, Guy stands between Lee and Gaara!

A cold-hearted end…!

Even his fatal Hidden Lotus was not enough to beat Gaara. Like a monster, the sand comes to devour the motionless Lee. Unable to bear it any longer, Guy intervenes and puts an end to this death match…

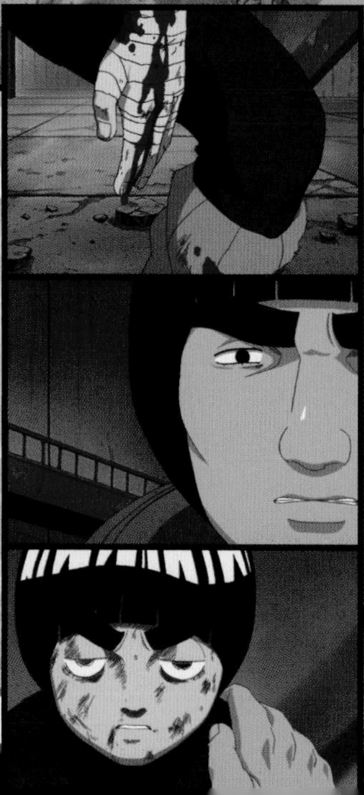

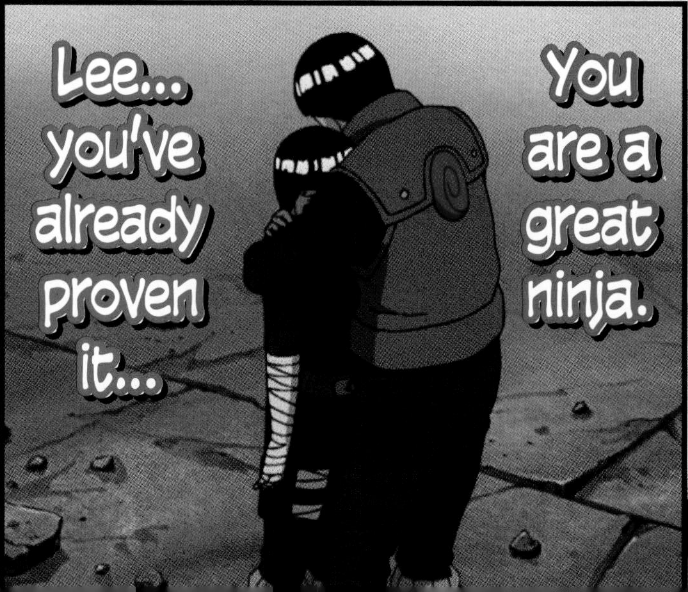
Lee… you've already proven it…
You are a great ninja.

⬅ Even though he's out cold, Lee gets to his feet.

A do-or-die goal now unattainable...

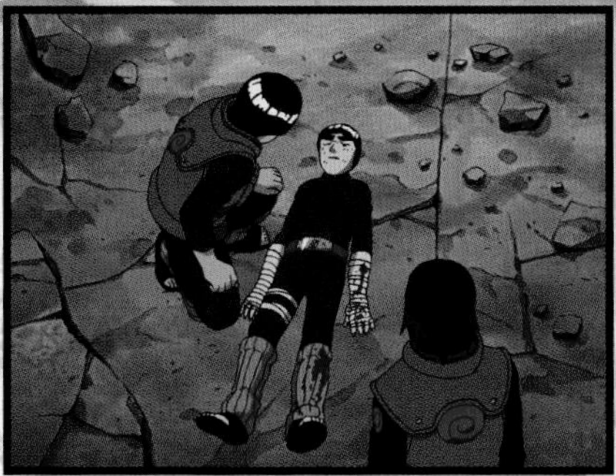

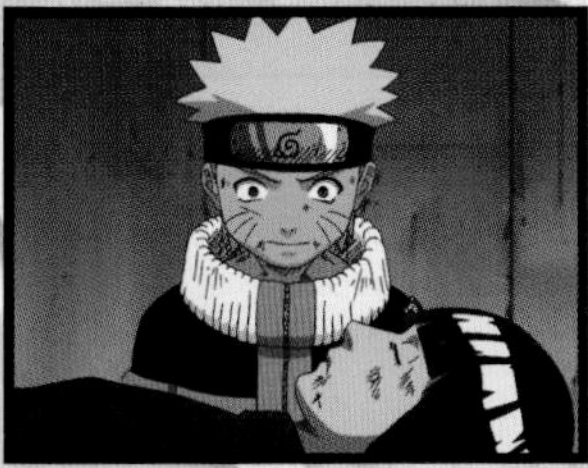

➡⬆ A cost too great. The diagnosis: Lee will "never be able to fight again"...

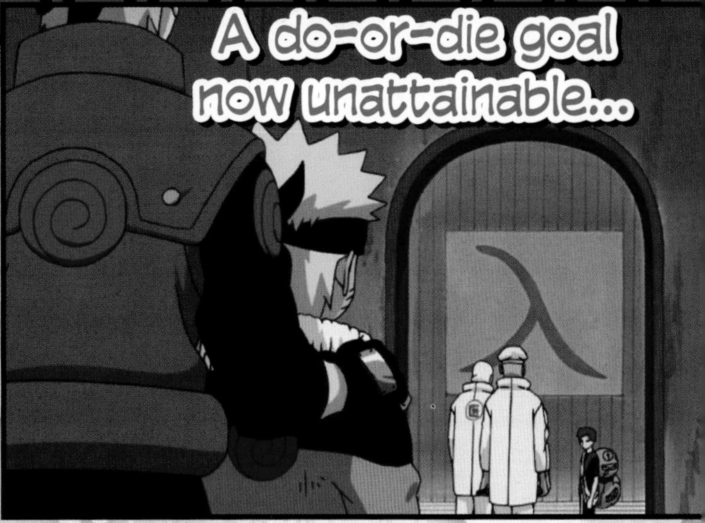

⬆ Aiming to prove oneself in combat against the very best... Naruto understands Lee's life-sacrificing aspiration.

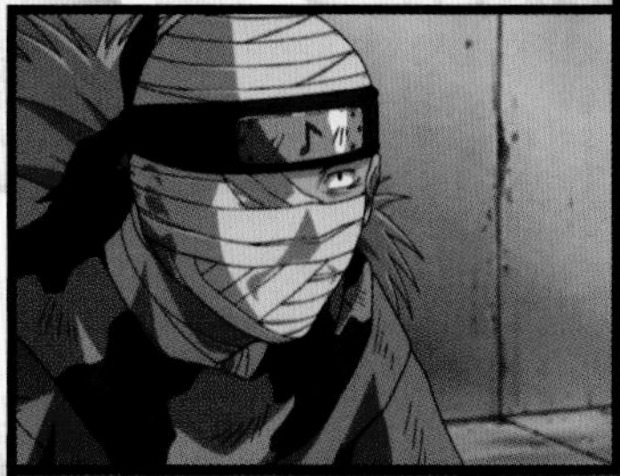

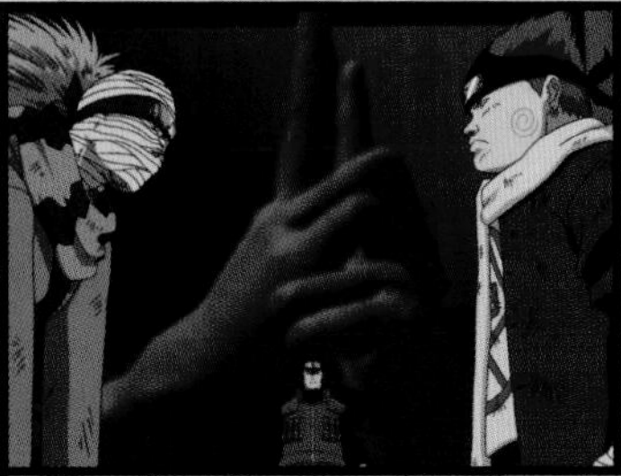

⬅ Choji is inspired by all-you-can-eat BBQ! But Dosu succeeds in stopping Choji's rolling Human Boulder Jutsu and blasts him with his sonic attack. Easy victory!

THE LAST MATCH IS AN ANTICLIMAX!

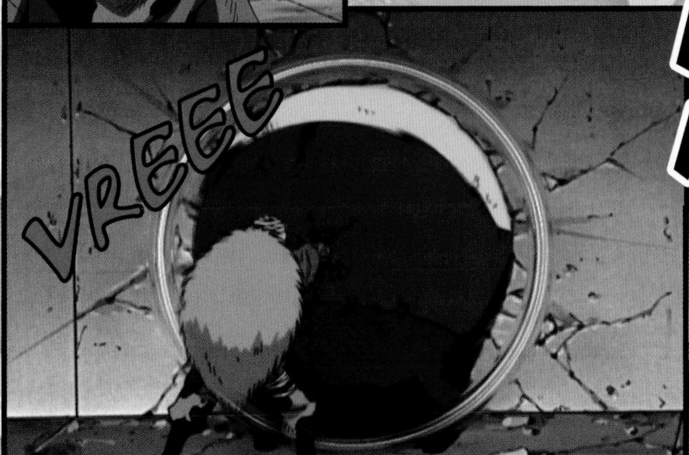
VREEE

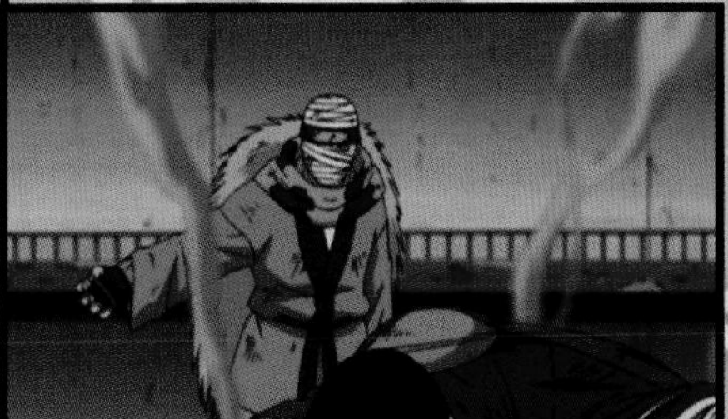

At last, into the final match! And...!

Lee exhibited a truly grand finale in his death struggle with Gaara. All who witnessed this spectacle are sure to have it etched deep into their memories. And in the afterglow of such a battle, the prelims finally reach the last match: Choji vs. Dosu.

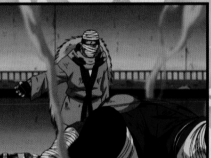

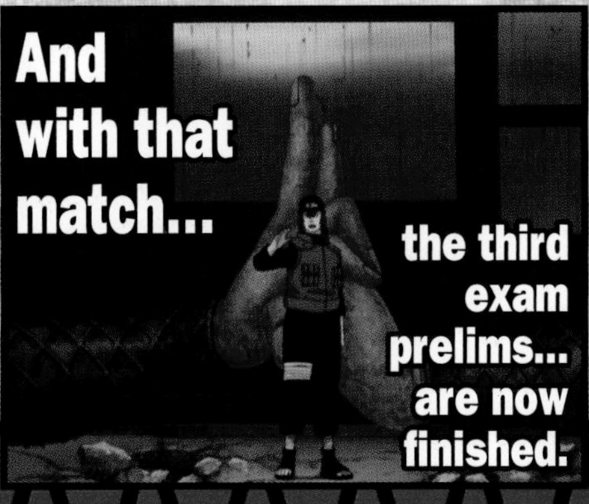
And with that match...
the third exam prelims... are now finished.

⬅ At last, nine participants for the final round are determined. One month to go until the finals!

Episode 51

Behind the Chunin Exams... A dark plot unfolds!

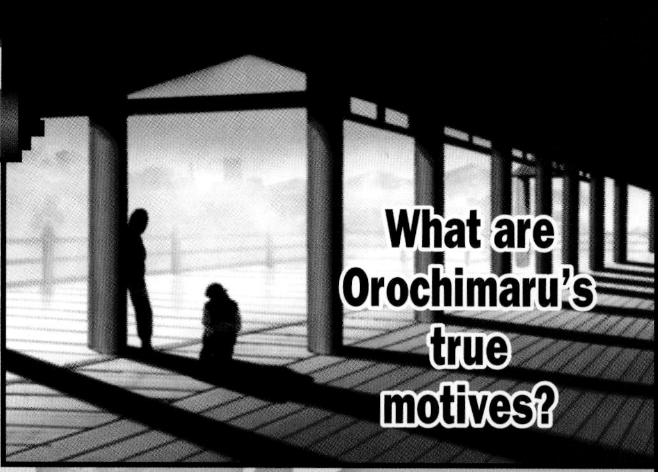

What are Orochimaru's true motives?

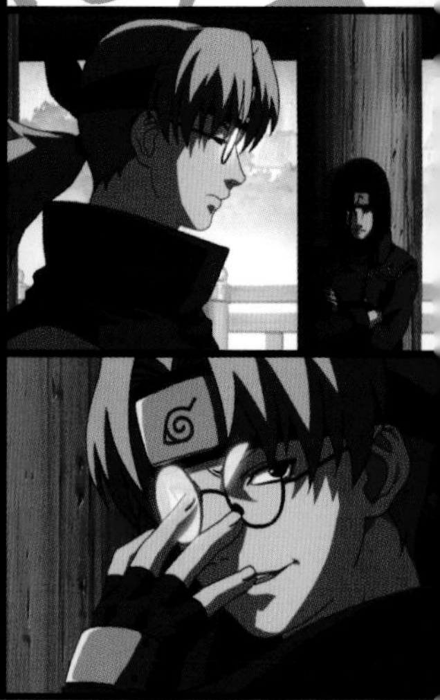

⬆➡ At a quiet temple, Orochimaru listens to Kabuto's report. What came to Orochimaru's mind as he stood in his hometown of the Hidden Leaf Village…?

Sound's shady secret schemes!

The third exam prelims have reached a satisfactory conclusion. The candidates for the final round have been chosen. But Kabuto, who bowed out of the prelims, and Orochimaru are holding a secret meeting in the shadows. What orders did Orochimaru hand down…?!

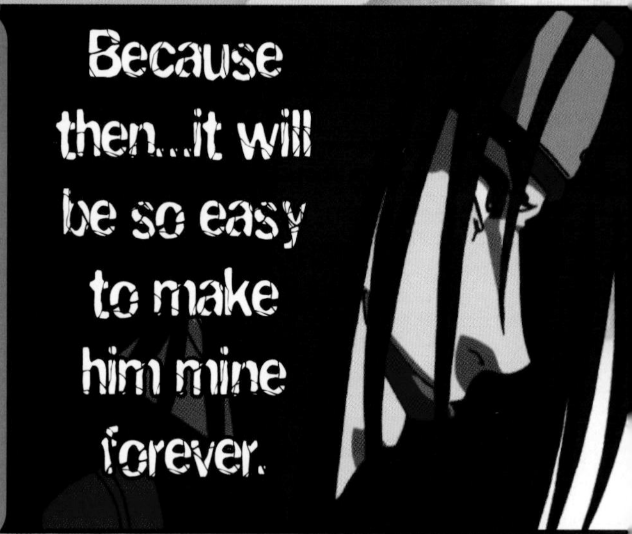
Because then...it will be so easy to make him mine forever.

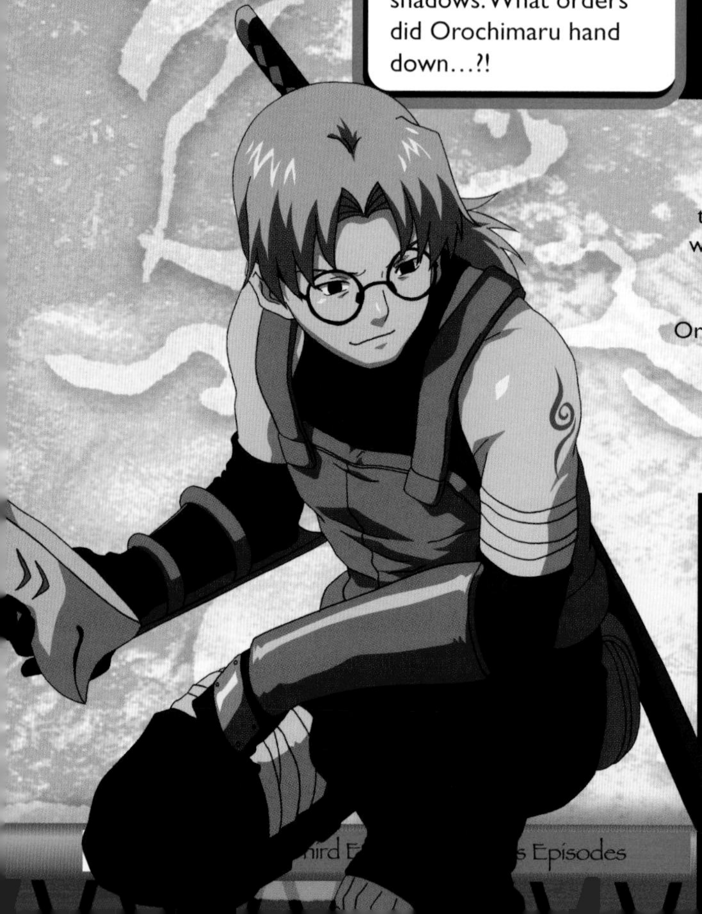

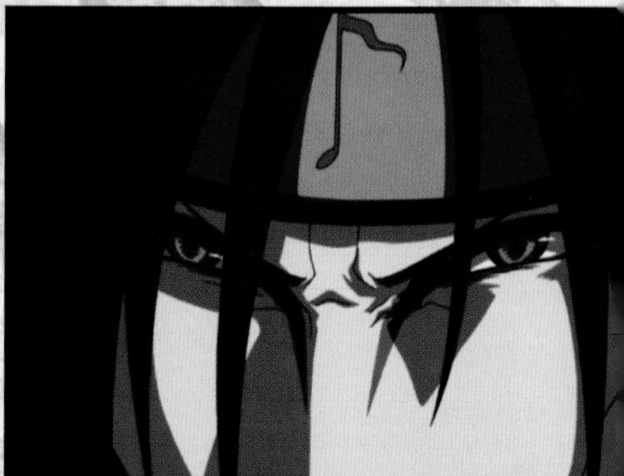

⬇➡ "And that's why I want you to go abduct him!" Is Orochimaru's interest Sasuke's blood?!

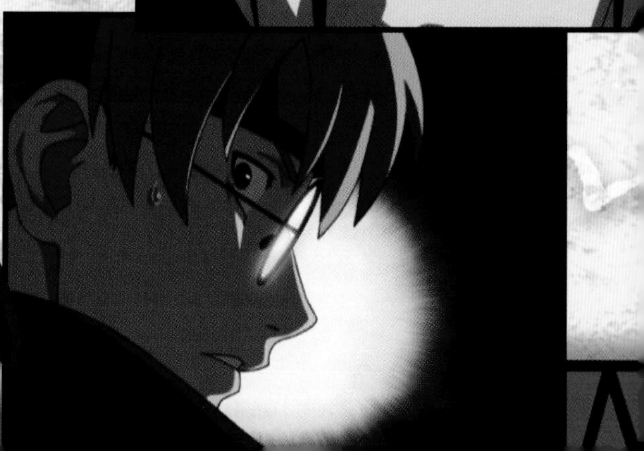

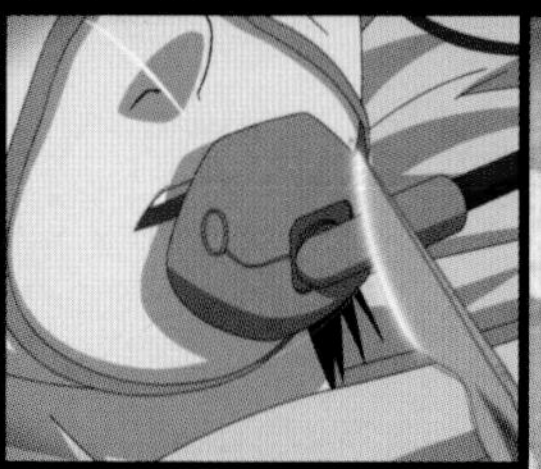

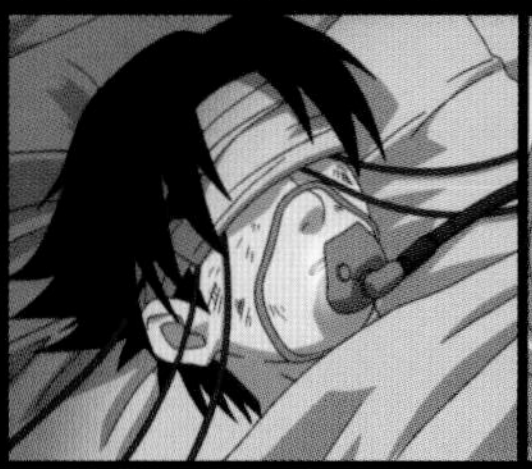

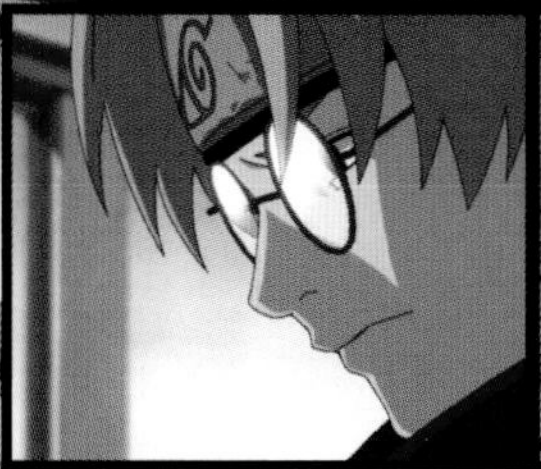

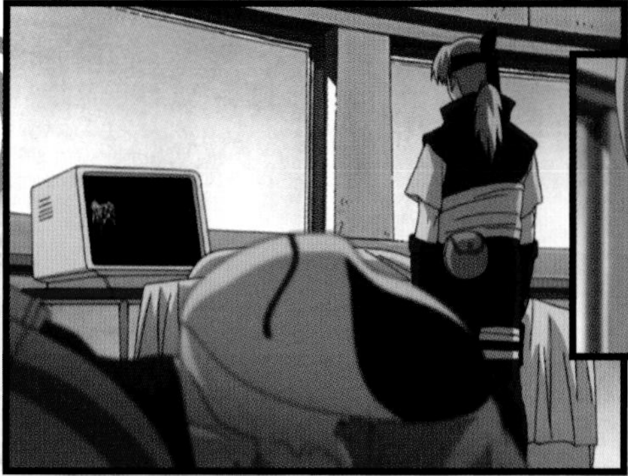

⬅⬆ What came to Kabuto's mind seeing the vulnerable, sleeping Sasuke? And what is the underlying truth in Kabuto's words, "We failed to avoid Orochimaru's watchful eye, and it's most unfortunate for both of us."

A calm, cold blade closes in on Sasuke!

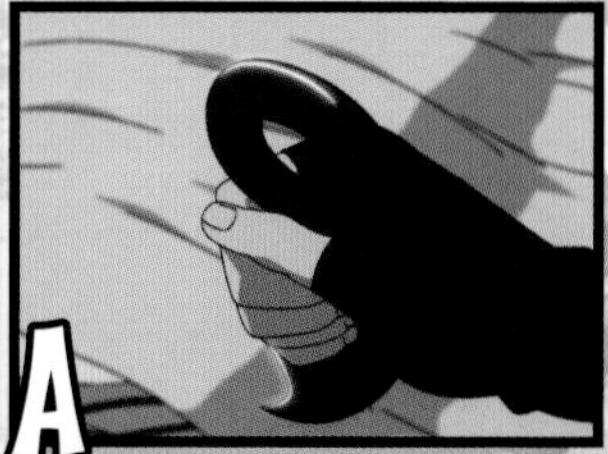

A strikingly skillful confrontation!

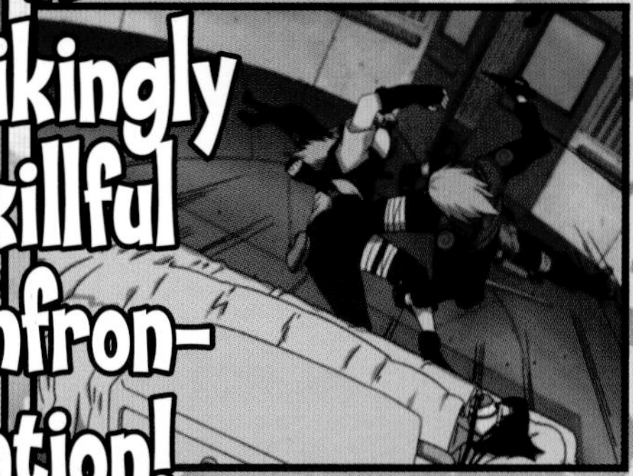

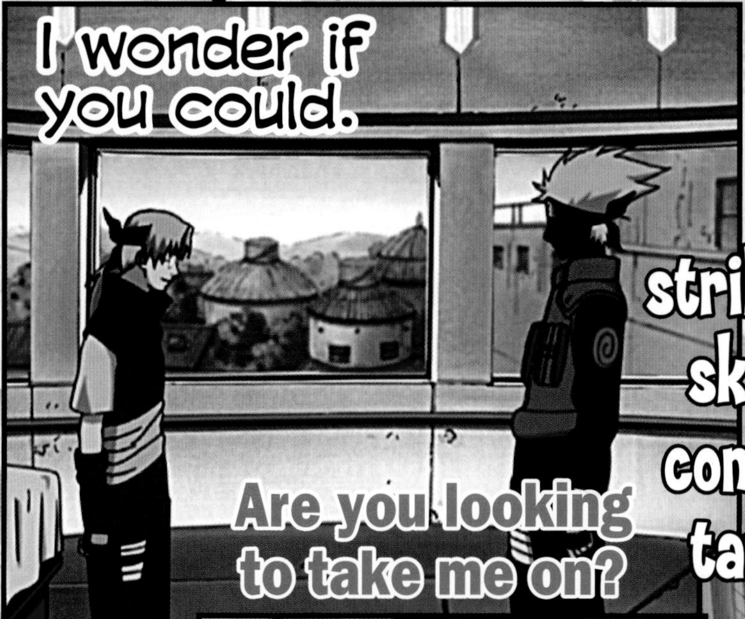
I wonder if you could.
Are you looking to take me on?

⬆ The predator and the protector face off. Kakashi demands to know what relationship Kabuto has with Orochimaru. Kabuto responds with sarcasm. Conflict is inevitable!

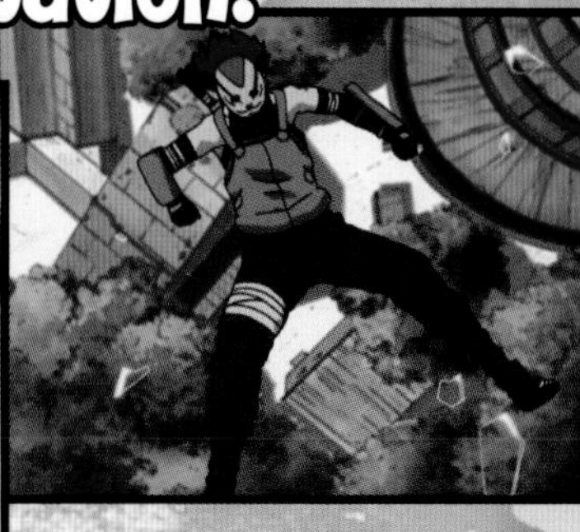

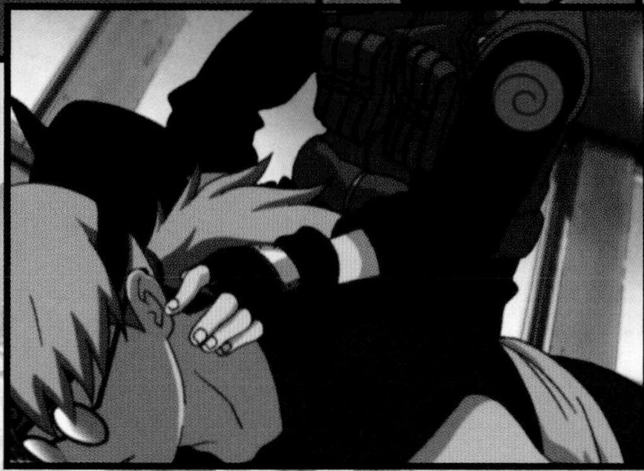

⬅⬆ It looked like Kakashi had the upper hand, but his opponents were all decoys that Kabuto created with his Dead Soul Jutsu, and Kabuto succeeds in making his escape from the hospital room.

An assassin sent to target Sasuke!

On assignment from Orochimaru, Kabuto sneaks into Sasuke's hospital room. After easily taking out several of the Anbu Black Ops, he closes in with his sharp blade pointed at Sasuke's throat… An instant later that blade is aimed at Kakashi.

A month to go until the final round!

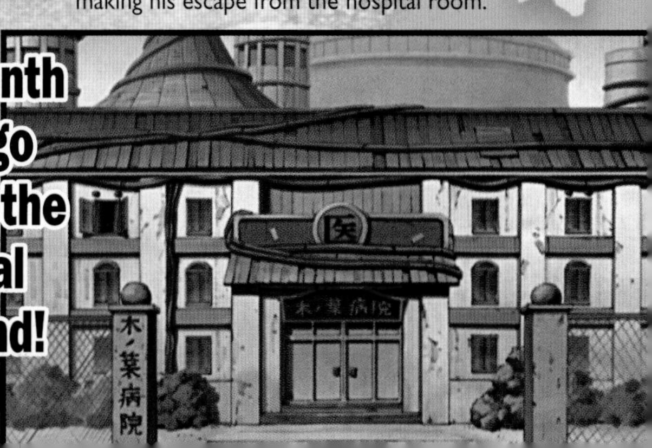
木ノ葉病院
医

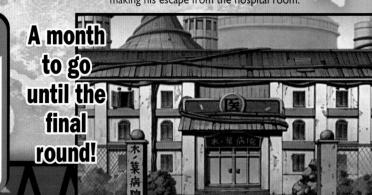

Where's the hidden truth?!
HIDDEN LEAF TRAINING QUIZ

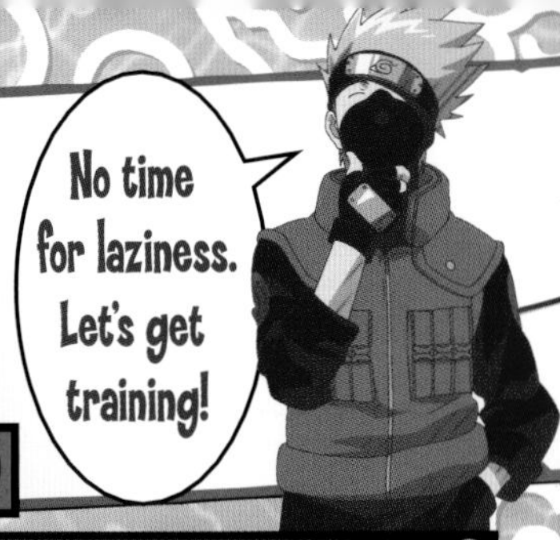
No time for laziness. Let's get training!

Part 1: See through the Multiple Shadow Clone Jutsu!

Find this Naruto!

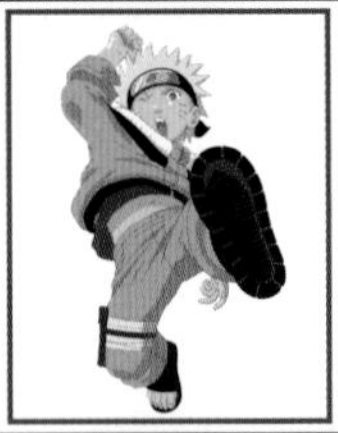

Naruto has created multiple shadow clones. Figure out how many Narutos there are in exactly the same pose as the one on the left. You've got 10 seconds. Well, start searching!

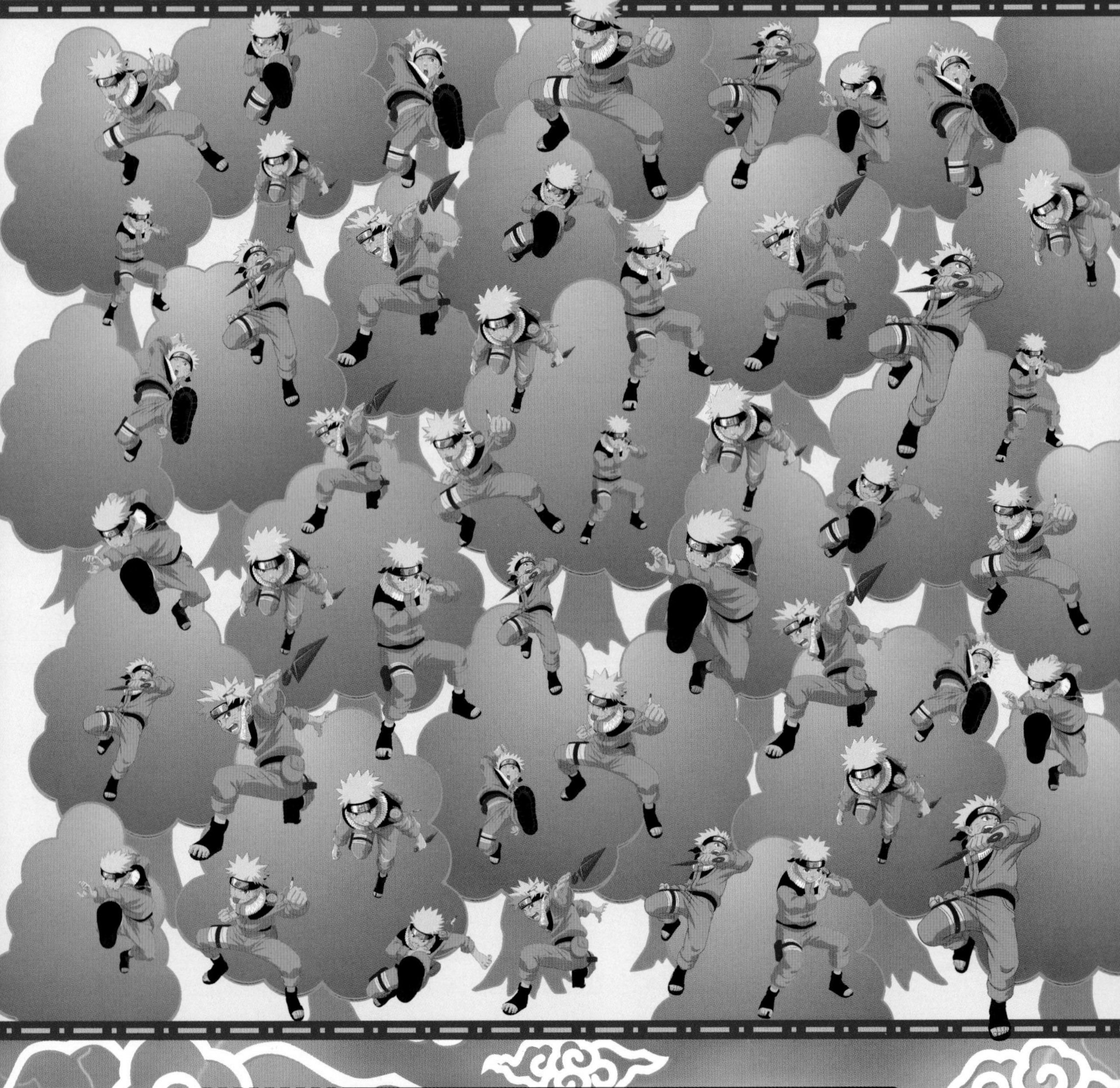

The answer is on page 280!

You closet perv!

Training for victory in the finals!

Ebisu returns!

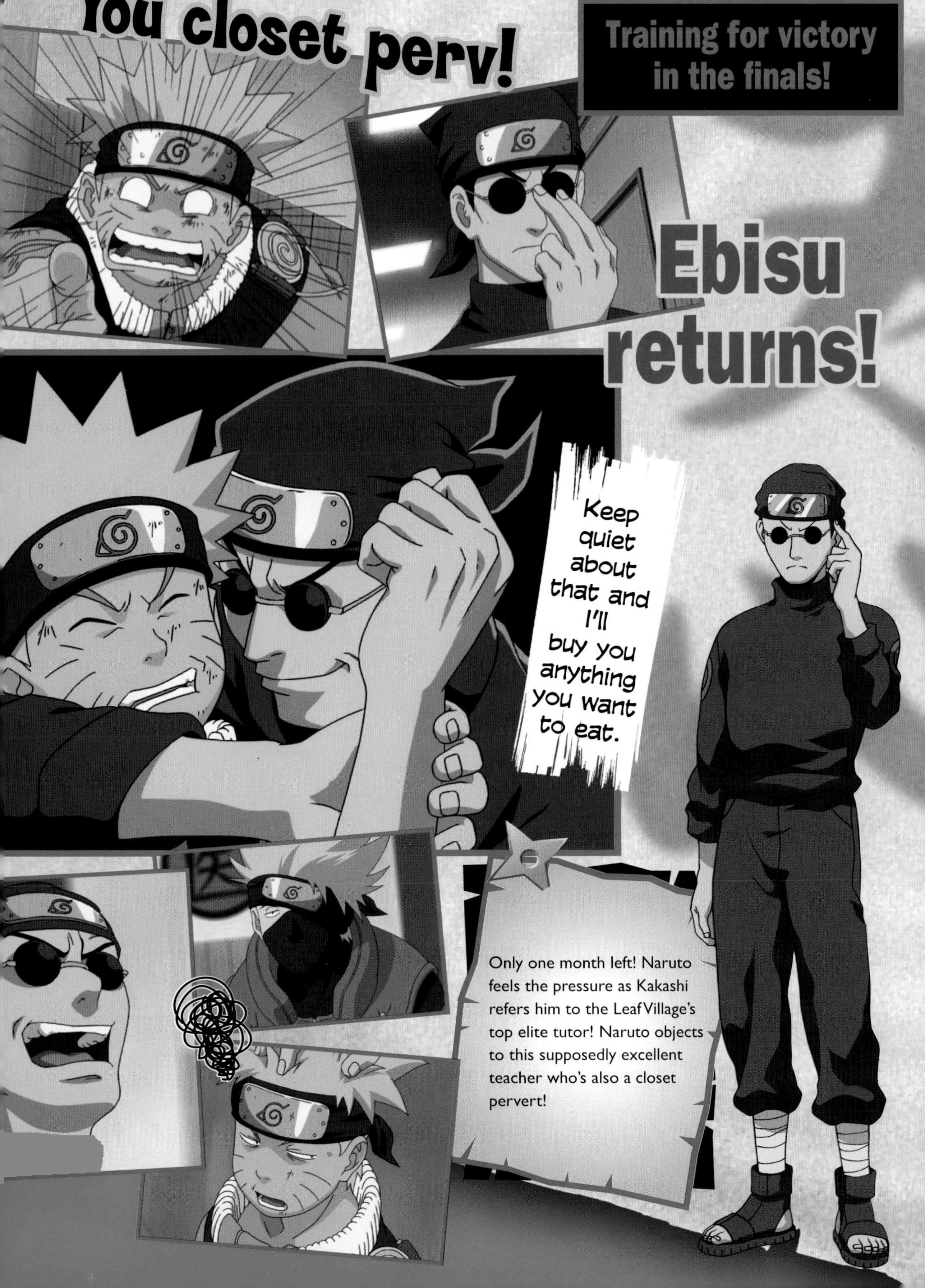
Keep quiet about that and I'll buy you anything you want to eat.

Only one month left! Naruto feels the pressure as Kakashi refers him to the Leaf Village's top elite tutor! Naruto objects to this supposedly excellent teacher who's also a closet pervert!

A mysterious intruder!

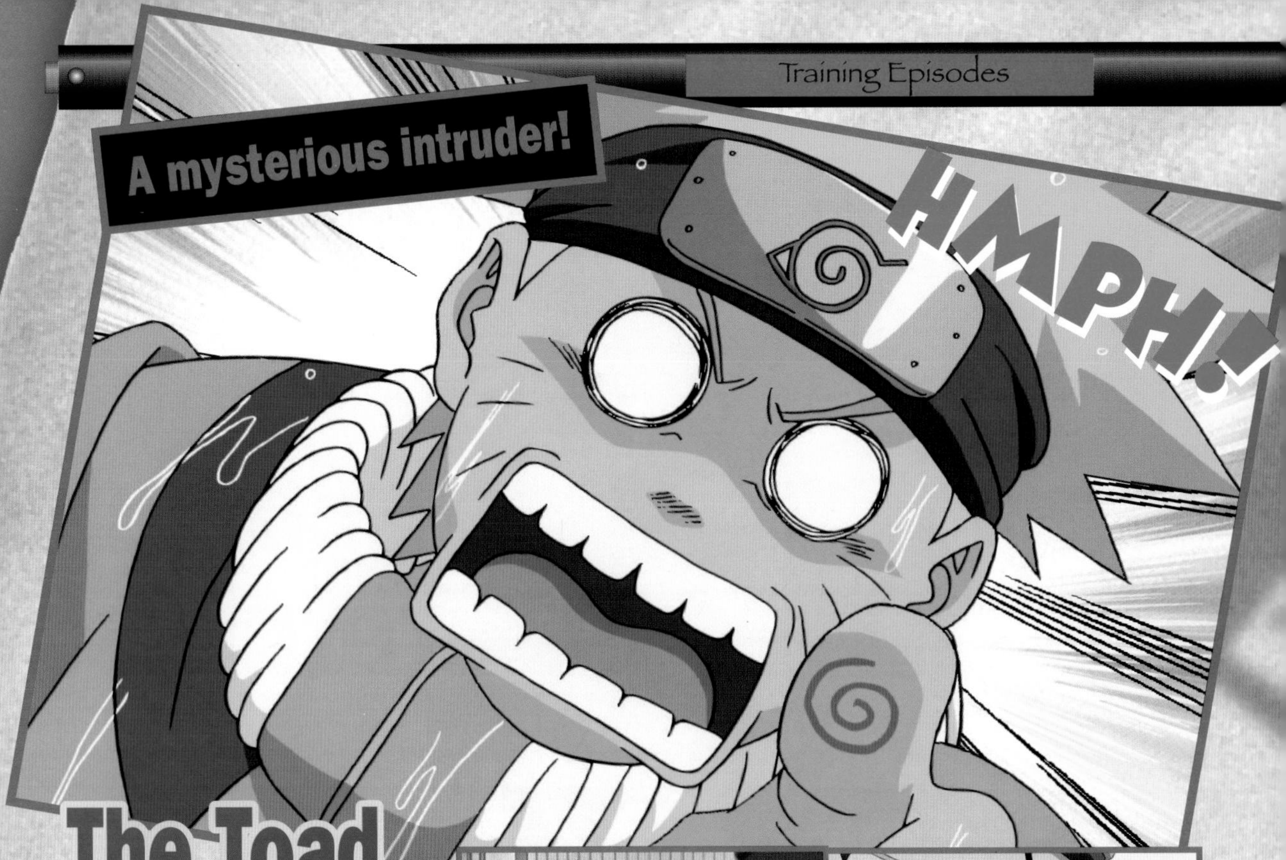
HMPH!

The Toad Sage makes his dynamic entrance!

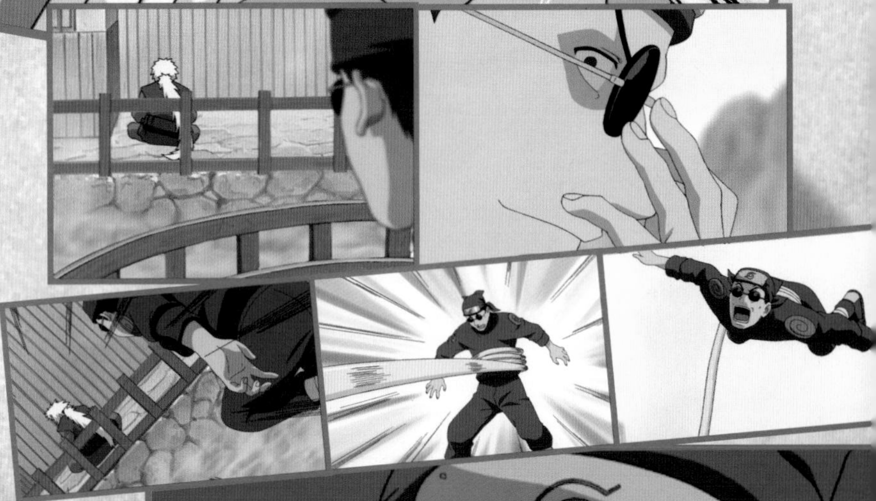

In the middle of being trained to walk on water, Naruto notices someone lurking around the women's bath. As an elite tutor, Ebisu is responsible for preventing any disreputable behavior. But as he moves to punish the perp…

The elite tutor gets flattened in return!

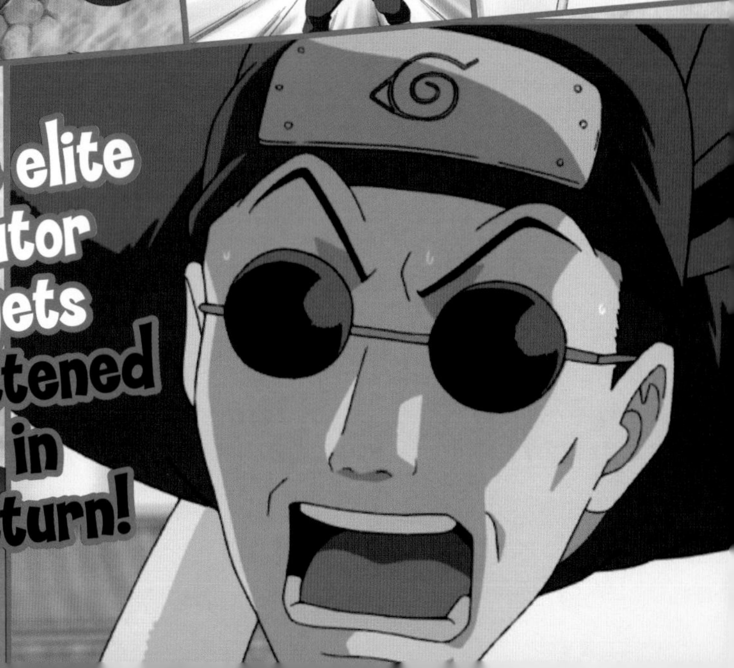

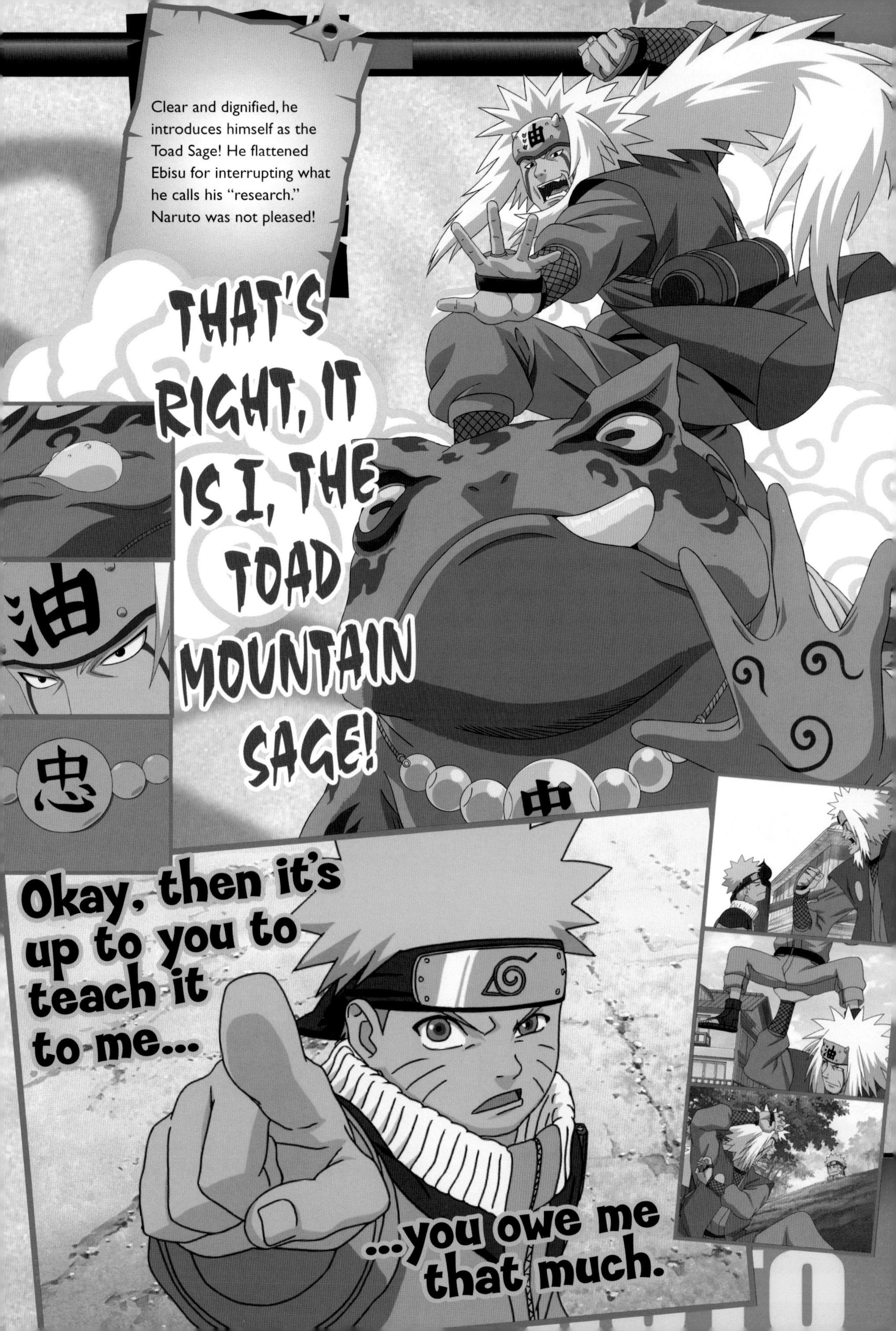
Clear and dignified, he introduces himself as the Toad Sage! He flattened Ebisu for interrupting what he calls his "research." Naruto was not pleased!
THAT'S RIGHT, IT IS I, THE TOAD MOUNTAIN SAGE!
油
忠
Okay, then it's up to you to teach it to me...
...you owe me that much.

The Perverted Sage, a great mentor?!

So far so good!

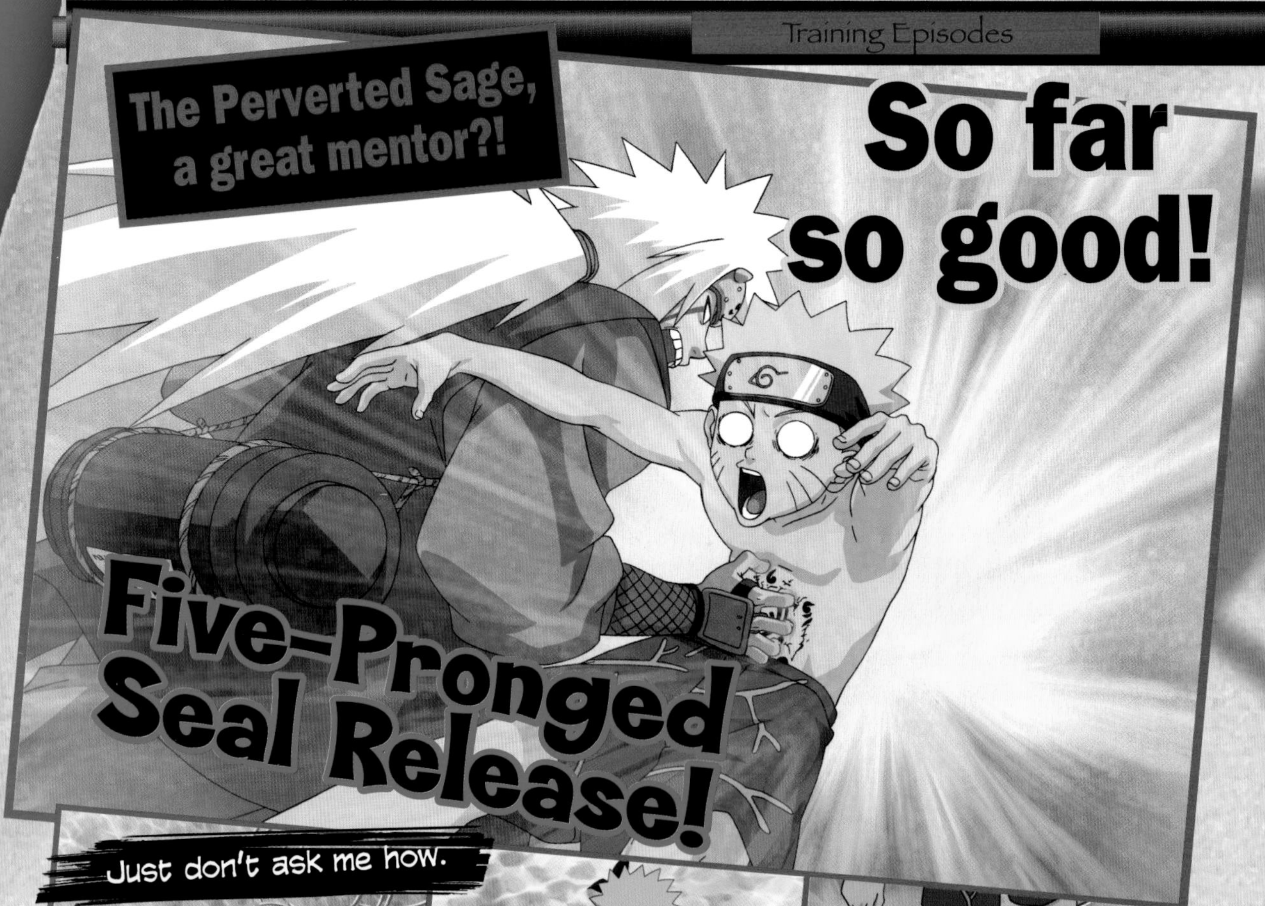
Five-Pronged Seal Release!

Just don't ask me how.

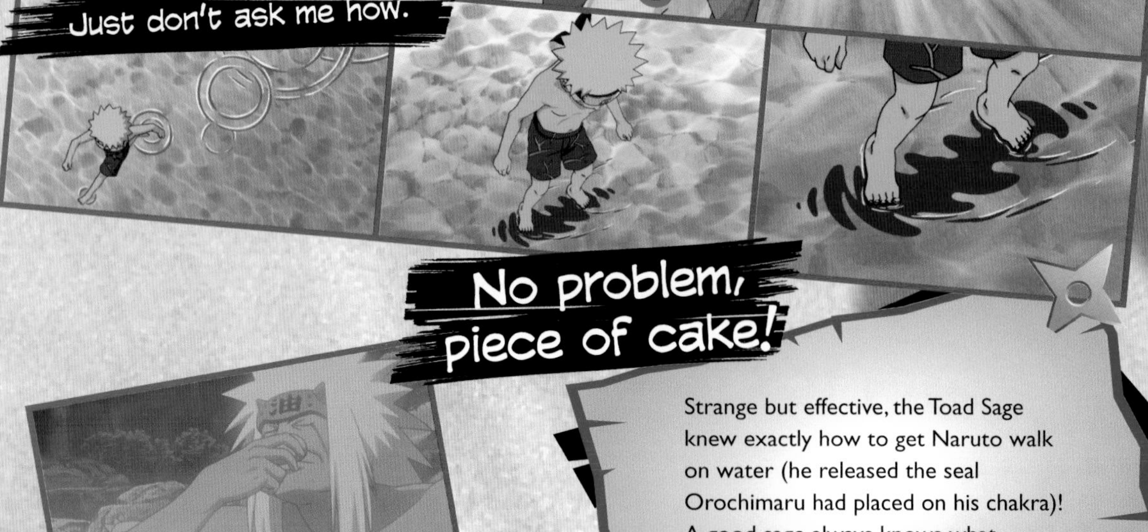

No problem, piece of cake!

Strange but effective, the Toad Sage knew exactly how to get Naruto walk on water (he released the seal Orochimaru had placed on his chakra)! A good sage always knows what buttons to push.

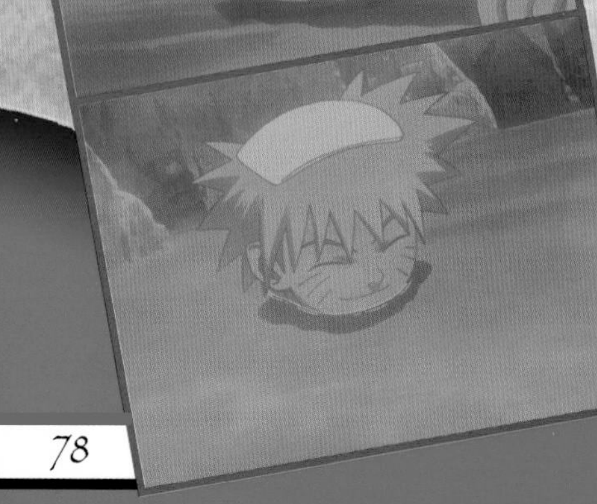

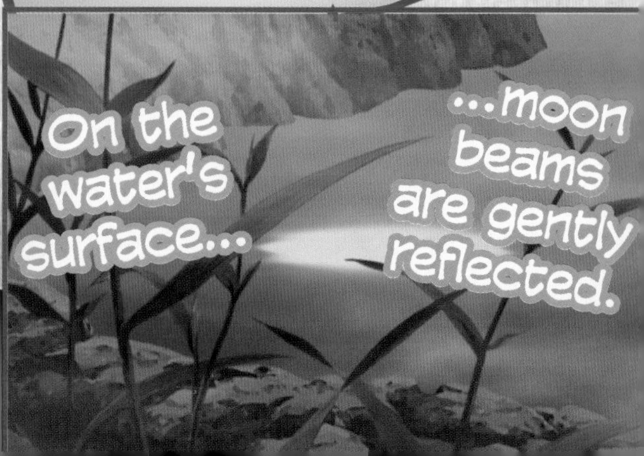
On the water's surface...
...moon beams are gently reflected.

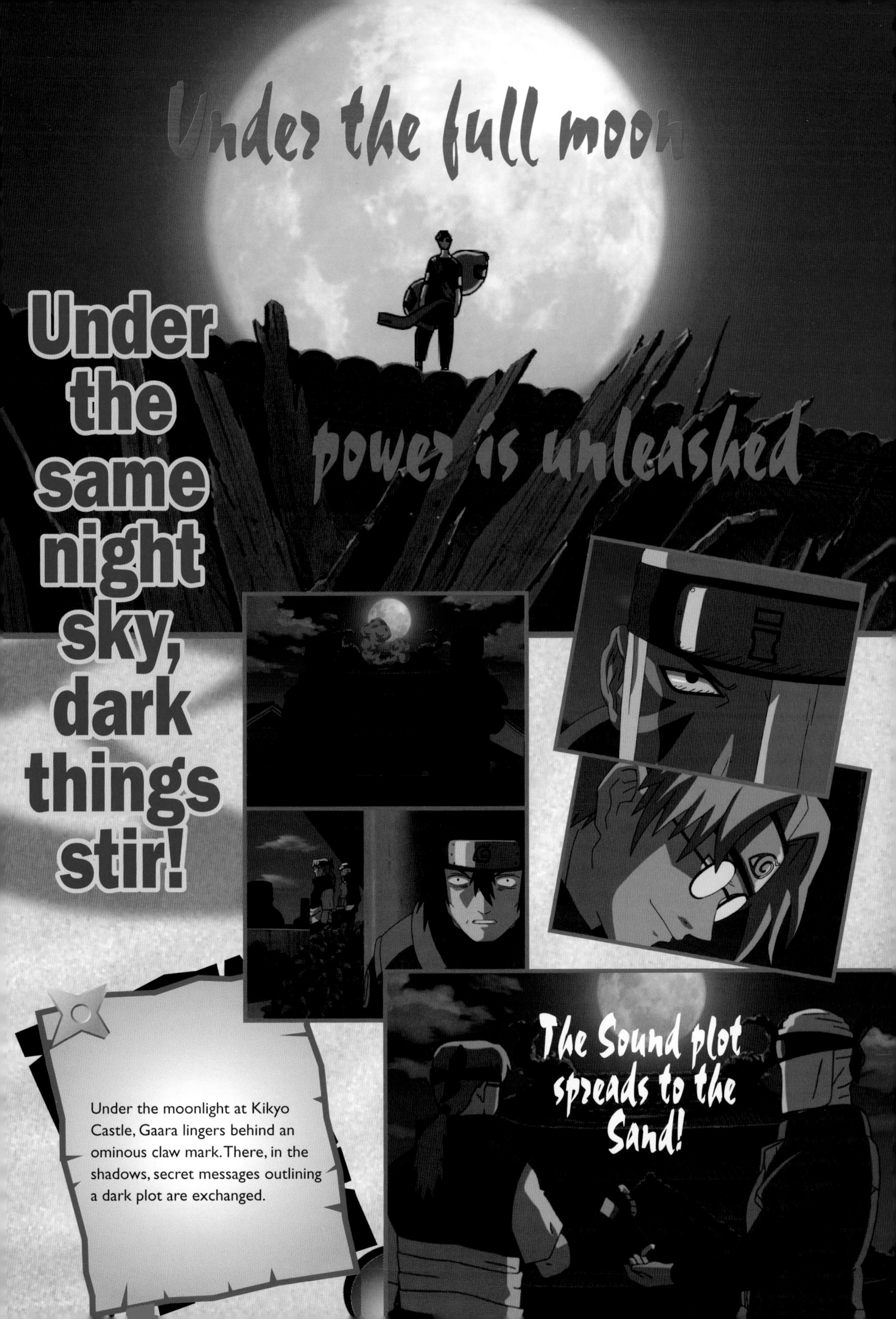
Under the full moon
power is unleashed
Under the same night sky, dark things stir!
The Sound plot spreads to the Sand!

Under the moonlight at Kikyo Castle, Gaara lingers behind an ominous claw mark. There, in the shadows, secret messages outlining a dark plot are exchanged.

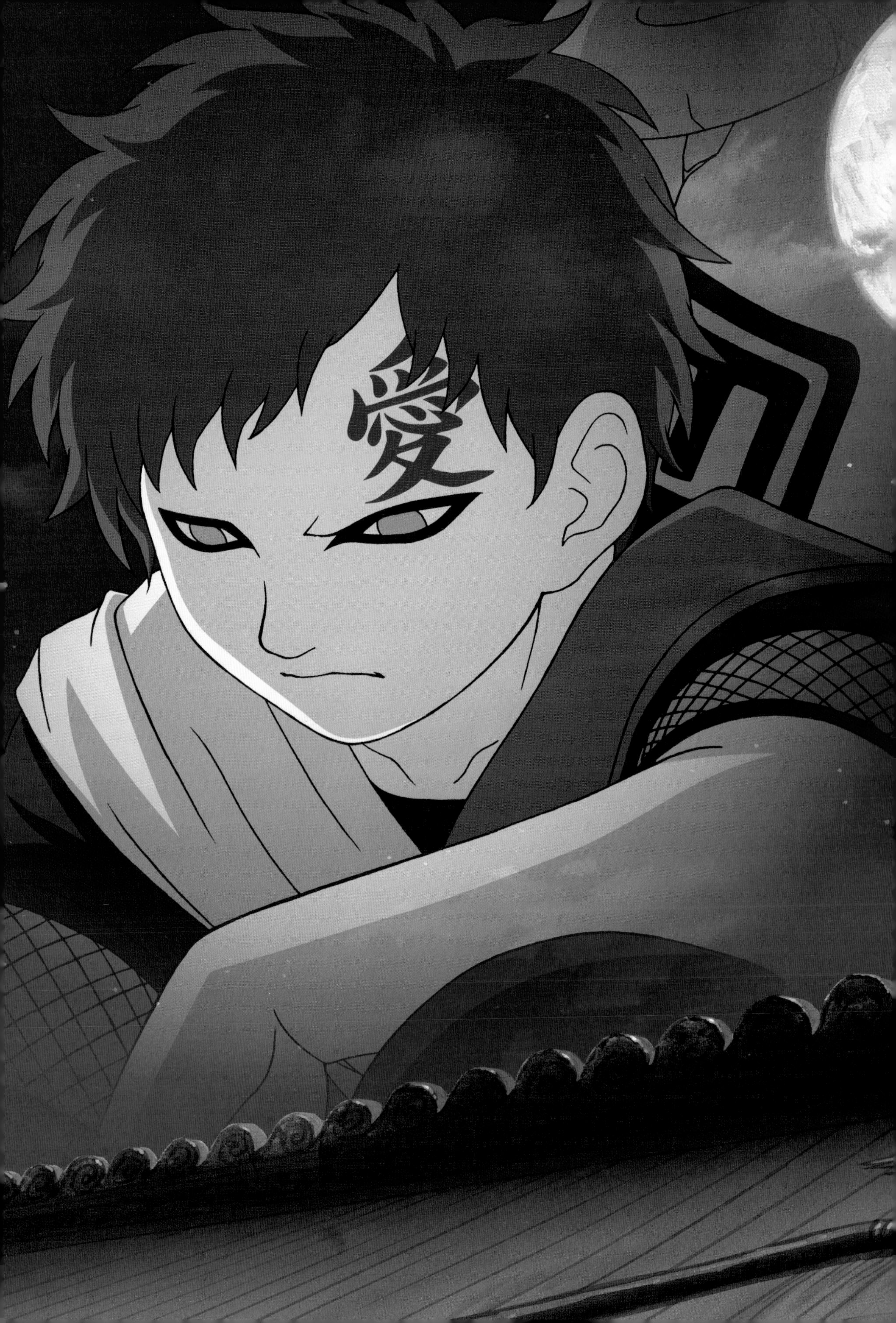

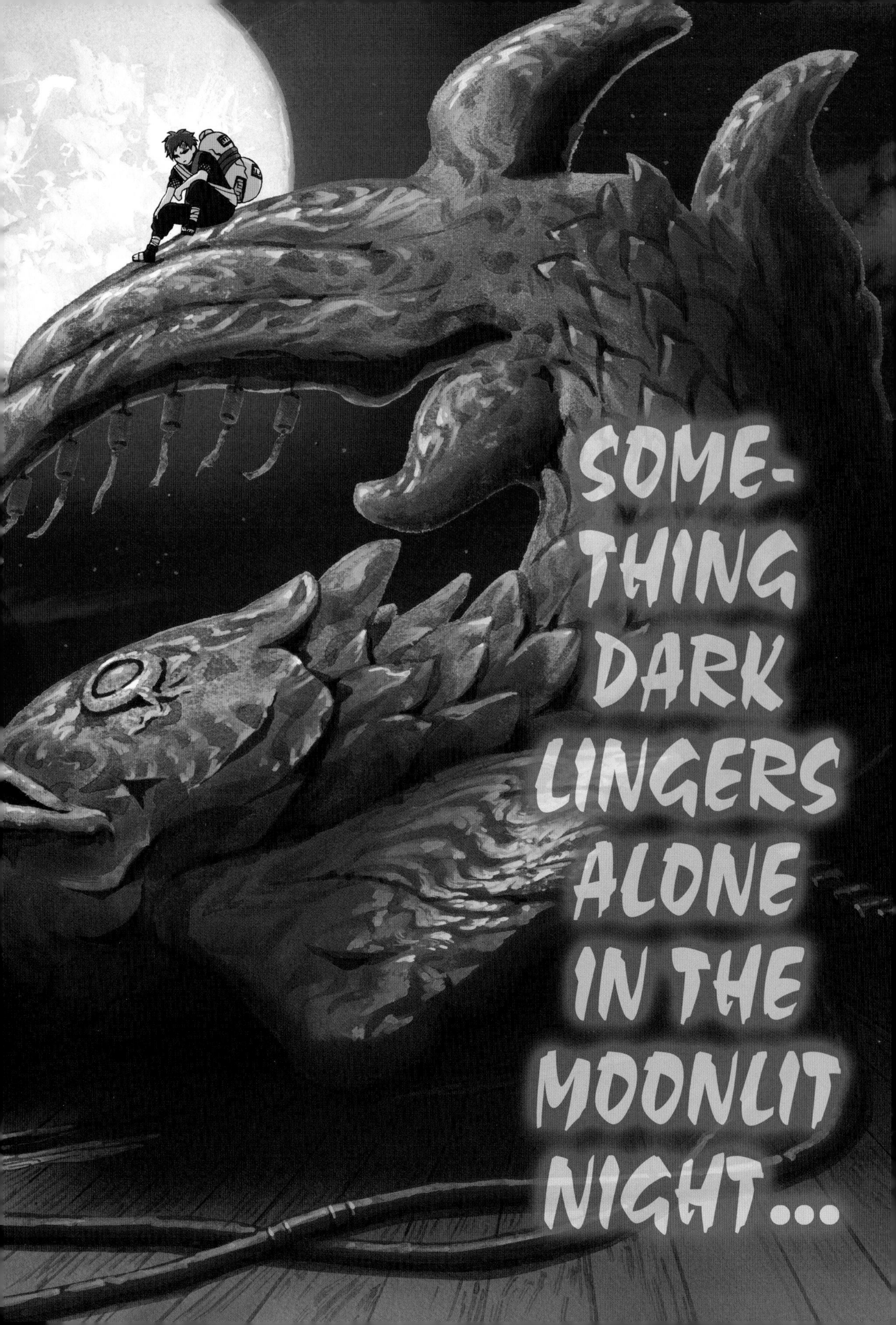
SOME-
THING
DARK
LINGERS
ALONE
IN THE
MOONLIT
NIGHT...

Let love bloom!

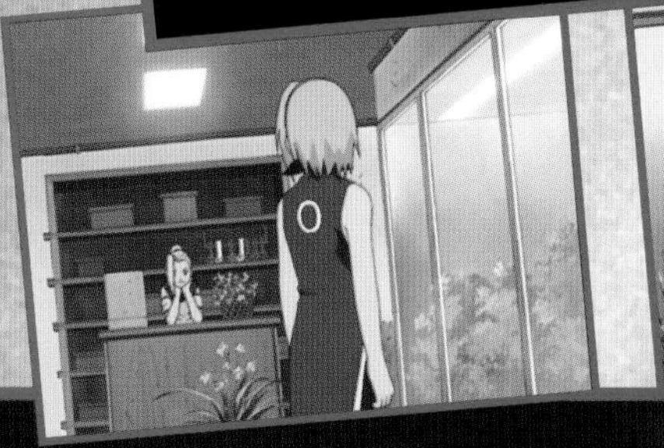

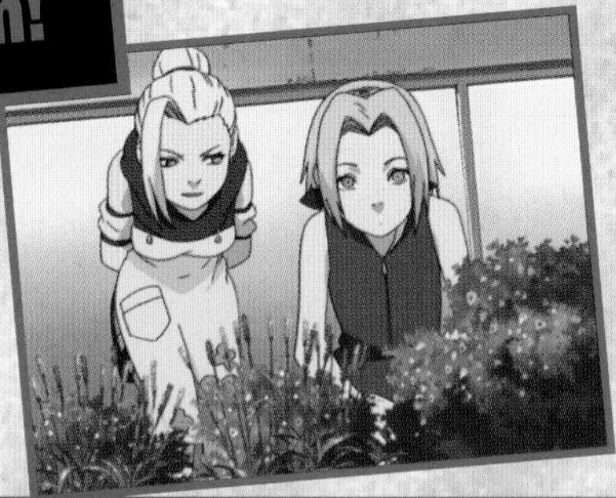

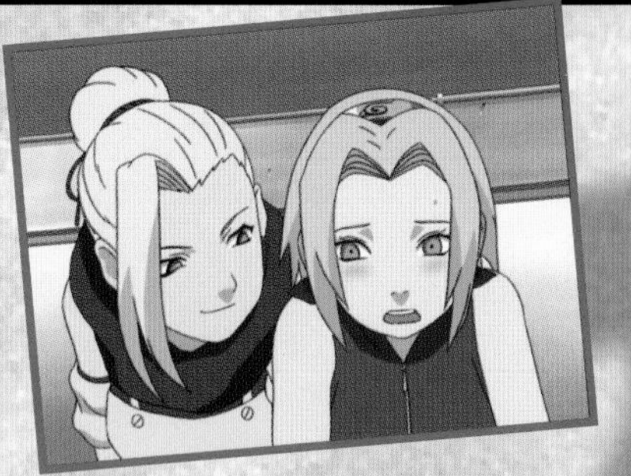

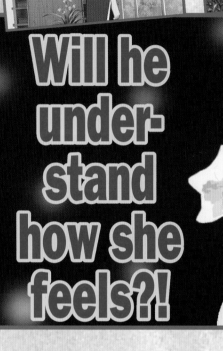

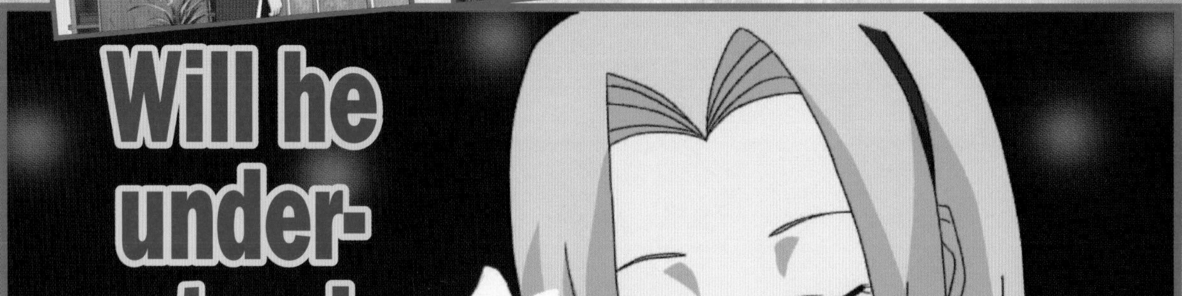
Will he under-stand how she feels?!
So much feeling in a single flower...

The Daffodil: a noble flower that bravely endures the long months of winter, waiting for the spring. Sakura wants to express her feelings with a daffodil and goes to visit Sasuke in the hospital. But Sasuke is missing.

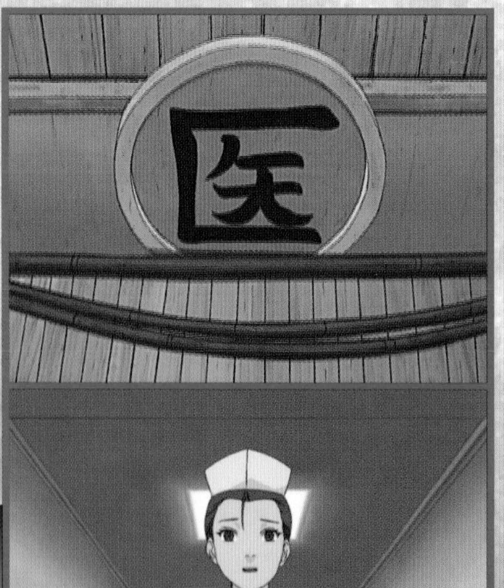
医

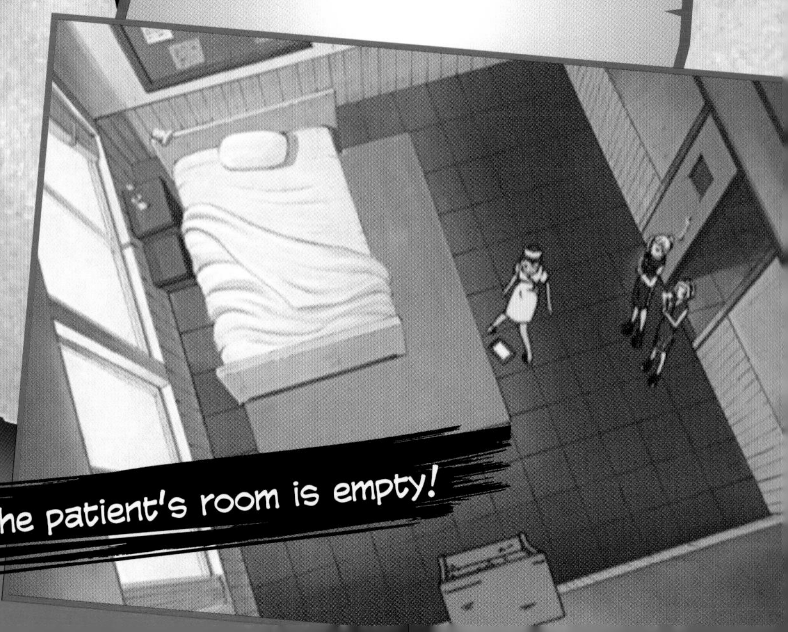

The patient's room is empty!

Individual battles...

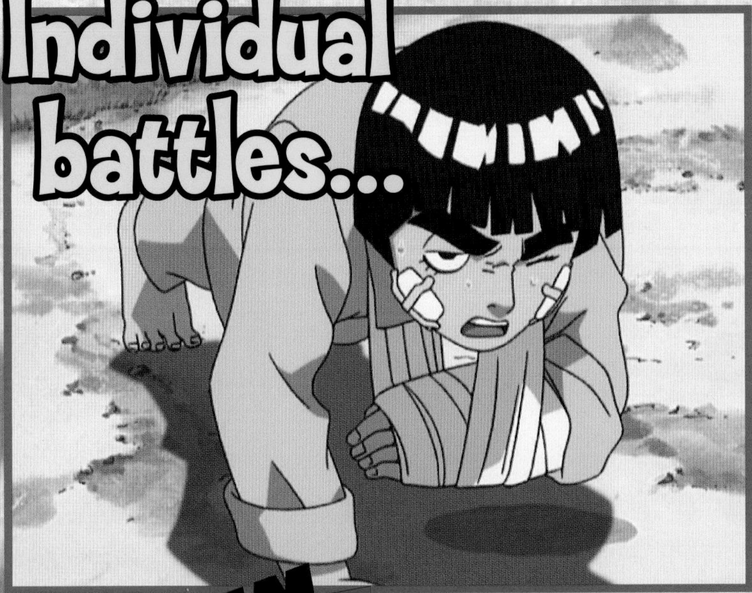

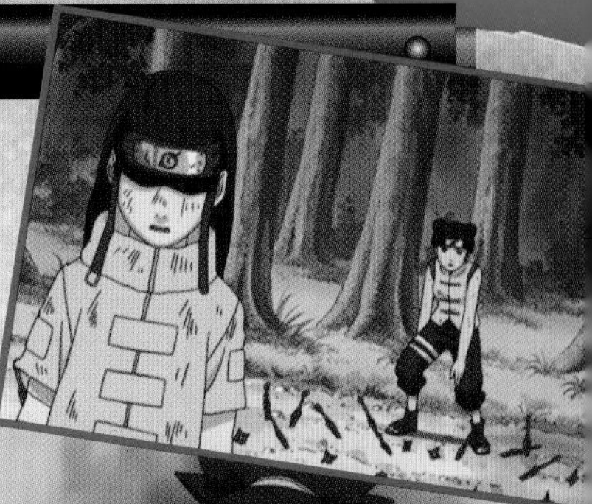

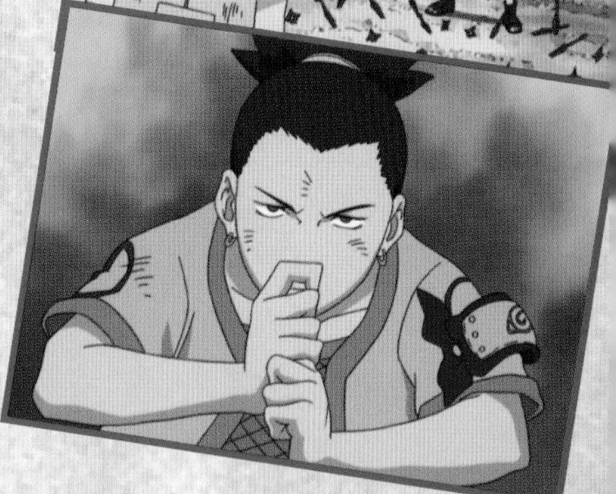

Even with severe injuries, Lee pushes on with his training. Everyone else steps it up as well, preparing for the final rounds. There's no time for hesitation now as they strive for true success…!

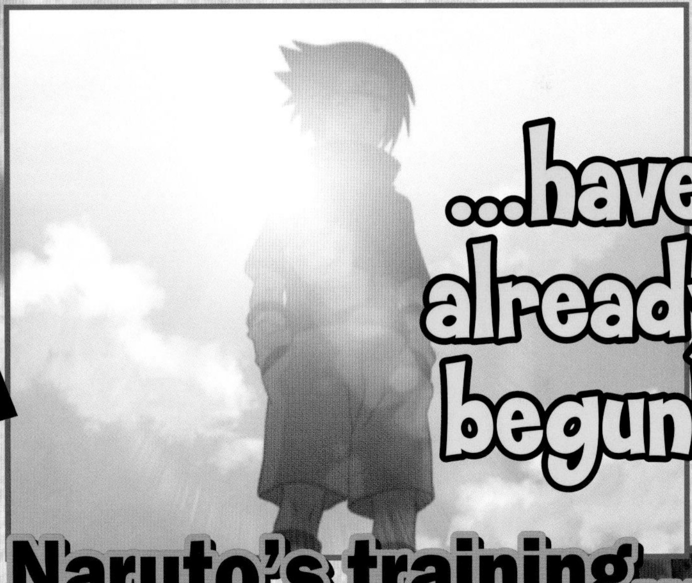

...have already begun!

But Naruto's training...

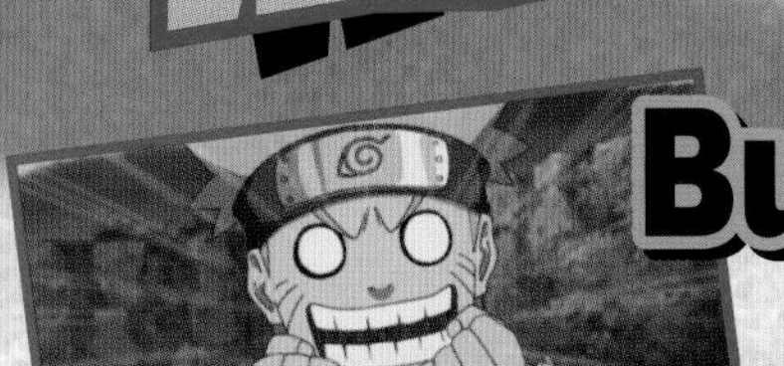

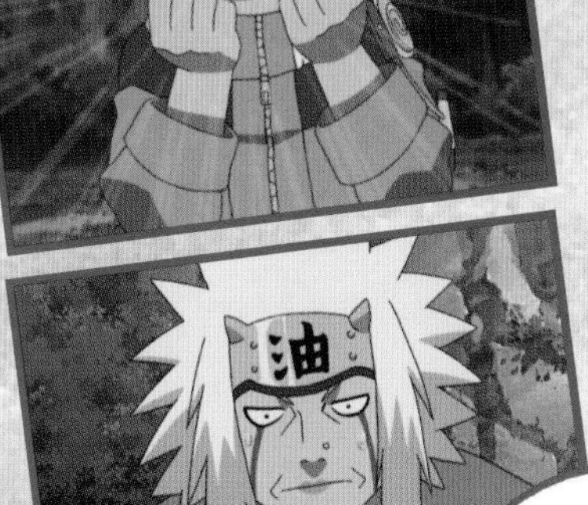

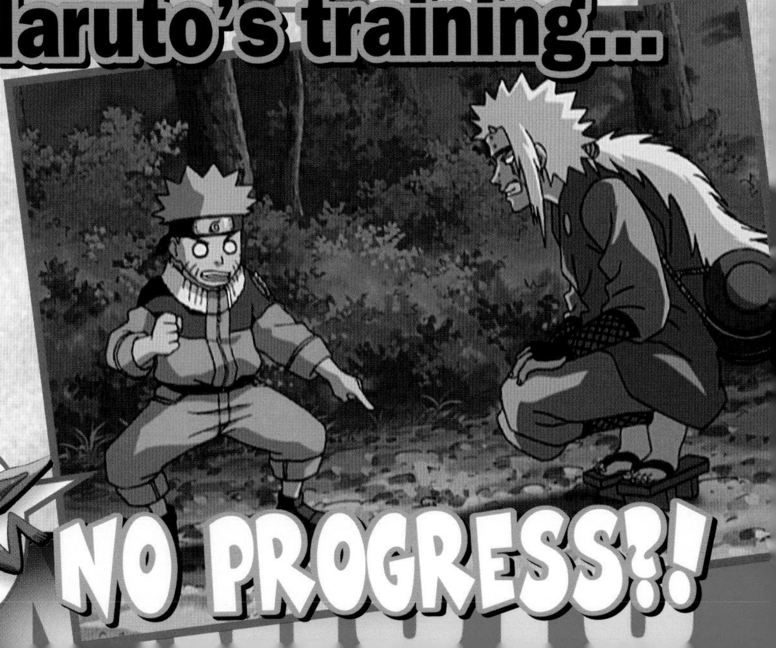

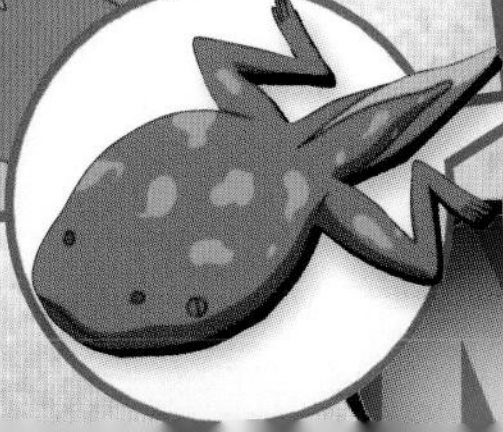

NO PROGRESS?!

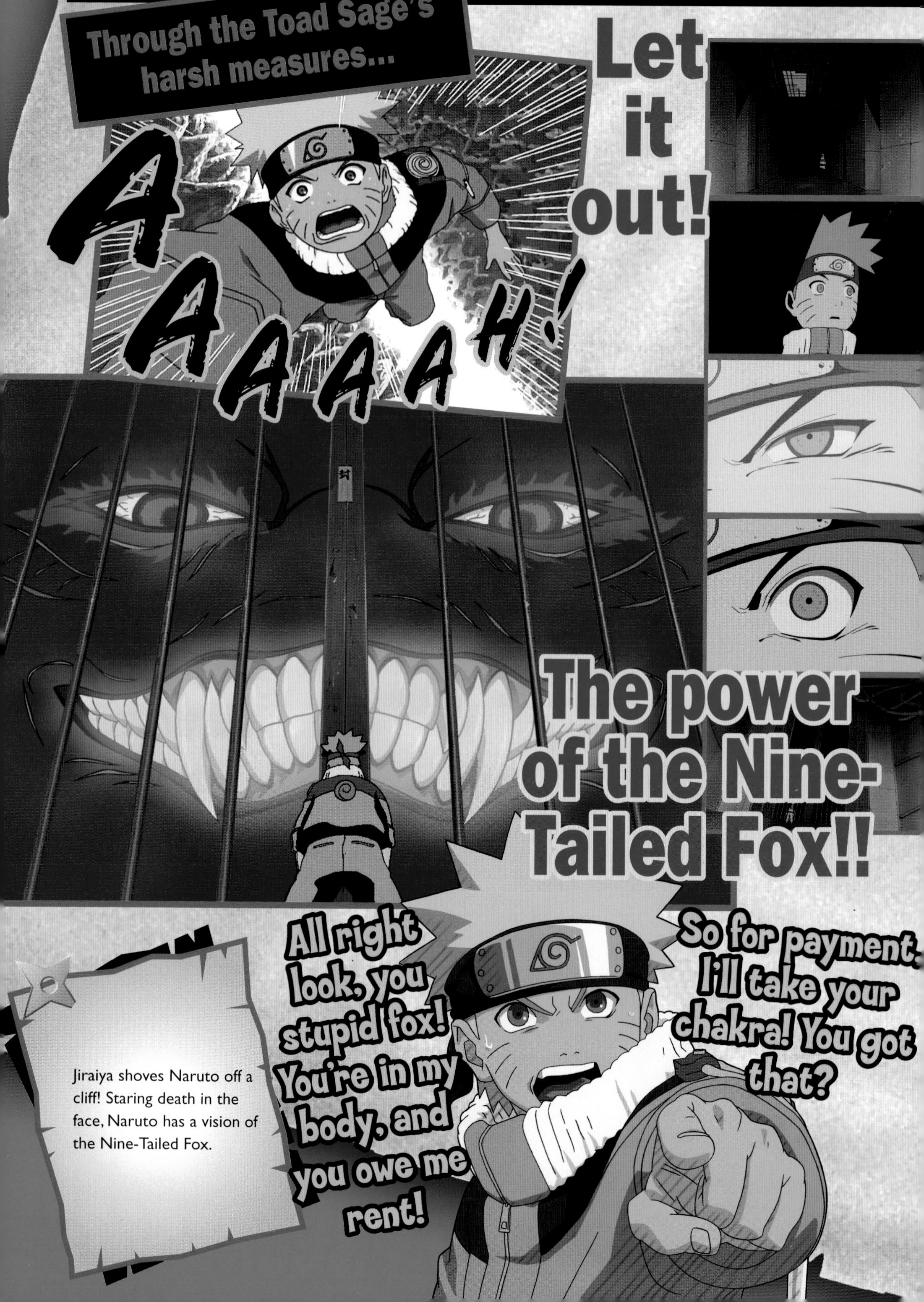
Through the Toad Sage's harsh measures...
Let it out!
AAAAAAH!
The power of the Nine-Tailed Fox!!
So for payment, I'll take your chakra! You got that?
All right look, you stupid fox! You're in my body, and you owe me rent!

Jiraiya shoves Naruto off a cliff! Staring death in the face, Naruto has a vision of the Nine-Tailed Fox.

Facing the enormous Nine-Tailed Fox head-on, Naruto makes its chakra his own! This is the power of the Nine-Tailed Fox – this is the power of Naruto! At last, the Summoning Jutsu succeeds. Enter Gamabunta!

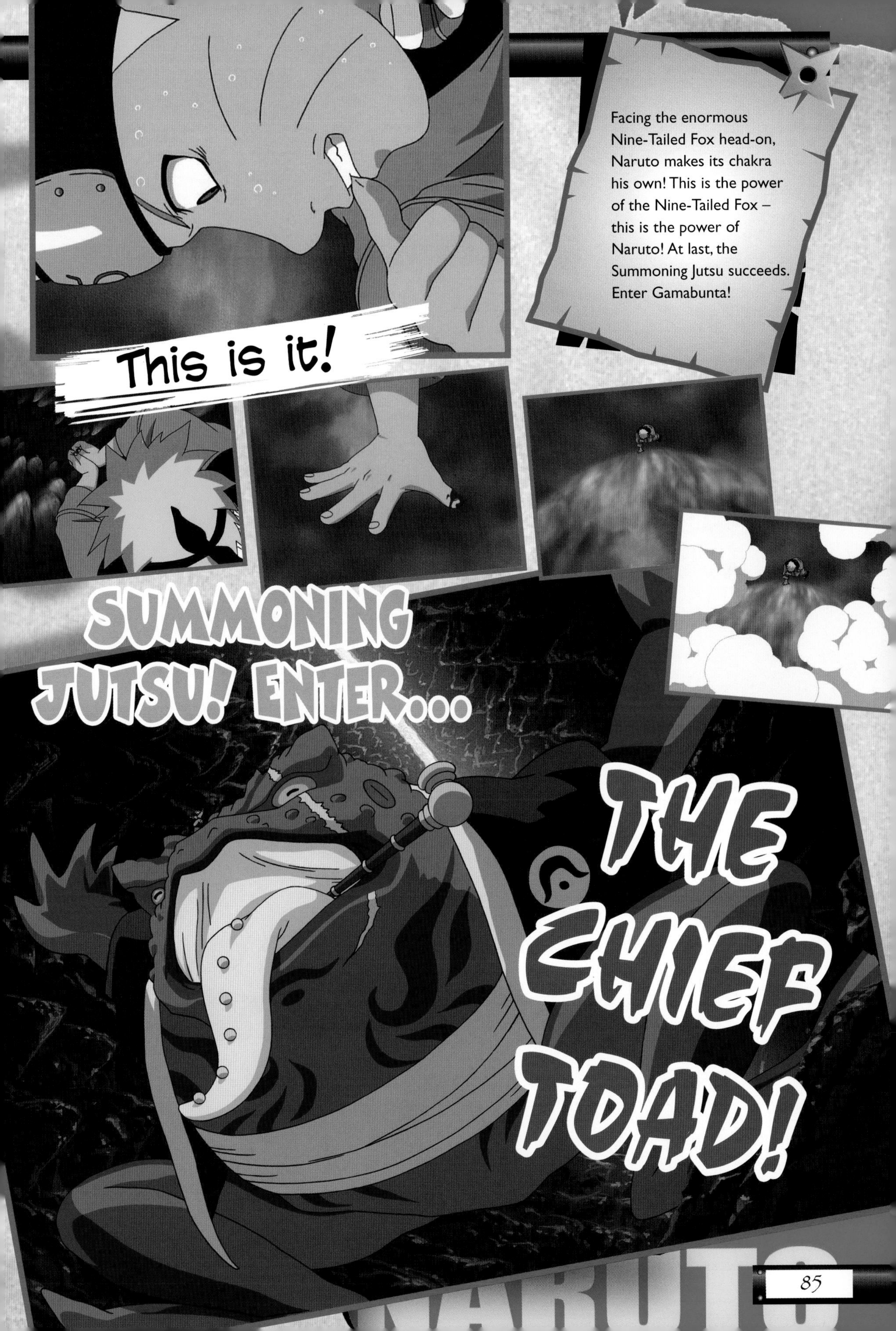
This is it!
SUMMONING JUTSU! ENTER...
THE CHIEF TOAD!
NARUTO

Jiraiya

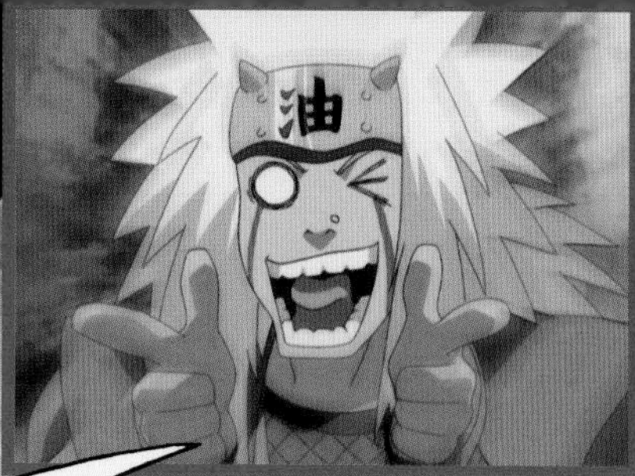

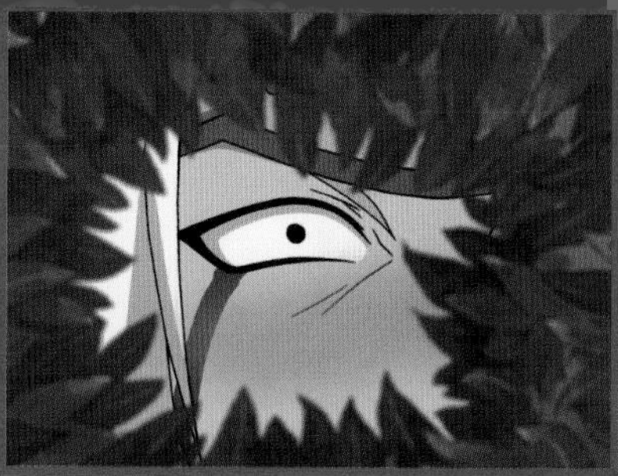

One of the legendary "Sannin," the great Toad Sage!

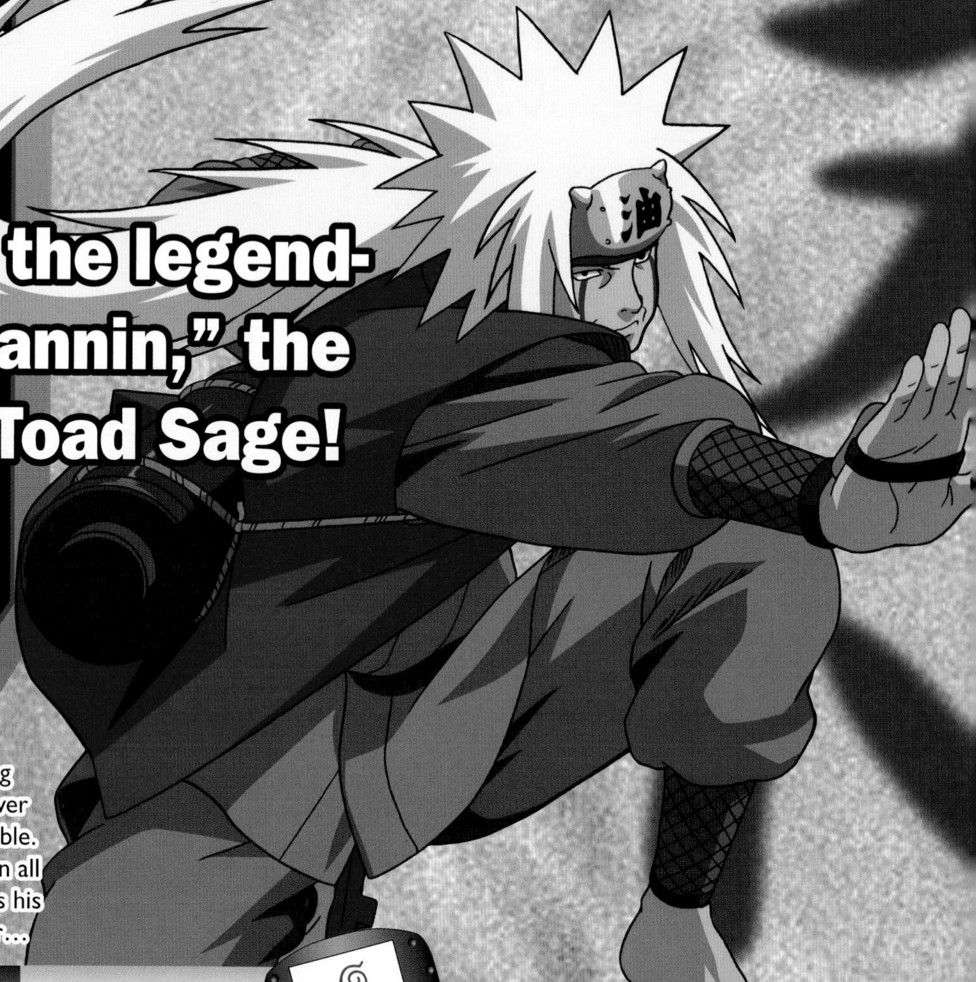

To have earned his reputation as a living legend, his true power must be immeasurable. But for some reason all people remember is his lecherous character...

PROFILE

Rank: —
Ninja Registration Number: 002301
Height: 191.2 cm (6' 3")
Weight: 87.5 kg (193 lbs.)
Birthday: November 11 (50 years old, Scorpio)
Blood type: B
Personality: Lecherous, bohemian

JIRAIYA

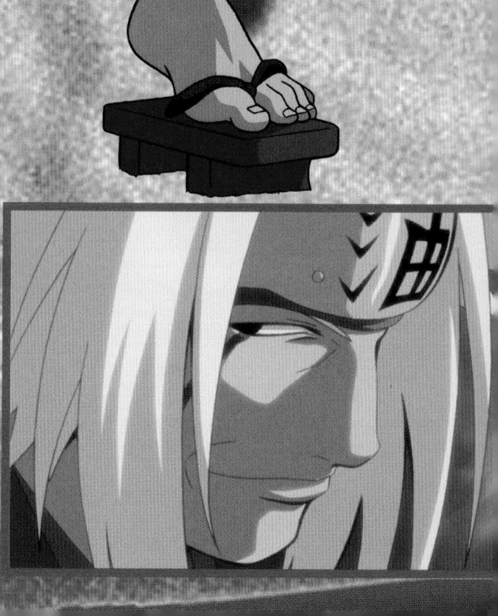

I am *not* a little pervert!

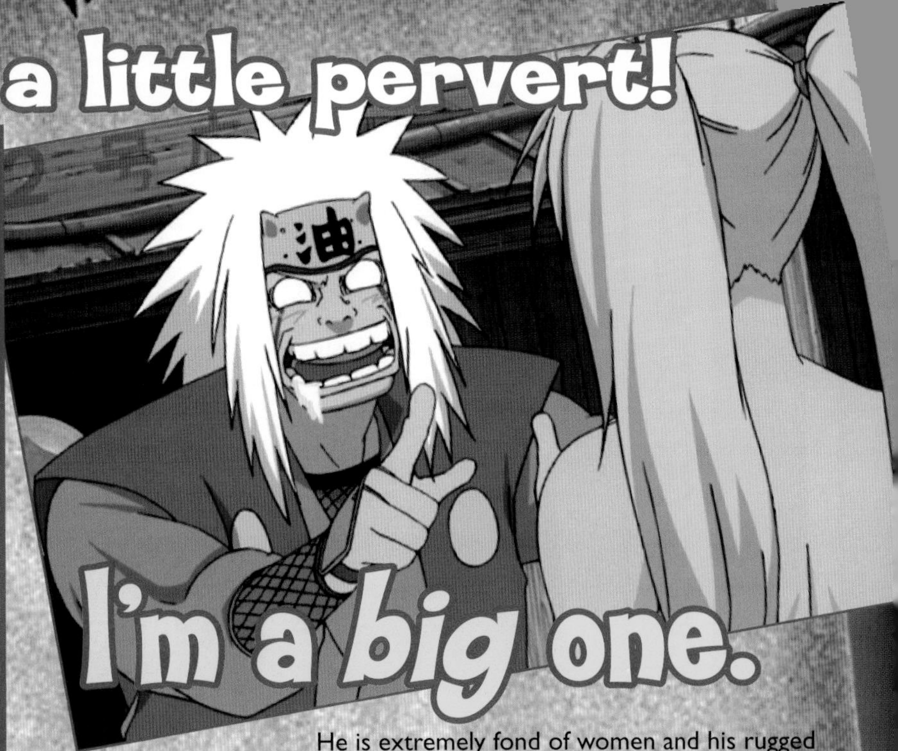

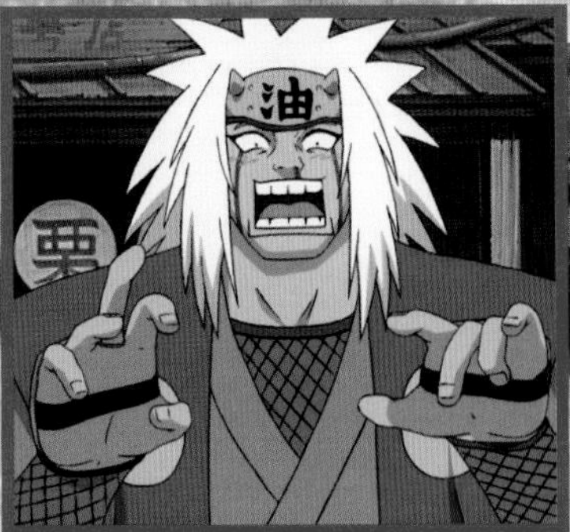

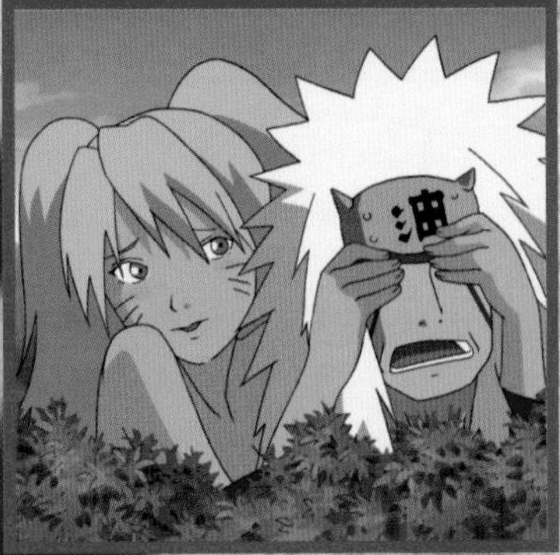

I'm a *big* one.

He is extremely fond of women and his rugged demeanor can melt away at the mere sight of a girl. His perv-power and passion for what he calls "researching" women is truly unparalleled!

He is free-spirited and rambunctious, but he watches over Naruto with a warm heart. What brought him back to the Hidden Leaf Village after all these years to become Naruto's mentor? We can only guess…

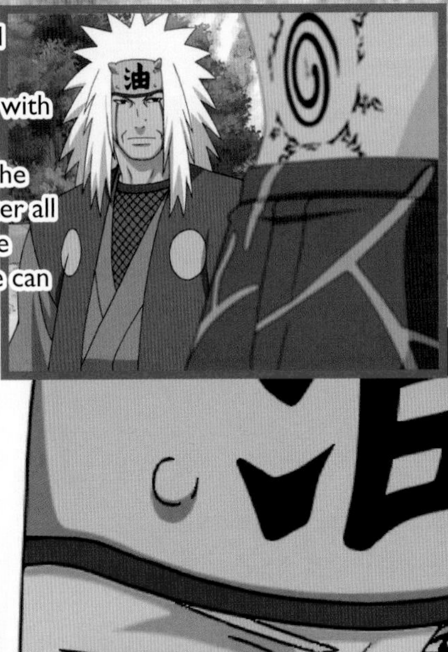

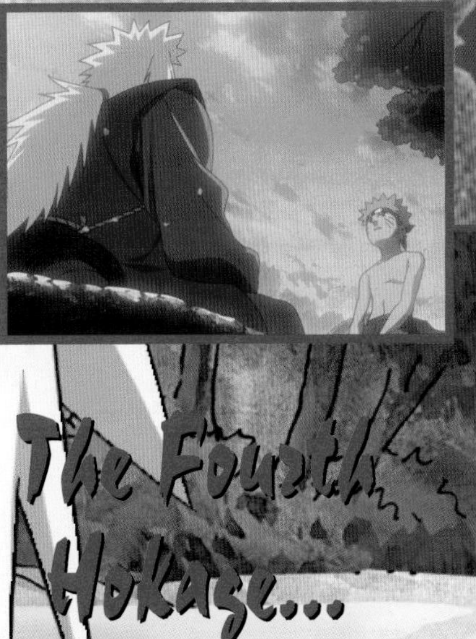

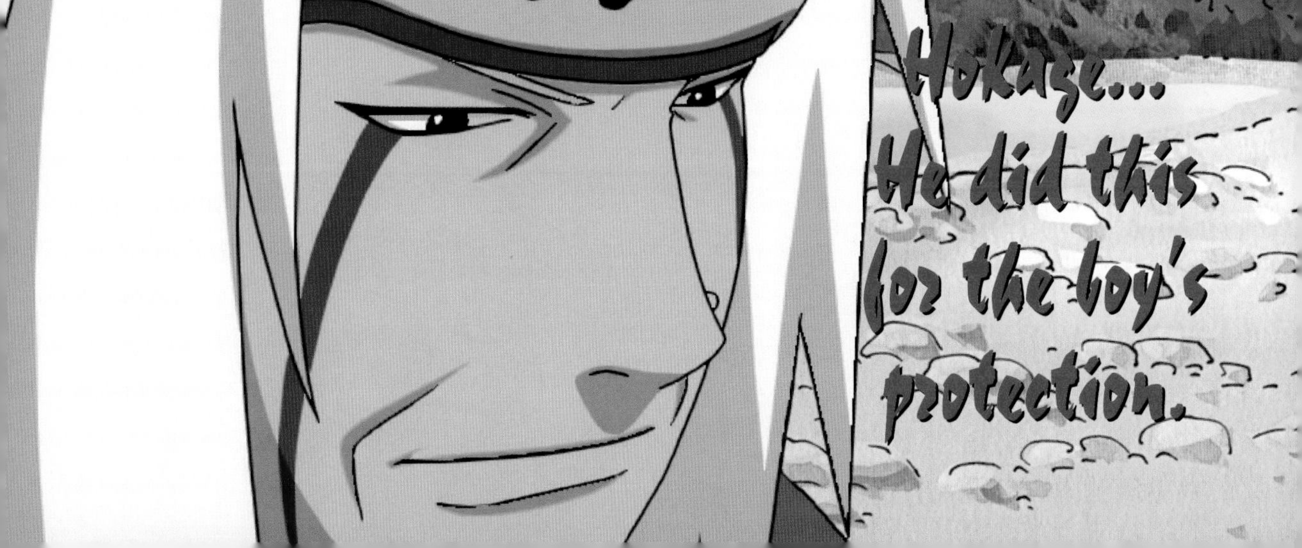

The Fourth Hokage… He did this for the boy's protection.

JIRAIYA'S RESEARCH NOTEBOOK ON KUNOICHI!

The novelist cuts us a sweet critique of the female ninja!

A legendary Sannin as well as a great writer, Jiraiya is undisputedly best known for being woman crazy! Data collected daily in his top secret Research Notebook is now finally exposed!

KURENAI YUHI♥

BIG WINNER

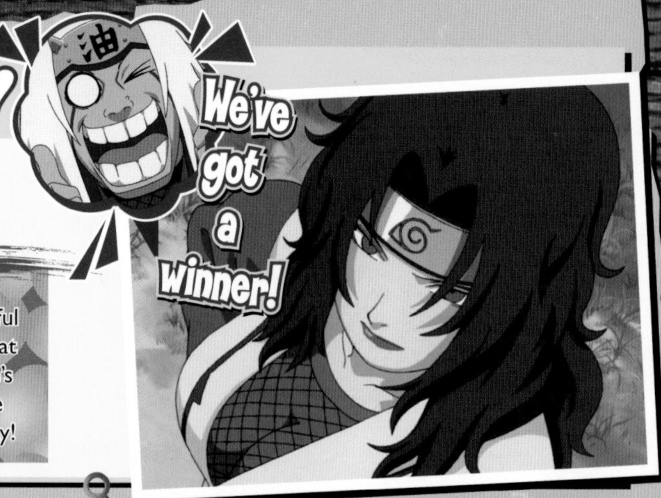
We've got a winner!

➡Whoa, what a beautiful sight! Especially with that steely glare of hers. She's truly incredible. An elite jonin and an elite beauty!

ANKO MITARASHI♥

MEGA WINNER

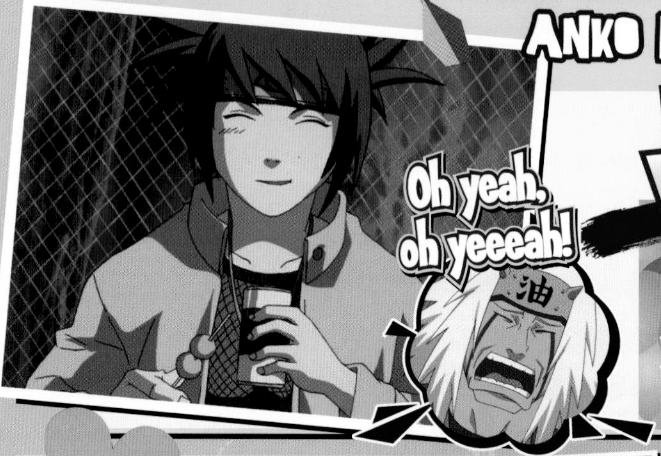
Oh yeah, oh yeeeah!

⬅Oh yeah—pretty tasty, huh? That tomboy Anko has grown into a gorgeous woman, holy smokes! I wish I were that dumpling…♥

YOUNG GENIN MAIDENS♥

ULTRA WINNERS

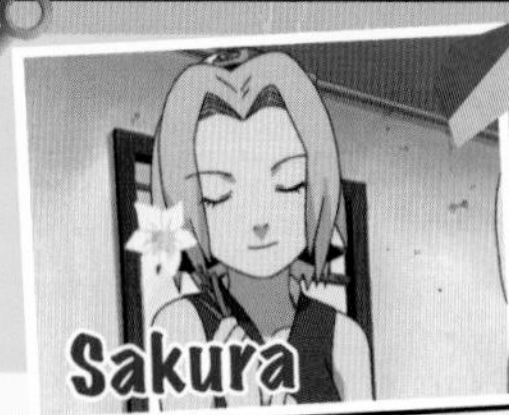
Sakura

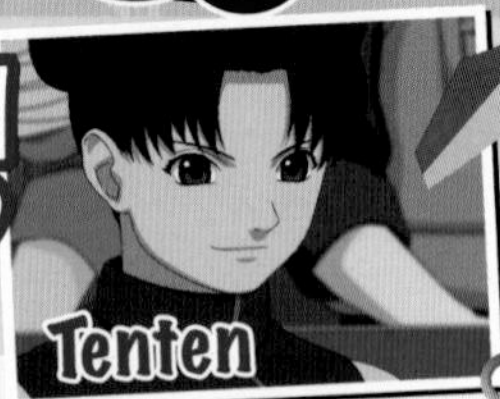
Tenten

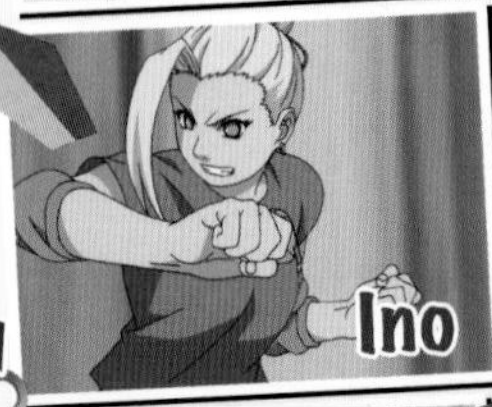
Ino

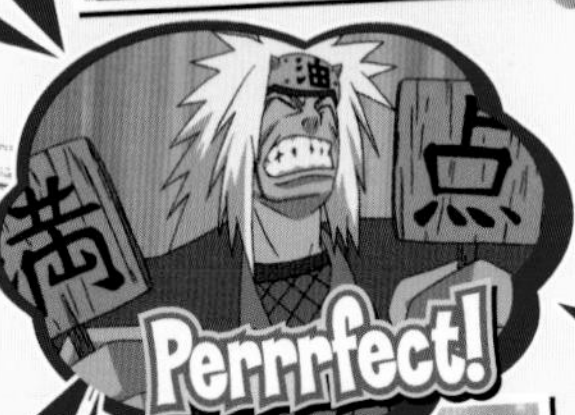
Perrrfect!

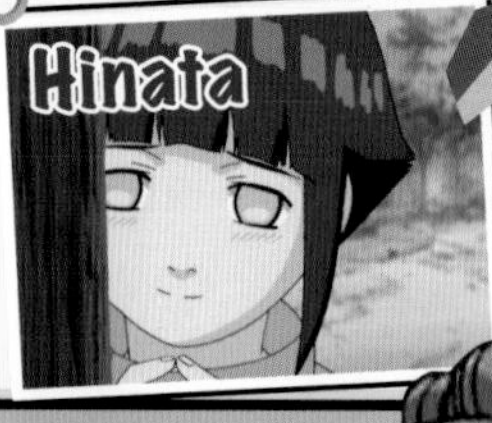
Hinata

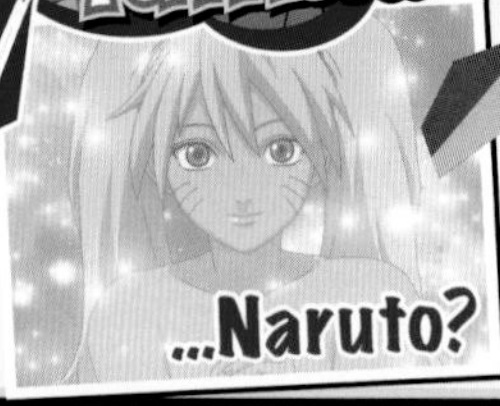
...Naruto?

➡I can't wait to see how these lovelies turn out. Maybe it's time I moved back home…No, can't do that! I need to conduct more research on girls all over the world for my next novel!

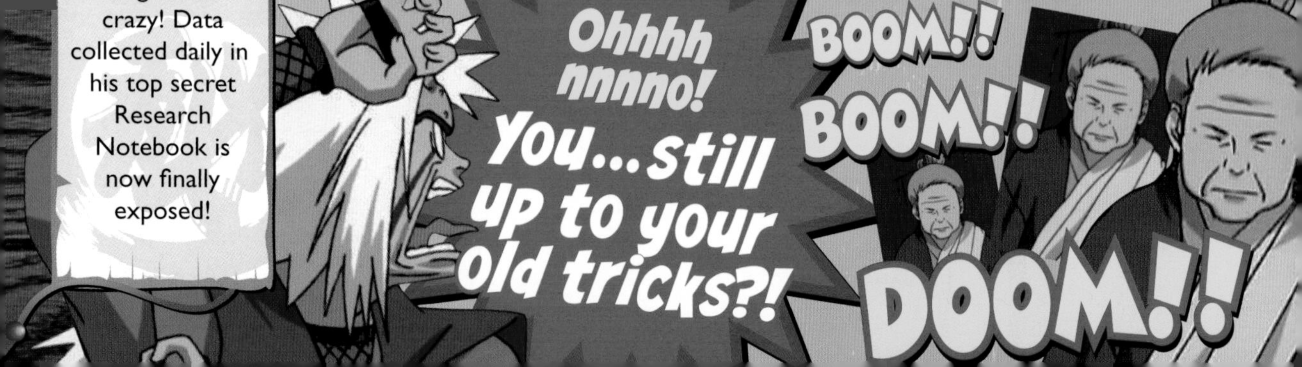
BOOM!!
BOOM!!
DOOM!!
Ohhhh nnnno!
You...still up to your old tricks?!

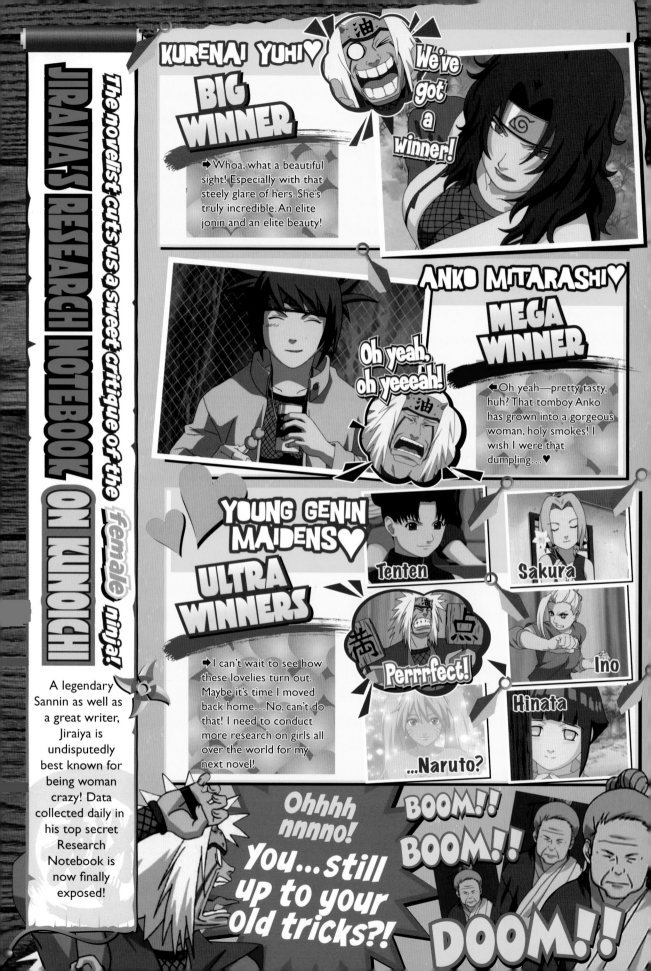

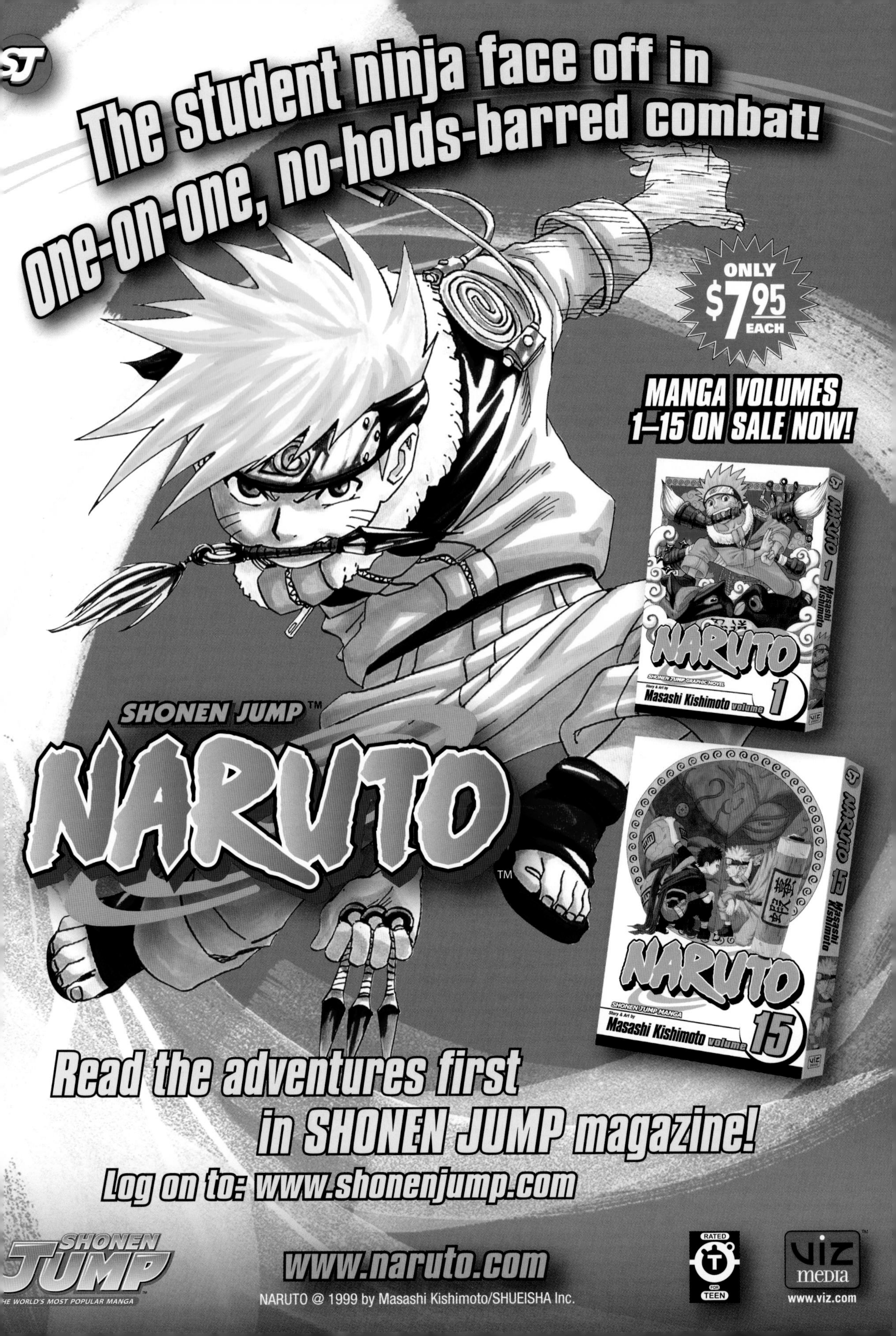

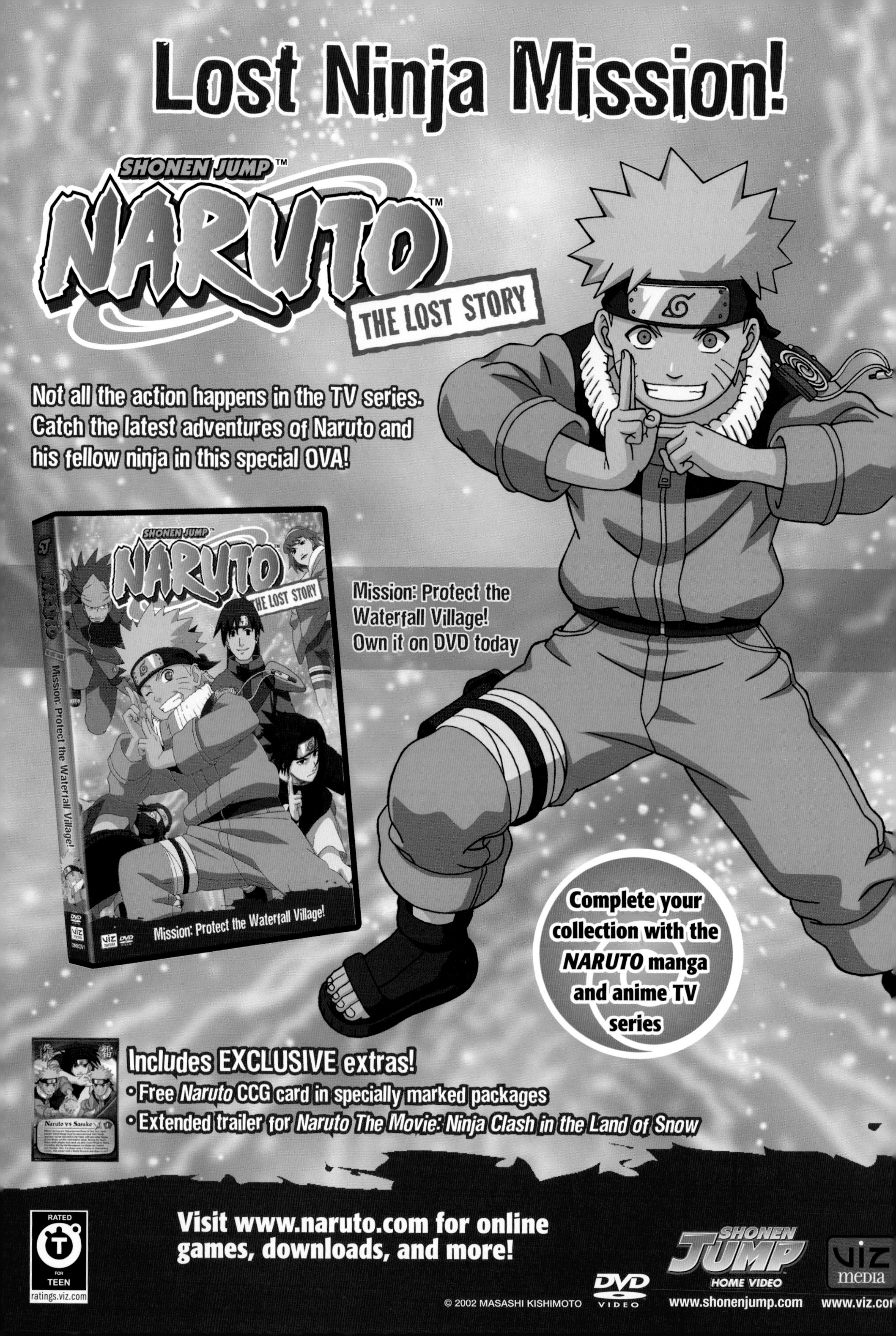
Lost Ninja Mission!
SHONEN JUMP™
NARUTO™
THE LOST STORY
Not all the action happens in the TV series. Catch the latest adventures of Naruto and his fellow ninja in this special OVA!
Mission: Protect the Waterfall Village! Own it on DVD today
SHONEN JUMP
NARUTO
THE LOST STORY
Mission: Protect the Waterfall Village!
Complete your collection with the NARUTO manga and anime TV series
Includes EXCLUSIVE extras!
• Free Naruto CCG card in specially marked packages
• Extended trailer for Naruto The Movie: Ninja Clash in the Land of Snow
Naruto vs Sasuke
RATED T FOR TEEN
ratings.viz.com
Visit www.naruto.com for online games, downloads, and more!
© 2002 MASASHI KISHIMOTO
DVD VIDEO
SHONEN JUMP HOME VIDEO
www.shonenjump.com
VIZ media
www.viz.com

The Ninja Way: Tales of Bravery

Training Episodes

Episodes 52 to 58: The prelims are over and Naruto prepares for the finals. Under the tutelage of reliable (?) mentor Jiraiya, training begins!

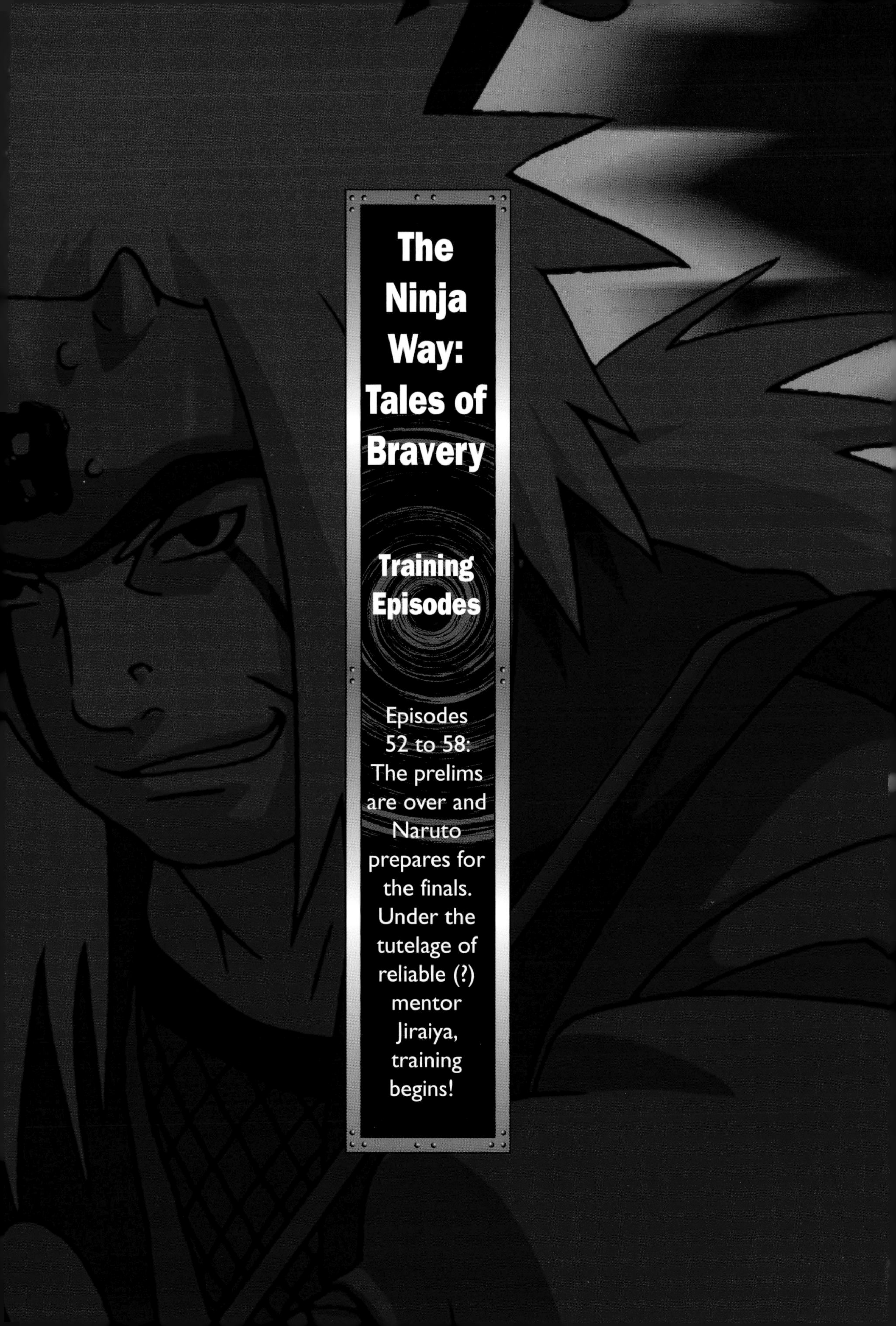

Episode 52 to Episode 58

Get strong! Hardcore chakra training!

Start with a warm-up?! A knock-down, drag-'em-out chase!

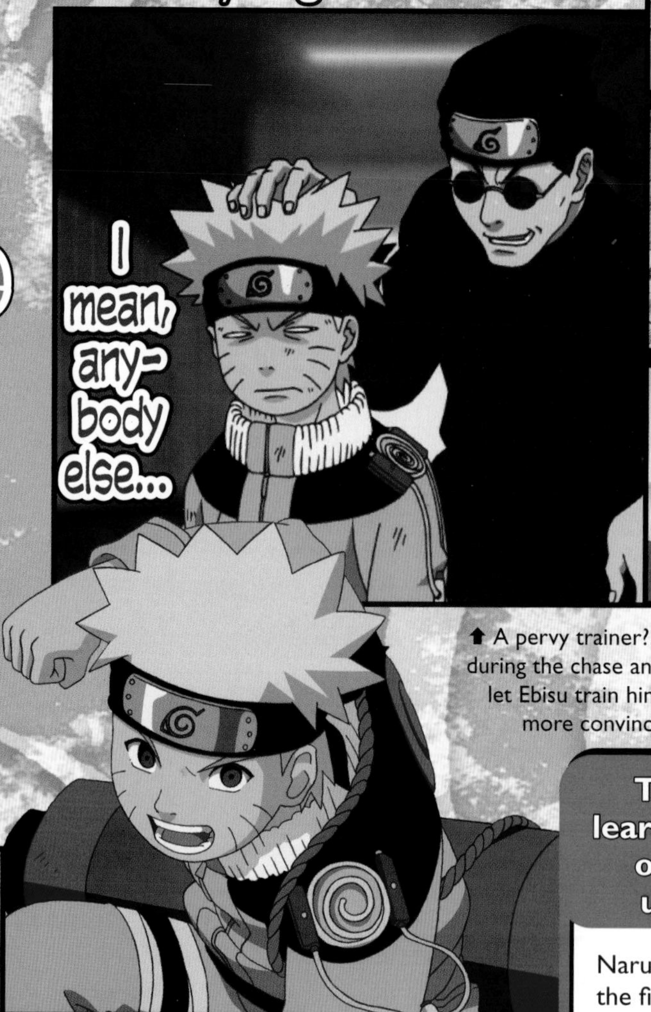
I mean, anybody else...

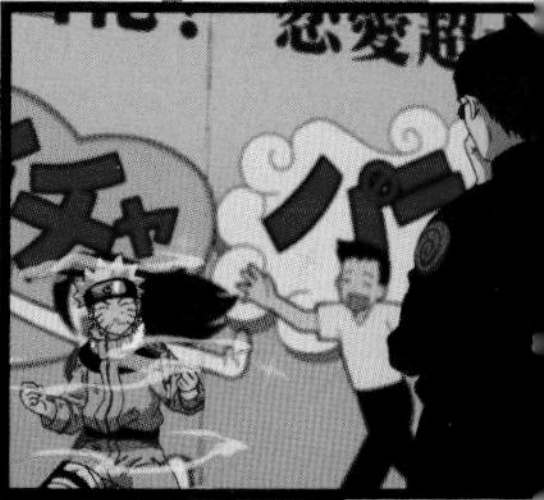

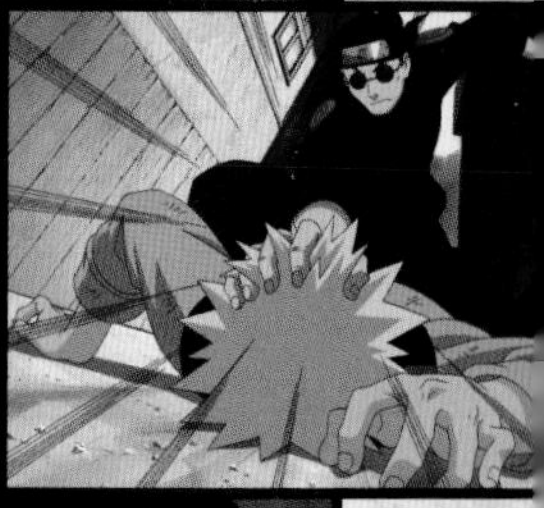

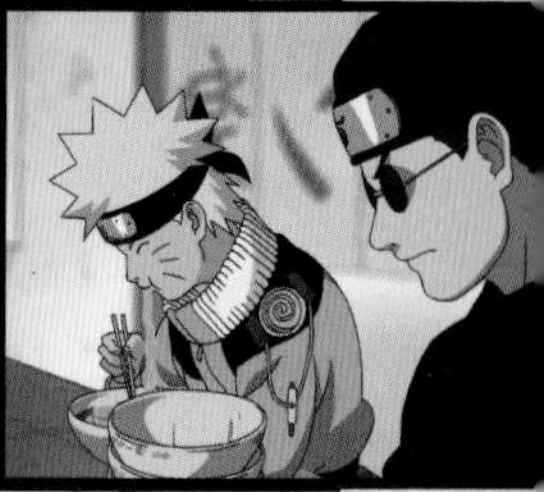

⬆ A pervy trainer?! Naruto gets beat bad during the chase and reluctantly agrees to let Ebisu train him, but only after a little more convincing at Ichiraku Ramen!

The task of learning to walk on water is underway!

Naruto is pumped for the finals! But the training that elite (?) teacher Ebisu assigns is walking…on hot water?! Chakra training in the hot springs district!

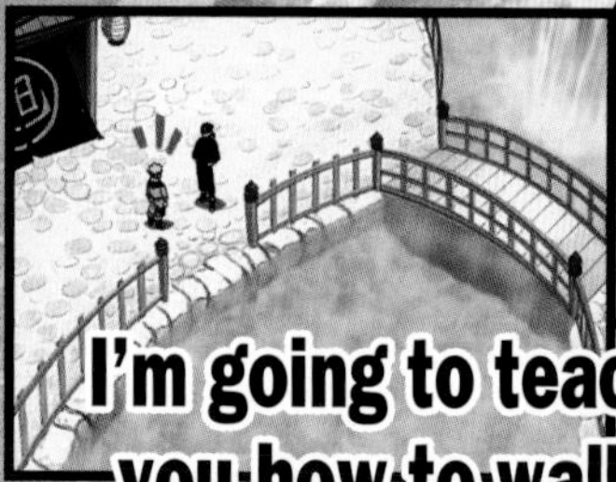

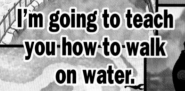

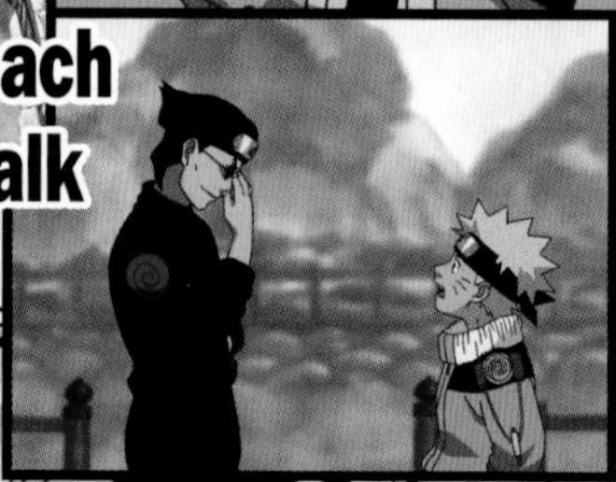
I'm going to teach you how to walk on water.

⬆➡ The key is to adjust your chakra to the water's shifting surface!

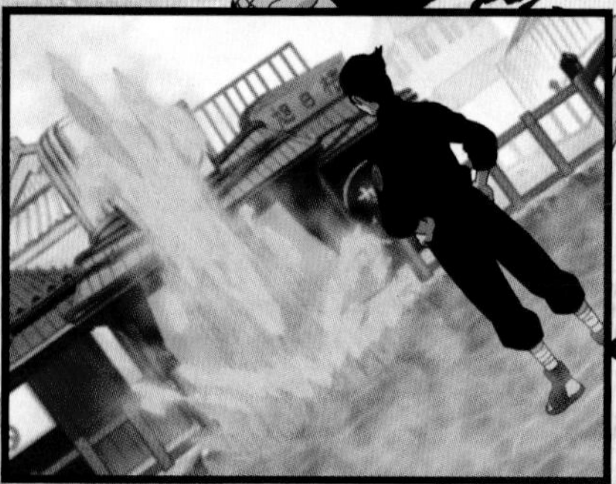

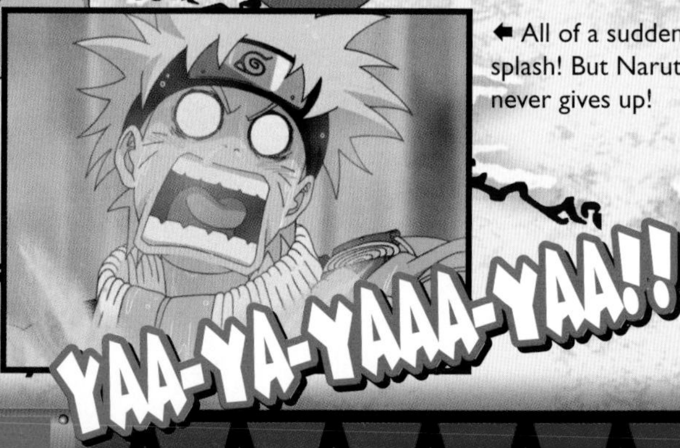
YAA-YA-YAAA-YAA!!

⬅ All of a sudden – splash! But Naruto never gives up!

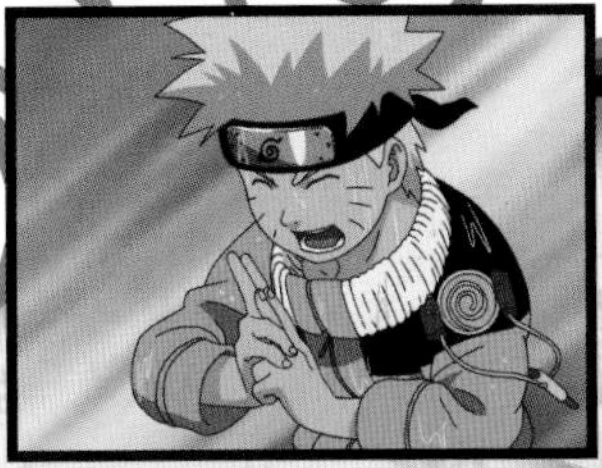

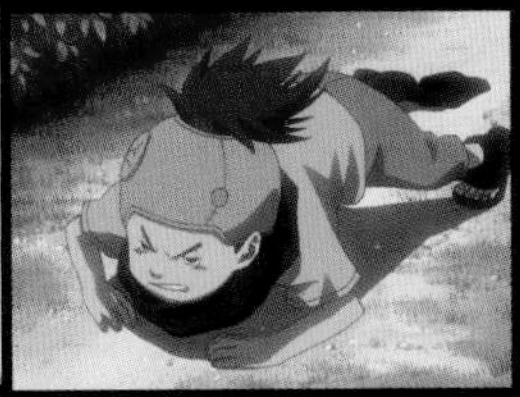

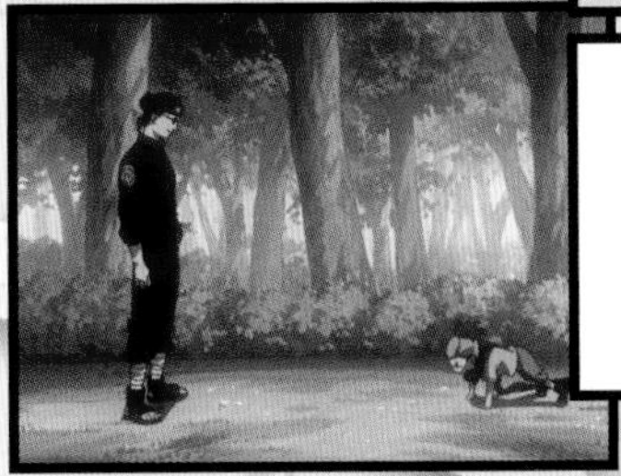

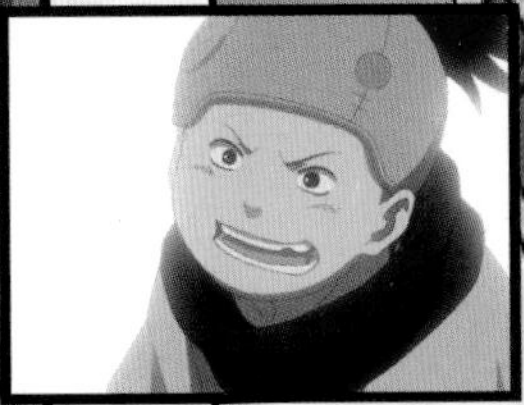

➡⬆ Seeing Naruto diligently push on with his training despite countless failures reminds Ebisu of Konohamaru, who is definitely showing improvement under Naruto's influence.

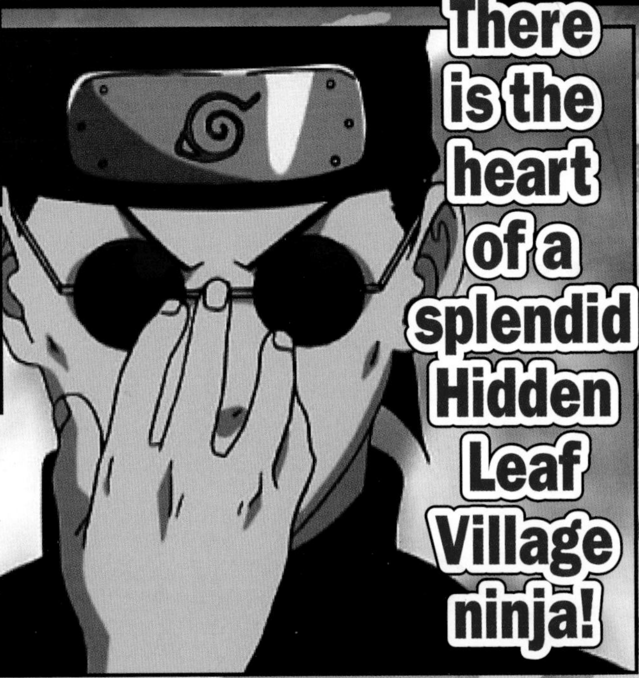

There is the heart of a splendid Hidden Leaf Village ninja!

A SUDDEN INTERRUPTION IN TRAINING?!

THE ENIGMATIC, SHAMELESS NINJA BURSTS ONTO THE SCENE!

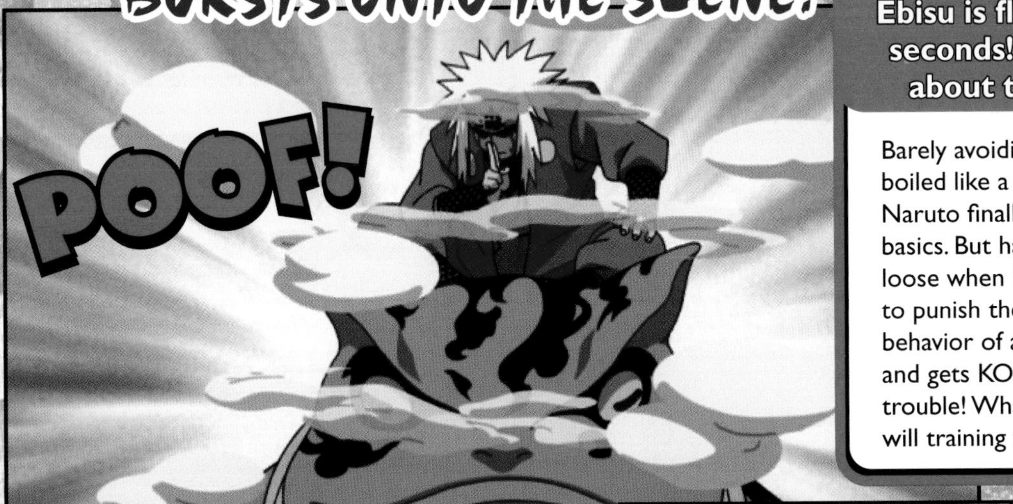
POOF!

The closet perv Ebisu is flattened in seconds! But what about training?!

Barely avoiding being boiled like a lobster, Naruto finally grasps the basics. But havoc breaks loose when Ebisu attempts to punish the disreputable behavior of a Peeping Tom, and gets KO'd for his trouble! What direction will training take now?!

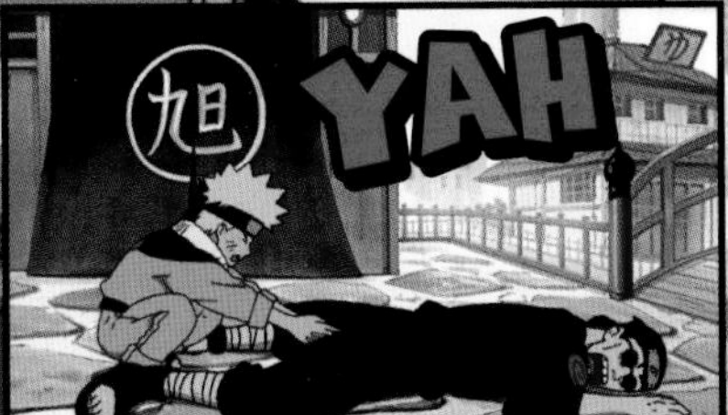
YAH

⬅ Leaving the intruder aside, Naruto gives Ebisu a finishing shot with A Thousand Years of Death!

Loud and proud, the Toad Sage!

His true identity?

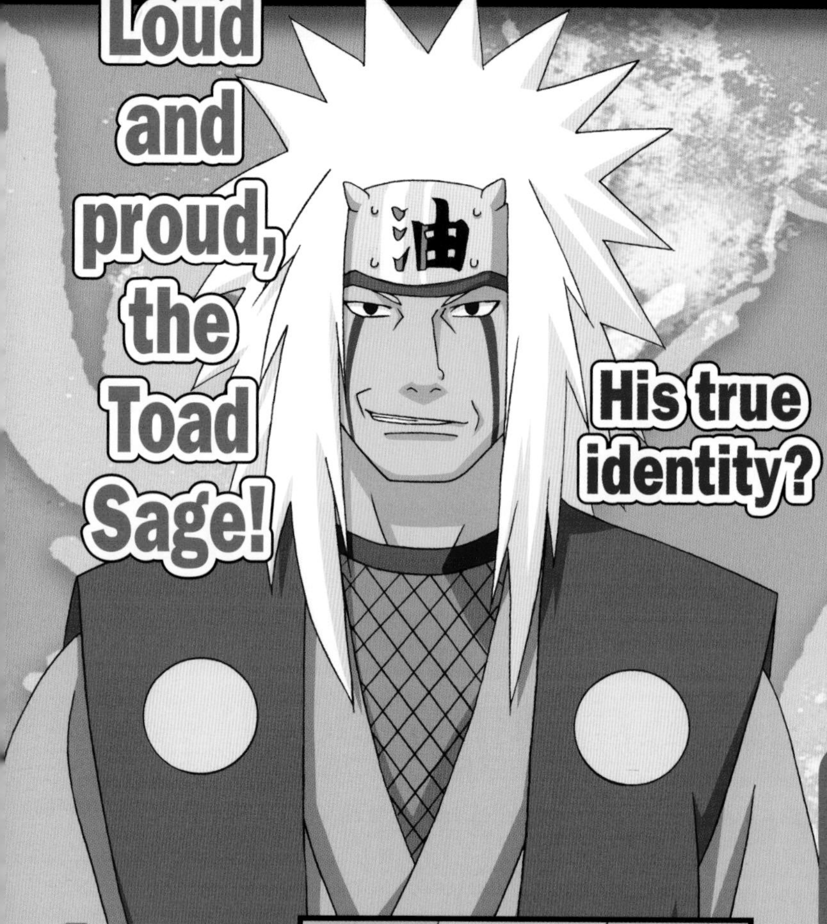

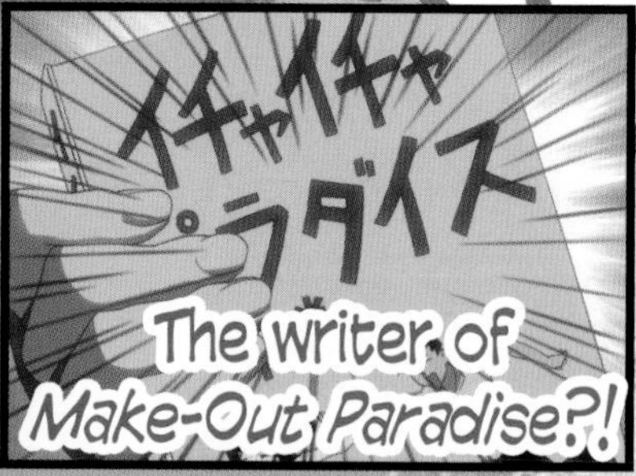
イチャイチャ
ラダイス
The writer of Make-Out Paradise?!

⬆ This self-proclaimed novelist-sage claims to be conducting research in the Hidden Leaf Village!

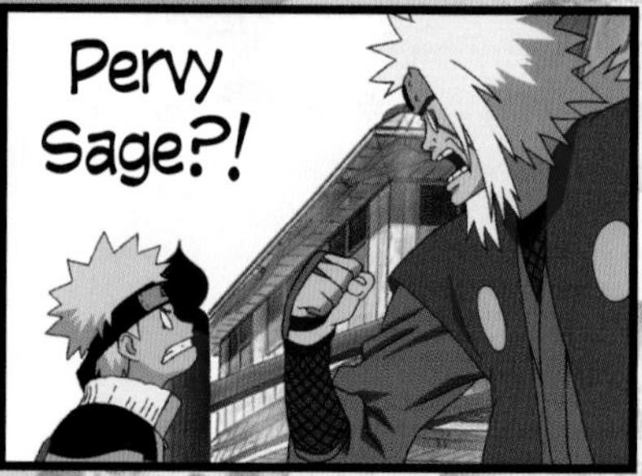
Pervy Sage?!

Who is he? Forget that—training is required!

The dubious Toad Sage flattened Ebisu?! Naruto tries to make him take responsibility for ruining his training, but he flatly refuses.

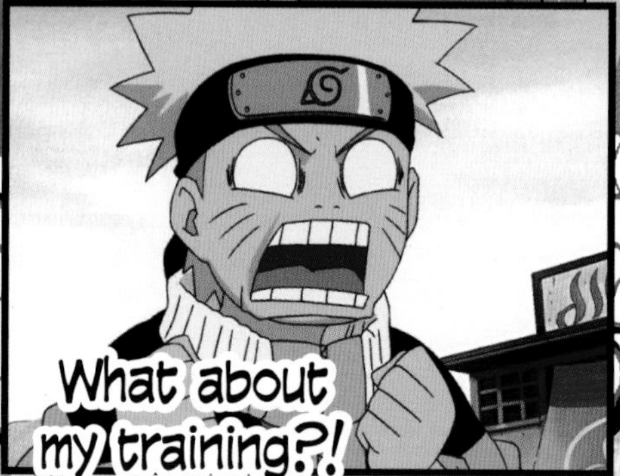
What about my training?!

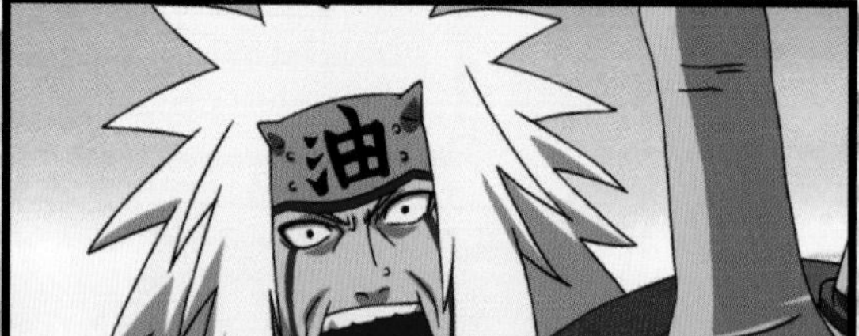
I don't like kids.

⬅⬇ Naruto has to do something to convince the Pervy Sage! Naruto brings up just what he wanted…sort of!

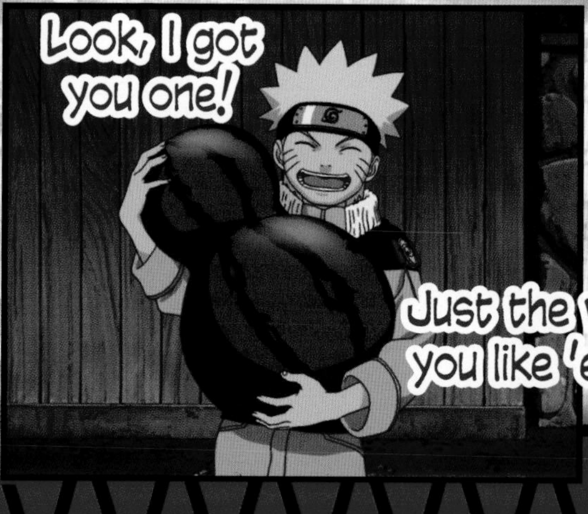
Look, I got you one!
Just the way you like 'em!

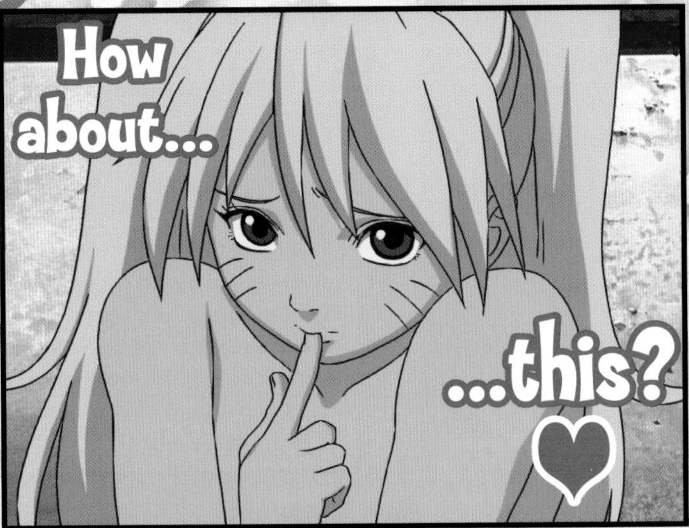
How about...
...this? ♥

⬆ No man can resist those angel eyes! Even the battle-hardened Sage's heart melts…♥

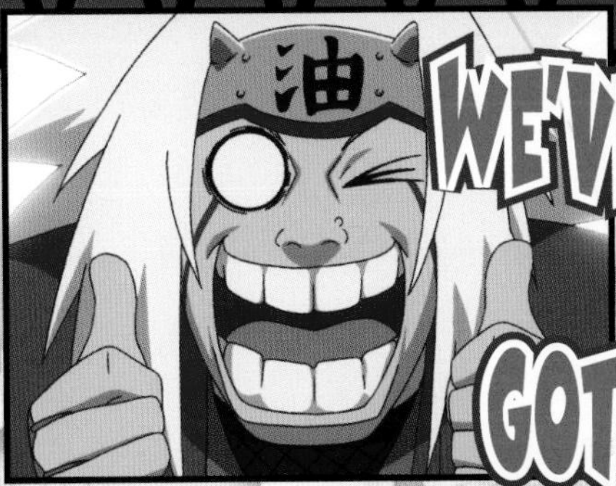
WE'VE
GOT

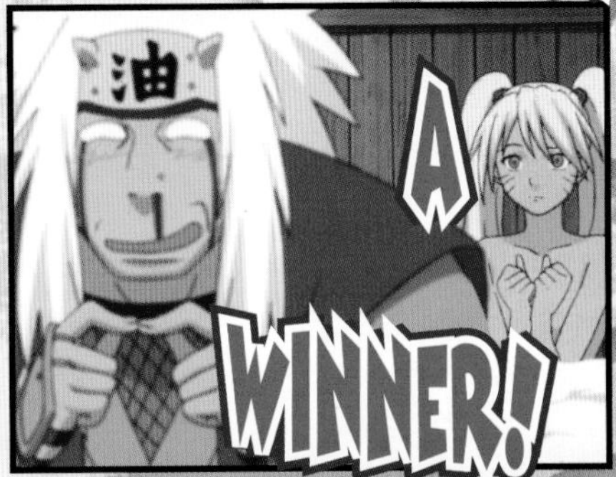
A
WINNER!

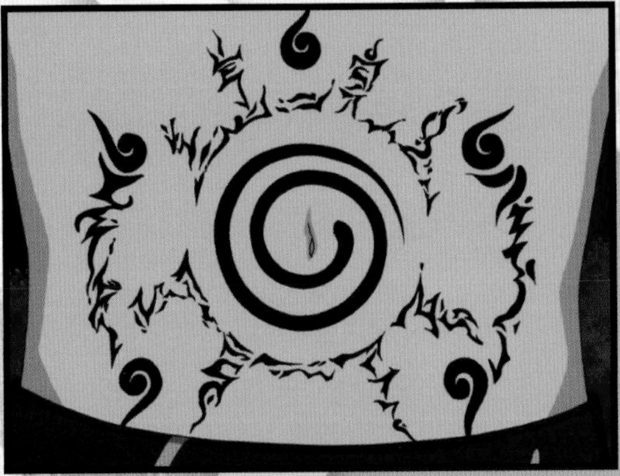

⬅ Orochimaru's Seal Sign is released with the Five Prong Seal Release! Naruto's chakra starts to flow stably, allowing him to accomplish the feat!

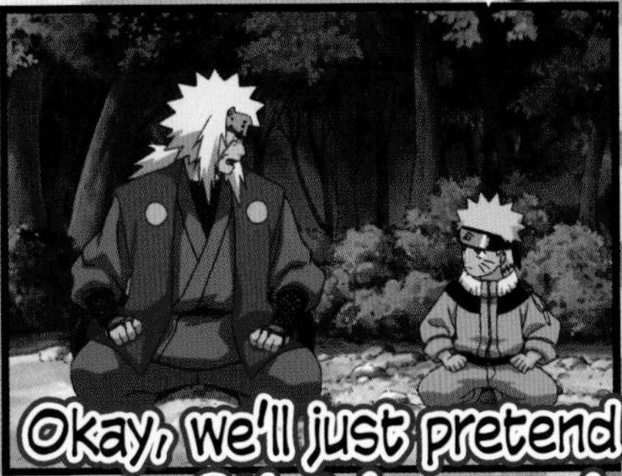
Okay, we'll just pretend none of that happened. Let's begin your training.

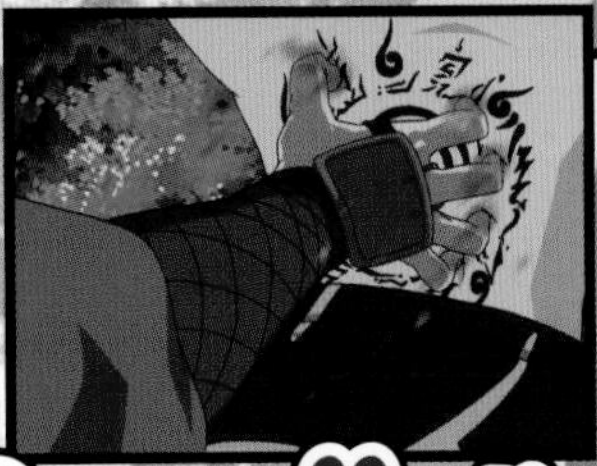

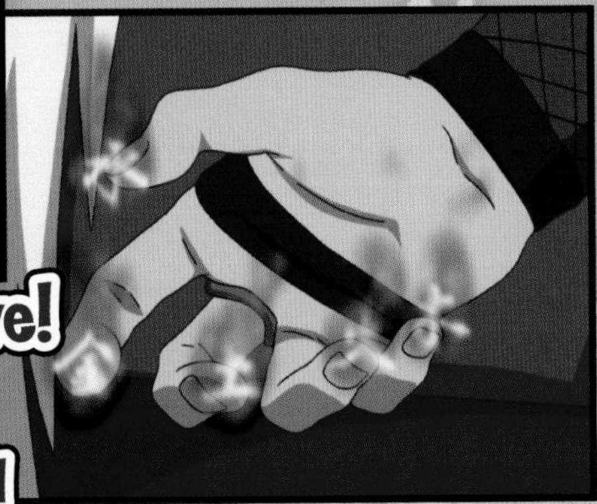
Super effective! Sage-style acupressure!

The Sage submits to the sexy impact!

Naruto tries his last resort, Sexy Jutsu! It works! The Pervy Sage agrees to train him.

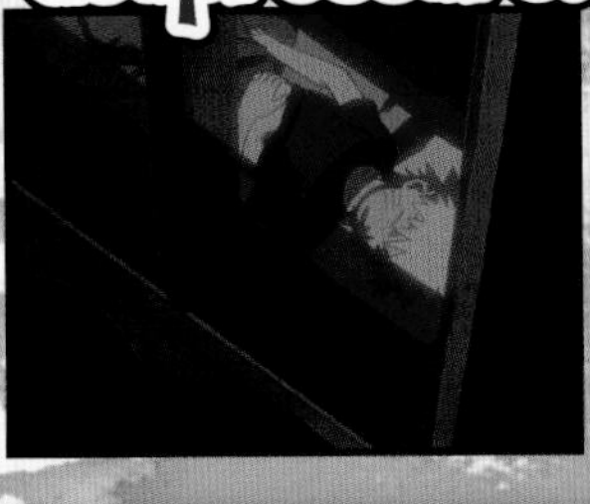

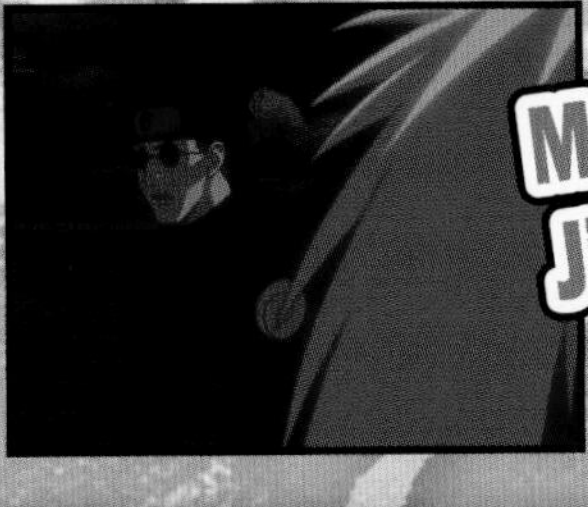

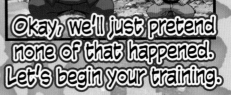

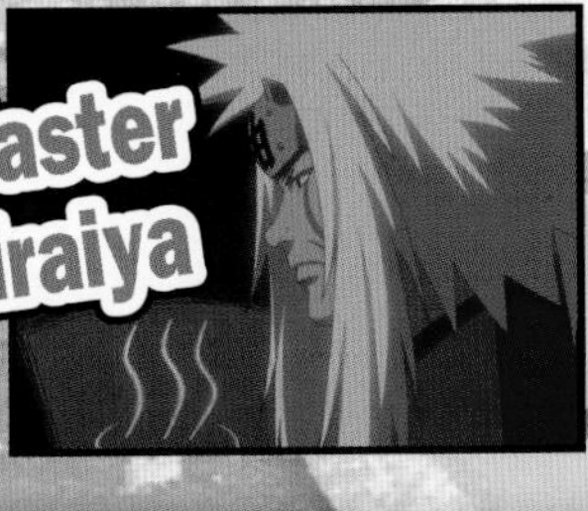
Master Jiraiya

⬅ Ebisu referred to the Sage by the name Jiraiya, one of the legendary Sannin.

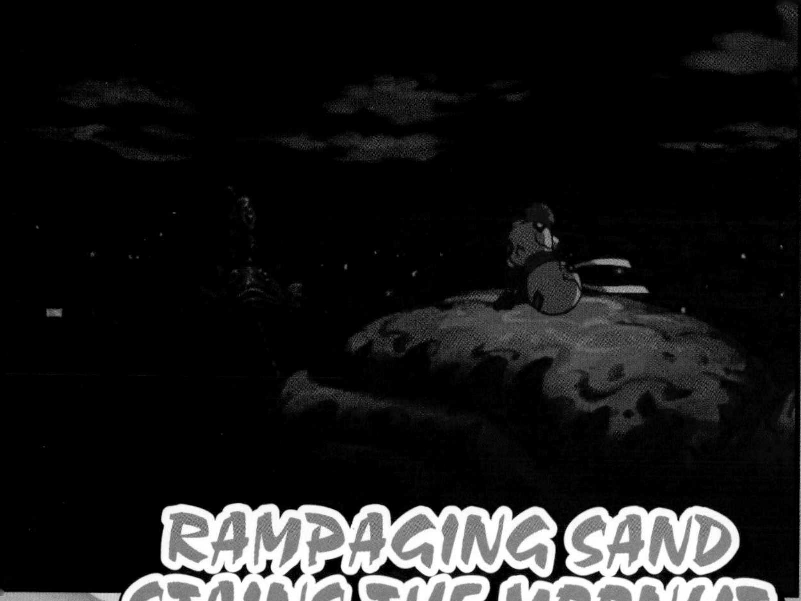

⬅ Gaara lurks, shrouded in the shadows of Kikyo Castle. On what does he fix his gaze?

This night is filled with plotting and murderous intent—

The Sound ninja Dosu shows up at Kikyo Castle to take out Gaara. What nightmare does Dosu encounter in his final living moment…? Meanwhile, Sand and Sound's disturbing plot is being revealed!

RAMPAGING SAND STAINS THE MOONLIT NIGHT WITH BLOOD!

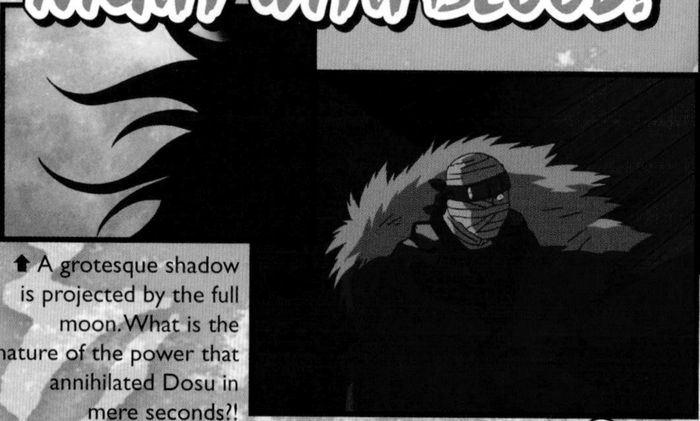

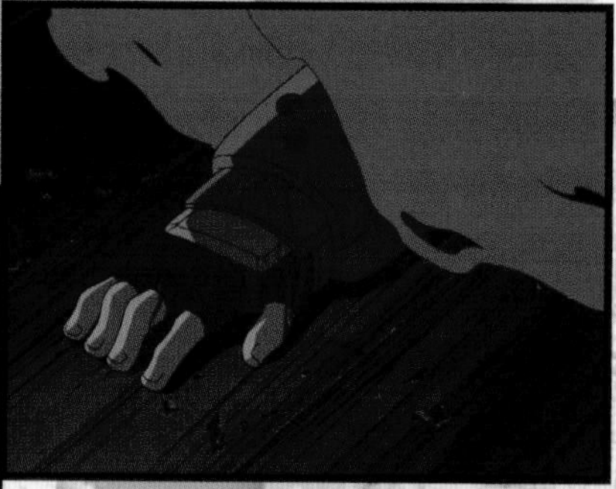

⬆ A grotesque shadow is projected by the full moon. What is the nature of the power that annihilated Dosu in mere seconds?!

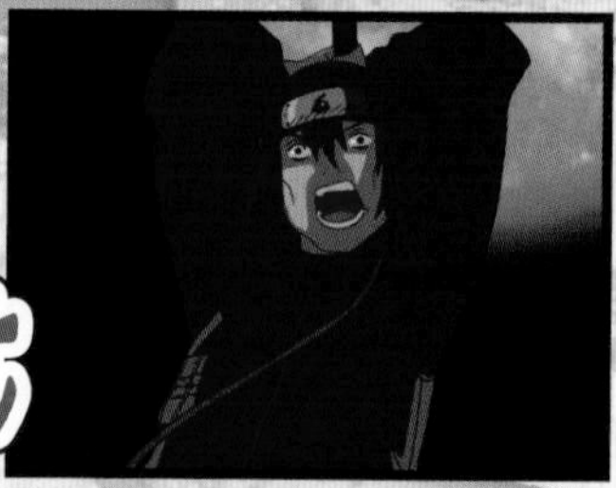

Crescent Moon Dance!

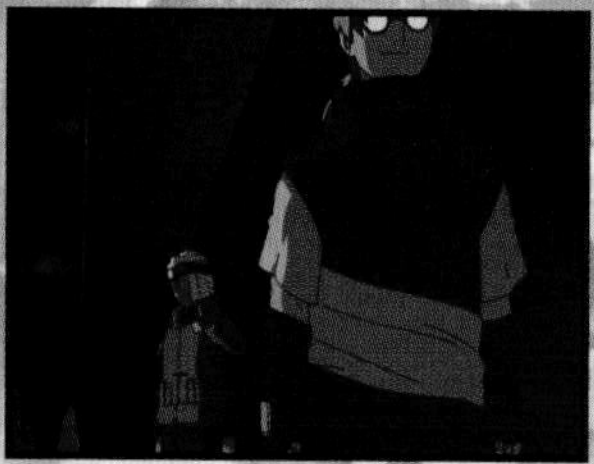

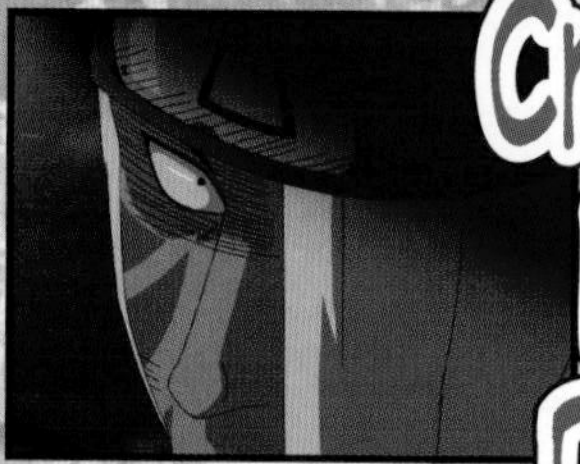

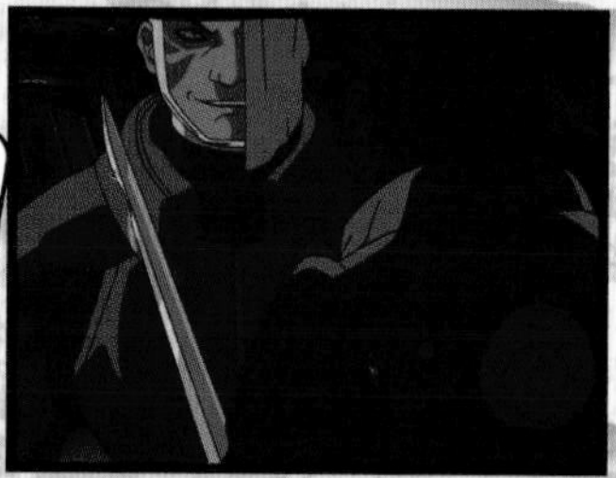

Sand and Sound collude!

➡ Hayate Gekko learns of Sand and Sound's plan. But he is discovered and now has no choice but to fight!

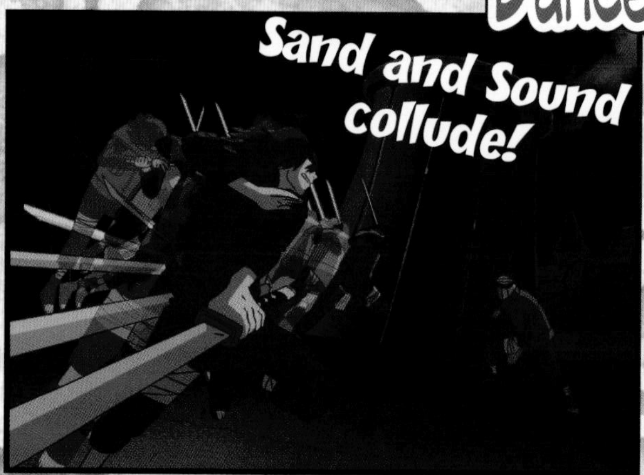

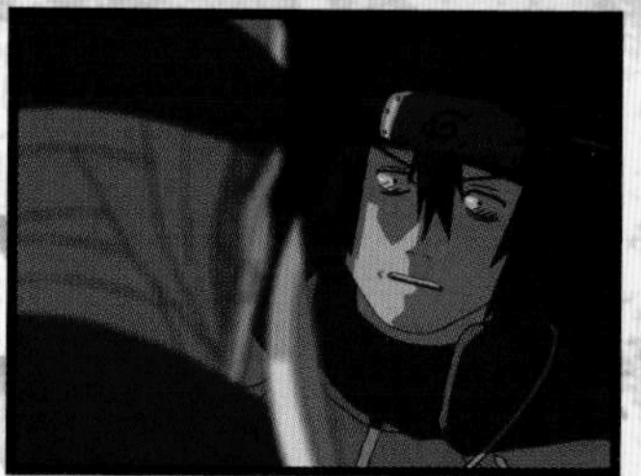

⬆ A perfect blow from a talented youth! It appeared that the dark plot had been cut down, but…

It's finally time to learn the secret technique!

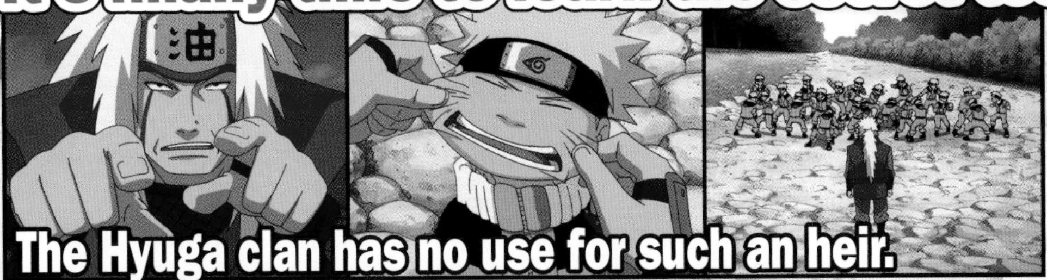
The Hyuga clan has no use for such an heir.

⬅ The first condition to initiate the summon is to burn off regular chakra. To achieve this—a giant battle royale among Naruto's Shadow Clones!

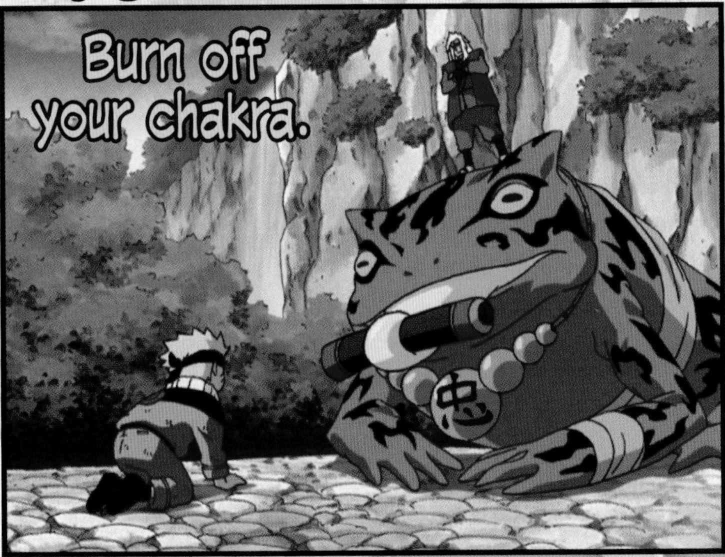
Burn off your chakra.

A reward for perseverance! Secret technique Summoning Jutsu lessons!

The day after Naruto succeeded in walking on water, training really gets intense! Jiraiya, the so-called Toad Sage, teaches Naruto the Summoning Jutsu!

➡⬆ Condition number two, signing a contract with the summoning toad is complete. Time to give it a try!

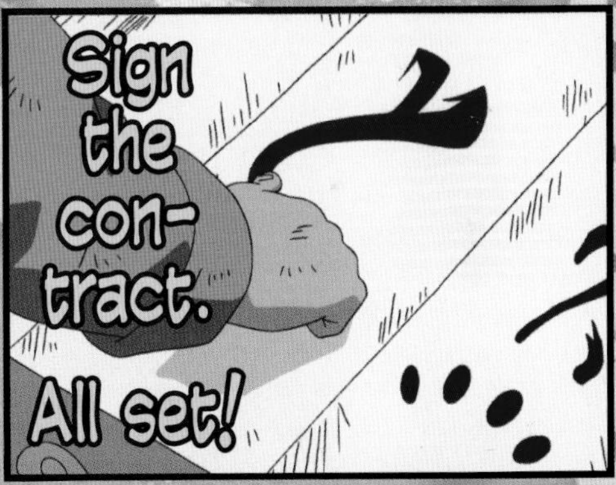
Sign the con-tract.
All set!

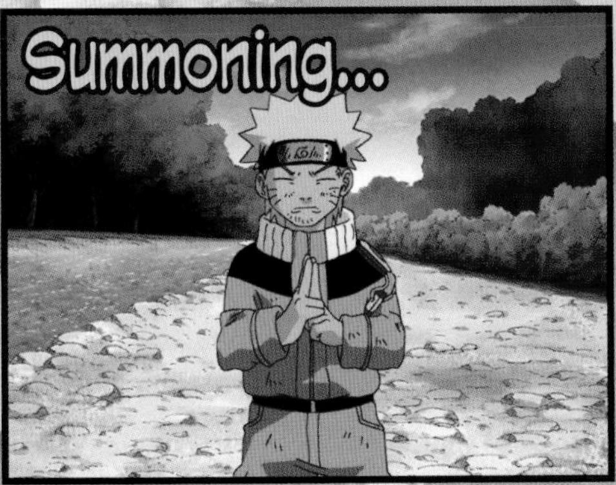
Summoning...

➡ And for his efforts… A tadpole?! This is no good at all!

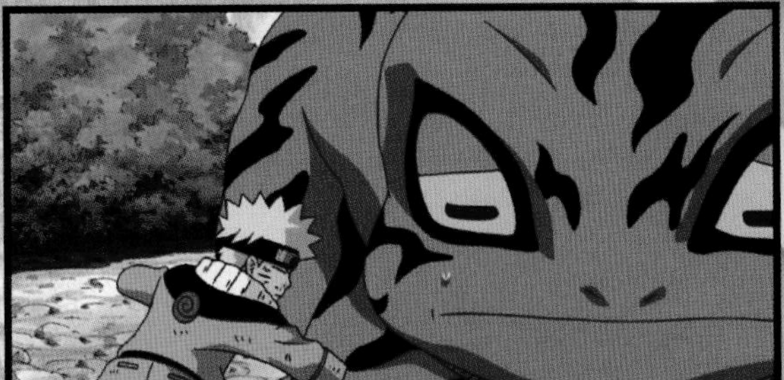

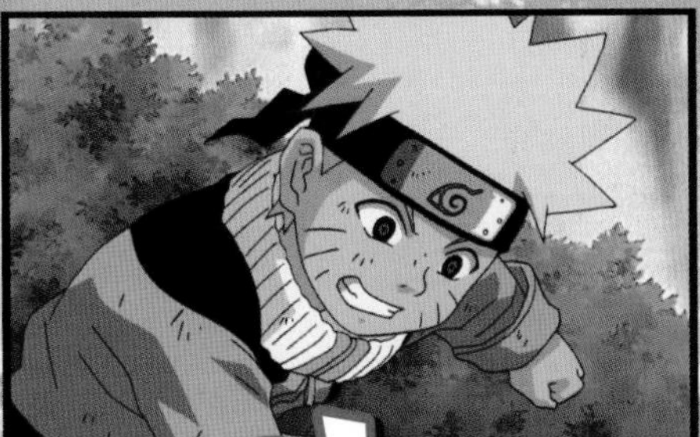

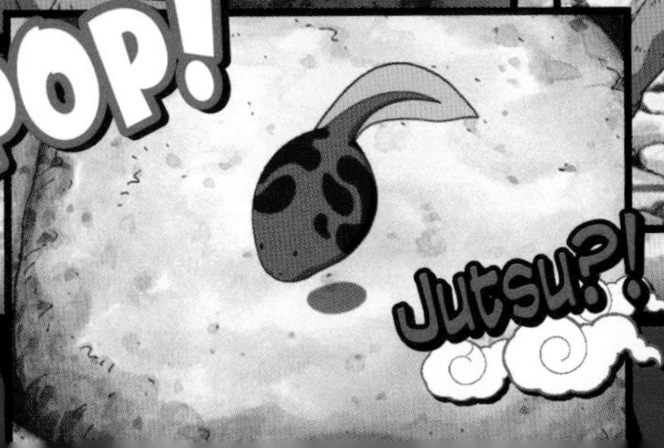
POP!
Jutsu?!

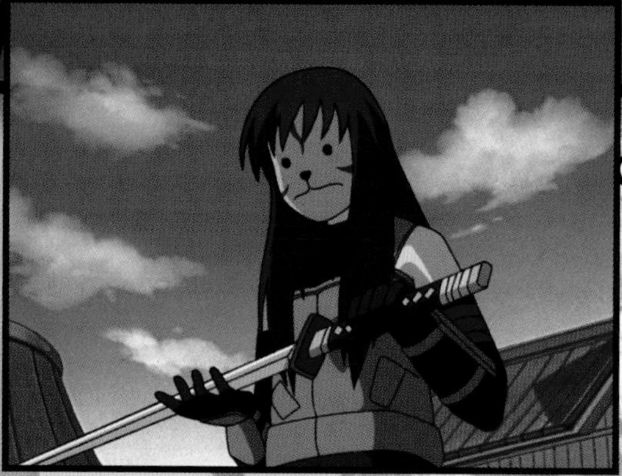

THE RIPPLES CAUSED BY THIS EVIL ROCK THE VILLAGE!

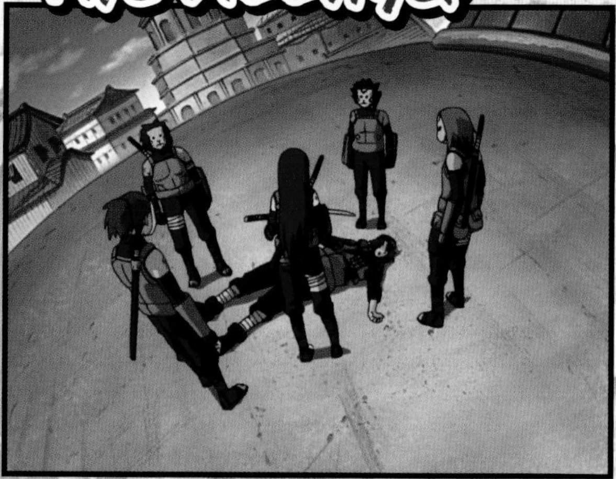

The aftermath of a hideous battle...The Hidden Leaf Village quakes!

Hayate, who was hot on the trail of Sound and Sand, is found in a tragic state. The highest-ranking ninja of the Village Hidden in the Leaves gather before the Hokage, who tells them...

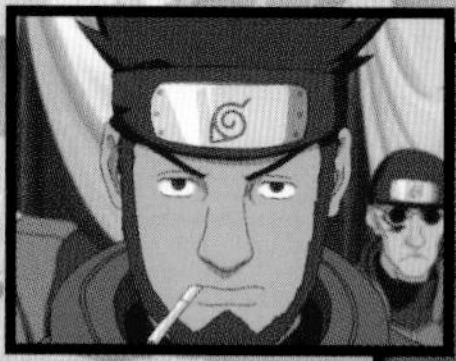
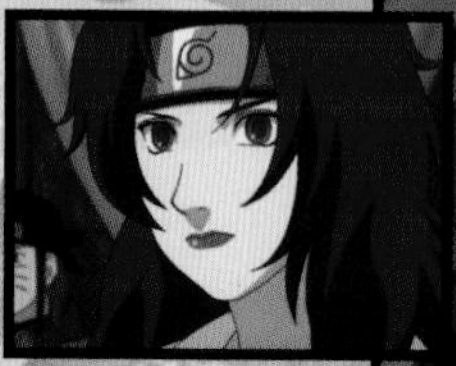
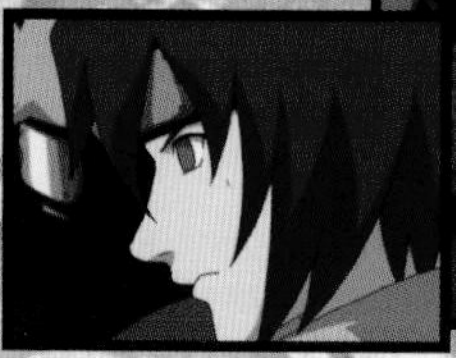

The elite ninja of the Hidden Leaf Village...

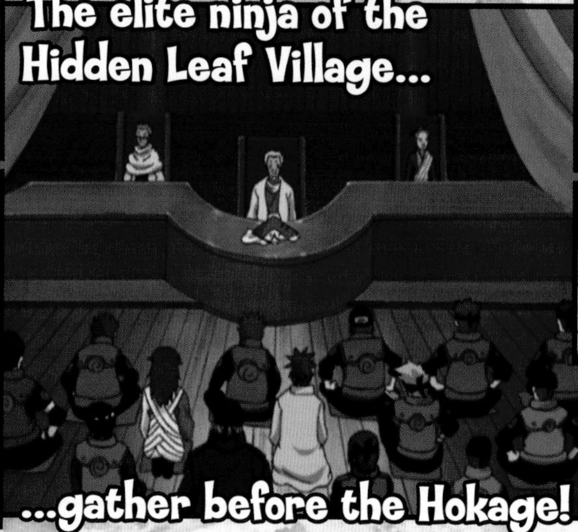

...gather before the Hokage!

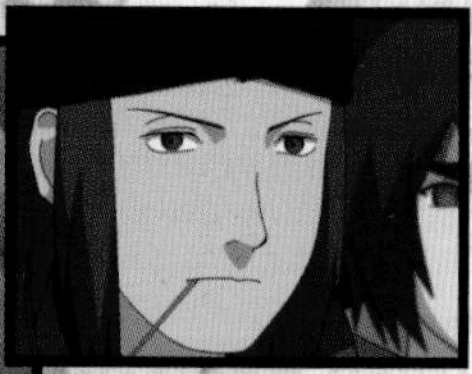
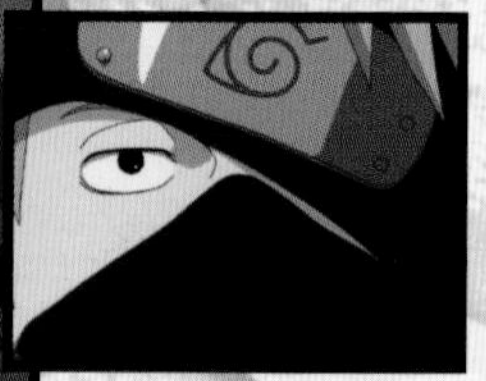

⬅⬆ The nations in alliance with Orochimaru conspire, but for what purpose?! Tension builds among the assembled ninja!

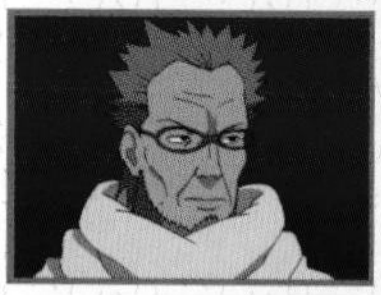

Homura Mitokado

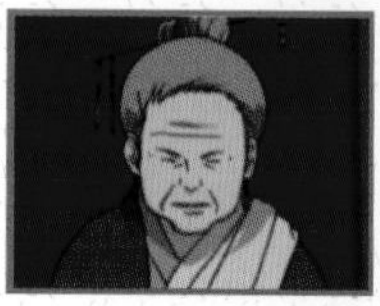

Koharu Utatane

The Reliable Elders!

Advisors

Like the Third Hokage, Homura and Koharu risked their lives during the war years. All of them, including the Hokage, lead the village with their vast knowledge, experience and advanced tactical abilities.

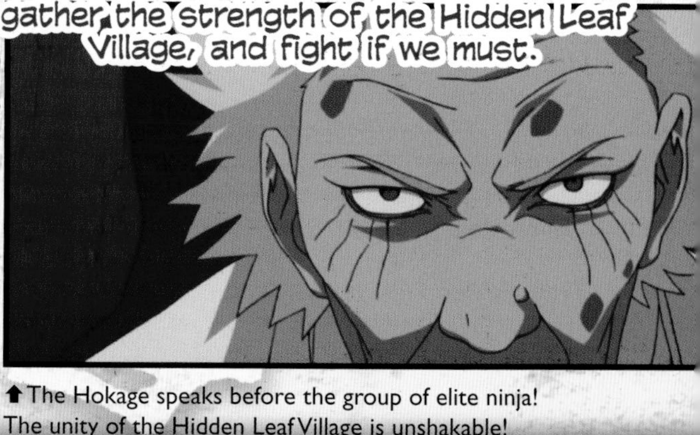
When and if the time comes, we will gather the strength of the Hidden Leaf Village, and fight if we must.

⬆ The Hokage speaks before the group of elite ninja! The unity of the Hidden Leaf Village is unshakable!

A confrontational hospital visit takes a touching turn?!

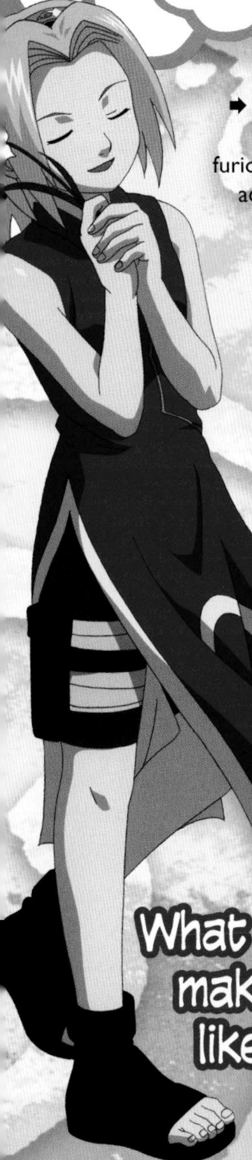

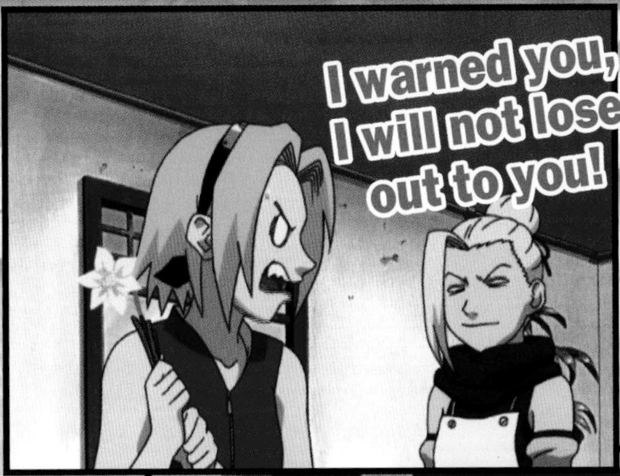
I warned you, I will not lose out to you!

➡ No tricks! Sakura is furious at Ino's accusations!

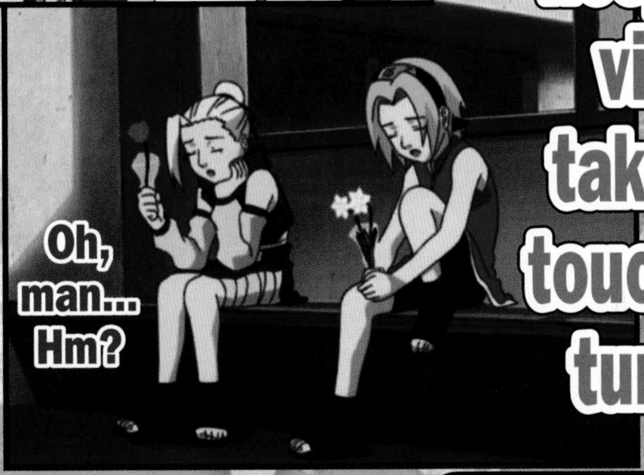
Oh, man... Hm?

➡ Sasuke's hospital room is empty?! Faint expectations turn to sighs.

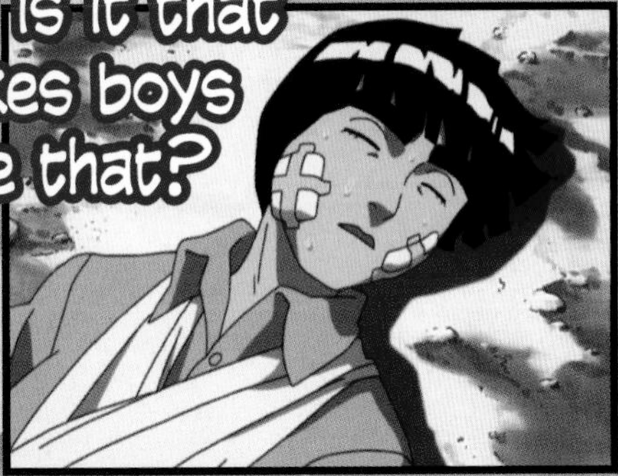
What is it that makes boys like that?

⬅ Despite his condition, Lee pushes on with his training…and collapses!

Always pushing things too far?

Sakura goes to visit Sasuke in the hospital ♥. But she ends up face to face with Ino. Jealousy ensues…

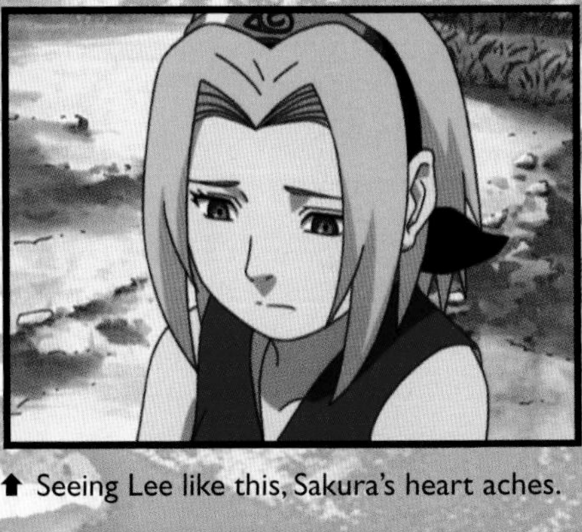

⬆ Seeing Lee like this, Sakura's heart aches.

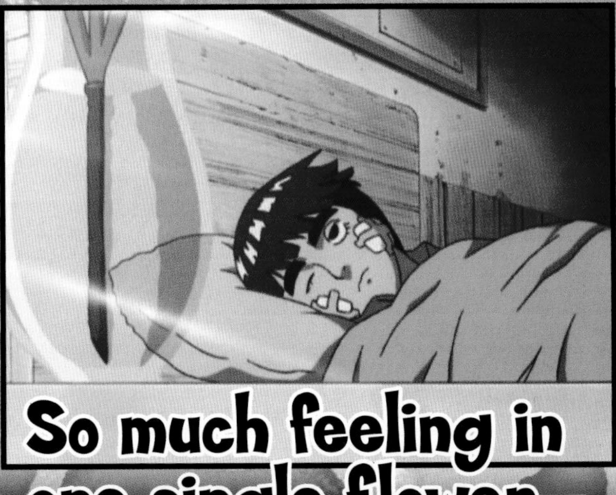

⬅ Lee wakes up in his hospital bed with Sakura's daffodil blooming by the window.

So much feeling in one single flower—

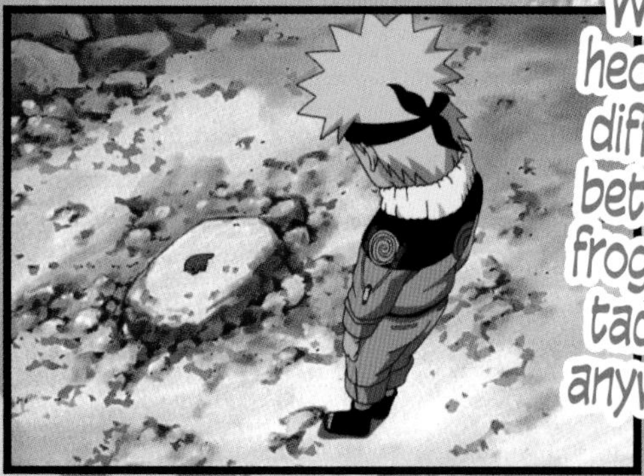

What the heck is the difference between a frog and a tadpole, anyway?!

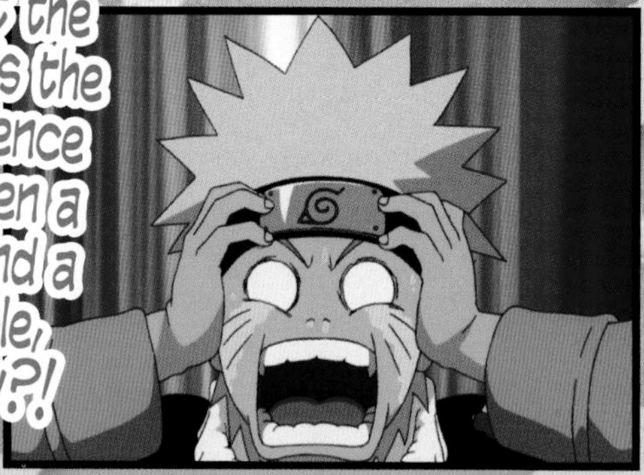

⬅ Still no frog?! A worn-out Naruto pushed to the limit!

Training continues. And he finally produces…a frog!

Bringing out talent with a little pampering?!

It's been three weeks since training began, but Naruto's Summoning Jutsu shows no improvement! Jiraiya attempts to force a breakthrough.

Relaxing at a hot spring!

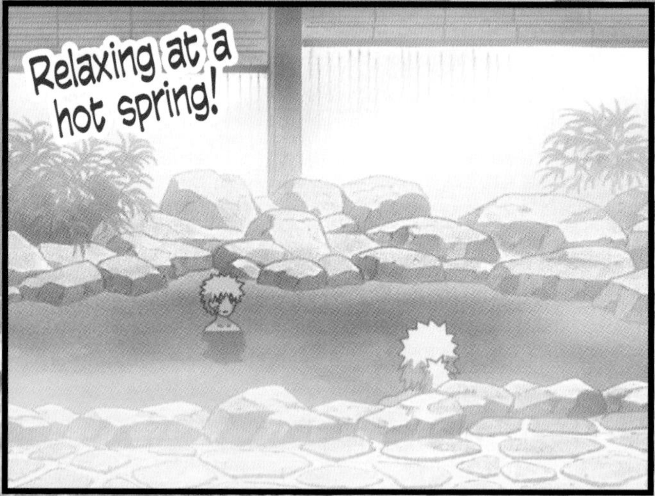

⬅ Jiraiya brings a discouraged Naruto to a hot spring bath. Heavenly relaxation… But be wary, Jiraiya's eyes are not smiling!

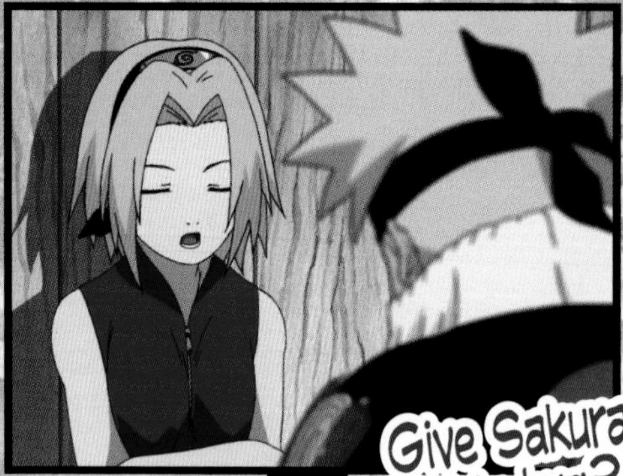

Give Sakura a big hug?

Is this part of training too?!

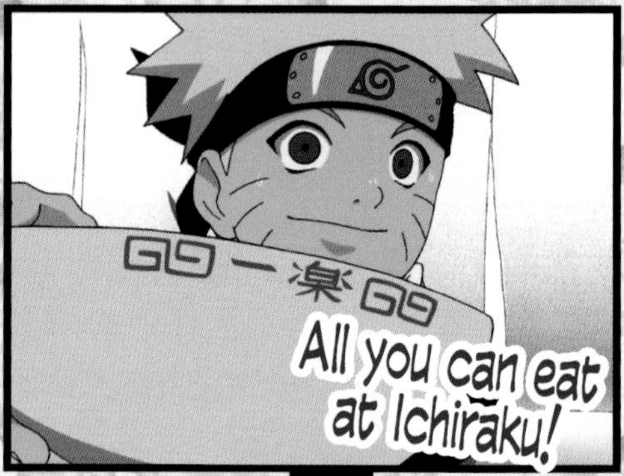
一楽

All you can eat at Ichiraku!

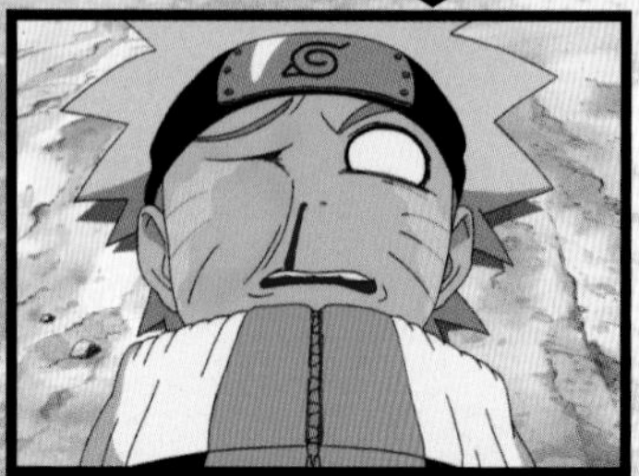

⬆⬅ The dream come true…is all just a dream!

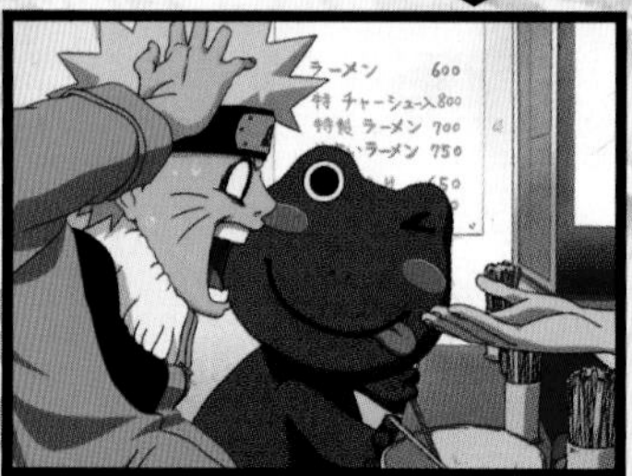

⬆⬅ Naruto eats his fill. But wait… Jiraiya expects Naruto to pick up the tab?!

A life-threatening ordeal...

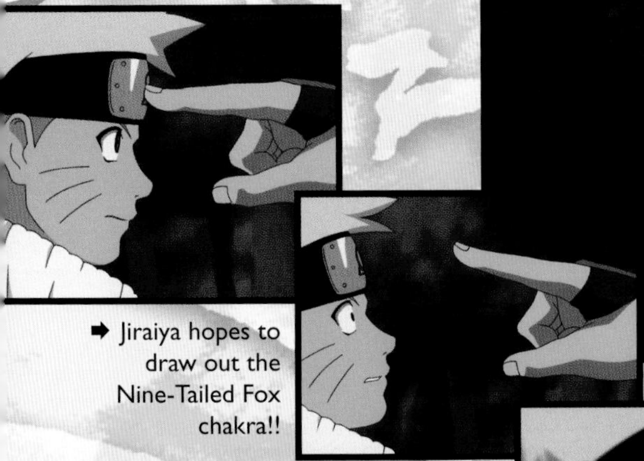

➡ Jiraiya hopes to draw out the Nine-Tailed Fox chakra!!

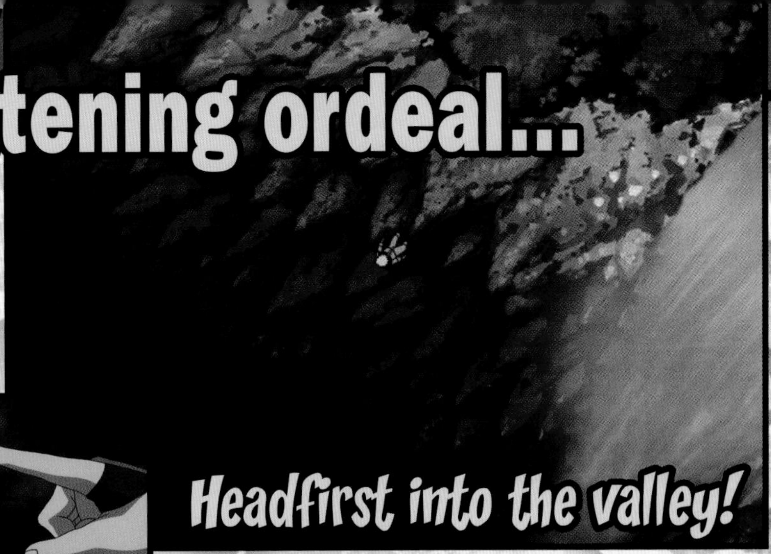
Headfirst into the valley!

⬆ The rocks are too slippery, even when using chakra!

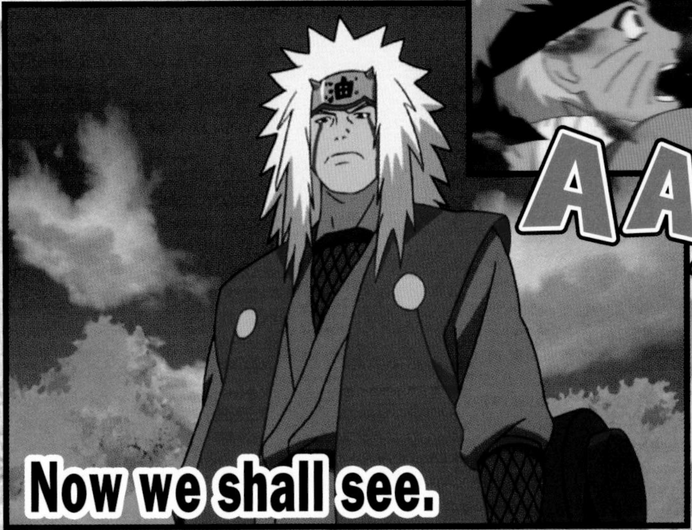
Now we shall see.

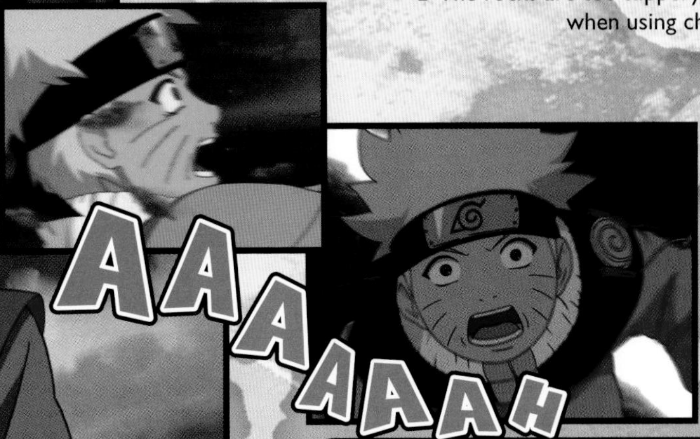
AAAAAAAH

Suddenly it's a matter of life or death! Naruto falls into the deep valley!

All the special treatment was so Naruto wouldn't die with any regrets! Sent over the edge by Jiraiya, Naruto plummets! It's time to do or die!

Meanwhile...

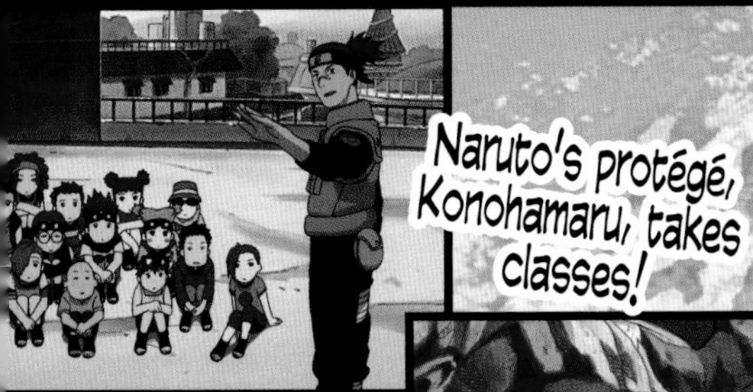
Naruto's protégé, Konohamaru, takes classes!

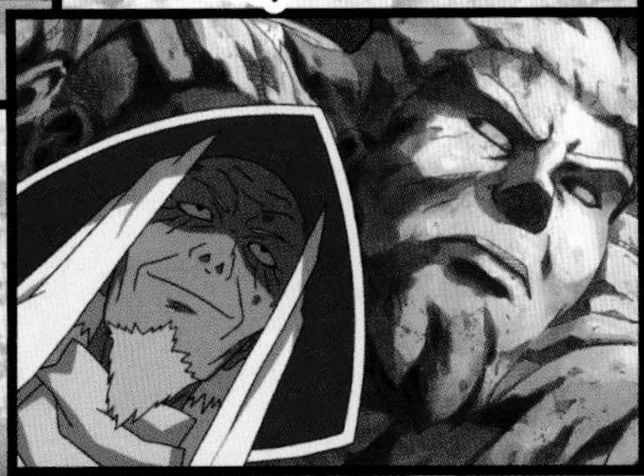

⬆➡ The Third Hokage joins history class. His younger face peers down from the carving in the rocks above.

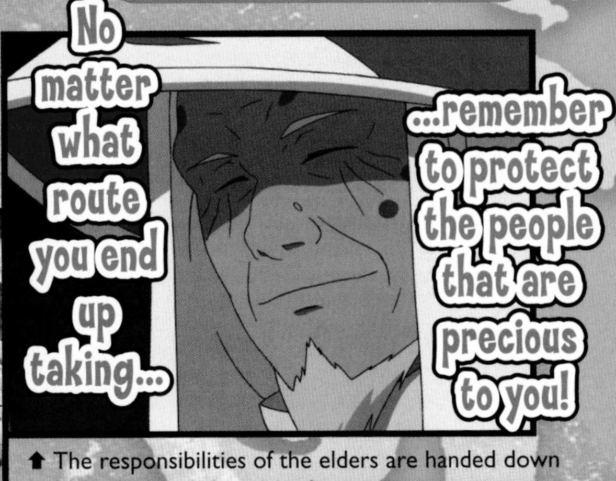
No matter what route you end up taking...
...remember to protect the people that are precious to you!

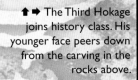

⬆ The responsibilities of the elders are handed down to those who will forge the future...

The power of the Nine-Tailed Fox is sealed within Naruto!

Now, the sealed power awakens!

Has Naruto traveled to a realm between dream and reality? The contract with the Nine-Tailed Fox Spirit sealed within his body provides Naruto with ultimate power!

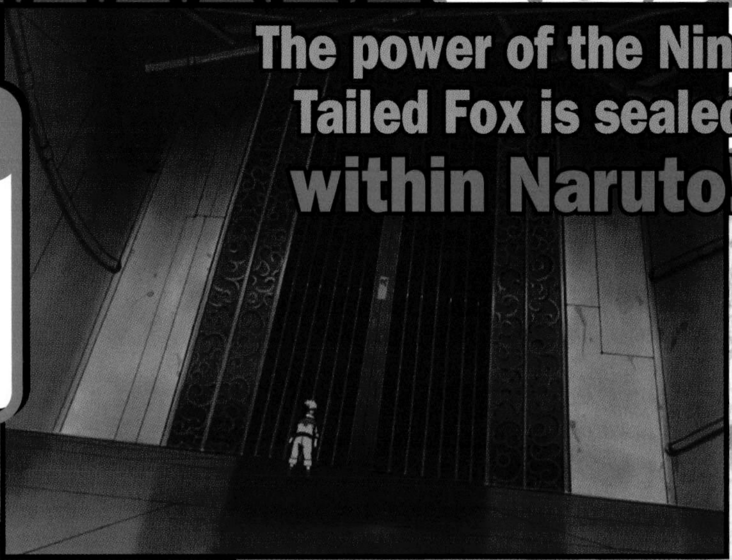

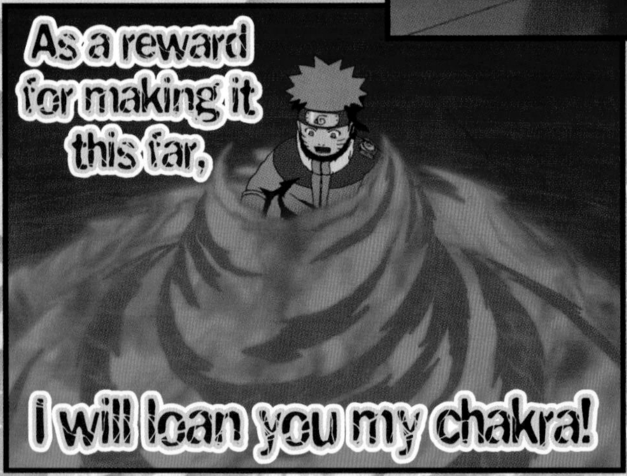
As a reward for making it this far,
I will loan you my chakra!

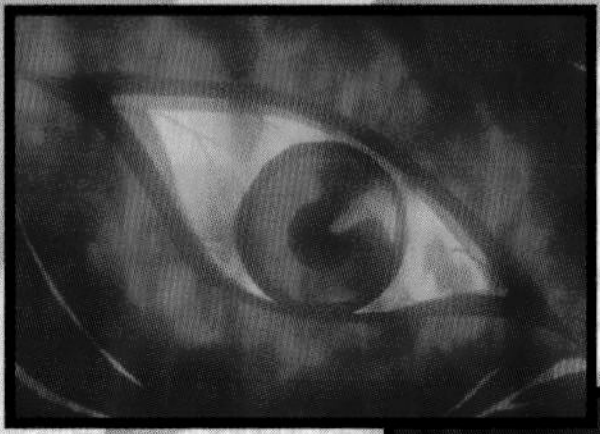

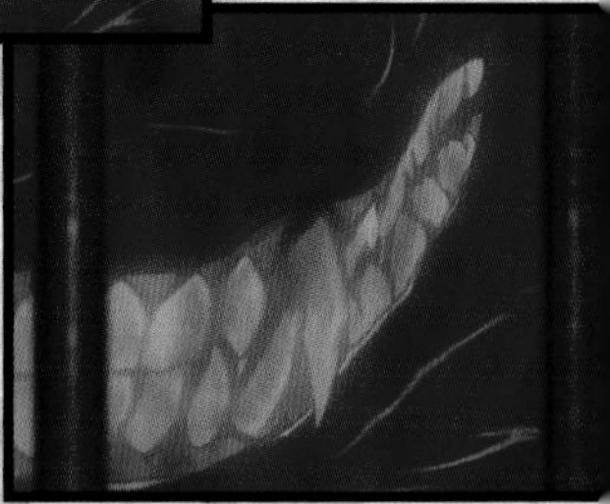

⬆➡ Naruto fearlessly demands that the monster he faces lend him its power.

Super giant! Enter the massive, ultra-powerful Gamabunta!

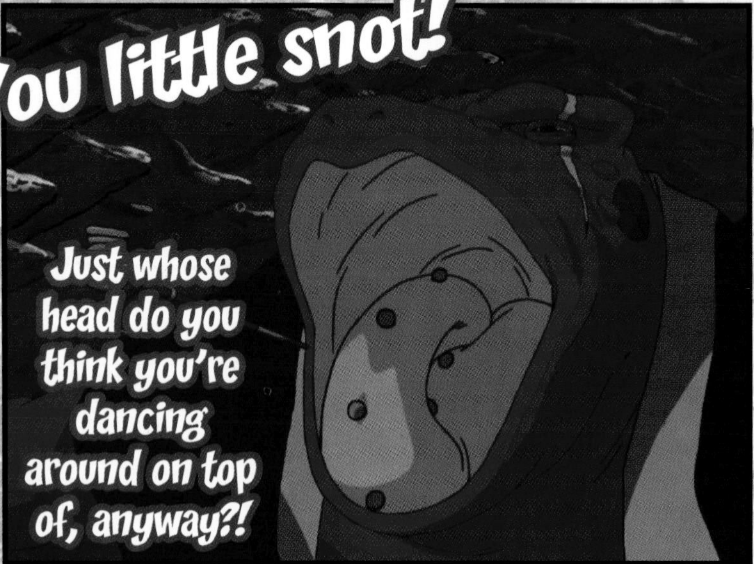
You little snot!
Just whose head do you think you're dancing around on top of, anyway?!

⬆ Got it! The Summoning Jutsu is a major success! But…Naruto gets scolded anyway?!

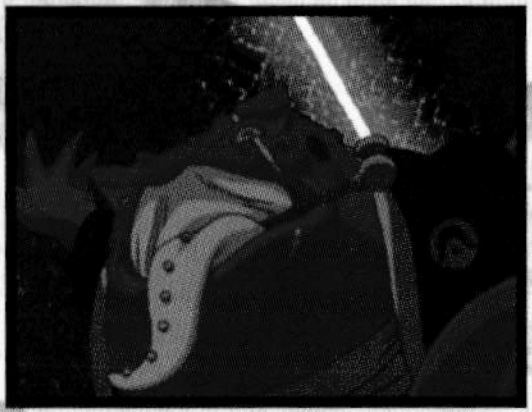

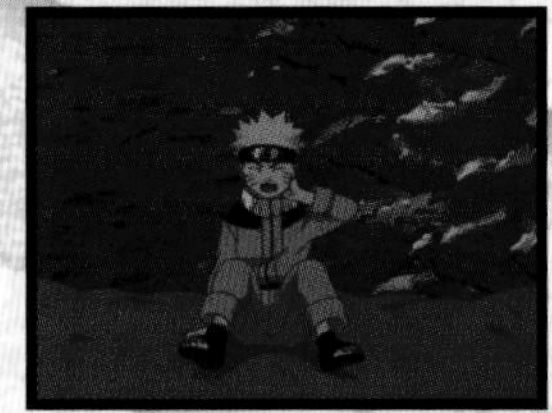

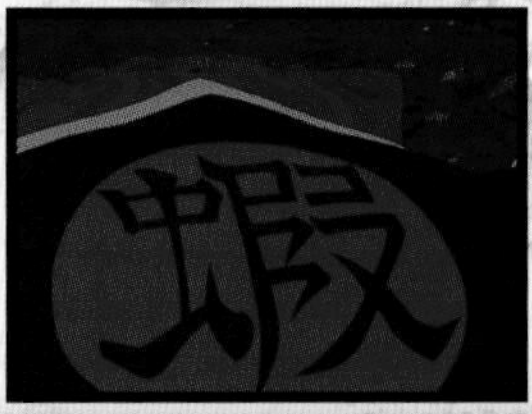

Never back down! A display of guts to show the Uzumaki spirit!

A battle of wills. Neither side gives an inch.

Naruto reels at the force of the giant toad! But he won't be made fun of -- that's not Uzumaki style!

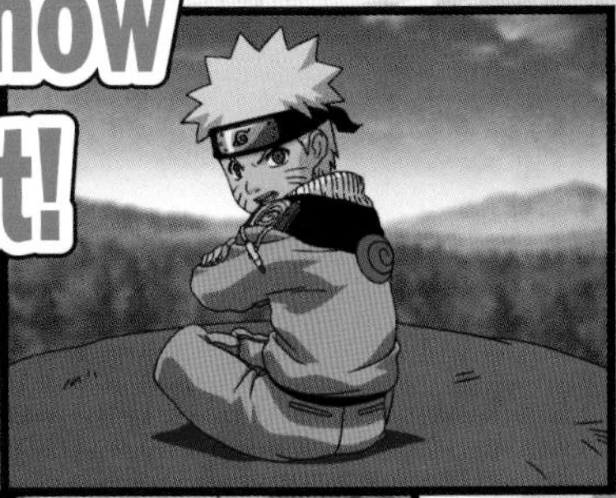

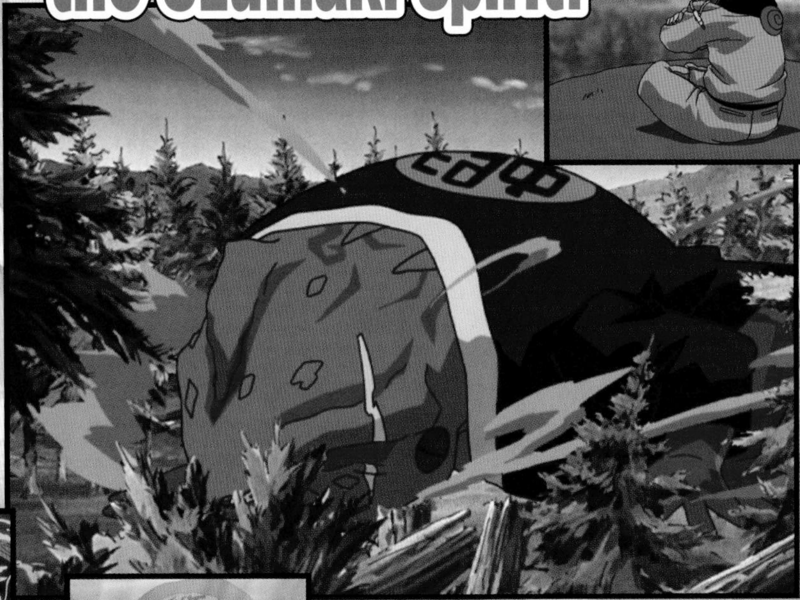

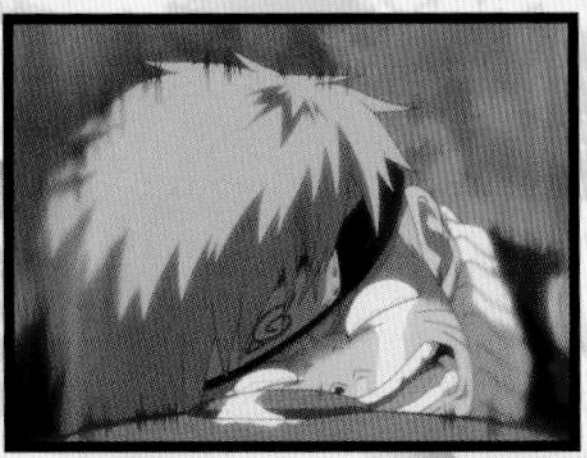

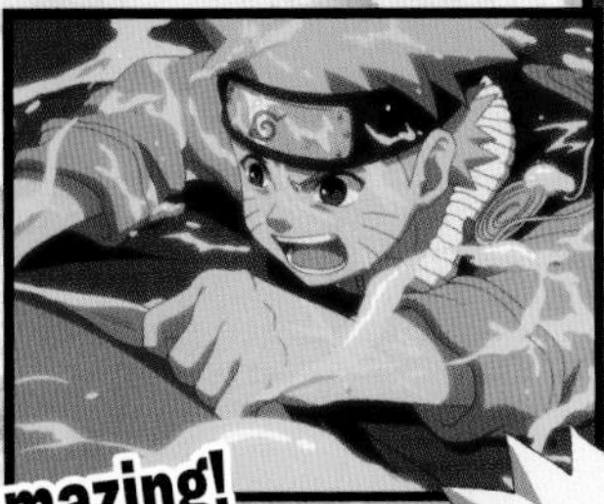

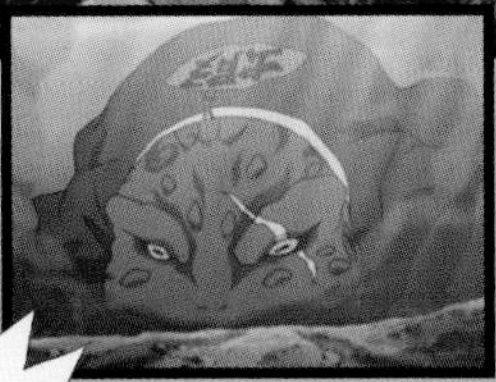

⬆ Naruto and Gamabunta in a clash of wills! Victory will be decided by whether or not Naruto can hang on while riding Gamabunta's back. The earth shakes with the titanic struggle. Who will prevail?!

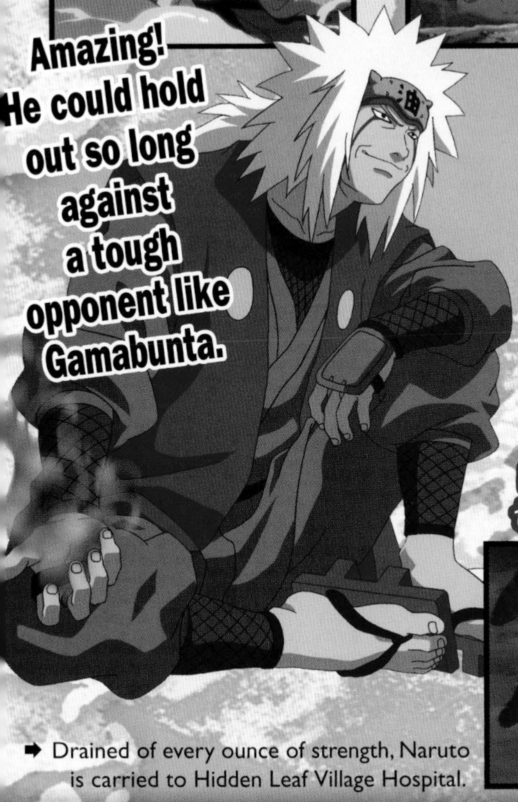

Amazing! He could hold out so long against a tough opponent like Gamabunta.

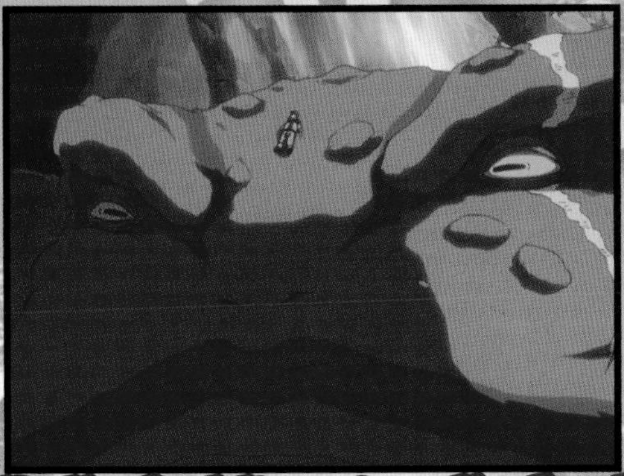

⬅ Naruto completely exhausts his strength, but Gamabunta acknowledges the spirit and guts he displayed.

It's the first time since the Fourth Hokage that someone dared to climb on my head.

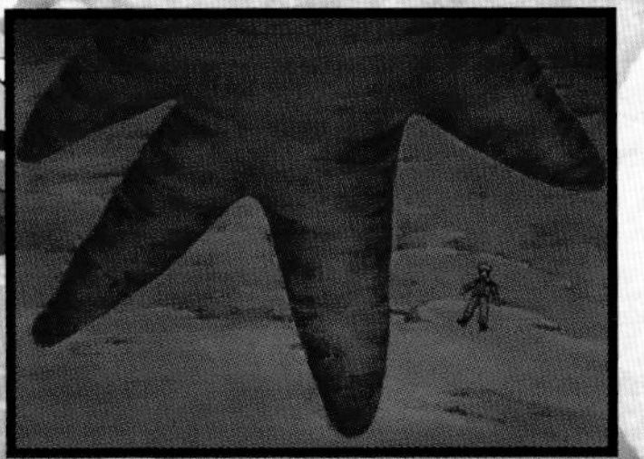

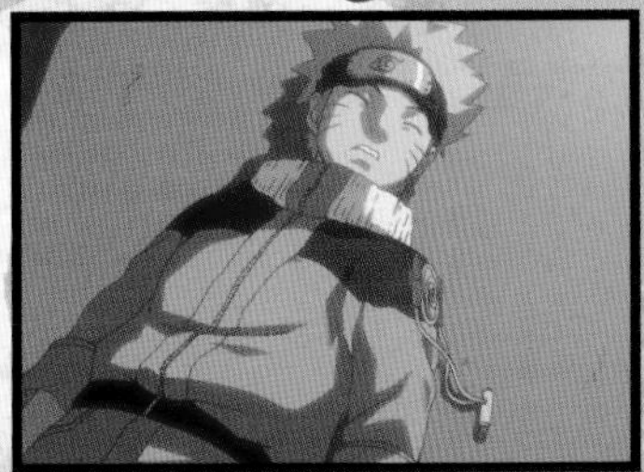

➡ Drained of every ounce of strength, Naruto is carried to Hidden Leaf Village Hospital.

Naruto and Shikamaru vs. Gaara?

One day before the final round, something lethal sneaks into the hospital and approaches Lee's room... Naruto and Shikamaru sense danger... and then encounter Gaara, plunging them into volatile conflict!

➡ Gaara of the desert silently lurks. No one can quell his deadly intent.

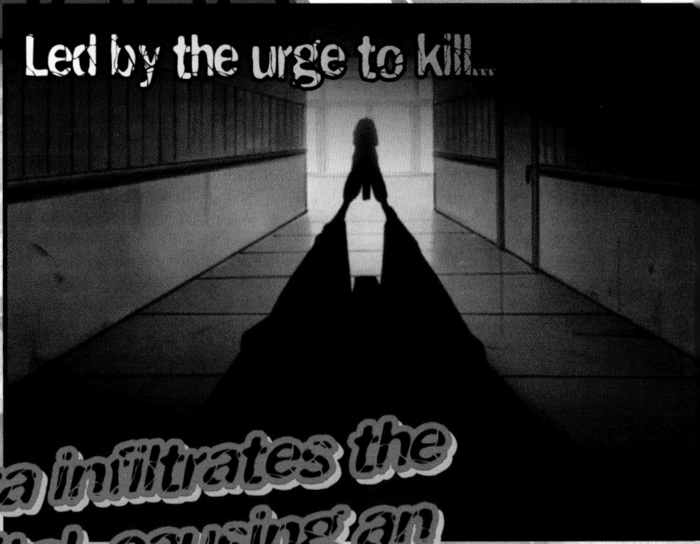
Led by the urge to kill...

Gaara infiltrates the hospital, causing an explosive situation!

➡ Gaara keeps his cool even though rendered motionless by the Shadow Possession Jutsu.

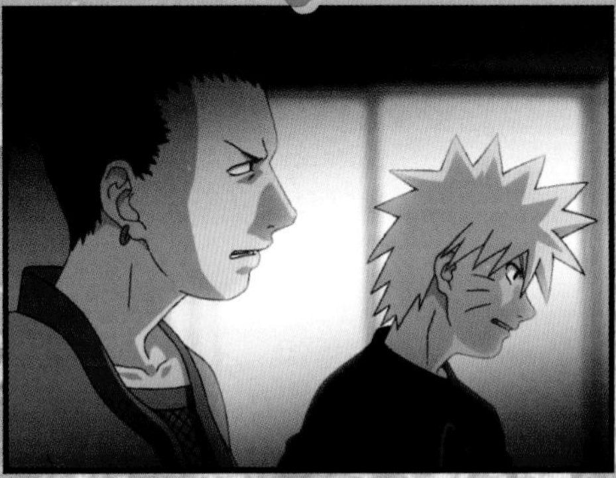

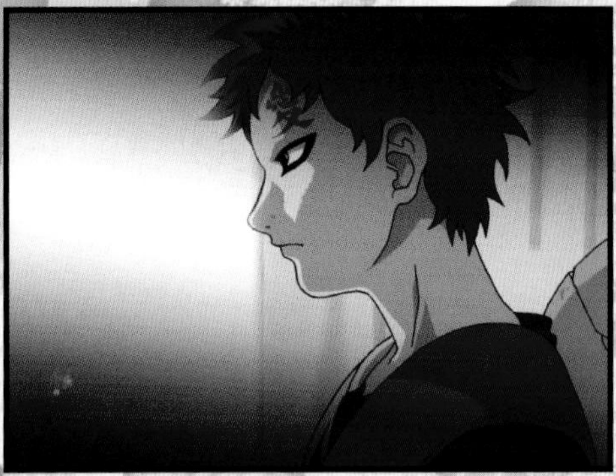

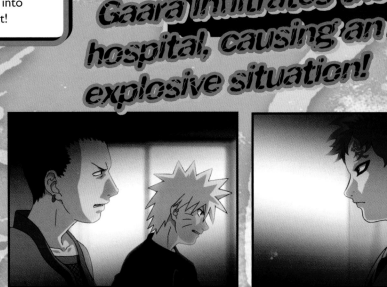

I was born a monster.

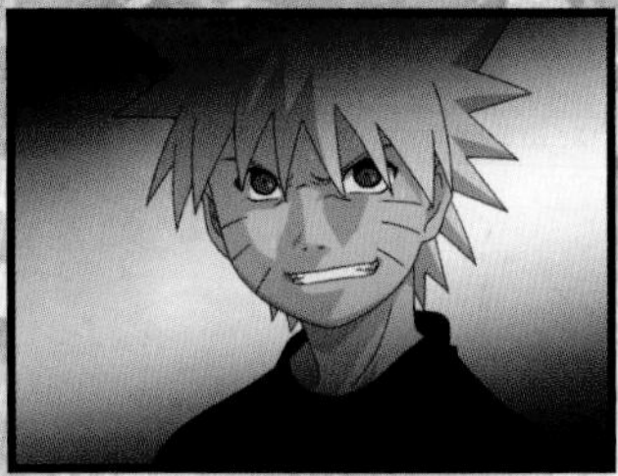

⬇⬆ He may act like a demon, but I got the real thing inside of me! Naruto provokes Gaara, but...?!

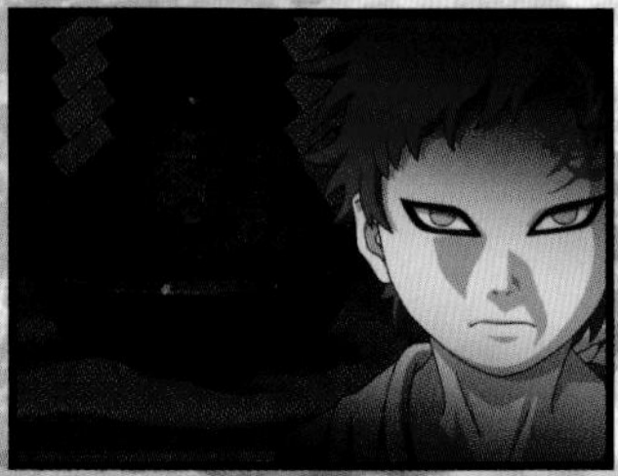

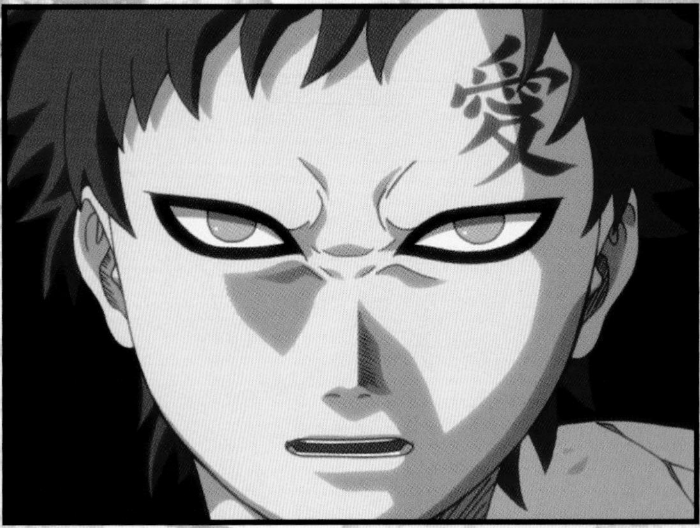

⬆ Gaara, the incarnation of sand, tells the shocking secret of his birth!

Gaara talks about the meaning of his life.

Far from being loved, Gaara was detested by his parents and had to live alone. He came to see that his reason for living was to kill others in order to fulfill his own existence. Such strength terrifies Naruto!

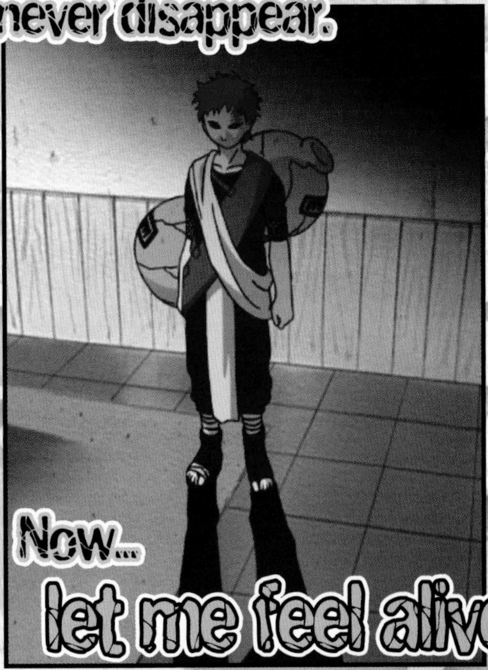
I will never disappear.
Now...
let me feel alive!

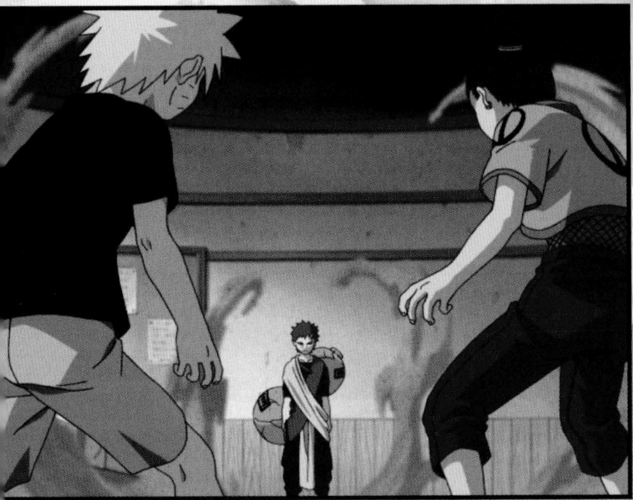

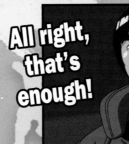

⬆ Gaara's sand is poised to strike! Would Naruto and Shikamaru be dead if Guy hadn't intervened?!

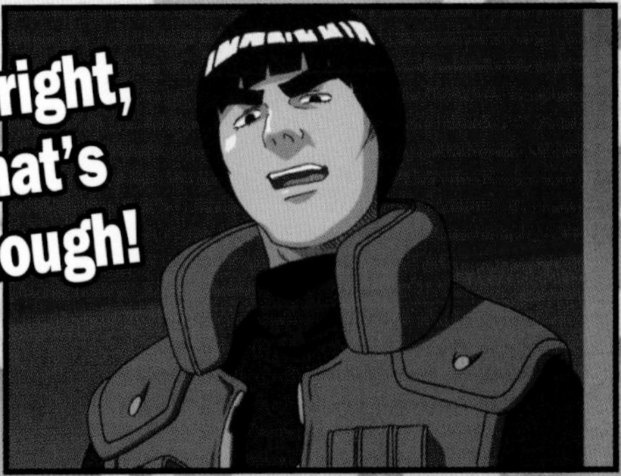
All right, that's enough!

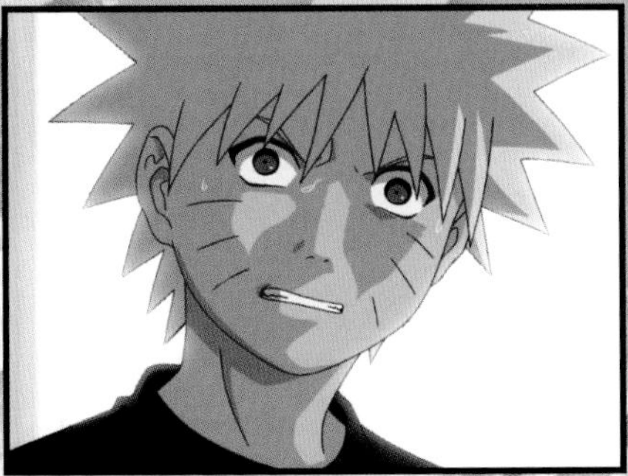

⬆➡ Knowing all too well about isolation, Naruto understands Gaara's strength. Naruto looks at Gaara with a fear in his eyes that he can't conceal.

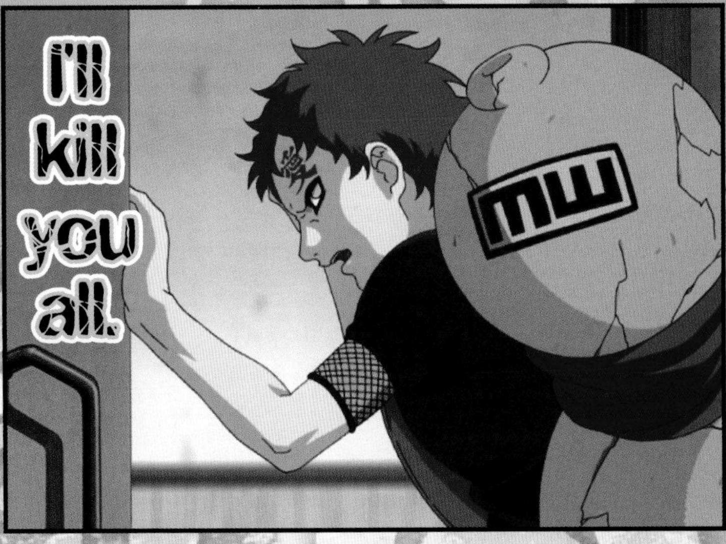
I'll kill you all.

And at last...
...the final round is tomorrow.

Anbu Black Ops Special Report

Part Four

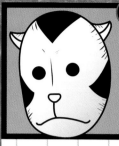

Orochimaru

On the occasion of the current Chunin Exams, Orochimaru returns to the village. What is the true intention of his scheming behind the scenes...?

⬆ Just one look into his glimmering evil eyes and you will see an image of your own death...

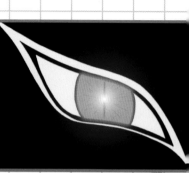

Report 1

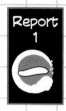

In the Hidden Leaf Village, there were once shinobi called the Legendary Sannin.

Orochimaru relished the reputation he shared with Jiraiya and Tsunade as a Sannin and enjoyed being recognized as the strongest. He exceeded the others in the intensity of his ninjutsu, but even more terrifying was his bloodcurdling stare.

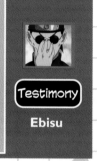

The mere sight of Orochimaru and his Giant Snake staining the battlefield with blood terrified even those from his own village. Some say that his abilities surpassed those of the Hokage. He was without a doubt the strongest and most feared figure of the time.

Testimony

Ebisu

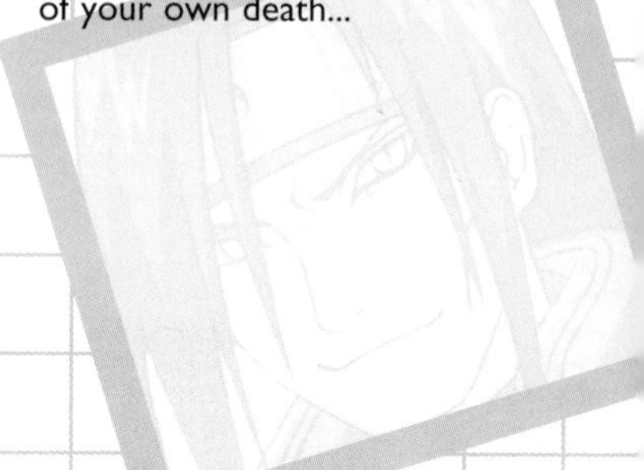

⬇ Orochimaru, disguised as a Grass ninja, lurks in the Forest of Death. Anko struggles in vain...

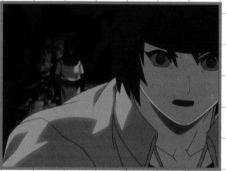

Report 2

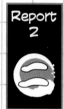

The Bingo Book's Level S Rank: Possessing extremely dangerous abilities.

Now he is on the Hidden Leaf Village's wanted list as a rogue ninja. The Anbu Black Ops have done their best, but they have never even found a single trace of him. Then, during the Chunin Exams, it turns out that Orochimaru has already infiltrated the village.

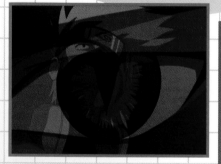

⬆ Even jonin Kakashi is frozen in the face of Orochimaru's fearful aura.

➡ Curse marks planted on the necks of Sasuke and Anko. The curse mark is capable of drawing out sinister power.

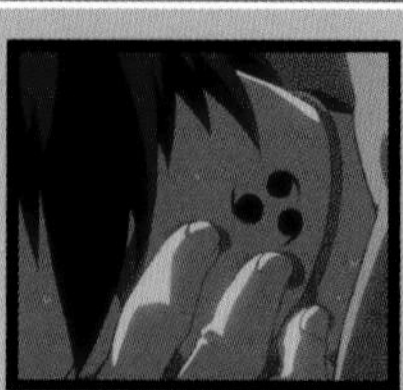

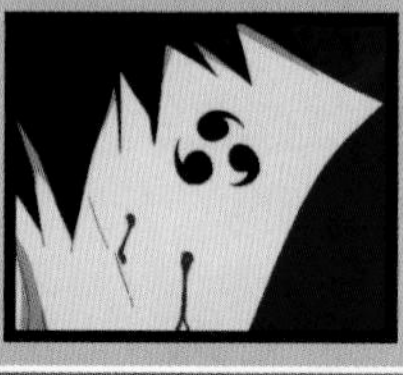

Being unable to defeat my ex-mentor Orochimaru was mortifying. In desperation I even used the Forbidden Jutsu he taught me. He appears to be interested in Sasuke Uchiha, and he planted a curse mark similar to mine on him. There must be another motive, something far more evil...

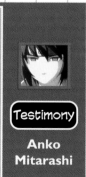

Testimony

Anko Mitarashi

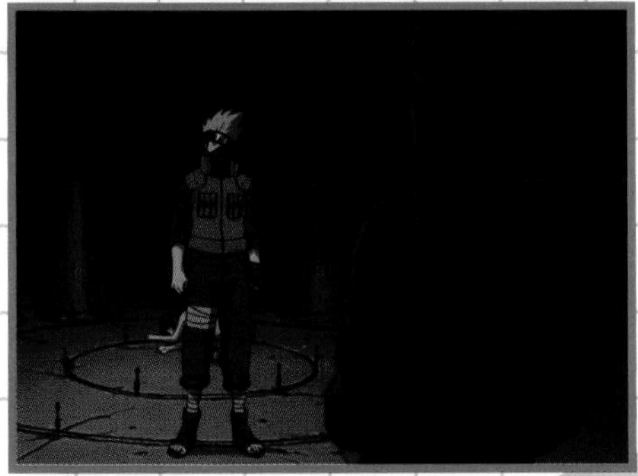

⬅ He appears before Kakashi once again, but does nothing and then disappears...

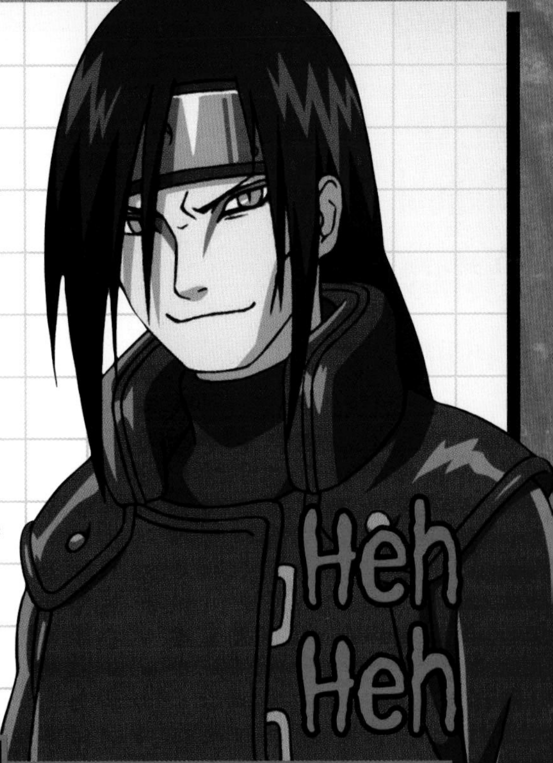
Heh Heh

Report 3

Orochimaru founded the Village Hidden in the Sound and concealed himself behind the scenes of the Chunin Exams.

Orochimaru confronts Kakashi during the Third Exam Prelims and admits that he's the leader of the Village Hidden in the Sound and that he sent the Sound ninja to the Chunin Exams. Orochimaru revels in pulling strings behind the scenes. It's now clear that his deadly fangs target the Hidden Leaf Village!

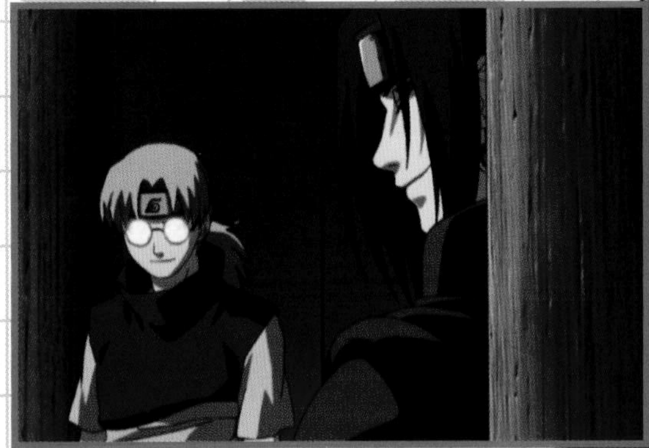

➡ Kabuto, a Medical Corps genin of the Hidden Leaf Village, is a spy in the service of Orochimaru!

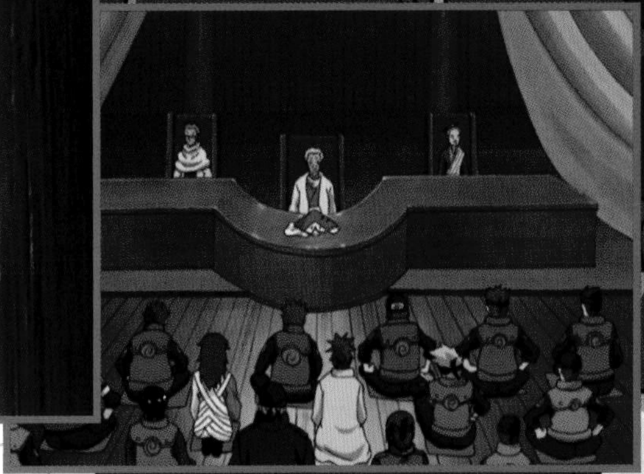

⬆ After the suspicious death of Hayate Gekko, a number of shinobi gather to take urgent measures to deal with the acts of Orochimaru and the Sound.

Kabuto Yakushi—another source of mischief in the shadows.

Kakashi's report reveals that Kabuto is a spy for Sound. He appeared to be just a member of the medical corps whose rank would never increase but... Now, like Orochimaru, his whereabouts are unknown.

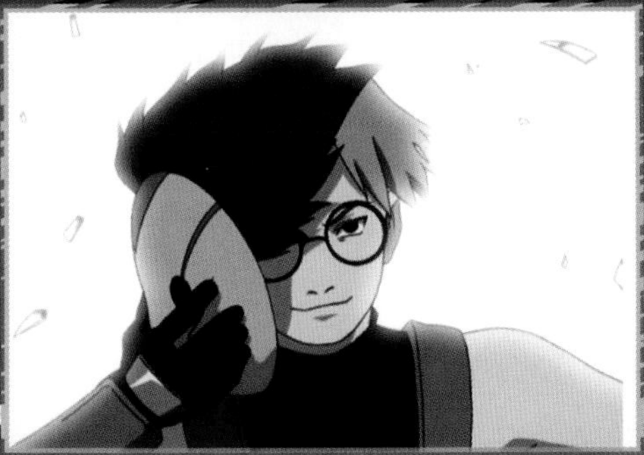

Summary Report

Orochimaru was once a Legendary Sannin. Now he is the ultimate threat to the village. The high-ranking ninja consider measures to deal with worst-case scenarios, including the possible assassination of the Hokage and the entire defeat of the Leaf Village. The final round begins despite deep anxiety felt by all.

Secret Shinobi Picture Album

Part Five

The Village Hidden in the Leaves

Let's take a tour with Naruto! Explore the Village Hidden in the Leaves, the largest of all the shinobi hidden villages!

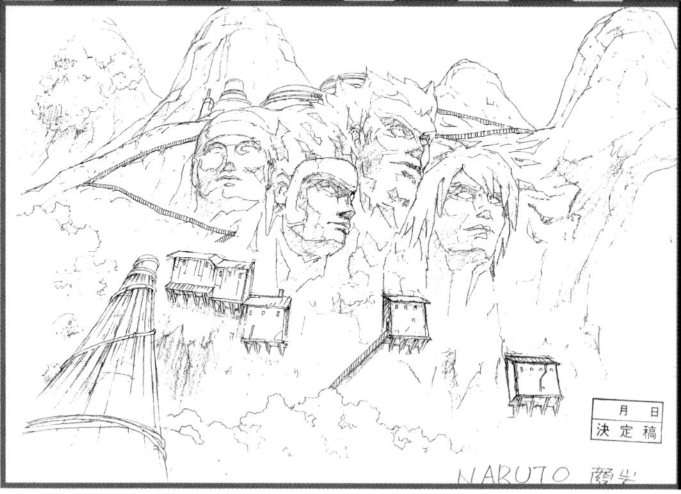

The Great Stone Faces

The biggest and best spot for graffiti. Come check out my art!

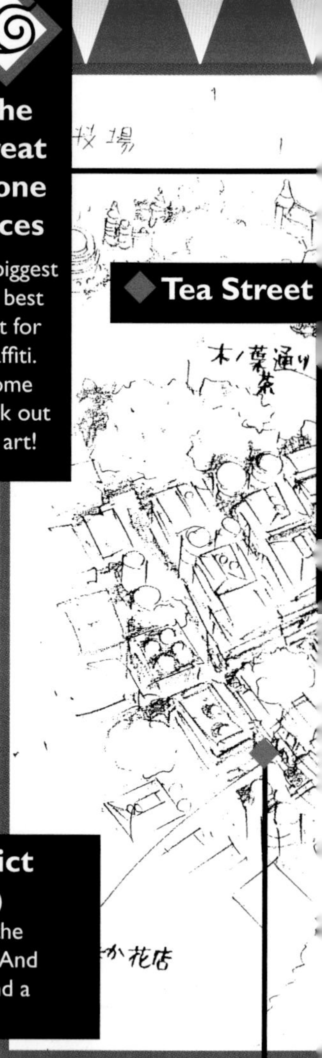

Tea Street

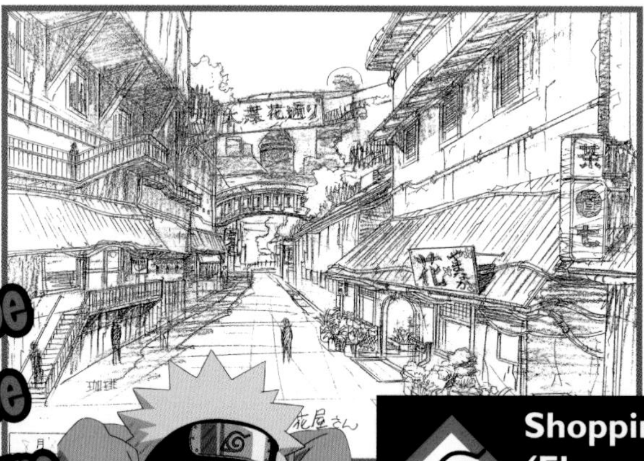

Shopping District (Flower Street)

Ino's flower shop is at the entrance to this street. And there's a coffee shop and a diner. Believe it!

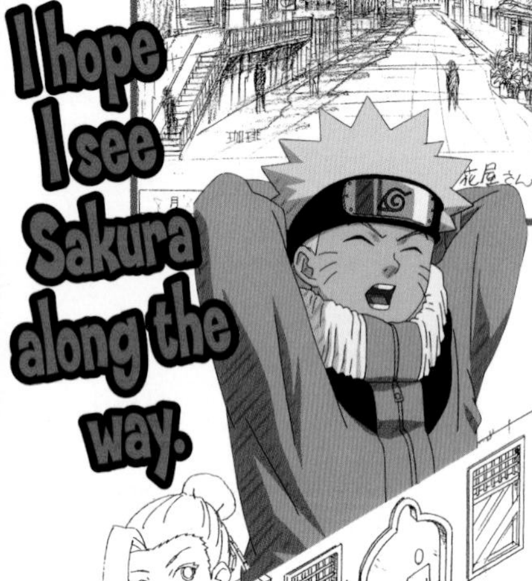
I hope I see Sakura along the way.

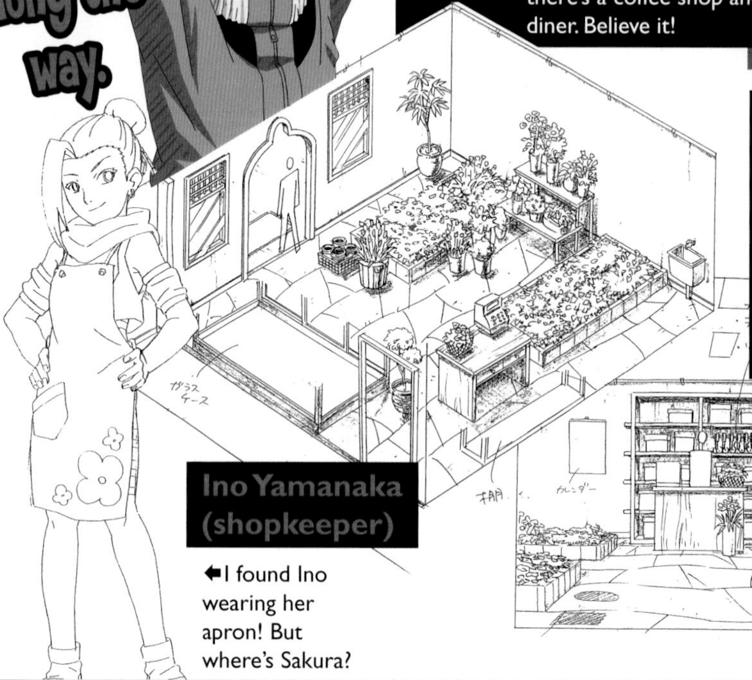

Ino Yamanaka (shopkeeper)

⬅I found Ino wearing her apron! But where's Sakura?

Yamanaka Flower Shop

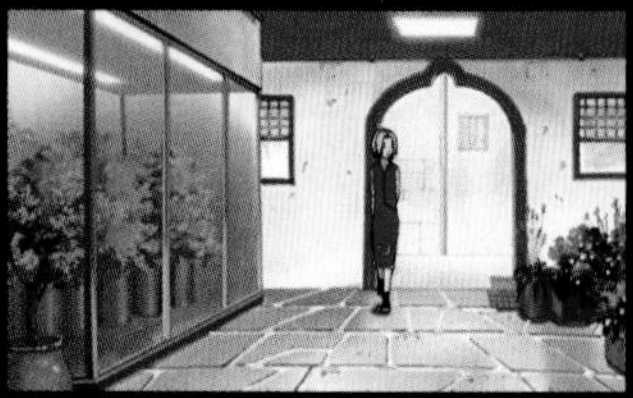

⬆The shop is filled with a rainbow of colored flowers. Seeing them makes me appreciate flowers!

A bird's-eye view of the Village Hidden in the Leaves

The Ninja Academy is at the foot of the Great Stone Faces, the focal point from where the streets fan out! There are tons of fun places!

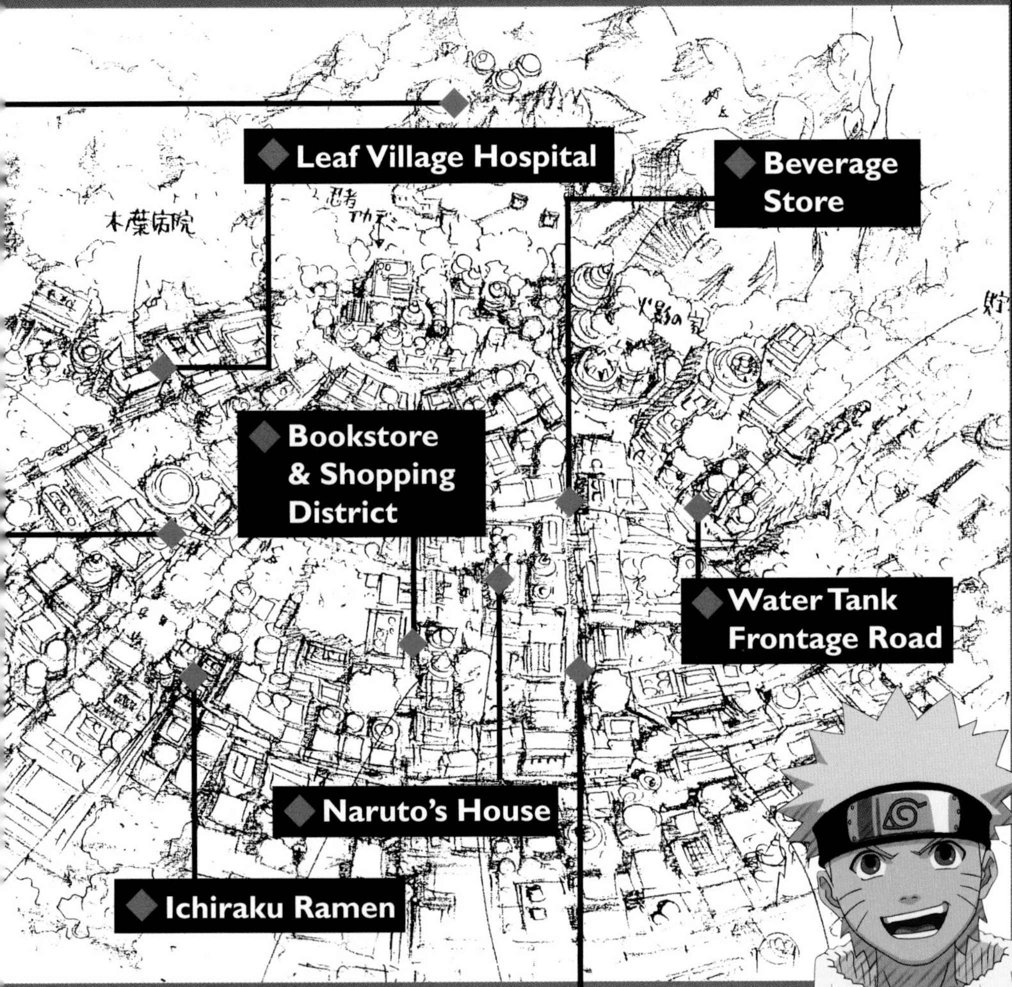

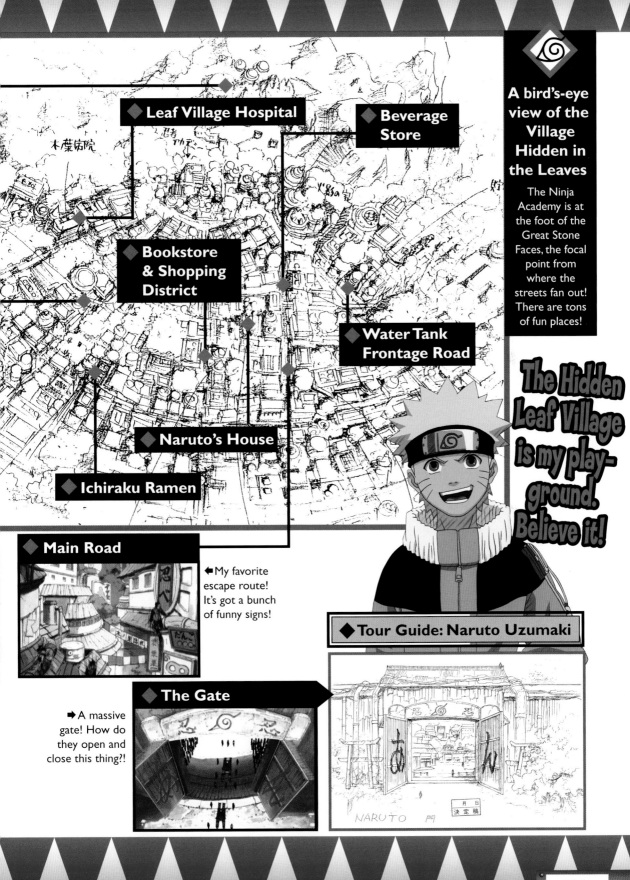

Leaf Village Hospital
Beverage Store
Bookstore & Shopping District
Water Tank Frontage Road
Naruto's House
Ichiraku Ramen
Main Road
The Gate

The Hidden Leaf Village is my play-ground. Believe it!

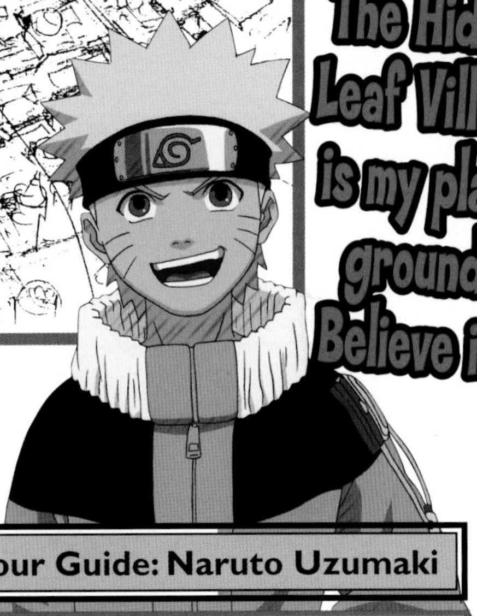

◆ Tour Guide: Naruto Uzumaki

◆ Main Road

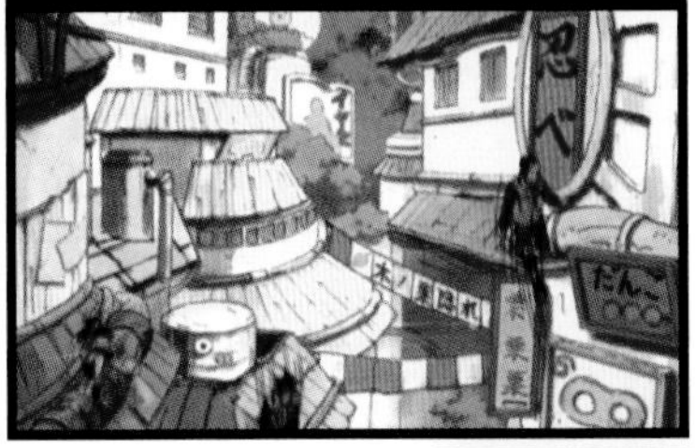

⬅My favorite escape route! It's got a bunch of funny signs!

◆ The Gate

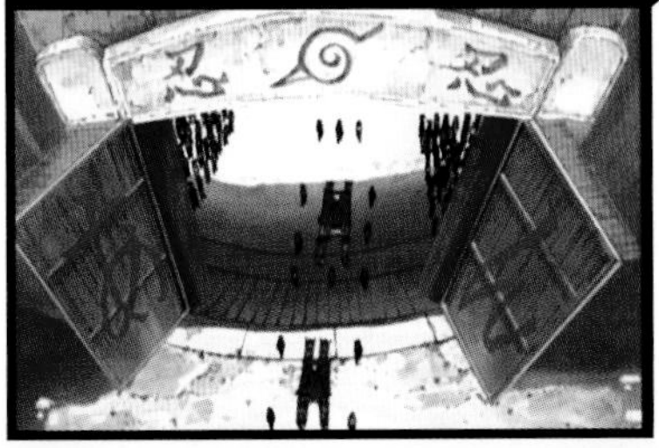

➡A massive gate! How do they open and close this thing?!

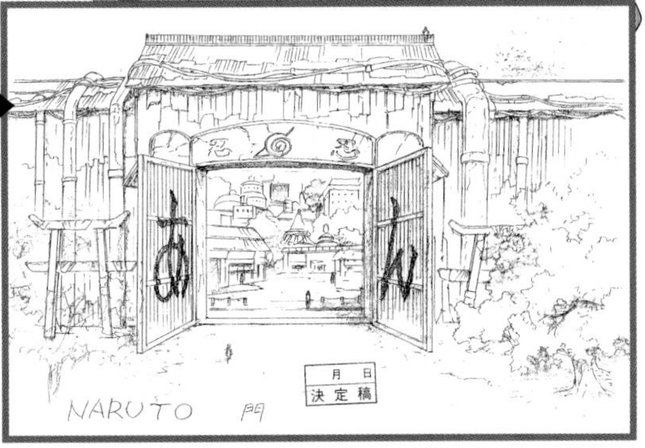

月 日
決定稿
NARUTO 門

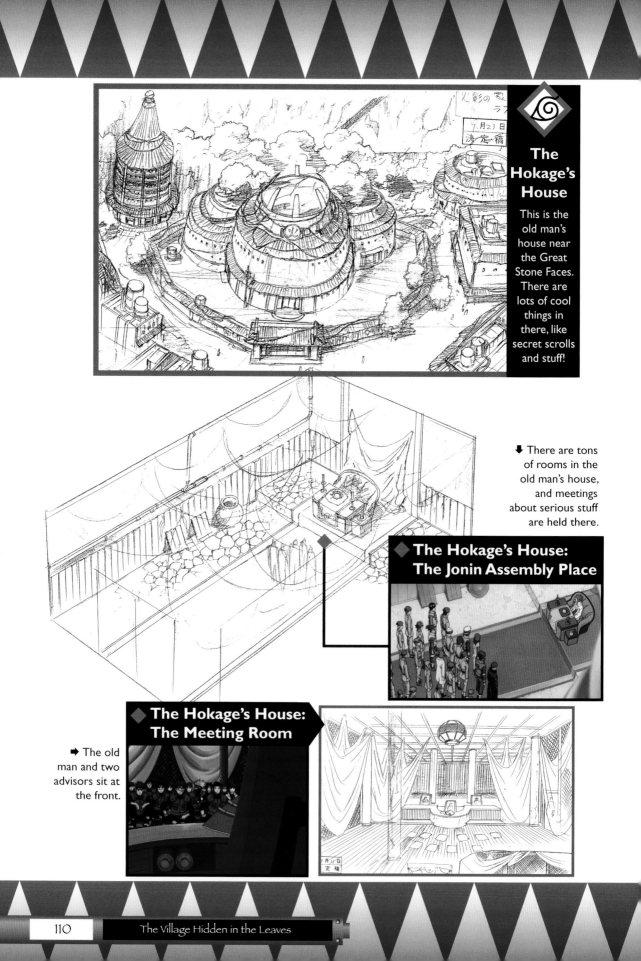

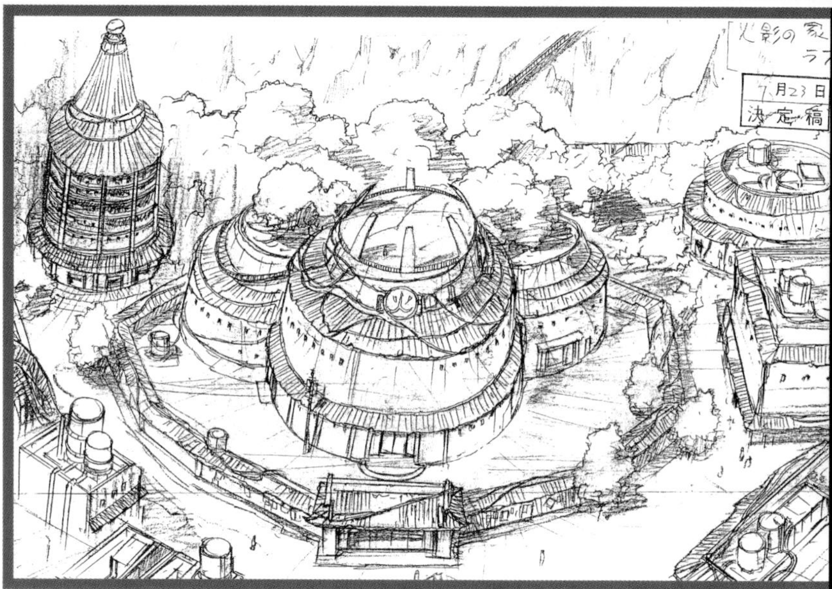
7月23日
決定稿

The Hokage's House

This is the old man's house near the Great Stone Faces. There are lots of cool things in there, like secret scrolls and stuff!

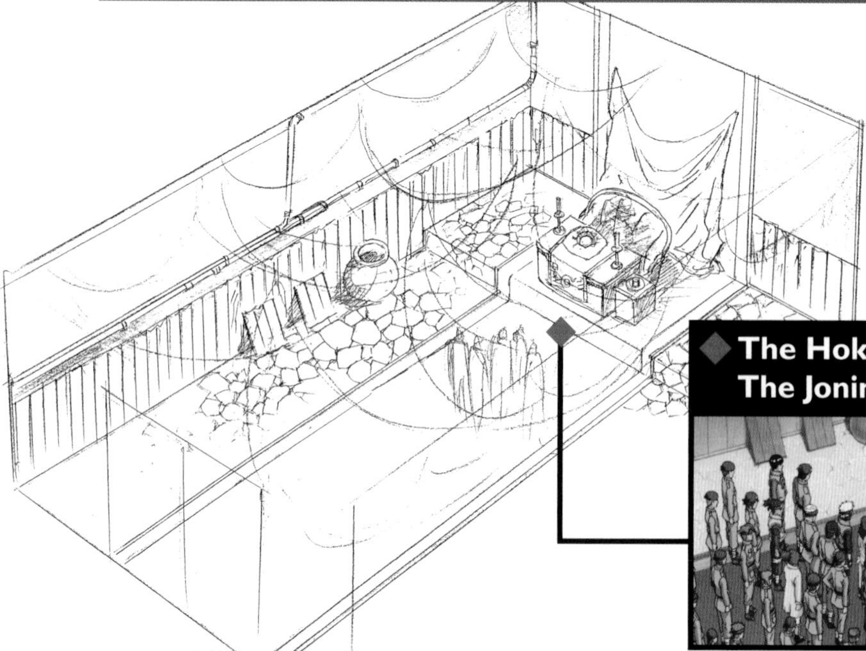

⬇ There are tons of rooms in the old man's house, and meetings about serious stuff are held there.

The Hokage's House: The Jonin Assembly Place

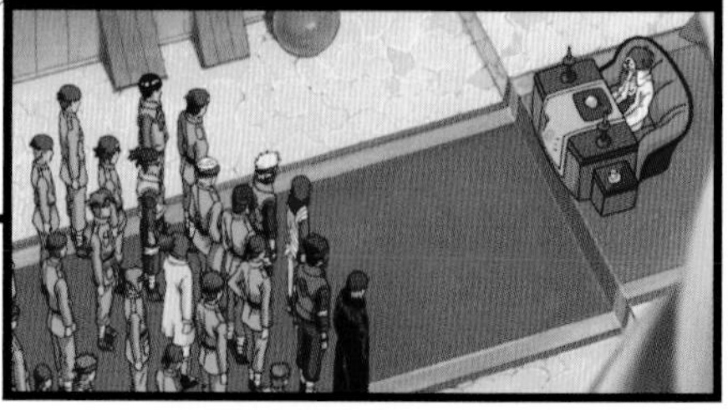

The Hokage's House: The Meeting Room

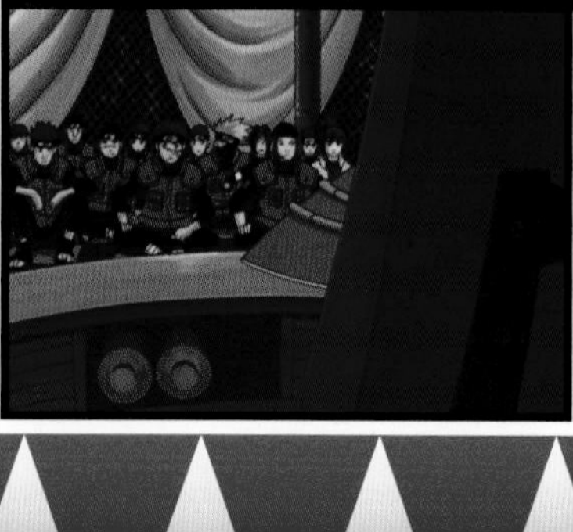

➡ The old man and two advisors sit at the front.

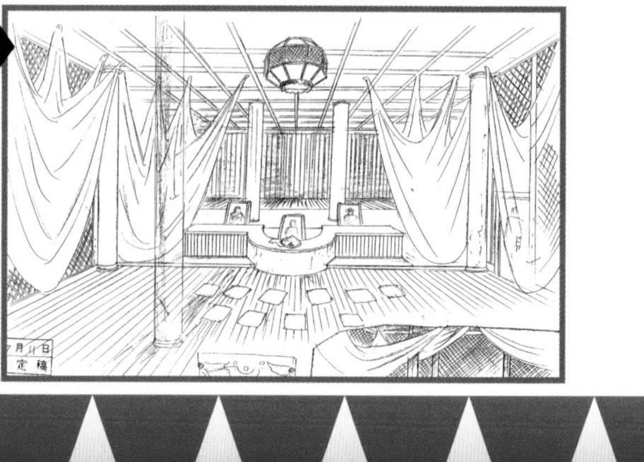

Where the heck is Sakura, anyway?!

The Temple

This temple is huge! But doing graffiti on the pillars, though... That's just kid stuff!

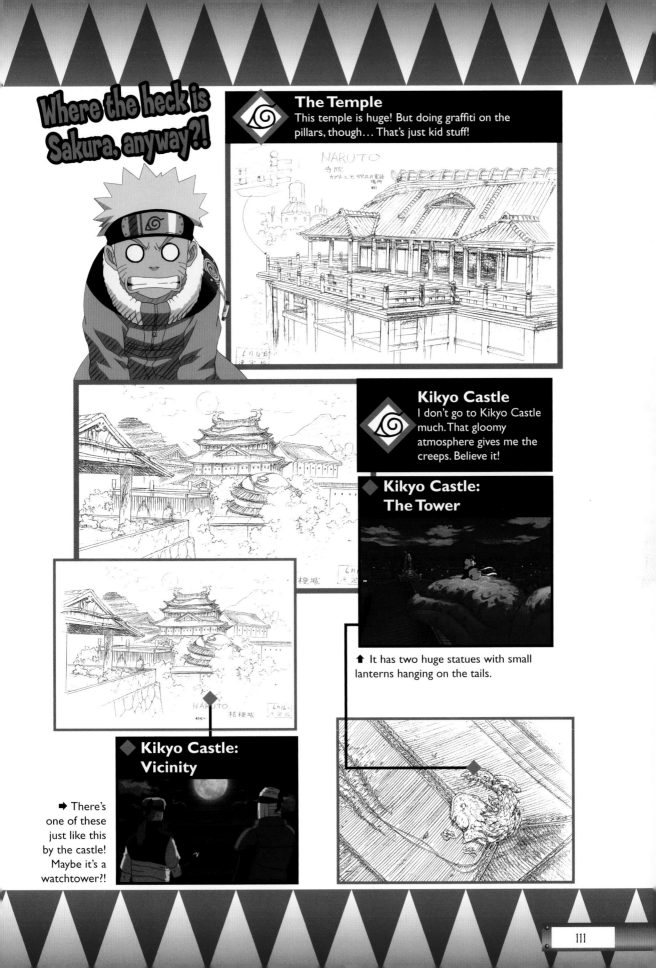

Kikyo Castle

I don't go to Kikyo Castle much. That gloomy atmosphere gives me the creeps. Believe it!

Kikyo Castle: The Tower

⬆ It has two huge statues with small lanterns hanging on the tails.

Kikyo Castle: Vicinity

➡ There's one of these just like this by the castle! Maybe it's a watchtower?!

Secret Shinobi Picture Album

Part Six

Places to Dine in the Leaf Village

Gourmet dining in Hidden Leaf Village! Chow down at all the best places with gourmet guide Choji!

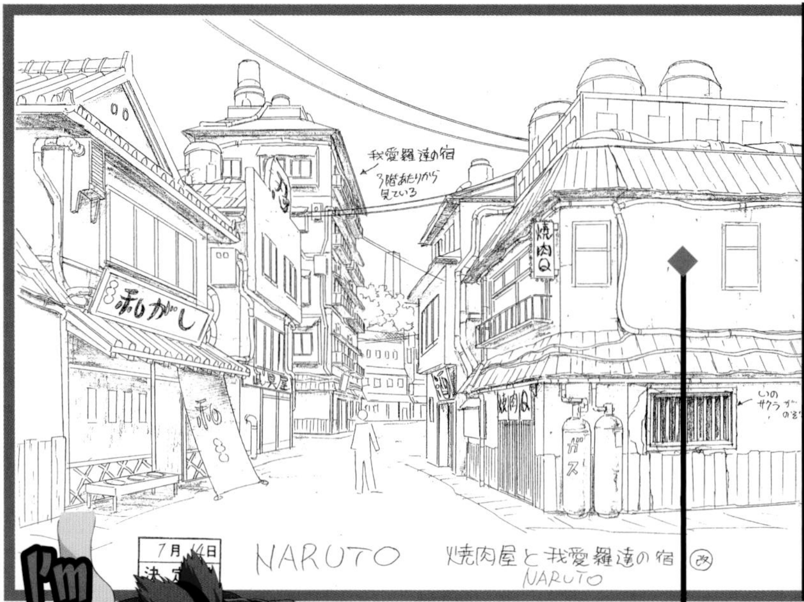

我愛羅達の宿
3階あたりから見ている
焼肉Q
NARUTO
焼肉屋と我愛羅達の宿

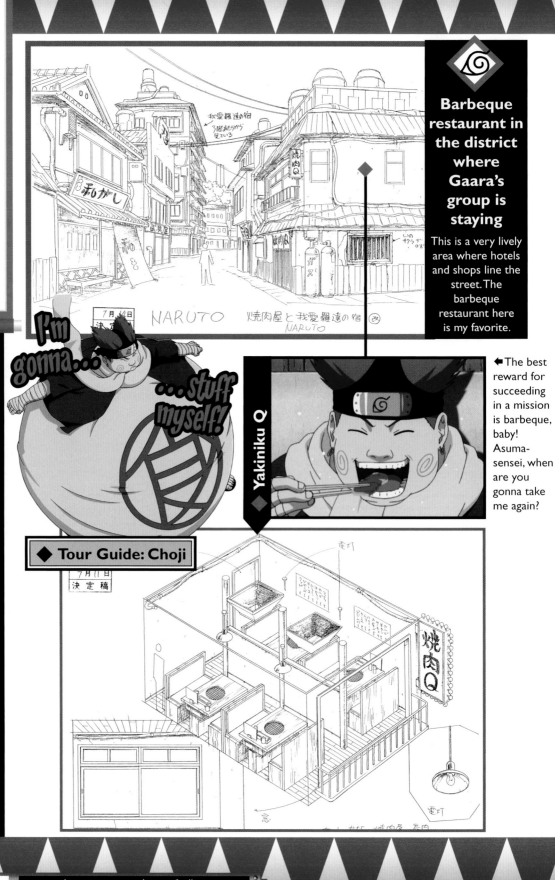

Barbeque restaurant in the district where Gaara's group is staying

This is a very lively area where hotels and shops line the street. The barbeque restaurant here is my favorite.

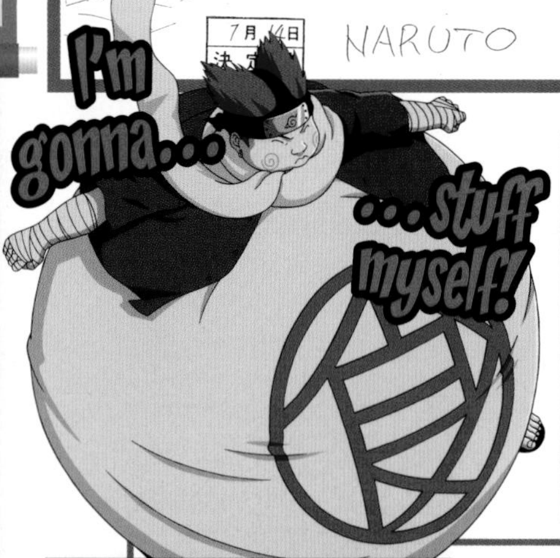

I'm gonna…
…stuff myself!

◆ Tour Guide: Choji

◆ Yakiniku Q

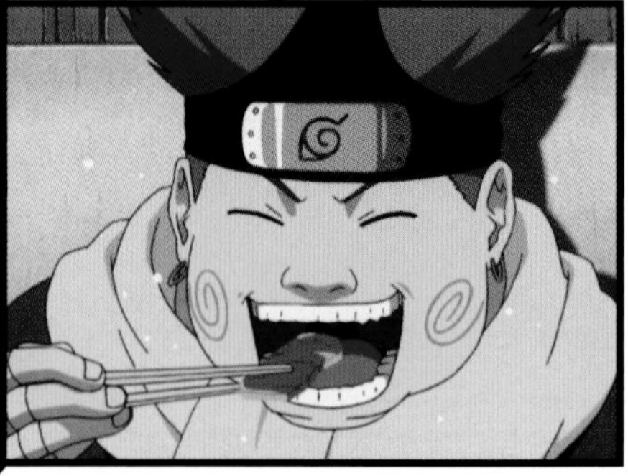

⬅The best reward for succeeding in a mission is barbeque, baby! Asuma-sensei, when are you gonna take me again?

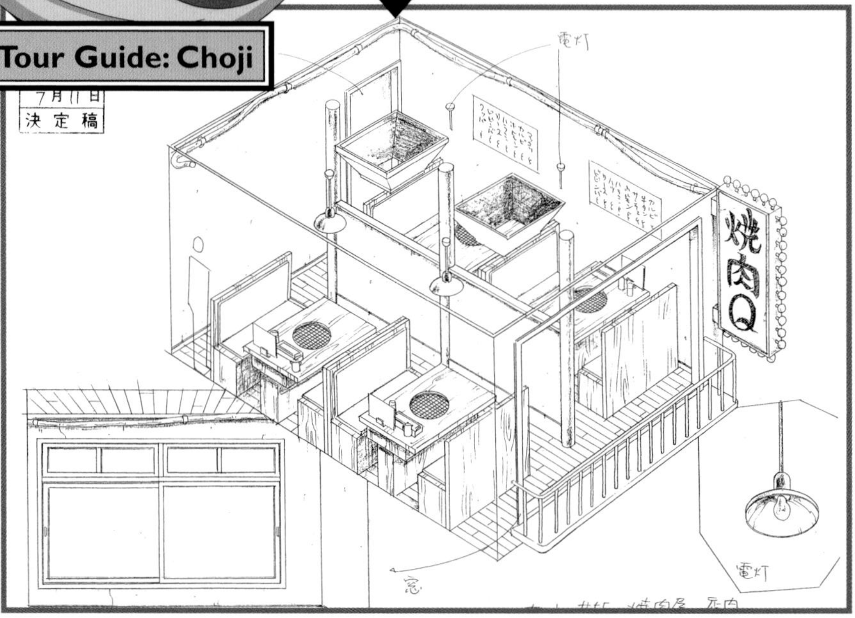

7月11日
決定稿
電灯
焼肉Q
窓

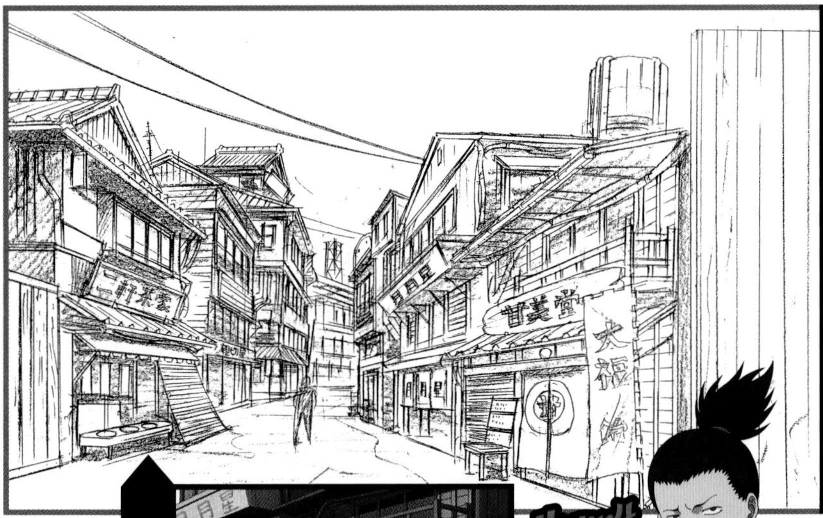

The Hot Spring District

When I hear hot springs, I think of manju, a steamed dumpling with sweet bean filling! There are lots of shops for sweets here!

Kanbido

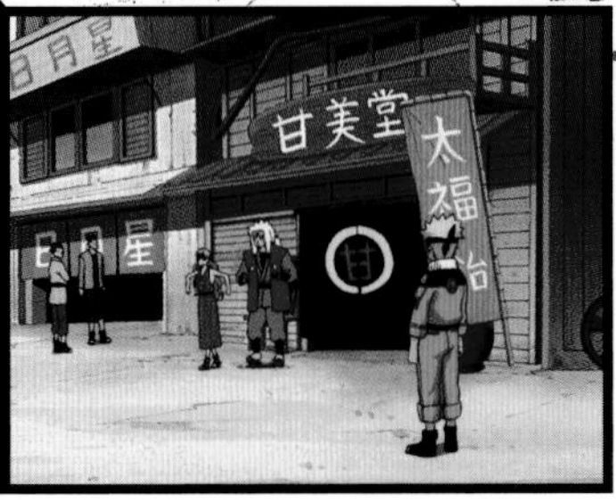
甘美堂

➡Huh? What are you doing, Naruto? You love this shop just like I do, don't you?

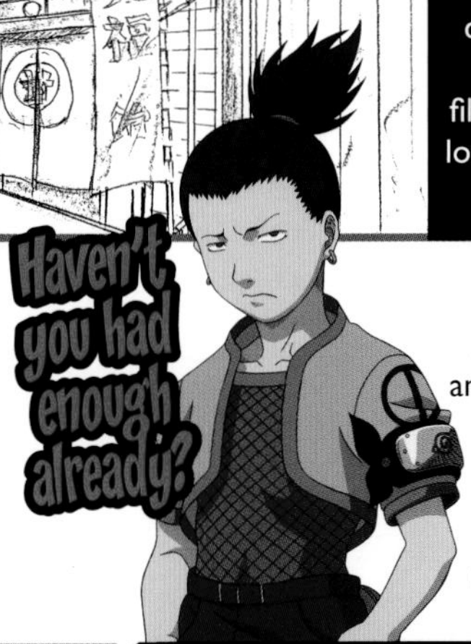
Haven't you had enough already?

⬇I like dango, or sweet dumplings, and mame-daifuku, a soft, round rice cake stuffed with sweet bean filling, too. But roasted-chestnut sweets rule!

Amaguriama: first shop

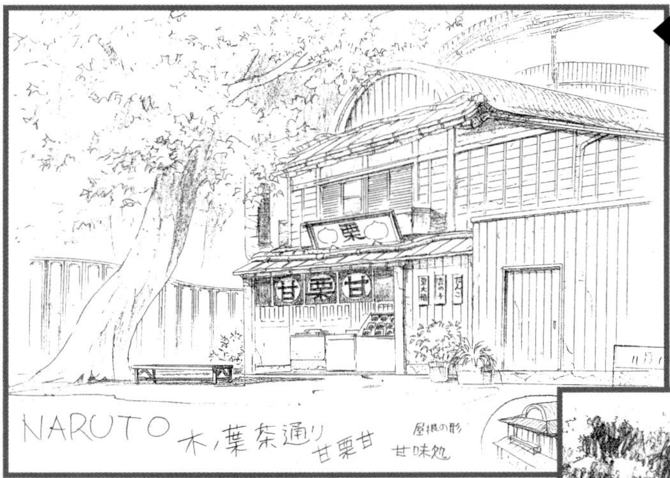
甘栗甘
NARUTO 木ノ葉茶通り 甘栗甘 甘味処

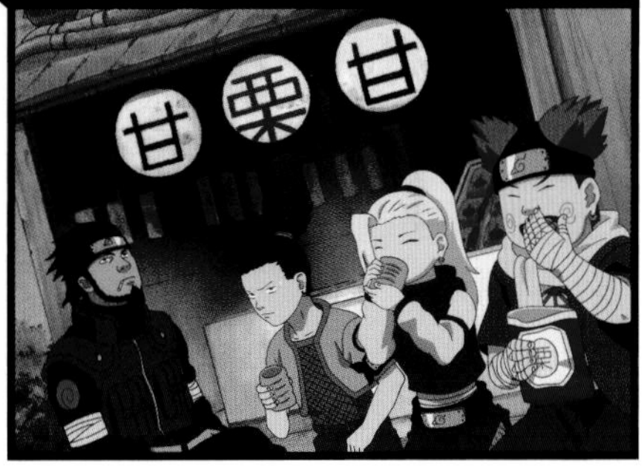
甘 栗 甘

Amaguriama: second shop

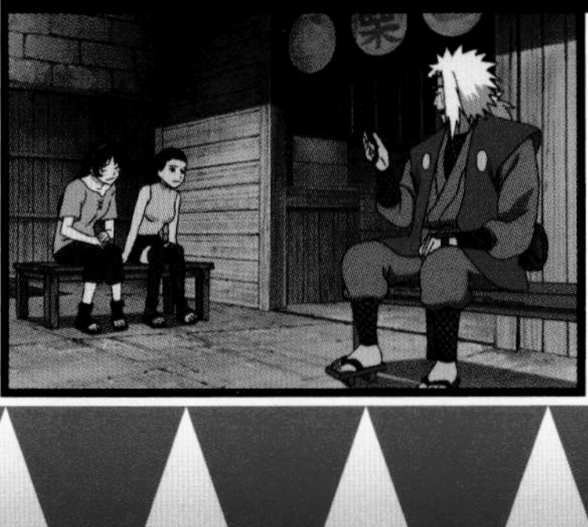

➡We can eat inside or outside at the second shop in the hot spring district.

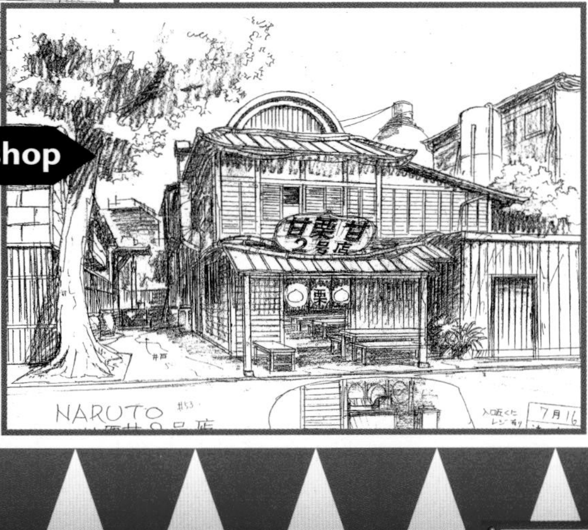
甘栗甘
NARUTO

Where's the hidden truth?!

HIDDEN LEAF TRAINING QUIZ

Training is youth! Youth is training!

Part 2: Jiraiya's Research at the Women's Spa!

Is Jiraiya peeping at women through his telescope? No way! Jiraiya isn't that kind of person! I'm a fool to even think that! Use all your youthful might to reveal the true identities of who's in the lens!

Woohoo! Today's another research day! ♥

WHAT DID JIRAIYA SEE...?!

Q1. Wow! A girl with milky-white skin that looks as smooth as silk! And she's all flushed from the sun. So what are we actually looking at here? Oh—Oh, yeah!

Q2. Whoopee! She's also as white as snow! ♥ Wait! Could this be...?!

Q3. Too bad it's blurry from the steam, but this must be a lady with a nice tan! Umm, is this her shoulder?

Q4. Oh, yeah! This is it! I see a belly button! Definitely a voluptuous beauty! No doubt about it!

This will make for some good literature!

Dash to page 280 for the answers!

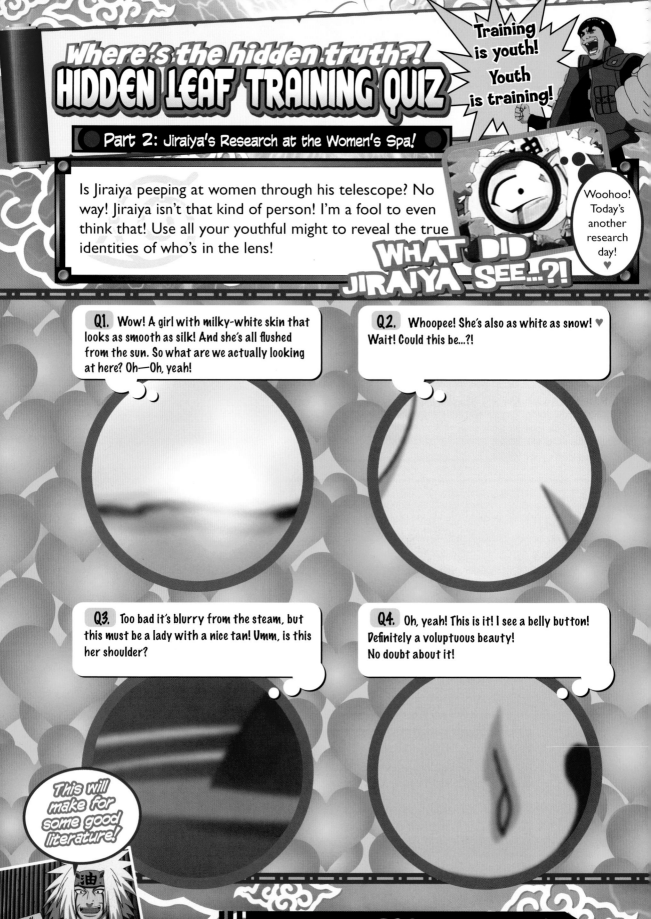

Hurry up!

The long way to the arena...

An underground tunnel?!

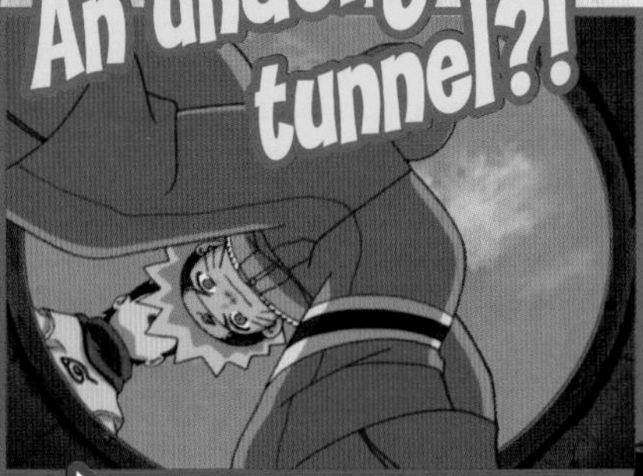

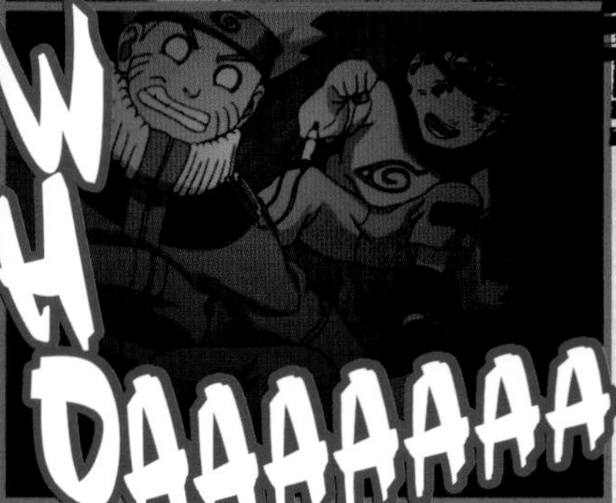
WH
DAAAAAAA

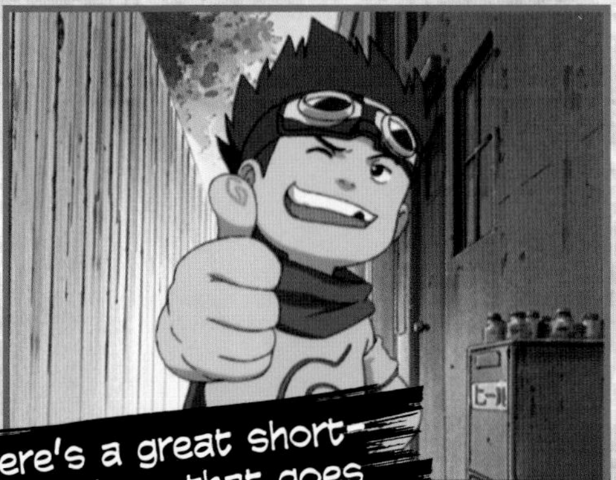
There's a great short-cut up here that goes straight to the arena!

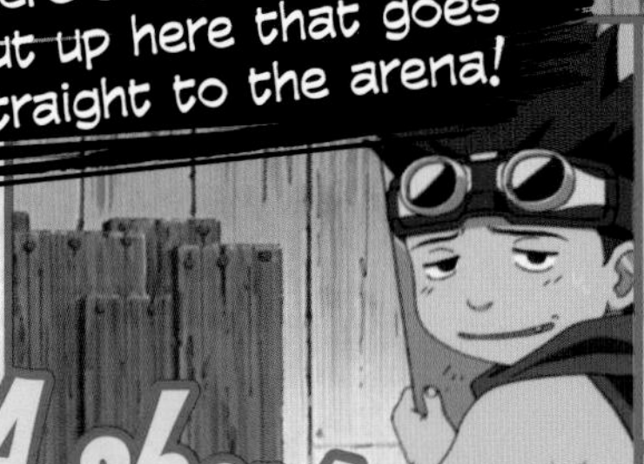

A shortcut?!

If that doesn't work...

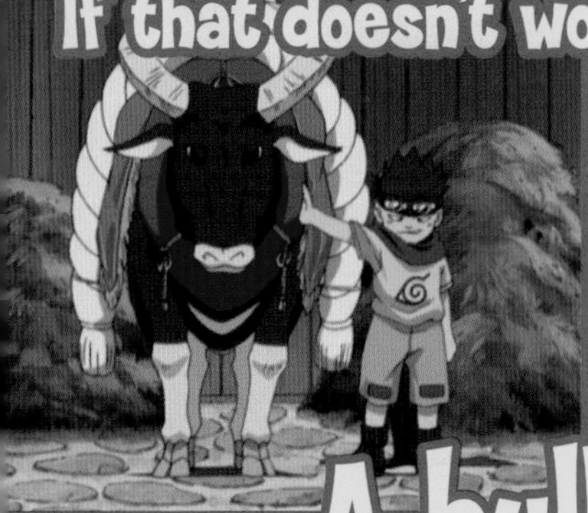

...A bull?!

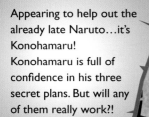

Appearing to help out the already late Naruto…it's Konohamaru! Konohamaru is full of confidence in his three secret plans. But will any of them really work?!

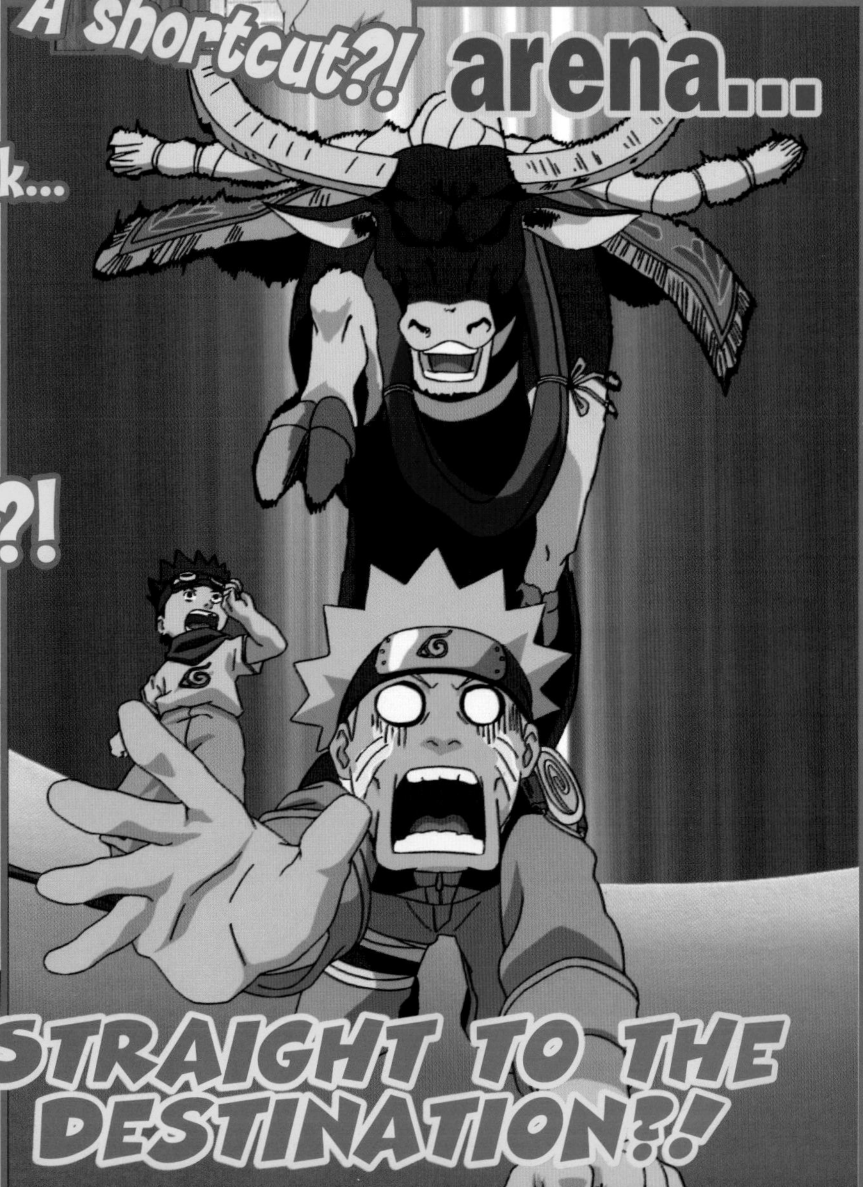

STRAIGHT TO THE DESTINATION?!

The Slacker vs. The Genius!

A clash of fates!

Neji pummeled Hinata in the prelims and Naruto wants some payback! Their fighting spirits are jacked up from the get-go. This clash of fates is dead serious!

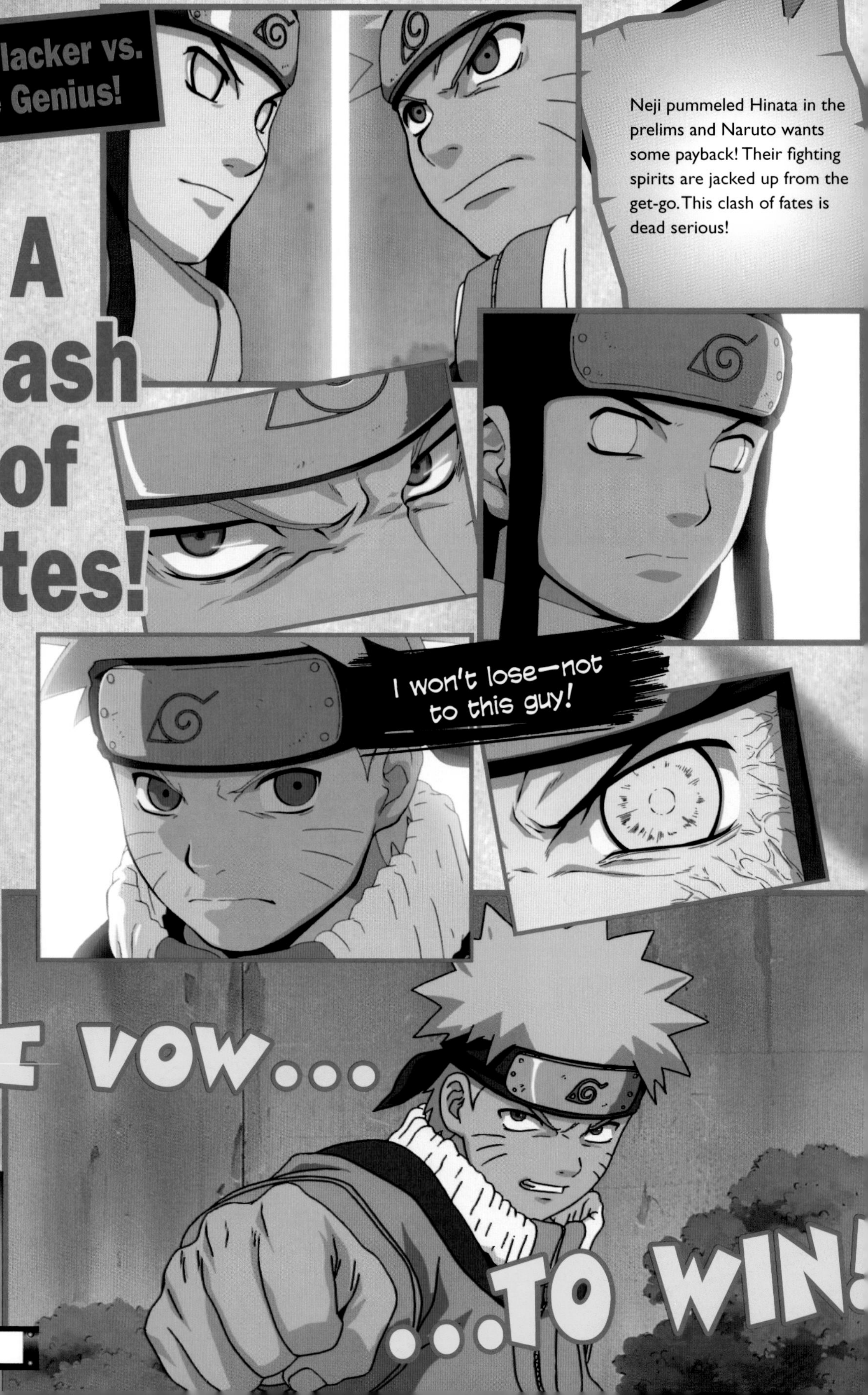
I won't lose—not to this guy!
I VOW...
...TO WIN!

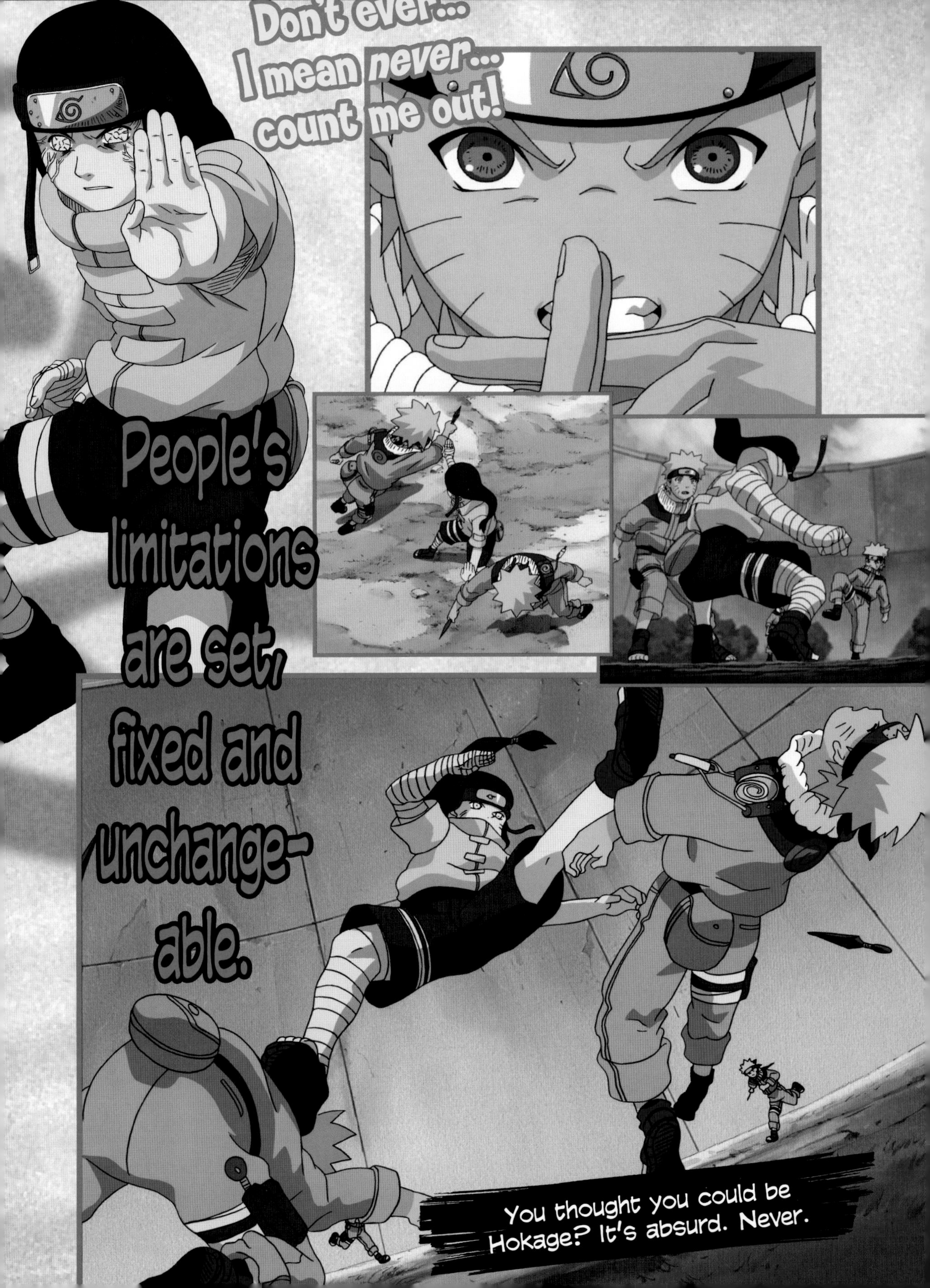
Don't ever...
I mean *never*...
count me out!
People's limitations are set, fixed and unchange-able.
You thought you could be Hokage? It's absurd. Never.

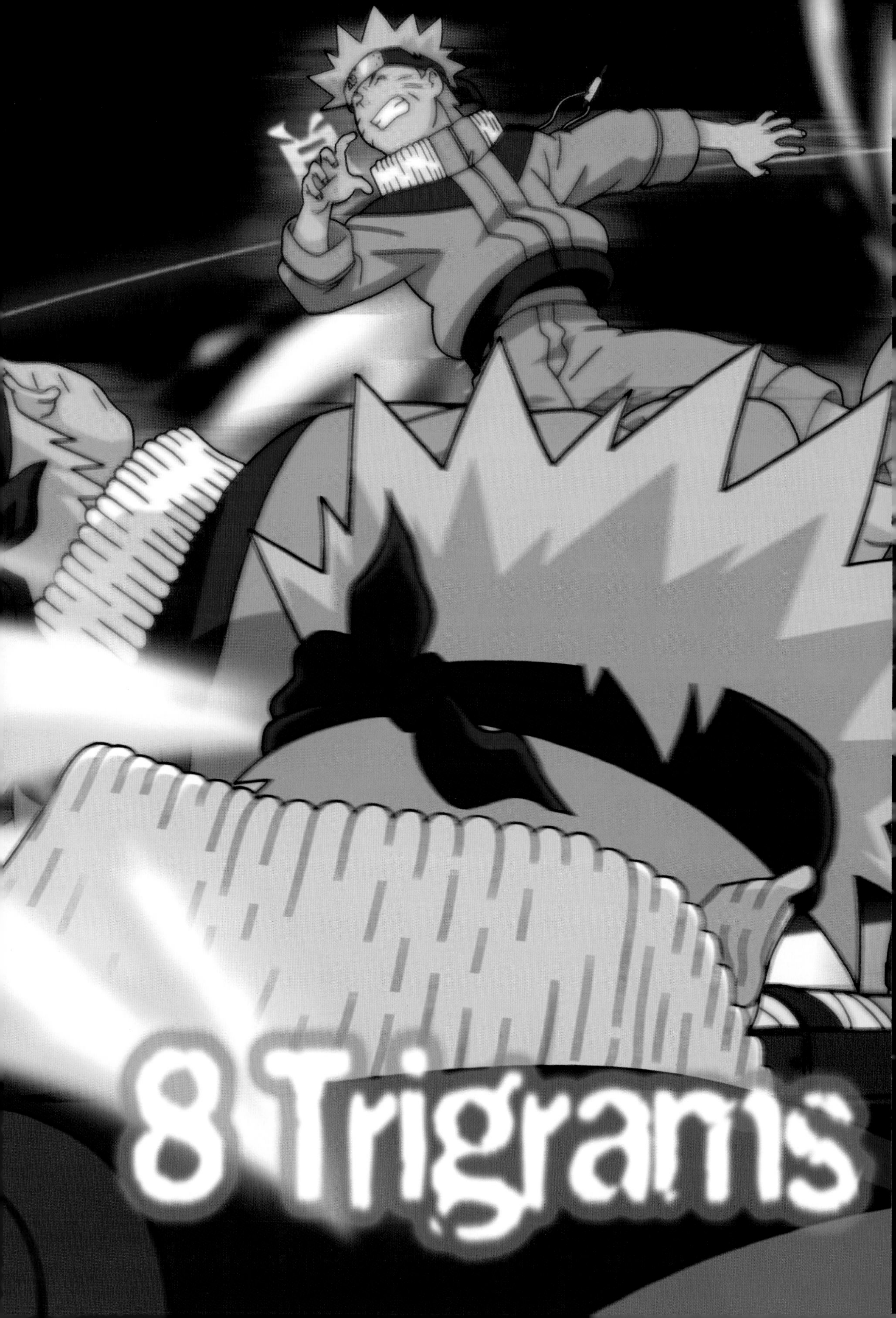
8 Trigrams

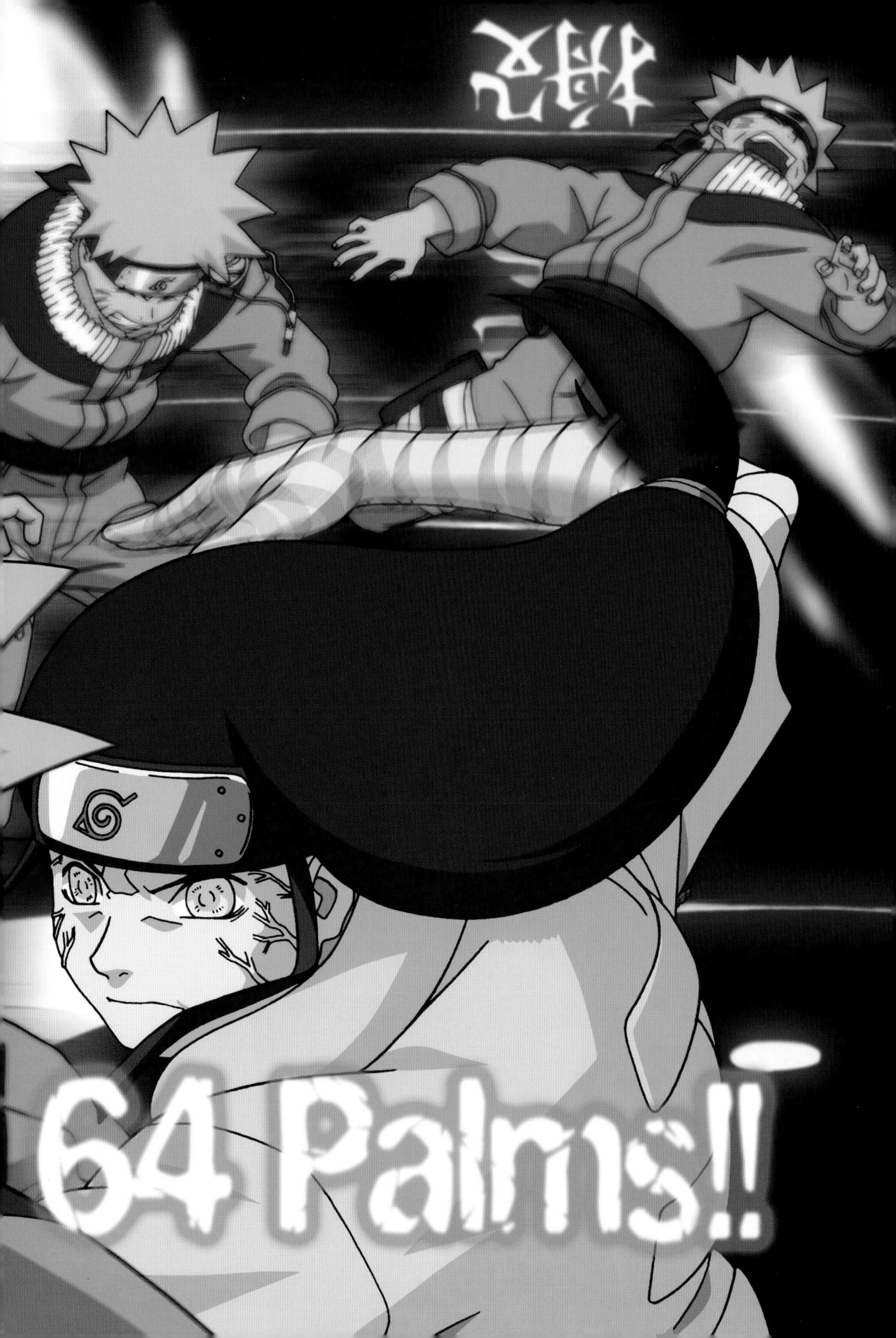
64 Palms!!

Like a bird trapped in a cage...

We are all given a destiny at birth...

The clan's dreadful destiny...

...and it's pointless...

...to fight against it.

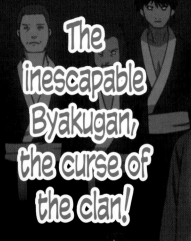

The inescapable Byakugan, the curse of the clan!

Neji shows his hated mark and reveals his past—a cruel fate in which his life and death are determined by the family he was born into.

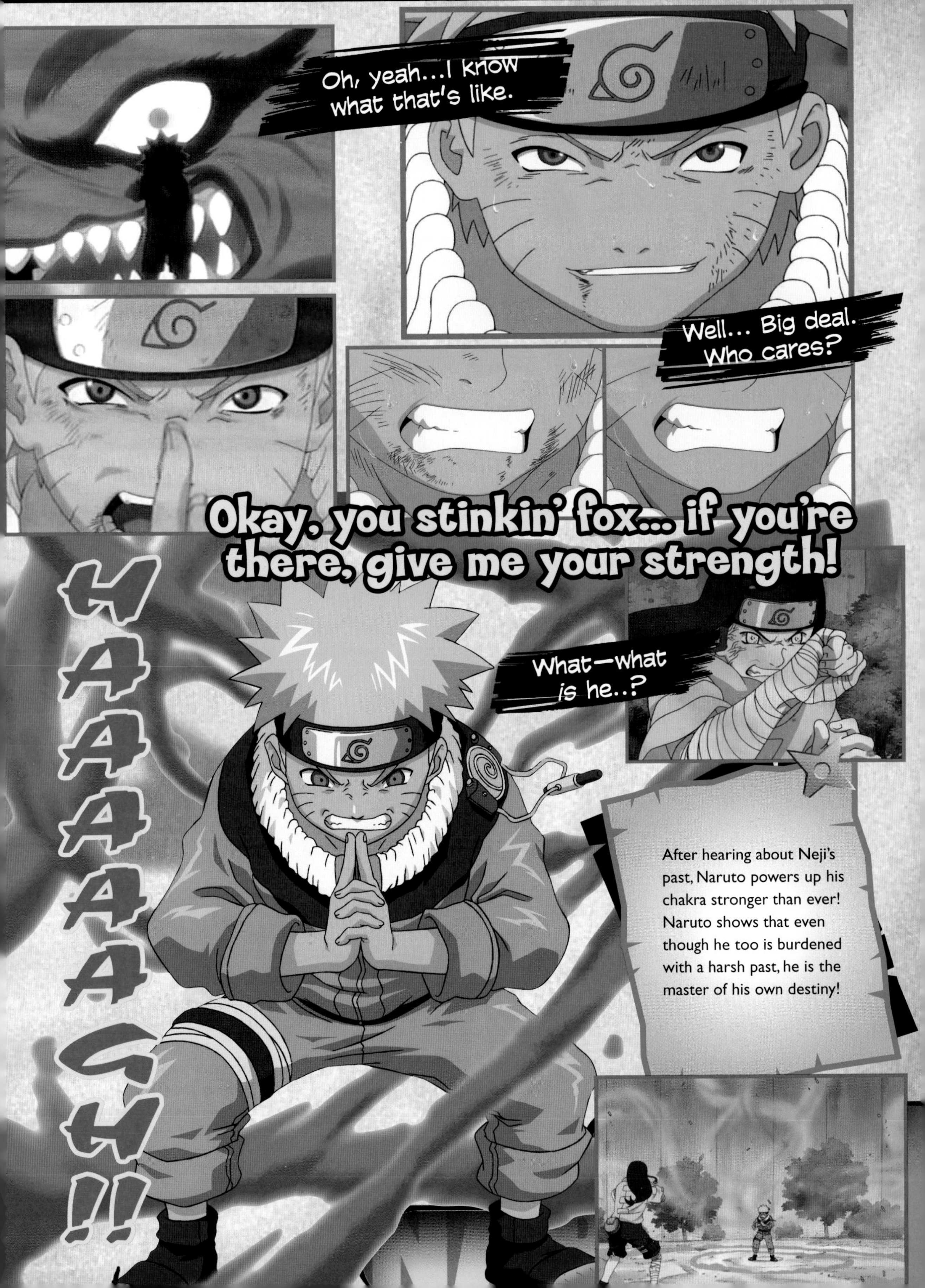
Oh, yeah...I know what that's like.
Well... Big deal. Who cares?
Okay, you stinkin' fox... if you're there, give me your strength!
HAAAAAAGH!!
What—what is he..?

After hearing about Neji's past, Naruto powers up his chakra stronger than ever! Naruto shows that even though he too is burdened with a harsh past, he is the master of his own destiny!

Zero motivation, but a 200-plus IQ!

Battle of wits and foresight!

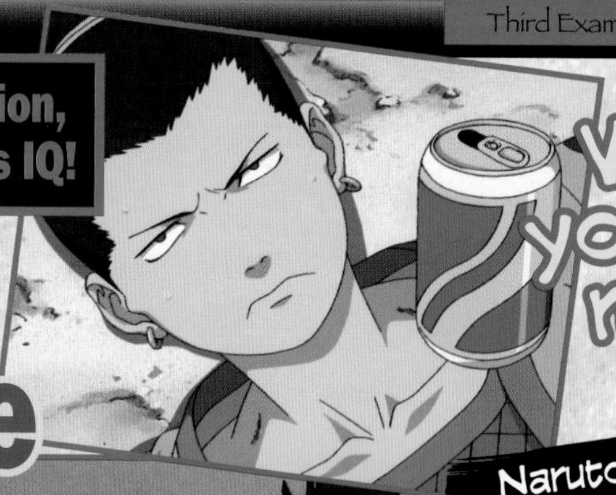
Naruto, you jerk...

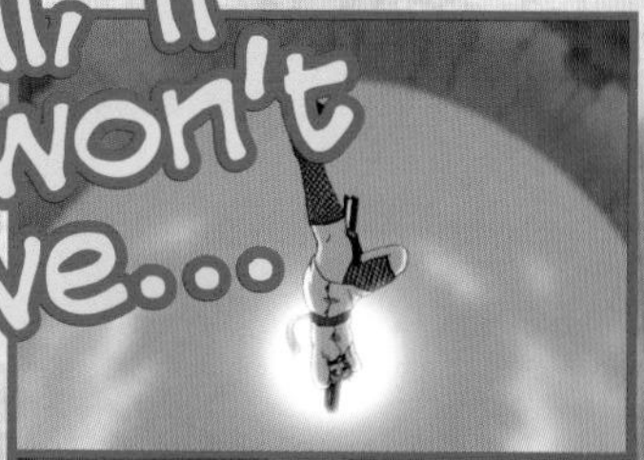
Well, if you won't move...

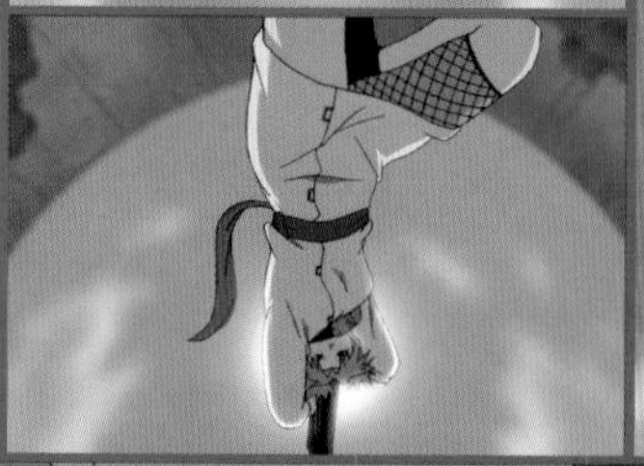

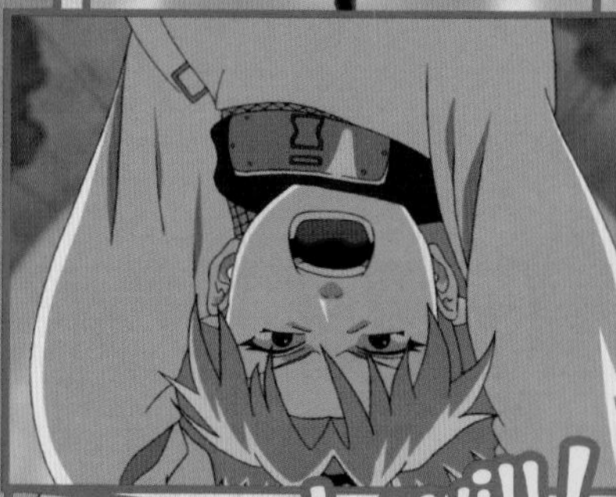

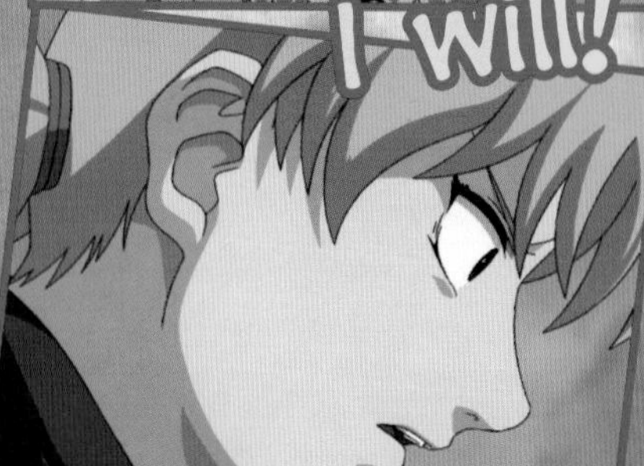
I will!

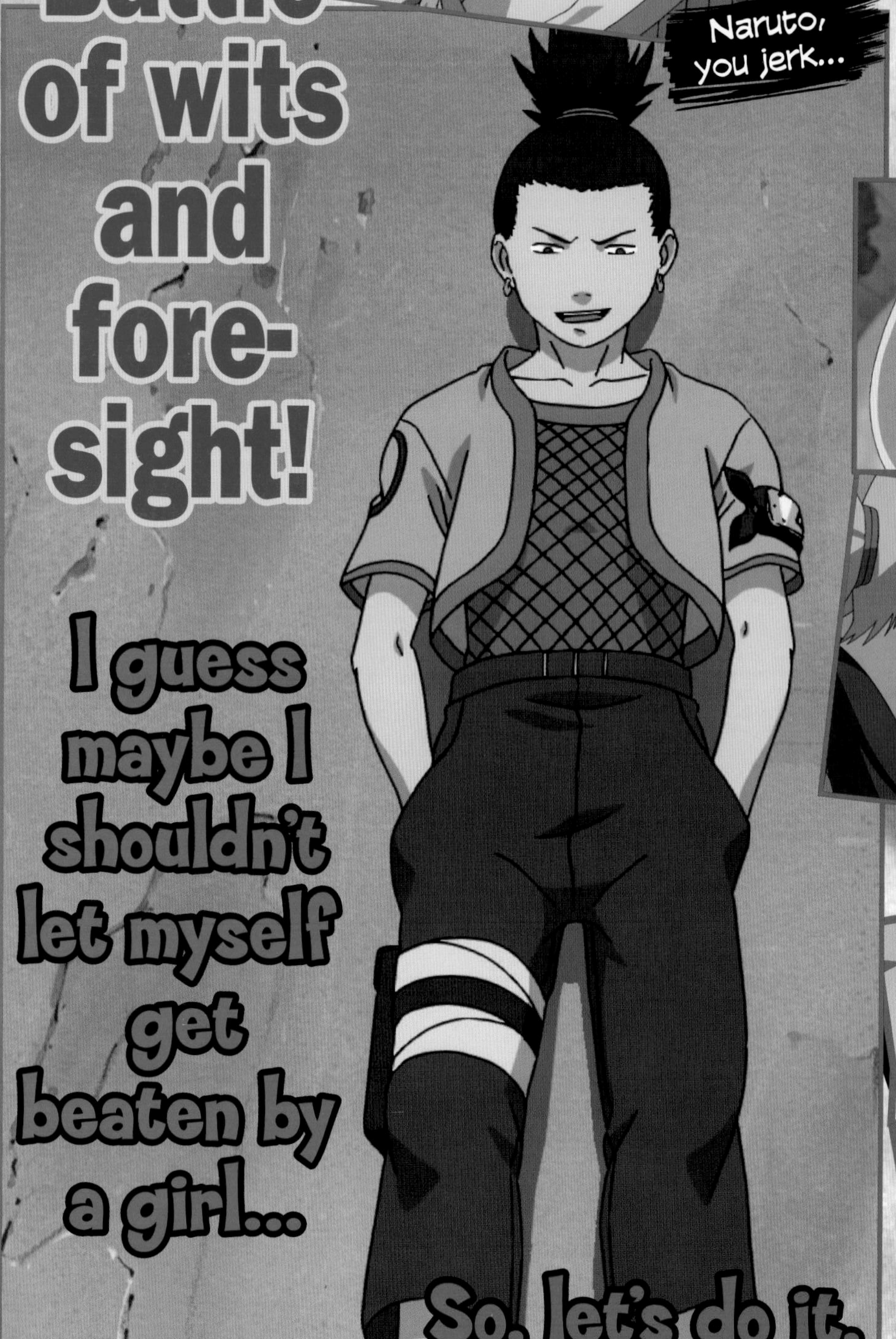
I guess maybe I shouldn't let myself get beaten by a girl...
So, let's do it.

Even during the match, Shikamaru shows no motivation. While Shikamaru faces Temari's wave of attacks, Asuma reveals a secret about him!

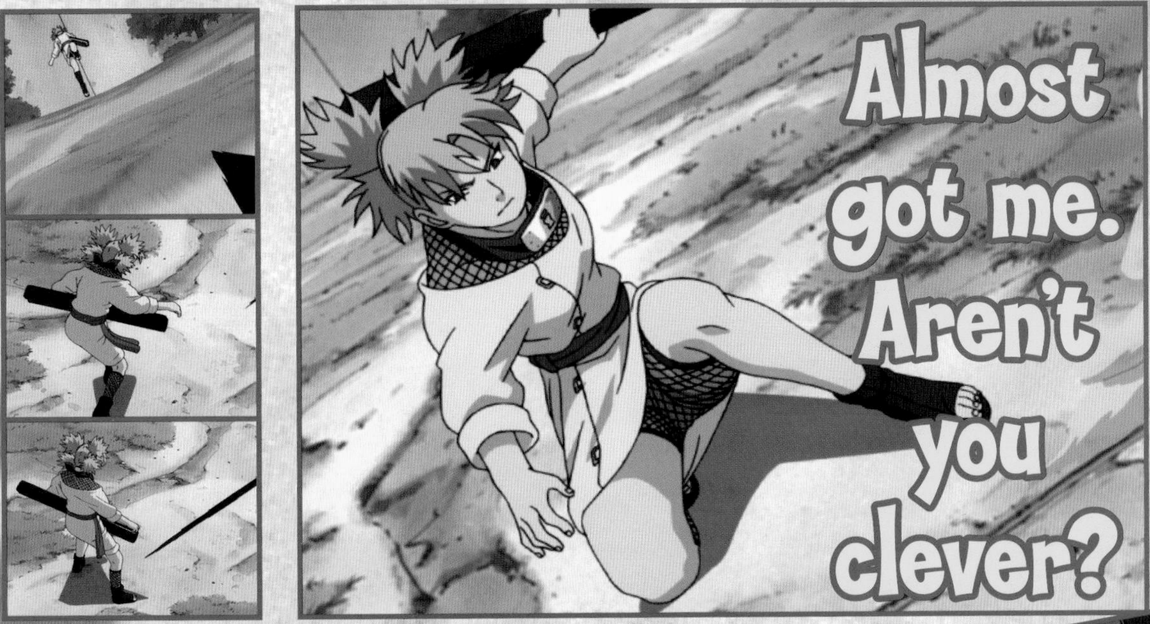
Almost got me. Aren't you clever?

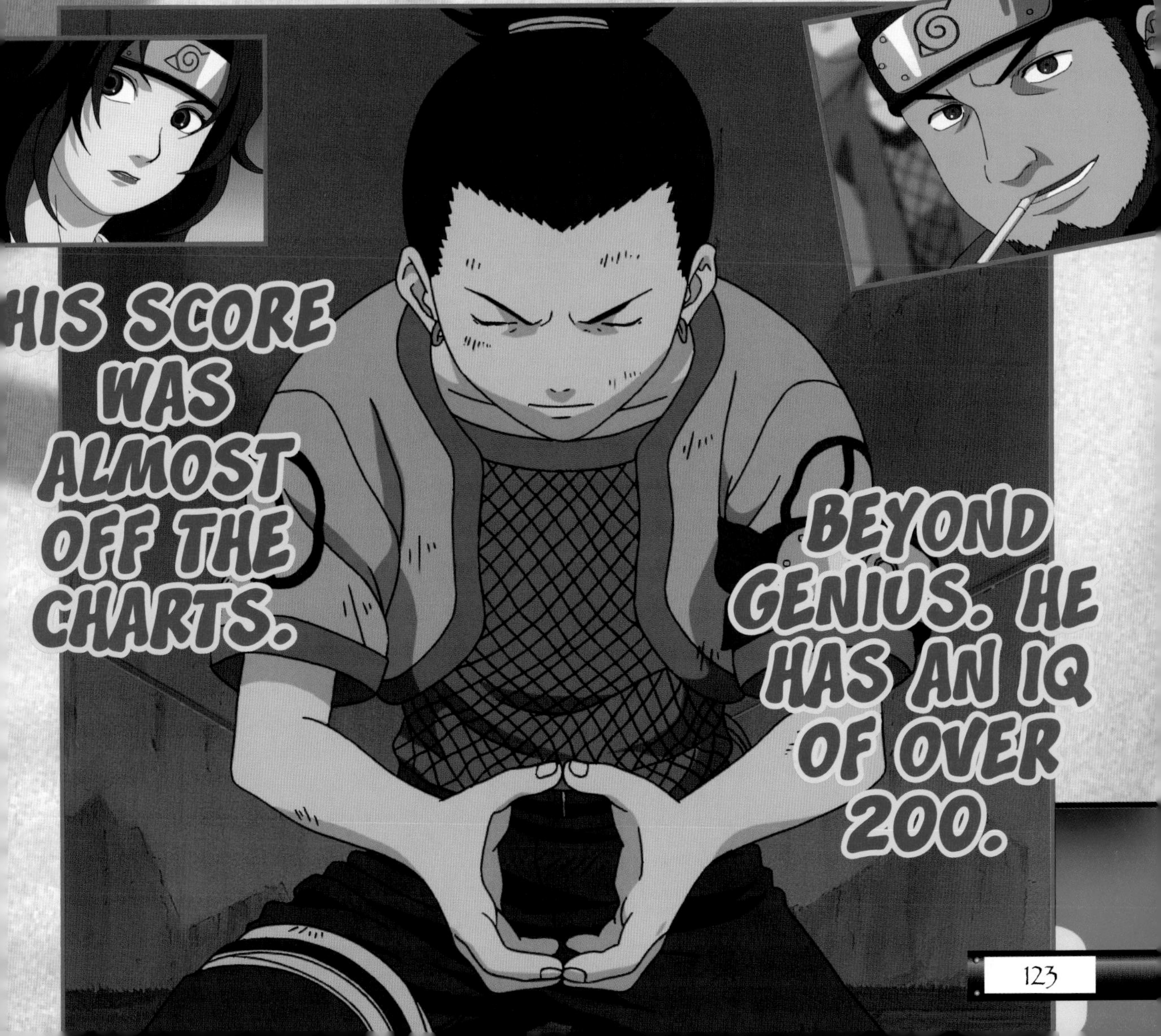
HIS SCORE WAS ALMOST OFF THE CHARTS.
BEYOND GENIUS. HE HAS AN IQ OF OVER 200.

With a gust of wind....

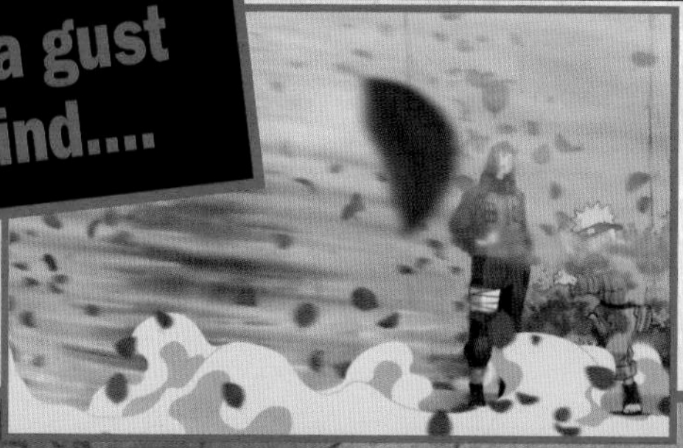

Amidst the whirlwind of leaves comes ...?!

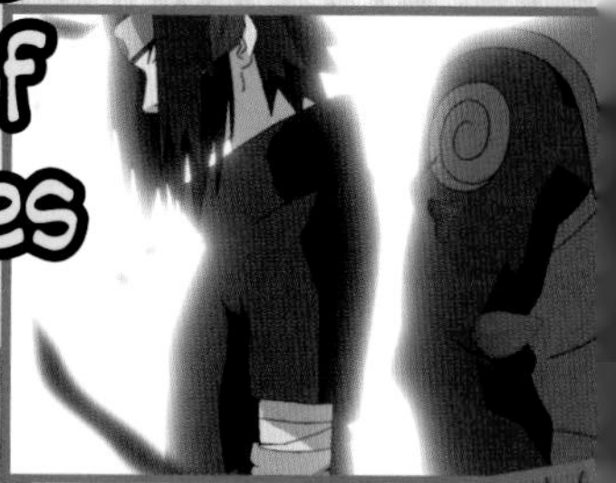

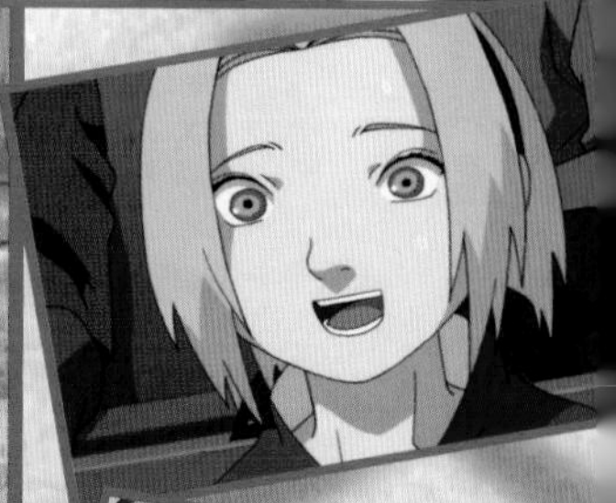

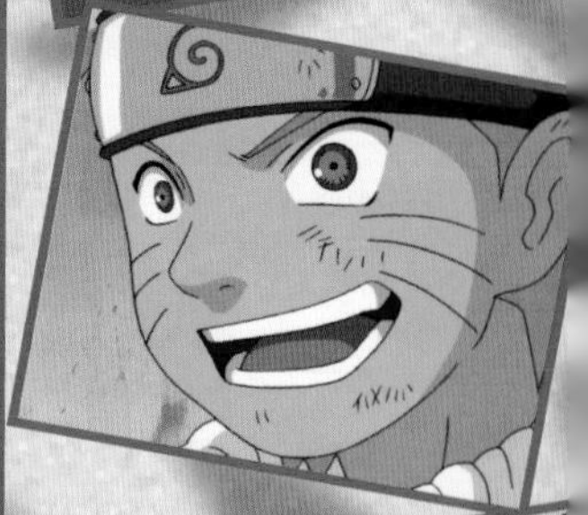

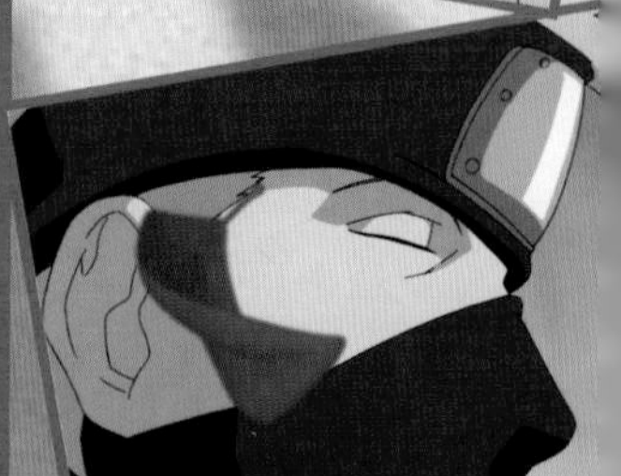

Sasuke arrives!

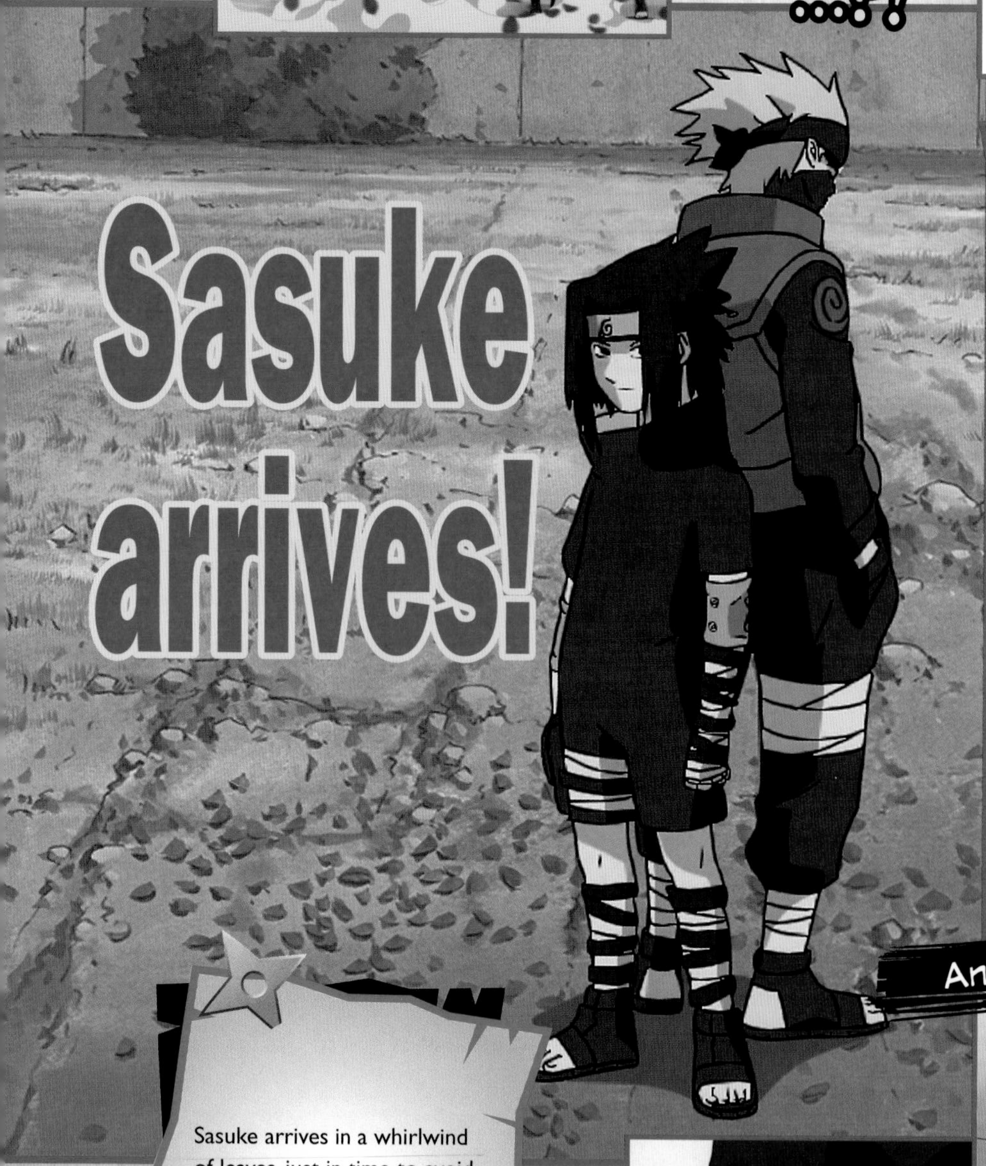

Sasuke arrives in a whirlwind of leaves, just in time to avoid being disqualified! Gaara grins at the sight. The confrontation between the best of the Sand and Leaves begins!

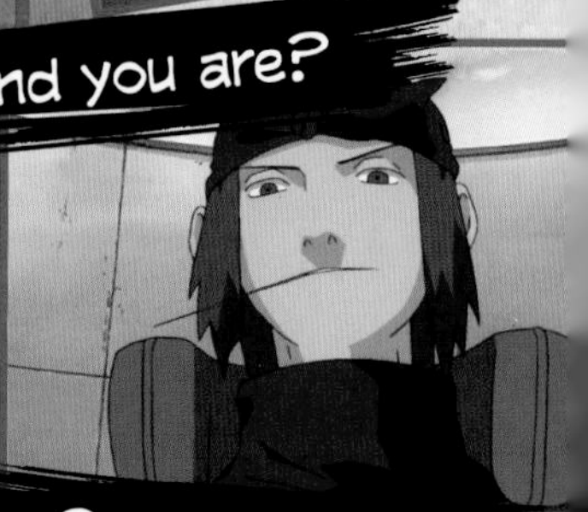
And you are?

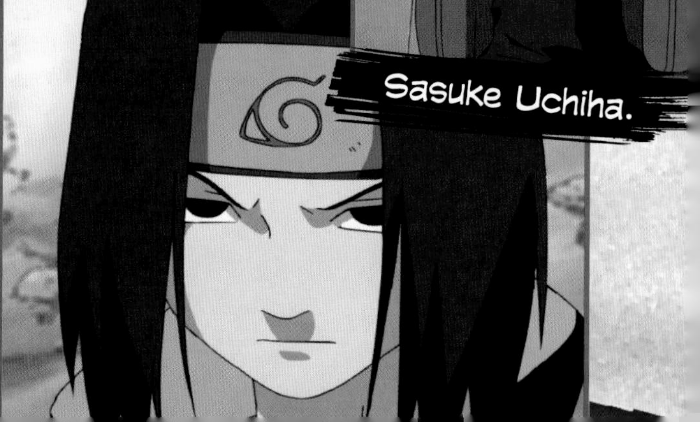
Sasuke Uchiha.

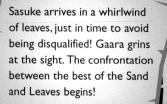

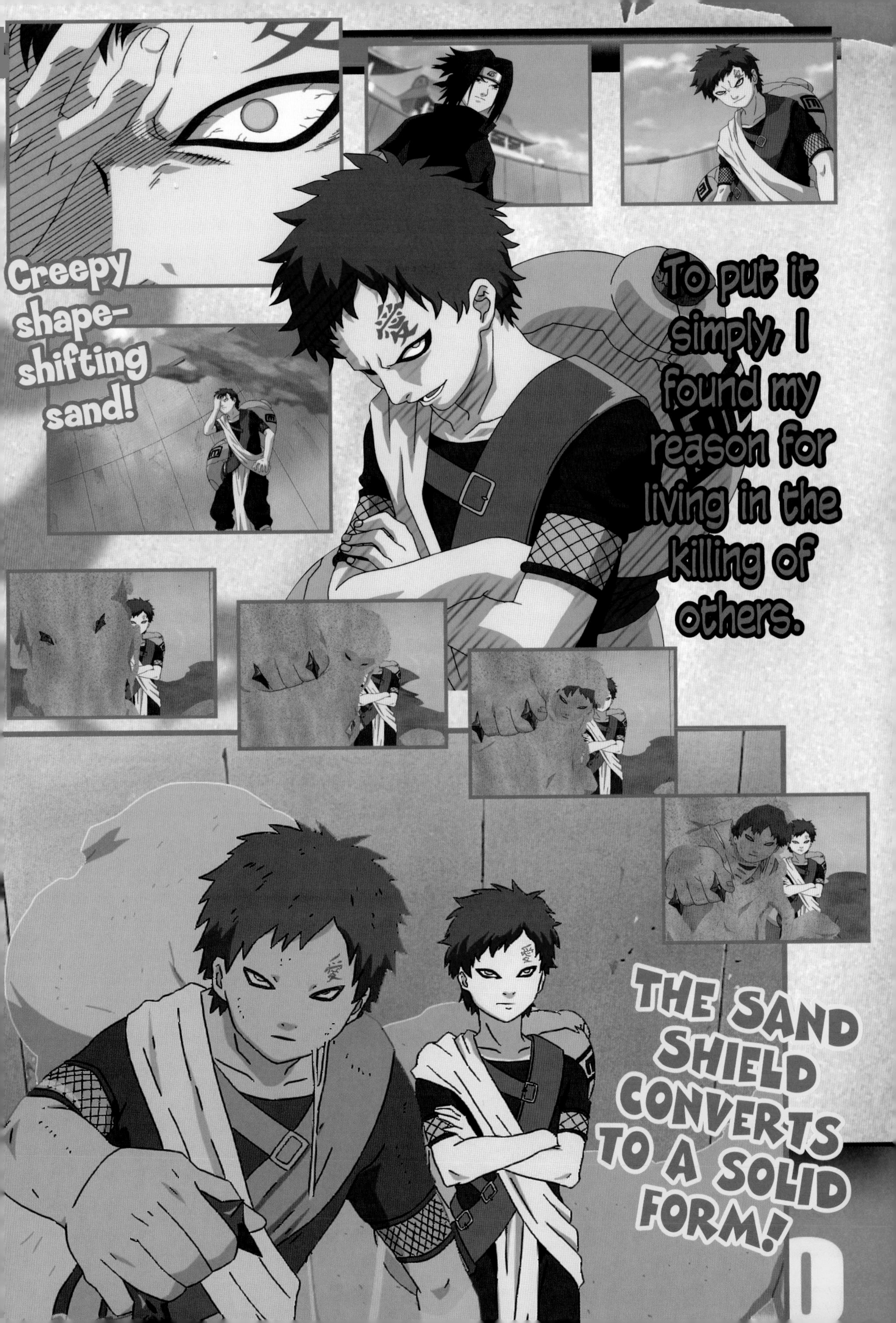
Creepy shape-shifting sand!
To put it simply, I found my reason for living in the killing of others.
THE SAND SHIELD CONVERTS TO A SOLID FORM!

Sasuke's onslaught!

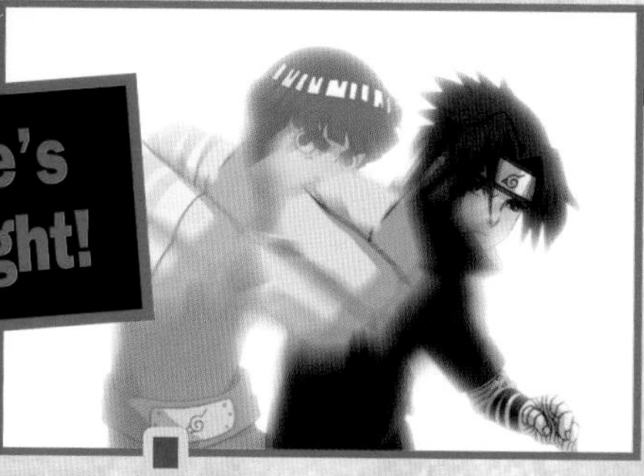

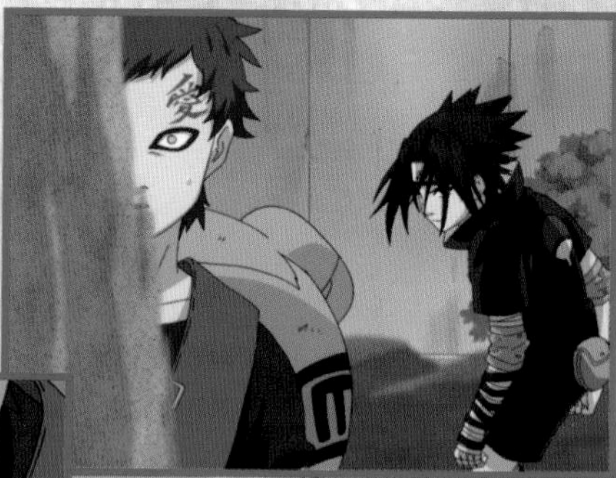

Gaara is cornered by Sasuke's incredible taijutsu!

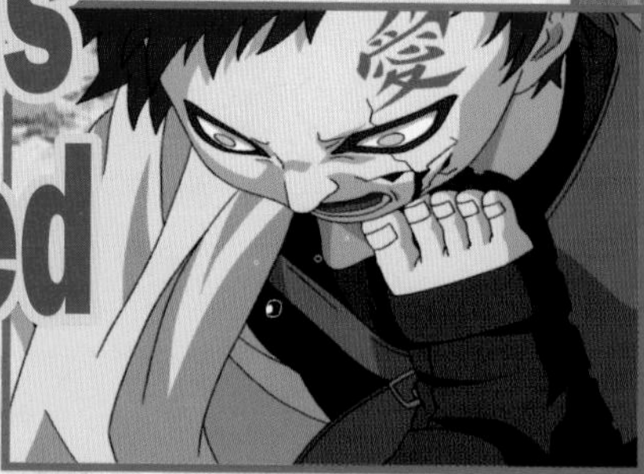

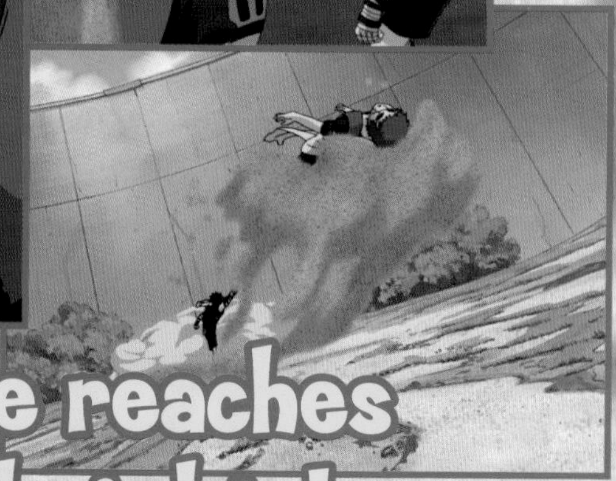

Sasuke reaches new heights!

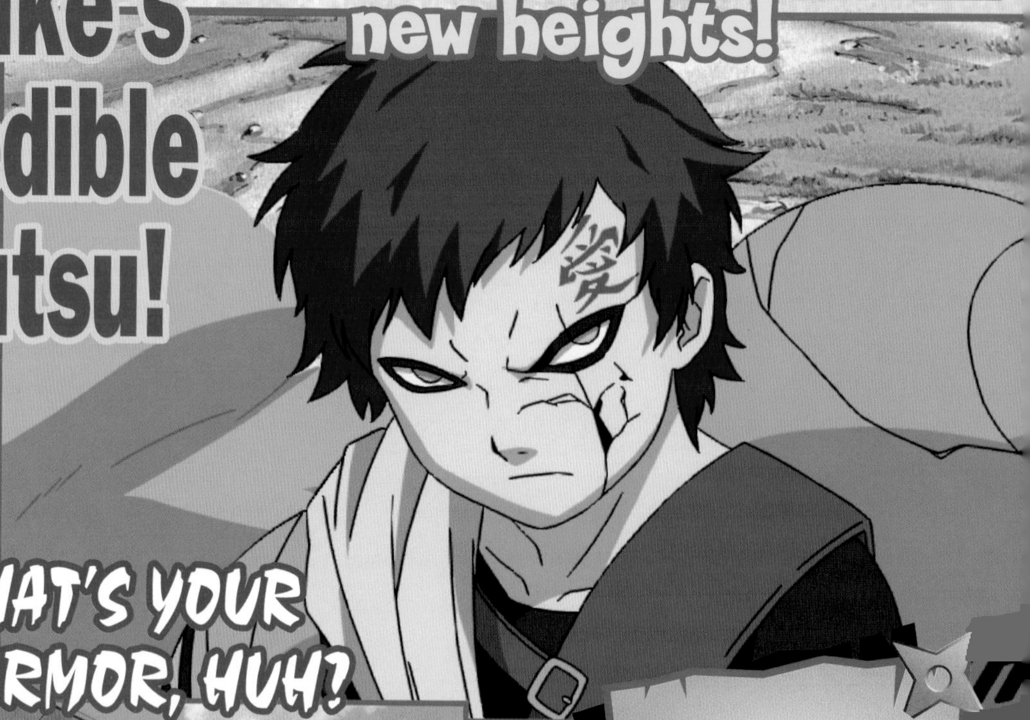

SO THAT'S YOUR SAND ARMOR, HUH?

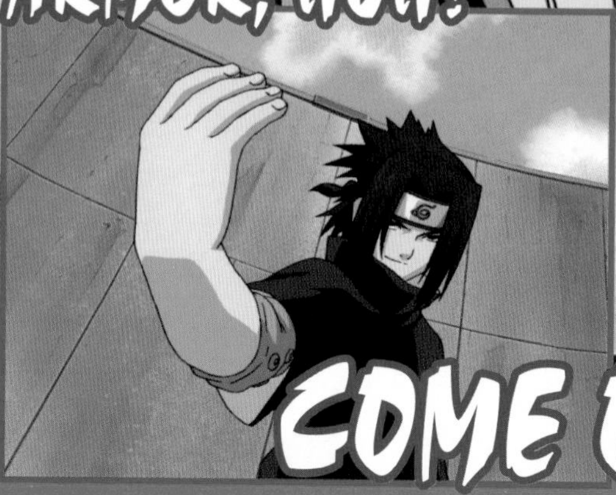

COME ON!

Even with his Sand Armor, Gaara is pinned down by Sasuke's ultra high-speed taijutsu. With Gaara in distress, his sand begins to encase him and an ominous hush falls over the arena.

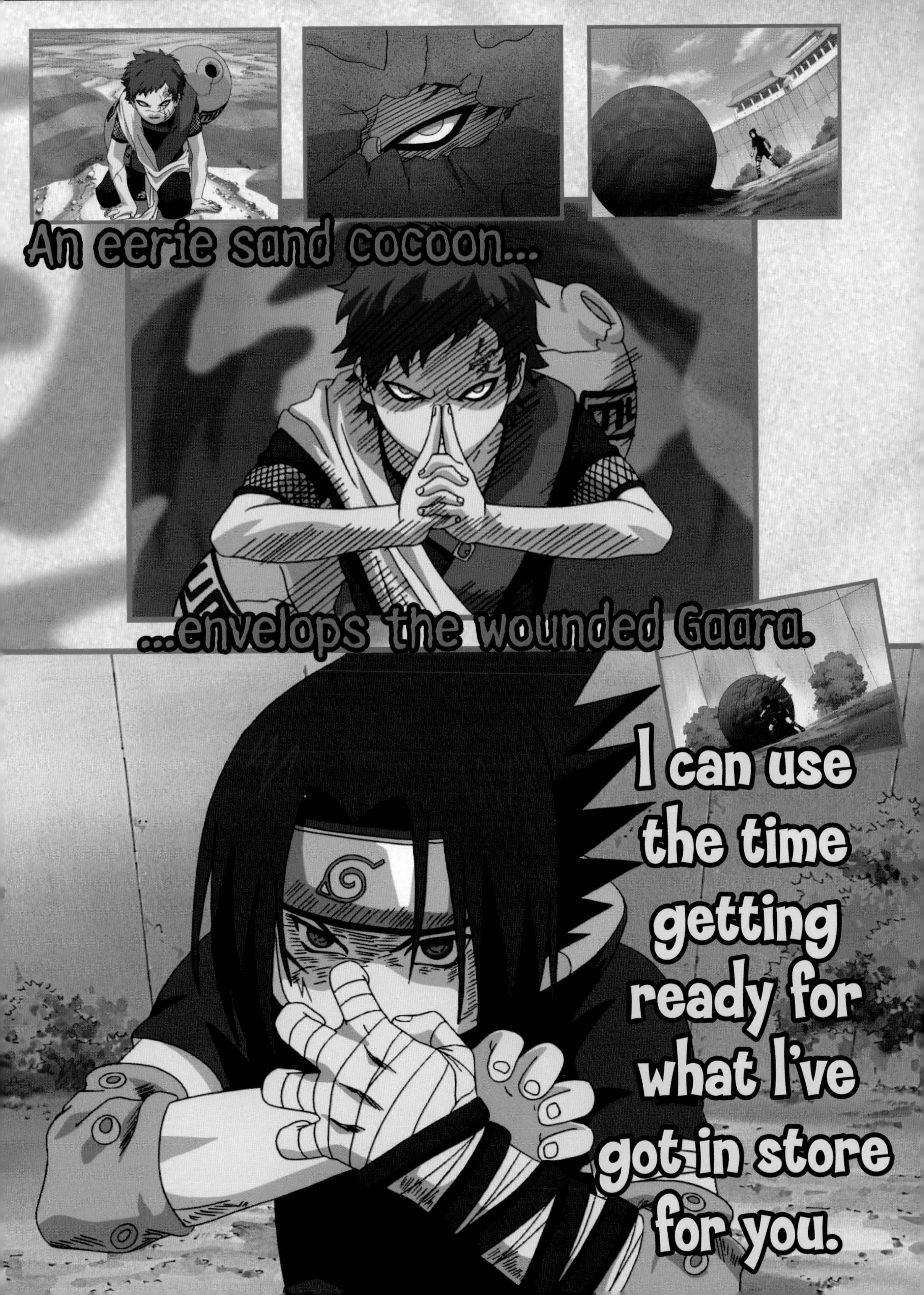
An eerie sand cocoon...
...envelops the wounded Gaara.
I can use the time getting ready for what I've got in store for you.

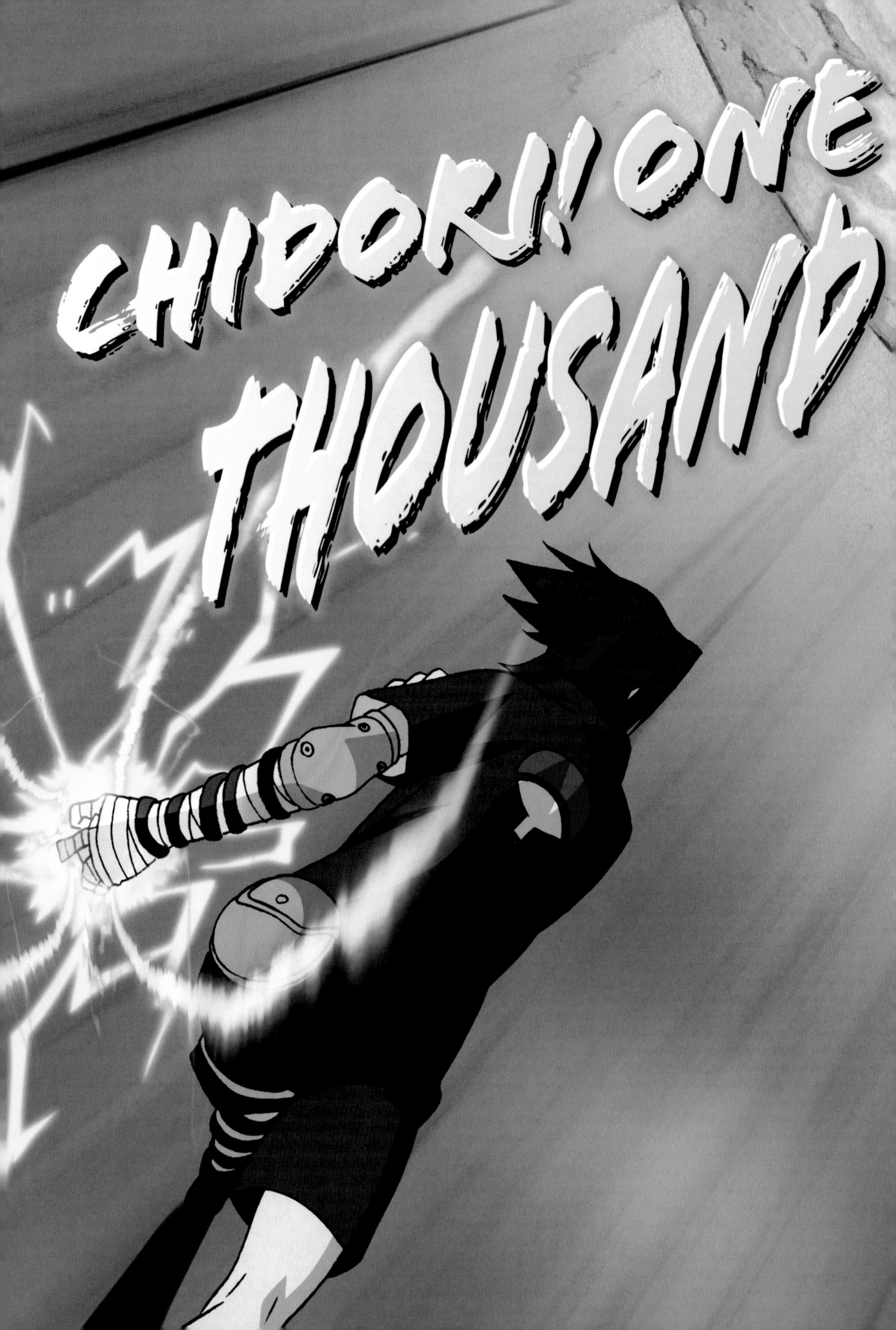
CHIDORI! ONE THOUSAND

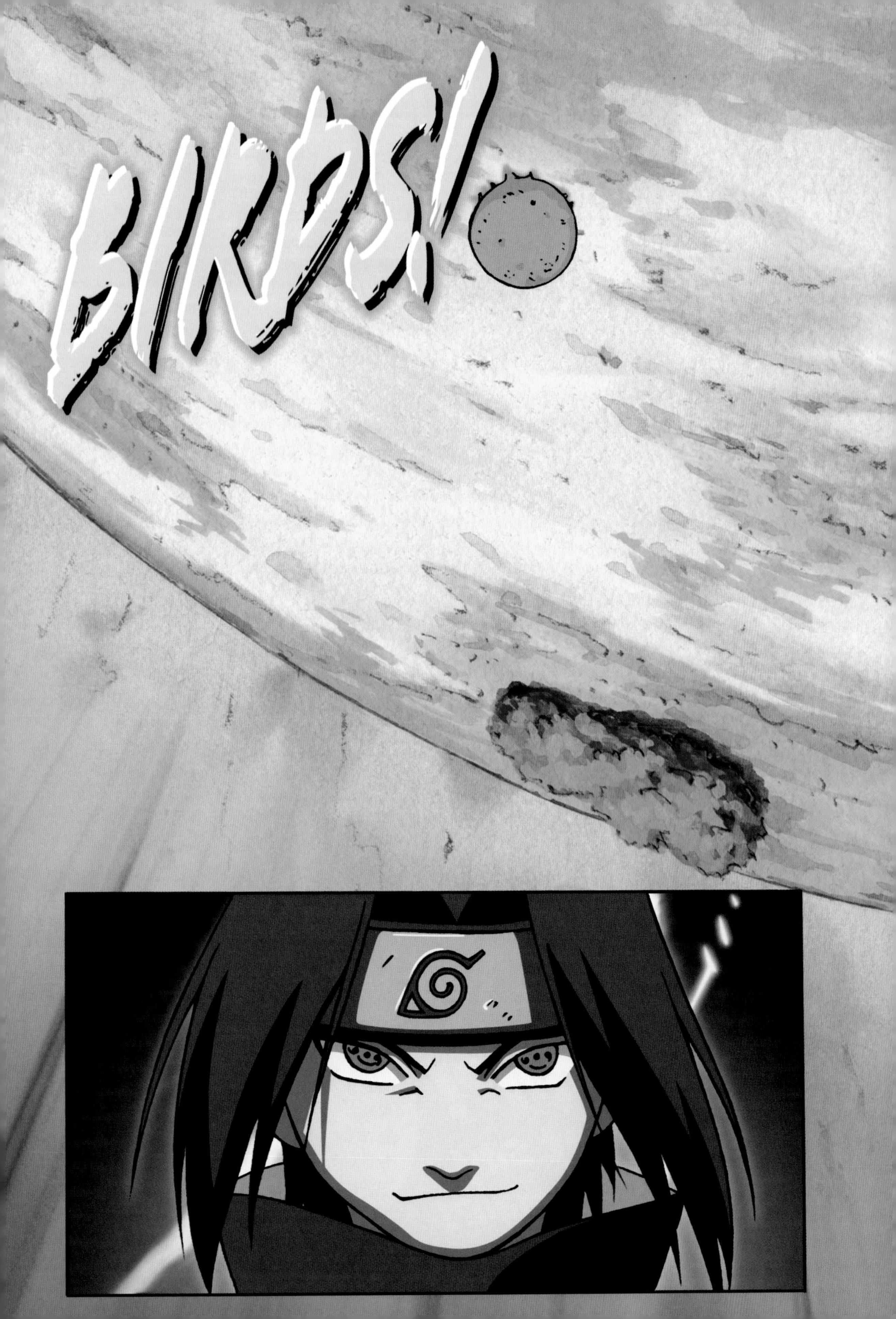
BIRDS!

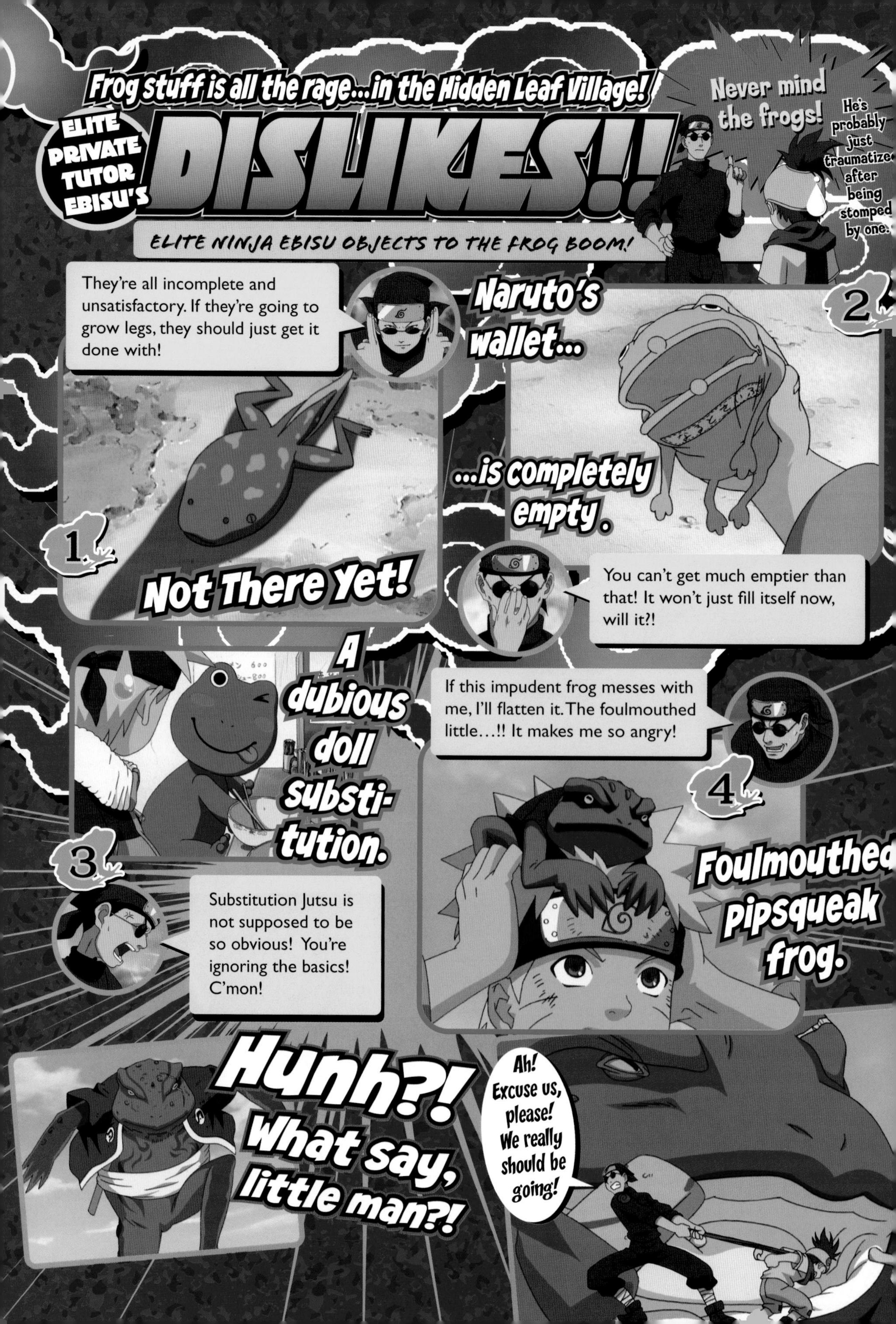

Frog stuff is all the rage...in the Hidden Leaf Village!
ELITE PRIVATE TUTOR EBISU'S
DISLIKES!!
ELITE NINJA EBISU OBJECTS TO THE FROG BOOM!
Never mind the frogs!
He's probably just traumatized after being stomped by one.
1
Not There Yet!
They're all incomplete and unsatisfactory. If they're going to grow legs, they should just get it done with!
2
Naruto's wallet...
...is completely empty.
You can't get much emptier than that! It won't just fill itself now, will it?!
3
A dubious doll substi-tution.
Substitution Jutsu is not supposed to be so obvious! You're ignoring the basics! C'mon!
4
If this impudent frog messes with me, I'll flatten it. The foulmouthed little…!! It makes me so angry!
Foulmouthed Pipsqueak frog.
Hunh?! What say, little man?!
Ah! Excuse us, please! We really should be going!

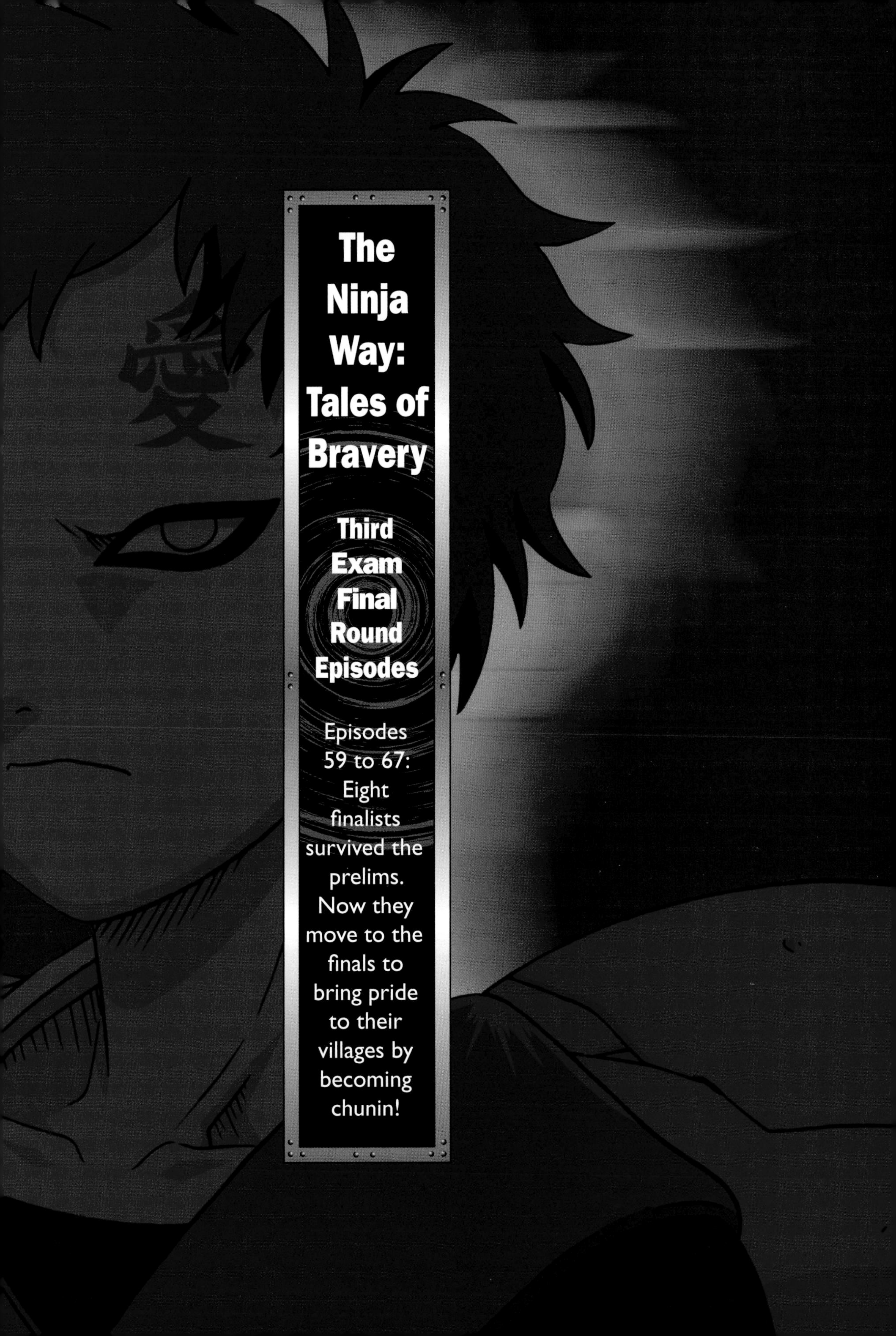

The Ninja Way: Tales of Bravery

Third Exam Final Round Episodes

Episodes 59 to 67: Eight finalists survived the prelims. Now they move to the finals to bring pride to their villages by becoming chunin!

Episode 59 to Episode 67

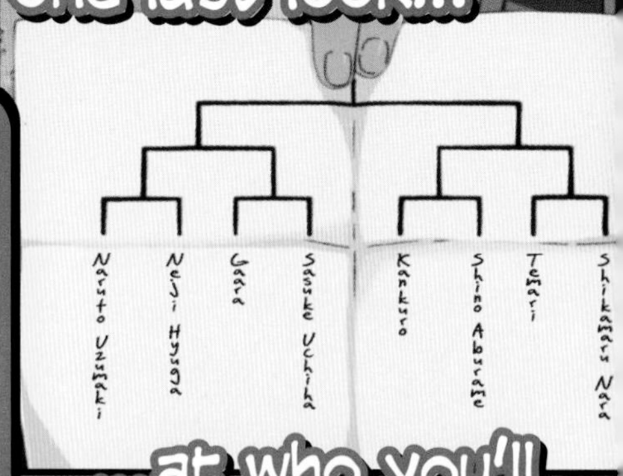

Merciless: The Chunin Exams! The final round is on!

Everyone take one last look...

Naruto Uzumaki
Neji Hyuga
Gaara
Sasuke Uchiha
Kankuro
Shino Aburame
Temari
Shikamaru Nara

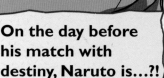

...at who you'll be facing.

Representing the best of every village, the top genin assemble!

Genma lets the eight finalists take one last look at the match-ups. The wait is over! With the pride and prestige of the villages riding on the outcome, the main event begins.

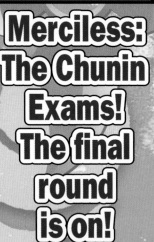

➡ Neji responds to Naruto's provocation with his Byakugan. This genius shows that he means business!

Are we gonna stand here talking all day?! Let's get going!

⬇ Naruto's first opponent is Neji. A mix of emotions keeps Naruto awake until late into the night.

⬆ An anxious Naruto isn't his usual lively self, even at Ichiraku, where the owner treats him to some specially made ramen.

On the day before his match with destiny, Naruto is...?!

Naruto gained confidence through his training with Jiraiya. But after confronting Gaara at the hospital, he realizes the outstanding level of skill possessed by his rivals. Naruto spends an uneasy night alone before the match.

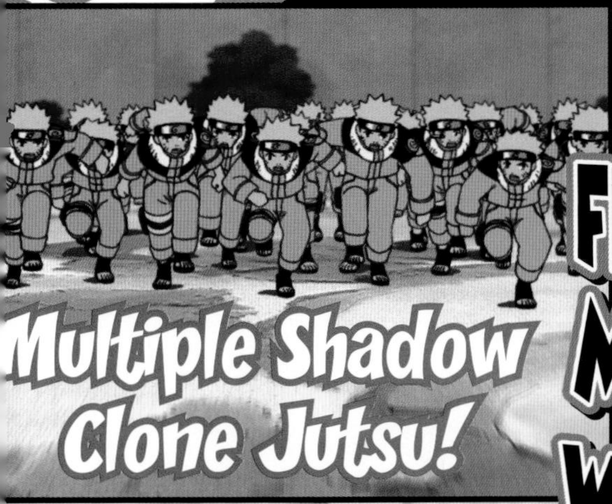

Multiple Shadow Clone Jutsu!

FIRST MOVE WINS!

Naruto wastes no time unleashing his best jutsu!

Neji's Byakugan detects chakra flow. Then, by striking at chakra points, he cripples the ability to activate jutsu, giving opponents little hope of victory! Naruto counters Neji's superior Taijutsu by attacking in a pack with Multiple Shadow Clone Jutsu.

⬆➡ A swarm of clones surround Neji! This is trouble even for a genius!

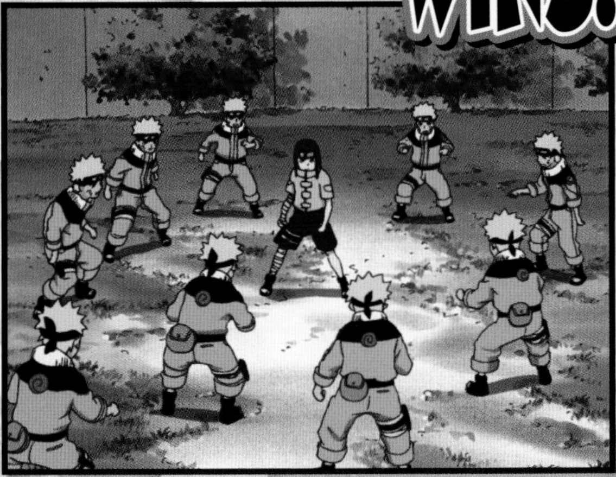

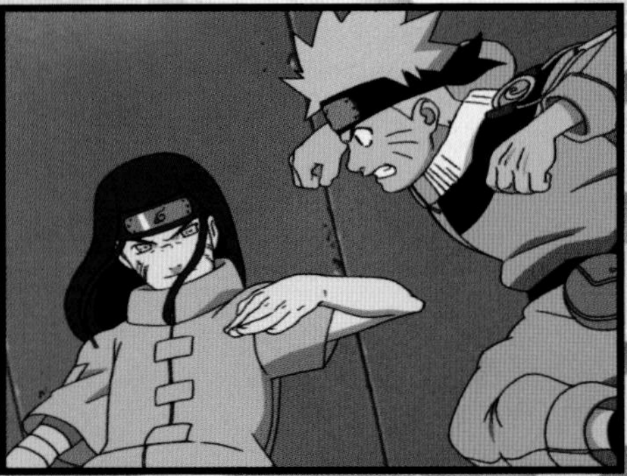

⬆ When Neji activates the Byakugan, he has a 360-degree field of view. Even sneak attacks from behind are useless.

Another ultimate defense that repels every attack:

Rotation!

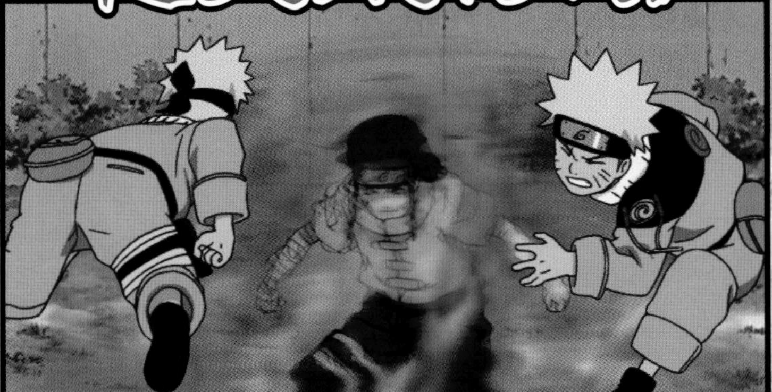

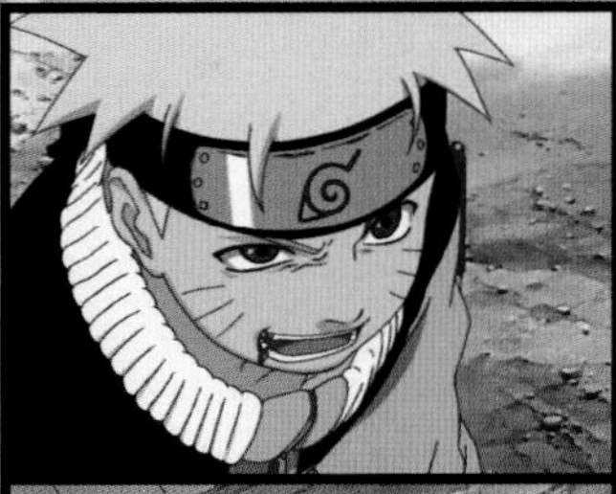

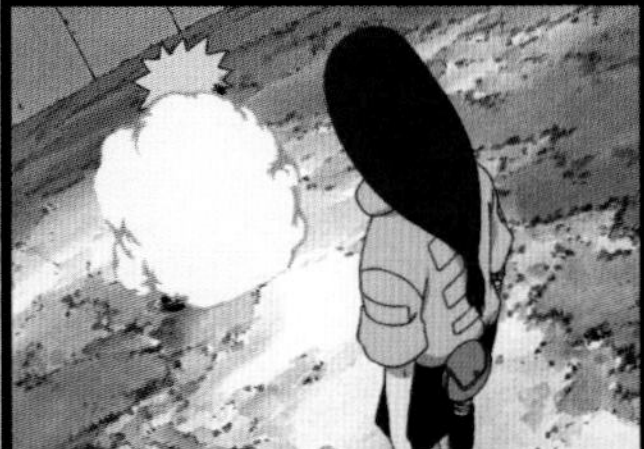

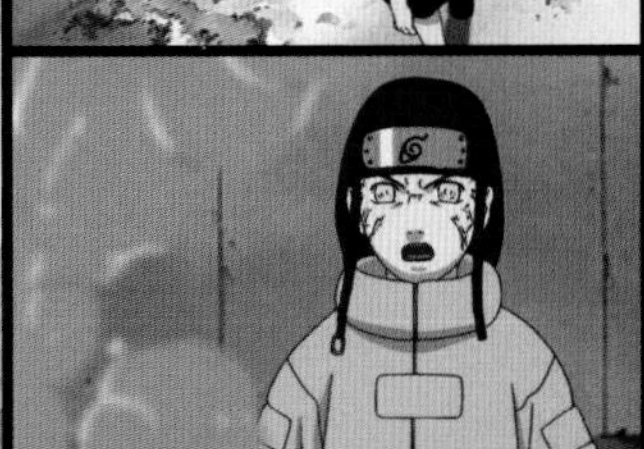

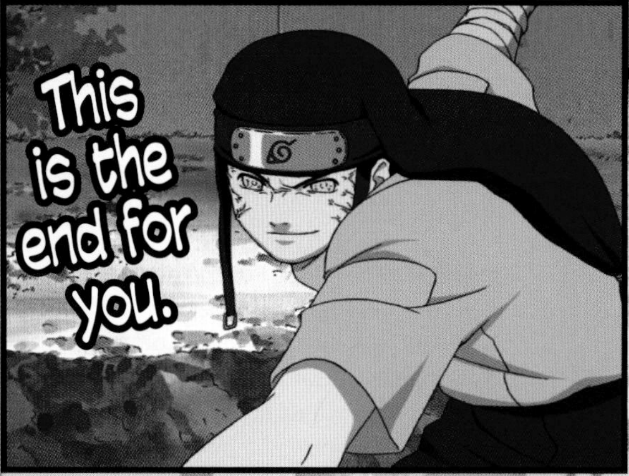
This is the end for you.

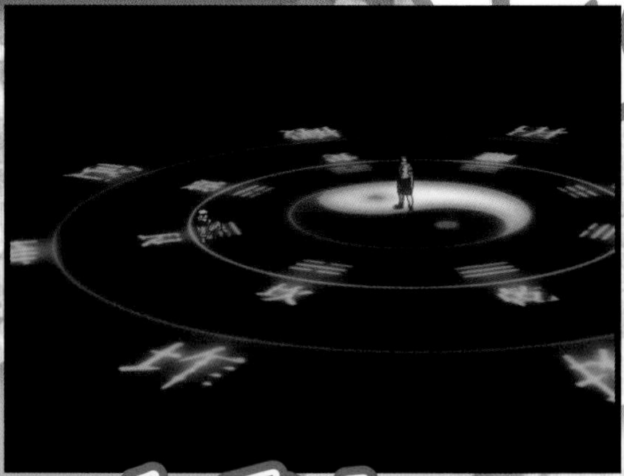

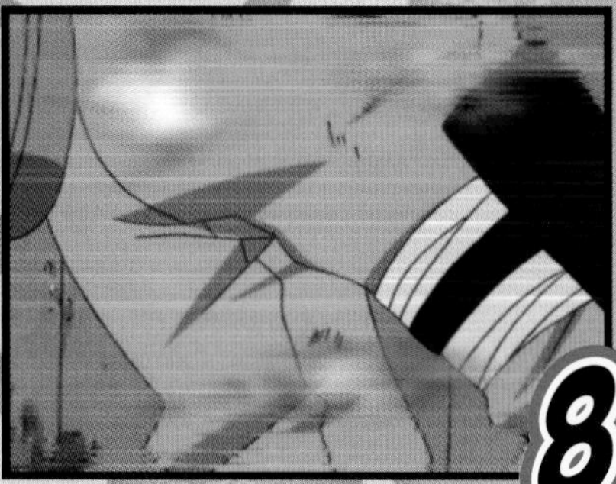

⬆ Neji strikes the body's 64 chakra points with furious, continuous attacks.

Gentle Fist: 8 Trigrams, 64 Palms!!

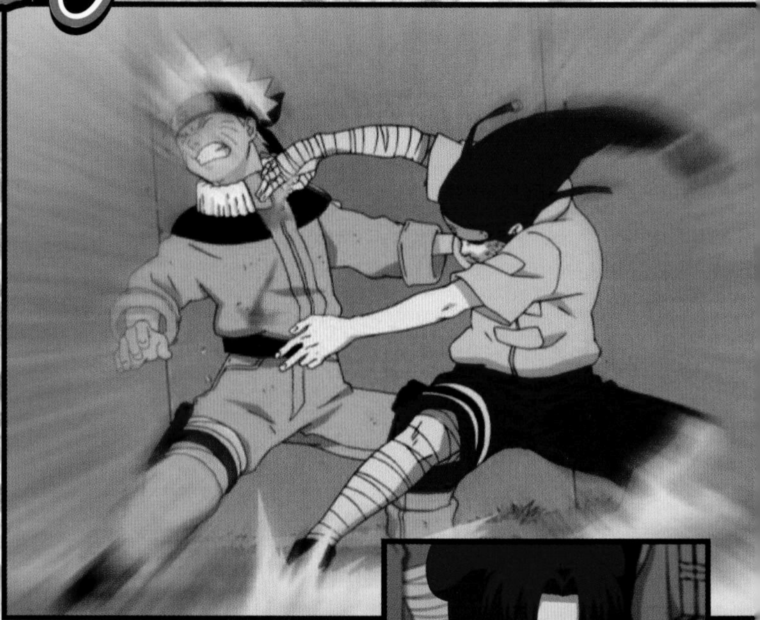

The gifted Neji releases the Main Branch's secret technique!

Neji displays the 8 Trigrams Palms Rotation and 8 Trigrams 64 Palms techniques passed down only in the Main Branch of the Hyuga Clan. Neji learned them without instruction from anyone.

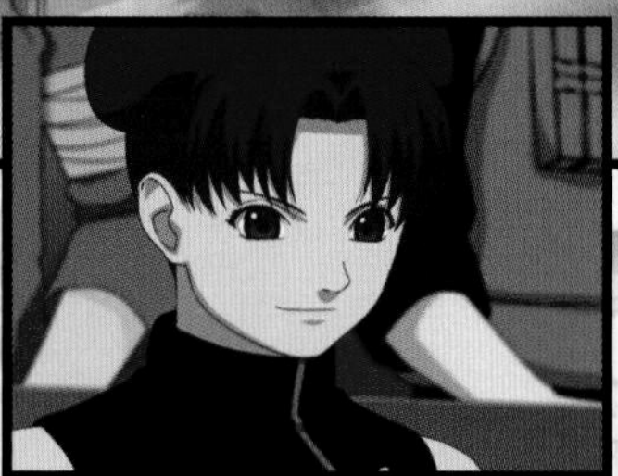

⬆ Tenten expects a complete victory from Neji.

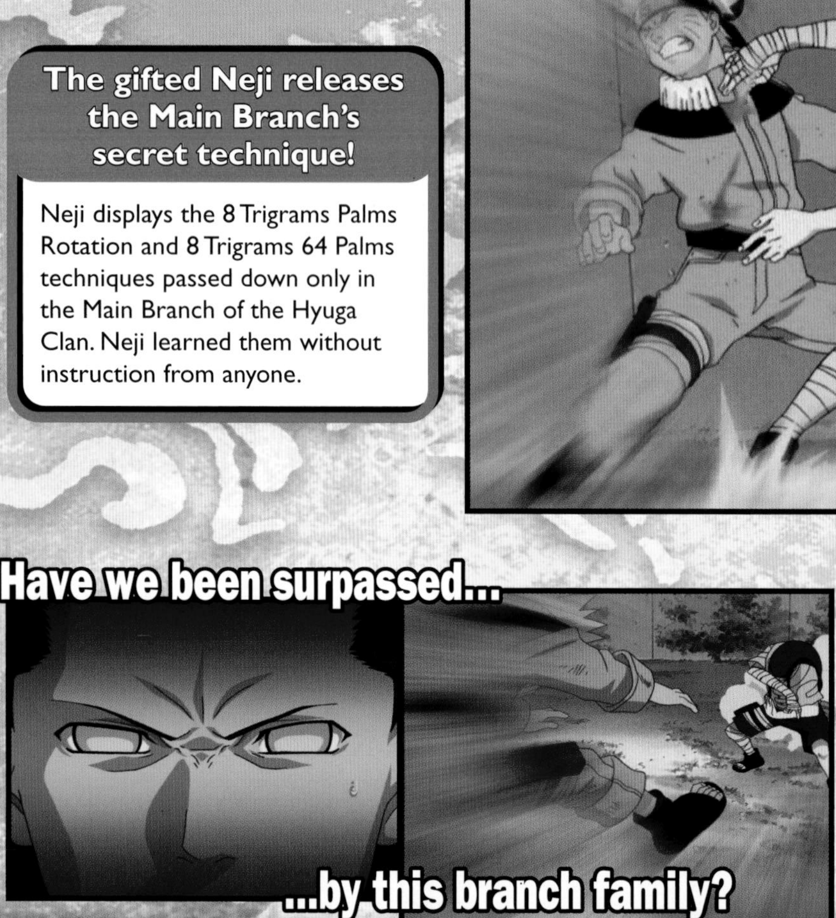
Have we been surpassed...
...by this branch family?

⬅ Even the head of the main branch, Hiashi, is astonished at Neji's talent.

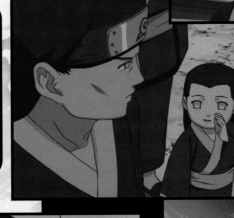

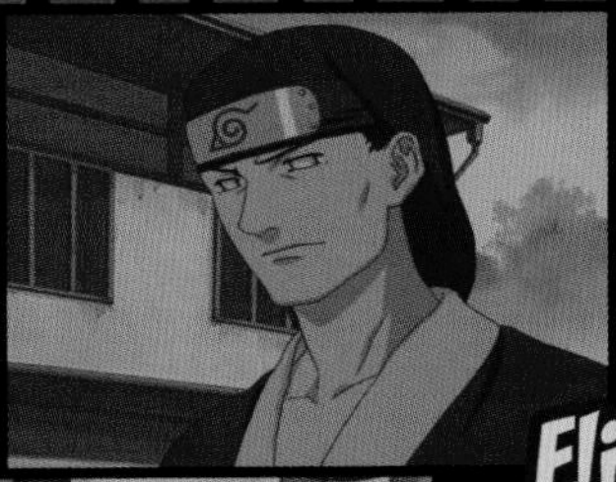

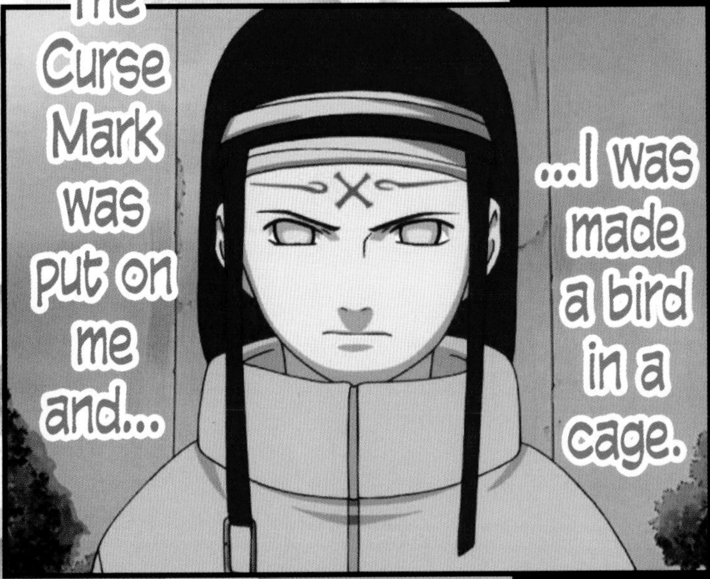

Elite bloodlines that breed tragedy!

⬇ Neji's tragedy began when he was only four years old.

The Main Branch and Side Branch, doomed by the clan's fatal enmity!

The Hyuga Clan possesses the unique power of the kekkei genkai. In order to protect their blood trait, all family members are bound by a strict code for how to use it.

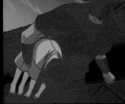

The Curse Mark was put on me and...
...I was made a bird in a cage.

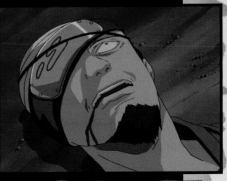

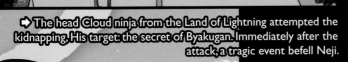

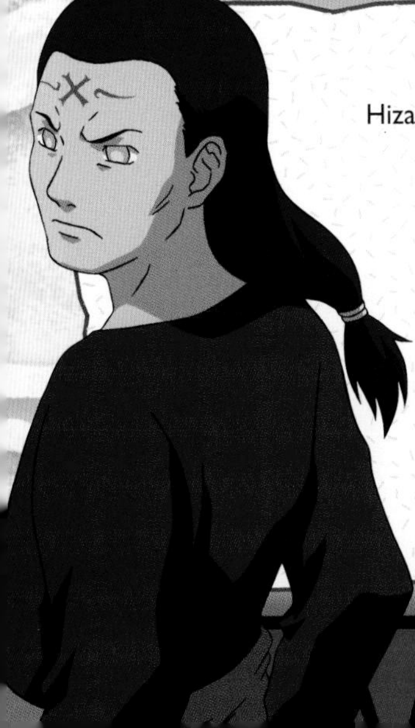

➡ The head Cloud ninja from the Land of Lightning attempted the kidnapping. His target: the secret of Byakugan. Immediately after the attack, a tragic event befell Neji.

⬆ Hinata, the heir to the main branch, was almost kidnapped by an unknown assailant.

➡ Neji's father Hizashi was killed to avert war.

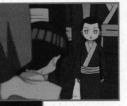

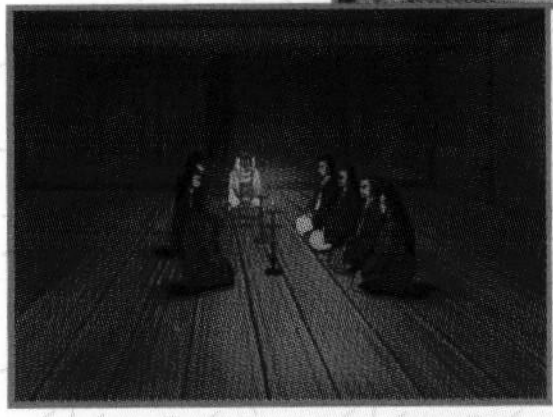

⬅ In childhood, Neji knew nothing of the destiny or the code of his clan.

The warped code of the Kekkei Genkai!

Without exception, all Side Branch members are branded with a mark on their forehead. The mark reacts to a secret sign from a Main Branch member and destroys the target's cerebral nerve, making the Side Branch members birds in a cage, unable to rebel.

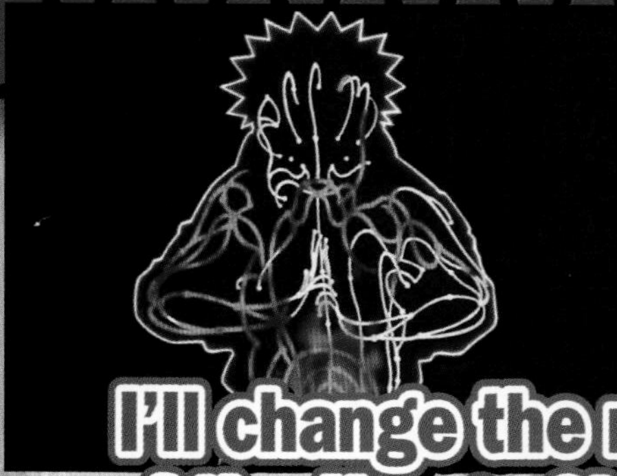

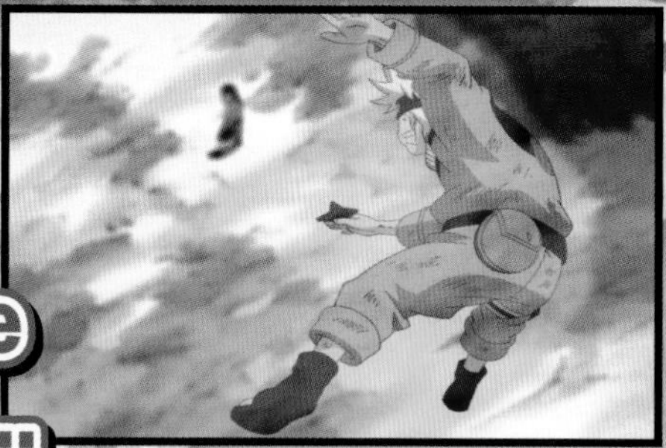

⬅ Naruto markedly improved his combat strength with the Nine-Tailed Fox's chakra.

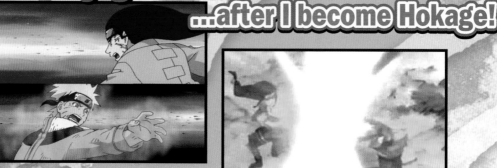

I'll change the role of the Hyuga Clan...

...after I become Hokage!

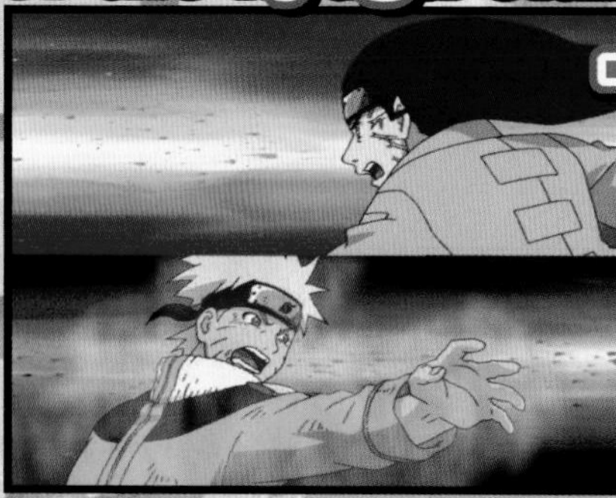

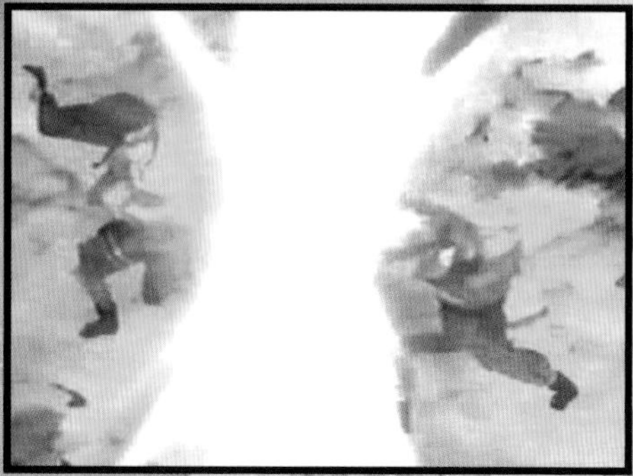

⬆➡ With his overflowing chakra, Naruto charges. At the same time, Neji counters by activating Rotation to evade the explosive attack!

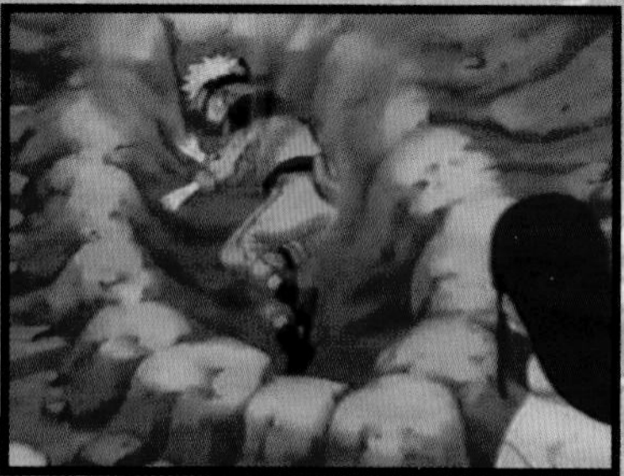

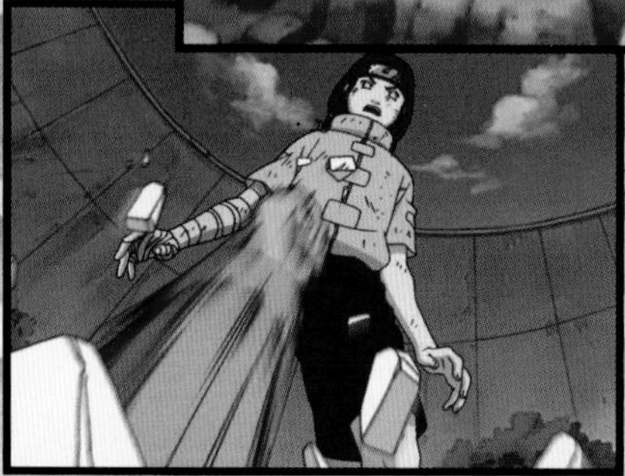

NARUTO'S FIST OF CONFI-DENCE!!

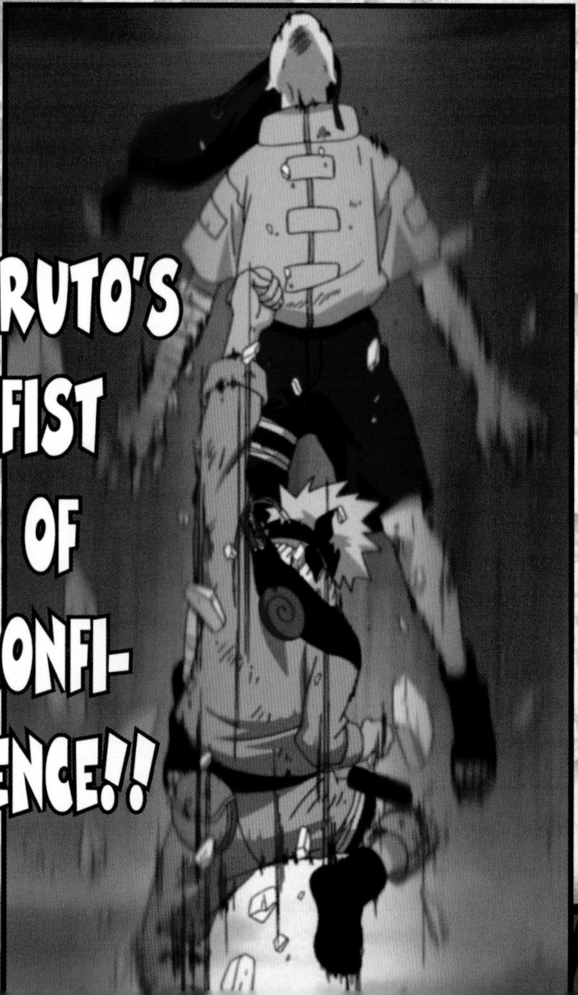

Naruto's mighty blow smashes through destiny!

After they collide, Neji is the first to stand and emerge from the cloud of dust. But at that very moment, when all were convinced of the winner, a mighty blow bursts up from underground and nails Neji. Believe in victory!

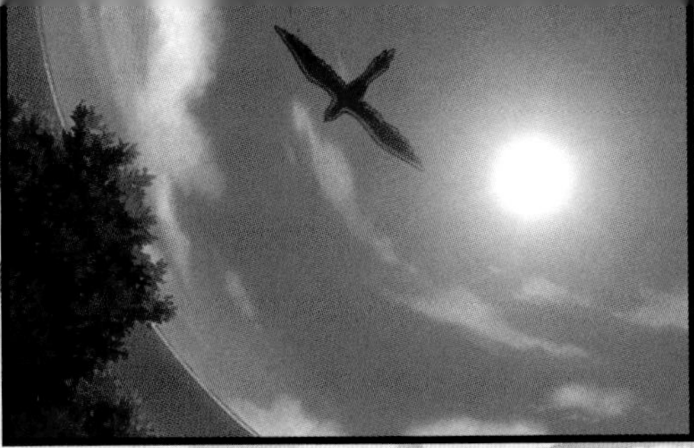

➡ Neji bears a deep wound in his heart. Since Naruto struggled through similar circumstances himself, he truly understands Neji's pain.

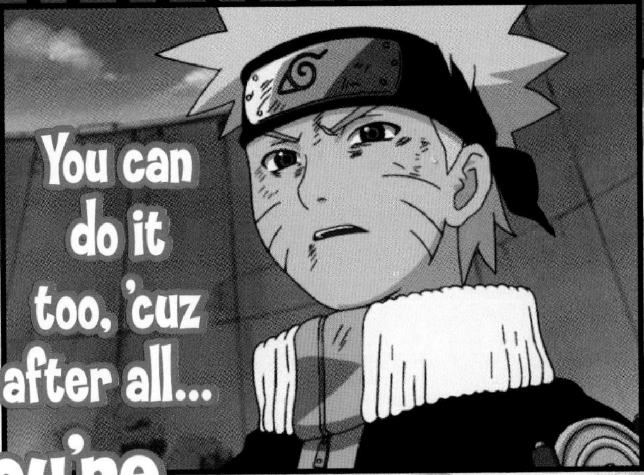

You can do it too, 'cuz after all... ...unlike me, you're not a failure.

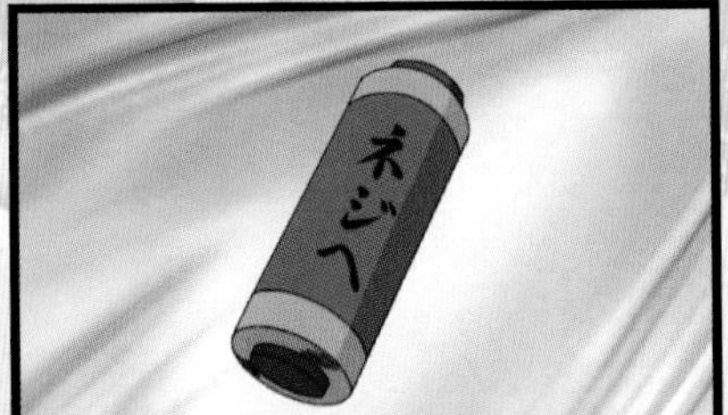

➡ There is no doubt this scroll, on which the truth of the tragic incident is recorded, was handwritten by Neji's father. *(Scroll says: To Neji)*

An unknown hero saved the Village Hidden in the Leaves!

Neji's father was looked upon as a victim who was used to protect the Hyuga Clan and avoid war. But the truth is that he sacrificed himself of his own free will. After the match, Hiashi visits Neji in the hospital and reveals the truth.

The truth revealed!

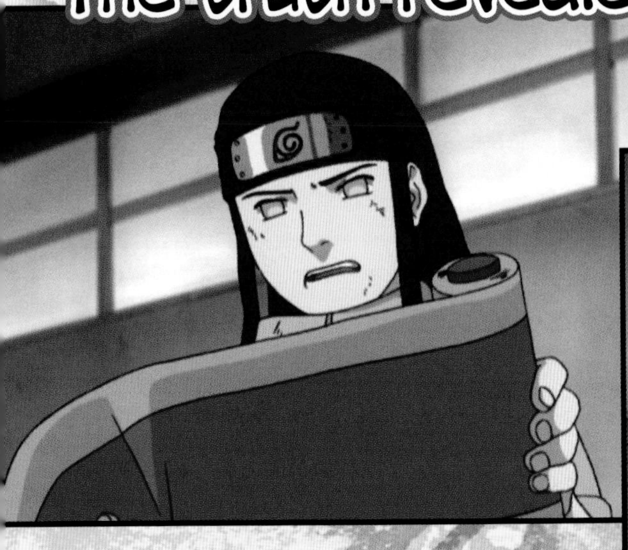

⬅⬇ Hizashi was not murdered. He voluntarily sacrificed his life to save the village. This memory is painful for Hiashi as well.

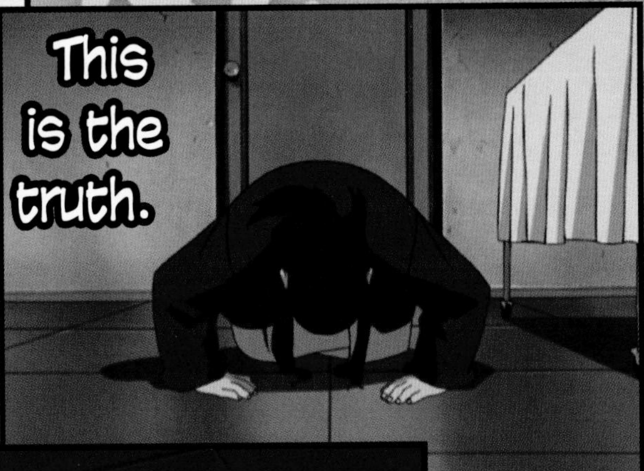
This is the truth.

The sky endlessly extends before Neji's eyes!

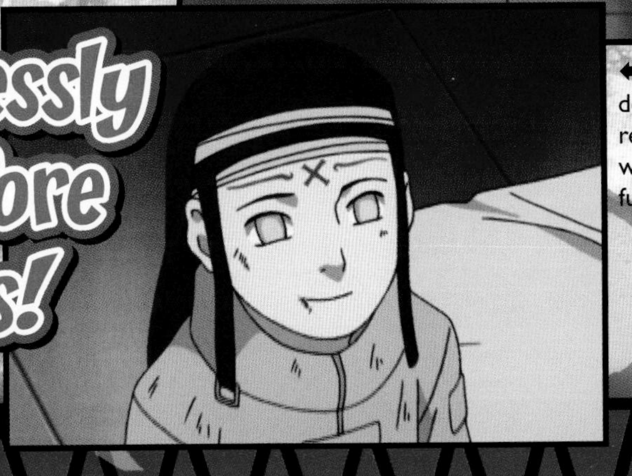

⬅ Opening the door of destiny reveals a wide-open future.

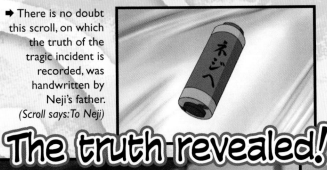

Showing his usual lack of motivation!

An out-standing battle of brains!

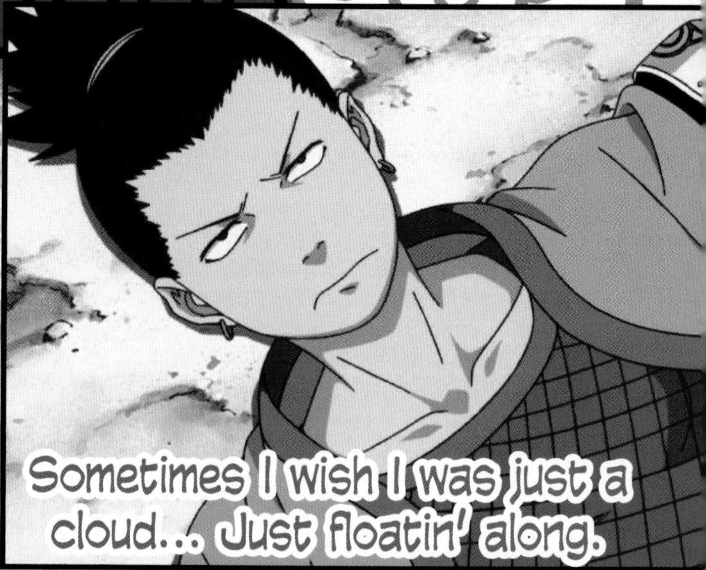
Sometimes I wish I was just a cloud... Just floatin' along.

⬆ Even after being thrown into the arena, Shikamaru is still half-asleep. Zero motivation from the very beginning!

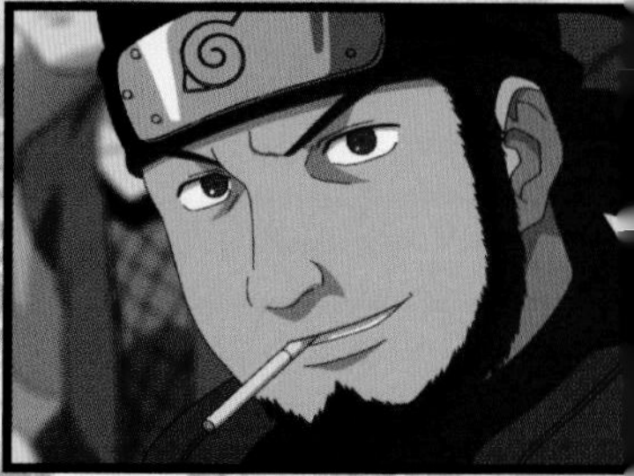

Squad 10 gives its full support.

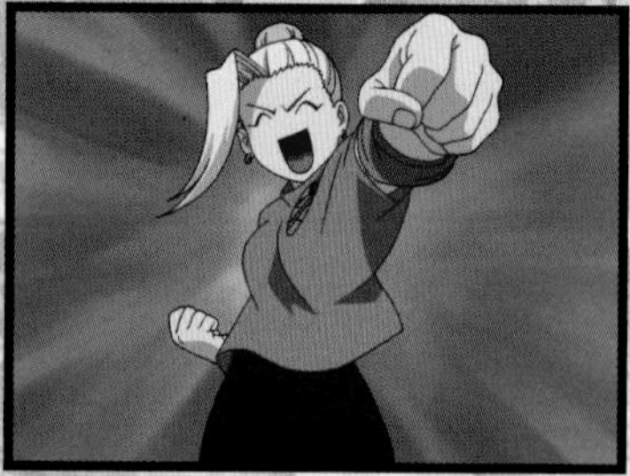

⬅⬋⬆ Despite Shikamaru's feelings, each member of Squad 10 watches intently!

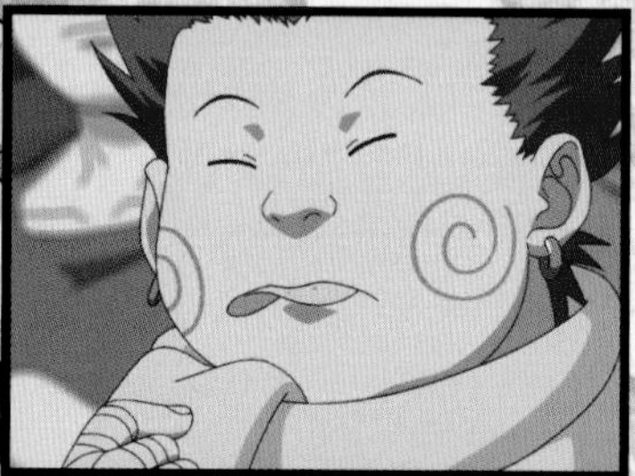

A slacker no more! Shikamaru gets serious?!

Shikamaru's words and expression show no motivation. However, now that he has survived and is in the final round, and with his opponent being one of the best of the Sand, he has no choice but to get serious?!

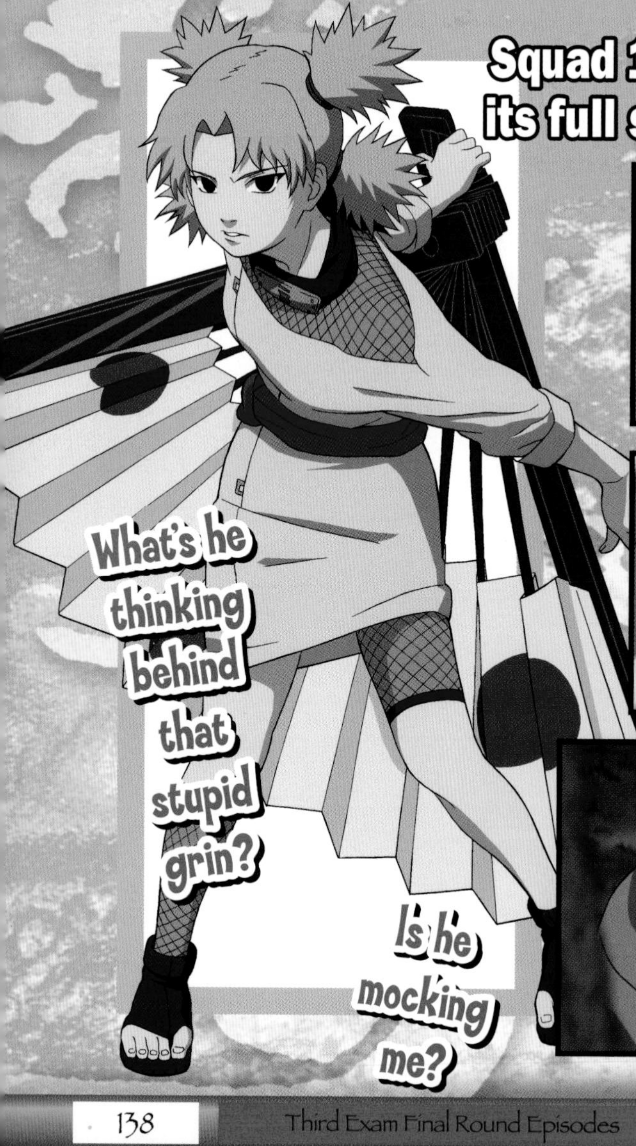
What's he thinking behind that stupid grin?
Is he mocking me?

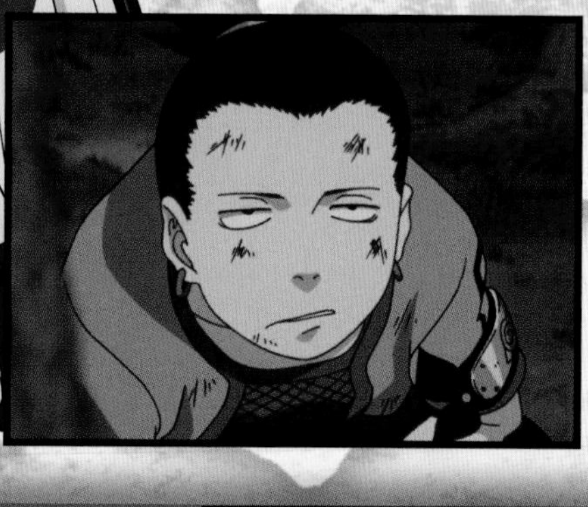

⬅ Shikamaru stares vacantly up at the sky. Temari thinks she's being mocked and attacks in a fit of rage.

An invisible blade slices through the air!

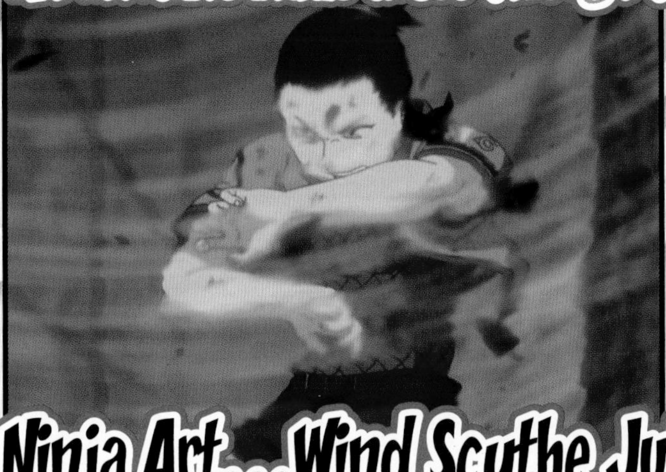

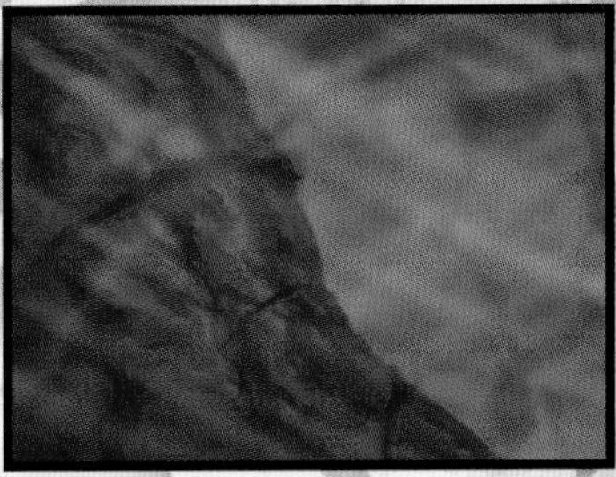

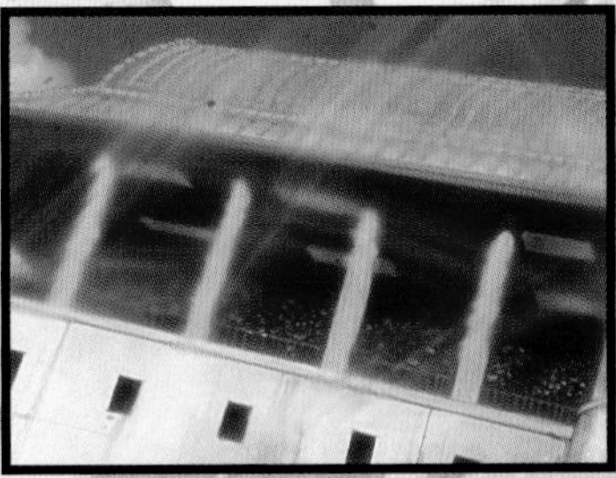

Ninja Art...Wind Scythe Jutsu!!

Are Shikamaru's hands tied by Temari's furious attacks?!

Temari continues the onslaught from a distance with her giant fan. Shikamaru looks for a chance to use Shadow Possession Jutsu but can't get into range. He has to hang on until a chance presents itself!

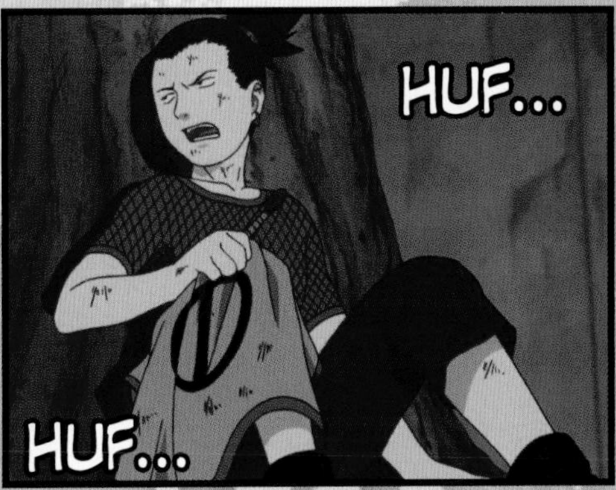
HUF...
HUF...

⬅ Shikamaru gets pinned down by Wind Scythe Jutsu and uses the trees as cover!

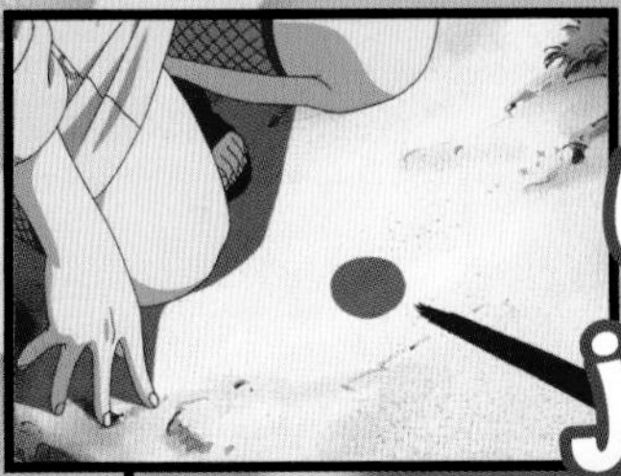

➡ Temari astutely estimates Shikamaru's attack range. It's just a few inches short.

Using a jacket...

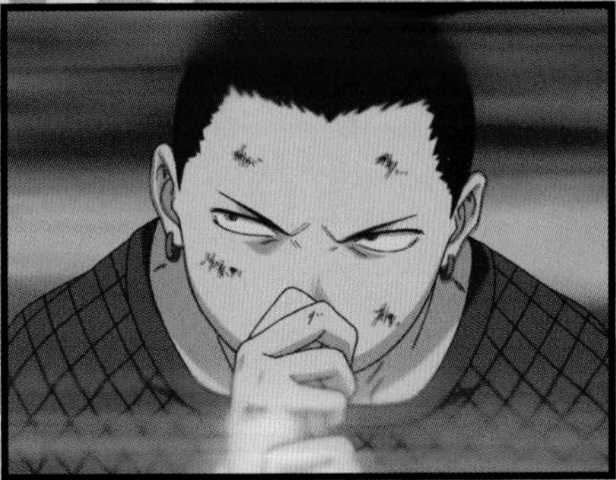

...as a parachute?!

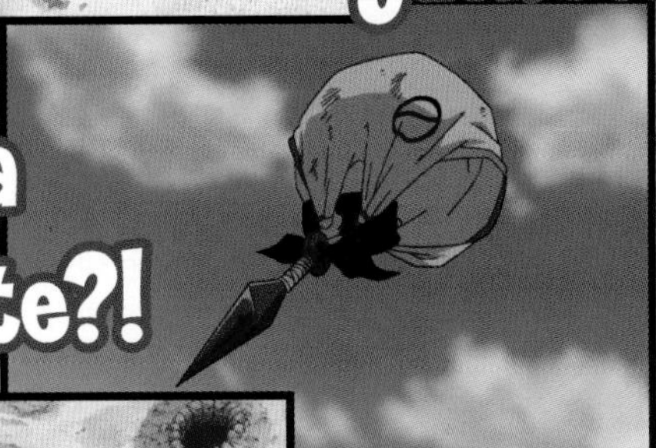

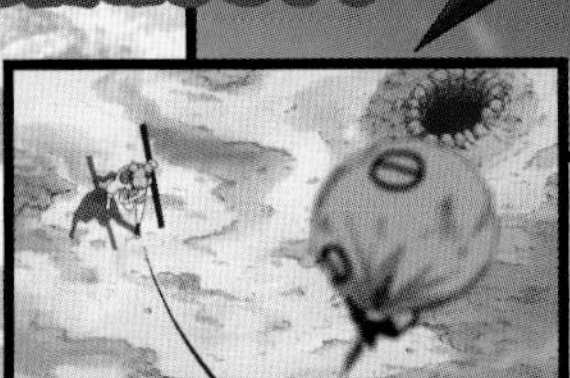

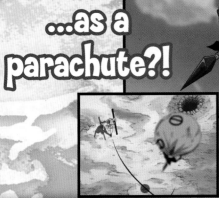

⬅ Amazingly, Shikamaru makes a shadow with his jacket, locking Temari into the range of his jutsu!

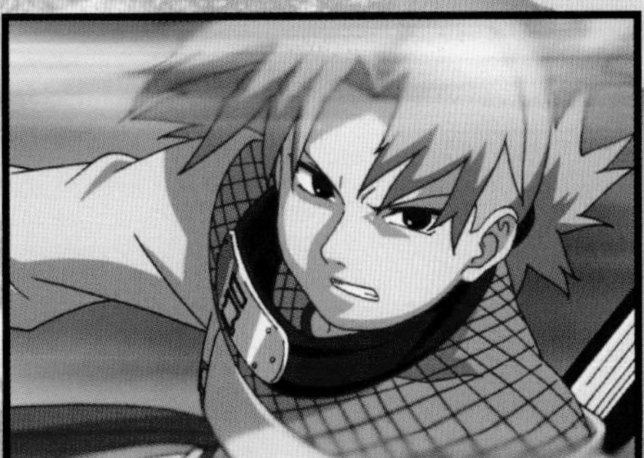

Shikamaru's tactic...

➡ The moment she attempts to launch an attack to seize victory, Temari is paralyzed.

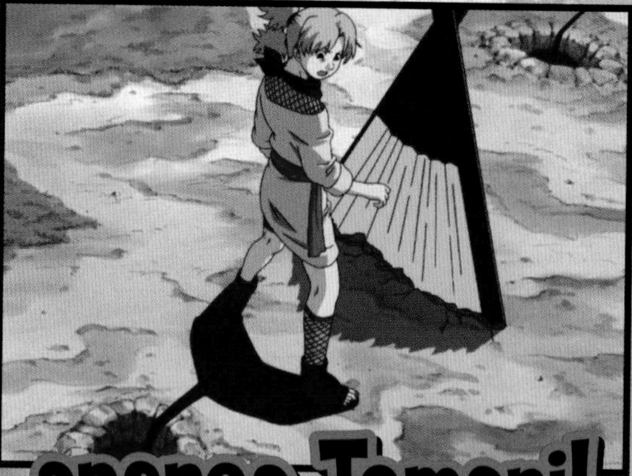

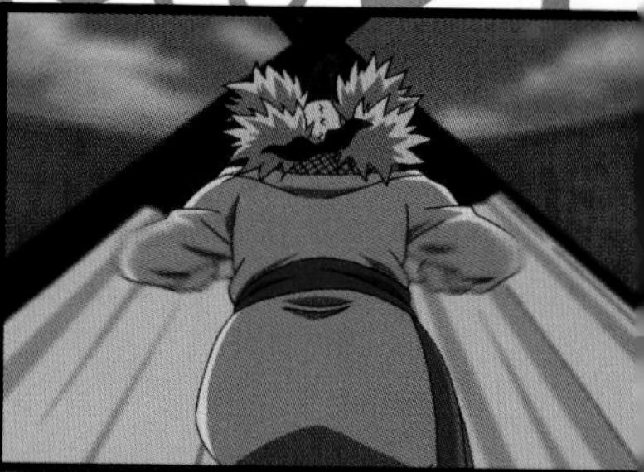

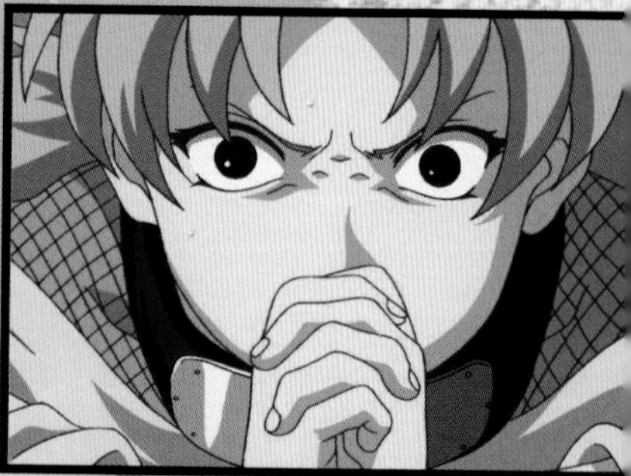

...snares Temari!

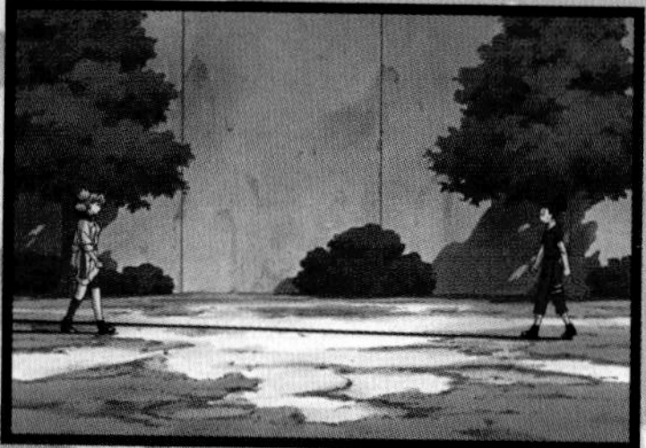

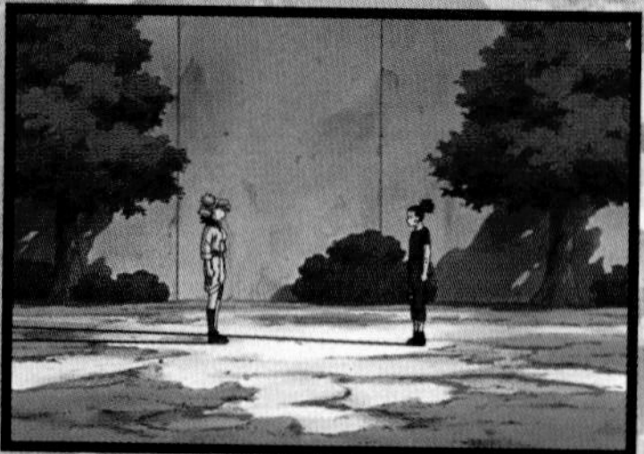

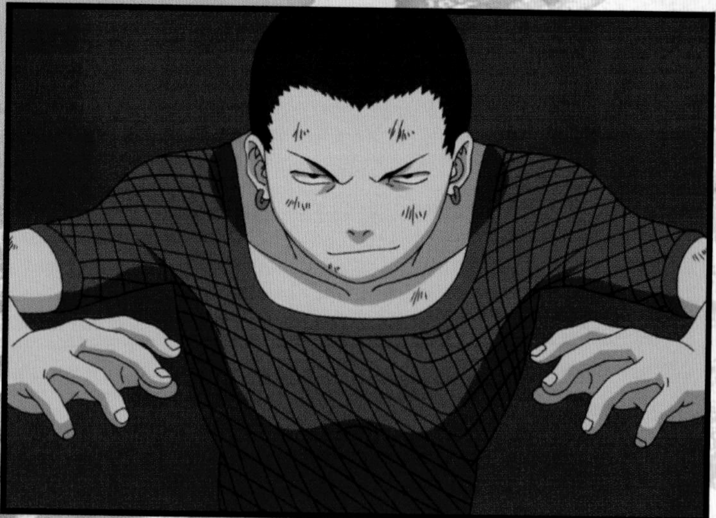

OK, THAT'S IT. I GIVE UP.

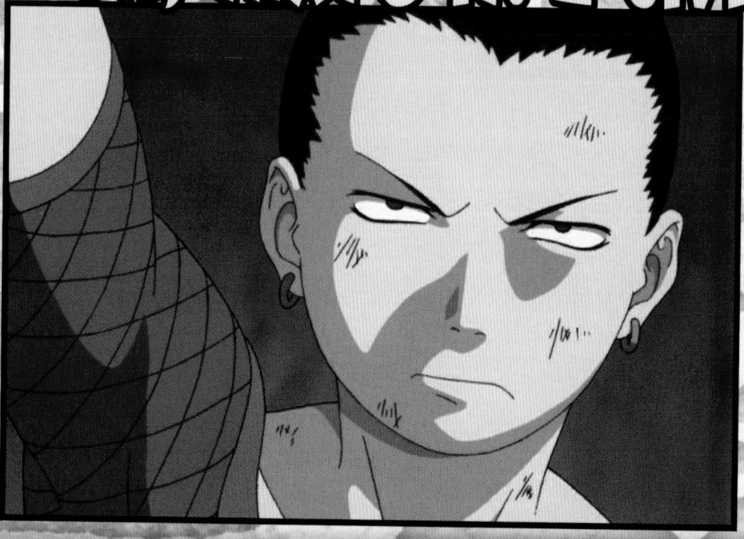

Shikamaru's victory is close at hand! But unbelievably he decides to...?!

After several feints, the Shadow Possession Jutsu finally does the job! The top tactician of the Leaf Village is poised to take down Temari and declare victory, but…?!

There's a flurry of speculation as the hotly anticipated match gets underway!

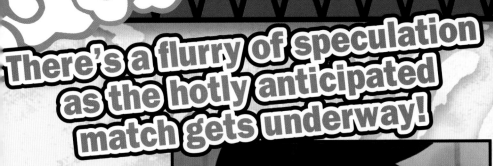

⬇ Spectators wager huge amounts of money on this super fight.

⬆ This match-up was actually destined to take place long before the Chunin Exams. Adversaries always eager to fight stronger opponents finally face each other in battle.

Sasuke arrives! Finally, the ultimate match!

The last descendant of the Hidden Leaf Village's legendary Uchiha Clan versus the son of the Sand Kazekage. The arena is fired up but Sakura cannot hide her anxiety.

⬅⬆ Lee looks well as he shows up with Guy, but deep down inside he is deeply hurt by his predicament.

What are Lee's feelings as he watches the finals?!

Lee, unable to use any ninjutsu, aimed to become a great shinobi by putting all his efforts into training in taijutsu. He longed to prove his taijutsu at the exams, but was injured in the prelims and now visits the Final Round Arena as a spectator.

141

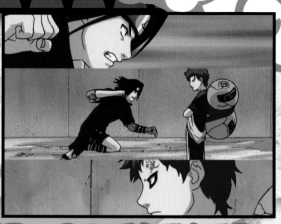

SUPER SPEED OBTAINED WITH THE SHARINGAN!

⬆ Through training, Sasuke succeeded in gaining speed equal to that of Lee.

Sasuke's ability overwhelms Gaara!

The battle finally commences! Gaara, with his arms folded in front in him, defends himself with his Sand Shield. But Sasuke suddenly and effortlessly accelerates his movements for a sneak attack on Gaara!

What's the matter, Gaara?

Is that all you've got?

⬆ The Sand Shield is unable to protect Gaara from Sasuke's attacks. Gaara makes hand signs and a massive amount of sand begins to close around him!

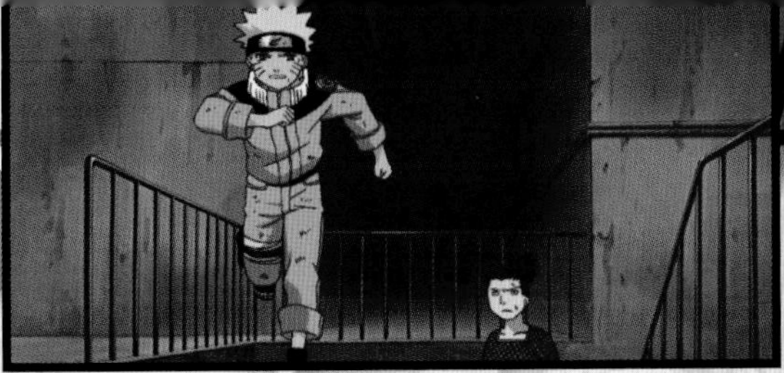

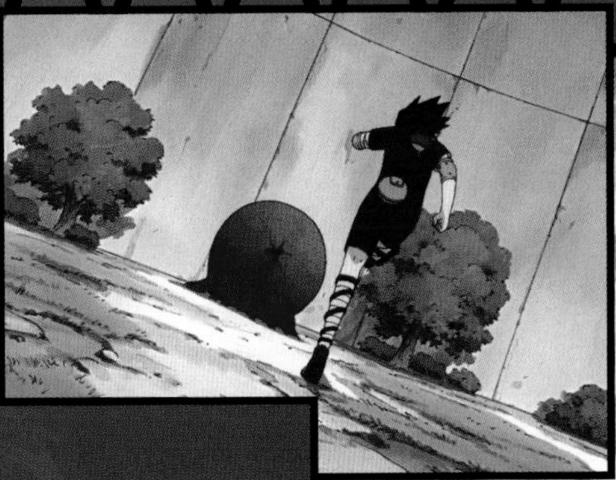

I'm going to stop this match!

The demonic sand encases Gaara and perplexes Naruto!

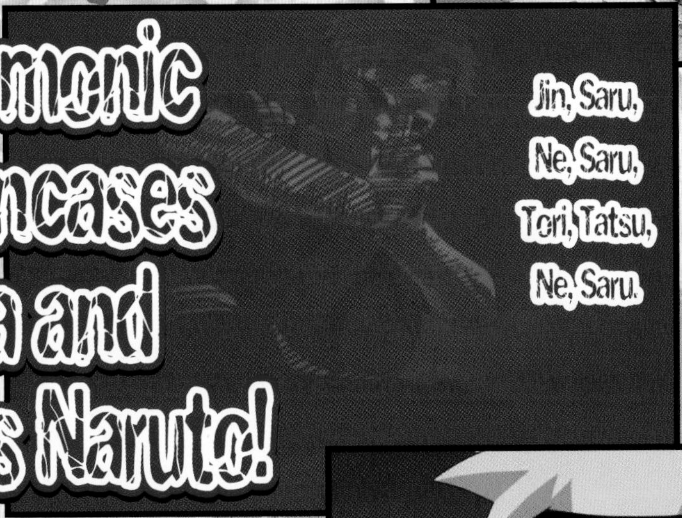
Jin, Saru, Ne, Saru, Tori, Tatsu, Ne, Saru.

⬅ Gaara's voice from within the sand cocoon can be heard as he makes hand signs. Naruto's anxiety grows while witnessing Gaara's morbid behavior.

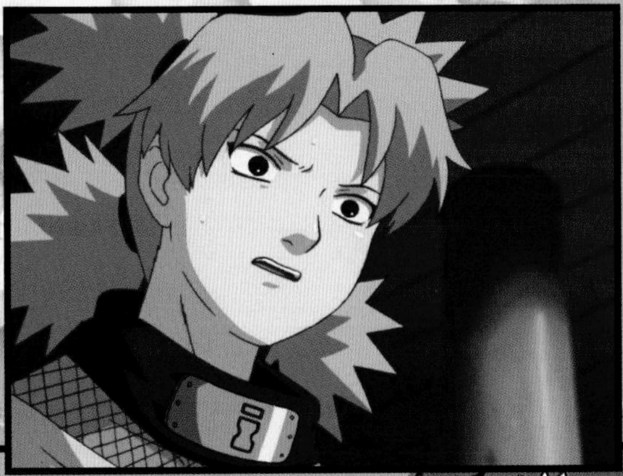

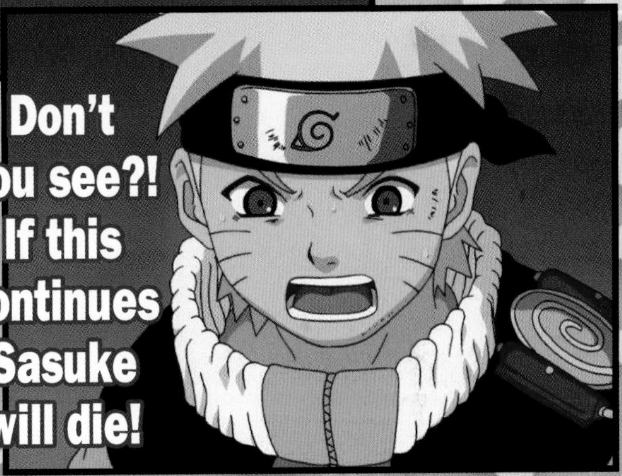
Don't you see?! If this continues Sasuke will die!

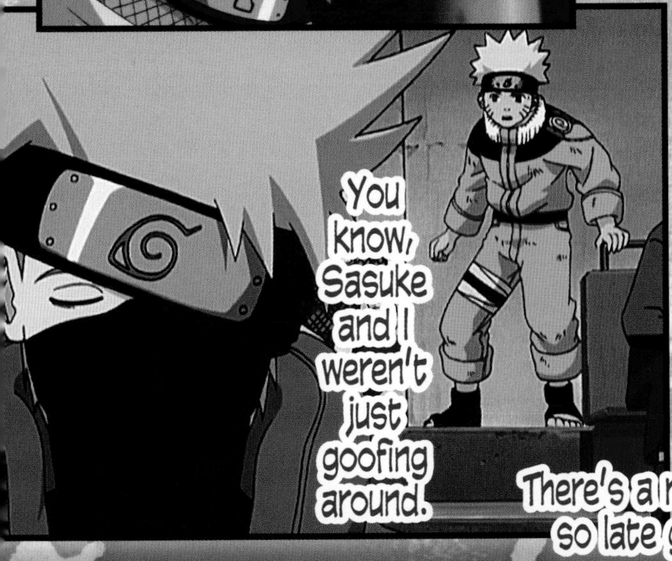
You know, Sasuke and I weren't just goofing around.
There's a reason we were so late getting here.

While Gaara is in full defense mode, Sasuke closes in!

A high-density sand cocoon, an ultimate defense that repels every attack! Sasuke continues to try and break the deadlock. Meanwhile Naruto, who knows Gaara's madness, struggles to try and stop Sasuke.

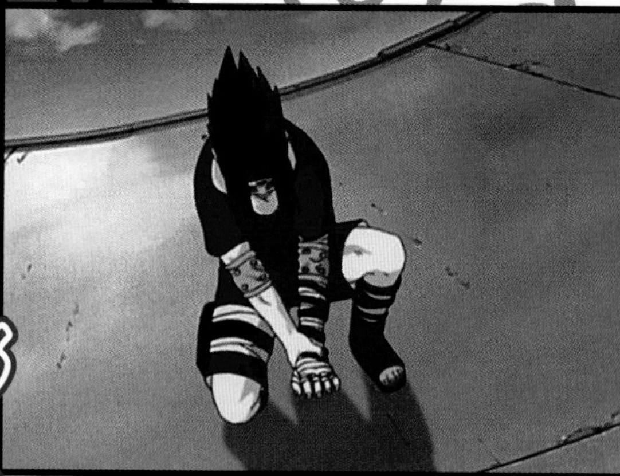

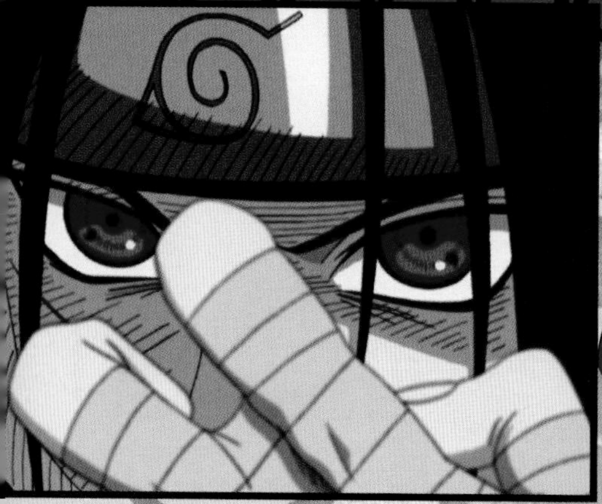

Chakra emanates from his arm with a chirping sound! It's the Chidori!

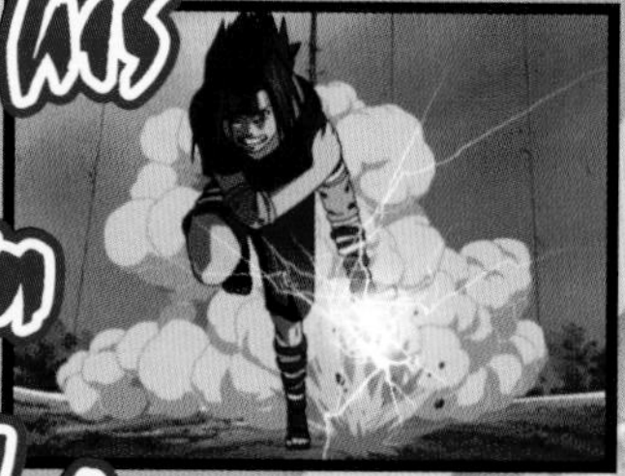

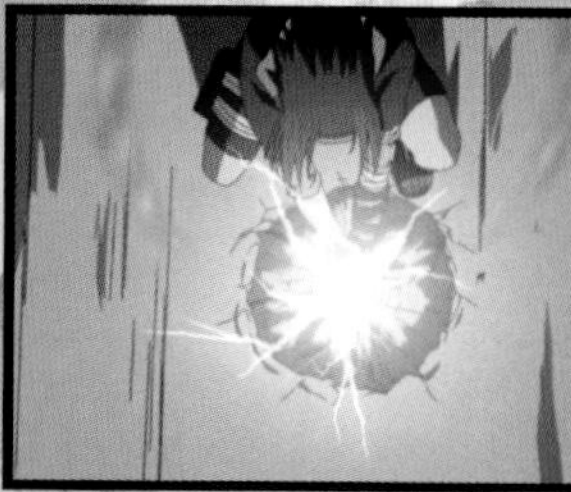

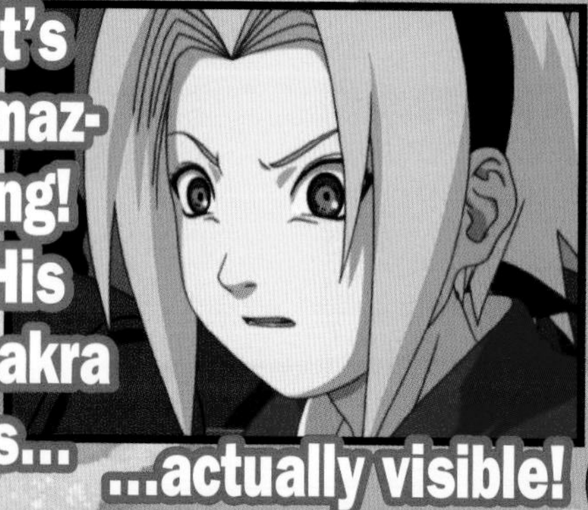

It's amazing! His chakra is...
...actually visible!

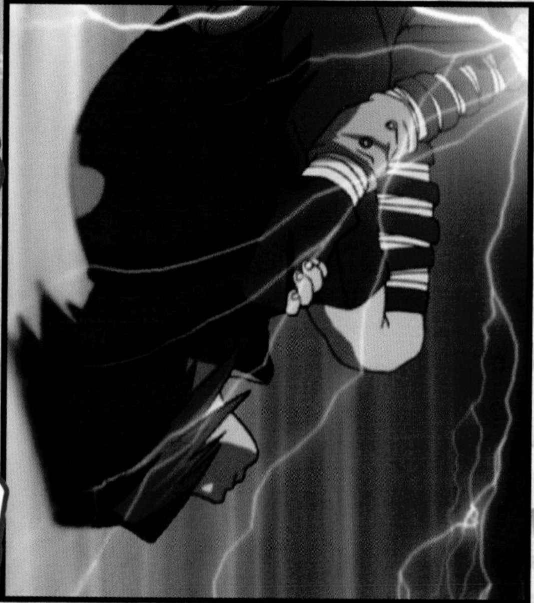

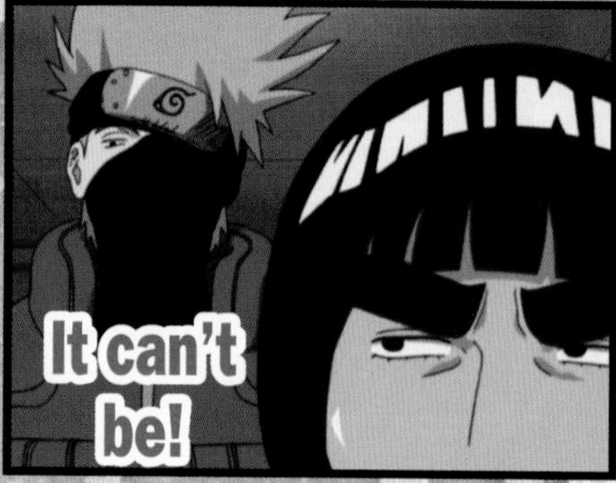
It can't be!

➡⬆ Sasuke begins to focus his chakra as the stunned spectators watch. At that moment his left arm emits light and he runs down the wall with incredible speed!

Awesome physical activation that tears up the defenses!

Sasuke decides to unleash his newly mastered secret technique, Chidori: One Thousand Birds, to break Gaara's defense! With ultimate physical activation and focusing an enormous amount of chakra into his left arm, he bores into the ground and rushes straight for Gaara!

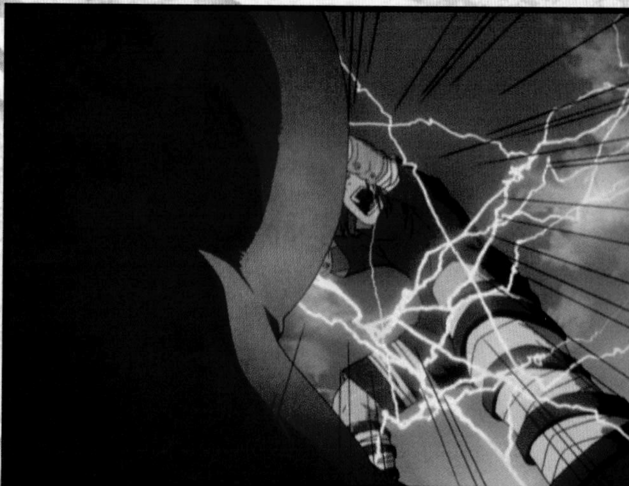

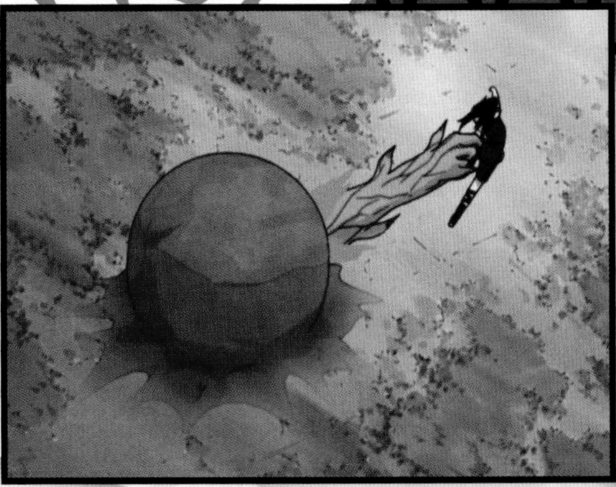

A grotesque arm extends from the sand cocoon!

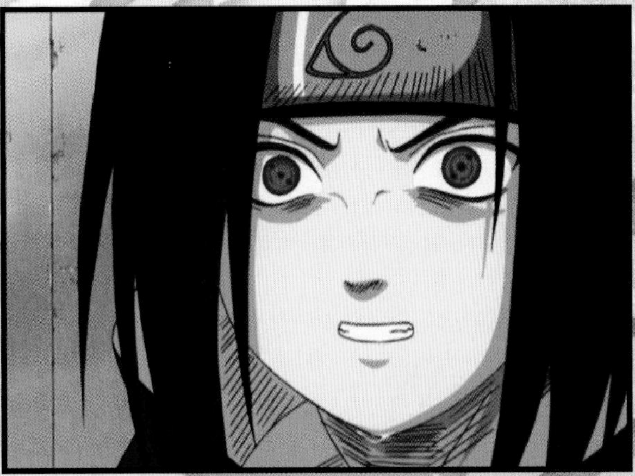

➡ Something stares out at Sasuke with heinous, murderous intent. What on earth is it?!

Gaara's armor comes down!

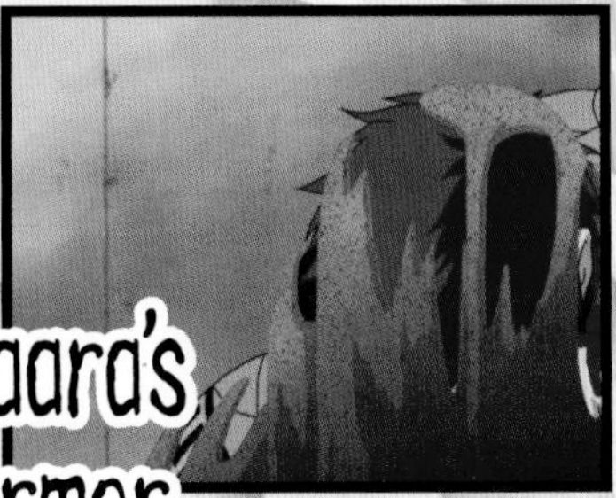

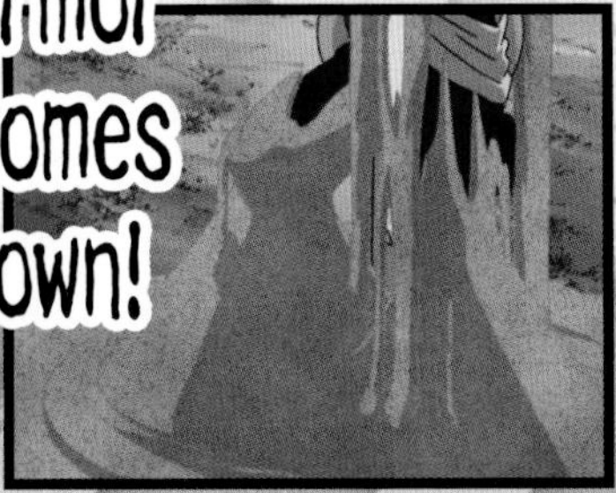

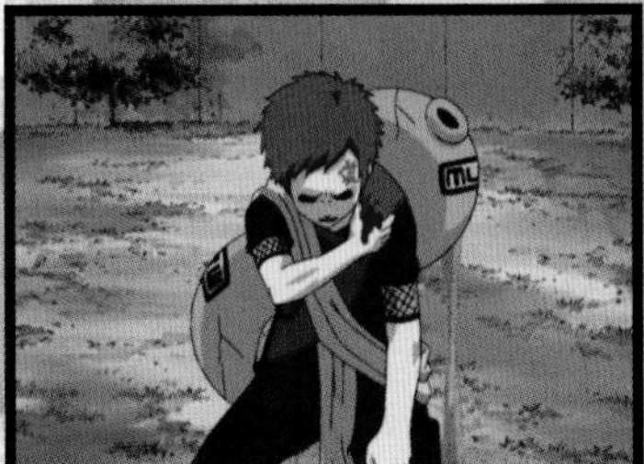

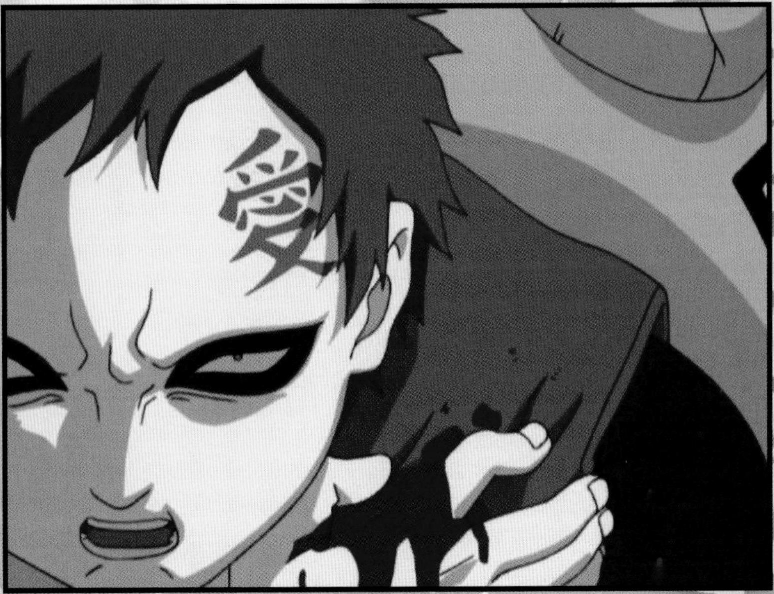

A brutal battle finally brought to an end! However?!

The ultimate defensive cocoon is breached and Gaara emerges, panting as if in pain and with his hand held to a wound on his left shoulder. It was obvious to everyone who won, but...!

Suddenly the arena is attacked by genjutsu...!

White feathers fall all around the arena and spectators start to drop one after another. But what about Sasuke and Gaara's match?

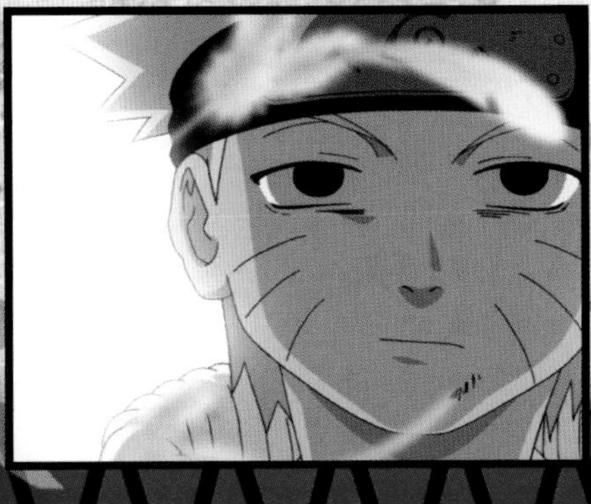

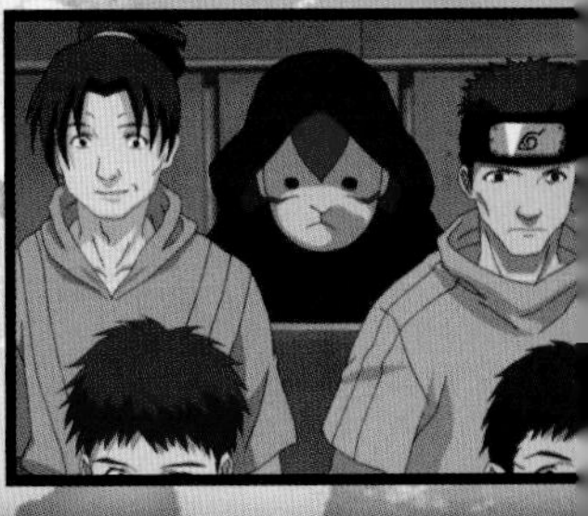

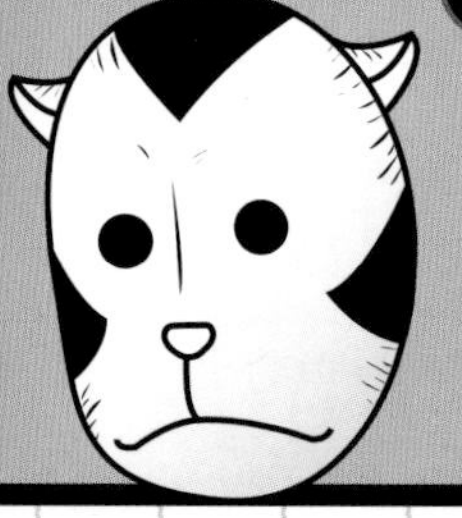

Anbu Black Ops Special Report

Leaf Village Squad 7

Squad 7 is led by Kakashi Hatake. The amazing growth of his three genin is reported here.

Naruto Uzumaki

He shows unexpected growth with each battle!

Naruto turned the tables and won his bouts in both the third exam prelims and the final round. In particular, his spur-of-the-moment ingenuity and vitality are remarkable.

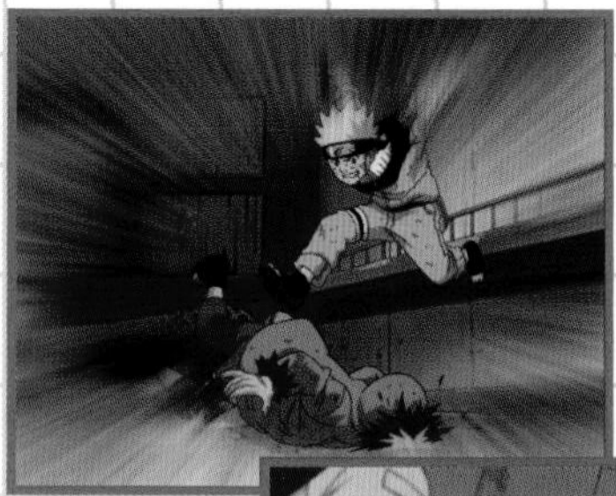

⬇ In the fight against Kiba, Naruto used a combination of the Shadow Clone Jutsu and taijutsu.

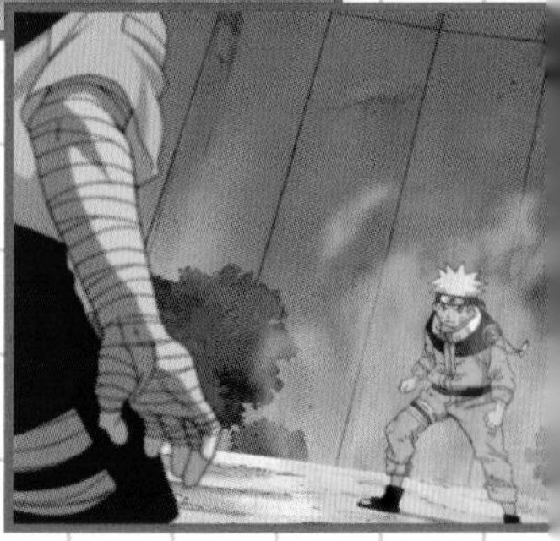

➡ In the latter half of the battle with Neji, he used totally different moves, almost like he was a different person.

Naruto has always been mischievous, like unleashing lewd jutsu or drawing graffiti on the Great Stone Faces. I never expected him to survive to the final round. I guess he'll always be unpredictable (ha ha).

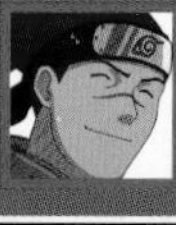

Testimony

Iruka

Report 1

What did he obtain from Master Jiraiya's training?!

It seems that Naruto had been training in the Hot Springs District for the 30 days before the final round. More than that, his mentor was none other than one of the legendary Sannin, Jiraiya! He must have really improved his chakra control through that training.

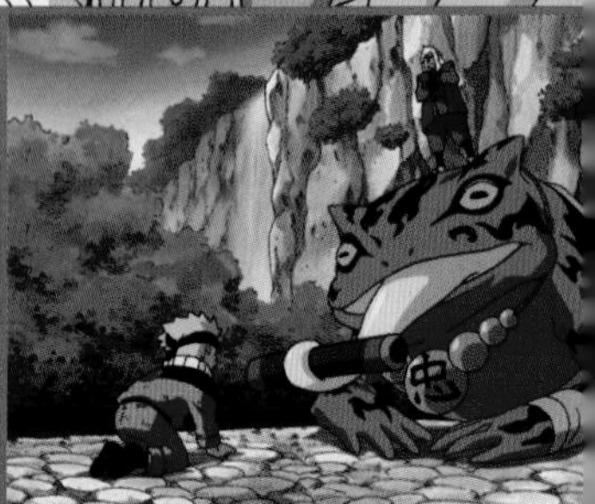

⬆ For some reason, he was constantly playing with the tadpoles What kind of training is that?

As a matter of fact, it was I that brought Naruto and Master Jiraiya together. I planned and executed it perfectly. Naruto's concentration is excellent. He even got the knack of the Summoning Jutsu, though of course, it's not perfect yet!

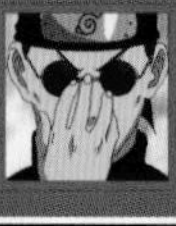

Testimony

Ebisu

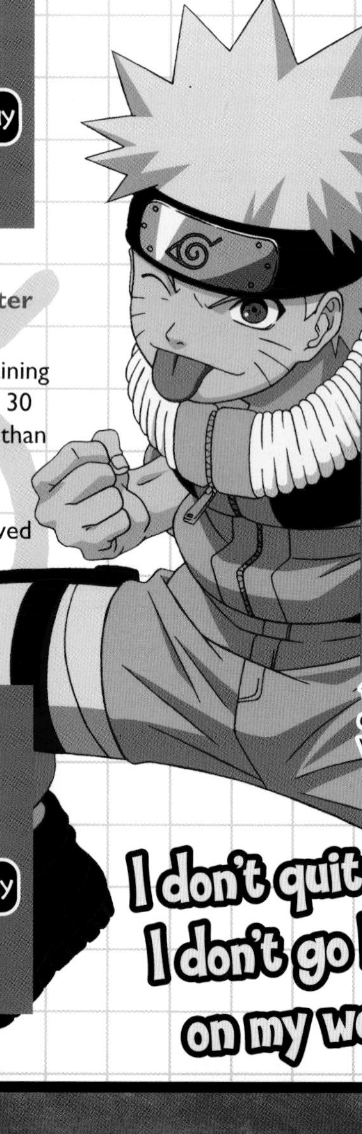

I don't quit. And I don't go back on my word.

A girl's gotta be tough if she's going to survive something like this!

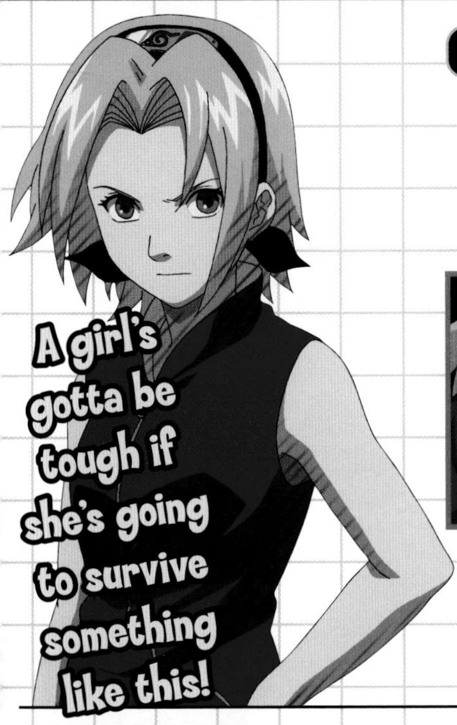

Sakura Haruno

The match showed her new potential!

Sakura Haruno faced the battle against Ino with more fighting spirit than ever before. Although it resulted in a draw, seeing her beat the Mind Transfer Jutsu with her strong willpower allows us a glimpse of what's in store for her in the future.

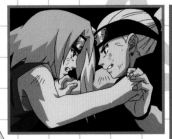

⬆ It was thought that she would exploit her forte and make it an intellectual battle, but…

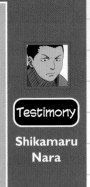

Those two were at each other's throats from the beginning, fighting over Sasuke. It was kind of scary hearing their voices echo around the arena as they shrieked at each other. But I wonder how serious they really are...?

Testimony

Shikamaru Nara

Sasuke Uchiha

The innate ability of the Uchiha Clan's bloodline on display in the final round!

Sasuke achieved the ultimate surprise attack—Chidori: One Thousand Birds—from training with Kakashi. With the Sharingan, he overcame the technique's weakness to counterattack. Sasuke displayed his new powers in the battle with Gaara.

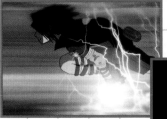

⬅ Kakashi's one and only original technique is perfectly reproduced.

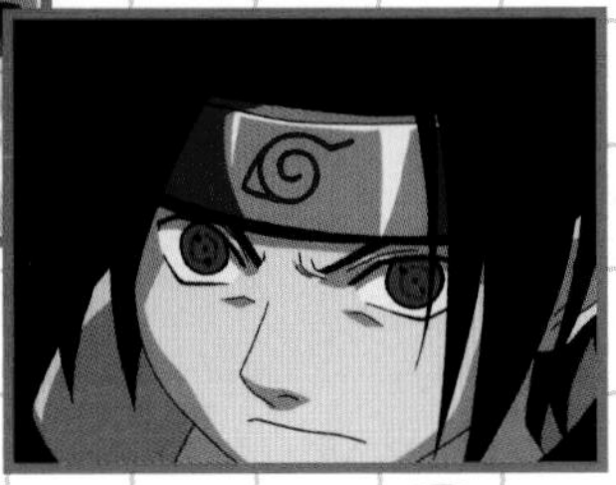

➡ Sasuke's curse mark was suppressed with Sealing Jutsu…

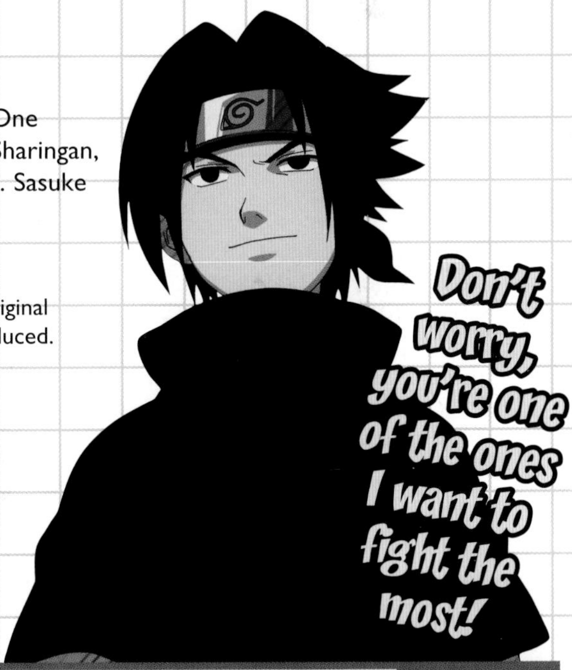

Don't worry, you're one of the ones I want to fight the most!

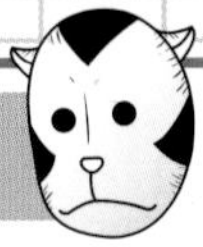

Overall Results

During the Chunin Exams, Naruto, Sasuke and Sakura reached milestones and continued to forge promising new paths! Training with excellent mentors definitely played a large role in the remarkable development of Naruto and Sasuke. Sakura has now met mentors that will continue to prepare her for the future as well. Much will be expected soon of these three young genin.

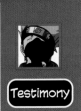

At this training session, I had him work intensely on improving his taijutsu, since his new jutsu, Chidori, requires that a tremendous amount of chakra be generated through physical activation. I'm just relieved he wasn't disqualified for being late. ♥

Testimony

Kakashi Hatake

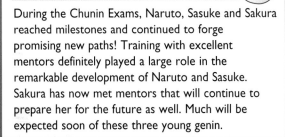

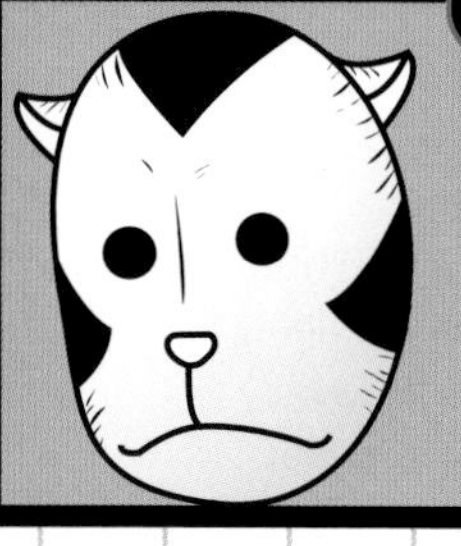

Anbu Black Ops Special Report

Part Six

Gaara

Gaara, a genin from the Hidden Sand Village, overcomes incredible obstacles with strange talents. What are the origins of Gaara's abilities and what is his true purpose?!

⬇ At the written test, he formed an eyeball in the air that linked with his optical nerve to spy on others.

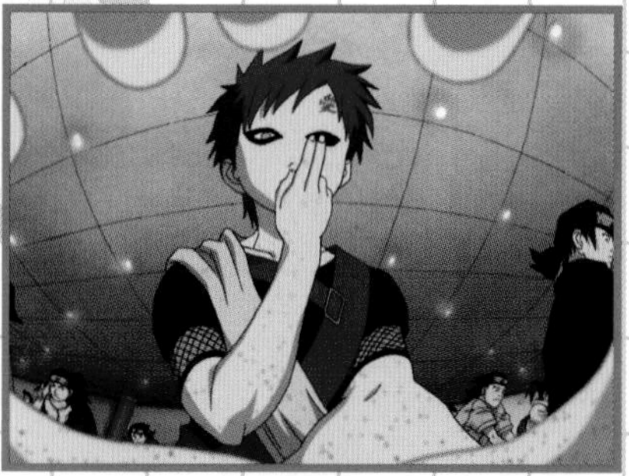

Report 1

The ability to manipulate sand!
Sand from his gourd changes shape as if alive, for attack, defense and even espionage.

➡ Gaara activates the Sand Shield via sheer willpower.

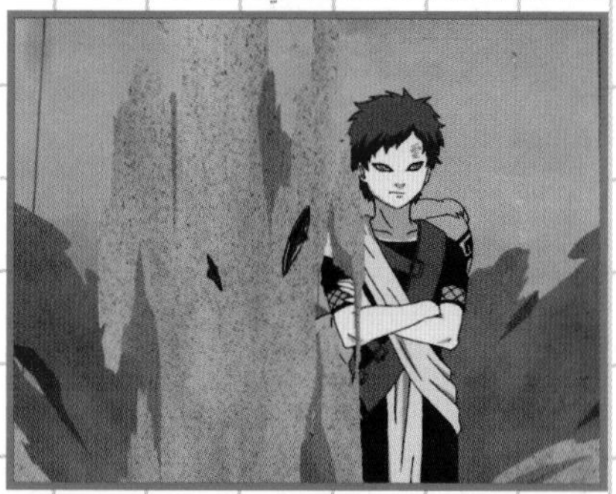

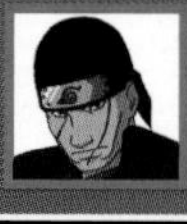

With many proctors present, myself among them, Gaara performed his jutsu without even the slightest change in expression. He also levitated sand and used it as a third eye. Very well done, for a novice.

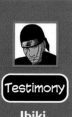

Testimony

Ibiki Morino

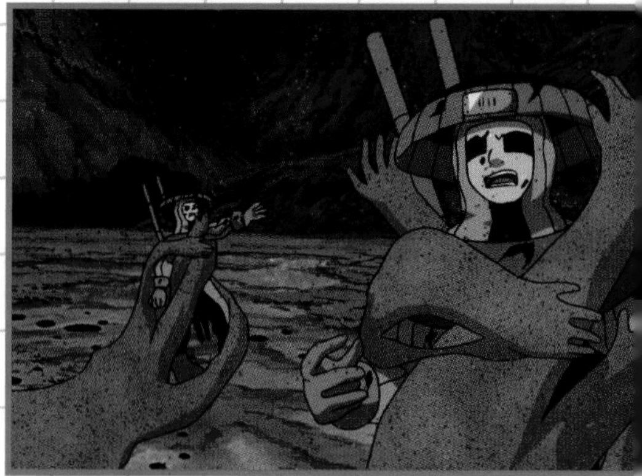

⬆ Sand Coffin, the jutsu that captures its opponents. The result of this battle is obvious but...

Report 2

Unknown and atrocious jutsu—!
During the Chunin Exams, Gaara displayed his dreadful Sand Burial ninjutsu attack. It's a vicious jutsu that captures the opponent and crushes them with high-density sand. This jutsu's inner mechanism and how it is activated is currently under investigation.

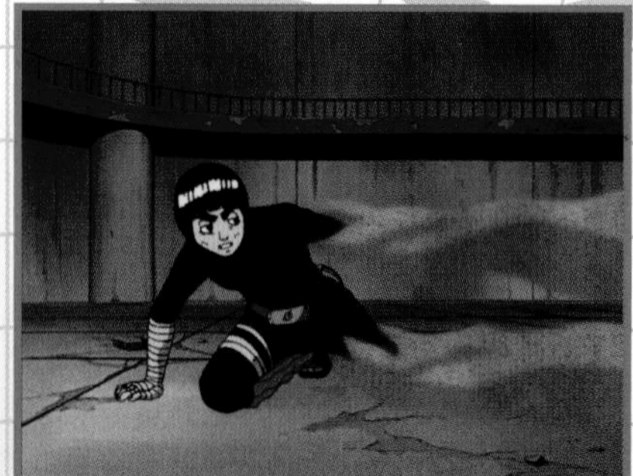

⬅ Sand Burial seriously wounded Lee's left arm and leg, hospitalizing him.

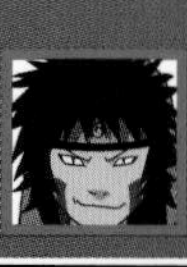

We saw it... The moment that creepy little guy from the Hidden Sand Village killed those three Rain ninja. Their begging for their lives was pointless... If Akamaru hadn't warned me, we probably would have ended up victims of his sand, too. Seriously.

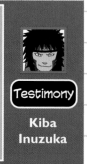

Testimony

Kiba Inuzuka

Report 3

A parched soul that is thirsty and out for blood!

Gaara shows mercy to no one. Without so much as a change in expression, he'll watch fresh blood spurt and slaughter like it's just a job. What lies at the core of his bloodthirsty heart?!

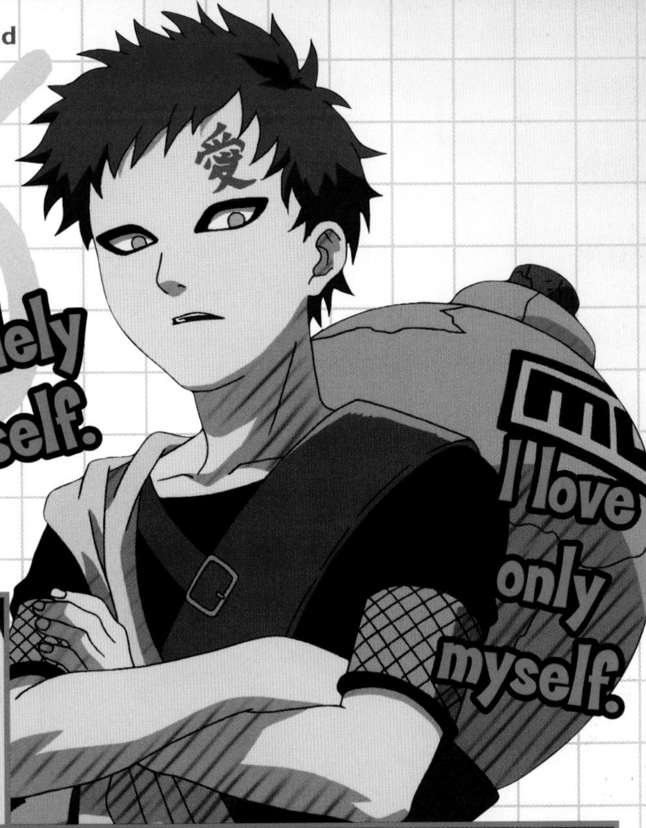
I live solely for myself.
I love only myself.

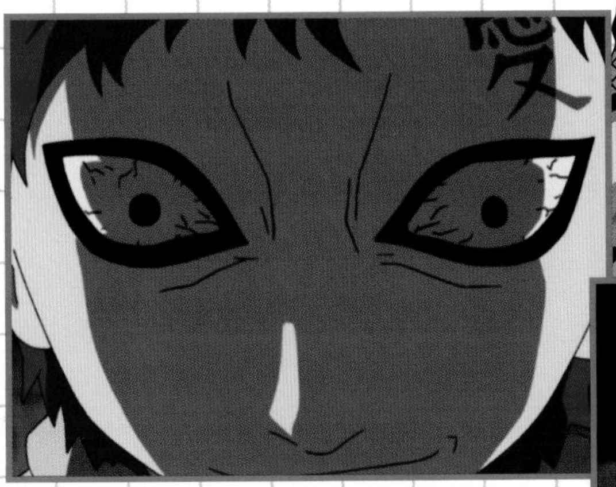

⬆ Right before the match against Sasuke he was unusually excited. What is the cause of his instability?

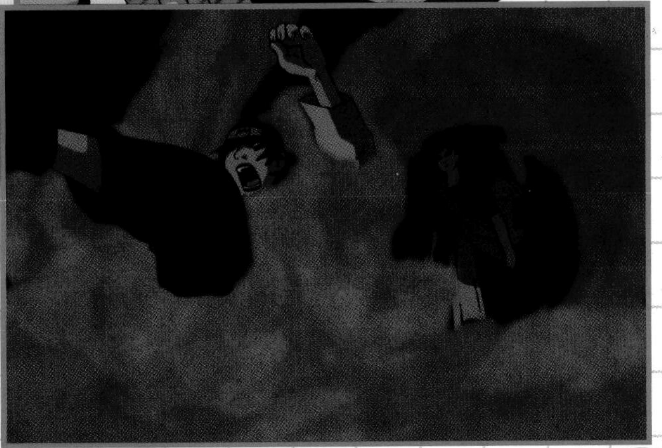

➡ Ice cold, even in battle against lower level opponents that have absolutely no ability to counter. Gaara pulls no punches.

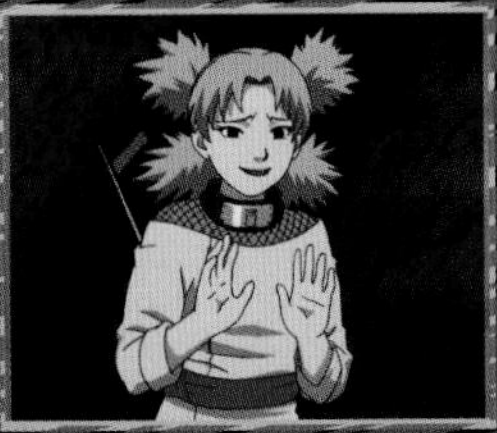

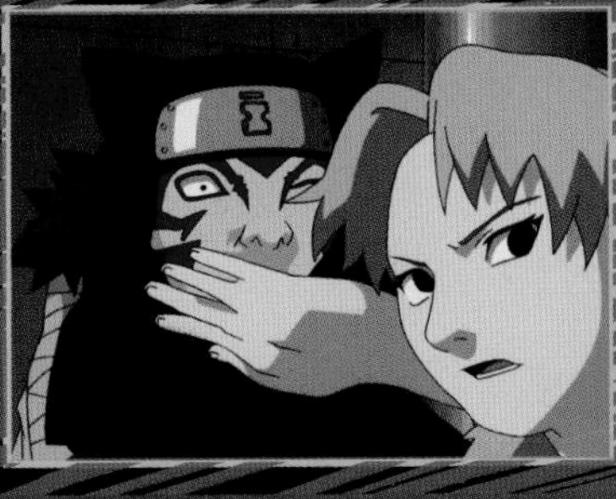

➡⬇ They sense Gaara's feelings so they can immediately avoid any life-threatening situations.

Even siblings have no safety guarantees!

Temari and Kankuro, participating in the exam along with Gaara, are real siblings, but they share no warm feelings. The other two are always sensitive to Gaara's moods because his immense power is so far out of their league.

Overall Results

He has ability far exceeding the genin level, is cruel in spirit, and possesses unknown jutsu. There are reports that he sneaked into Lee's hospital room to attack him. We cannot rule out the possibility of there being some kind of plot behind Gaara coming to the village. We must maintain a close watch on him, as well as on his siblings.

Secret Shinobi Picture Album

Part Seven

The Hidden Leaf Village Hospital

Injuries come with the territory for shinobi, but here comes one who never needs a doctor—Guy! He will show us around while he visits his beloved student!

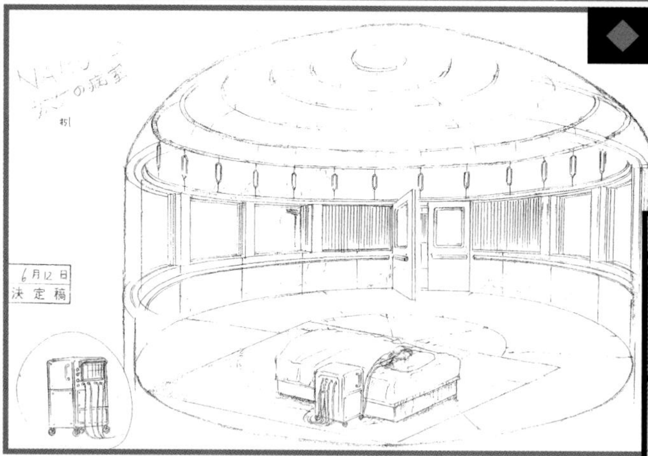

6月12日
決定稿

◆ The Intensive Care Unit

The room used by Sasuke right after the prelims. It has the most advanced medical treatment that the village has to offer!

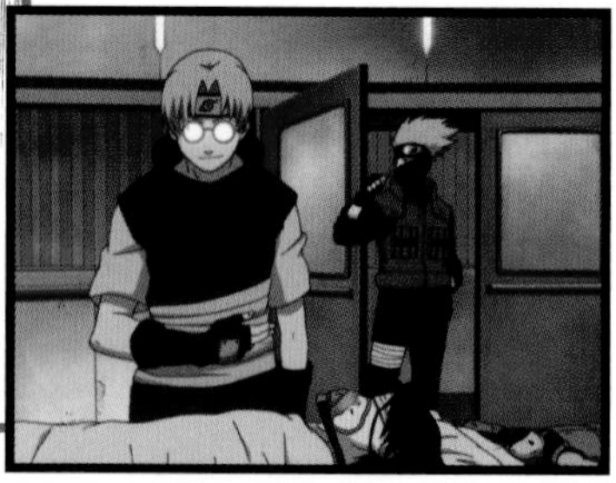

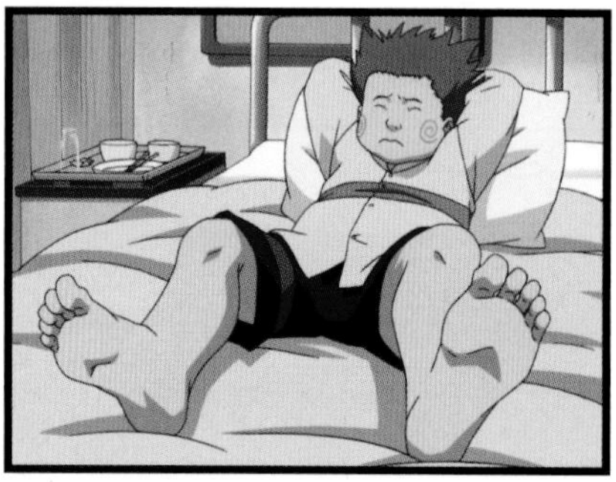

⬆ A standard room, like the one Choji was in when he was hospitalized with a stomachache. Hey! Doing sit-ups?! Good for you!

◆ Patient room (private)

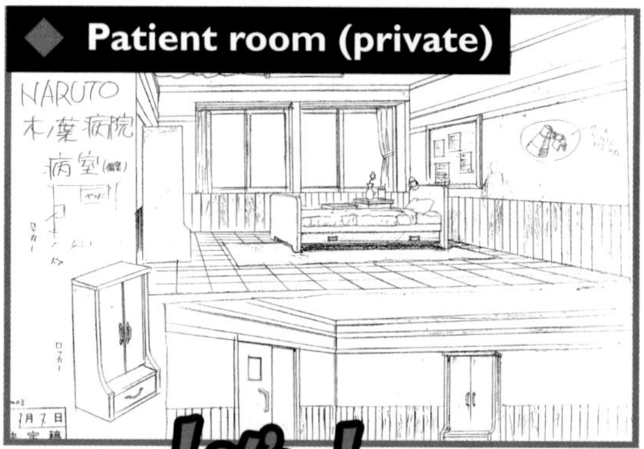

NARUTO

◆ Reception

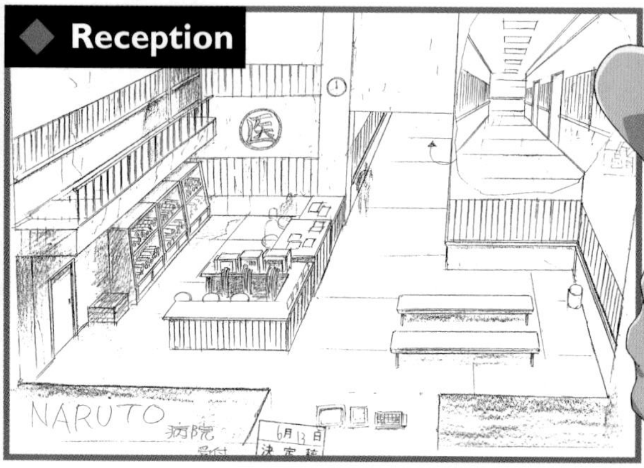

NARUTO
6月13日

➡ A modern reception area with a gorgeous chandelier. Hi, Naruto. Are you here to visit my little Lee?

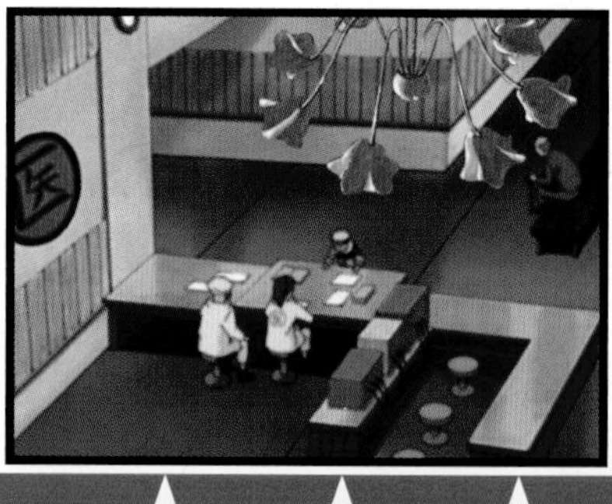

Let's drop in on a sneak visit to Lee!

◆ Tour Guide: Guy

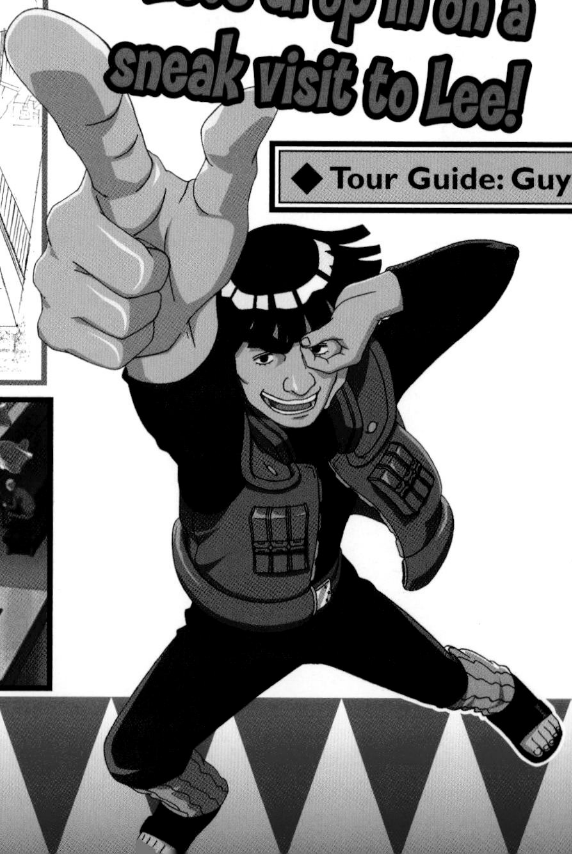

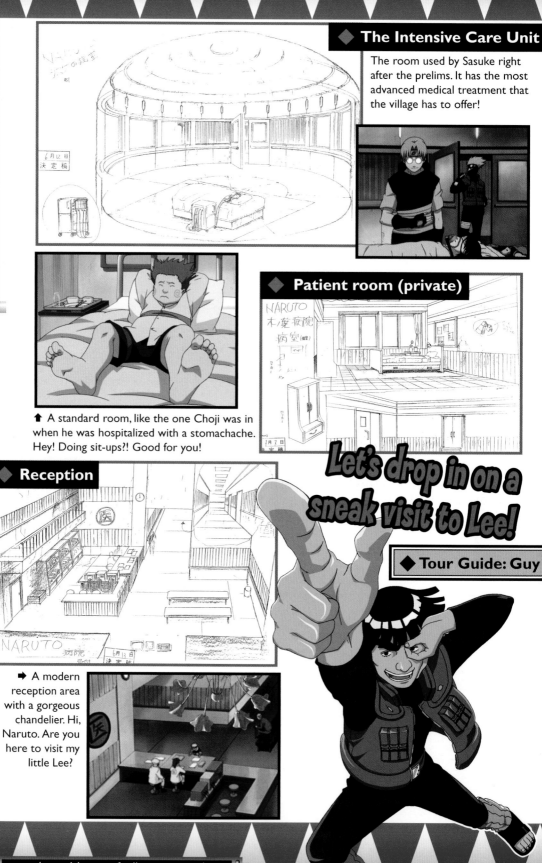

An exterior view of Hidden Leaf Village Hospital

This is the hospital's main entrance! It has a dignified look and many shinobi have visited it throughout its long and distinguished history!

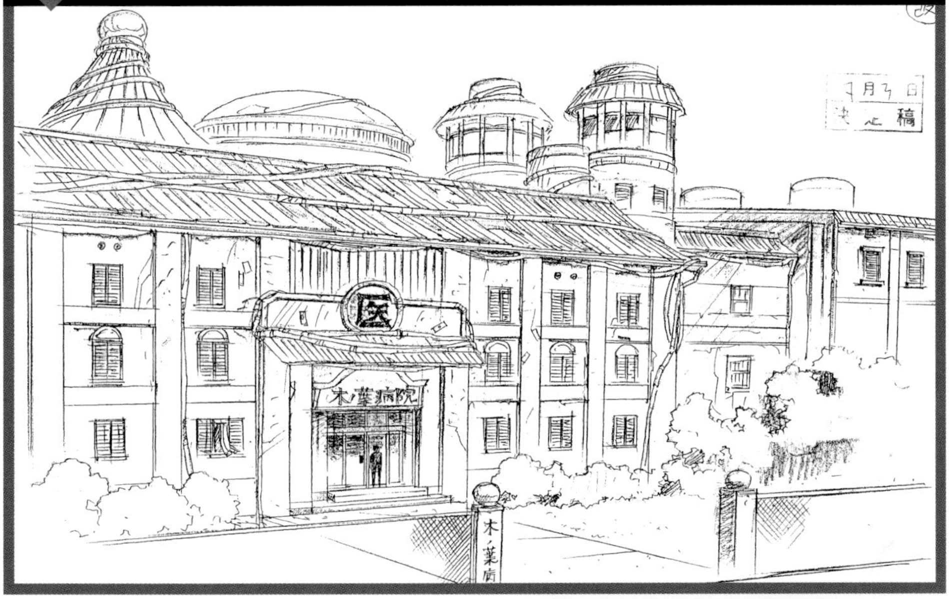

Hospital wards

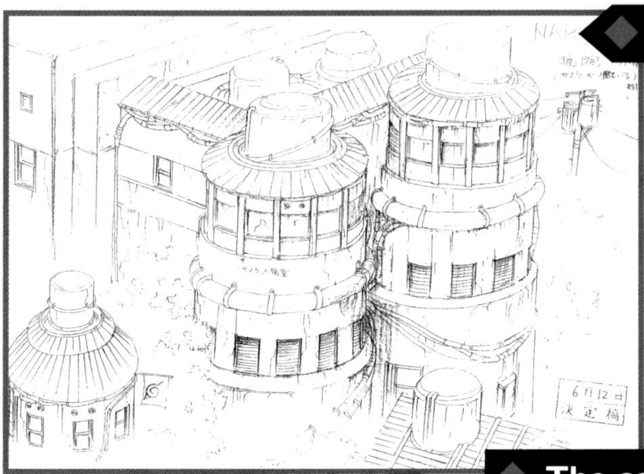

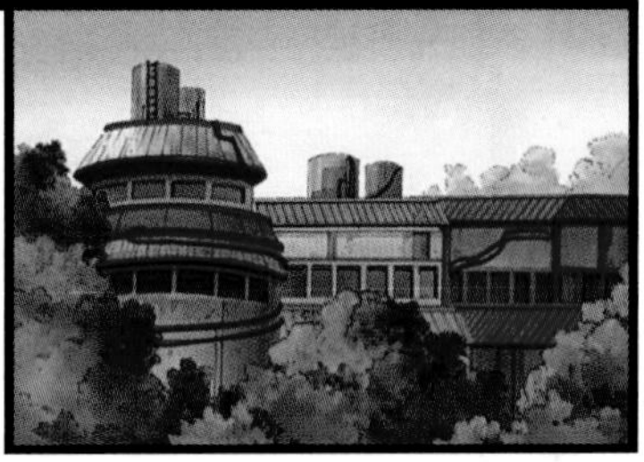

⬆ The intensive care ward! Sasuke is hospitalized on the top floor.

The courtyard

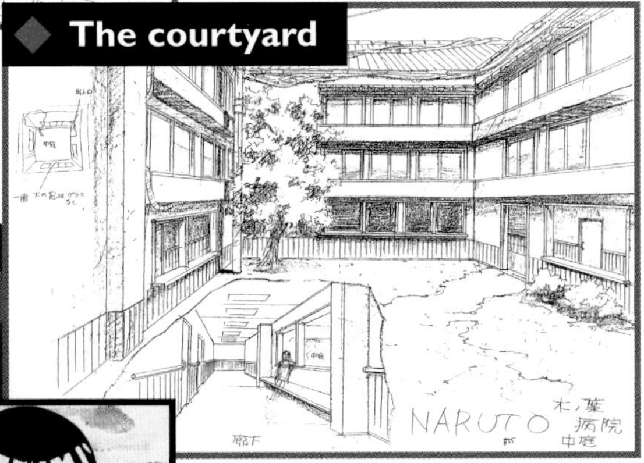

⬆ The courtyard is filled with greenery. Lee trained so hard here…sob! Oooh!

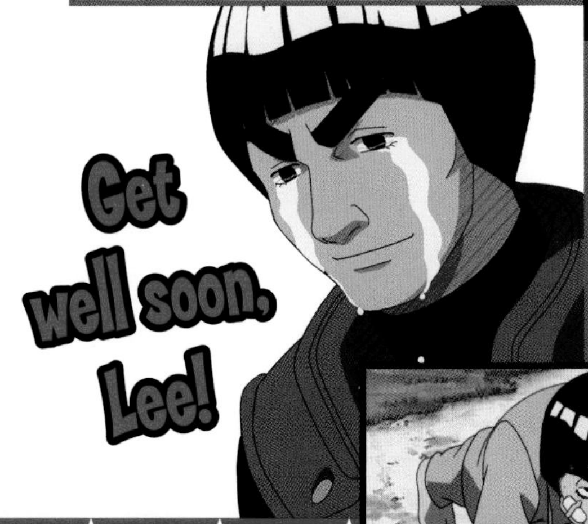
Get well soon, Lee!

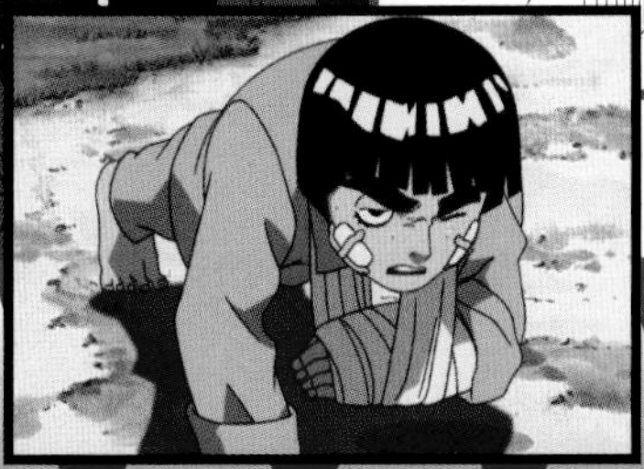

Secret Shinobi Picture Album

Part Eight

The Final Round Arena

The arena for the final round of the third Chunin Exam. Many famous battles have taken place here. The prominent proctor Genma is in charge!

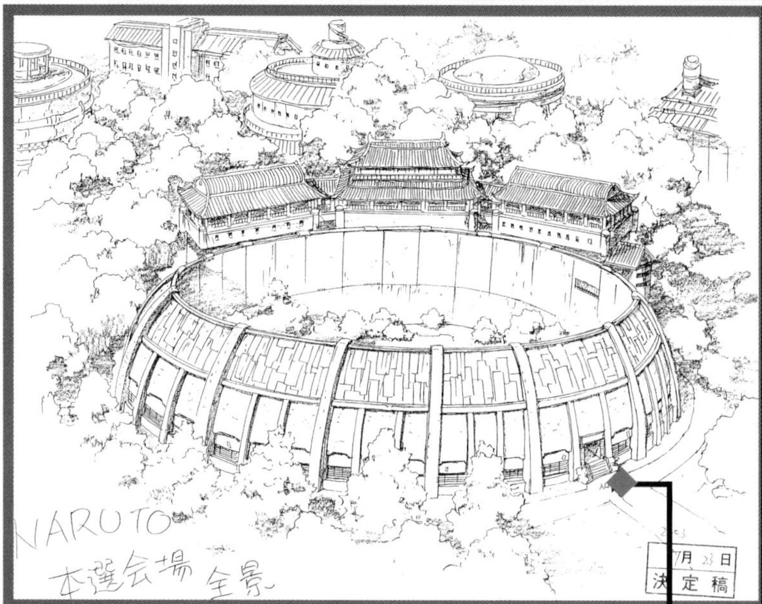
NARUTO
本選会場 全景
2003
7月23日
決定稿

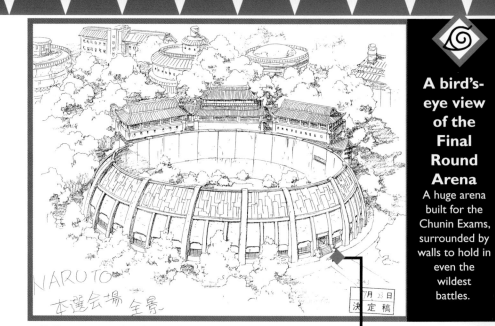

A bird's-eye view of the Final Round Arena

A huge arena built for the Chunin Exams, surrounded by walls to hold in even the wildest battles.

⬇ Two security shinobi stand guard. The roof entrance allows observation of visitors from the upper level.

◆ Arena Entrance

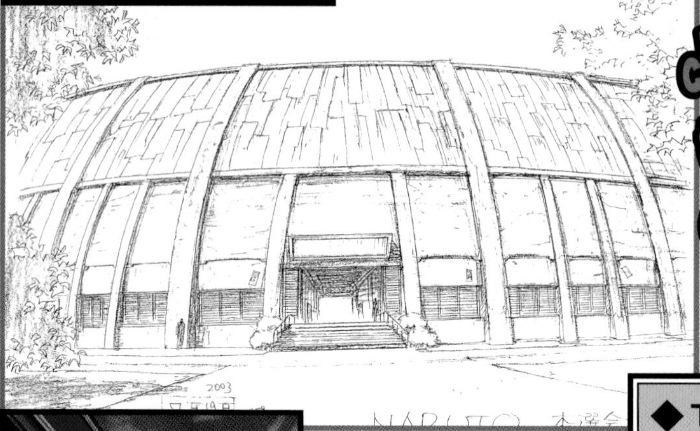

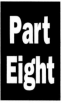

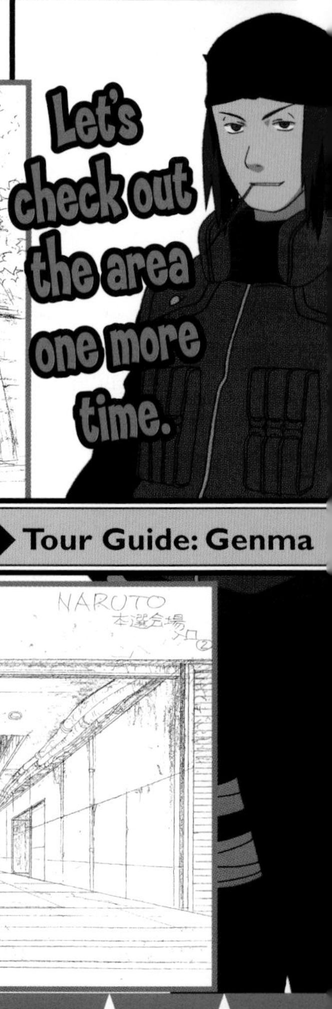
Let's check out the area one more time.

◆ Tour Guide: Genma

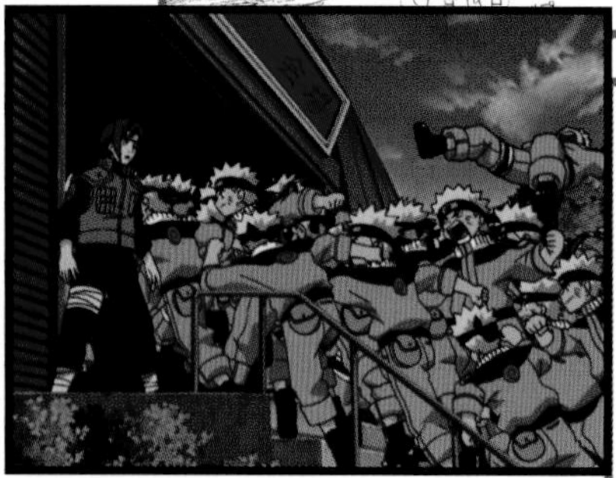

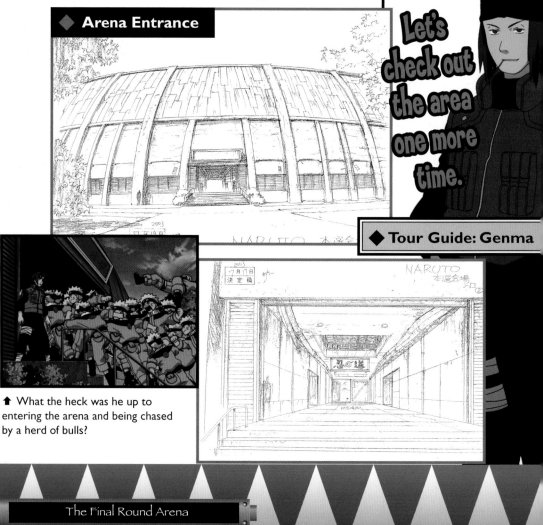

⬆ What the heck was he up to entering the arena and being chased by a herd of bulls?

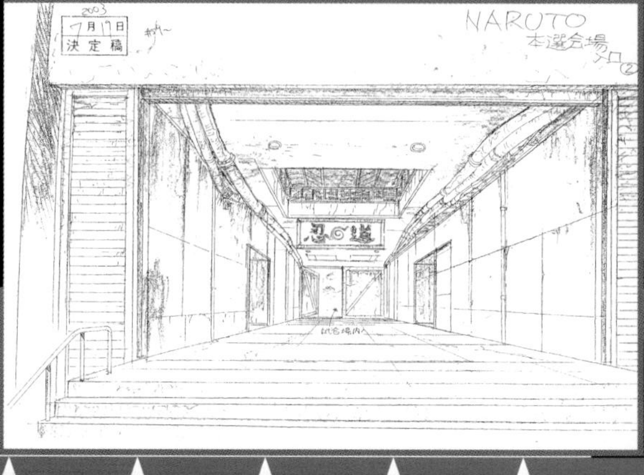
2003
7月17日
決定稿
NARUTO
本選会場

The VIP seats

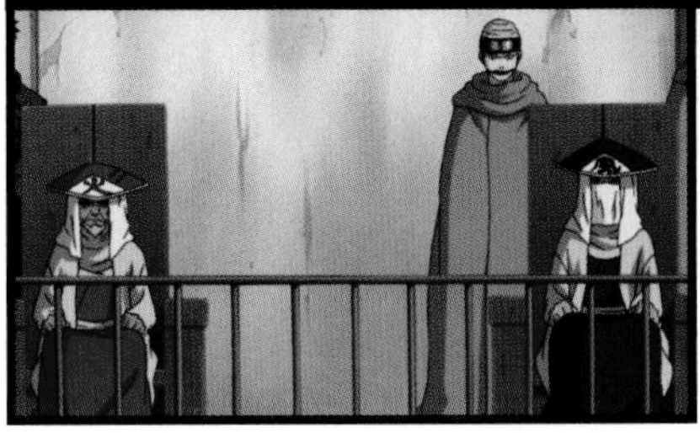

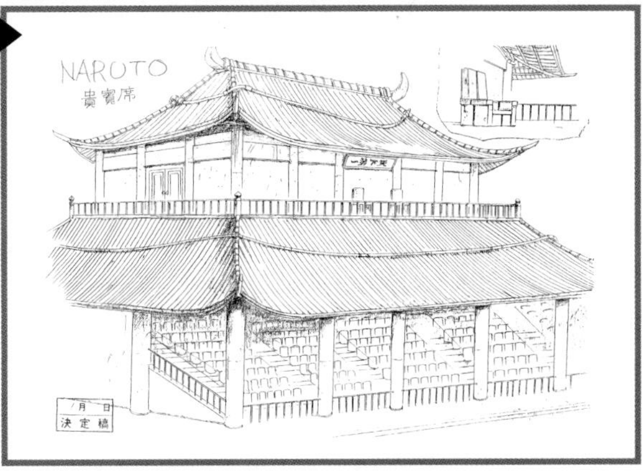
NARUTO
貴賓席
決定稿

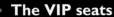

⬆ These are seats for honored guests, where the leaders of all the nations, including our Hokage, watch the action. The waiting room for the examinee brats is directly below this area.

Arena Seating

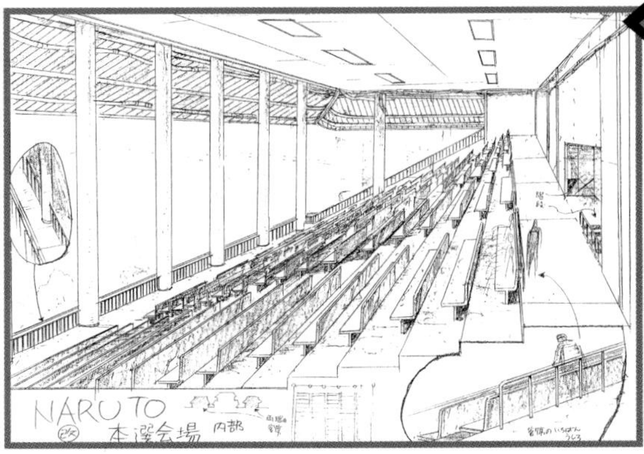
NARUTO
本選会場 内部

⬆ Spectator seating. Seats are aligned on a coliseum-style slope to provide the best possible view of the arena below.

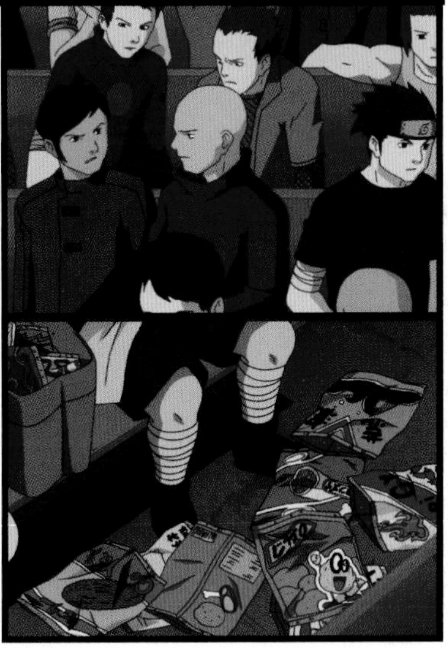

⬅ There's a relaxed mood in the main spectator seating area. Eating and drinking is not prohibited but…isn't that more than enough already?

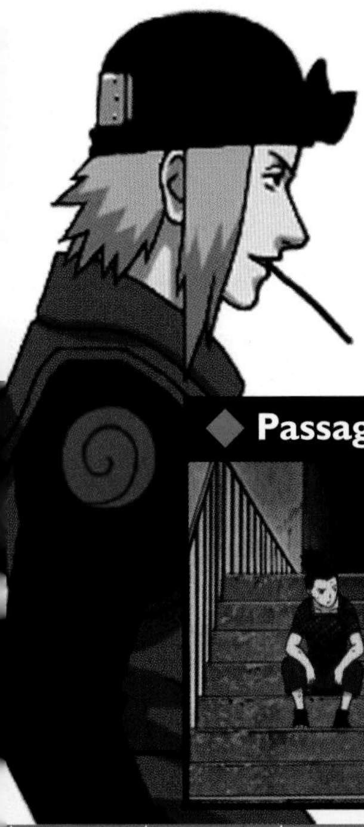

A lot of drama has taken place here.

Passages within the arena

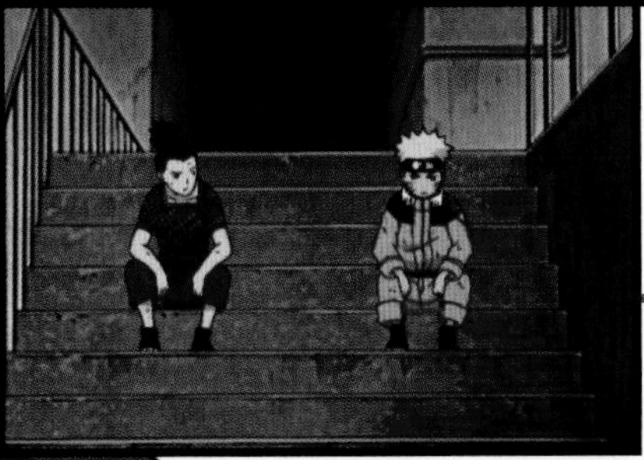

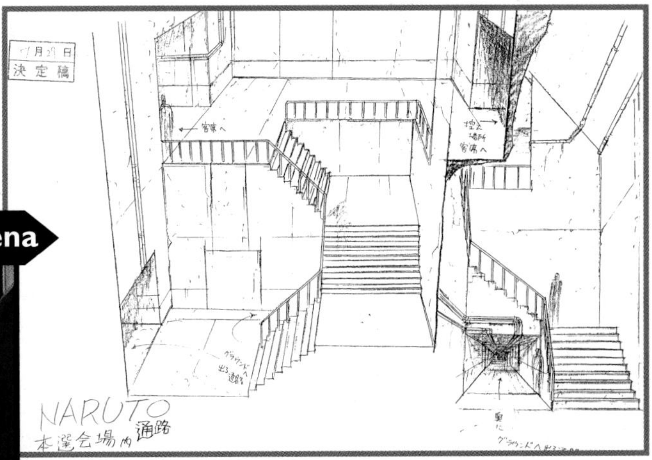
決定稿
NARUTO
本選会場内 通路

⬅⬆ Passages that connect the seats, waiting rooms and the battlefield. You guys get off the steps. Guests have to go through there, you know.

Where's the hidden truth?!

HIDDEN LEAF TRAINING QUIZ

You won't be able to solve these problems unless you really use your head!

Part 3: Find the similarities!

The characters in problems 1 to 4 are lined up based on certain common points! Figure out the common point and choose the appropriate character from the list below to fill in the blank! The problems go from easy to very difficult. Can you solve all four?

Problem 1

?

Problem 2

?

Problem 3

?

Problem 4

?

The answers are on page 280, but don't look before giving it a shot!

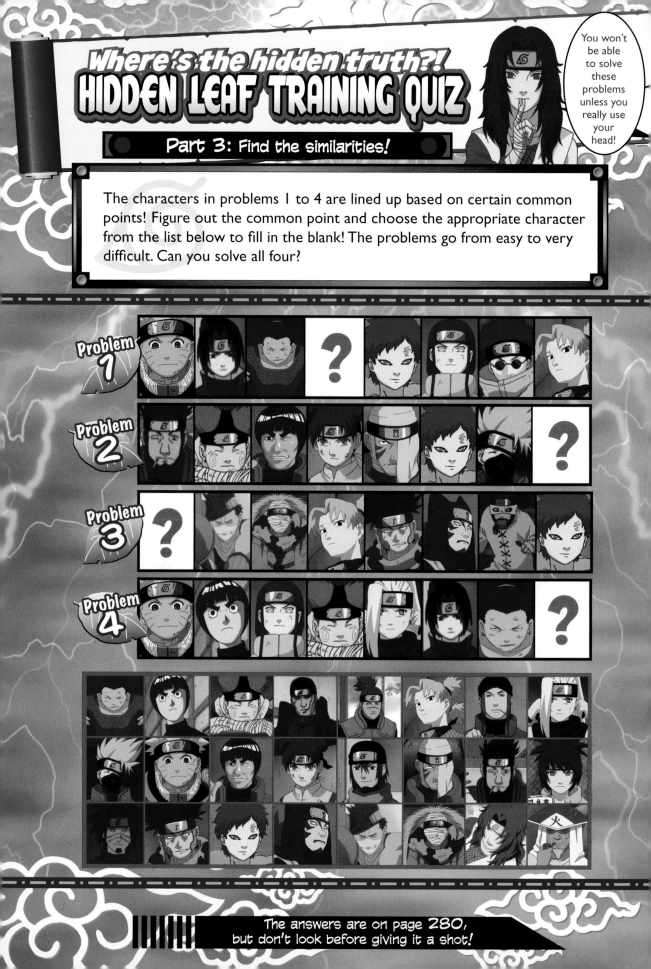

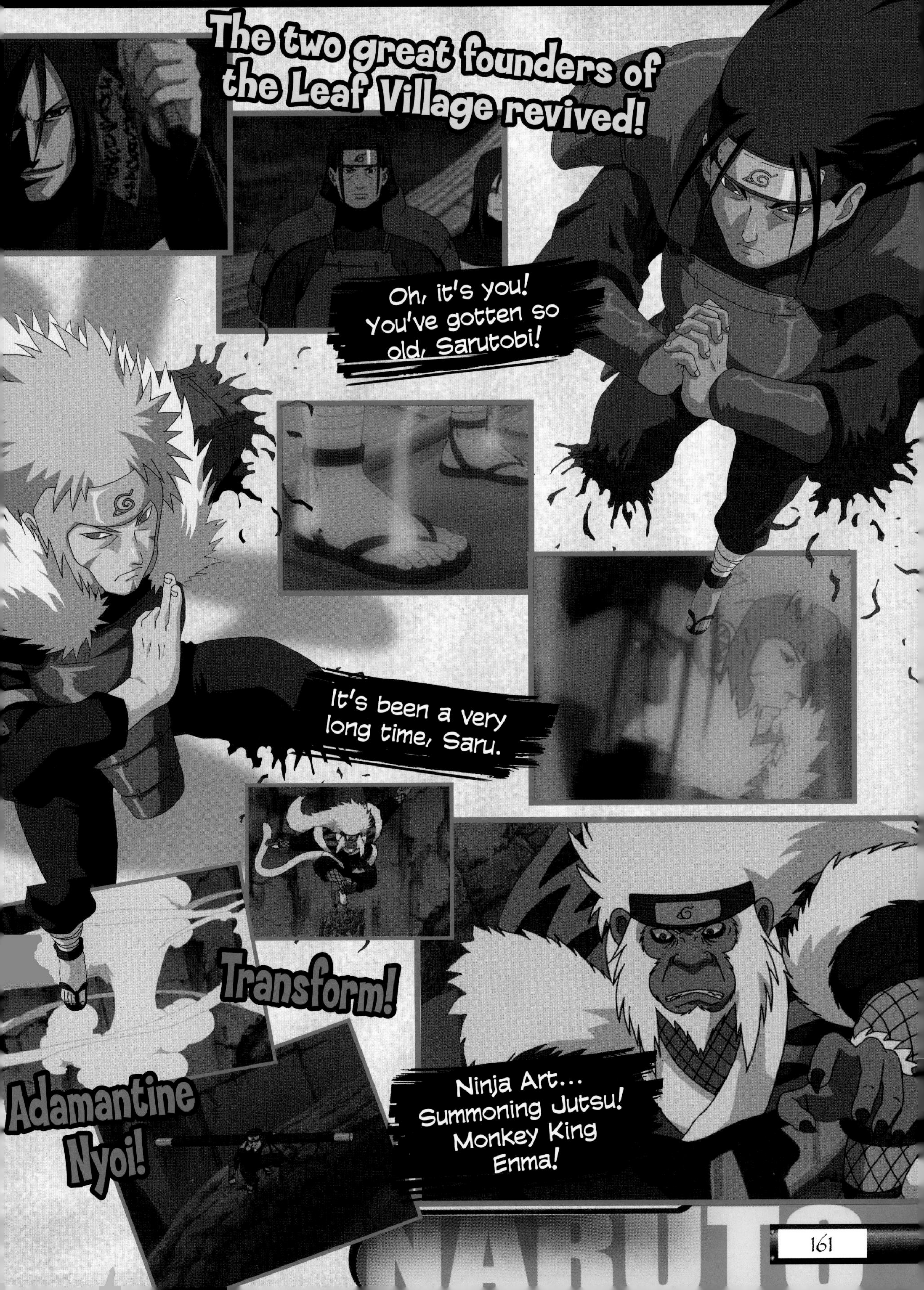
The two great founders of the Leaf Village revived!
Oh, it's you! You've gotten so old, Sarutobi!
It's been a very long time, Saru.
Transform!
Ninja Art... Summoning Jutsu! Monkey King Enma!
Adamantine Nyoi!
NARUTO

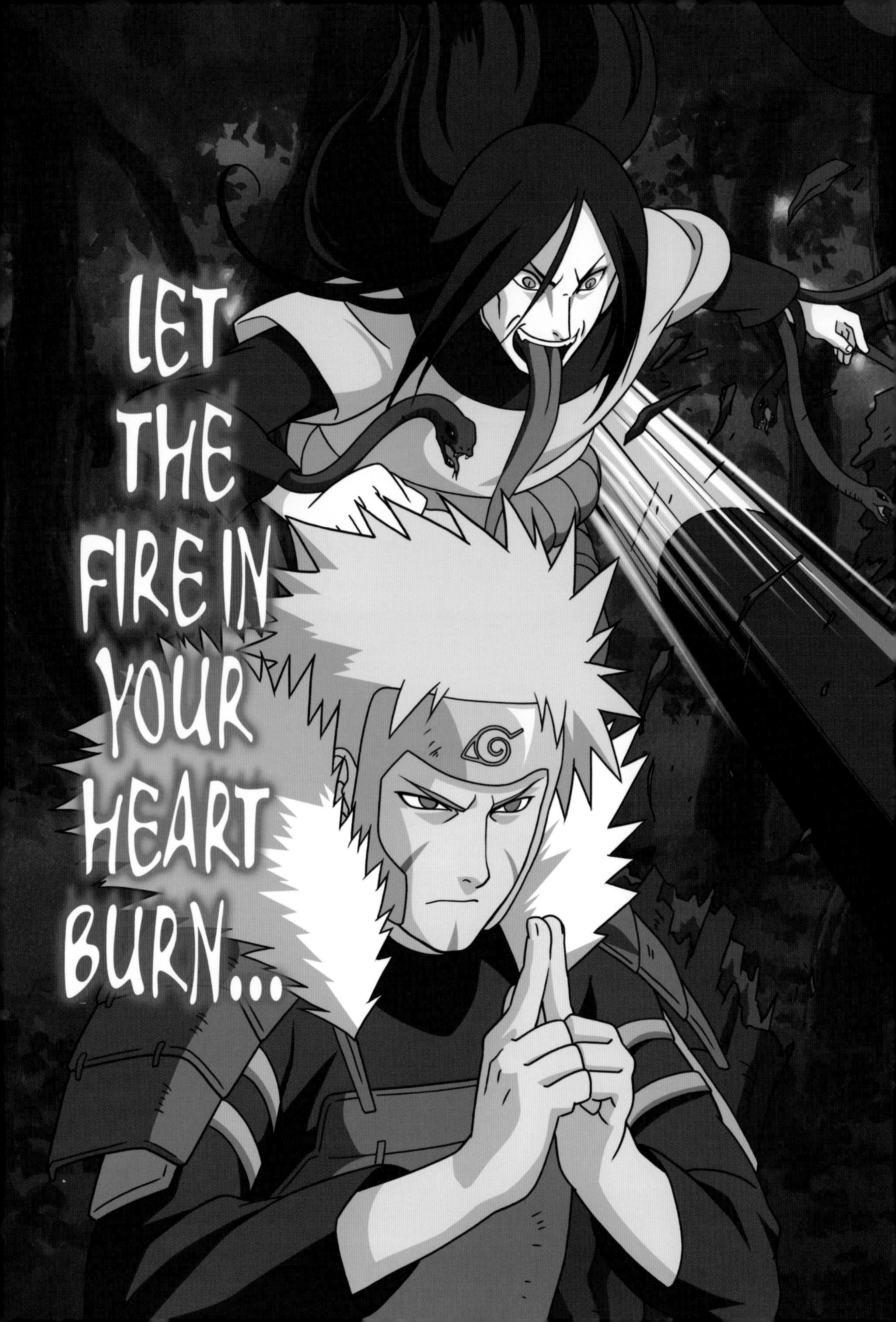
LET THE FIRE IN YOUR HEART BURN...

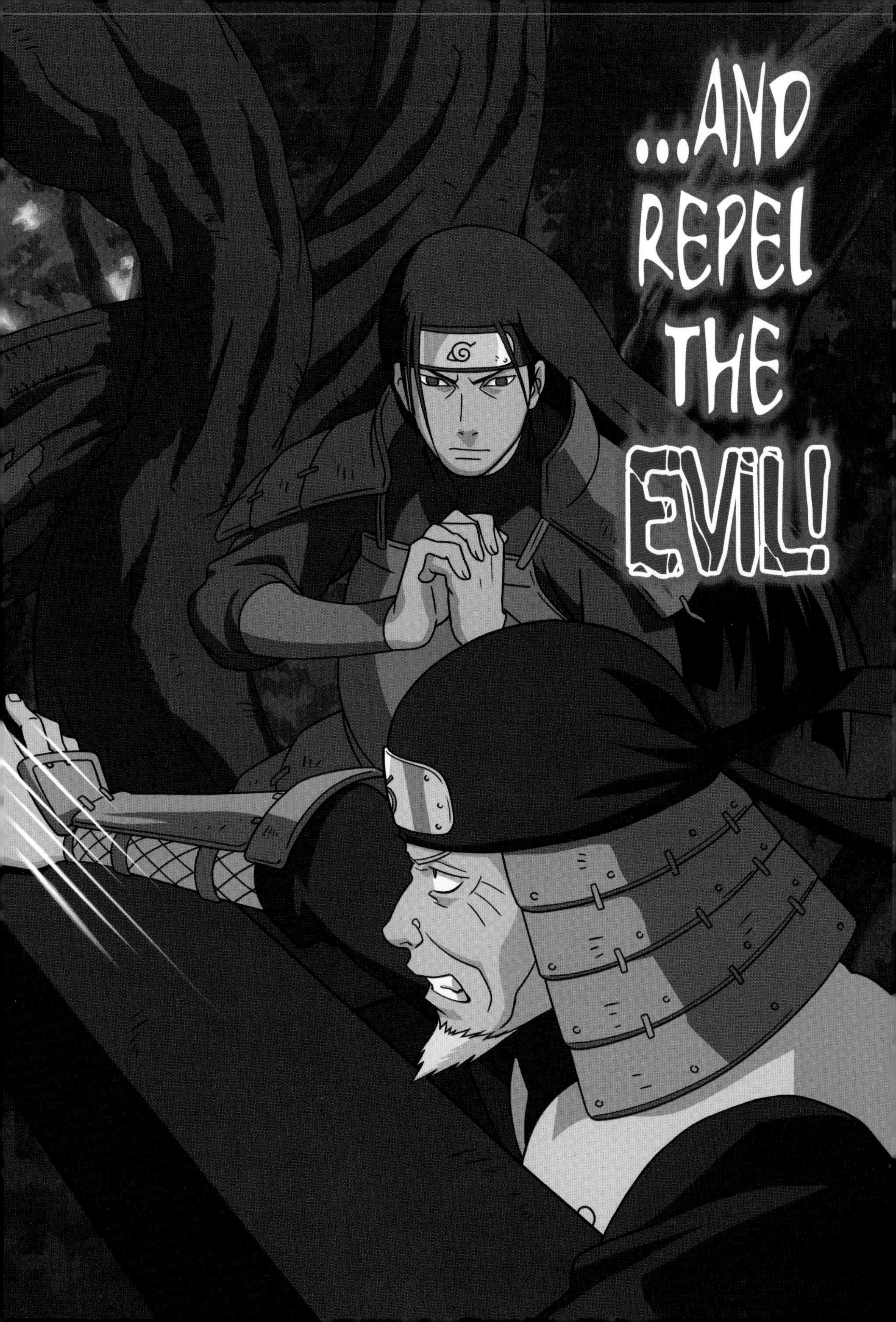
...AND REPEL THE EVIL!

Shino Aburame enters the battle!

Face to face! The Puppet Master vs. The Insect Tamer!

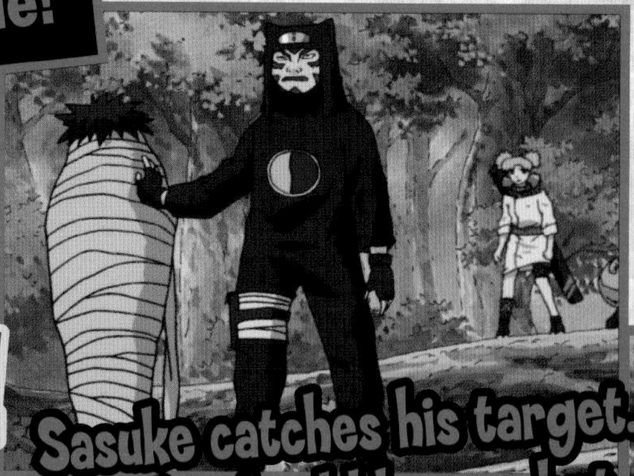

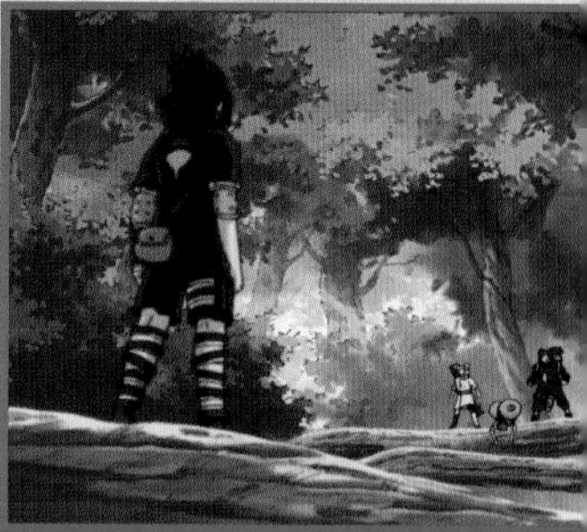

Sasuke catches his target. Then who should he see but...?

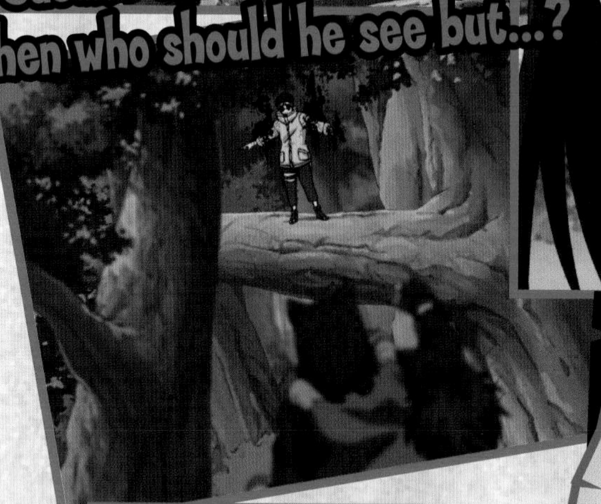

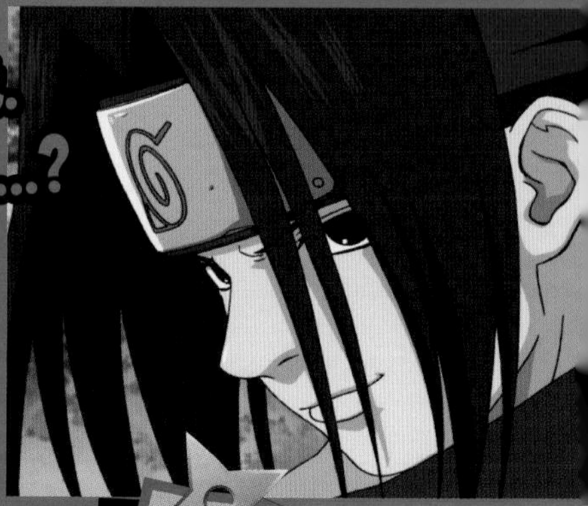

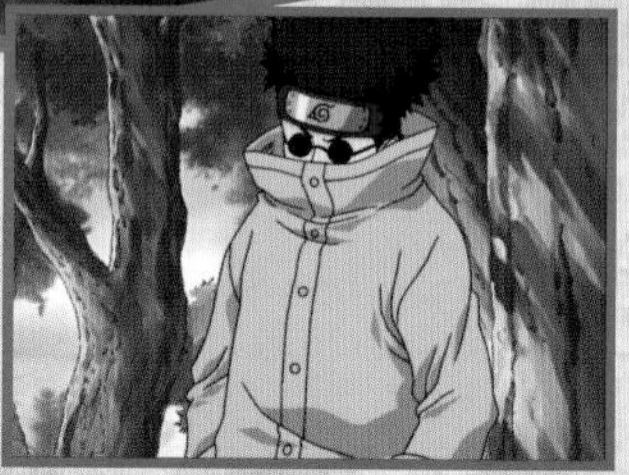

Standing in Sasuke's way is Kankuro! But Shino appears and covers for Sasuke. Where will this deathmatch between the Insect Tamer and the Puppet Master end?!

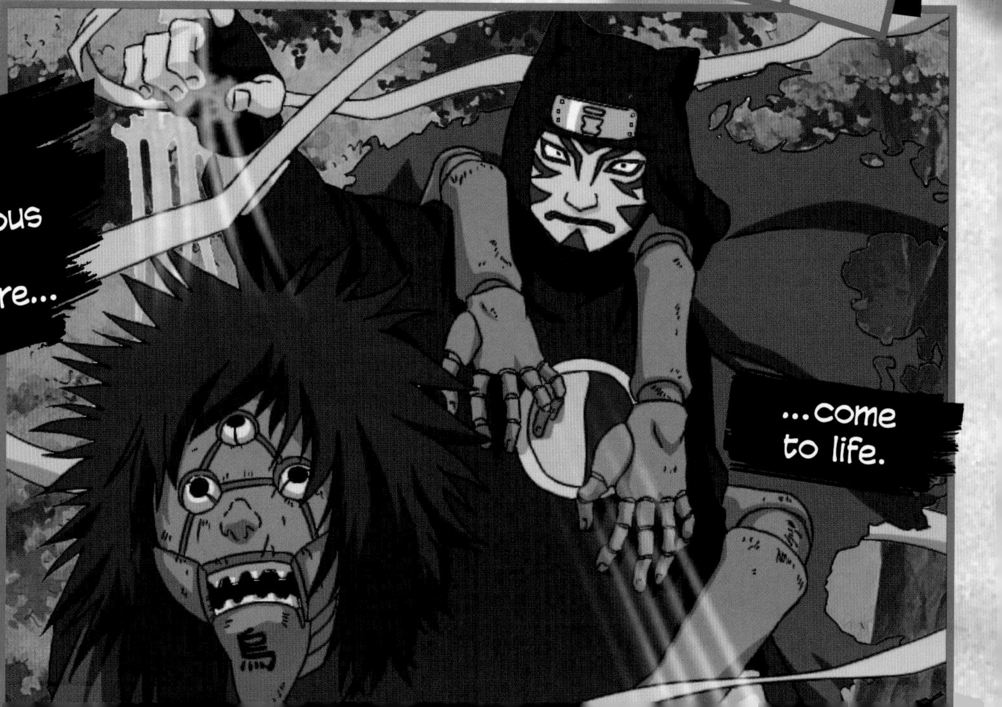

Imagine something more monstrous than your worst nightmare...

...come to life.

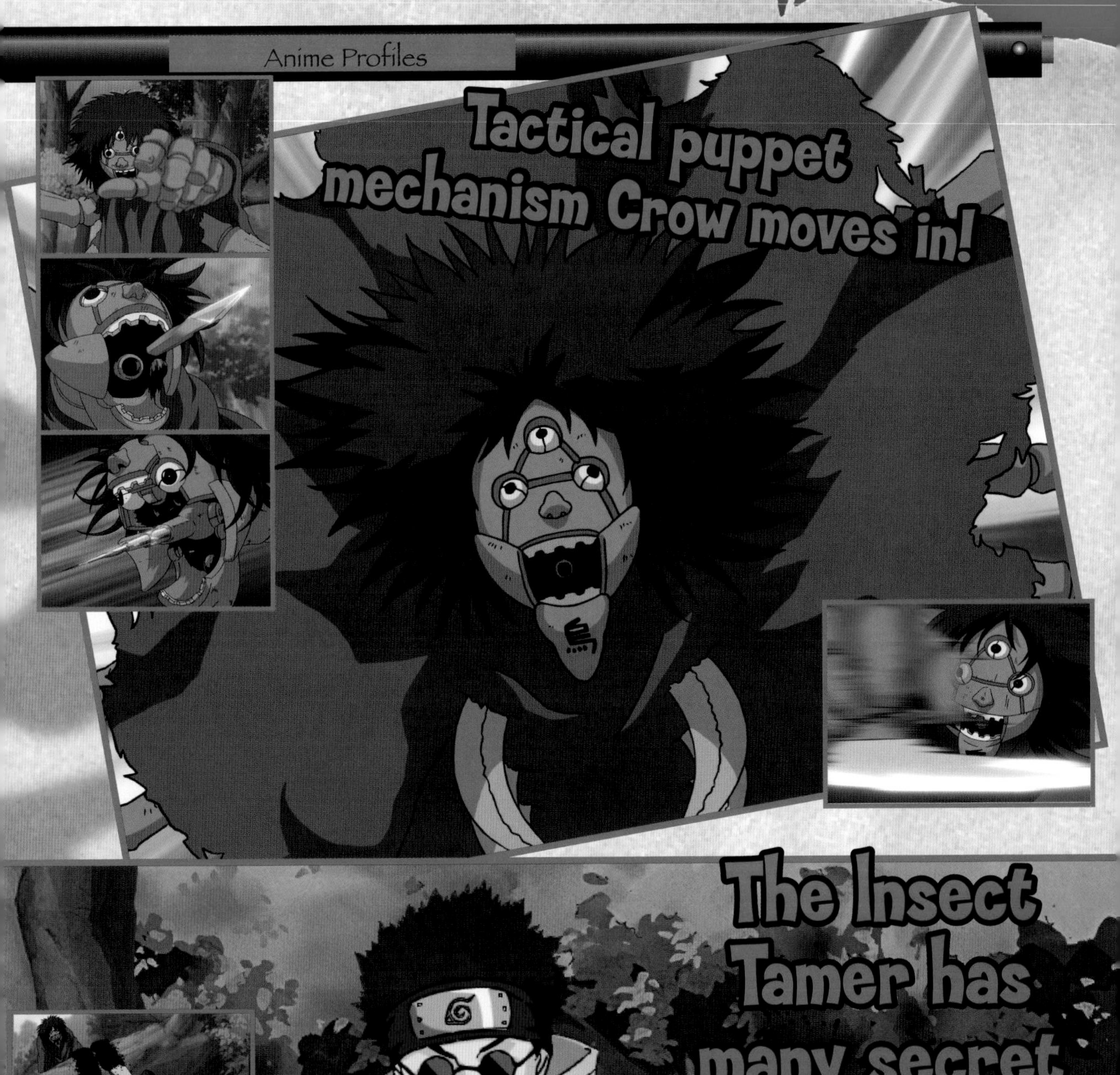
Tactical puppet mechanism Crow moves in!

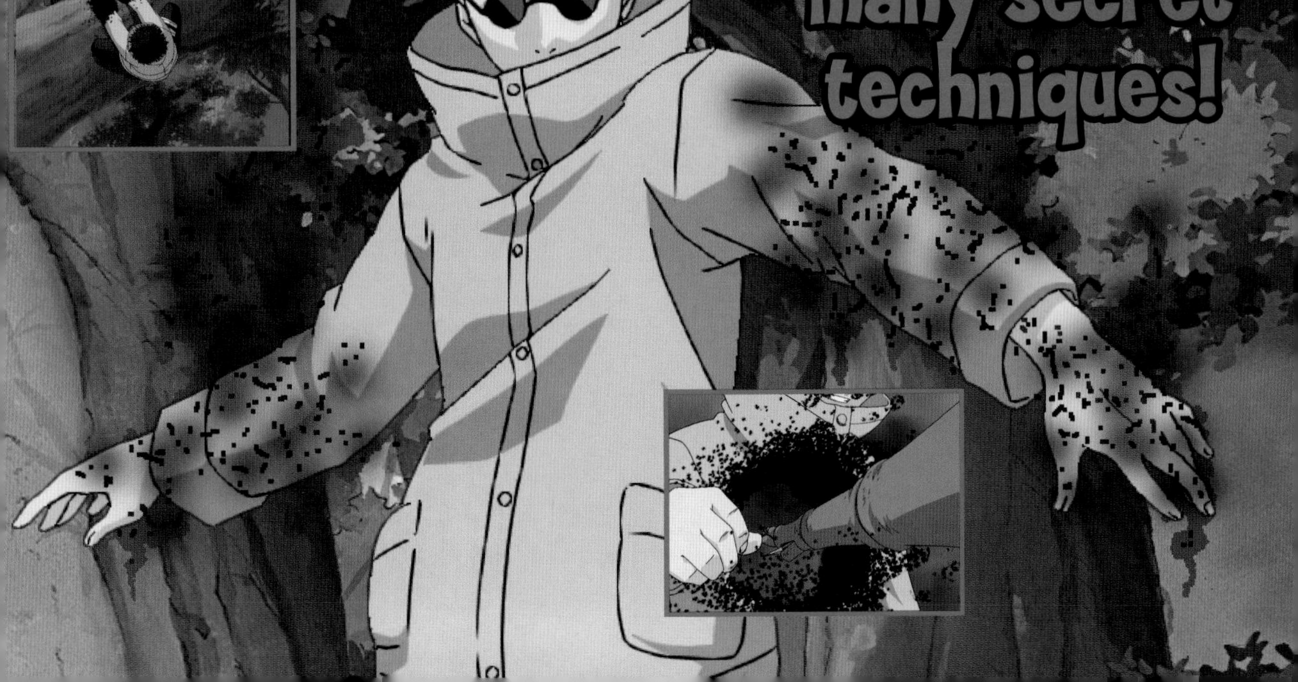
The Insect Tamer has many secret techniques!

Time to atone!

At last, the ultimate Sealing Jutsu is unleashed!

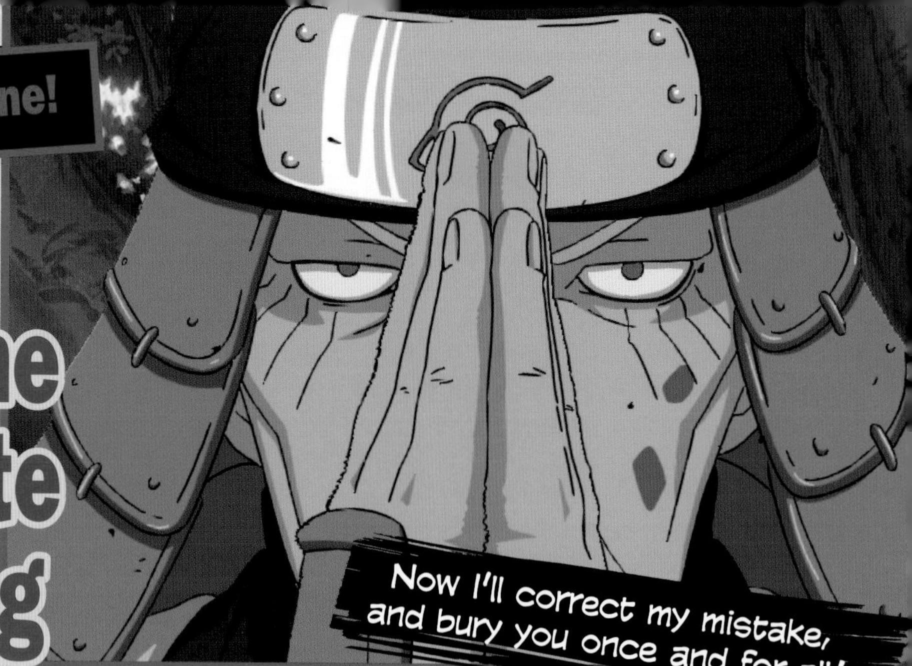
Now I'll correct my mistake, and bury you once and for all!

In the midst of battle, the Third Hokage is haunted by remorse. He unleashes the Sealing Jutsu: Reaper Death Seal to seal the two previous Hokage and thwart Orochimaru's ambition!

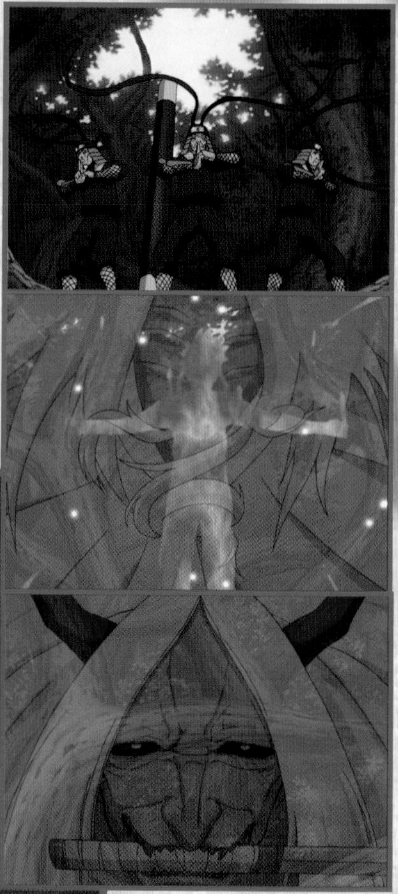

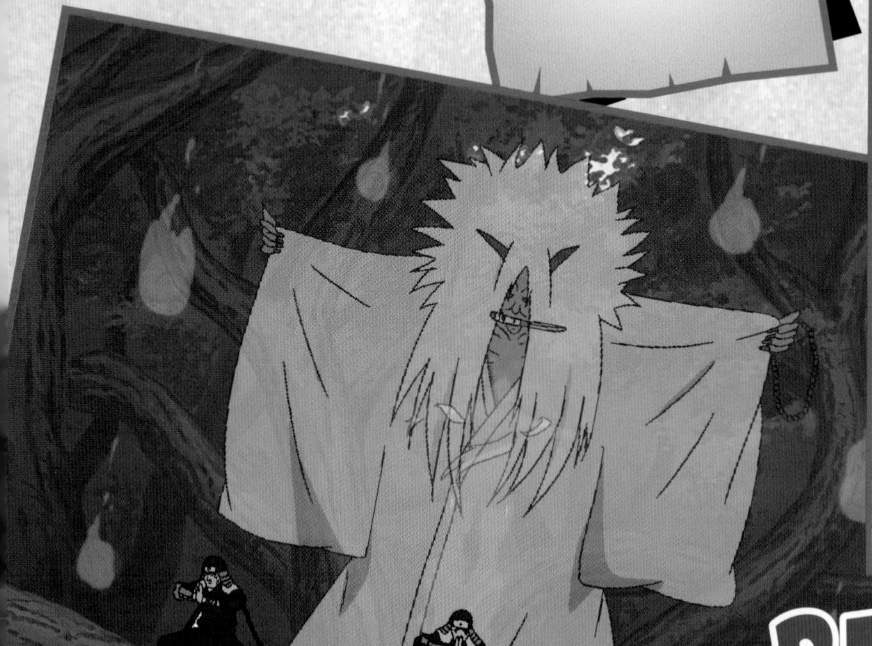

BEHOLD! SEALING JUTSU: REAPER DEATH SEAL!

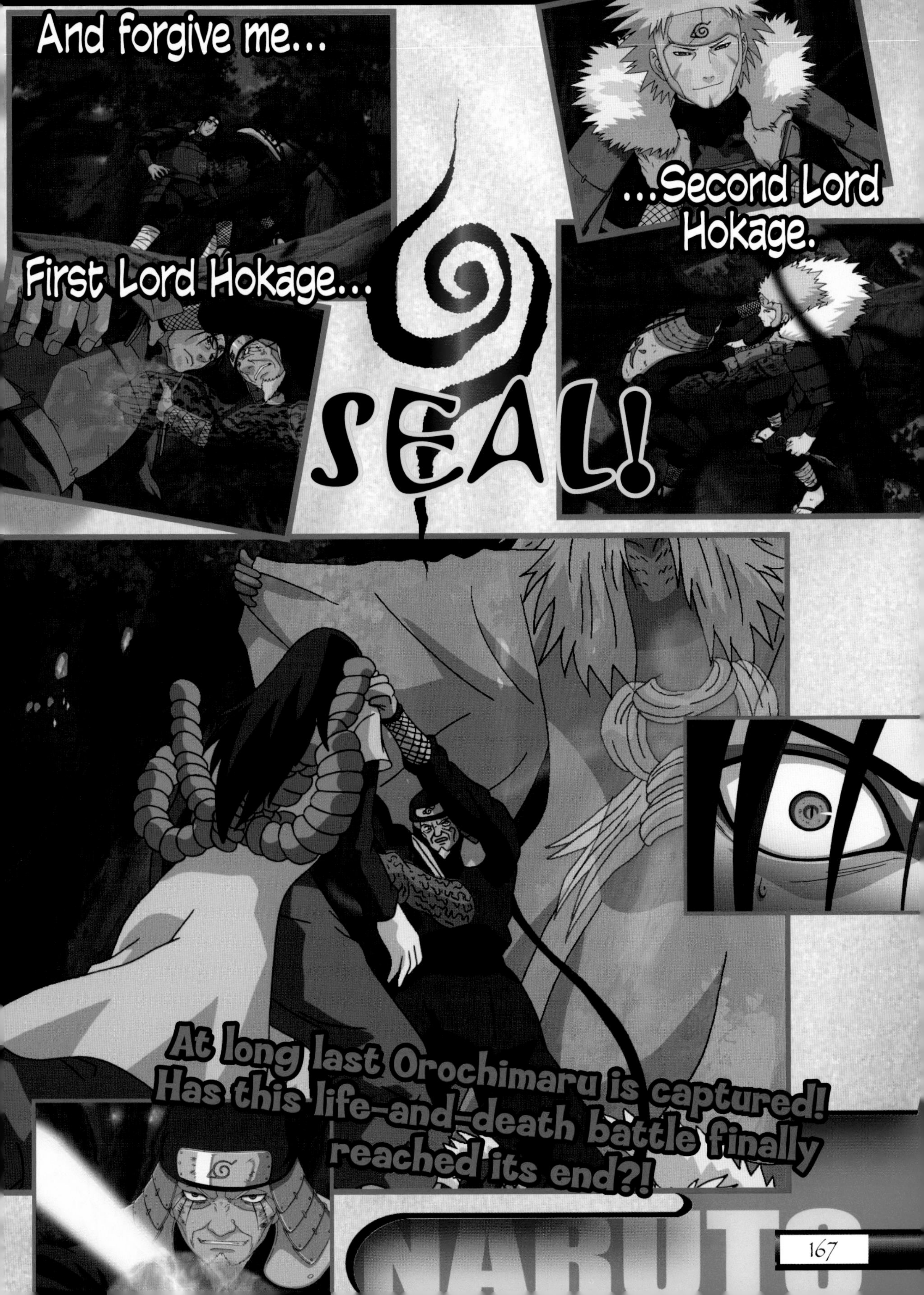
And forgive me...
First Lord Hokage...
...Second Lord Hokage.
SEAL!
At long last Orochimaru is captured! Has this life-and-death battle finally reached its end?!

Insanity!

Gaara's ghastly transformation!

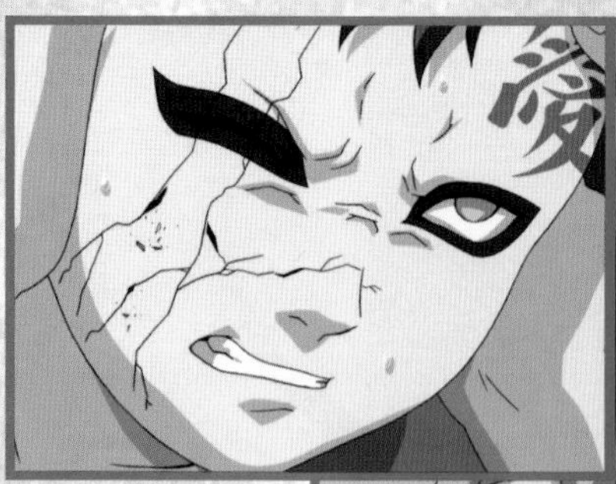

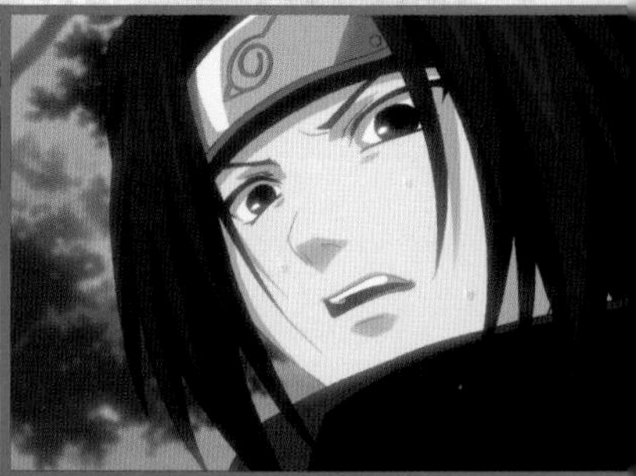

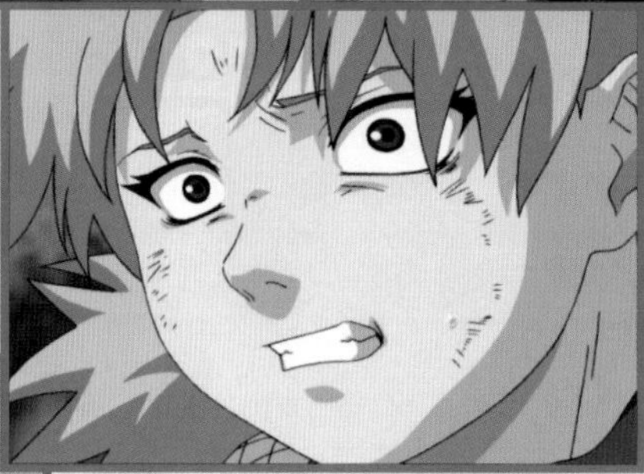

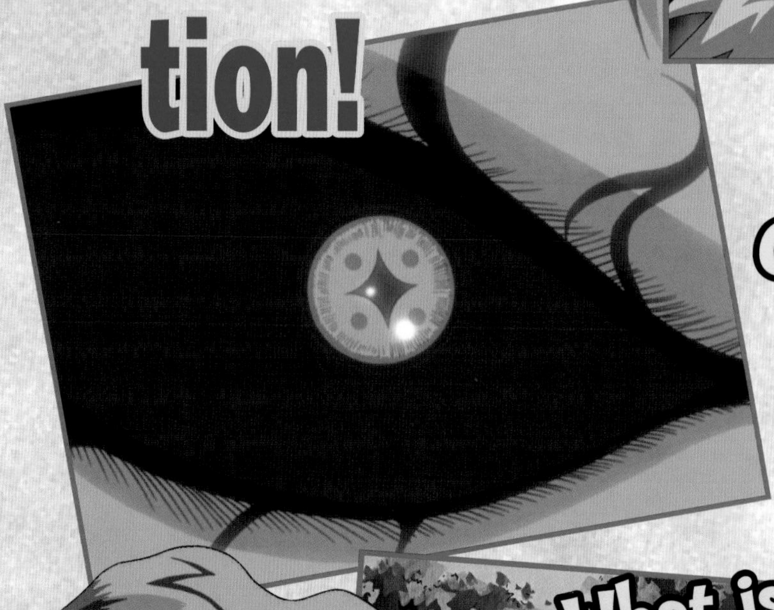

An ice-cold glare!

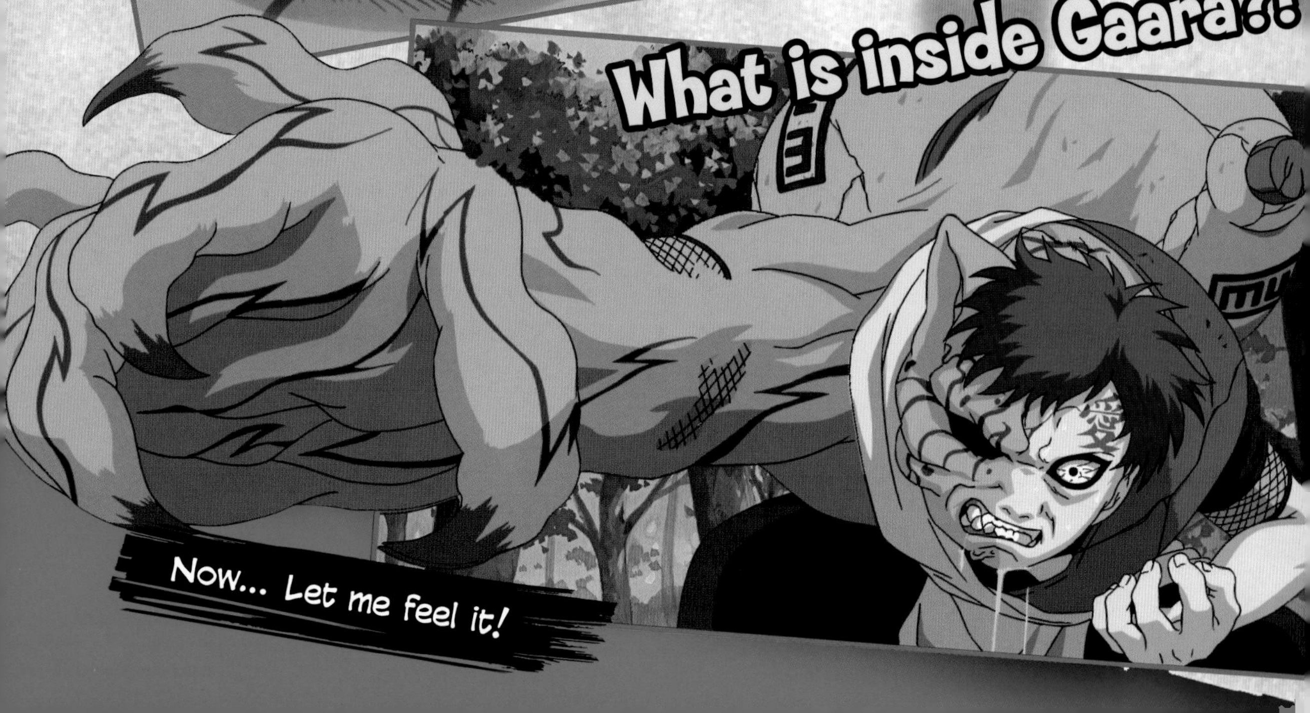

What is inside Gaara?!

Now... Let me feel it!

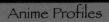

Sasuke catches Gaara and awakens something terrifying inside of him! The mutating Gaara attacks!

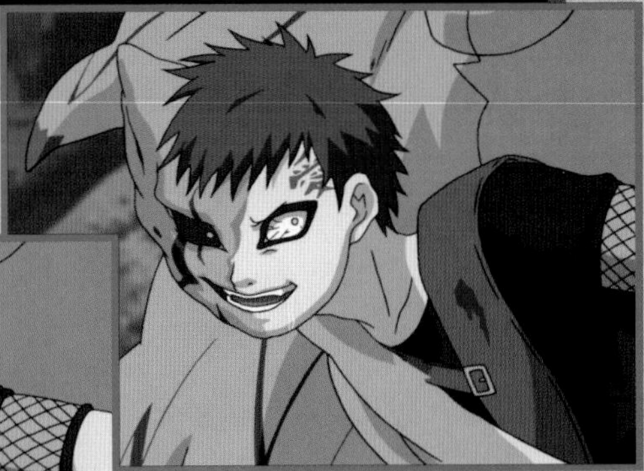

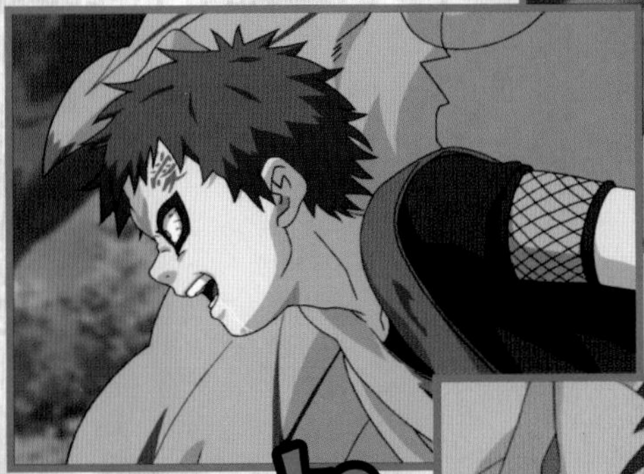

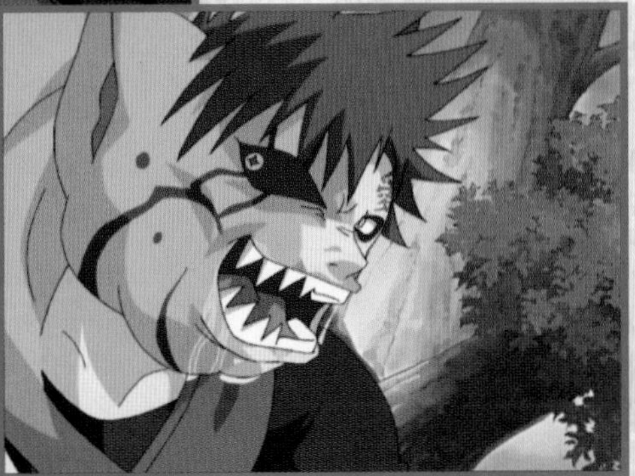

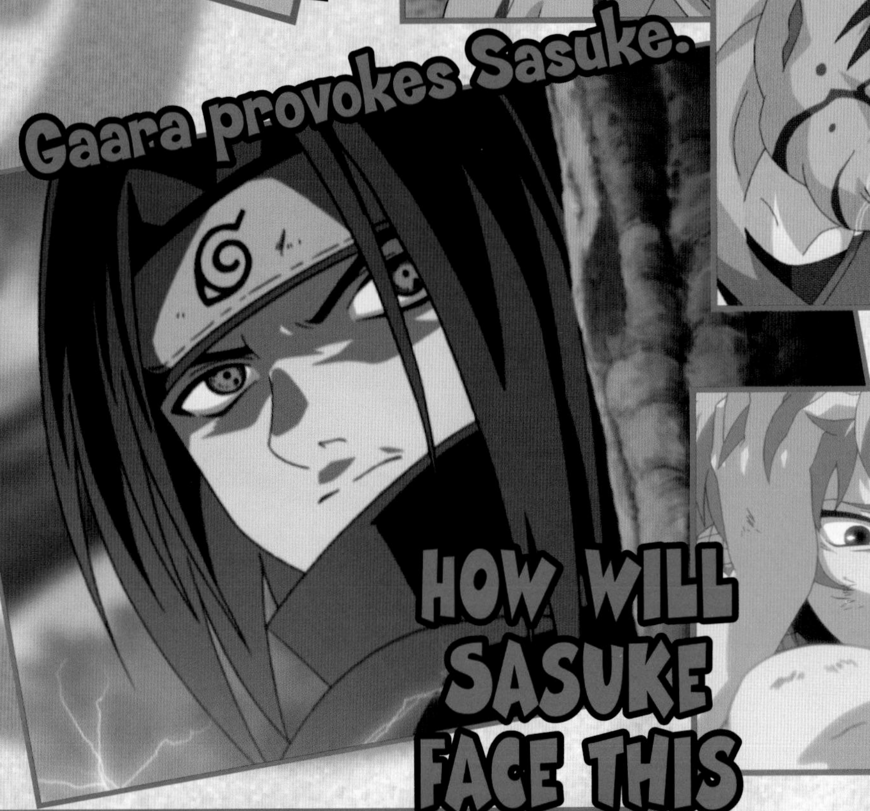
Gaara provokes Sasuke.
HOW WILL SASUKE FACE THIS BATTLE?

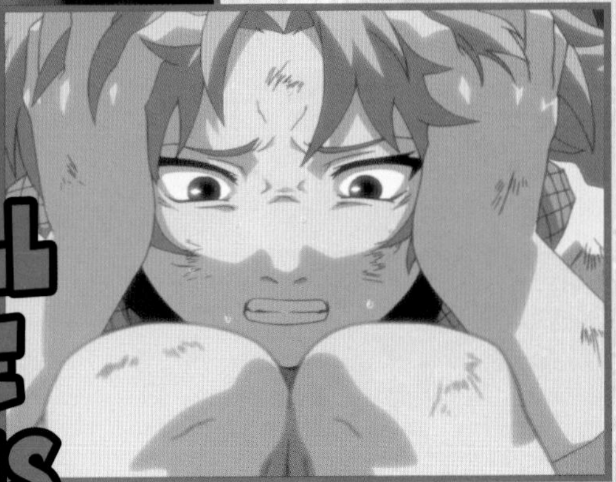

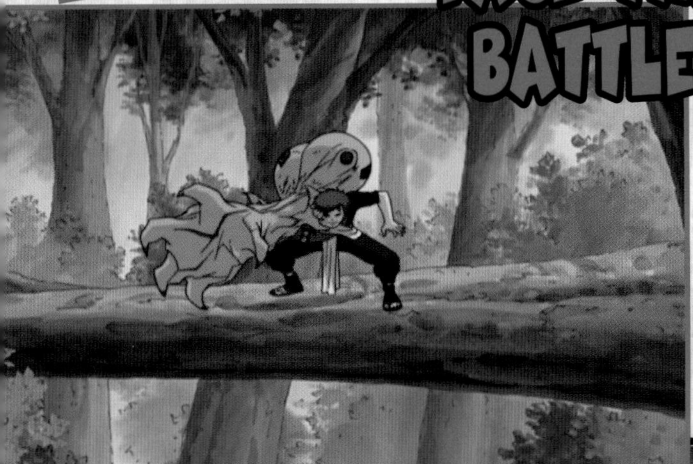

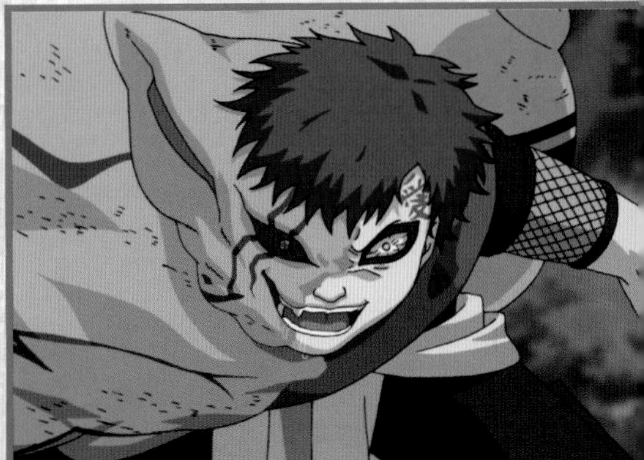

A flash of light slices the sand!

Once again the chirping of Chidori rings out.

"Prove that your existence is stronger than mine! You will never know unless you fight me! You will never feel it!" At Gaara's invitation, Sasuke gathers his strength and once again unleashes Chidori, staking his life on it.

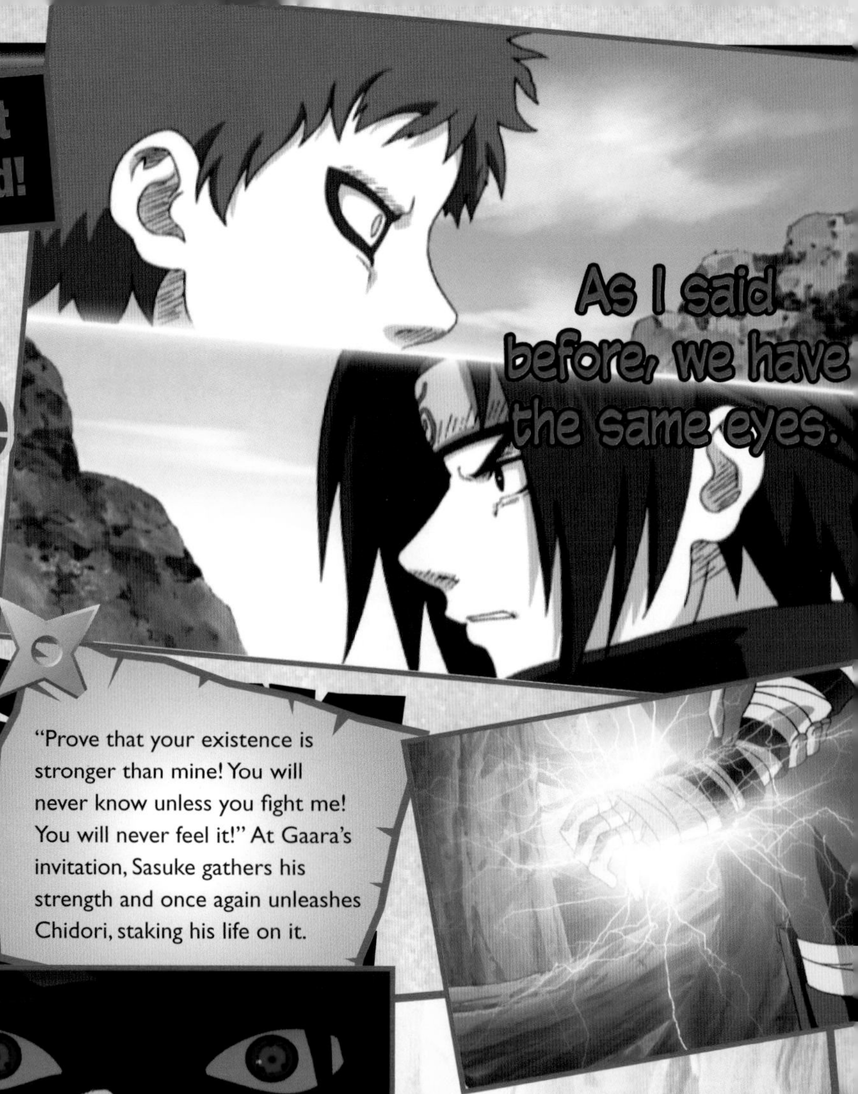
As I said before, we have the same eyes.

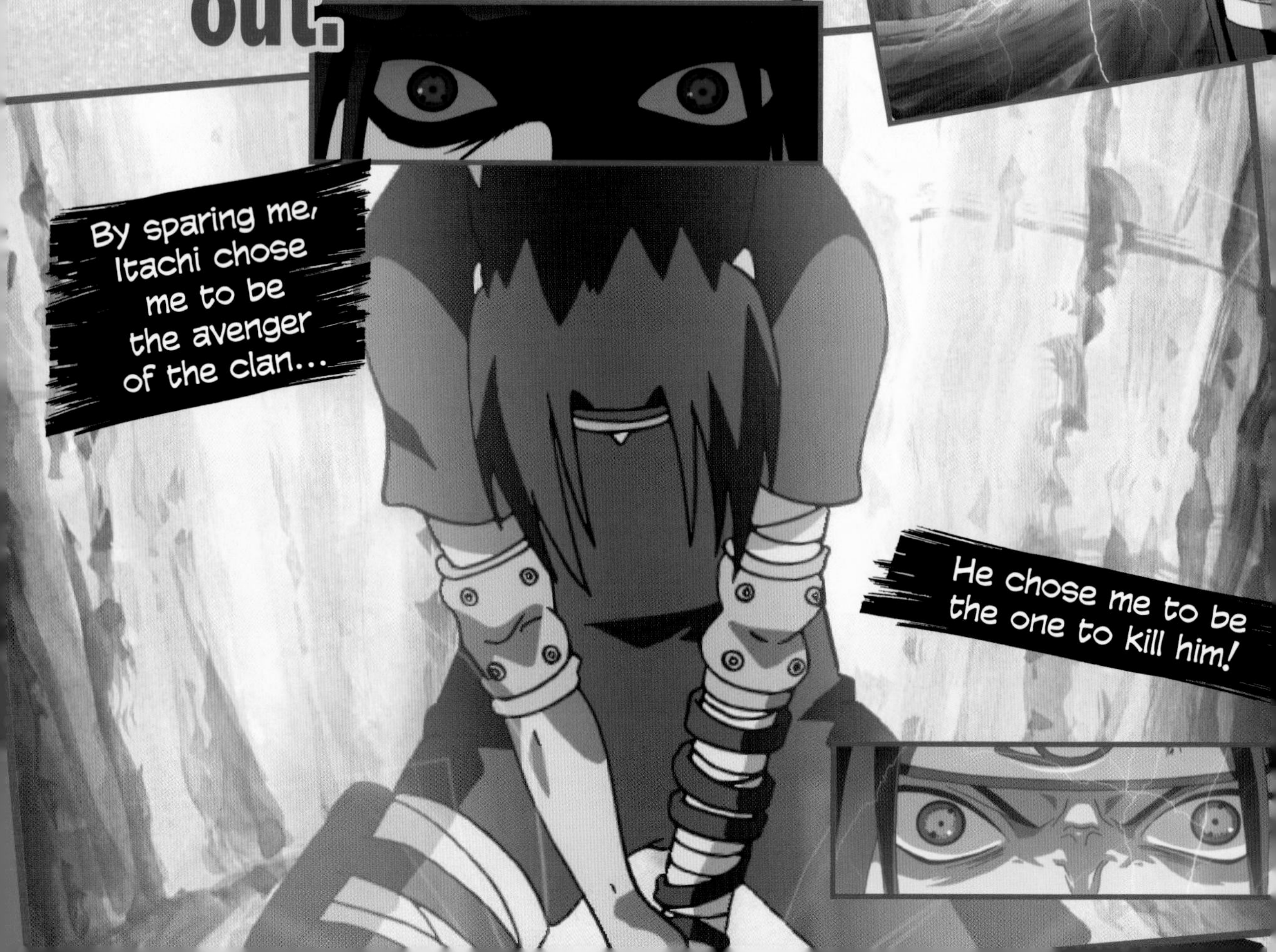
By sparing me, Itachi chose me to be the avenger of the clan...
He chose me to be the one to kill him!

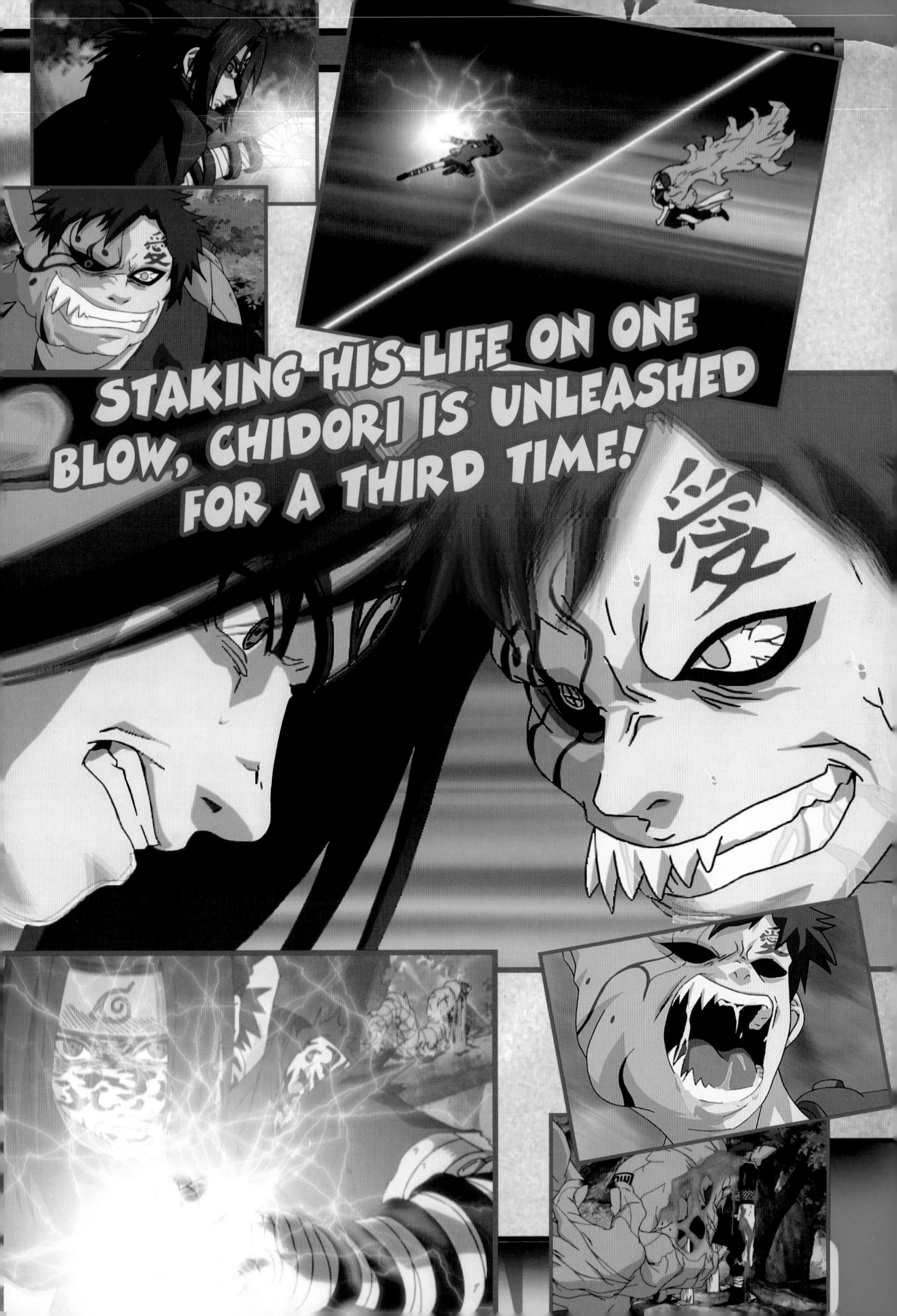
STAKING HIS LIFE ON ONE BLOW, CHIDORI IS UNLEASHED FOR A THIRD TIME!

Tragedy on a moonlit night!

The tragedy responsible for the "love" symbol inscribed on Gaara's forehead.

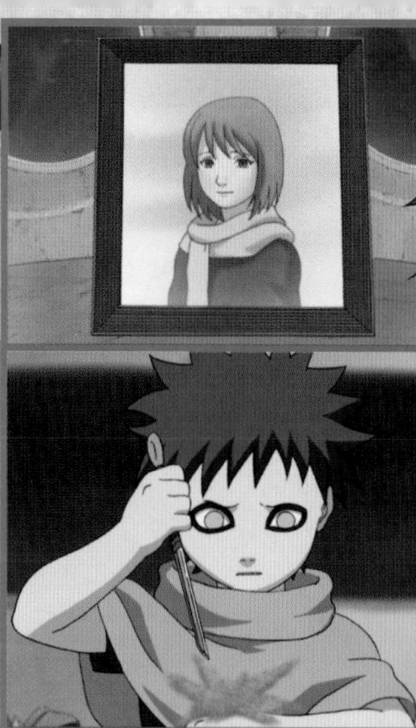

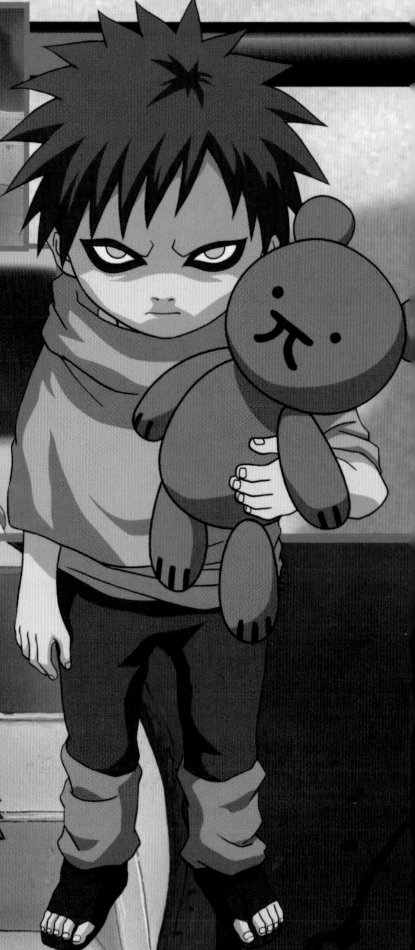

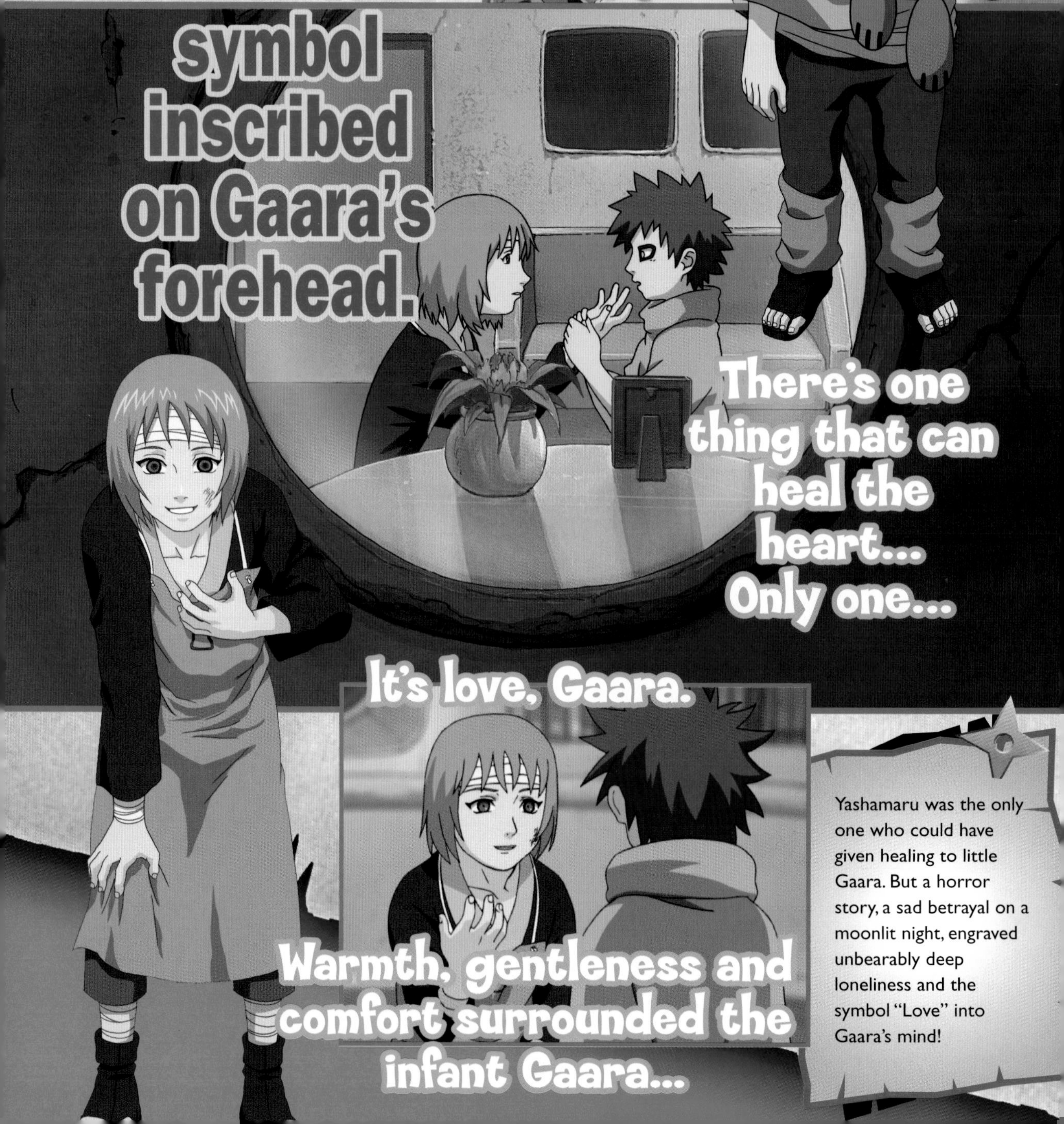

There's one thing that can heal the heart... Only one...

It's love, Gaara.

Warmth, gentleness and comfort surrounded the infant Gaara...

Yashamaru was the only one who could have given healing to little Gaara. But a horror story, a sad betrayal on a moonlit night, engraved unbearably deep loneliness and the symbol "Love" into Gaara's mind!

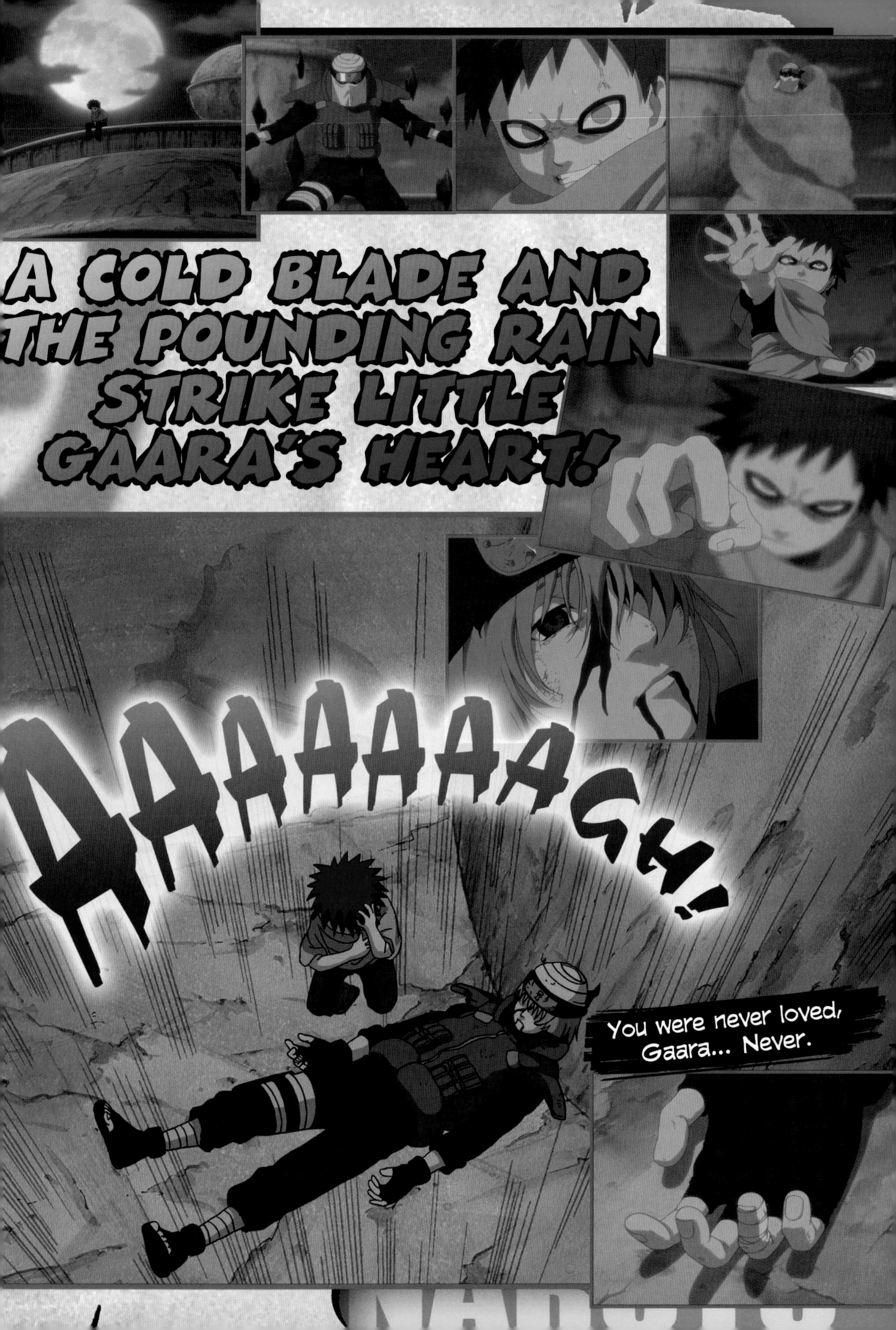
A COLD BLADE AND THE POUNDING RAIN STRIKE LITTLE GAARA'S HEART!
AAAAAAAGH!
You were never loved, Gaara... Never.

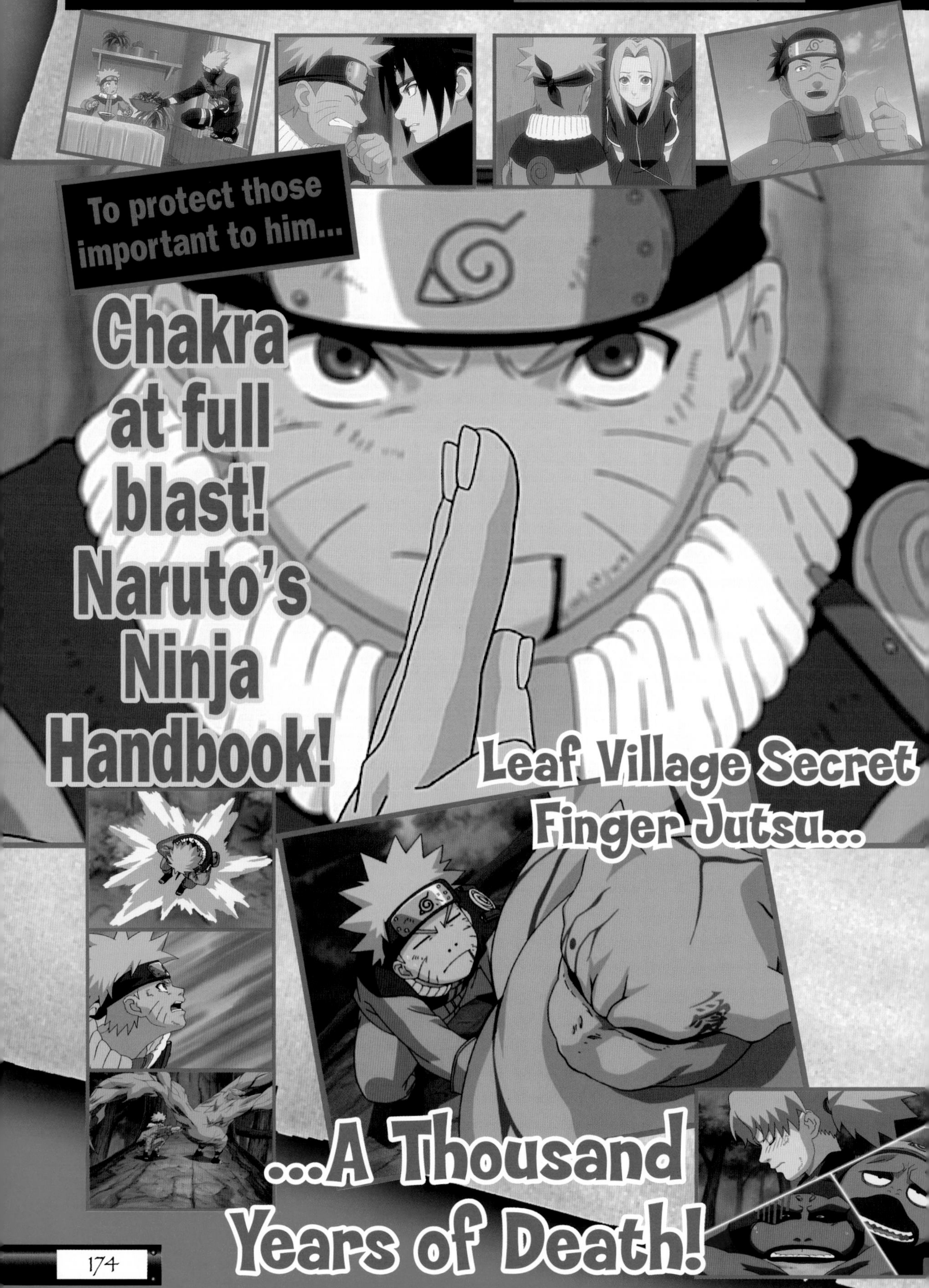
To protect those important to him...
Chakra at full blast! Naruto's Ninja Handbook!
Leaf Village Secret Finger Jutsu...
...A Thousand Years of Death!

Naruto manipulates his chakra to the max to confront the continuously transforming Gaara! He has to protect his friends, mentors and the Hidden Leaf Village. So it's time for everyone to find out what secret moves are in Naruto's Ninja Handbook!

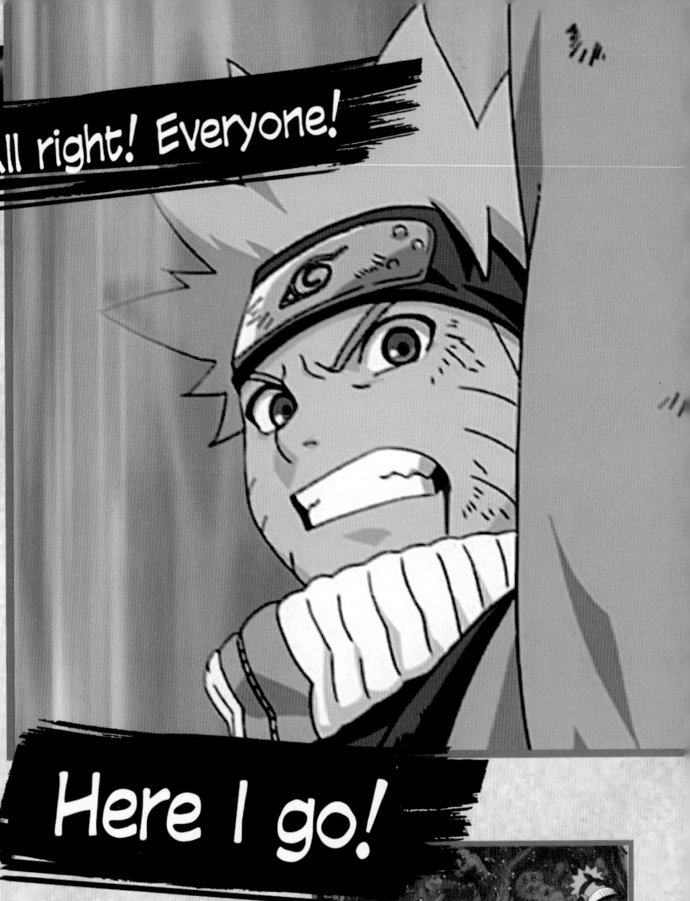
All right! Everyone!
Here I go!

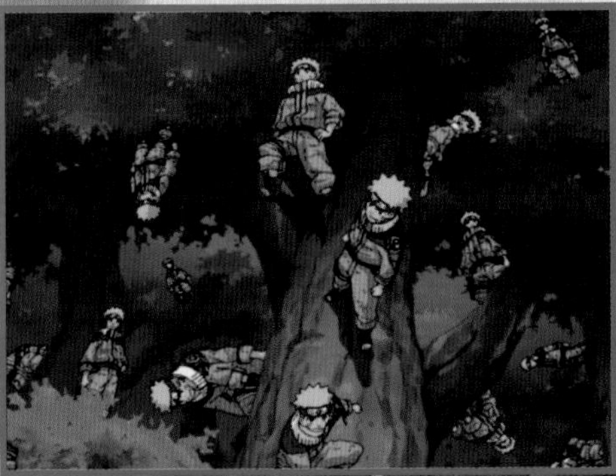

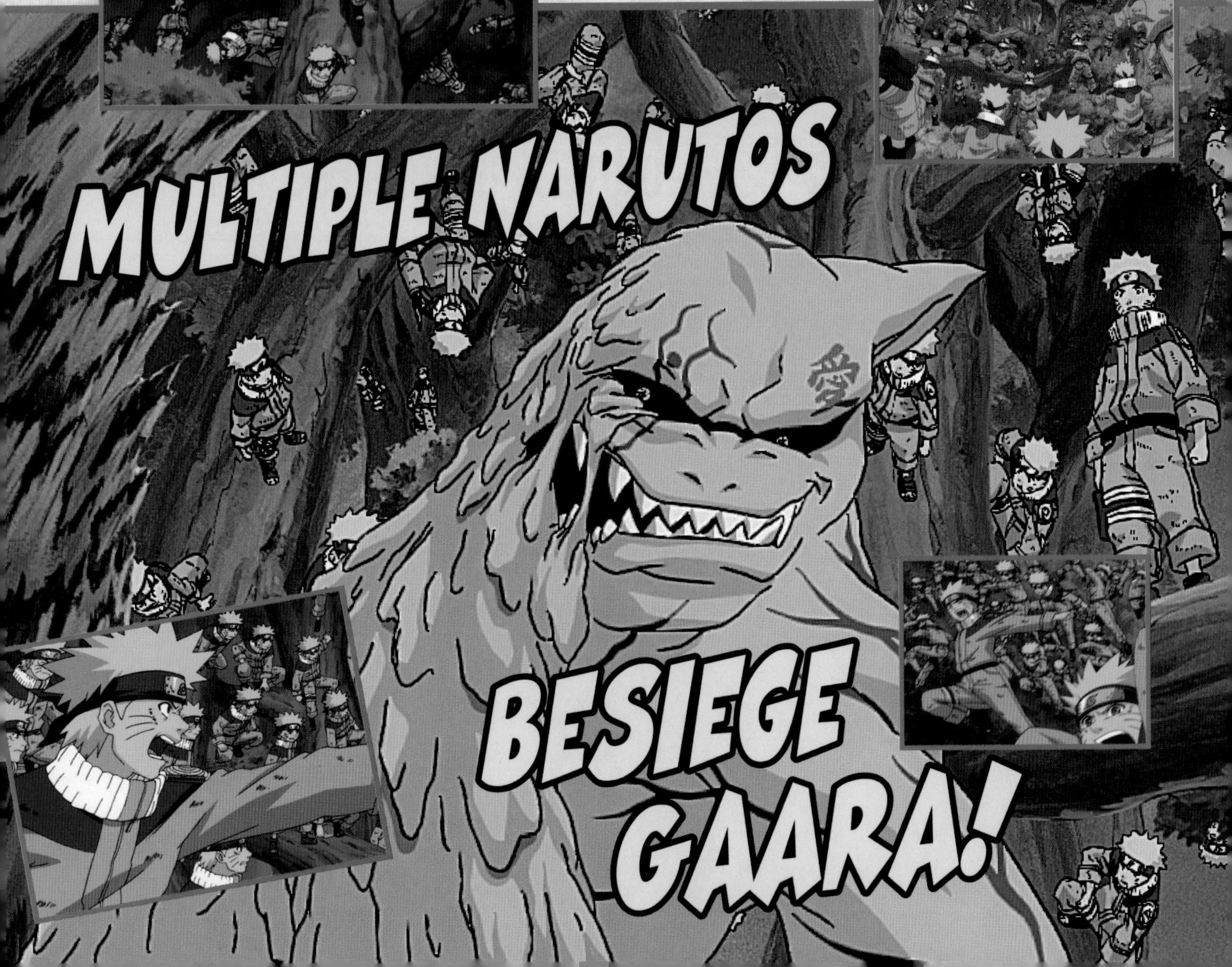
MULTIPLE NARUTOS
BESIEGE
GAARA!

An unprecedented battle!

Shukaku vs. Gama-bunta!

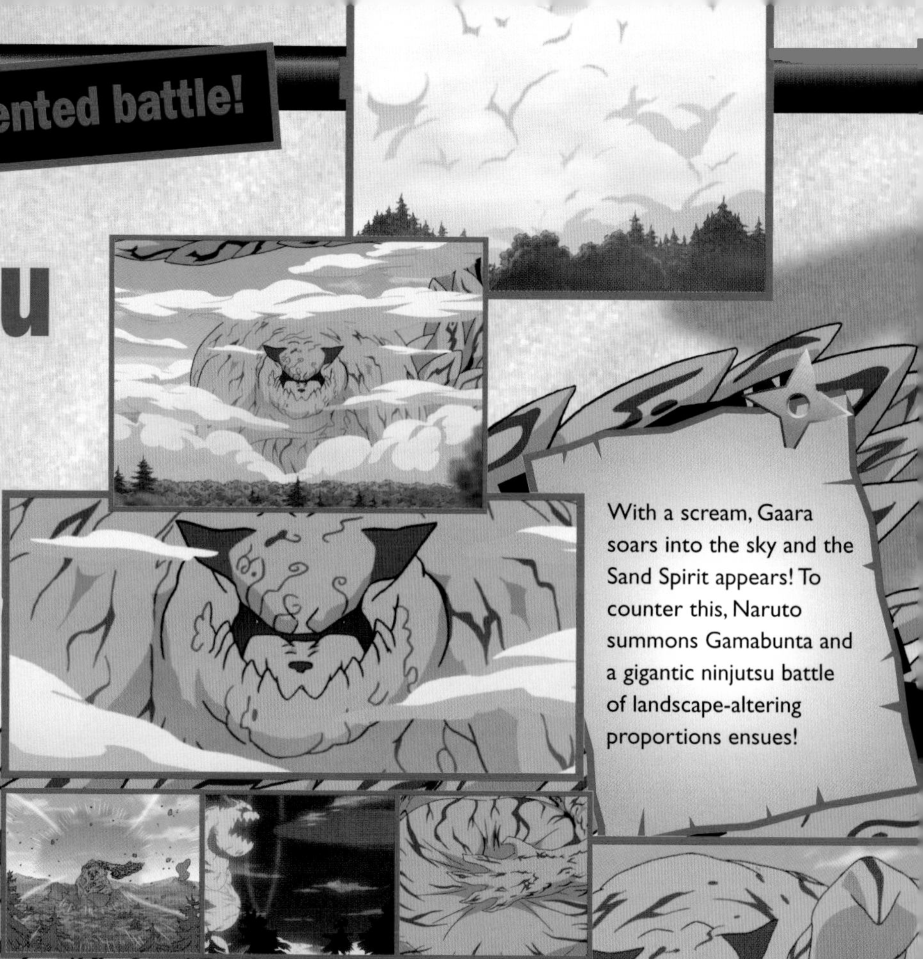

With a scream, Gaara soars into the sky and the Sand Spirit appears! To counter this, Naruto summons Gamabunta and a gigantic ninjutsu battle of landscape-altering proportions ensues!

Ultimately, its final form...

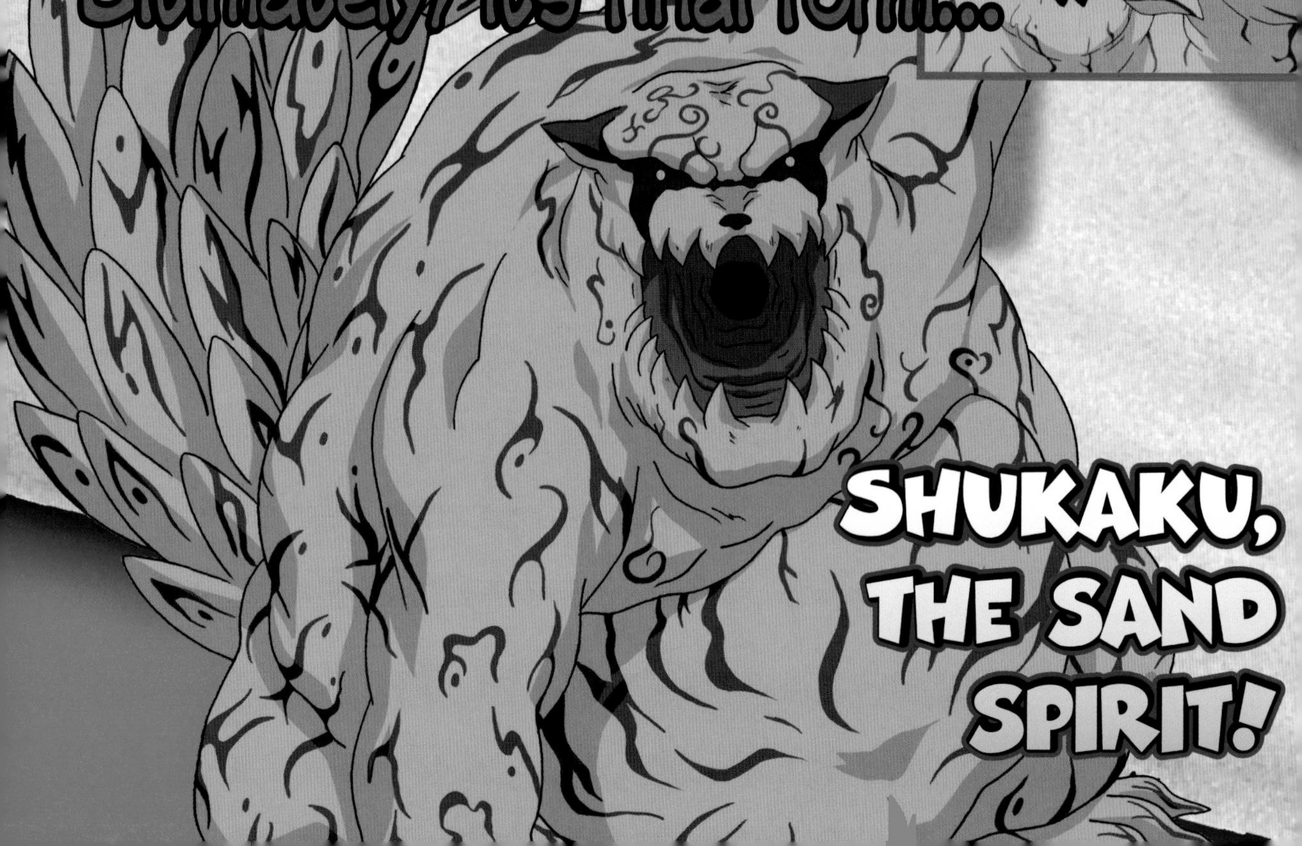

SHUKAKU, THE SAND SPIRIT!

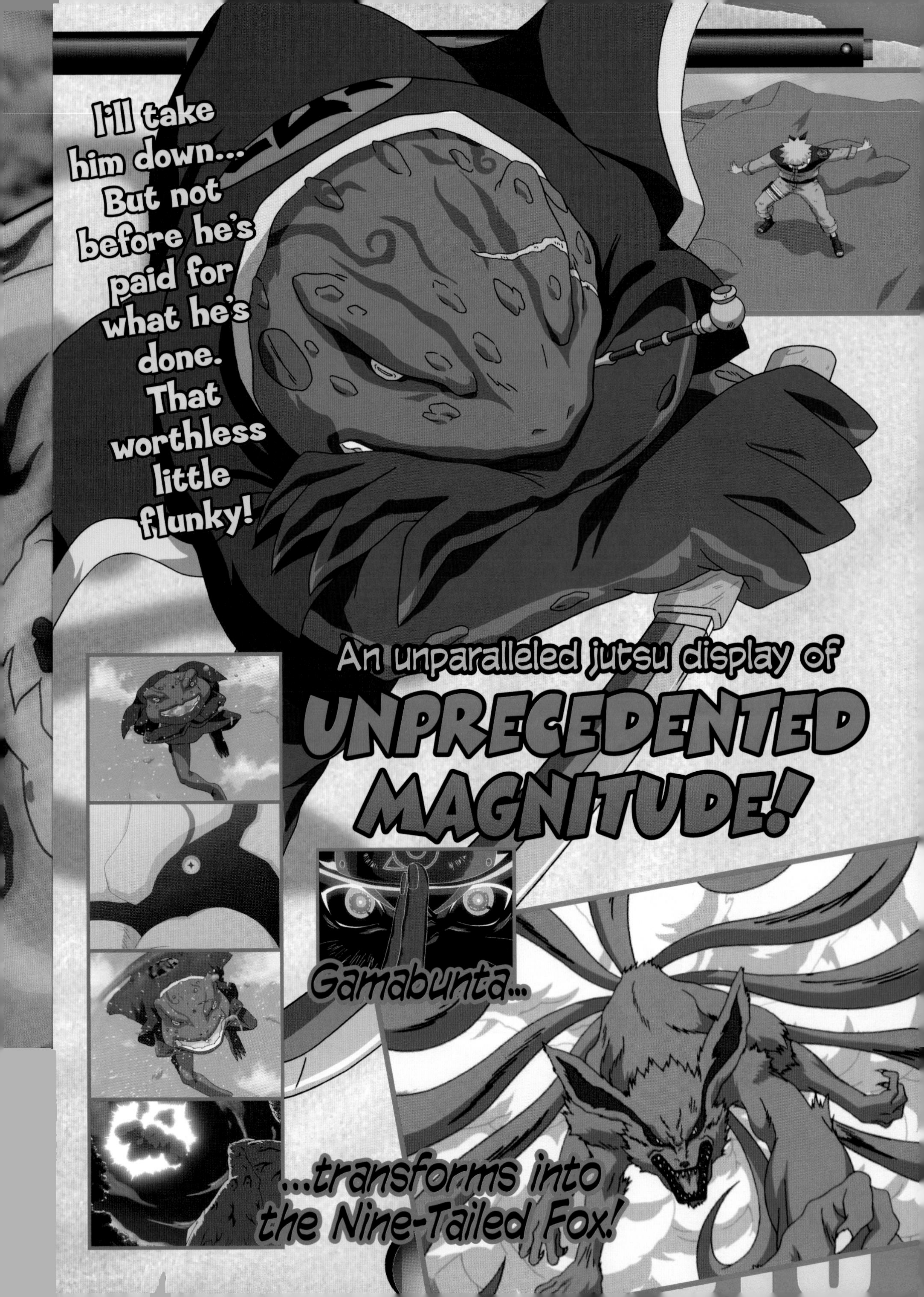
I'll take him down... But not before he's paid for what he's done. That worthless little flunky!
An unparalleled jutsu display of
UNPRECEDENTED MAGNITUDE!
Gamabunta...
...transforms into the Nine-Tailed Fox!

The Barrier of Four Flames keeps even the Anbu Black Ops from interfering!

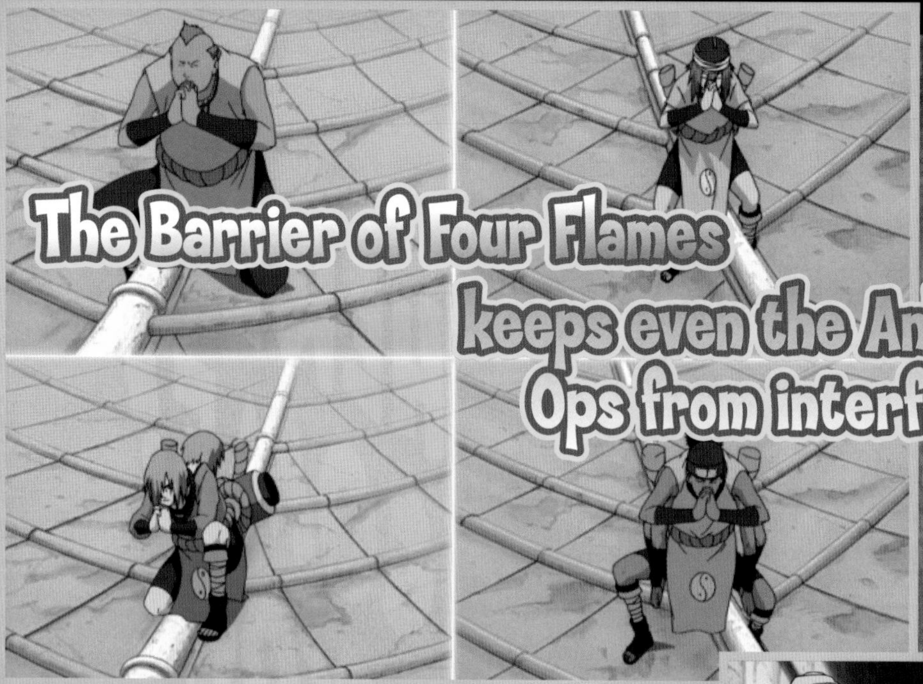

The four sneaked into the Hidden Leaf Village using their ninjutsu to disguise themselves as attendants of the Kazekage. With their Barrier Jutsu they set the stage for the decisive battle between Orochimaru and the Third Hokage: The Four Flames Formation.

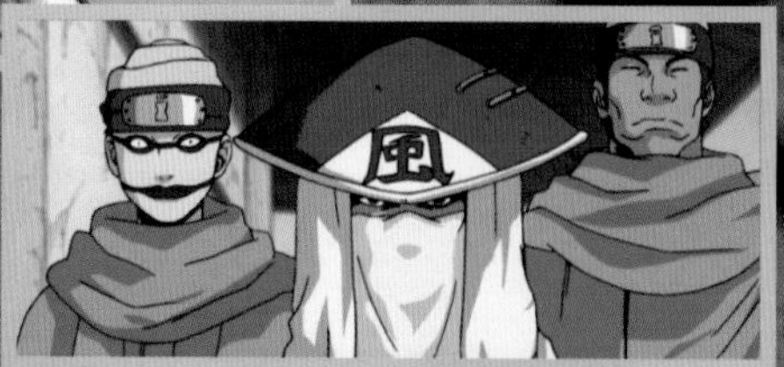

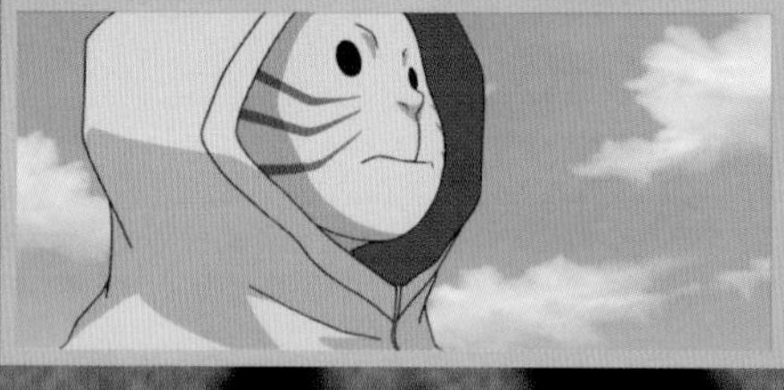

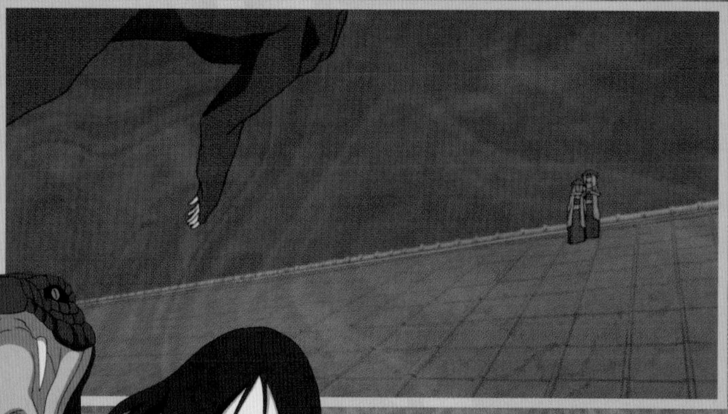

Touching this barrier would instantly incinerate even the elite Anbu Black Ops!

Shinobi of the Hidden Sound Village swear allegiance to Orochimaru!

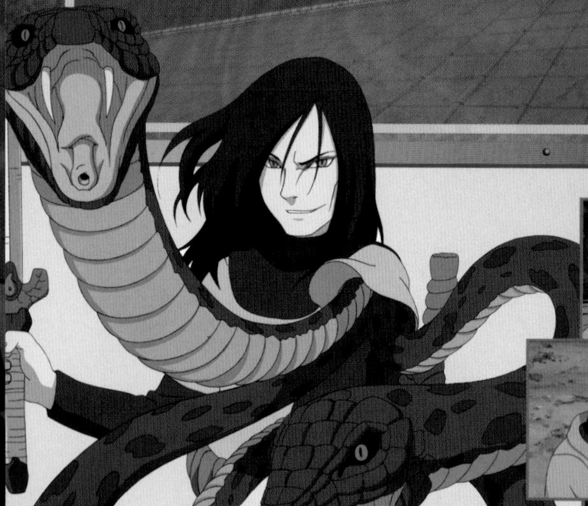

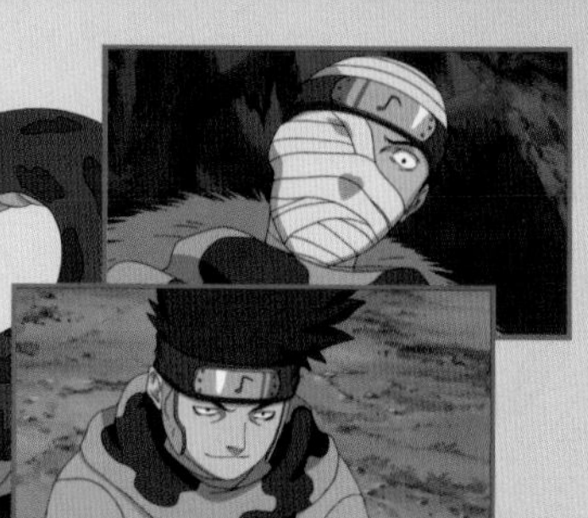

Sound ninja belong to the Hidden Sound Village and serve Orochimaru. Unlike work units consisting of the likes of Dosu, Zaku and Kin, who officially participated in the Chunin Exams, these elite four ninja of the Sound village seem to be figures central to Orochimaru's plan.

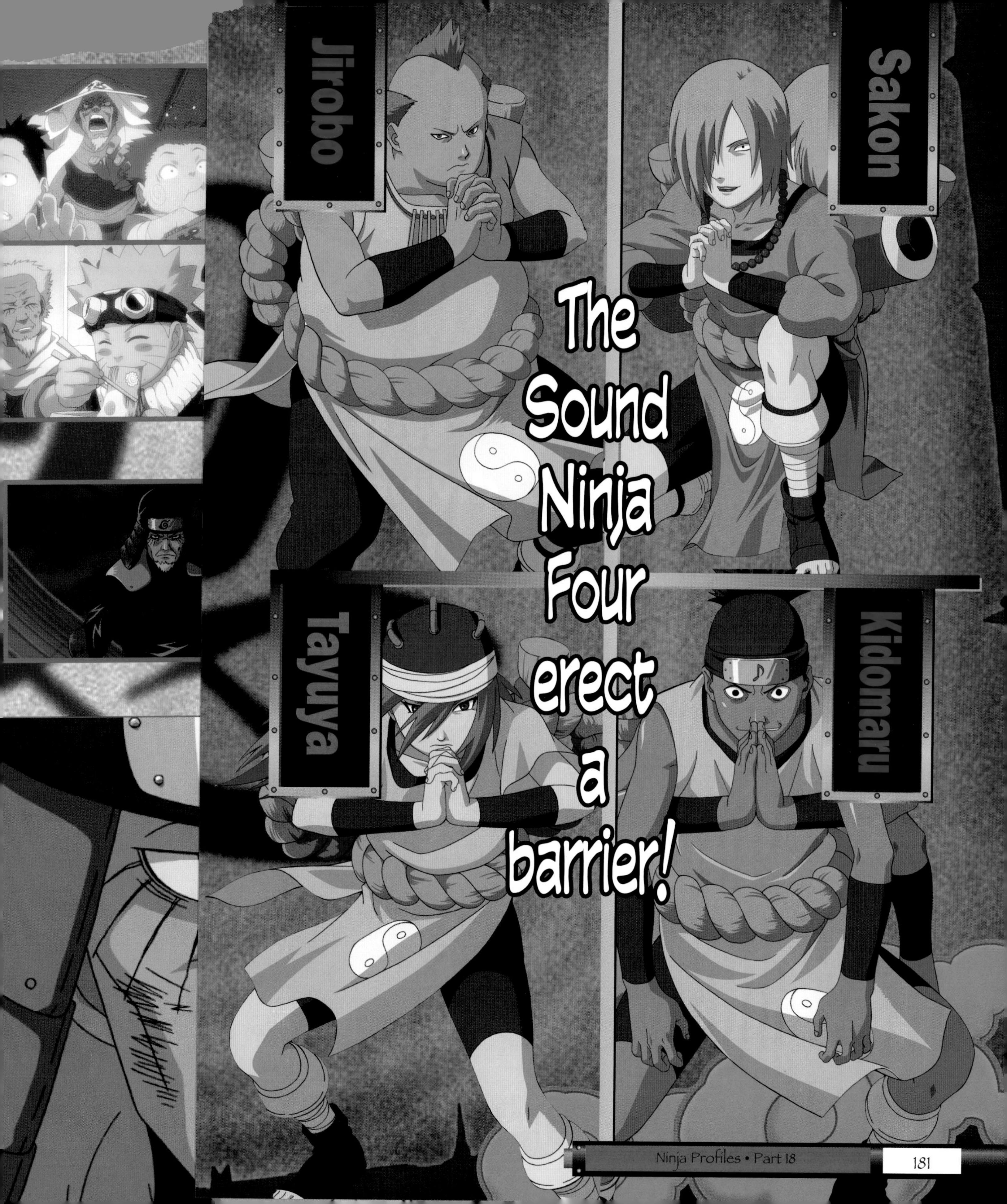
Jirobo
Sakon
Tayuya
Kidomaru
The Sound Ninja Four erect a barrier!

The Third Hokage

tai 体 nin 忍 gen 幻

The leader entrusted with complete authority over the Village Hidden in the Leaves. Once a distinguished professor, he is a ninja genius. He is often spoken of as possibly being the strongest Hokage ever.

Monkey

An aged monkey with a long, shared history with the Hidden Leaf Village and the Third Hokage. His wrinkles are just one mark of his vast experience. His piercing eyes match those of the Hokage. And he can transform into Adamantine Nyoi, enabling powerful combination attacks with the Third Hokage. His fate is directly linked to the Third Hokage and Orochimaru.

MONKEY KING ENMA

Of all animals, monkeys have intelligence and physical form closest to humans. Enma's extreme abilities are displayed in the battle alongside the Third Hokage against the threat posed by Orochimaru.

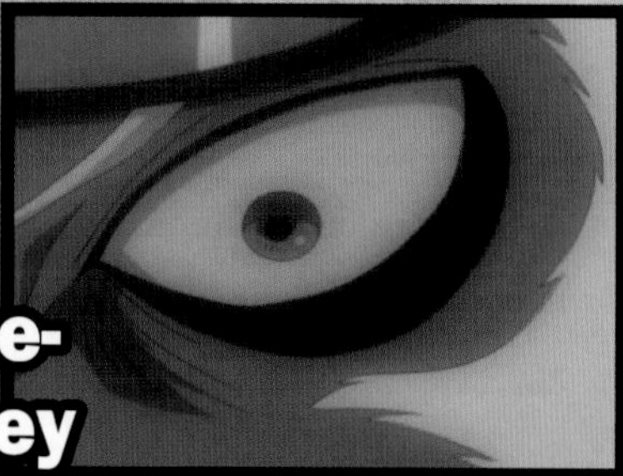

The old white-haired monkey survived turbulent times with the Third Hokage!

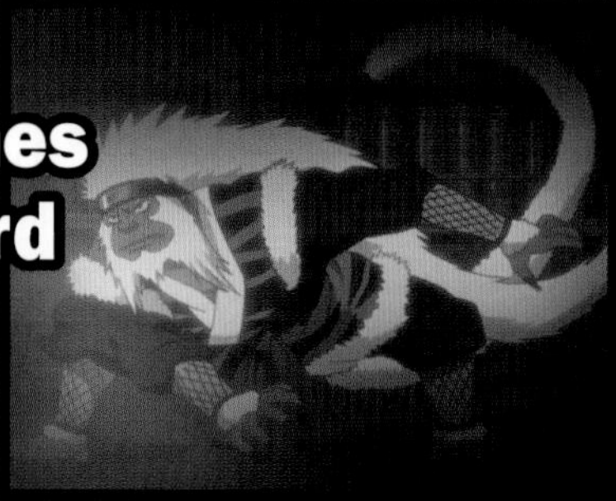

With his giant body and assertive manner, he lives in a world of gangster-like chivalry!

Toad

Through Naruto's painstaking effort, the biggest and strongest toad is finally summoned, with an attitude so arrogant that even Jiraiya says it's "beyond control."

GAMAKICHI

Gamabunta's son. Still just a kid, but his personality definitely resembles his father's.

Toads appear under the blood contract with the Summoning Jutsu user. There are toads with various personalities, from ones very loyal and devoted to their master to overbearing ones like Gamabunta and his son.

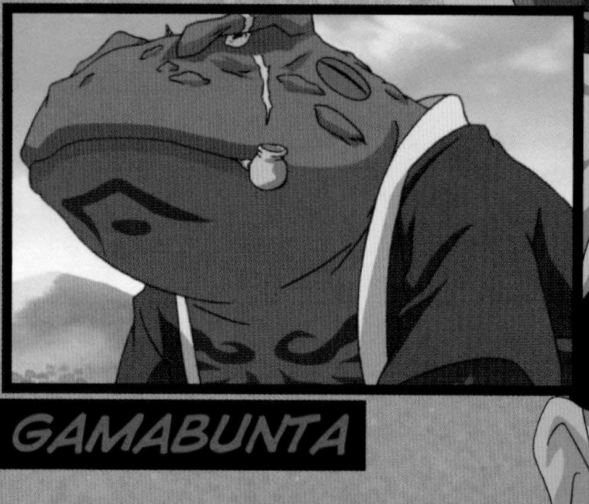

GAMABUNTA

Dog

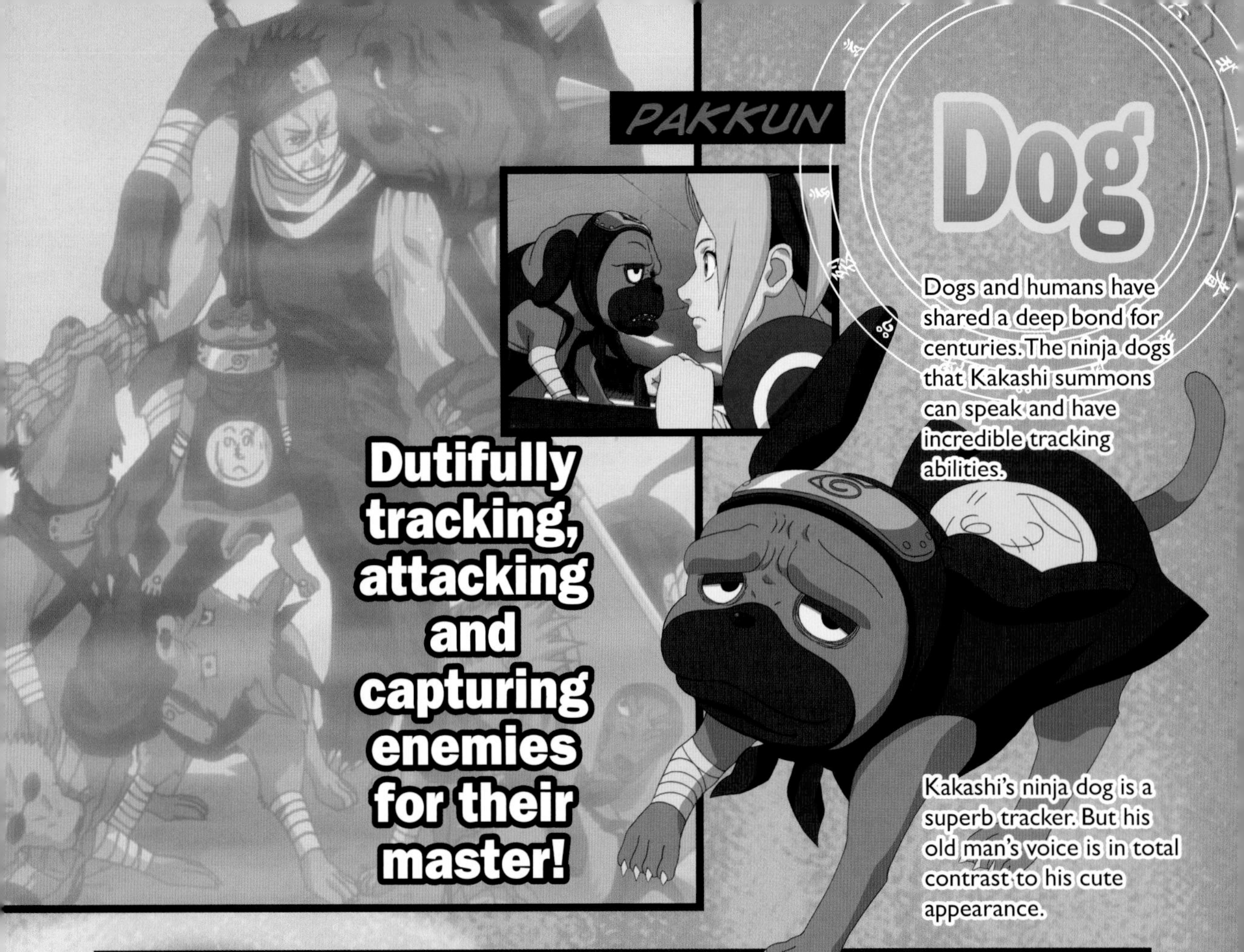
PAKKUN

Dogs and humans have shared a deep bond for centuries. The ninja dogs that Kakashi summons can speak and have incredible tracking abilities.

Dutifully tracking, attacking and capturing enemies for their master!

Kakashi's ninja dog is a superb tracker. But his old man's voice is in total contrast to his cute appearance.

Snake

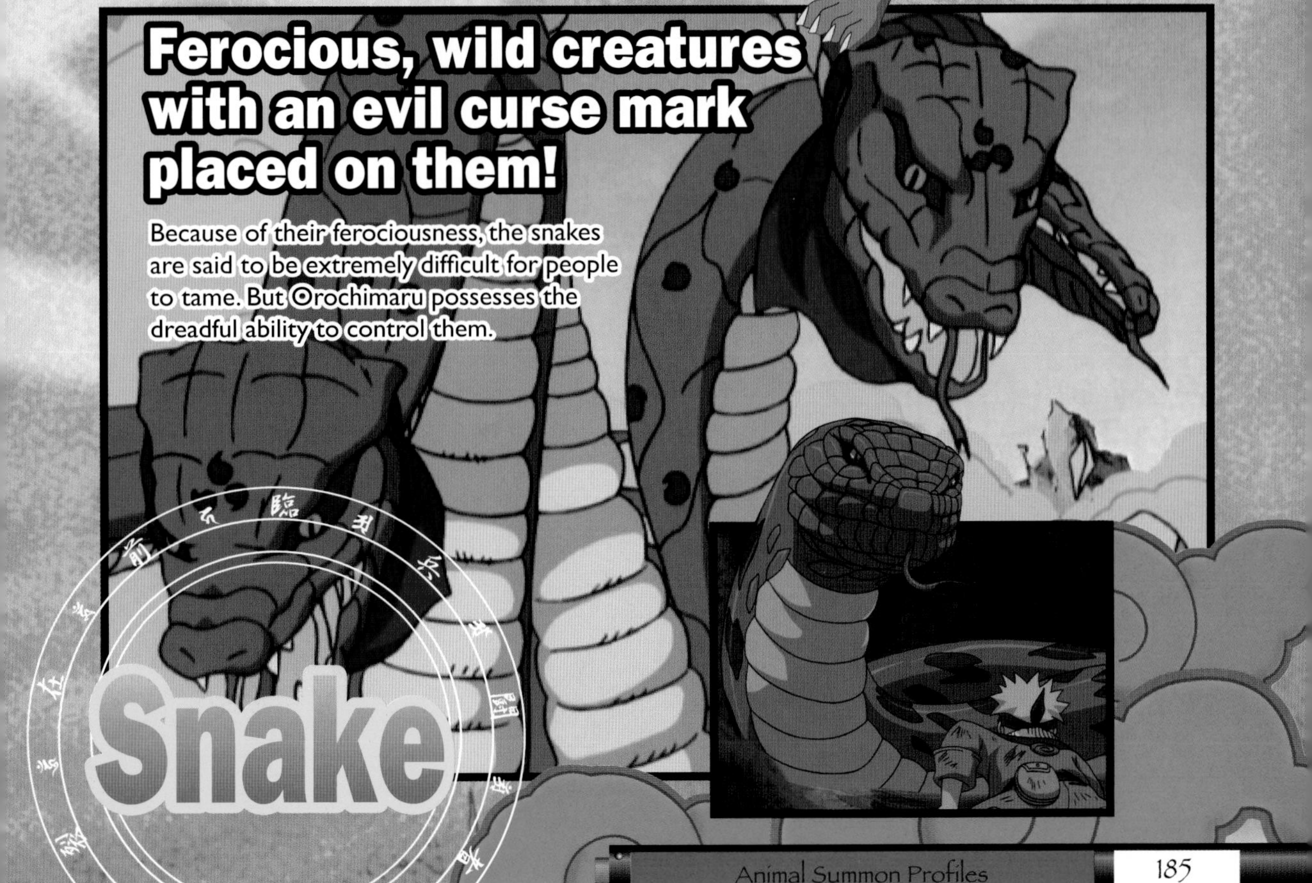

Ferocious, wild creatures with an evil curse mark placed on them!

Because of their ferociousness, the snakes are said to be extremely difficult for people to tame. But Orochimaru possesses the dreadful ability to control them.

Record of the SAND's insanity!

The entity that possesses Gaara…

THE SAND SPIRIT!

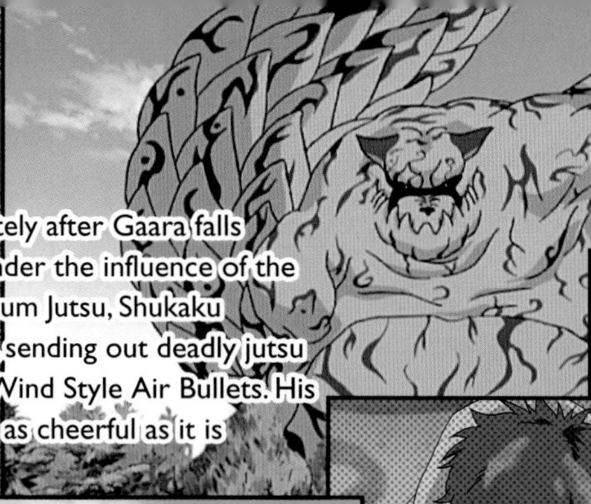

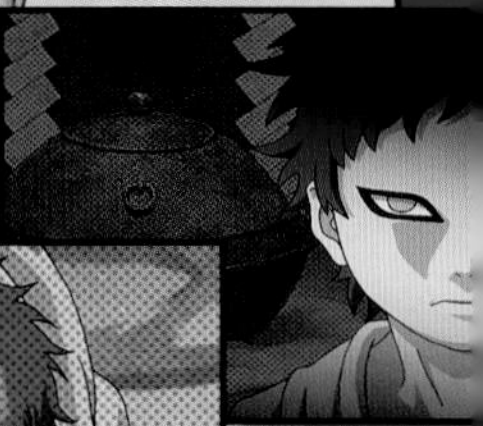

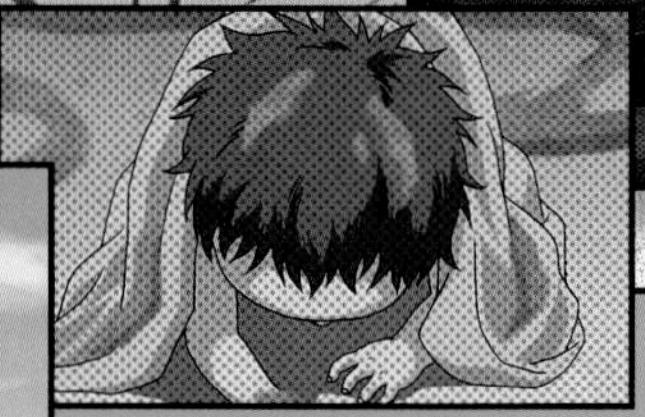

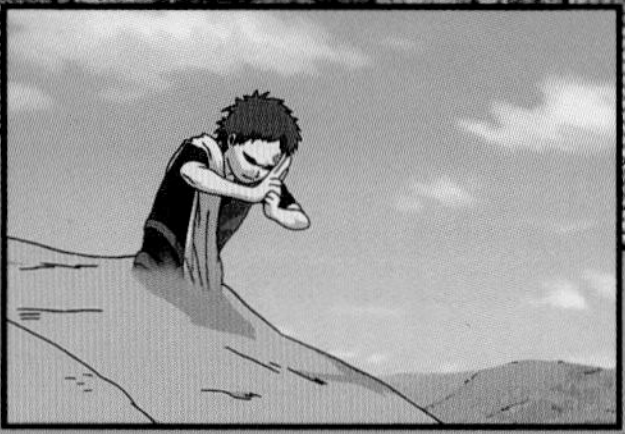

Immediately after Gaara falls asleep under the influence of the Play Possum Jutsu, Shukaku emerges, sending out deadly jutsu such as Wind Style Air Bullets. His nature is as cheerful as it is brutal.

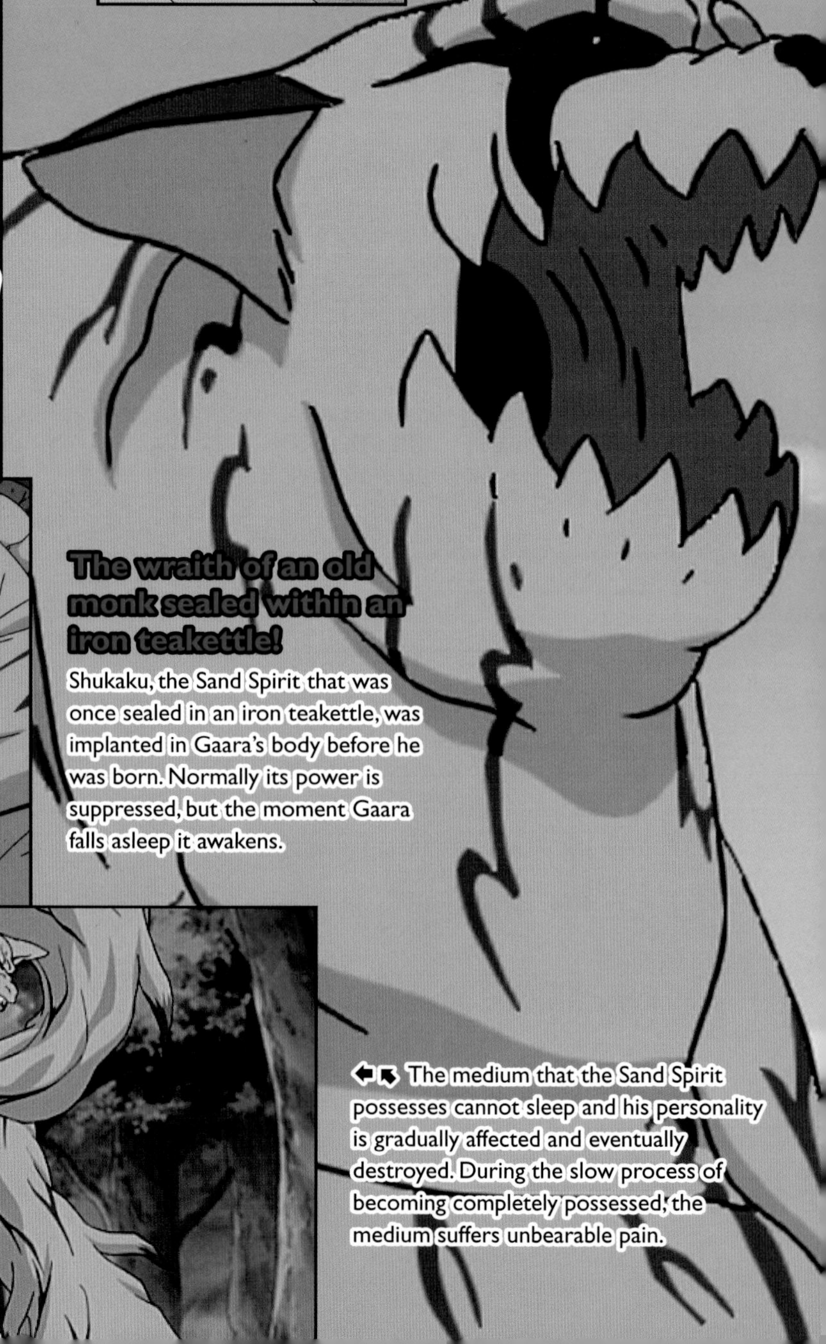

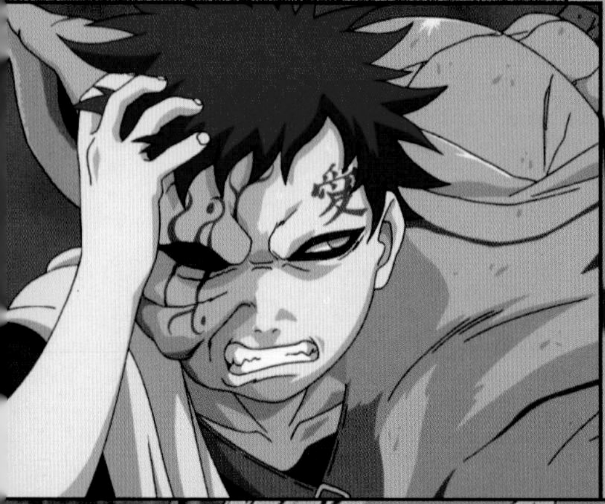

The wraith of an old monk sealed within an iron teakettle!

Shukaku, the Sand Spirit that was once sealed in an iron teakettle, was implanted in Gaara's body before he was born. Normally its power is suppressed, but the moment Gaara falls asleep it awakens.

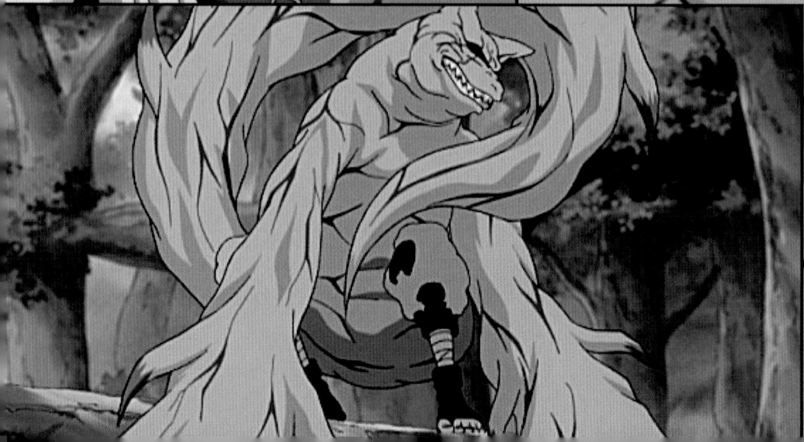

⇦⬊ The medium that the Sand Spirit possesses cannot sleep and his personality is gradually affected and eventually destroyed. During the slow process of becoming completely possessed, the medium suffers unbearable pain.

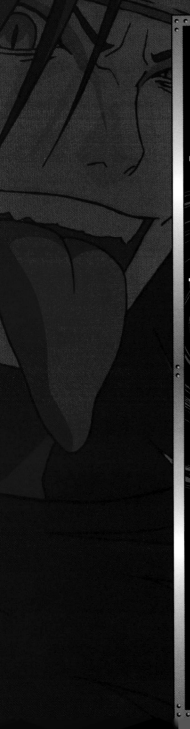

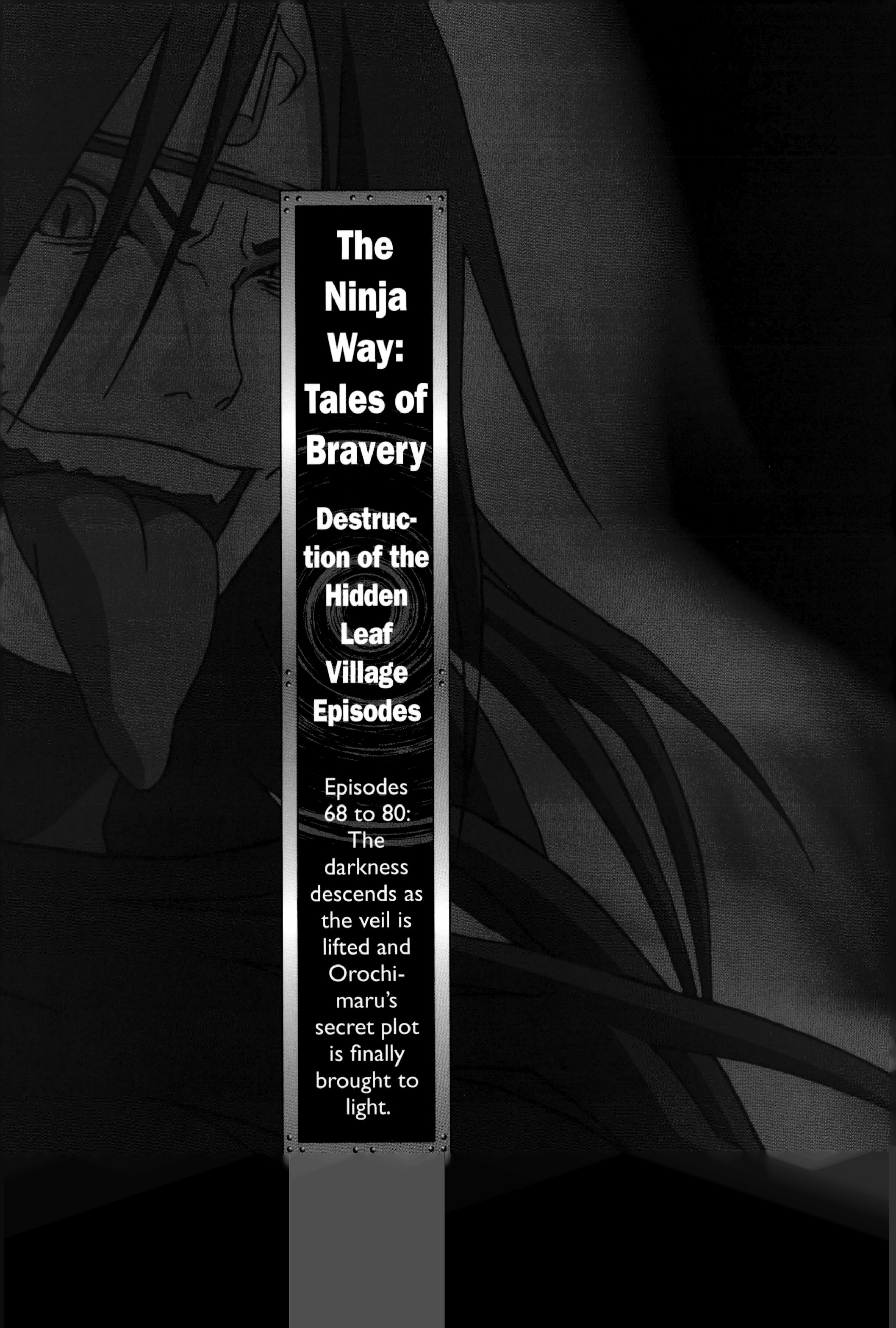

The Ninja Way: Tales of Bravery

Destruction of the Hidden Leaf Village Episodes

Episodes 68 to 80: The darkness descends as the veil is lifted and Orochimaru's secret plot is finally brought to light.

Episode 68 to Episode 80

The Destruction of the Hidden Leaf Village

The horror begins!

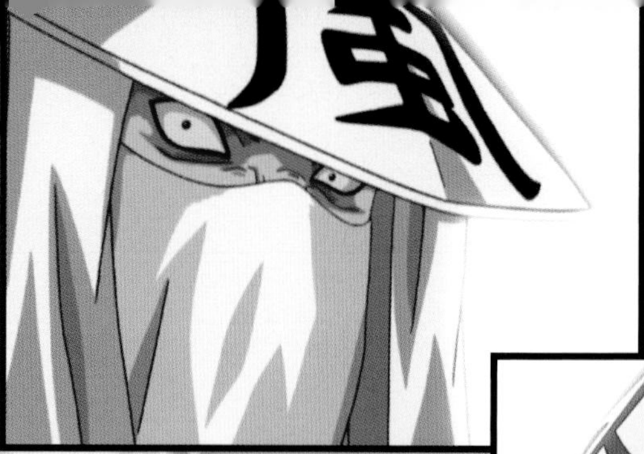

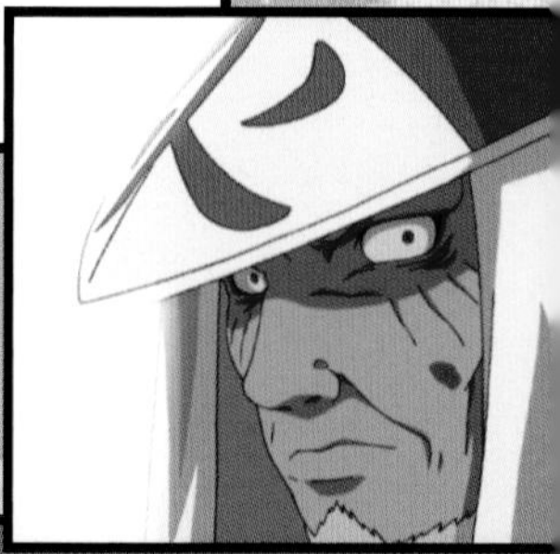

⬆ Amidst the confusion, with the glint of conspiracy in his eyes, the Kazekage stares at the Hokage.

➡ Sensing something amiss, the Third Hokage looks back at the Kazekage and, at that very moment, the destruction of the Hidden Leaf Village begins!

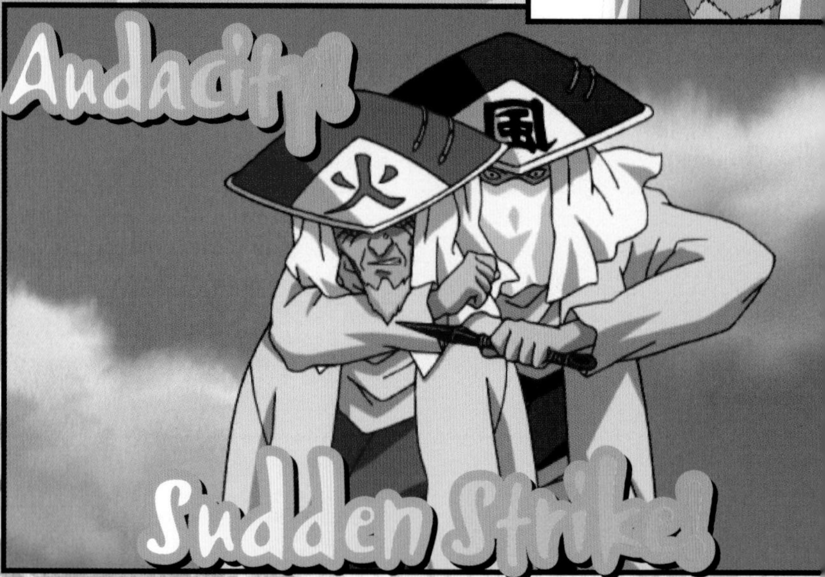
Audacity!
Sudden Strike!

⬆ The Kazekage takes the Hokage hostage with a kunai knife, and in the blink of an eye he moves to the roof.

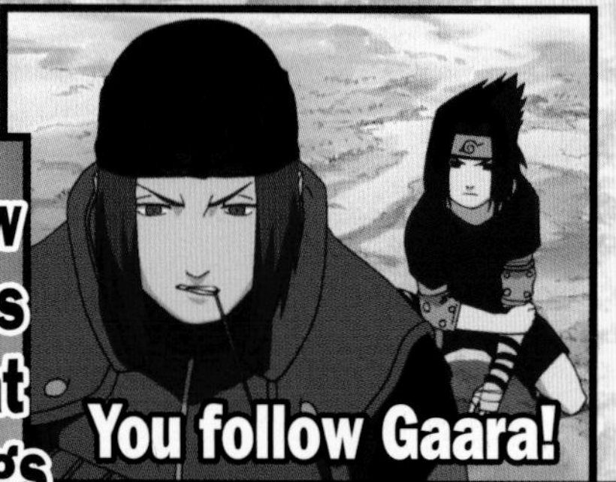
You follow Gaara!

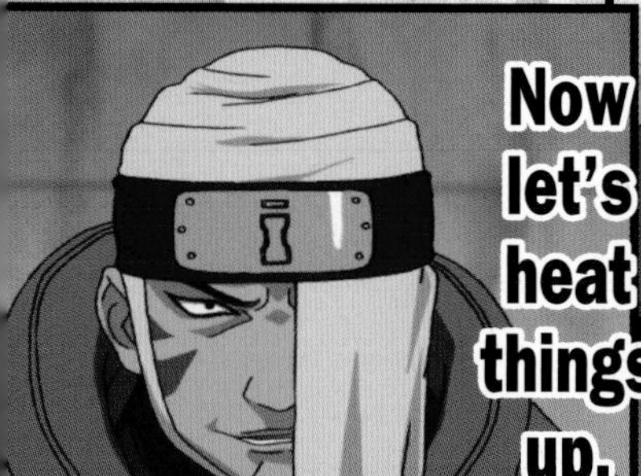
Now let's heat things up, huh?

⬆ Genma gives Sasuke an assignment, and then confronts Baki!

The true identity of the Sand Village's Kazekage is revealed!

The Kazekage suddenly takes action, bringing an abrupt halt to Sasuke and Gaara's match. Simultaneous, all-out assaults by the Sound and the Sand confront the Village Hidden in the Leaves with unprecedented danger.

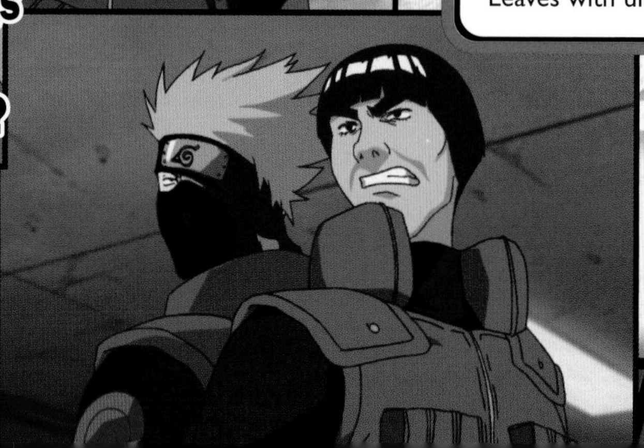

⬅ Kakashi and Guy also sense danger in the stunning turn of events at the Chunin Exam arena.

Sound and Sand shinobi suddenly attack!

The plot to topple the Hidden Leaf Village takes shape! At the Chunin Exam arena, which is now a battlefield, Kakashi gives Sakura, Naruto and Shikamaru an assignment to track down Sasuke and then wait for further orders.

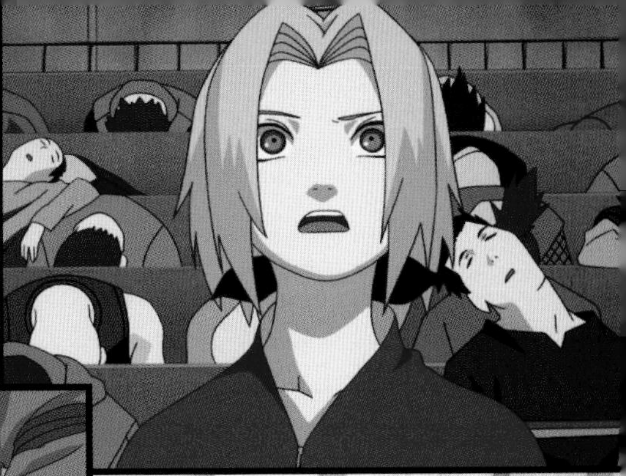

➡ Sakura immediately notices the genjutsu cast on the arena and protects herself with Genjutsu Reflection! She is astonished as her surroundings turn into a battlefield!

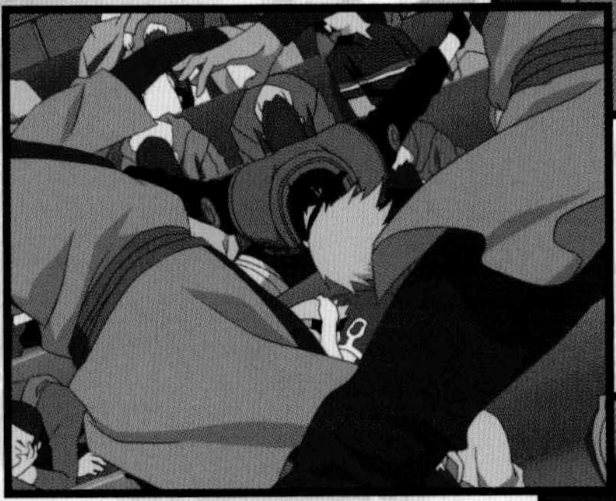

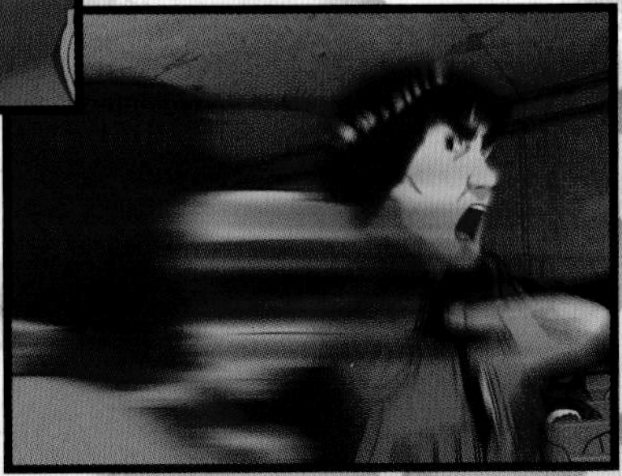

⬅⬇ With their superior skills, Kakashi and Guy get busy taking out the rebel shinobi.

⬇ Kakashi announces an assignment. He is well aware of Gaara's creepy chakra.

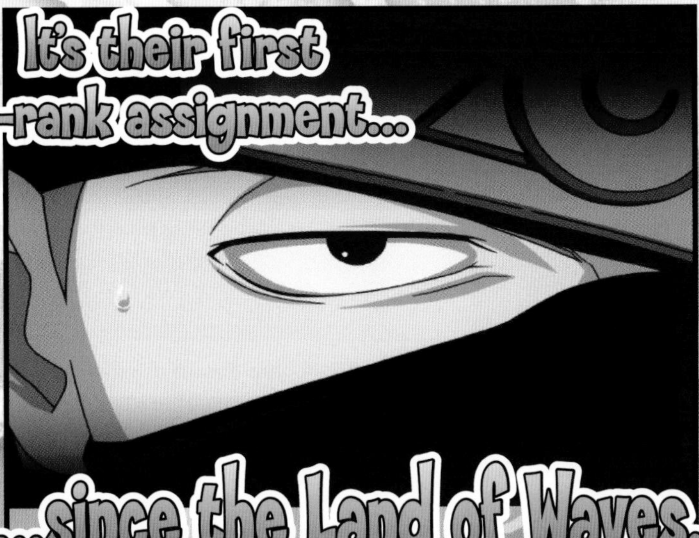
It's their first A-rank assignment...
...since the Land of Waves.

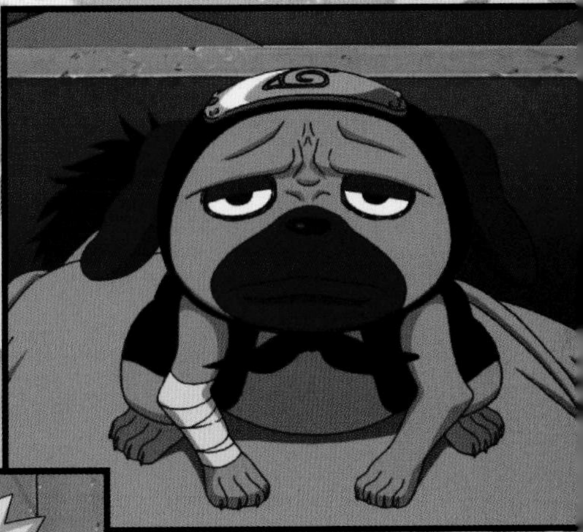

⬆ Pakkun has superior tracking ability.

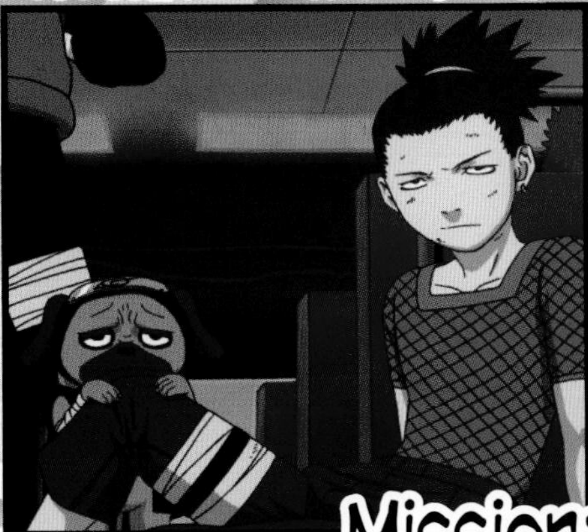

⬆ Shikamaru, who was pretending to be asleep, is rousted with a bite from Pakkun.

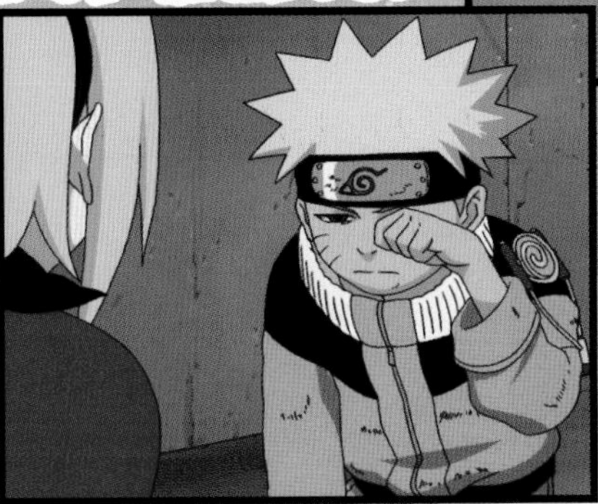

⬅ Awakened by Sakura, Naruto can barely grasp the situation.

Mission: Track down Sasuke and stop him!

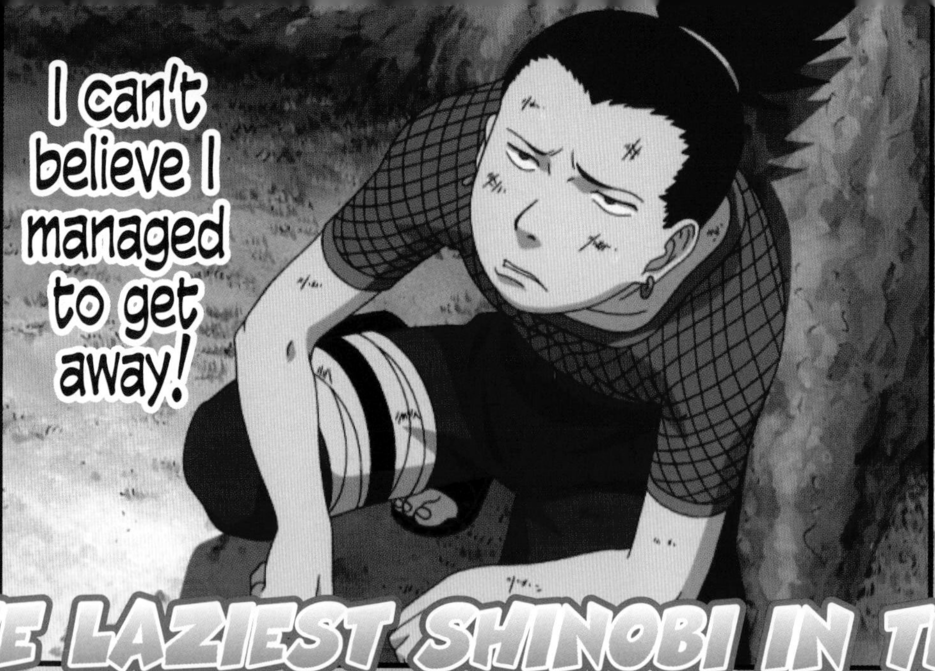
I can't believe I managed to get away!

THE LAZIEST SHINOBI IN THE HIDDEN LEAF VILLAGE FACES THE TASK OF A LIFETIME!

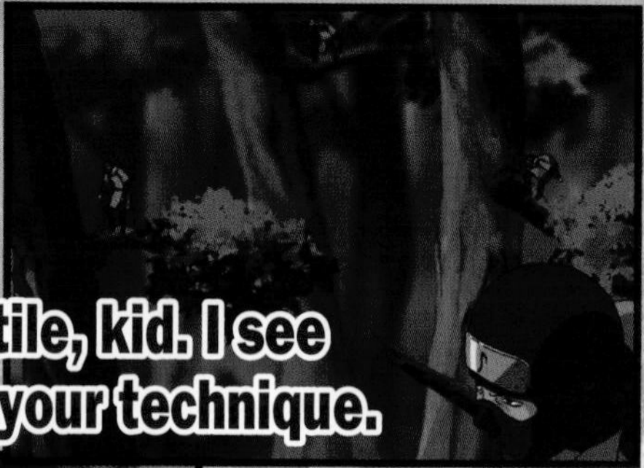
It's futile, kid. I see through your technique.

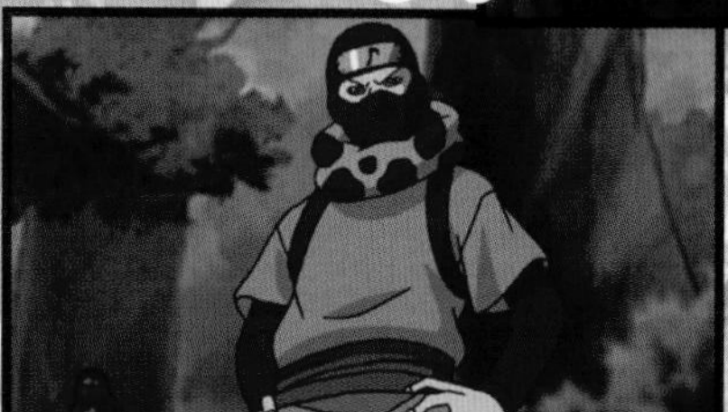

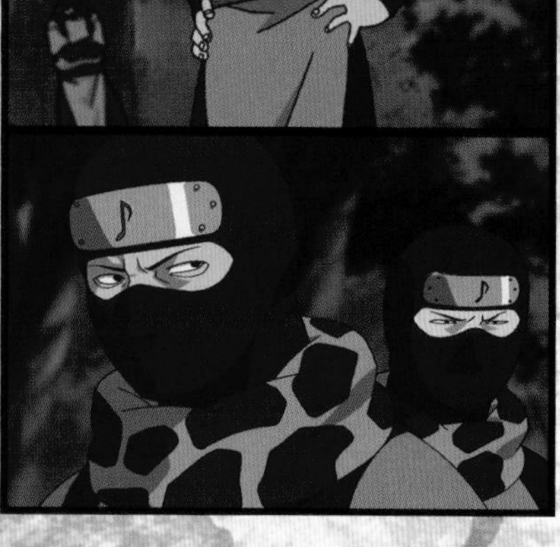

⬆⬅ The Sound shinobi follow footprints left on the ground. Shikamaru's plan succeeds and he traps them with the Shadow Possession Jutsu. But he has very little chakra left!

Shikamaru's cunning plan allows him to get the drop on the Sound ninja!

Noticing the Sound shinobi pursuing them, Shikamaru offers to play decoy to shake them off. His plan succeeds, but Shikamaru ends up surrounded by eight Sound shinobi!

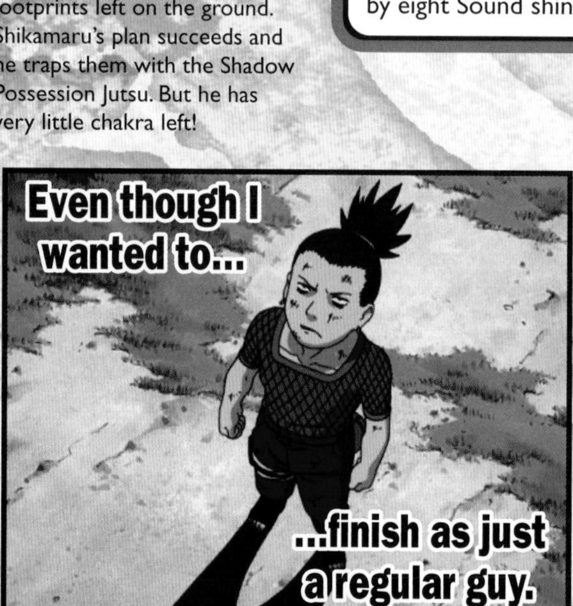
Even though I wanted to...
...finish as just a regular guy.

⬅ Looking up at the sky, Shikamaru laments his misfortune. All he wants is to live an ordinary life.

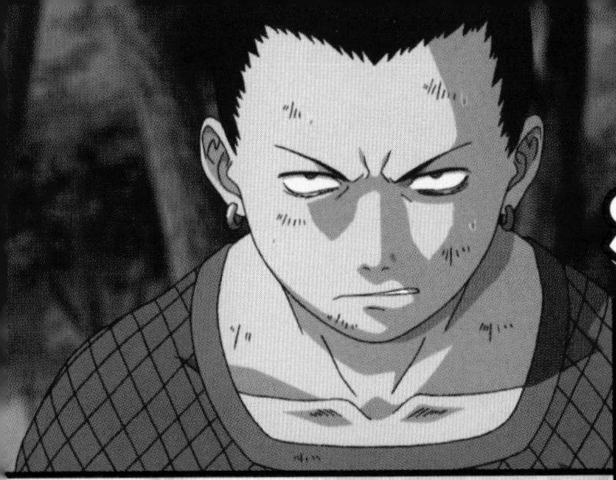

Goodbye ordinary life?! Shikamaru's in a tight spot!

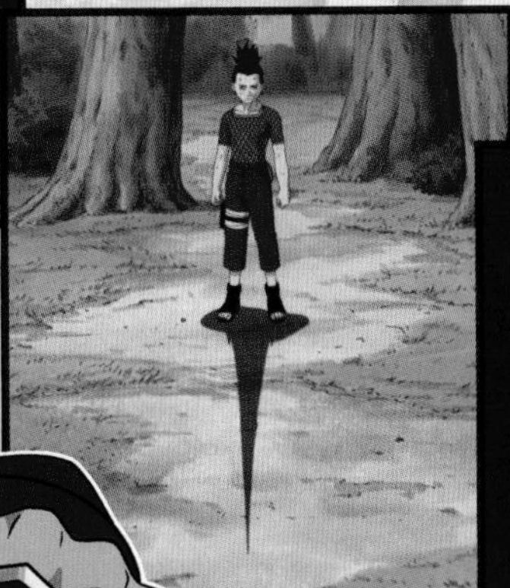

⬇ His chakra runs out and he's forced to release his Shadow Possession Jutsu. Is it time to concede defeat?!

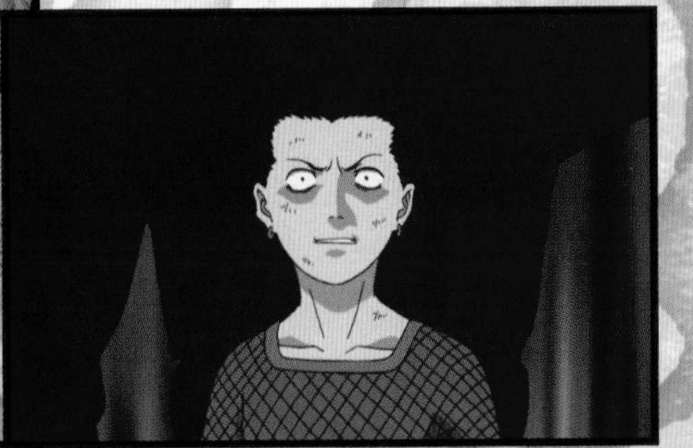

⬆➡ A shadow rises from behind and a chill runs down Shikamaru's spine!

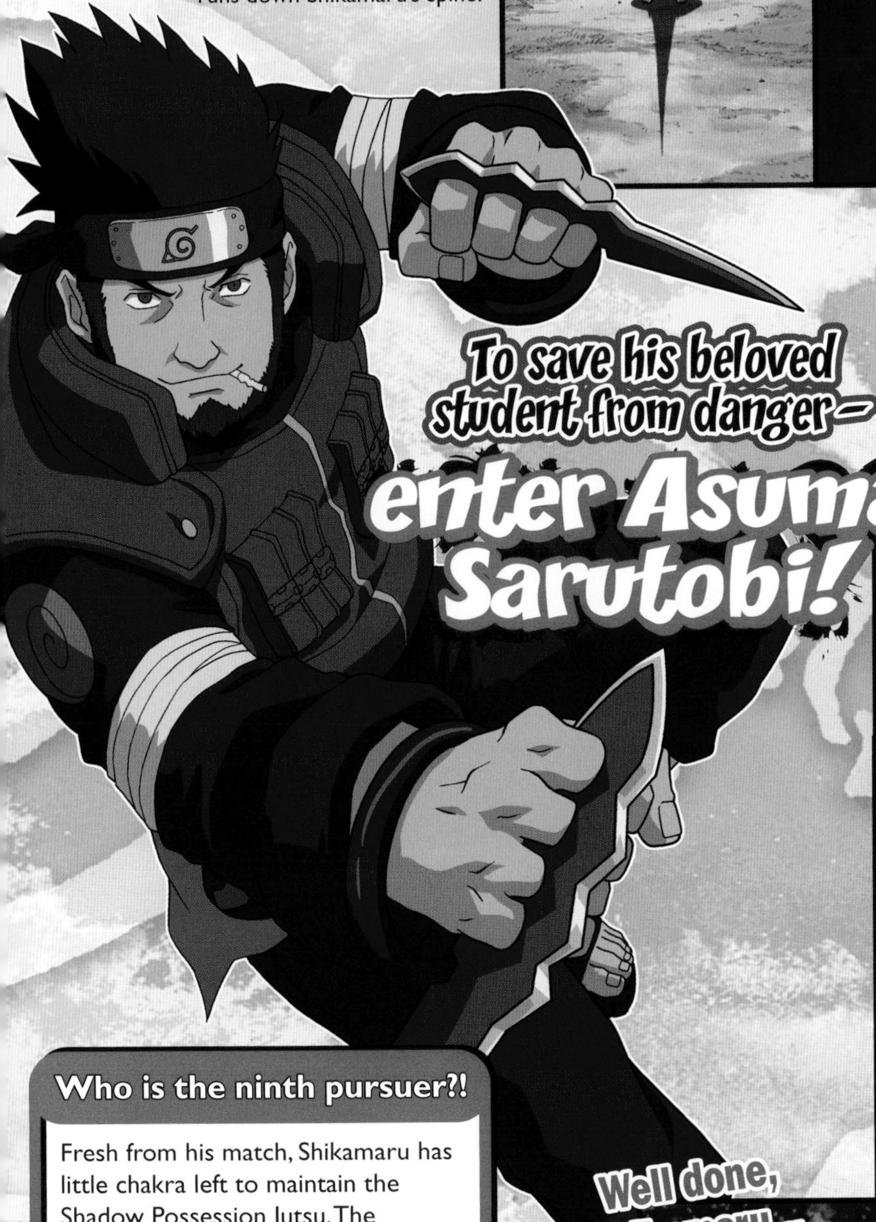

To save his beloved student from danger—enter Asuma Sarutobi!

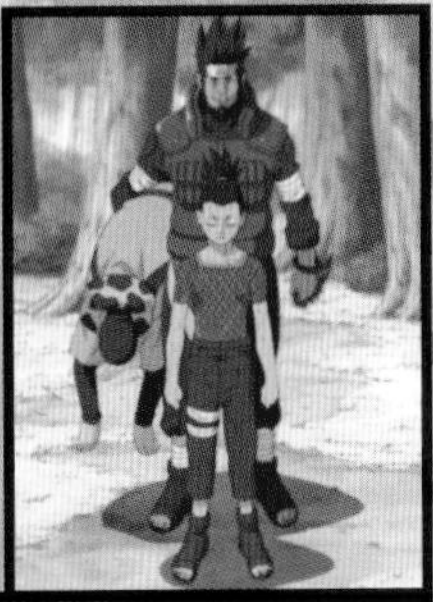

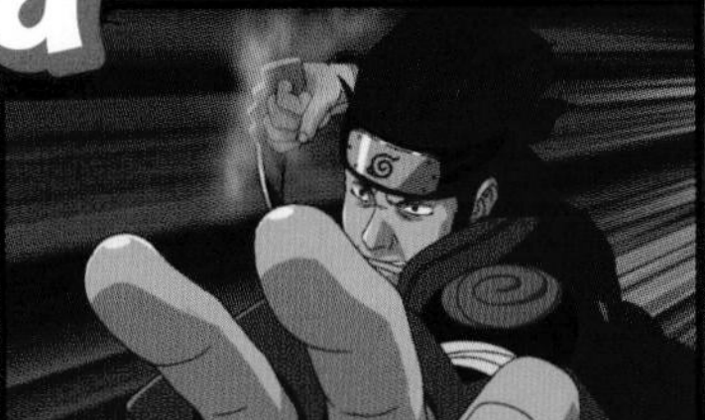

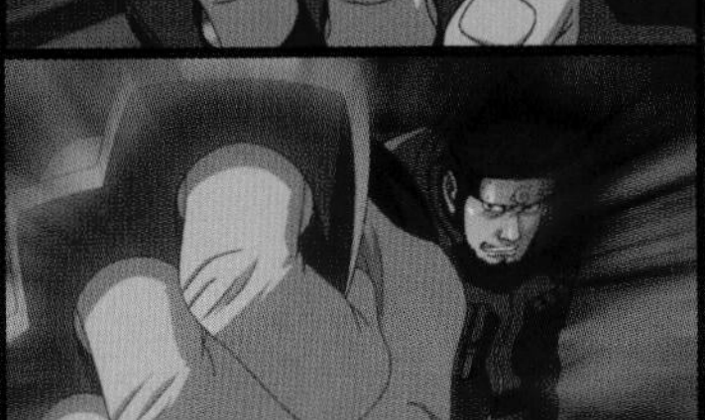

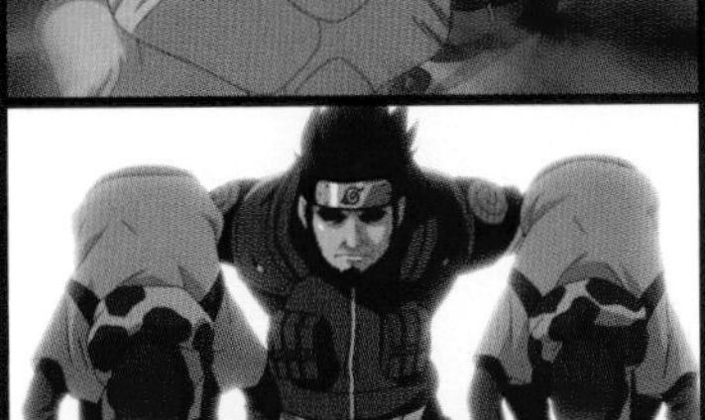

Who is the ninth pursuer?!

Fresh from his match, Shikamaru has little chakra left to maintain the Shadow Possession Jutsu. The moment Shikamaru loses control, the ninth pursuer comes up behind him. Surprisingly, it's his teacher, Asuma Sarutobi!

Well done, Shikamaru...

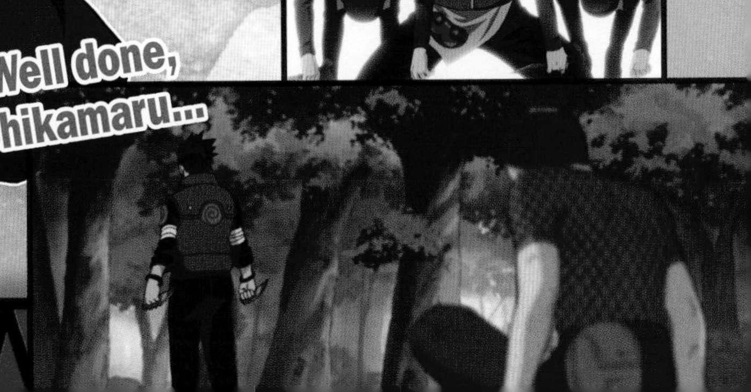

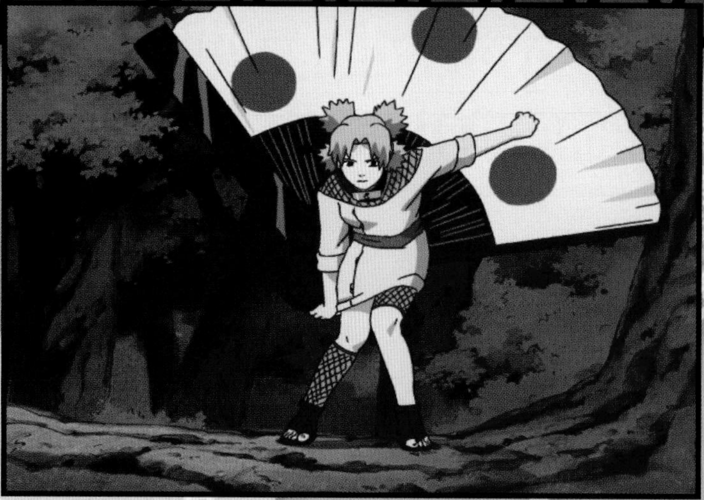

⬇⬅ Temari slashes down the trees with the Wind Scythe Jutsu, while Sasuke tries to conserve his chakra. Saving the Chidori, Sasuke fights back with the Fire Style Jutsu.

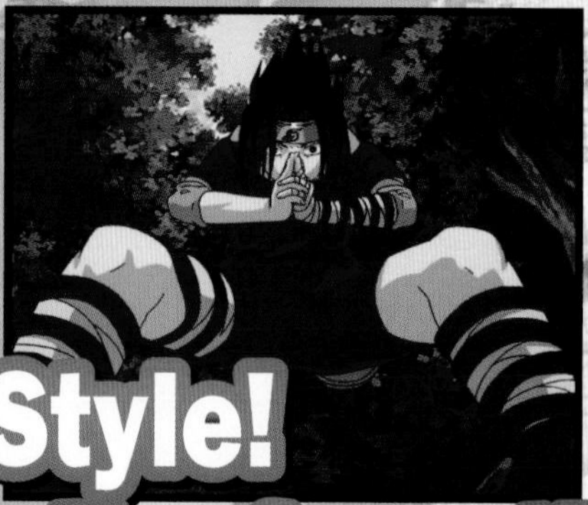

Wind Style vs. Fire Style! A blast wave covers the forest!

Temari's effort to pin down Sasuke is futile!

Sasuke slips through various traps and catches up with Gaara's party, but then must face Temari, who is determined to shake Sasuke off of Gaara's trail. The clash between fire and wind gets intense, and soon the forest is engulfed in fire blasts!

➡ Sasuke unleashes the Fireball Jutsu in response to Temari's offensive. But was Temari anticipating this?!

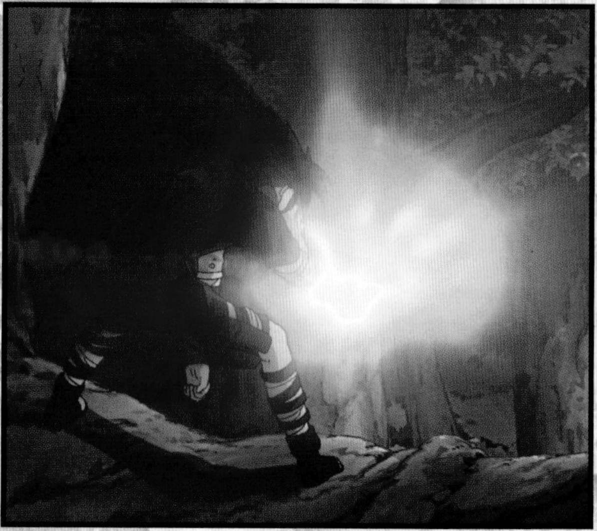

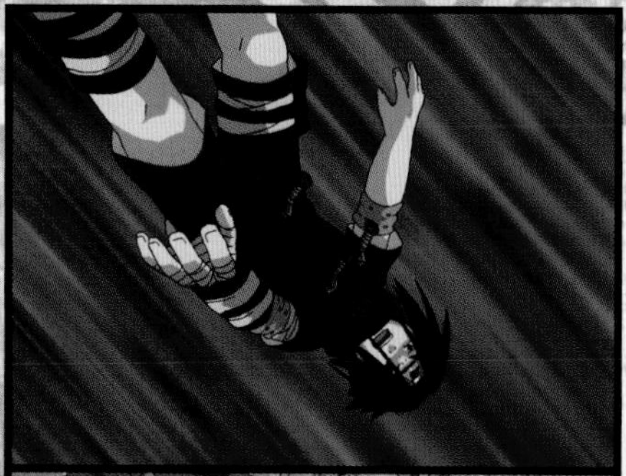

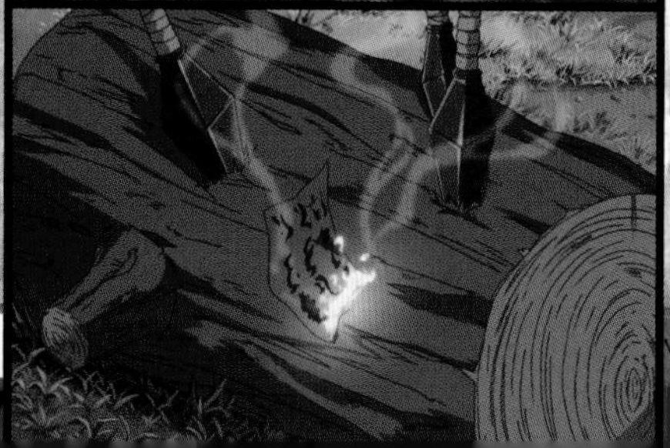

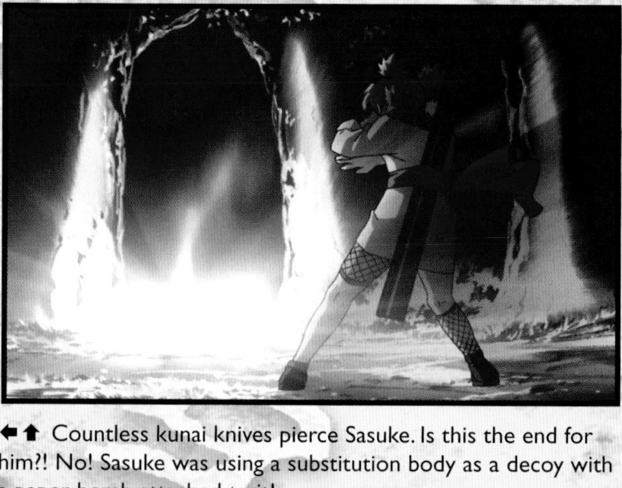

⬅⬆ Countless kunai knives pierce Sasuke. Is this the end for him?! No! Sasuke was using a substitution body as a decoy with a paper bomb attached to it!

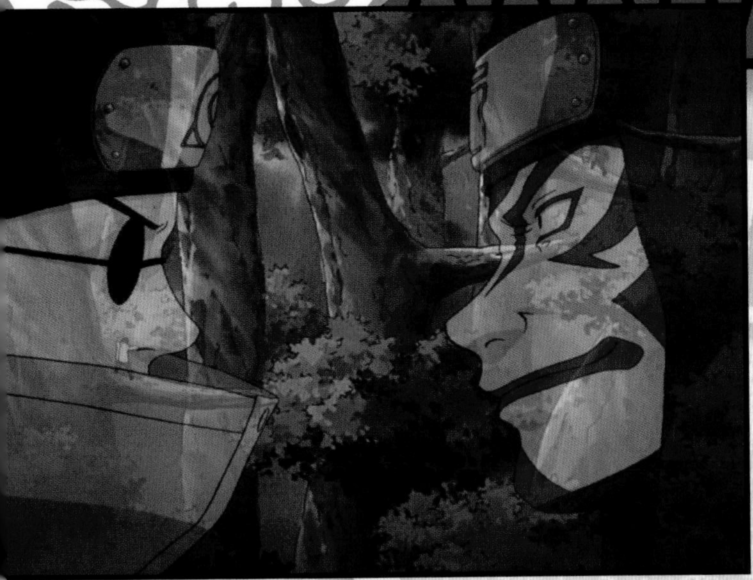

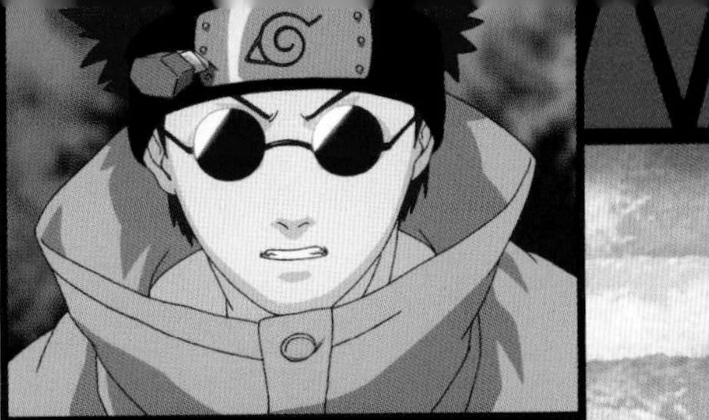

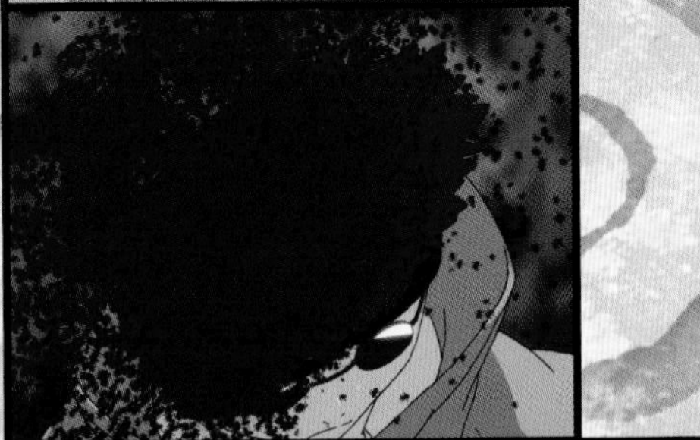

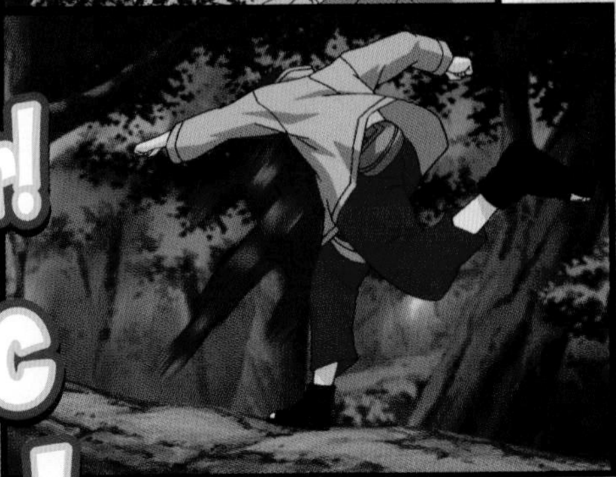

Insect Tamer vs. Puppet Master!
A phantasmagoric one-on-one battle!

⬆ Kankuro barely dodges Shino's fist in close-quarter combat, but..?!

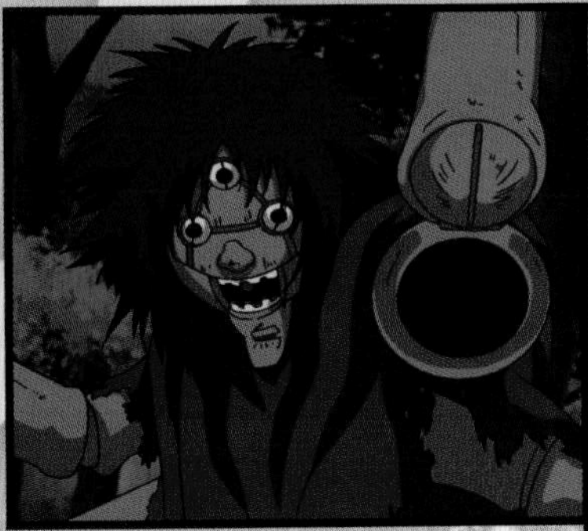

➡ The Crow, stocked with numerous lethal weapons, methodically corners Shino!

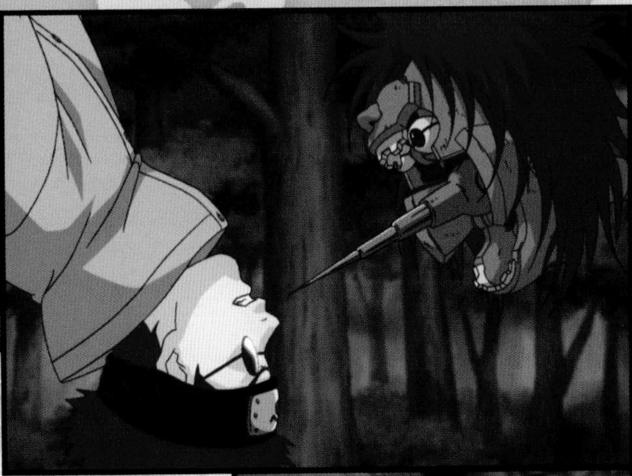

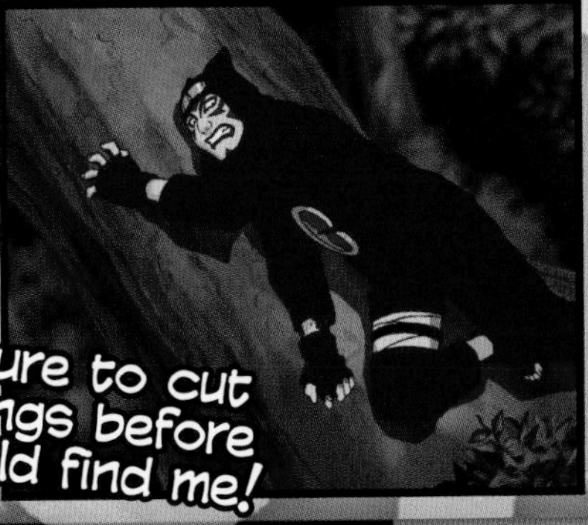
I was sure to cut the strings before they could find me!

➡ Shino's unexpected counterattack! Countless parasitic insects assail Kankuro!

A mind-boggling tactical death struggle!

Kankuro attacks Sasuke, who easily got past Temari! But Shino Aburame, who was secretly following them, bursts from the shadows and takes over the fight! Kankuro deploys his tactical puppet and Shino fights back with his parasitic insects. How will this battle between unyielding opponents play out?!

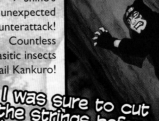

The ultimate battle!
The Third Hokage vs. Orochimaru!
A sad reunion...

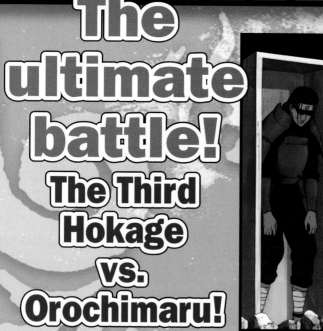

⬇ ⬅ The Hokage unleashes the Shuriken Shadow Clone Jutsu, but coffins suddenly appear and block it. Though the Hokage succeeds in stopping a third coffin, the lids of the other two open and, astonishingly, the First Hokage, the founder of the Hidden Leaf Village, and the Second Hokage emerge!

...with his predecessors!

Former Hokage are summoned!

Orochimaru summoned the Third Hokage's mentors who originally established the Village Hidden in the Leaves. To the Third Hokage's horror, his predecessors have been made into pawns that mercilessly attack their beloved student!

➡ The First Hokage flexes his powerful arms! The Hidden Leaf Village's founder—now a would-be destroyer of the village—attacks the Third Hokage.

⬅ The Second Hokage attacks with fists of steel! He holds nothing back!

Laying his life on the line to save the village!

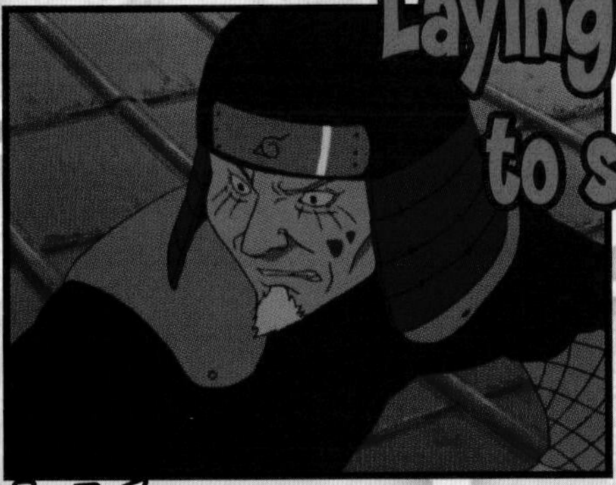

➡ The Third Hokage attacks Orochimaru with the Adamantine Nyoi. His skill fighting with a staff is magnificent!

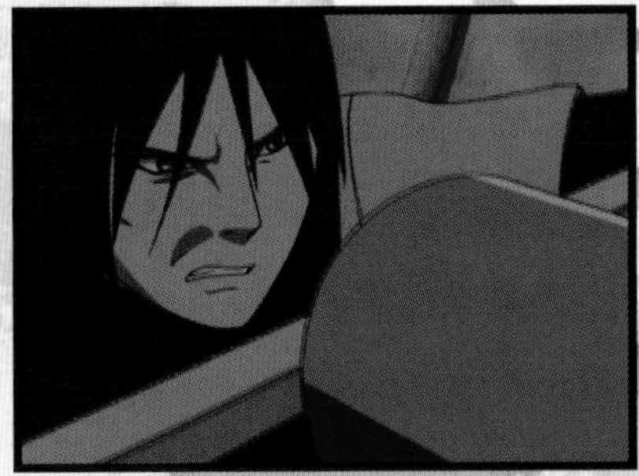

⬇ Orochimaru counters the Adamantine Nyoi with his Snake Sword!

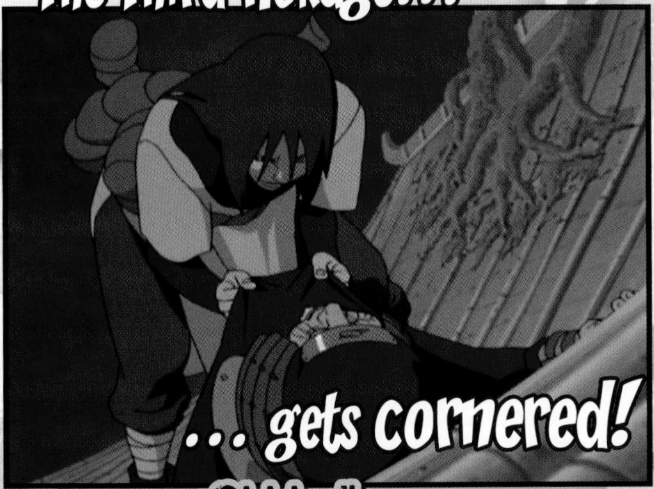
The Third Hokage...
... gets cornered!

⬆ Although possessing taijutsu equal to Orochimaru's, the Third Hokage's technique appears to be lacking. Has age caught up with him?!

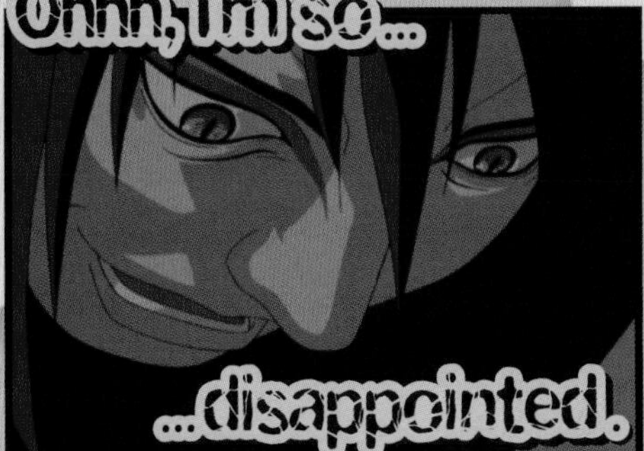
Ohhh, I'm so...
...disappointed.

⬅ Orochimaru expresses disgust at the decay of his ex-teacher's skills.

Former teacher and pupil cross swords!

Wielding the Adamantine Nyoi, the Third Hokage takes on Orochimaru, the betrayer of the Hidden Leaf Village. Burning with ambition, Orochimaru gradually corners the Third Hokage with his relentless attacks. Still, the Hokage resists!

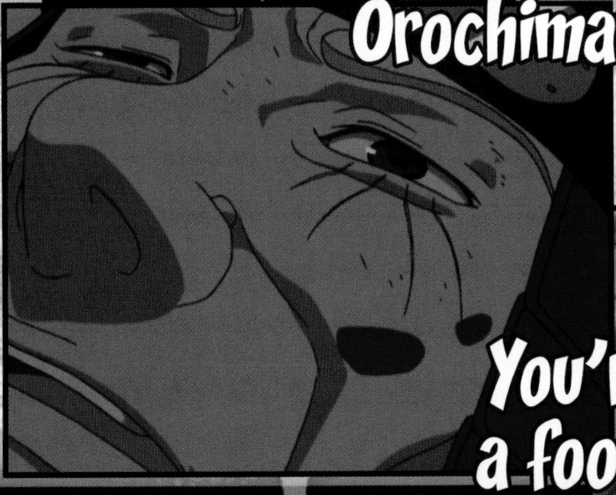
Orochimaru!

➡ Tears of remorse trail down the Third Hokage's cheek as he's pinned down by Orochimaru...

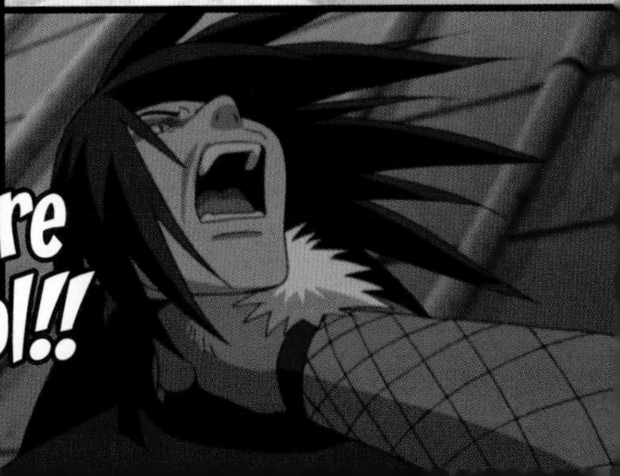
You're a fool!!

⬇ Responding to Enma's encouragement, the Third Hokage shifts to offense and seizes Orochimaru by the throat!

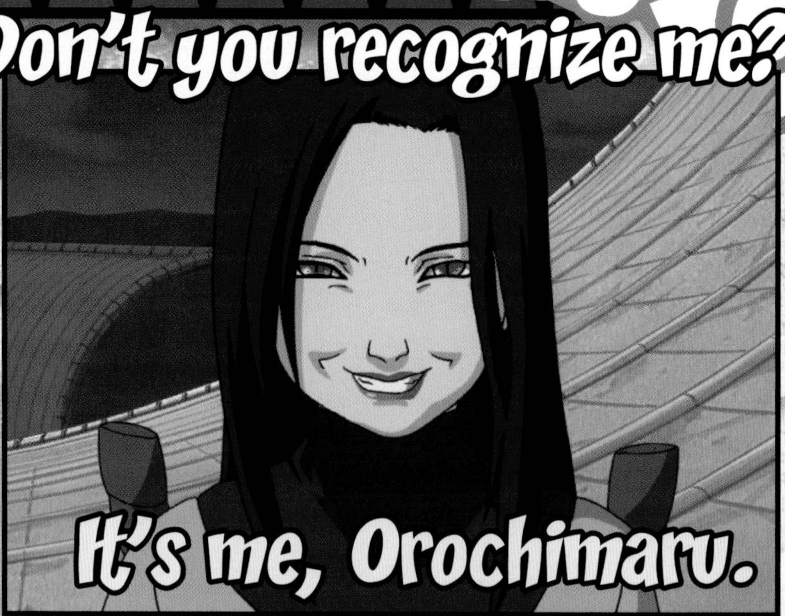
Don't you recognize me?
It's me, Orochimaru.

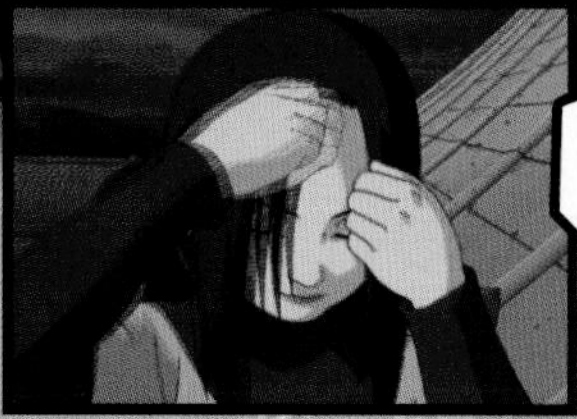

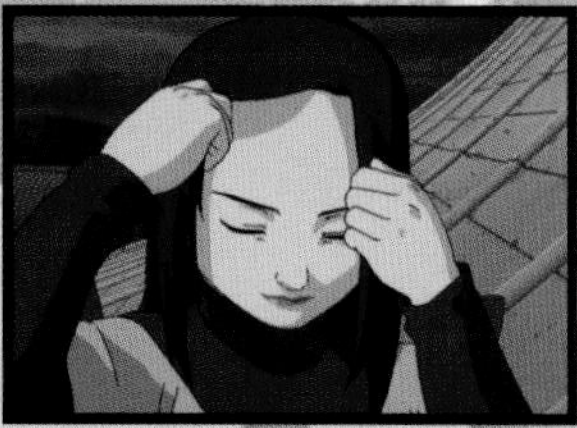

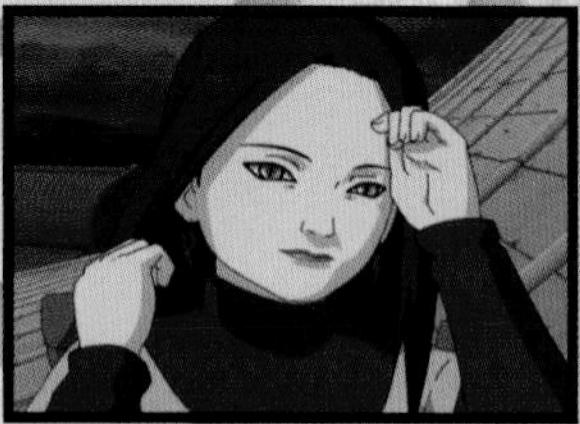

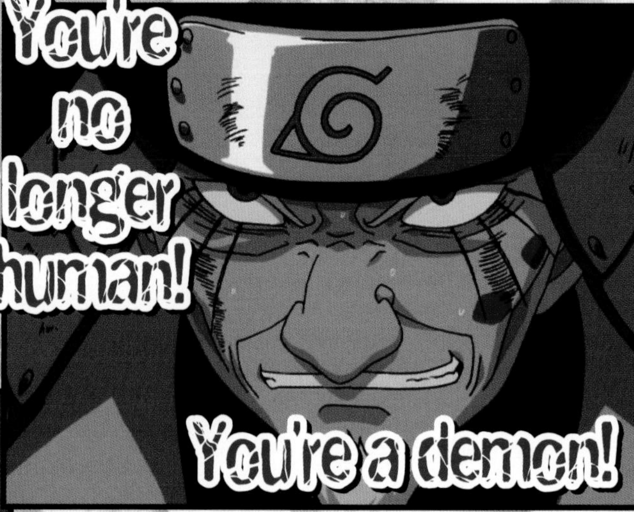
You're no longer human!
You're a demon!

⬆ Astonished at Orochimaru's fiendish actions, the Third Hokage recalls an incident from the past and could not help but utter bitter words.

Orochimaru completes the forbidden jutsu!

Orochimaru's face appears young and handsome. There is no doubt that he has completed the forbidden Immortality Jutsu that he had been researching.

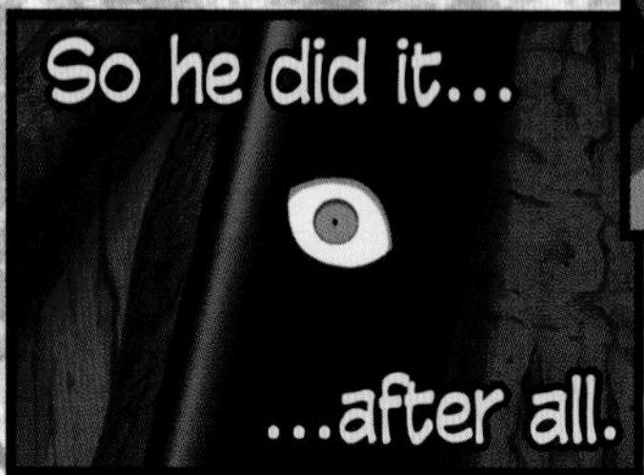
So he did it...
...after all.

➡ Enma is also shocked to learn of the forbidden jutsu's completion!

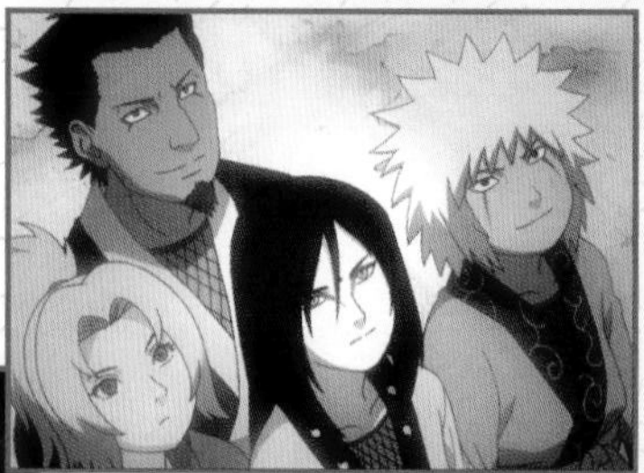

⬅ The Third Hokage was always fully aware of the potentially deadly mix of ambition and intelligence shining brightly in the eyes of Orochimaru, even as a child.

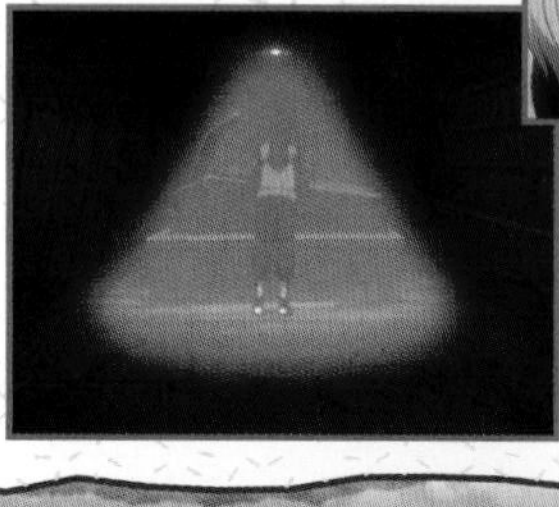

➡ Orochimaru researched the forbidden jutsu deep in the subterranean chambers under the village. He was once cornered but...

The Third Hokage's regret

A mistake from the past

After witnessing the extraordinary abilities Orochimaru possessed since childhood, the Third Hokage had great expectations for him. But Orochimaru devoted himself to forbidden jutsu to advance his own ambitions and left the village. The Hokage once nearly caught Orochimaru, but failed because of the affection he still had as his teacher. He has regretted it ever since.

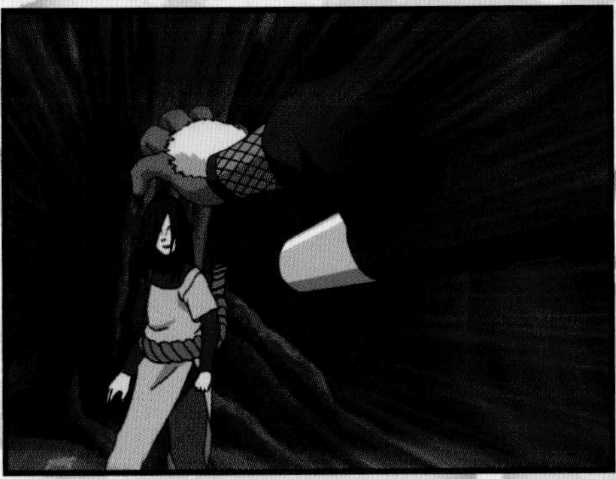

➡ In the darkness, the Third Hokage finally gets ahold of Orochimaru!

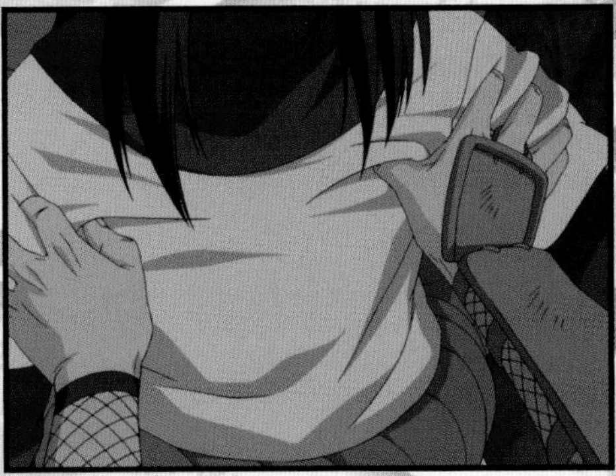

The Third Hokage's... ...greatest and final secret jutsu!

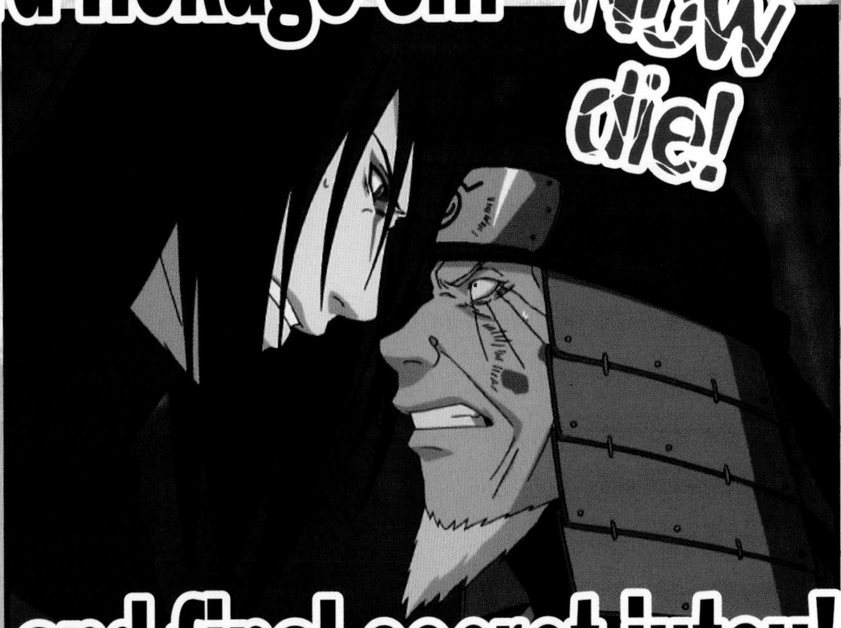
Now die!

The sealing jutsu Reaper Death Seal is unleashed! Has the fatal struggle reached its end?

The Third Hokage uses a secret jutsu to correct his mistake and finish it all. He succeeds in sealing the two former Hokage and finally capturing Orochimaru! The fatal struggle reaches its end?!

⬇ For both the Third Hokage and the Fourth Hokage, the Reaper Death Seal becomes their final jutsu.

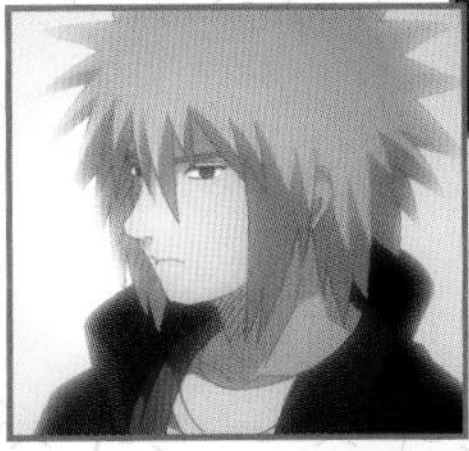

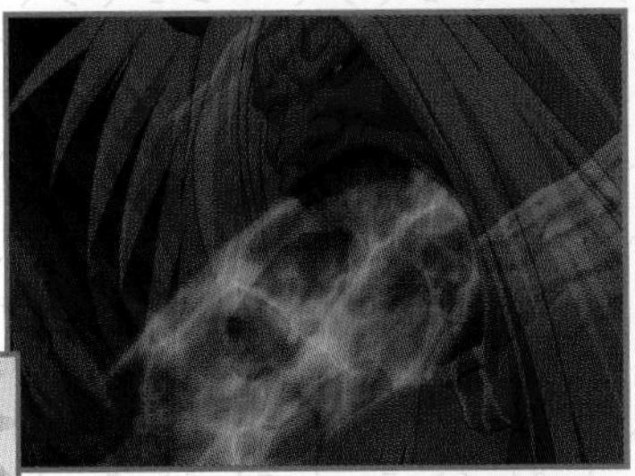

⬆ The Reaper devours the soul of its target. The user of the jutsu and its target are doomed to forever battle within the Reaper's belly!

The same jutsu the Fourth Hokage used to seal the Nine-Tailed Fox!

Sealing Jutsu: Reaper Death Seal

The sealing jutsu the Third Hokage uses in the fatal battle against Orochimaru is a dreadful jutsu in which a Reaper is summoned—through the sacrifice of the user's own soul—that devours the soul of its target. This is the jutsu that the Fourth Hokage, the hero who saved the Hidden Leaf Village, used to seal the Nine-Tailed Fox.

With one blow...

...I'll finish this!

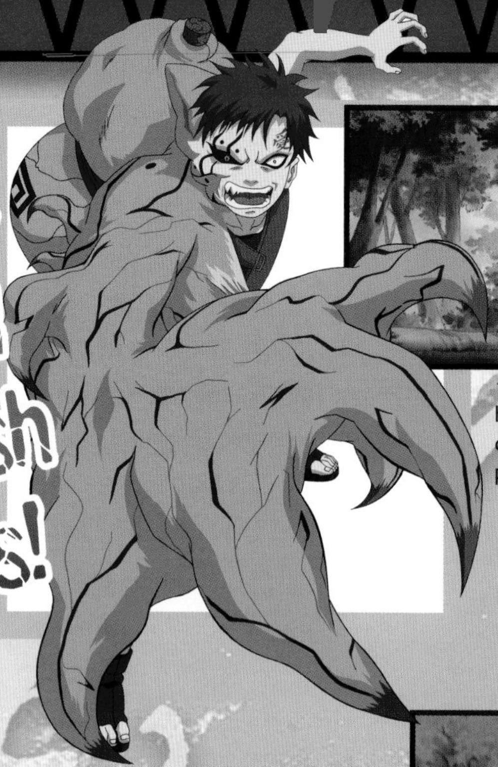

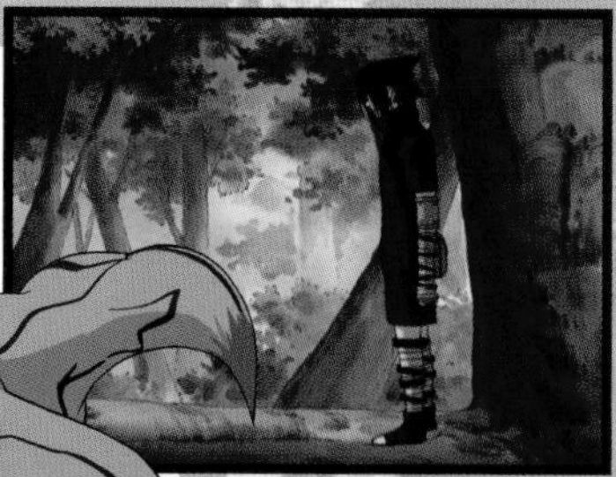

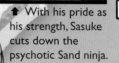

⬆ With his pride as his strength, Sasuke cuts down the psychotic Sand ninja.

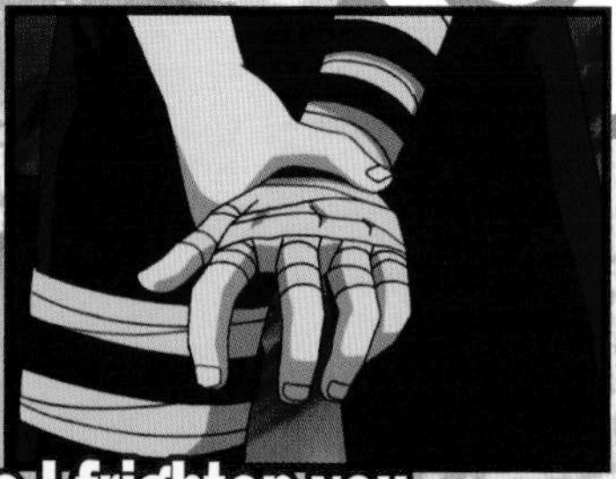

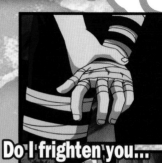

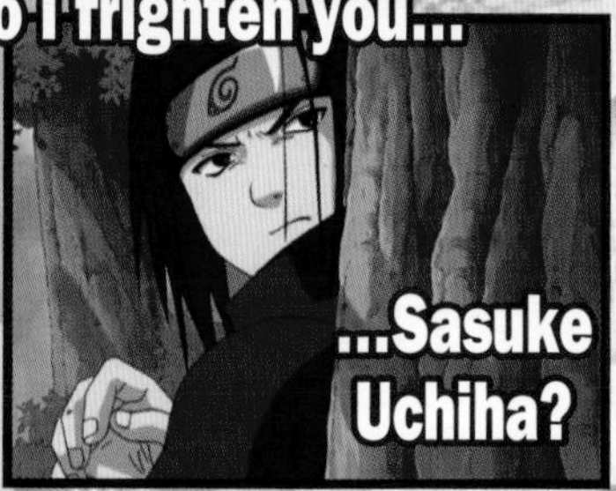
Do I frighten you...
...Sasuke Uchiha?

➡ With the capacity to use Chidori only once more, Sasuke puts everything into it!

As Gaara provokes him, Sasuke stands and makes a hand sign in response.

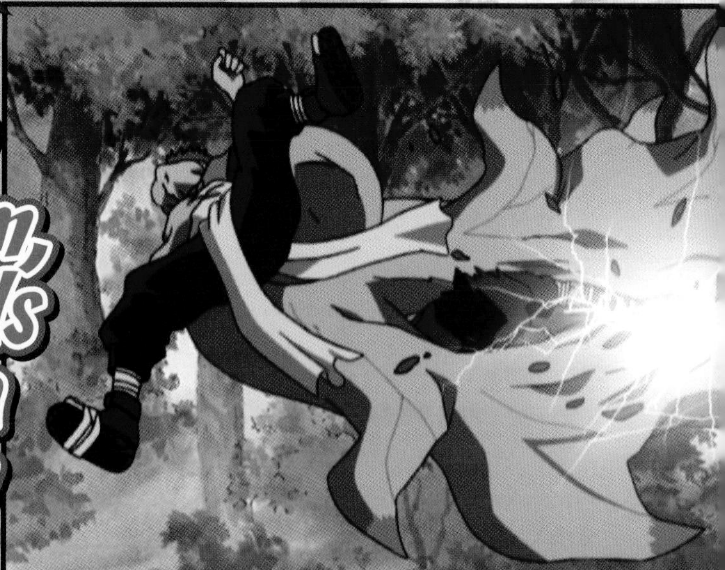

⬆ Sasuke's full-power blow punches clean through Gaara!

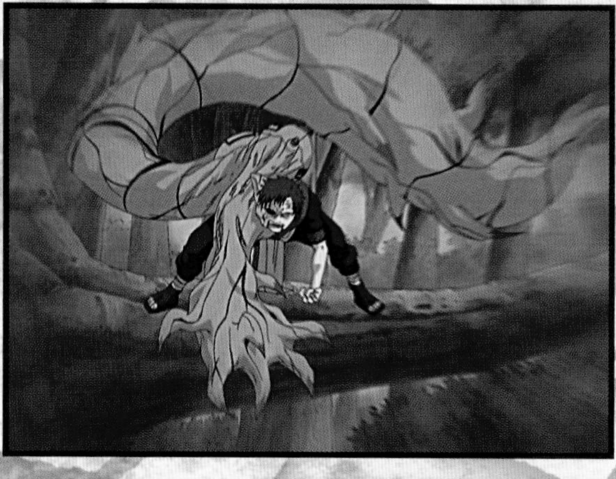

➡ Now a grotesque tail appears! Even after a direct hit from the Chidori, Gaara's transformation continues.

No one can stop him! Gaara transforms into a monster!

Gaara questions Sasuke incessantly, while Sasuke stakes his very life on a second Chidori shot to cut him down! However, it only serves to progress Gaara's transformation!

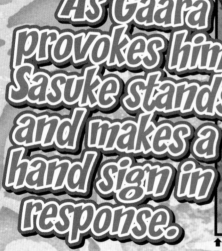

Well, for one thing, it wouldn't work...

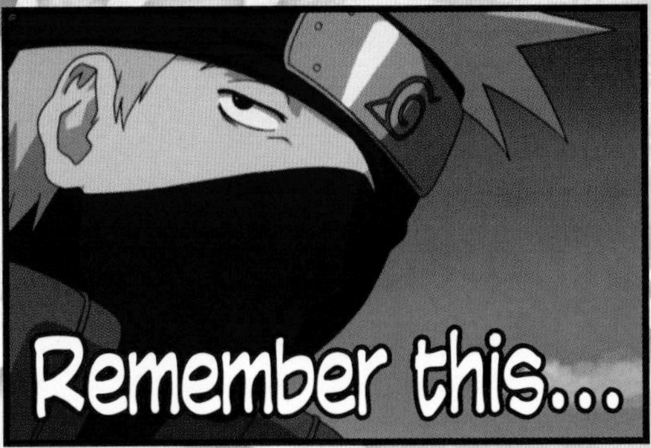
Remember this...

⬆ With his back now against the wall, the warning from his sensei, Kakashi, echoes in Sasuke's mind...!

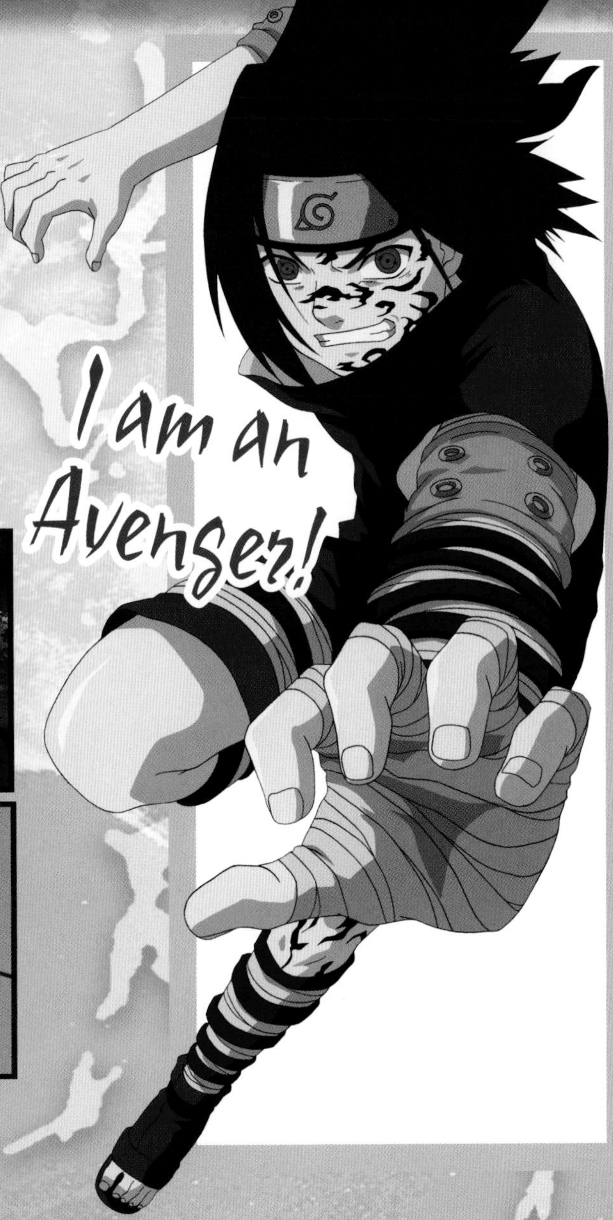
I am an Avenger!

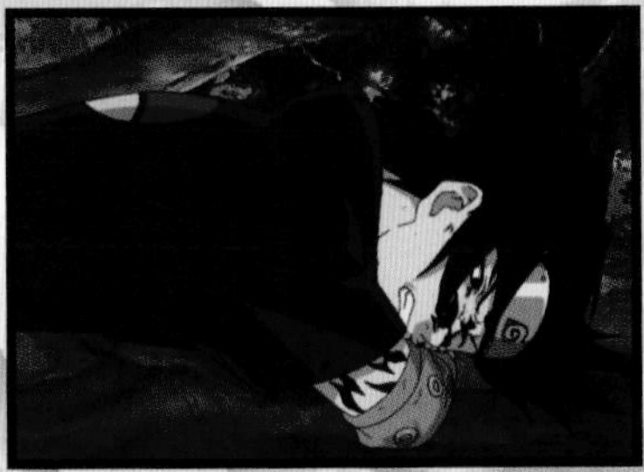

➡ Sasuke is paralyzed as the curse mark is activated!

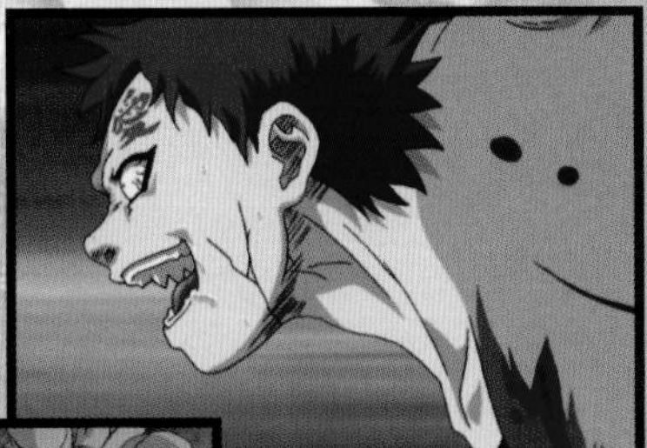

➡ A third blow of the Chidori fails and Gaara bares his fangs.

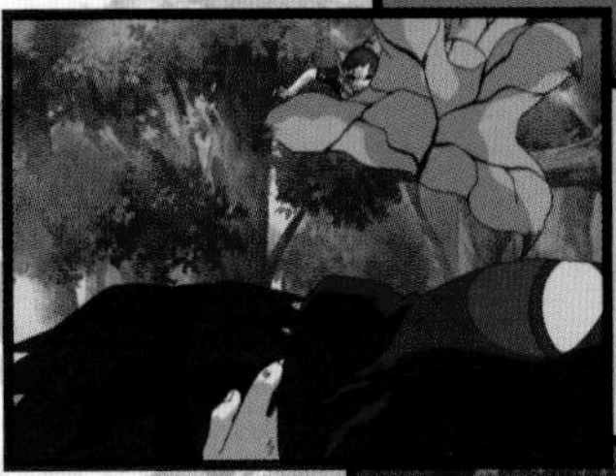

⬅ Gaara rushes in to finish Sasuke off.

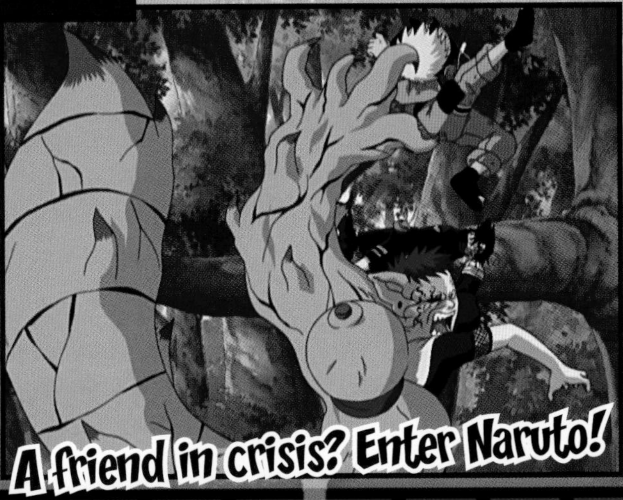
A friend in crisis? Enter Naruto!

➡ All seems lost! But at that very instant someone bursts onto the scene! To Sasuke's rescue—with a flying kick—comes Naruto!

A bluish white spark breaks the obstruction!

To confront the ever more atrocious and powerful transformed Gaara, Sasuke's only resort is to exceed his limit with a third Chidori blow! It's a gamble far too risky. Kakashi forbade it, and it is uncertain whether it will even work at all.

SAKURA SHIELDS SASUKE!

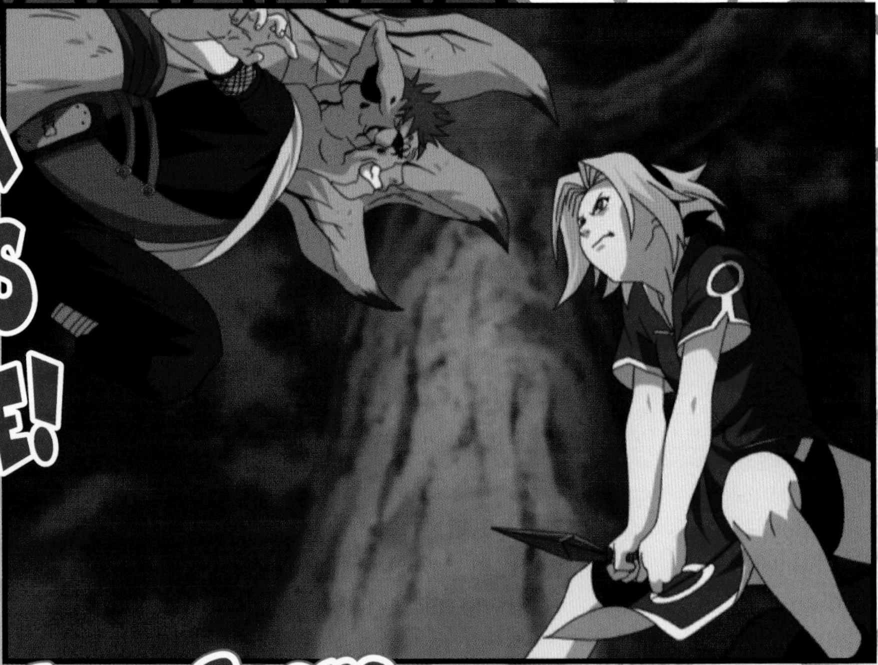

➡ With only one kunai knife in her hand, Sakura stands between Sasuke and Gaara.

Why does Gaara reel in pain?

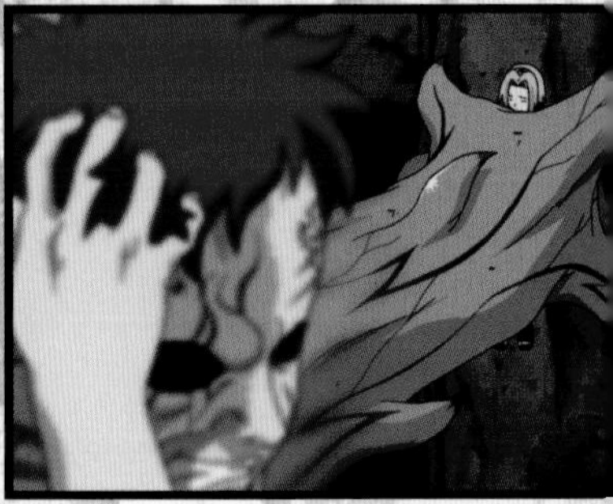

➡ Sakura triggers a memory!

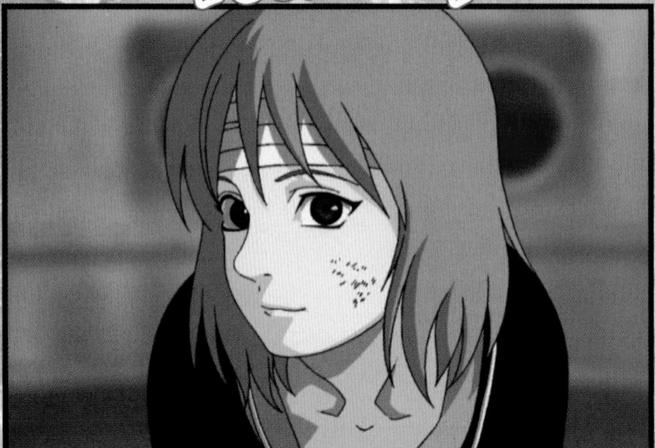

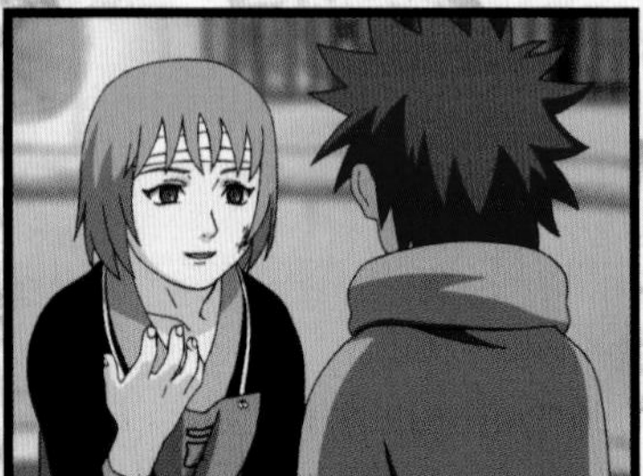

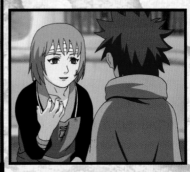

⬅ Yashamaru was the one who taught Gaara the meaning of love.

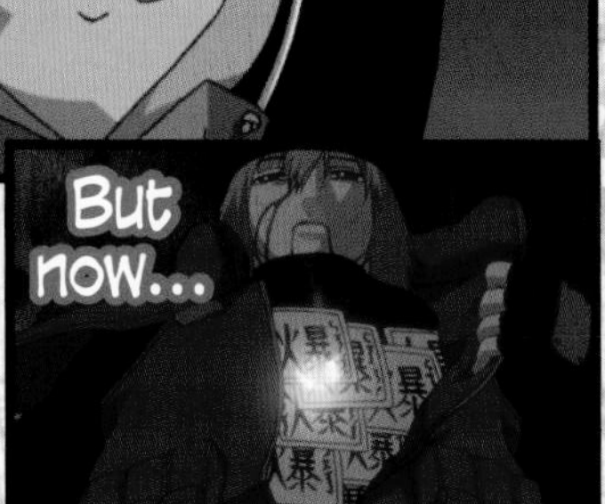
But now...
This is the end...

⬆ Cruel words from the one who taught him love cause little Gaara's heart to shudder.

⬇ The intense emotions that carved the symbol on Gaara's forehead explode!

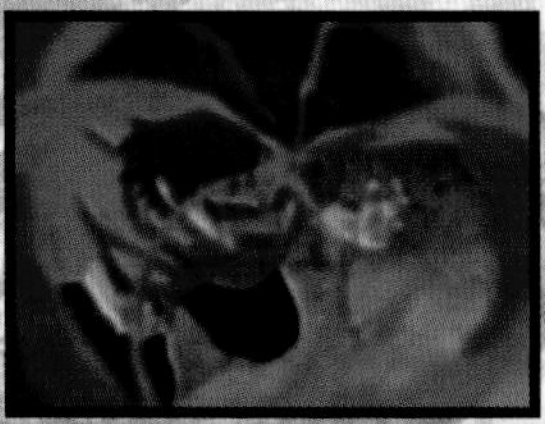

A horrible memory bubbles to the surface!

Gaara is hurt and confused when Sakura stands to protect Sasuke. Tragic, gruesome memories of the past replay in his mind!

Nice, kid... Not too shabby.

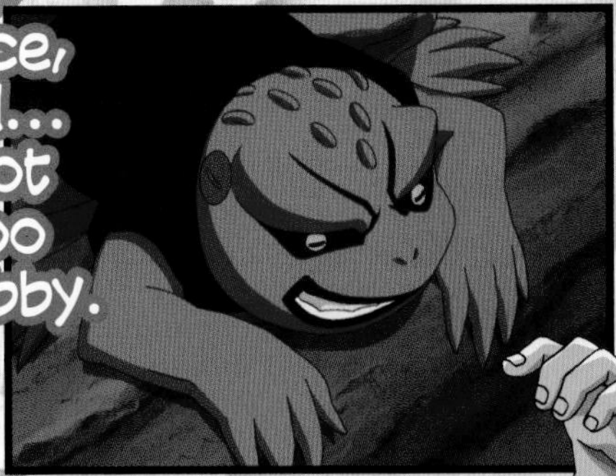

⬆ Gamakichi gives his approval of Naruto's grand offensive!

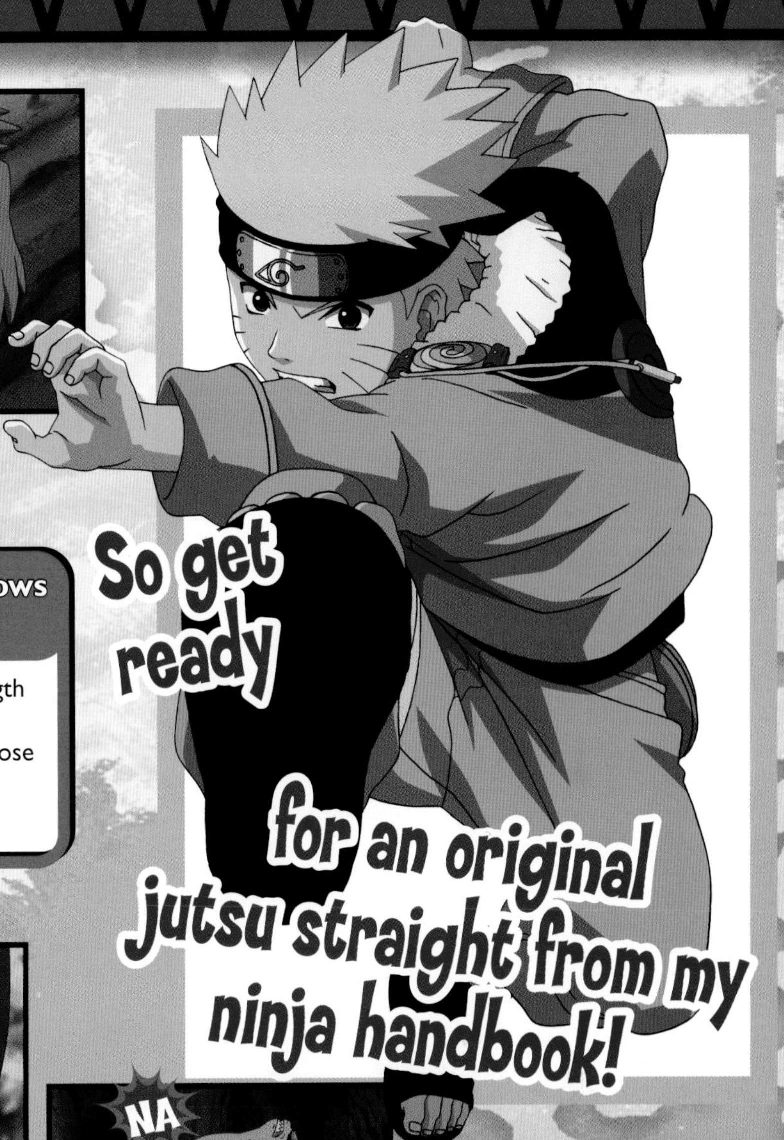

So get ready for an original jutsu straight from my ninja handbook!

Naruto's chakra overflows for his dear friends!

Naruto realizes what true strength is and decides what to do! To protect Sasuke, Sakura and all those he loves, he charges with every ounce of chakra!

Unbelievable...Is that Naruto?!

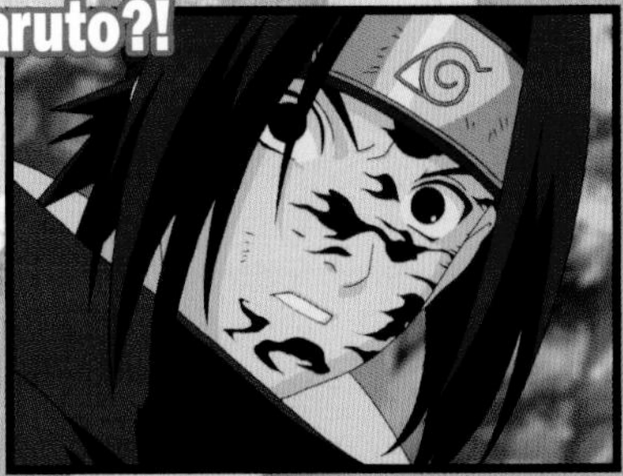

⬆ Sasuke is startled as he witnesses Naruto's tremendous growth!

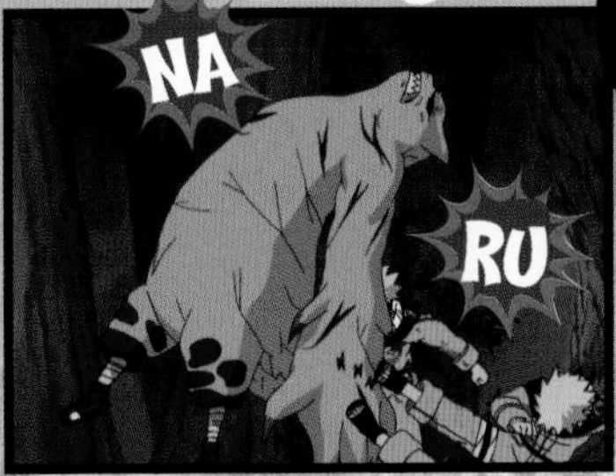
NA
RU

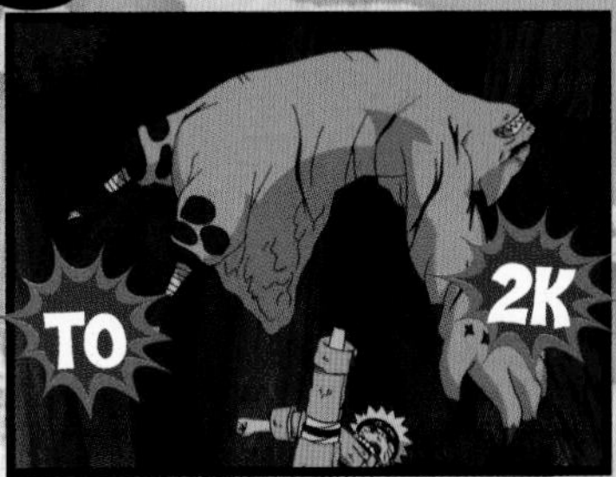
TO
2K

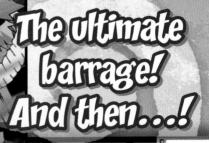

⬆ A thousand Narutos pummel Gaara with flying kicks and punches. It's an Uzumaki 2K Barrage!

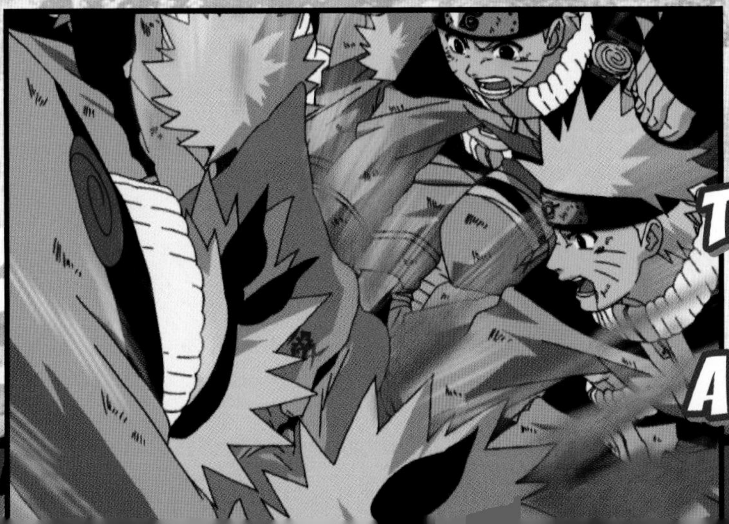

The ultimate barrage! And then...!

True terror lunges toward the heavens. The Sand Spirit Emerges!

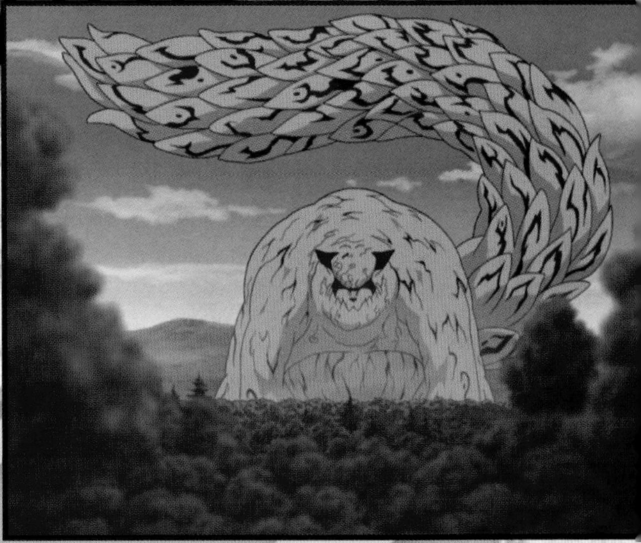

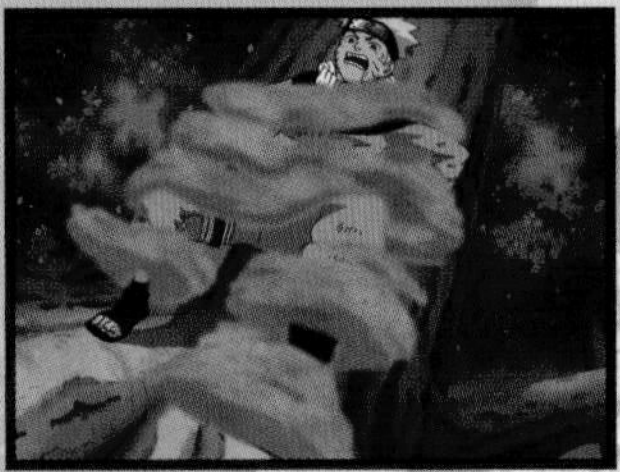

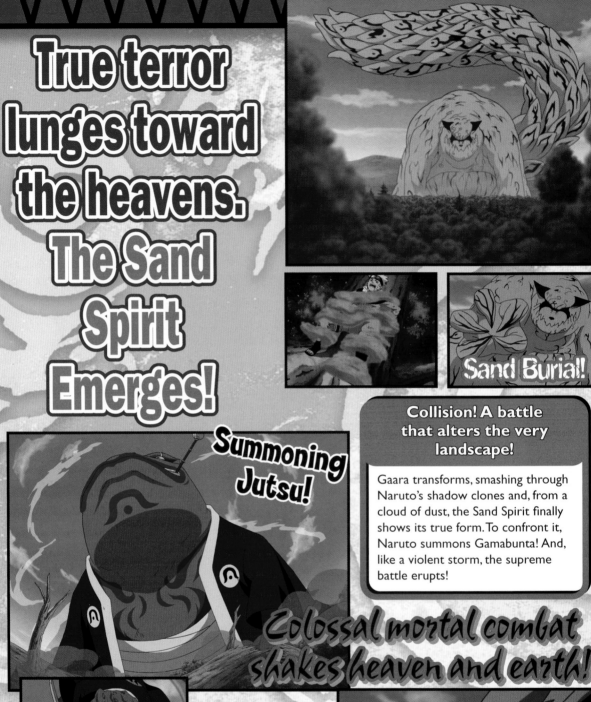

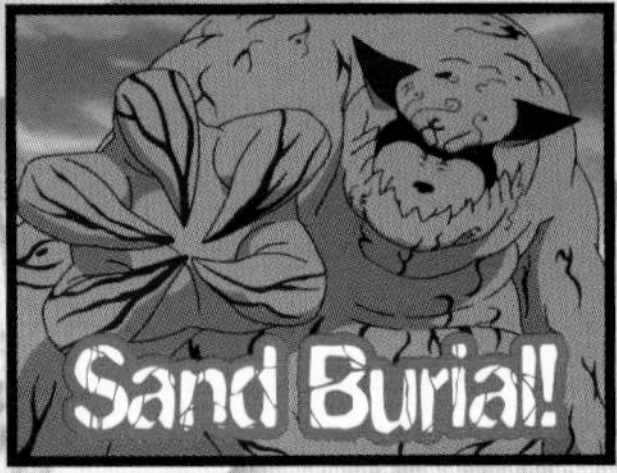
Sand Burial!

Collision! A battle that alters the very landscape!

Gaara transforms, smashing through Naruto's shadow clones and, from a cloud of dust, the Sand Spirit finally shows its true form. To confront it, Naruto summons Gamabunta! And, like a violent storm, the supreme battle erupts!

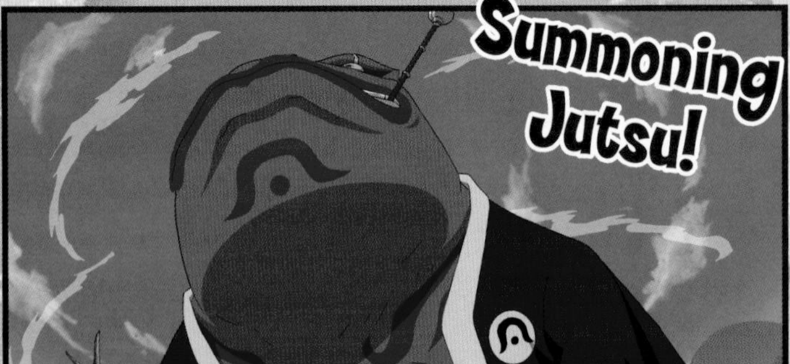
Summoning Jutsu!

Colossal mortal combat shakes heaven and earth!

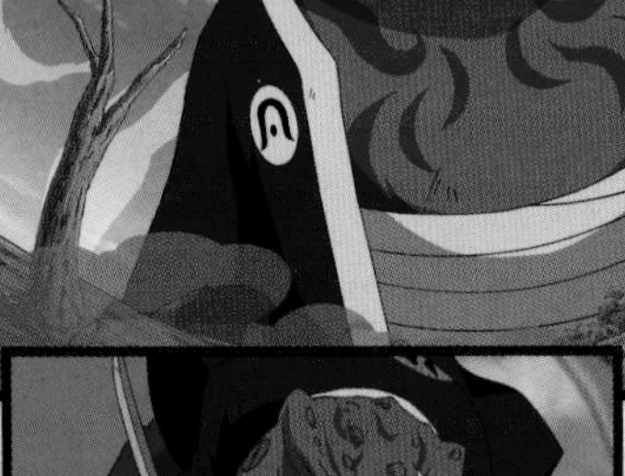

⬅ Gamabunta lunges at Shukaku, the Sand Spirit, with his short sword.

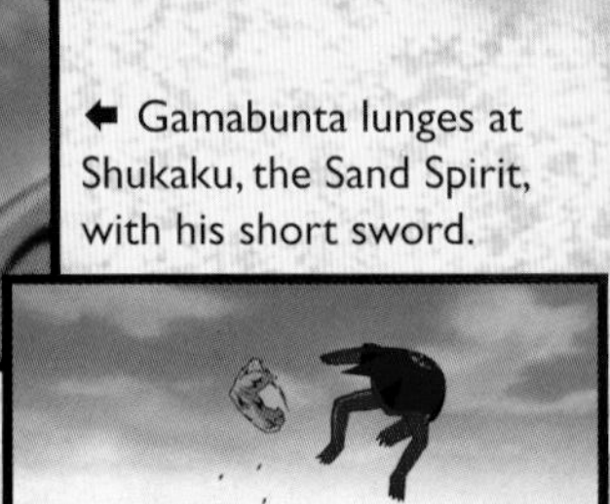

➡ Gamabunta's Toad Blade Slash slices the Sand Spirit's right arm clean off.

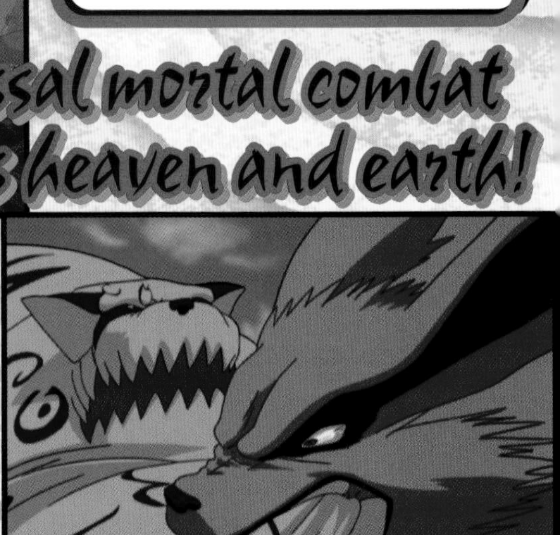

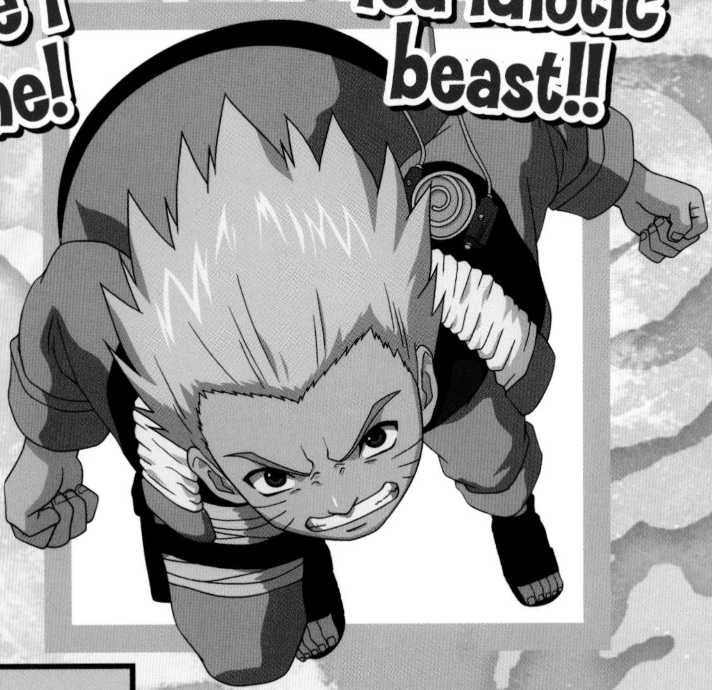
You idiotic beast!!

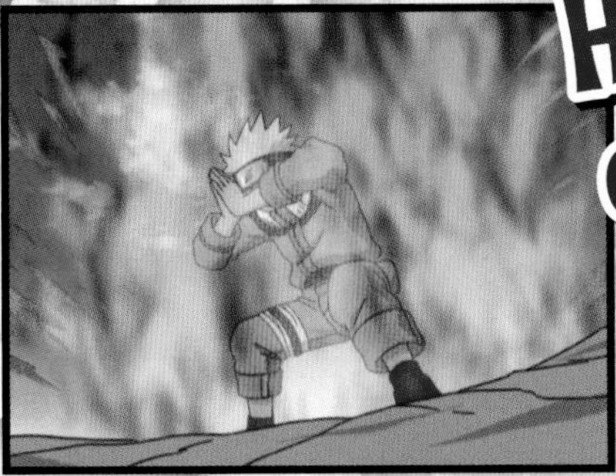
Here I come!

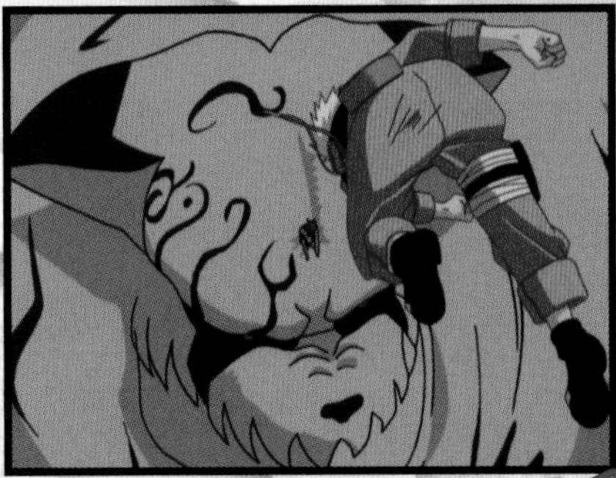

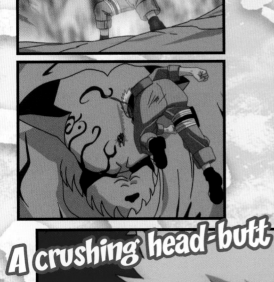

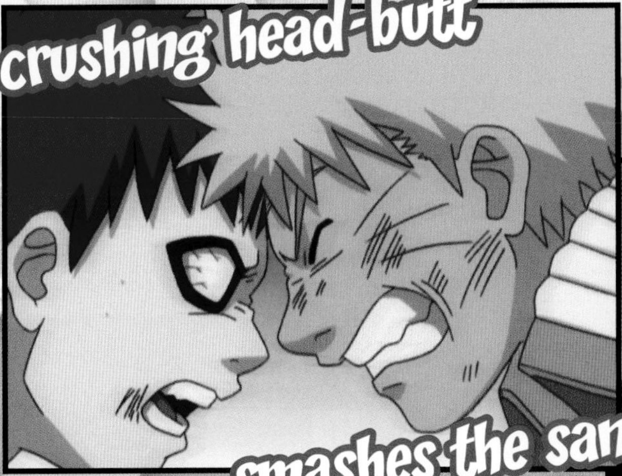
A crushing head-butt
smashes the sand!

⬅ A clumsy head-butt from Naruto finally takes out Shukaku!

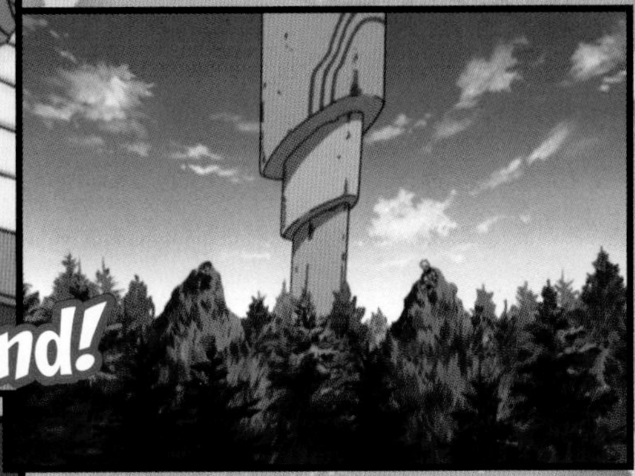

⬆ Gamabunta also disappears, restoring silence...

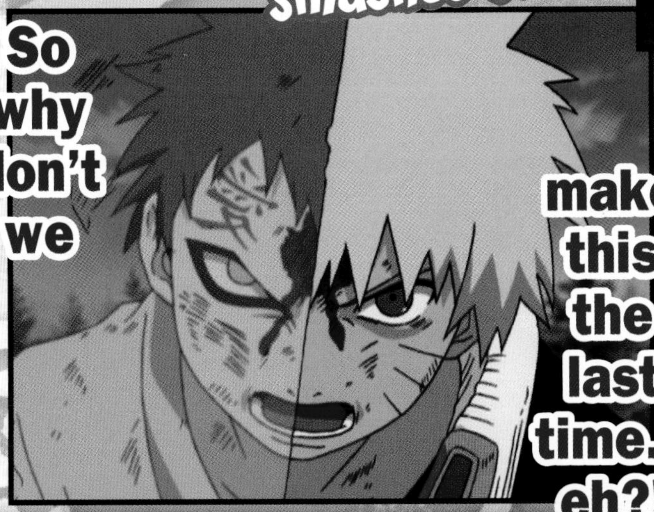
So why don't we
make this the last time... eh?!

The decisive final blow.

To suppress the Sand Spirit, Naruto charges at Gaara with only his body. Out of chakra, both the Sand Spirit and Gamabunta disappear. To bring it to an end, Naruto and Gaara hit the ground.

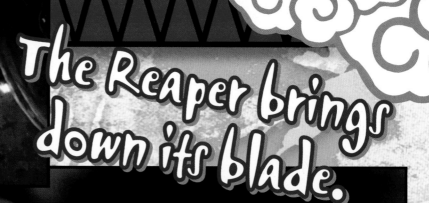

The Reaper brings down its blade.

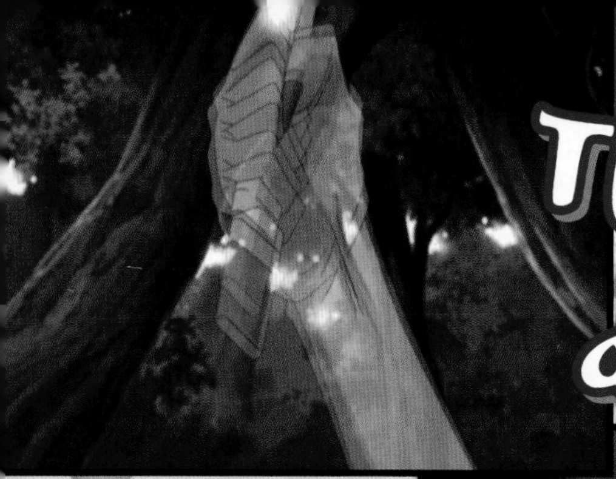

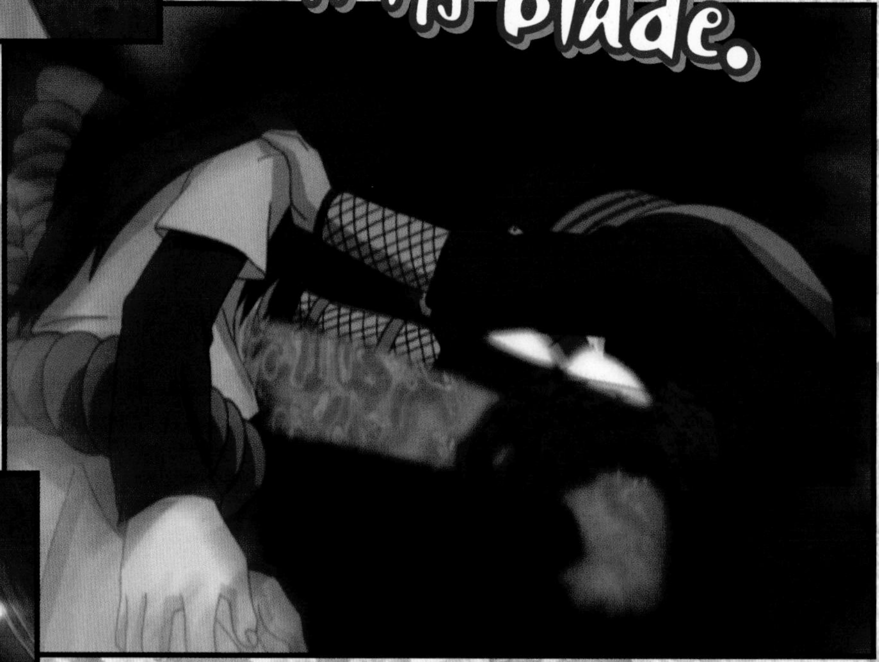

⬆➡ The Third Hokage, with only minimal power remaining, decides to cut Orochimaru's arms to disable his jutsu.

⬇ Both Orochimaru's arms are severed by the blade and sealed!.

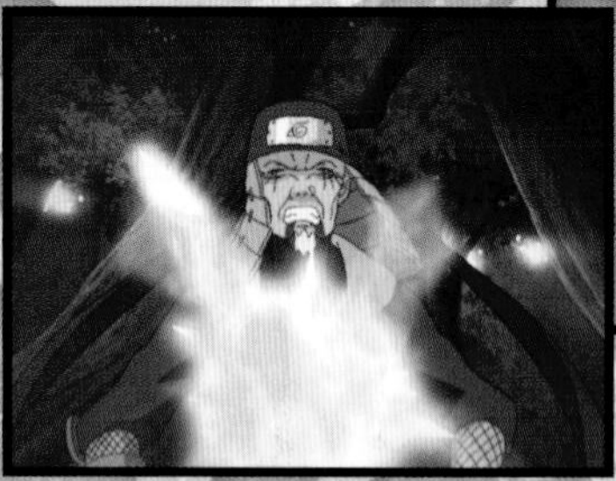

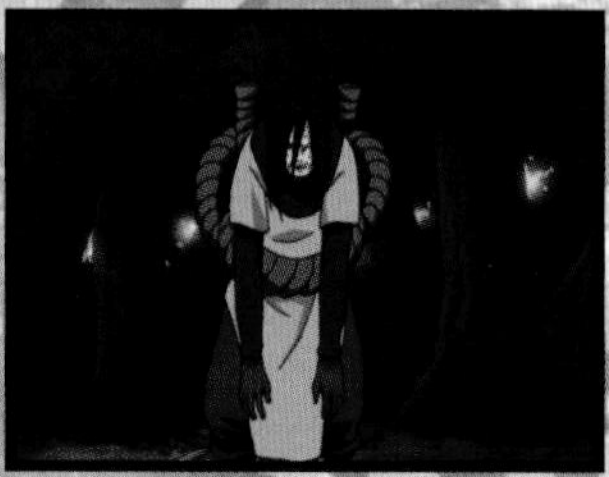

⬆ Rendered unable to use his arms to make hand signs, Orochimaru will never be able to use jutsu again.

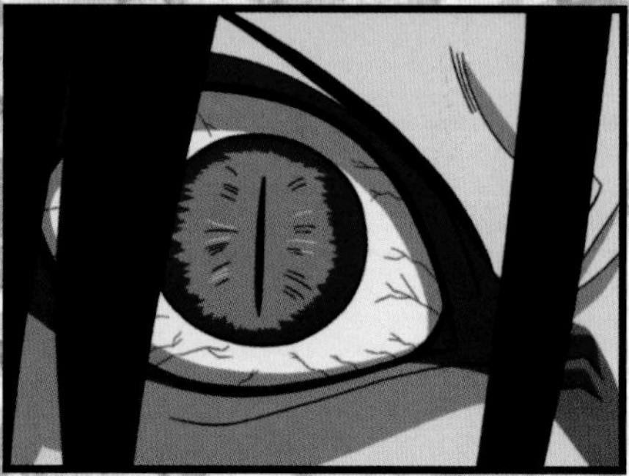

⬆ Realizing the tenacity of the Hokage, Orochimaru feels fear!

⬇ What is reflected in the Third Hokage's eyes in the final moment of his life when the sealing jutsu is complete?!

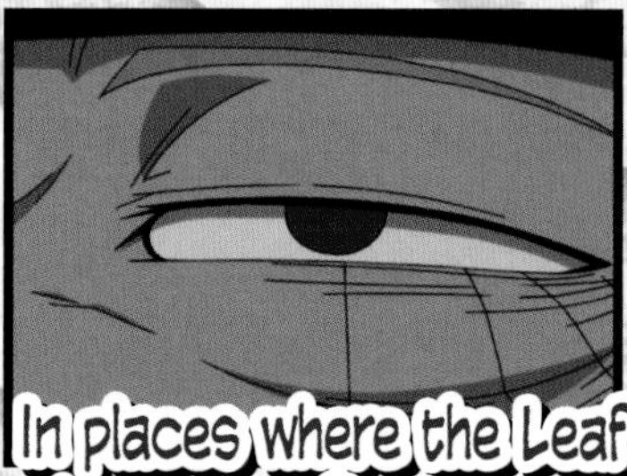

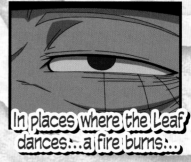

In places where the Leaf dances…a fire burns…

Heroic ending! A vile ambition is thwarted.

The Reaper's blade severs Orochimaru's arms, a most cruel punishment for one so addicted to jutsu. Unfortunately, the Third Hokage passes away, entrusting the future of the Hidden Leaf Village to the next generation.

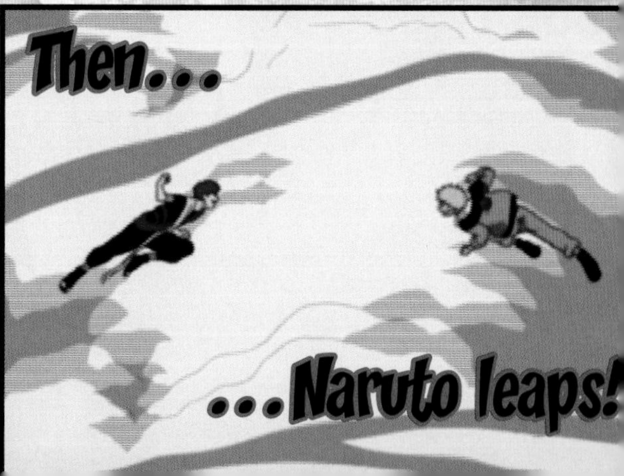
Then…
…Naruto leaps!

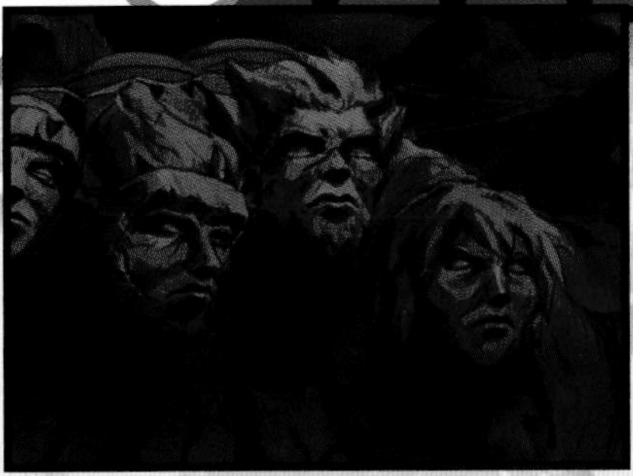

⬆ The ceremony takes place on the Ninja Academy's rooftop where the craggy Great Stone Faces are in clear view.

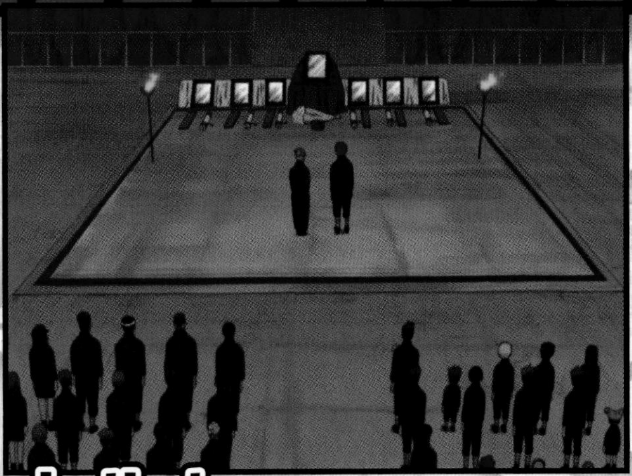

⬆ The funeral is held in the steadily falling rain. The shinobi of the Hidden Leaf Village gather to offer flowers to the casualties of war.

Sorrow turns to rain that drenches the Hidden Leaf Village.

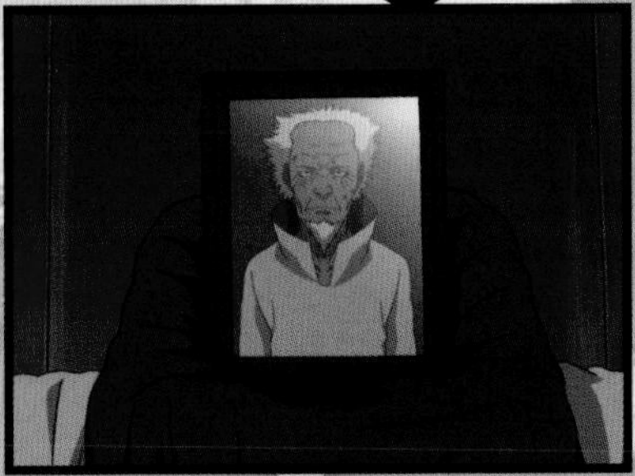

⬅ The memorial image of the Third Hokage will continue to watch over each and every member of the village family.

The Will of Fire is passed down…

Two days following the destruction of the Hidden Leaf Village, all the shinobi of the village gather. In the pouring rain, Naruto and the rest of the assembled bereaved firmly assume the mantle of the Third Hokage's Will of Fire as they come to terms with the losses of life.

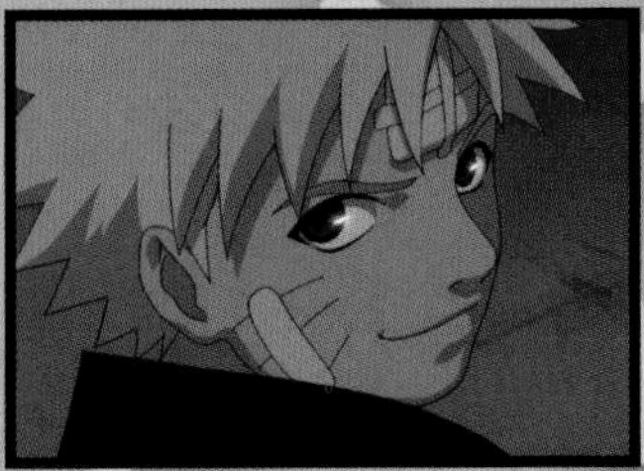

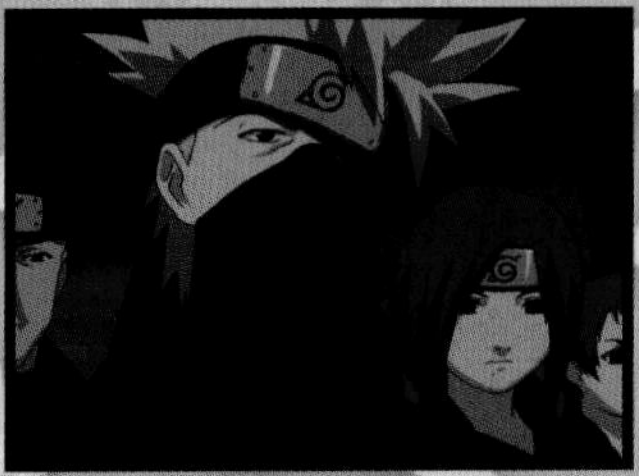

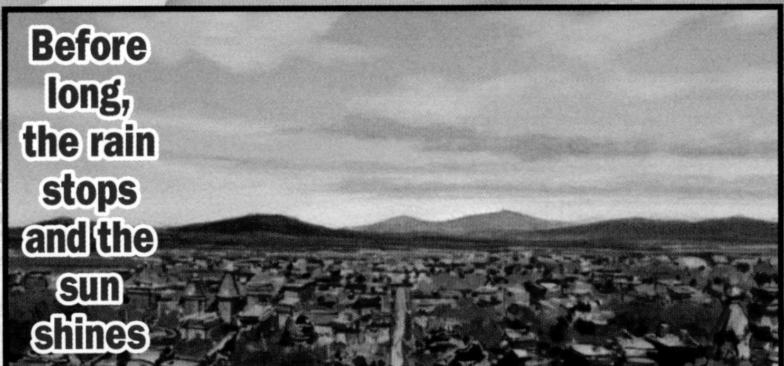

Before long, the rain stops and the sun shines once again.

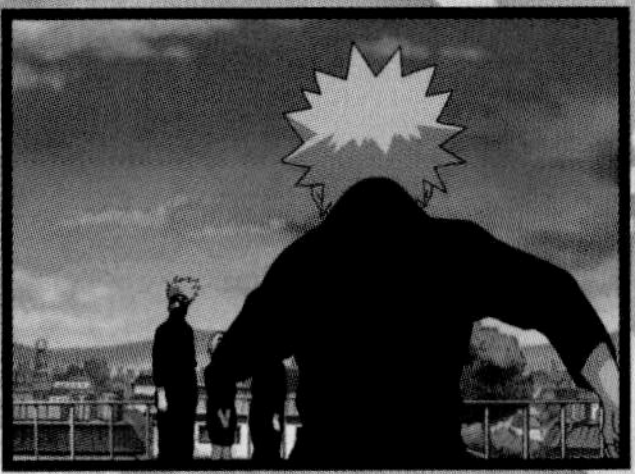

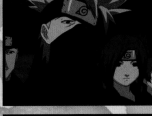

⬆ Inheriting the Will of Fire, Naruto charges toward tomorrow!

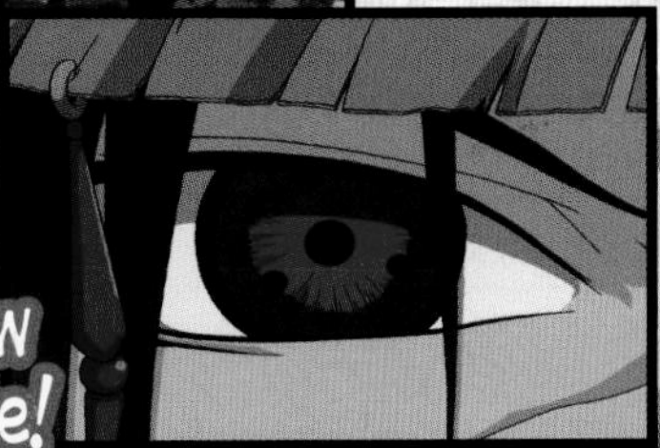

⬅ Whose red eyes peer down on the village?!

But eyes that hold a new danger now look down upon the Hidden Leaf Village!

Secret Shinobi Picture Album

Part Nine

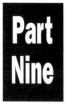

The Hot Spring District

Research with Jiraiya at the hot springs, the best training spot and a place to heal the body and soul!

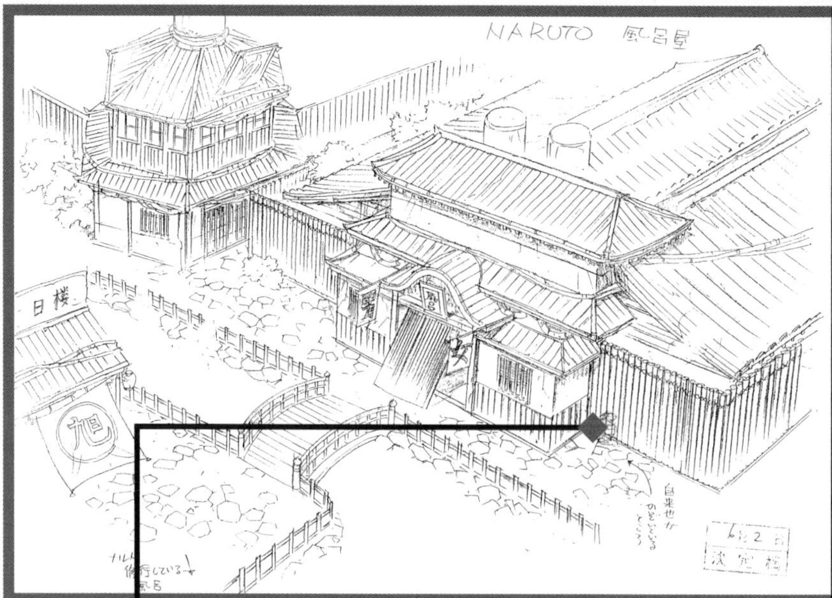

NARUTO 風呂屋

The bathhouse

The bathhouse in the hot spring district. This bamboo fence is really easy to peep through!

Bathhouse

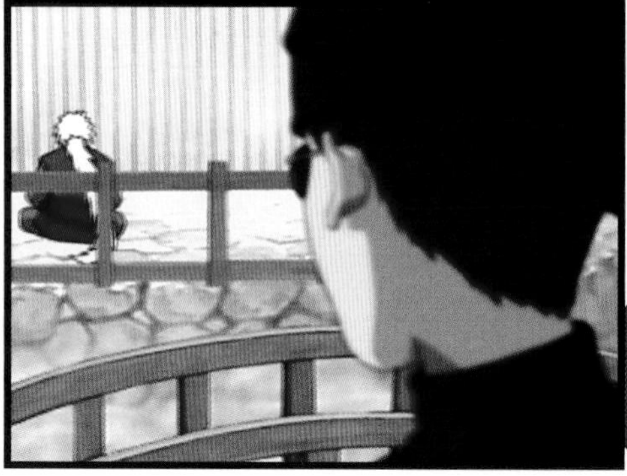

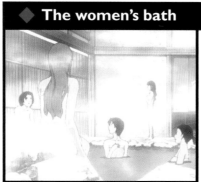

⬆ I sense a fervid gaze watching me as I pe...research. It's getting hot in here! Wait, is that Ebisu staring at me?! I'm not interested in men!

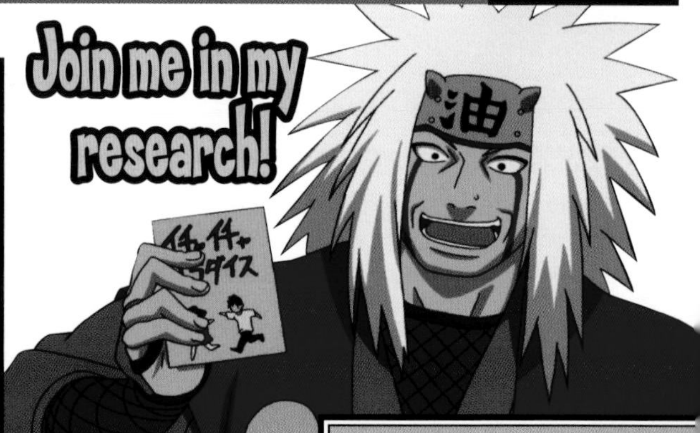

Join me in my research!
油

◆ Tour Guide: Jiraiya

The women's bath

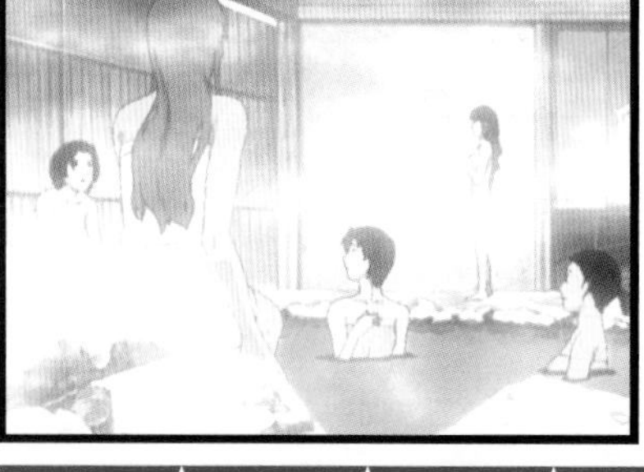

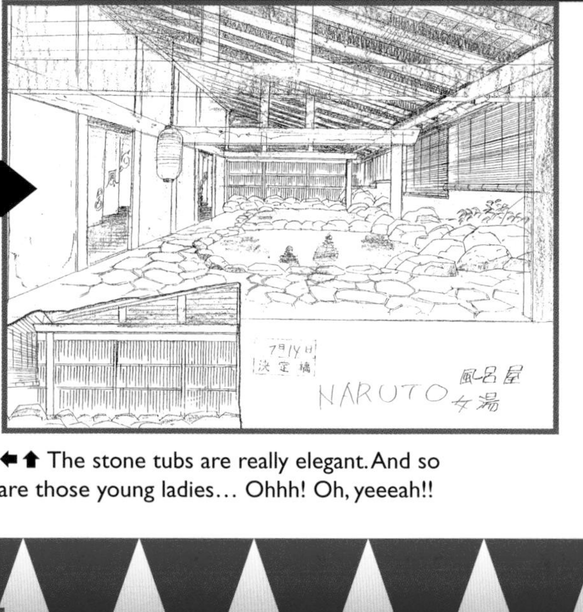

NARUTO 風呂屋 女湯

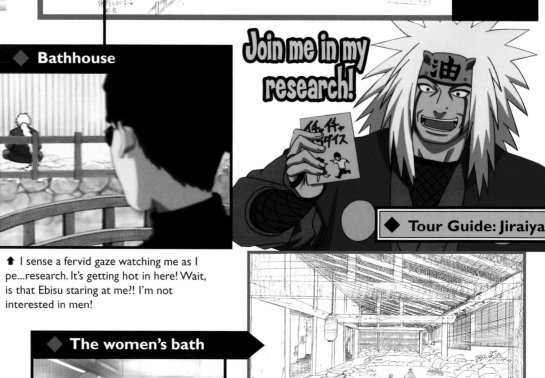

⬅⬆ The stone tubs are really elegant. And so are those young ladies… Ohhh! Oh, yeeeah!!

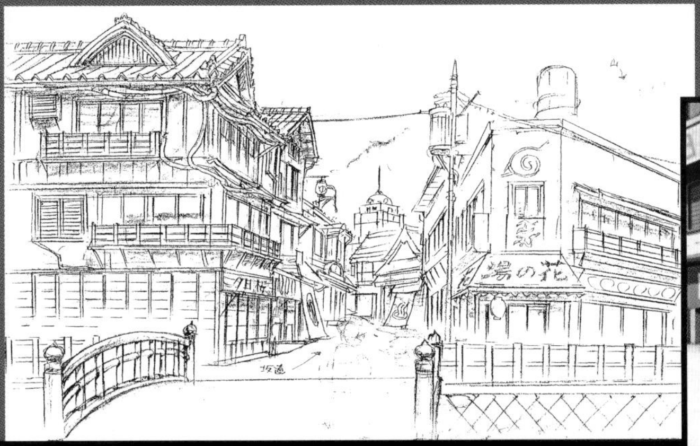

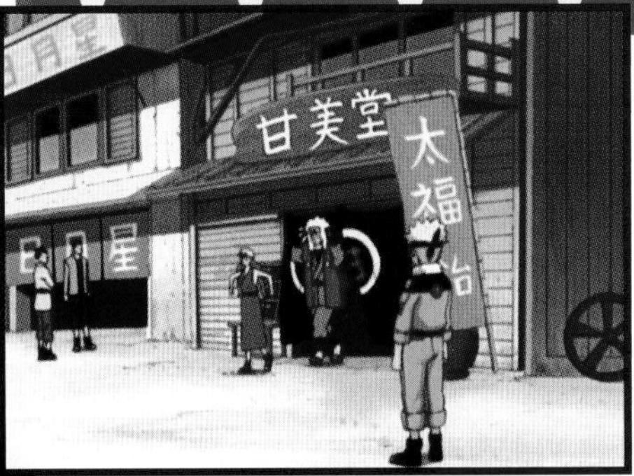
甘美堂

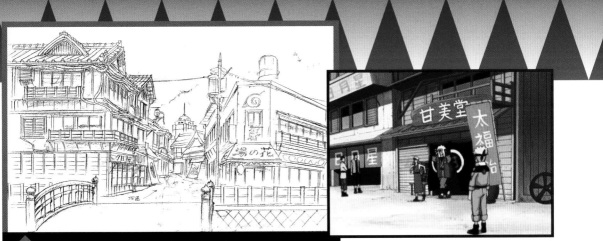

The Hot Spring District

Many bathhouses line the streets here. With so many different kinds of shops, it's a great place for sightseeing.

⬆ Candy shops are where all the cute girls hang out. That makes me instinctively want to drop by.

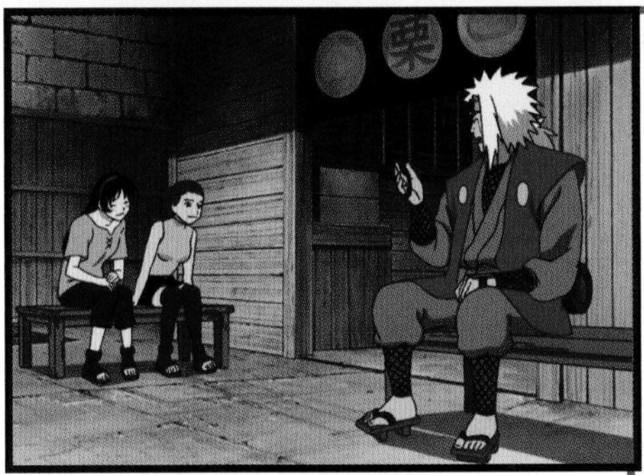

⬆ Soothing women's minds with slick conversational skills is my forte.

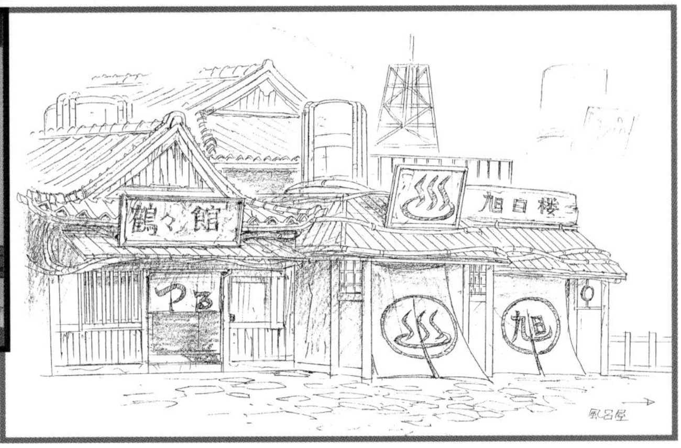
鶴々館

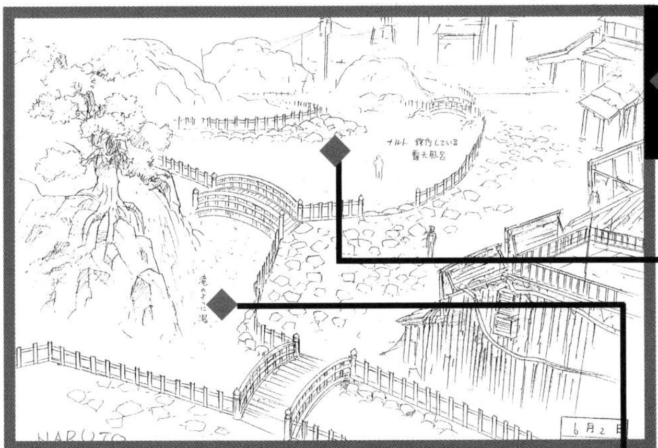

The hot spring source

The hot waters flow down like a waterfall. Most of Naruto's training took place here.

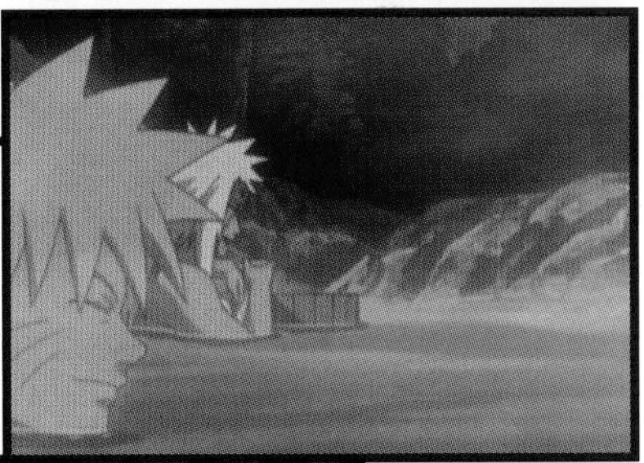

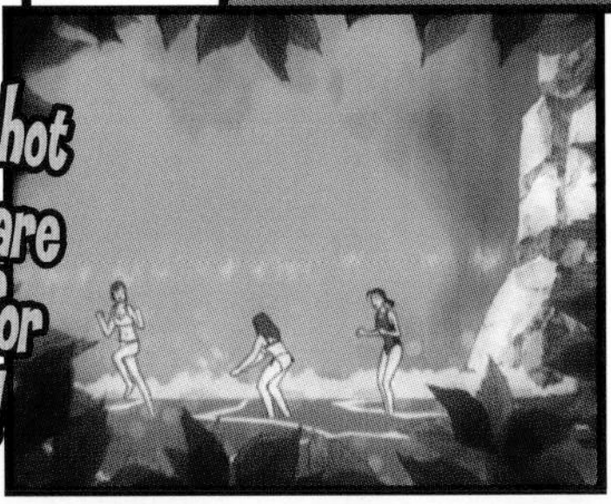

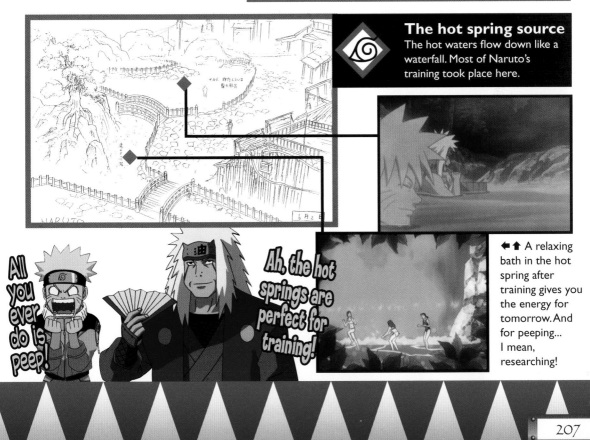

⬅⬆ A relaxing bath in the hot spring after training gives you the energy for tomorrow. And for peeping... I mean, researching!

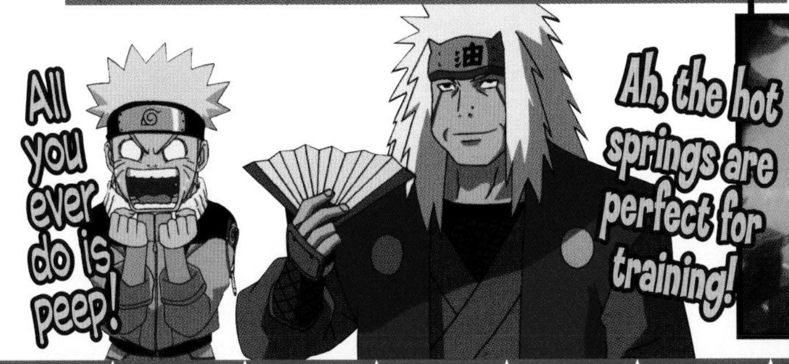
All you ever do is peep!
Ah, the hot springs are perfect for training!

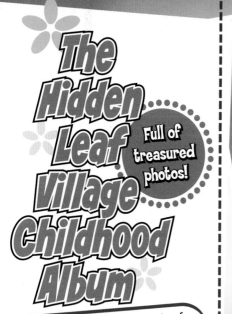

The Hidden Leaf Village Childhood Album

Full of treasured photos!

Memories of the Hidden Leaf Village are revealed! Enjoy taking a close-up look at treasured photos of ninja in their youth!

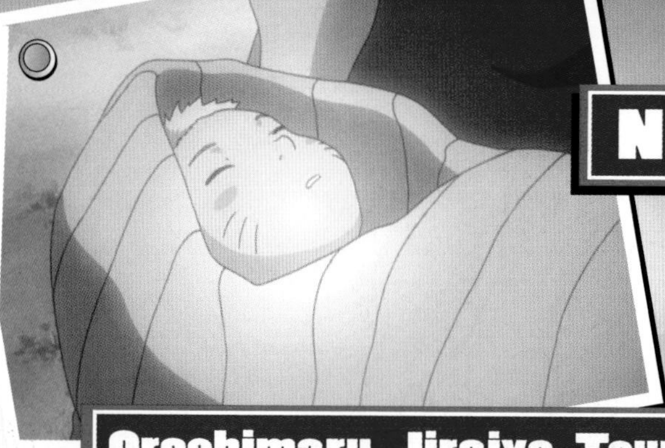

Naruto

←The face of the infant Naruto is dappled with sunshine…but who is holding him?

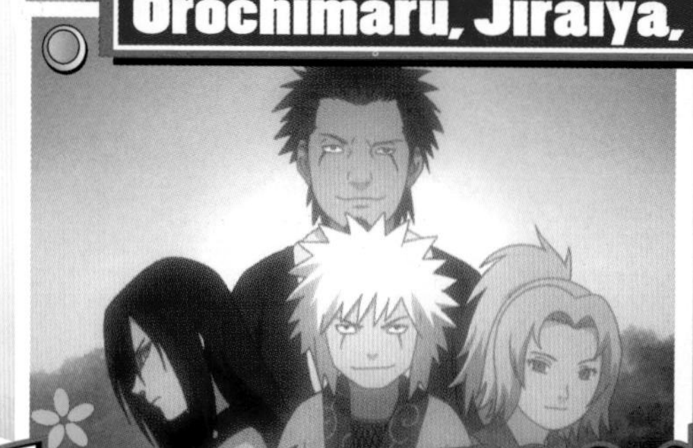

Orochimaru, Jiraiya, Tsunade

←A powerful mentor with his protégés! The Third Hokage stands proud with his students, the leaders of the next generation.

Everyone was a child once!!

Whatever the future held, all ninja were kids at one time. Images captured on film remain unchanged throughout the ages.

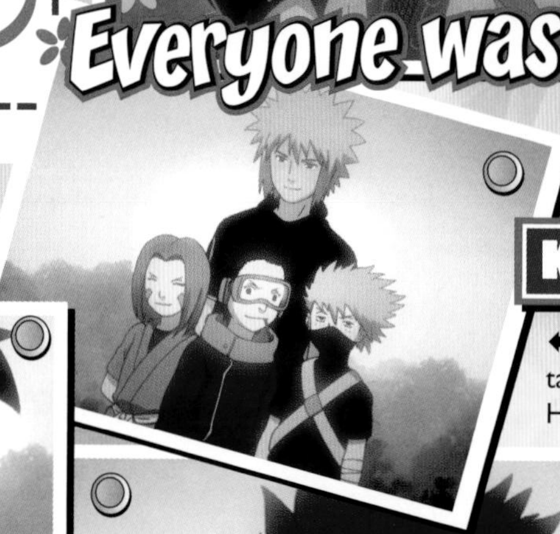

Kakashi Hatake

←Kakashi cherishes this photo taken with his teacher, the Fourth Hokage, and keeps it at his bedside.

↓Although still a child, sincerity shows in his face. He's always had that scar.

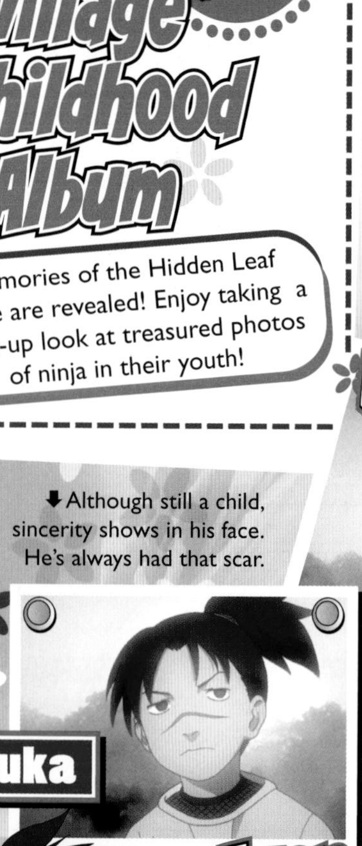

Iruka

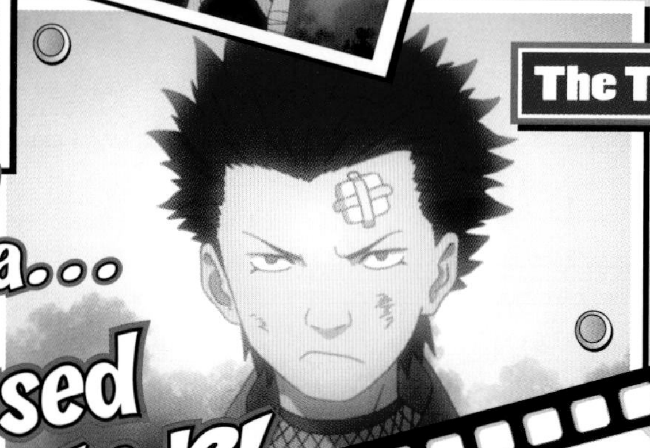

The Third Hokage

←Even the Third Hokage, renowned as the most powerful of all, got injured when he was a child?!

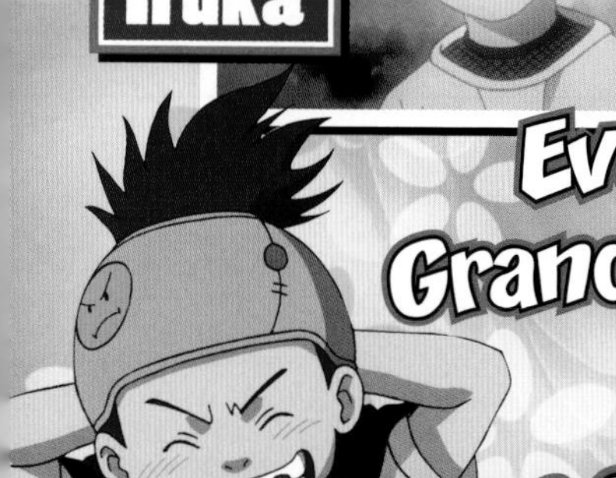

Even Grandpa…

…used to be a kid?!

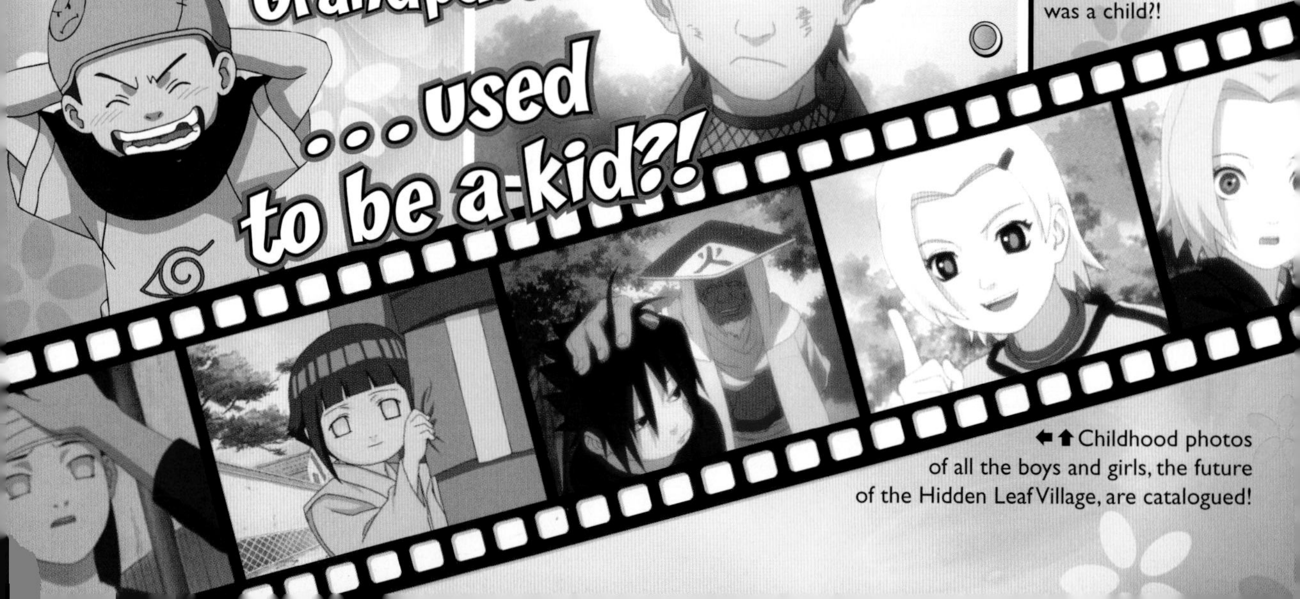

←↑Childhood photos of all the boys and girls, the future of the Hidden Leaf Village, are catalogued!

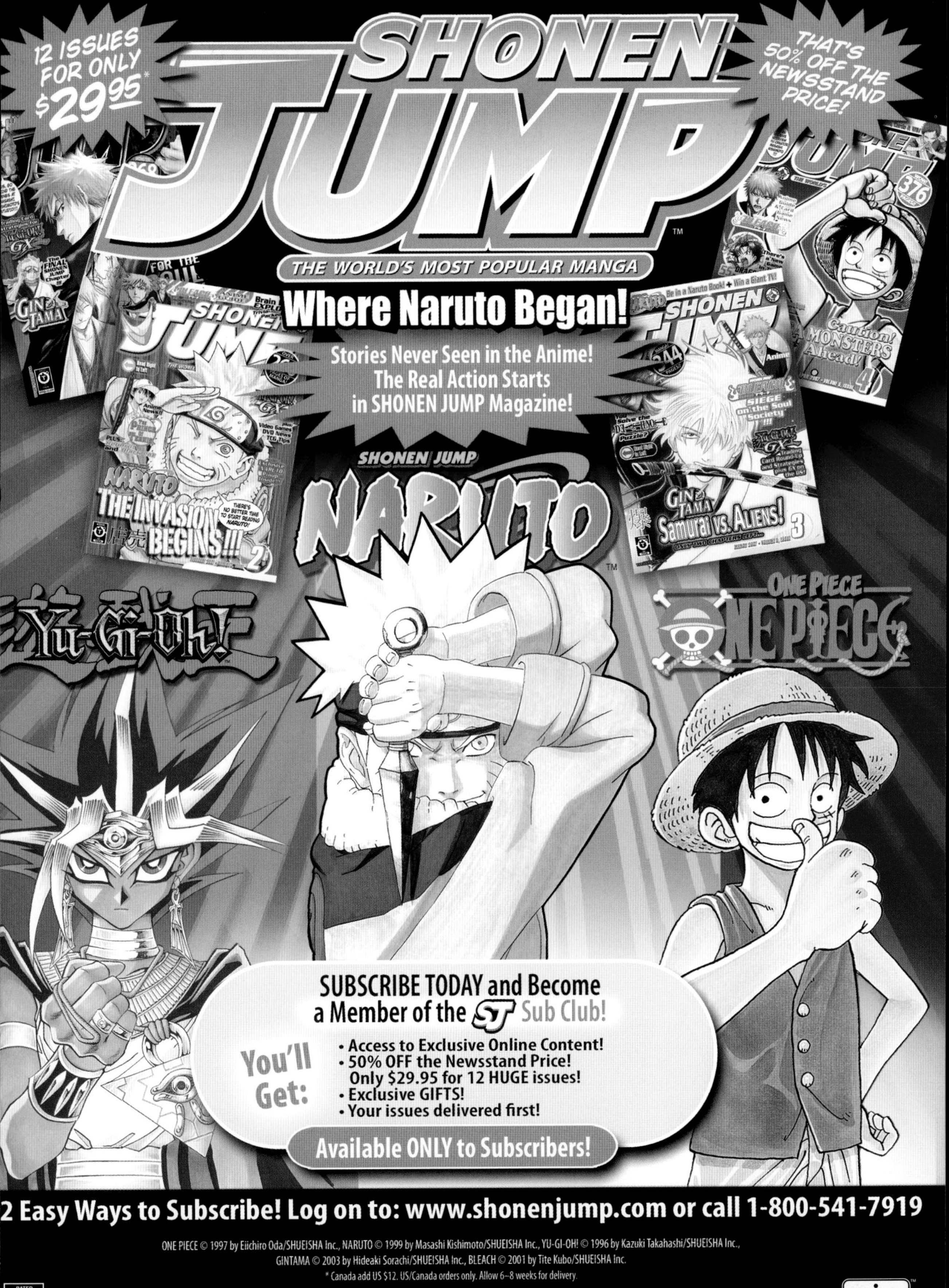
12 ISSUES FOR ONLY $29.95*
SHONEN JUMP
THAT'S 50% OFF THE NEWSSTAND PRICE!
THE WORLD'S MOST POPULAR MANGA
Where Naruto Began!
Stories Never Seen in the Anime!
The Real Action Starts
in SHONEN JUMP Magazine!
SHONEN JUMP
NARUTO
YU-GI-OH!
ONE PIECE
SUBSCRIBE TODAY and Become
a Member of the SJ Sub Club!
You'll Get:
• Access to Exclusive Online Content!
• 50% OFF the Newsstand Price!
Only $29.95 for 12 HUGE issues!
• Exclusive GIFTS!
• Your issues delivered first!
Available ONLY to Subscribers!

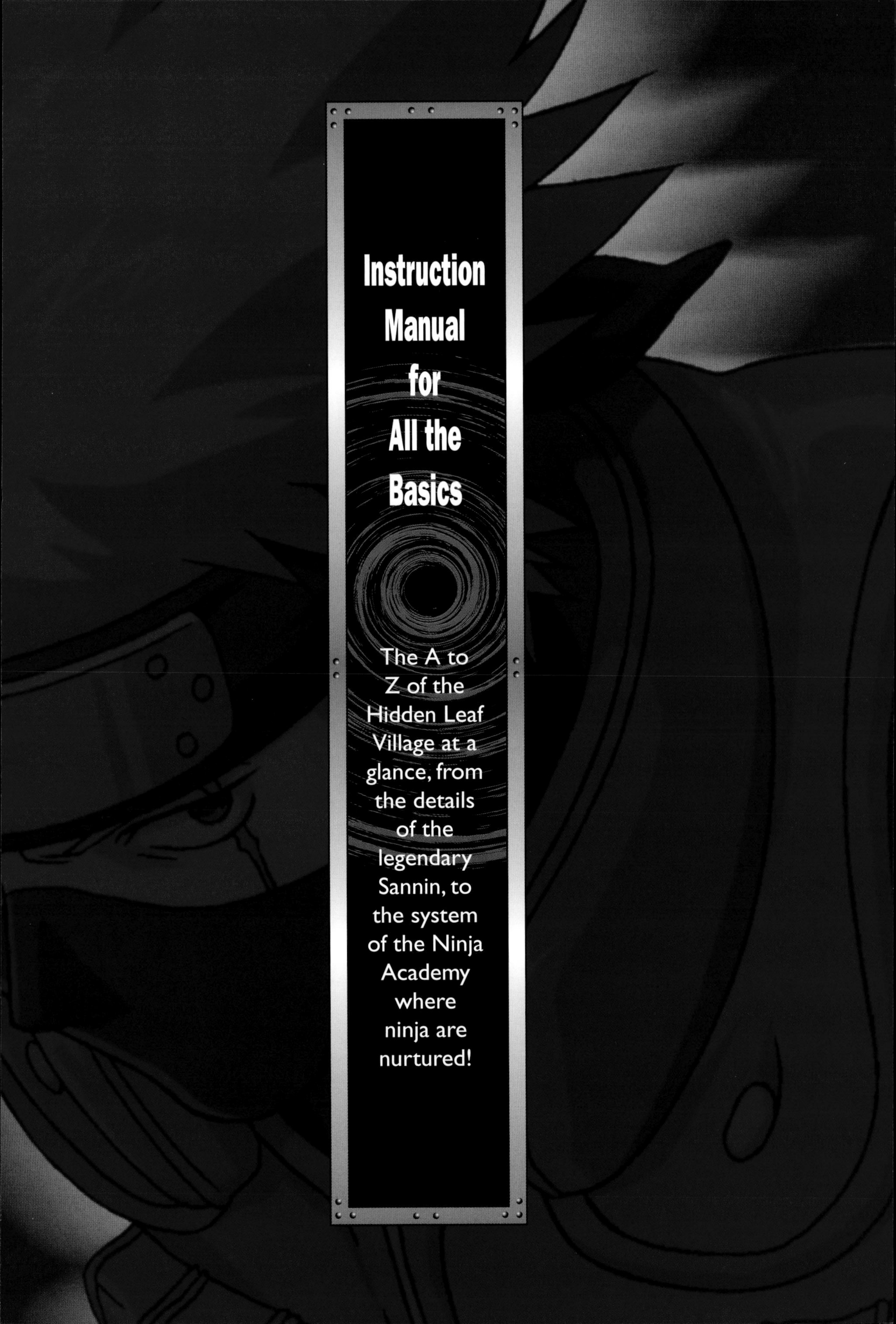

Instruction Manual for All the Basics

The A to Z of the Hidden Leaf Village at a glance, from the details of the legendary Sannin, to the system of the Ninja Academy where ninja are nurtured!

The Legendary Sannin

Unprecedented tales of bravery from the Hidden Leaf Village passed down from generation to generation!

Three shinobi with astounding abilities that are the stuff of legend. Now separated and departed from the village, some lead a vagabond's lifestyle and some exist as a threat.

Jiraiya

None can match this freewheeling and insatiable perv, the intrepid toad-master. He's a remarkable teacher, as shown by the prowess of the Fourth Hokage.

Orochimaru

Orochimaru was a genius who displayed superb abilities even in childhood, and the Third Hokage held high hopes for his future. However, corrupted by ambition, he turned his fangs on the Hidden Leaf Village.

Chart of Mentor-Student Relationships

The Third Hokage, who was brought up by the First and the Second Hokage brothers, mentored the Sannin. His talent as a great teacher is reflected here.

The First Hokage

The Second Hokage

The Third Hokage

Jiraiya

Orochimaru

Tsunade

And Tsunade...

Tsunade is the only female Sannin and the strongest kunoichi, brilliantly standing out in village history. Her whereabouts at present, including whether or not she's alive, are unknown.

➡ Tenten admires Tsunade and wants to be just like her.

Behold, the Eating Kings! Another legendary Sannin!

Jiraiya, Orochimaru and Tsunade are not the only legendary trio of ninja! In the Hidden Leaf Village there are eating kings diligently dedicated to the art of gluttony! These Sannin are legendary—in their own way—and feared throughout the food industry!

Dango legend

Anko Mitarashi

⬆ The village queen of sweets, she can eat fifty skewers of dango with sweet azuki soup in one sitting.

Ramen legend

Naruto Uzumaki

⬆ He ate nine full bowls of ramen with a smile, showing no concern for Ebisu, who had to pay for them.

BBQ legend

Choji Akimichi

⬆ Unbeatable! The ultimate glutton, he has caused the closure of countless barbecue restaurants.

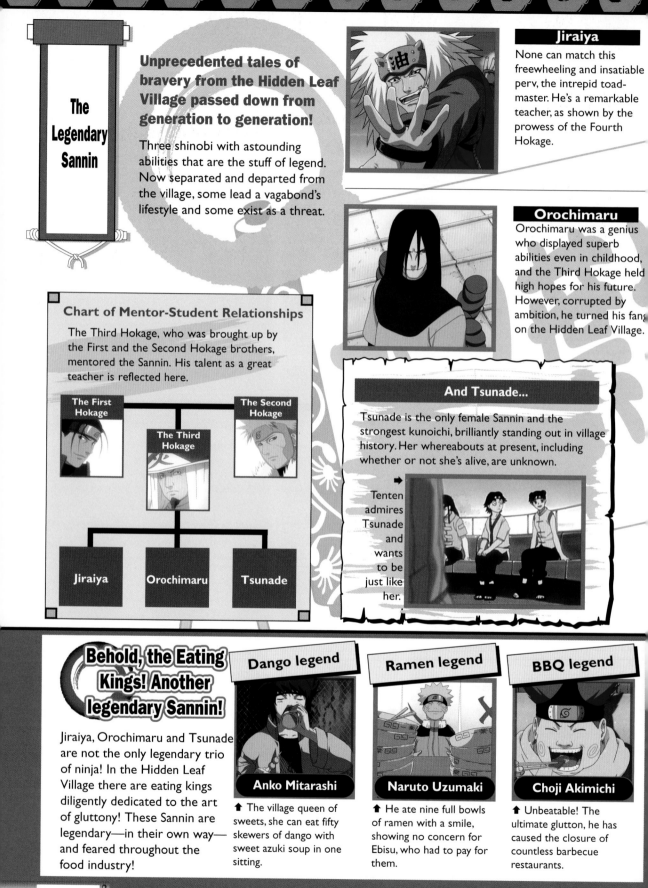

Anbu

➡ Responsible for everything in the village, the Hokage is a capable leader of the Anbu Black Ops.

A select unit that moves in the shadows under the direct supervision of the Hokage!

Their formal name is "Anbu: Assassination and Battle Tactics Special Unit." Missions, which come directly from the Hokage, are dangerous and difficult ones, such as assassination and espionage. Everything, including the content and results of missions, is top secret.

Rescue of a Special Jonin.

➡ Saving Anko in the Forest of Death. Their abilities are immeasurable.

The true image of the shadowy Anbu agents!

Only the Hokage fully understands the organization and battle prowess of the Anbu... Just as their faces are hidden under masks, their true identities are cloaked in mystery.

⬆ Haku was a member of the unit that tracks rogue ninja.

Other nations also have special units!

Much like the Hidden Leaf Village's Anbu, apparently hidden villages of other nations also have shinobi in charge of special missions.

⬇ Anbu are unconcerned with gender, so of course there are female members as well.

There are also Female Anbu.

Kakashi too!

⬆ In the battle against Zabuza, Kakashi confessed that he is ex-Anbu, too.

The Anbu Mask Gallery!

The Anbu engage in secret missions and always wear masks to hide their identities. It seems that their masks tend to portray some kind of animal. Let's take a look at some examples!

⬆ This mask with a protrusion like a beak appears to represent a bird.

⬇ A mask portraying a dog. The whiskers and cute mouth are distinctive features.

⬆ The shading around the eyes and stubby upturned nose tell us that it's a monkey.

The Ninja Academy

Ninja training institution established to maintain military strength.

The Second Hokage, believing the most urgent task was ensuring the military strength of the village and the enrichment of educational activities, founded the Ninja Academy as a training institute during the chaotic times. After the Second Hokage passed away, the Third Hokage upgraded the educational facilities.

The Founder

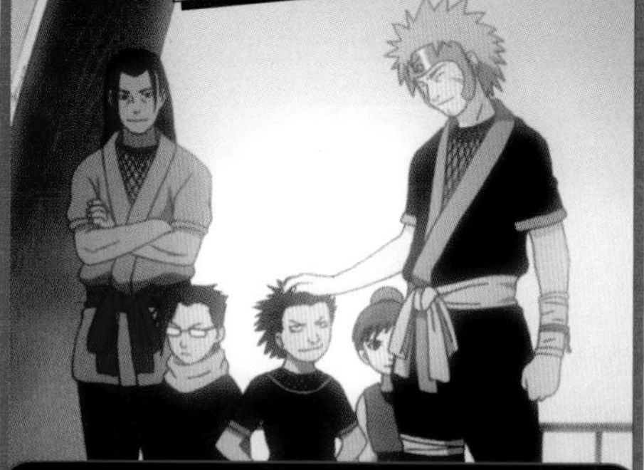

The Second Hokage

➡ The Second Hokage, younger brother of the First Hokage, is the founder. His three subordinates later became key people in the Hidden Leaf Village.

Chronology of the Hidden Leaf Village Ninja Academy

Years ago	Event
60 years ago	Founding
	First 36 graduates
50	Adopted formal name "Ninja Academy"
	First teacher-selection exam held
40	First major expansion
	Kunoichi classes established
30	Second major expansion
	First joint exercises with the Hidden Sand Village
20	School buildings partially destroyed by the Nine-Tailed Fox
	Following year, restoration work
10	Third major expansion
	Present

Conditions for Admission

1. A person with love for the Hidden Leaf Village who resolves to protect its peace and prosperity.
2. A person possessing an unyielding spirit who continuously puts in unceasing effort and training.
3. A person with sound mind and body.

These are the three prerequisites for admission.

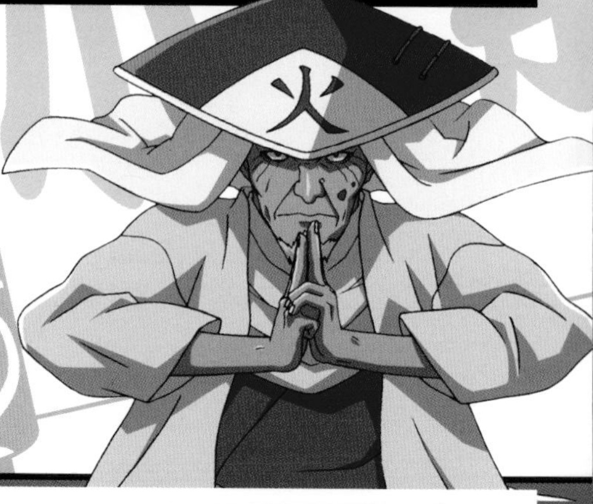

➡ The Third Hokage put special effort into raising educators, forming the basis of today's Ninja Academy.

Allow me to introduce the Ninja Academy teachers!

All the teachers of the Ninja Academy are unique. While having their own missions too, as educators they take charge of leading the students, on whose shoulders the future of the village rests.

Suzume-sensei

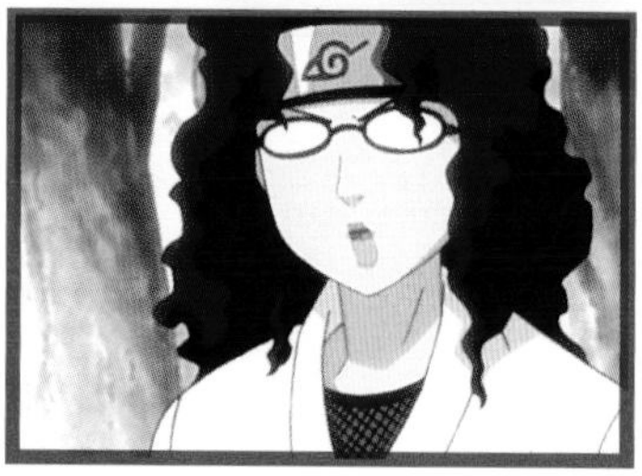

⬆ It is important for a shinobi to become highly refined during their Academy days. I'll see to that!

Iruka-sensei

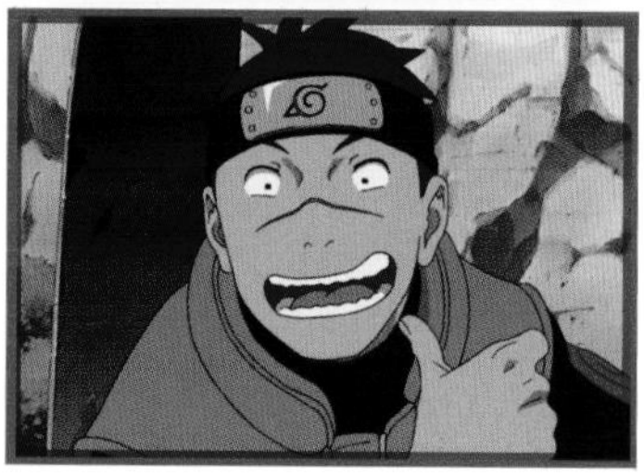

⬆ Nothing makes me happier than seeing a student firmly adhering to his own ninja way.

Basics, drills, practical application... and outdoor classes!

At the Ninja Academy, lessons are held not only in classrooms but also occasionally outside.

Refinement

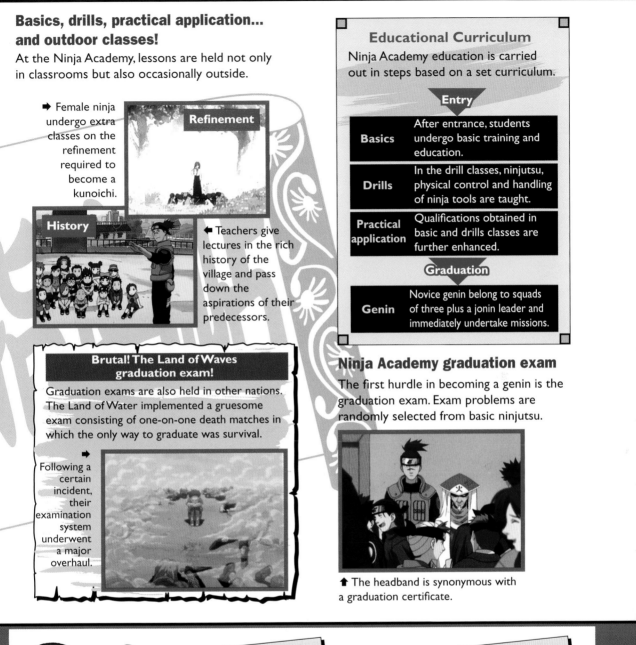

➡ Female ninja undergo extra classes on the refinement required to become a kunoichi.

History

⬅ Teachers give lectures in the rich history of the village and pass down the aspirations of their predecessors.

Educational Curriculum

Ninja Academy education is carried out in steps based on a set curriculum.

Entry	
Basics	After entrance, students undergo basic training and education.
Drills	In the drill classes, ninjutsu, physical control and handling of ninja tools are taught.
Practical application	Qualifications obtained in basic and drills classes are further enhanced.
Graduation	
Genin	Novice genin belong to squads of three plus a jonin leader and immediately undertake missions.

Brutal! The Land of Waves graduation exam!

Graduation exams are also held in other nations. The Land of Water implemented a gruesome exam consisting of one-on-one death matches in which the only way to graduate was survival.

➡ Following a certain incident, their examination system underwent a major overhaul.

Ninja Academy graduation exam

The first hurdle in becoming a genin is the graduation exam. Exam problems are randomly selected from basic ninjutsu.

⬆ The headband is synonymous with a graduation certificate.

Answers from a graduate on his top three worst subjects.

Being skillful in both literary and military arts is the very basis of becoming a shinobi! But everyone has weak areas. The village's hope, anonymous boy N, shows his three weakest subjects.

Practical Exam

⬆ I finally make a clone but...it's got no soul!

Exercises

⬇ As you can see, I fell into a trap! The blood's rushing to my head!

Reading & Writing

⬆ Reading alone makes me dizzy. My brain's gonna melt...Believe it!

Sealing Jutsu

Jutsu that suppresses chakra with a sign!

Jutsu that seal the target's chakra with a sign are called Sealing Jutsu. A Seal Formula mark emerges on the body of the victim. There are even- and odd-number formulas used, with each working differently. This type of jutsu is still full of mysteries.

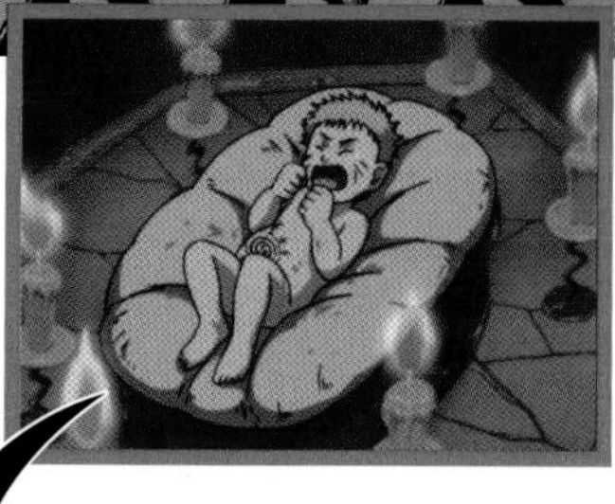

➡ Orochimaru's Odd-Numbered Seal was placed over the Fourth Hokage's Even-Numbered Seal, causing the sealing effect to become disordered.

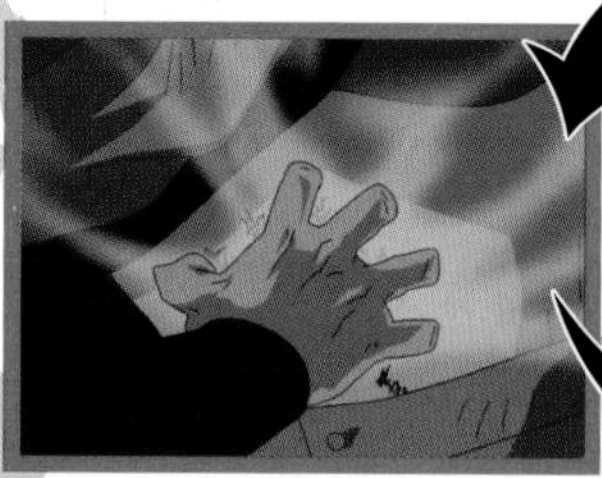

⬅ The Fourth Hokage, using a life-sacrificing Sealing Jutsu, sealed the Nine-Tailed Fox within Naruto's body.

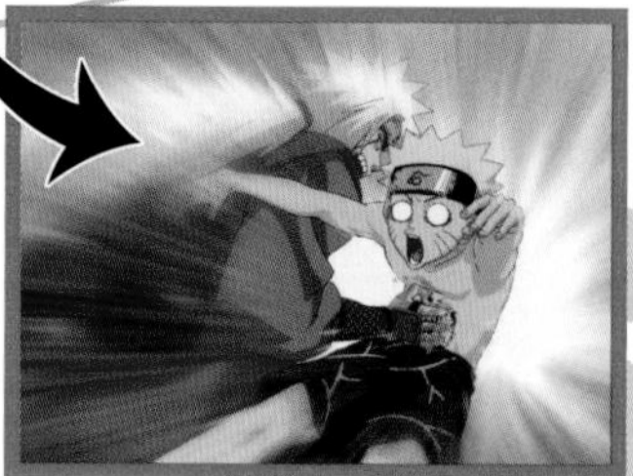

➡ Jiraiya released Orochimaru's Odd-Number Seal with the Five-Pronged Seal Release, enabling Naruto to control his chakra more easily.

Curse Mark Jutsu

A curse jutsu that engraves a mark on the mind and body to capture them!

Jutsu that manipulate their target through a sign are called Curse Mark Jutsu. A curse mark emerges on the target's body and reacts to secret signs made by the user. It's also possible to cause the victim mental and physical pain at the jutsu user's will.

⬇➡ The Secret Curse Mark of the Hyuga Clan Main Branch is a control measure placed, with no exceptions, on all members of the Side Branch.

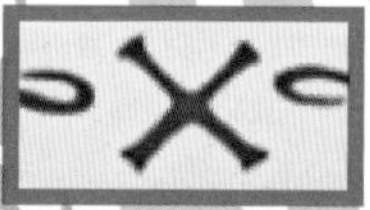

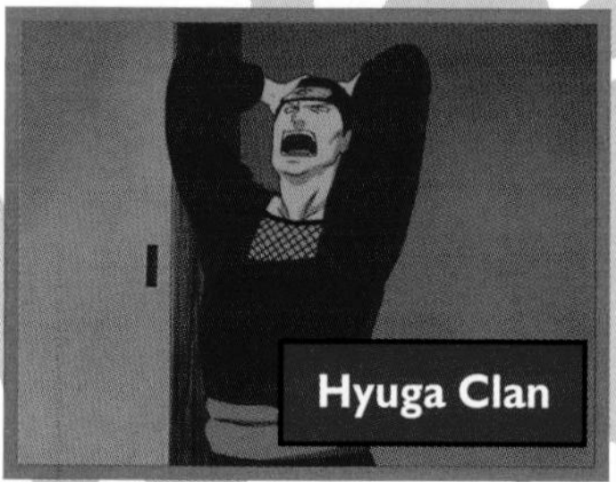
Hyuga Clan

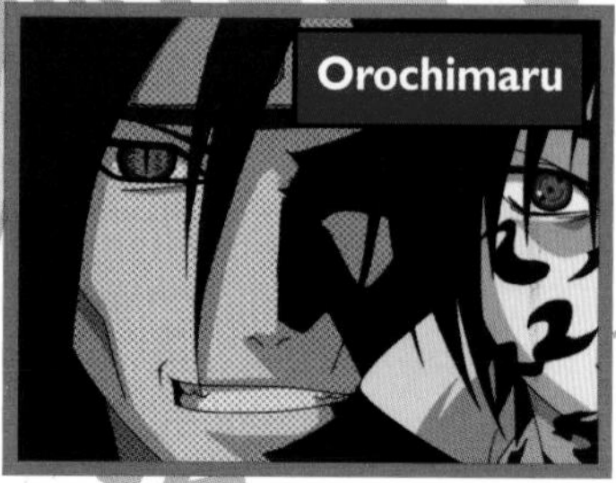
Orochimaru

⬅⬇ Orochimaru put his curse mark on Sasuke to draw out his evil side.

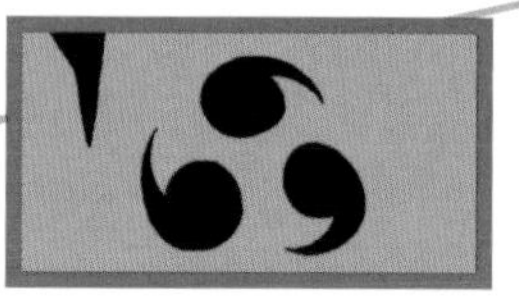

Seal release?! A thorough examination of the Inner Sakura!

Just as the Nine-Tailed Fox is sealed within Naruto, an Inner Sakura surely exists within Sakura, often demonstrating its formidable power. Let's take a closer look!

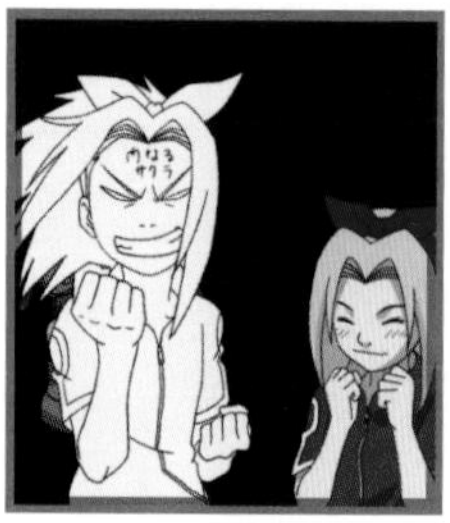

⬆ The heart of a woman has two sides like a coin! She may act cute, but inside her heart it's...s-s-scary…

⬇ When Ino snuck into her mind, she transformed into a giant to teach the invader a lesson. Massively scary!

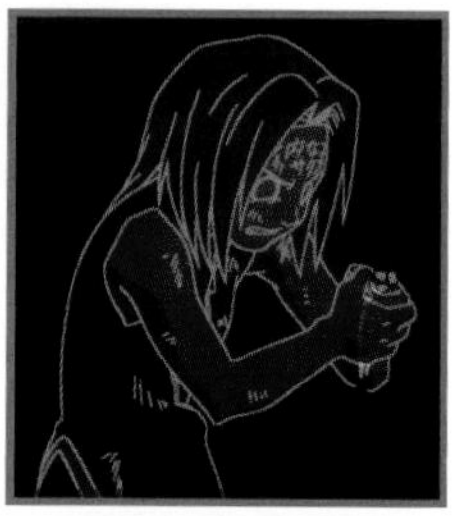

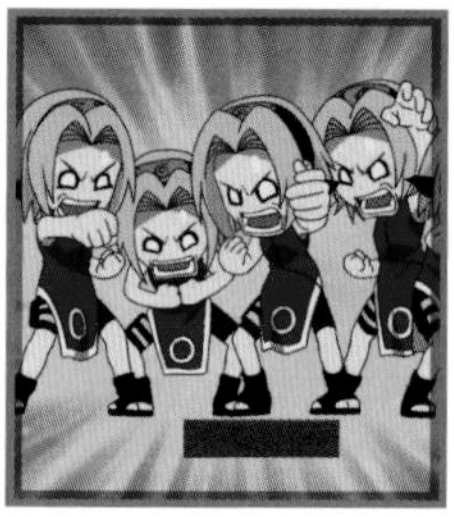

⬆ Finally she produced a pack of clones and they shouted "Cha!" in unison! S-s-seriously scary!

Expansion Jutsu

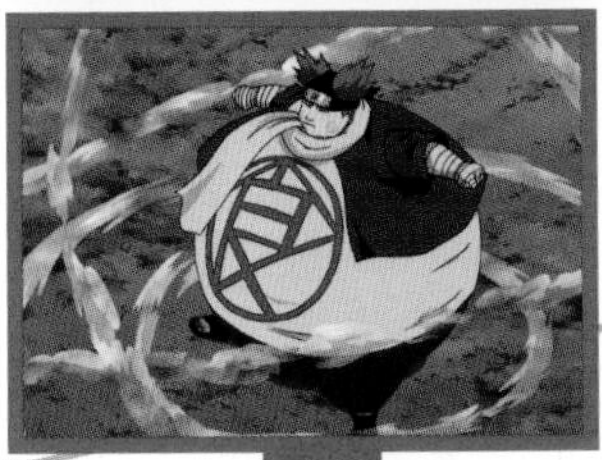

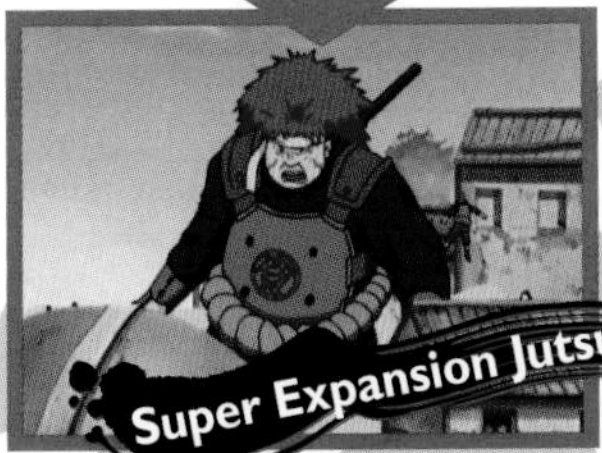
Super Expansion Jutsu!!

⬆ The user doesn't just expand, but completely transforms into a giant form with Super Expansion!

Shadow Possession Jutsu

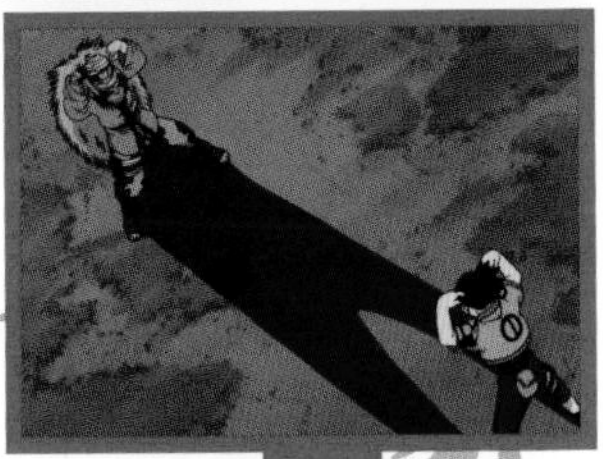

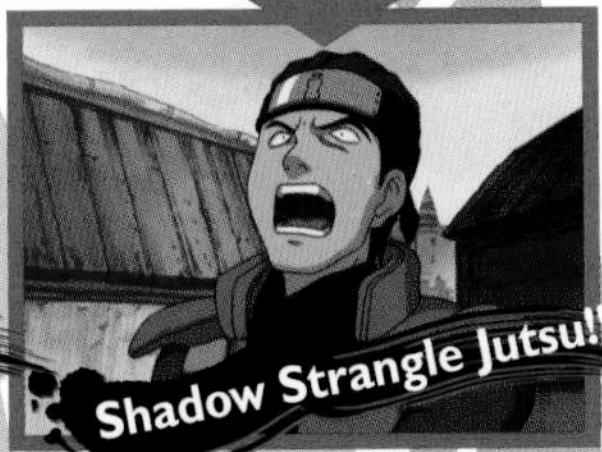
Shadow Strangle Jutsu!!

⬆ Shadow Possession, used to trap opponents, is ideal with assassination skills like Shadow Strangle!

Secret techniques

Secret jutsu handed down for posterity!

Secret techniques are jutsu handed down orally only among clans or groups living in certain areas. Except for ones like Kekkei Genkai, most of these techniques do not require specific blood traits or innate talent. The types and effects of these secret techniques appear to differ greatly based on the user's level.

Jutsu with hazardous effects

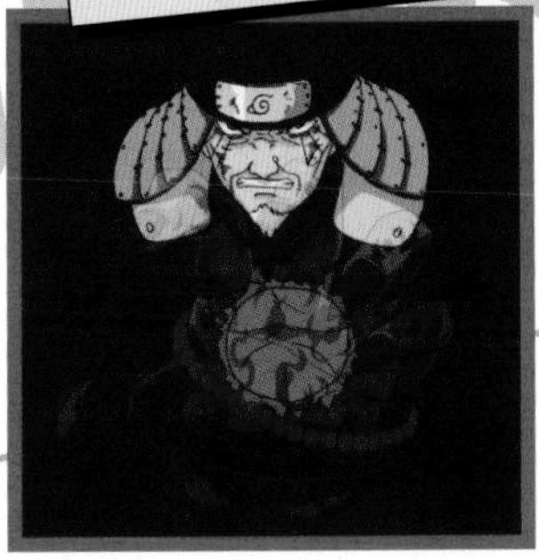

⬆ Reaper Death Seal, a jutsu that summons a Reaper and allows it to devour the souls of both the jutsu user and its target.

Jutsu that threaten the user's life

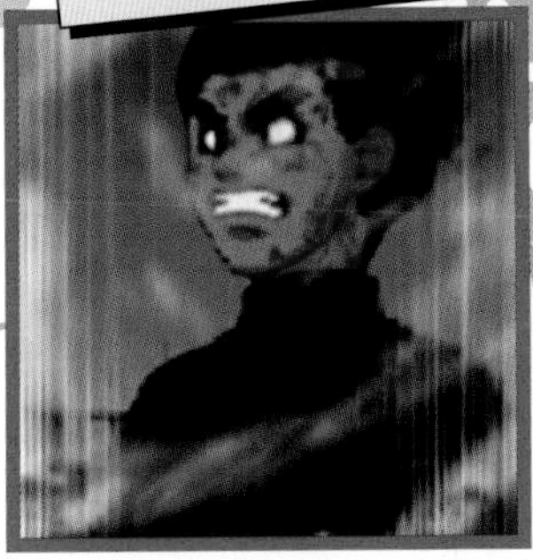

⬆ The Hidden Lotus calls forth superhuman power by forcing open gates within the body called the Eight Inner Gates.

Forbidden Jutsu

Dangerous jutsu that have been sealed by predecessors!

Jutsu that threaten the life of the user or have hazardous effects that defy the rules of heaven and earth. Forbidden jutsu are roughly divided into those two categories. In most cases their scrolls have been sealed, particularly those with hazardous effects.

Is this training, too? Fierce discipline.

Training is not only honing the body and amassing knowledge. The best in the Hidden Leaf Village take on daily training that's difficult to comprehend. At first glance it may not look like training at all, but it really is genuine training... probably...maybe!

Confession of love

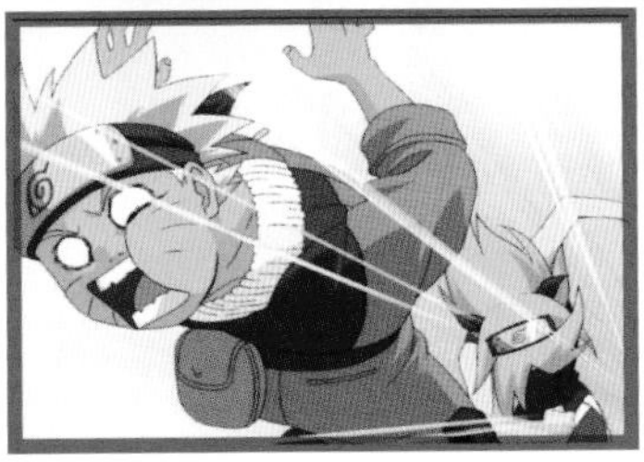

⬆ In training assigned by Jiraiya, Naruto makes up his mind and tries to confess his feelings to Sakura, but gets K.O.'d for it! That's gotta hurt!

Ferocious, violent, explosive eating!

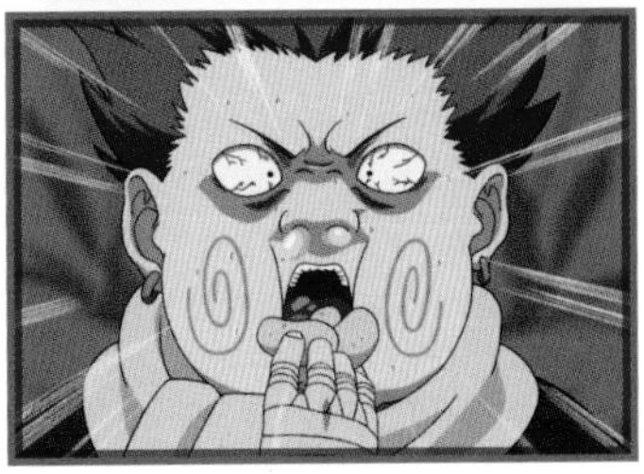

⬆ Expansion Jutsu consumes major calories. The reason Choji's always eating?! This is tough training, too.

Fero-cious Fist

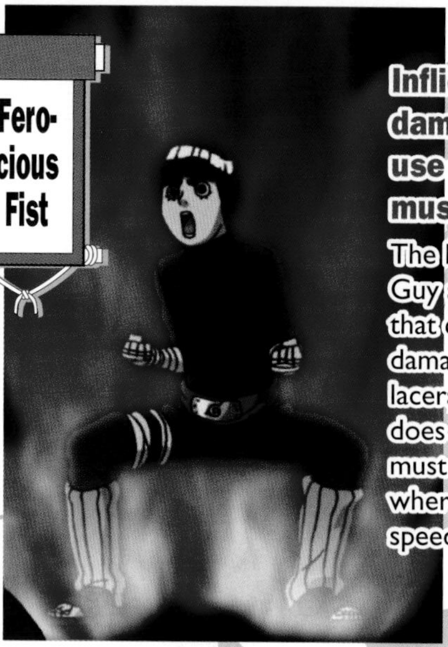

Inflicting physical damage through optimum use of highly developed muscular power!

The Ferocious Fist, which Guy and Lee wield, is taijutsu that causes massive physical damage, such as fractures and lacerations, to an opponent. It does not require chakra, but must be used at close range, where attack strength and speed are also required.

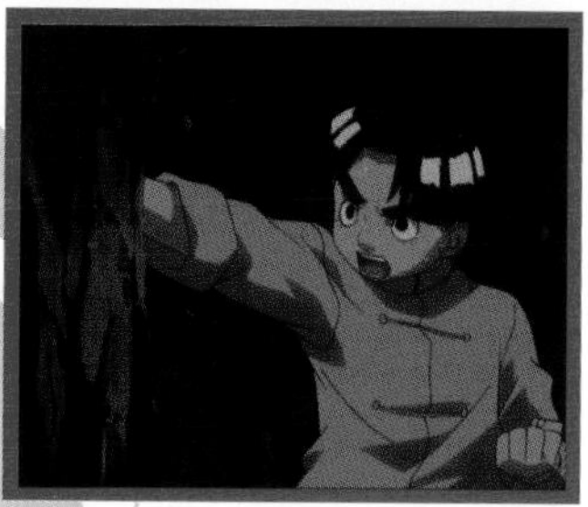

⬅ Since the Ferocious Fist can be accomplished by anyone, the key lies in training.

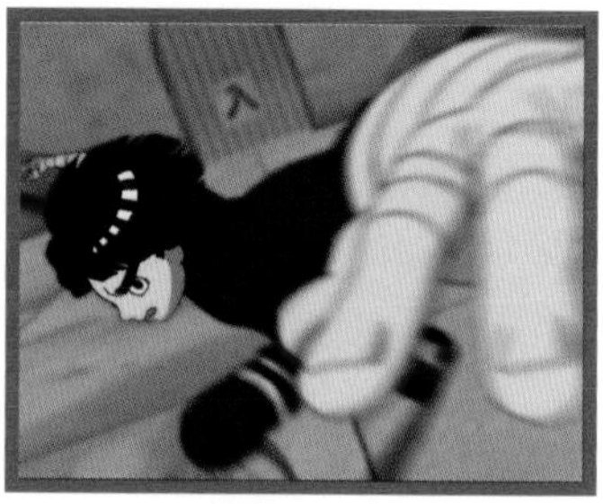

➡ Lee excels at the Ferocious Fist. It is the fruit of his efforts.

Gentle Fist

Inflicting internal damage with well-focused chakra!

The Gentle Fist, which Neji and Hinata use, is a taijutsu that uses chakra to cause direct damage to an opponents' internal energy flow or organs. It is even possible to stop chakra flow using Byakugan, the Kekkei Genkai of the Hyuga Clan.

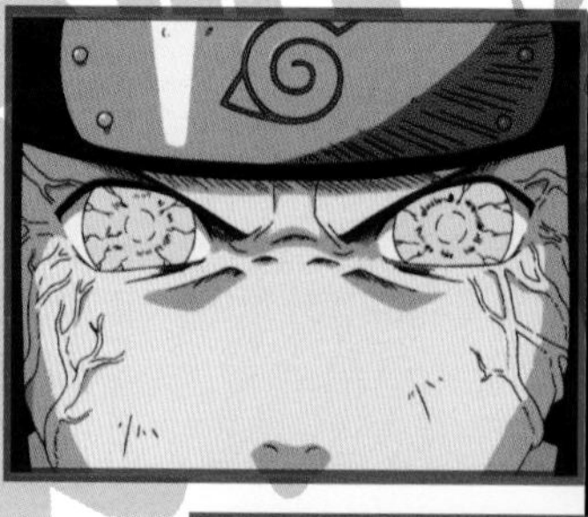

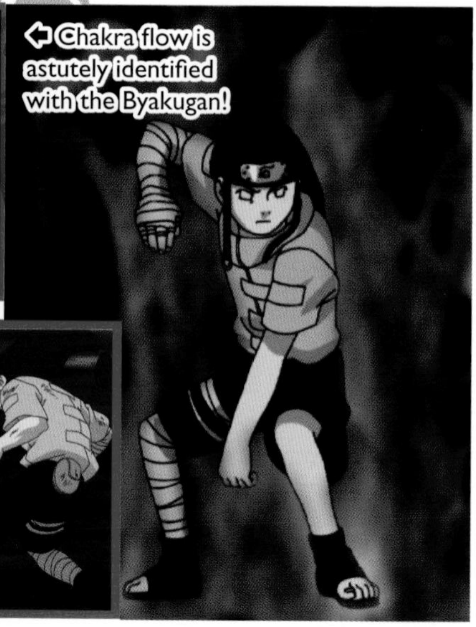

⬅ Chakra flow is astutely identified with the Byakugan!

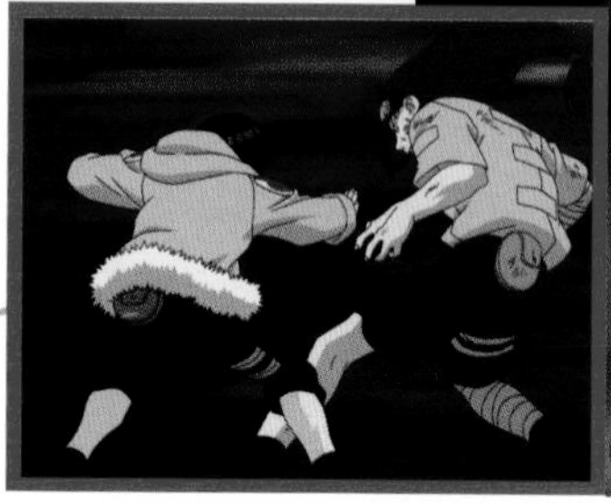

➡ A breathtaking battle between Gentle Fist users Hinata and Neji!

Guy and Kakashi. Major rivals of the Hidden Leaf Village talk face to face!

The most famous of the many competitive relationships in the Hidden Leaf Village is probably Kakashi and Guy's. According to Guy, in matches they have a record of 50 to 49, with Guy being one up! Will this competition ever see an end?!

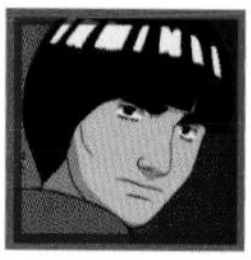

Heh-heh...a debate?! Looks like our hardy rivalry will take center stage!

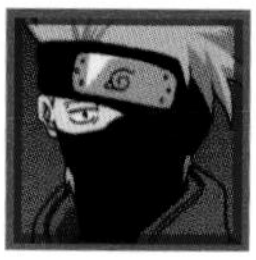

A rivalry is good to have. I think it's a good, manly relationship ♥.

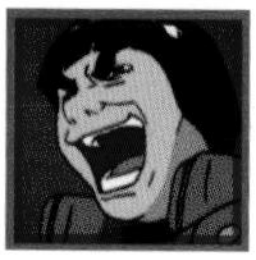

It's a hot-blooded relationship, like the one between my adorable Lee and Neji! But this time I would like to put a clear end to our...

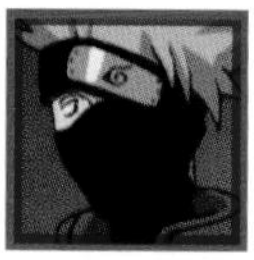

You and me wanna make some fireworks, too. Fireworks of passion… This story's heating up...Mmm, hm.

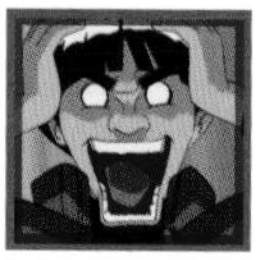

Yes, it sure is heating...hey, Kakashi! Close that dirty book of yours right this minute!

The Secret Scroll of the Purple Lightning Slash!

Never cease to train your body, to become faster and more skilled! Shot like a spark, vivid as lightning, secret techniques are divulged!

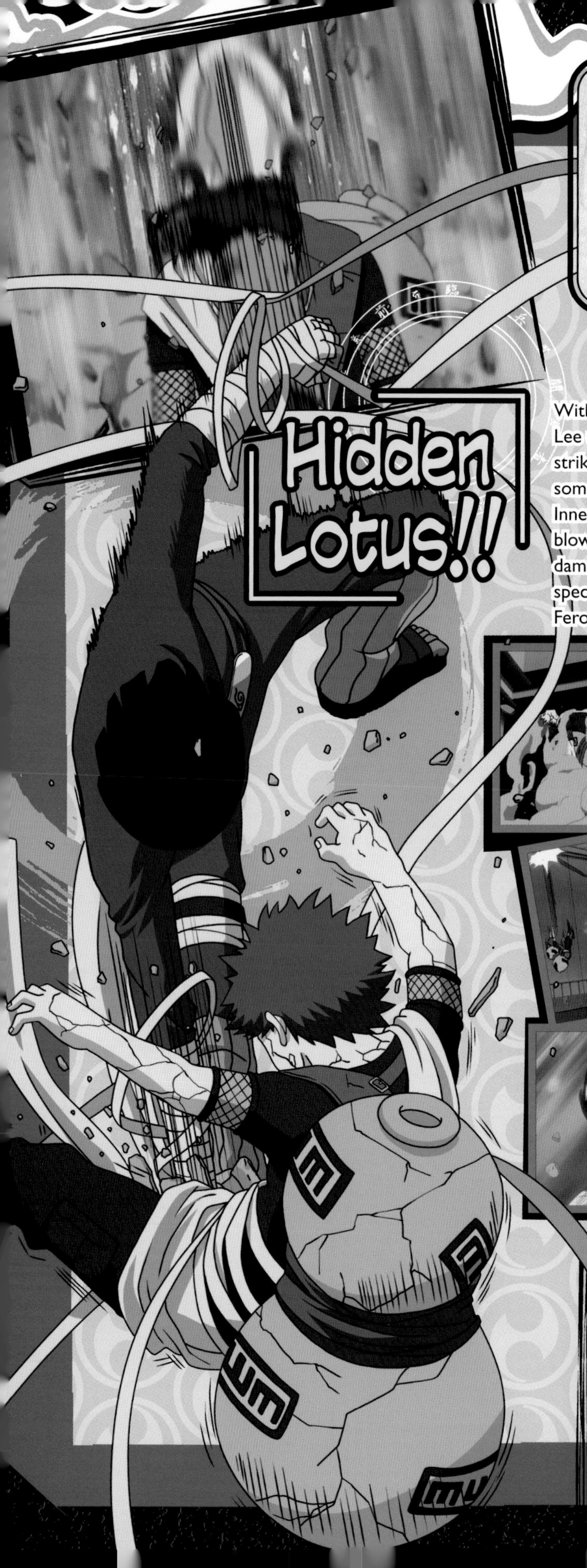
Hidden Lotus!!

With superhuman speed, Lee unleashes a series of strikes by forcing open some of the forbidden Eight Inner Gates. The finishing blow, while inflicting a damaging physical toll, is the spectacular height of the Ferocious Fist!

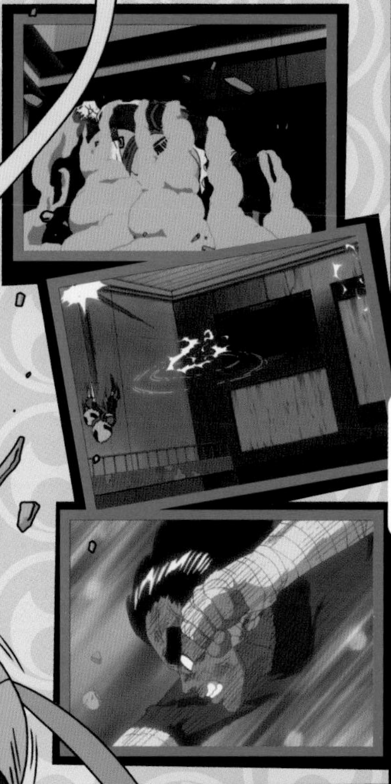

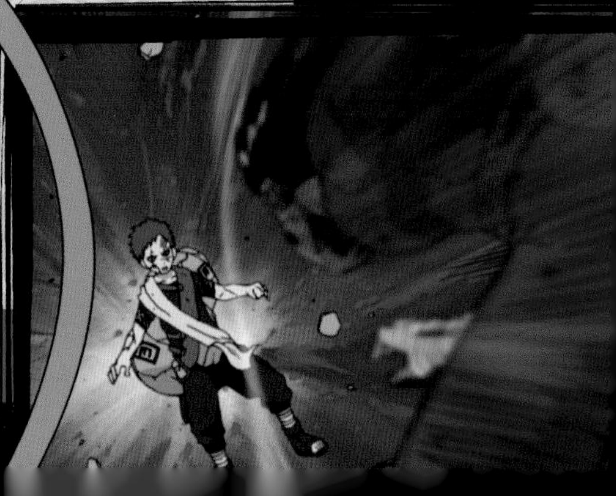

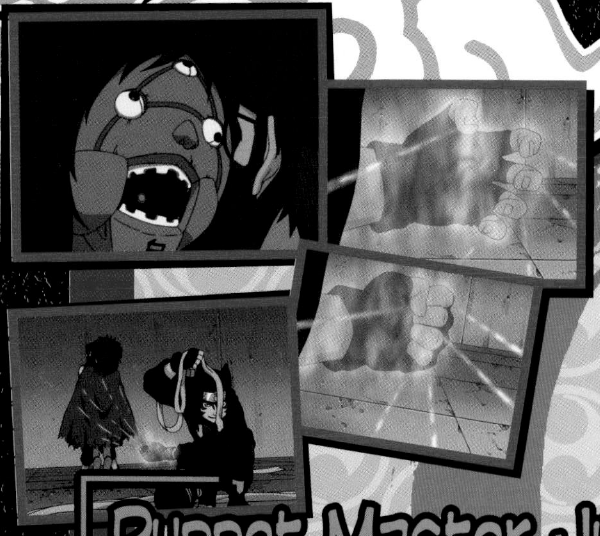

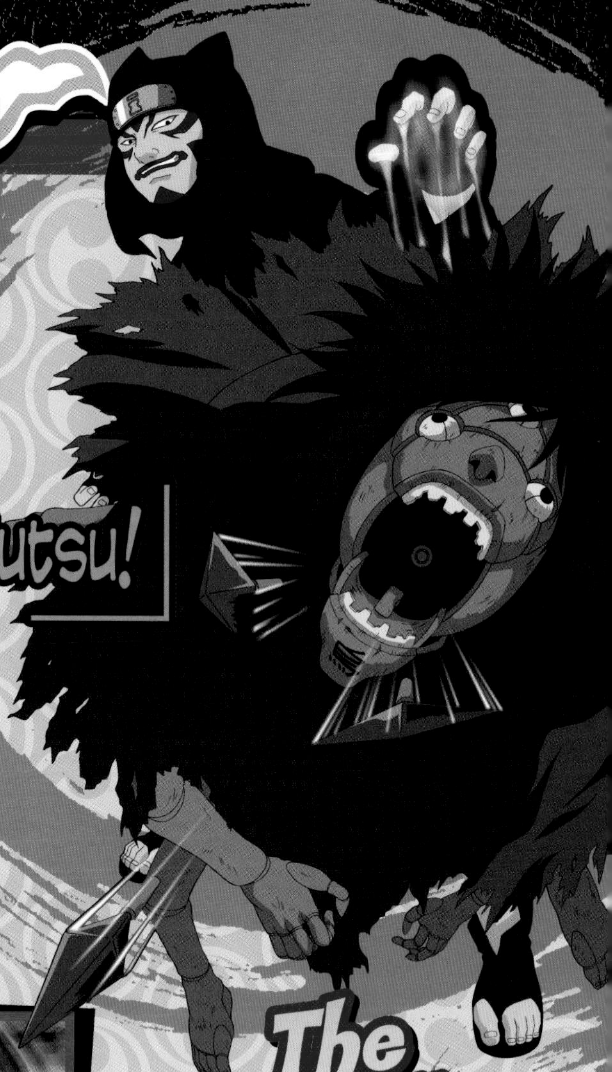

Puppet Master Jutsu!

Considerable skill and ability is required to manipulate a puppet as if it were alive. The eerie but awesome Puppet Master Jutsu demonstrated by Kankuro is evidence of his skill as a puppeteer.

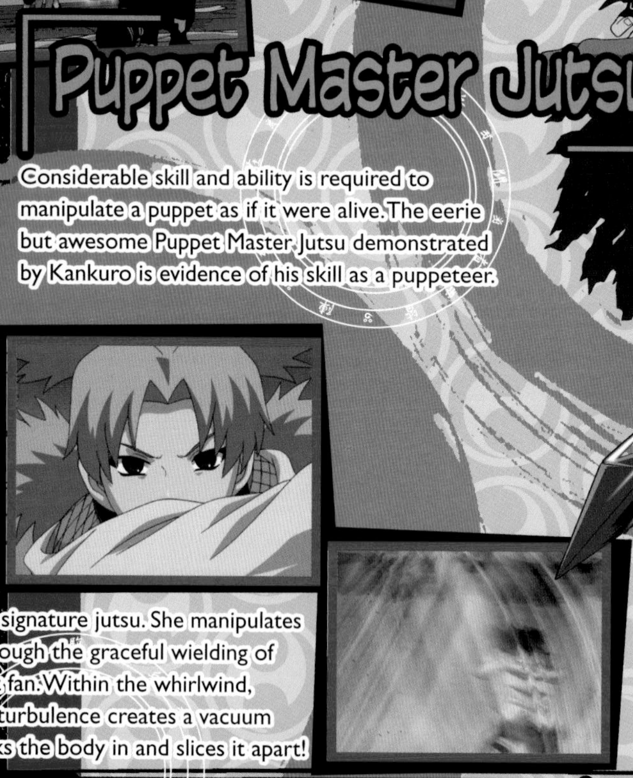

Temari's signature jutsu. She manipulates wind through the graceful wielding of her giant fan. Within the whirlwind, clashing turbulence creates a vacuum that sucks the body in and slices it apart!

Wind Scythe Jutsu!

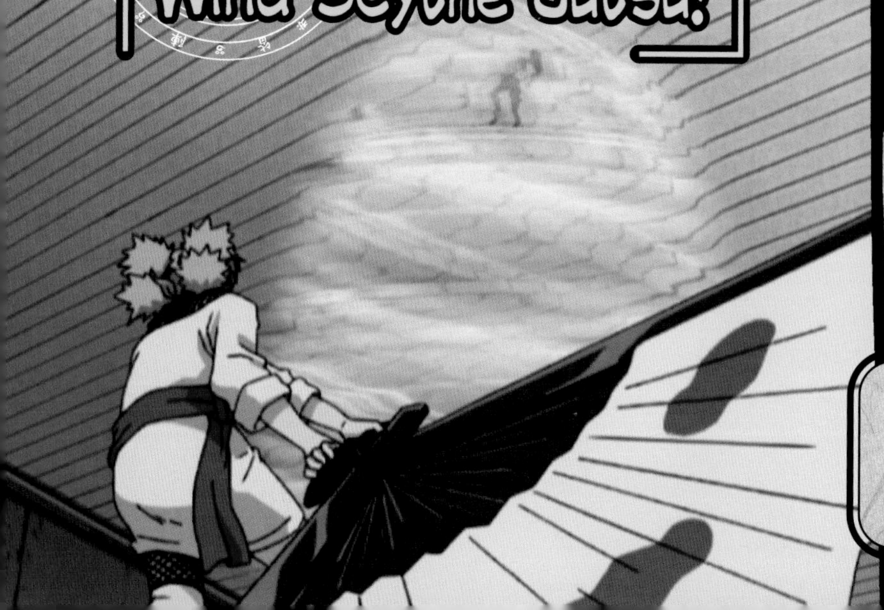

The deadly techniques of the young shinobi bloom!!

Youth makes them fearless and daring. They clash head-on with everything they've got! Witness the incredible jutsu they magnificently display during the Chunin Exam!

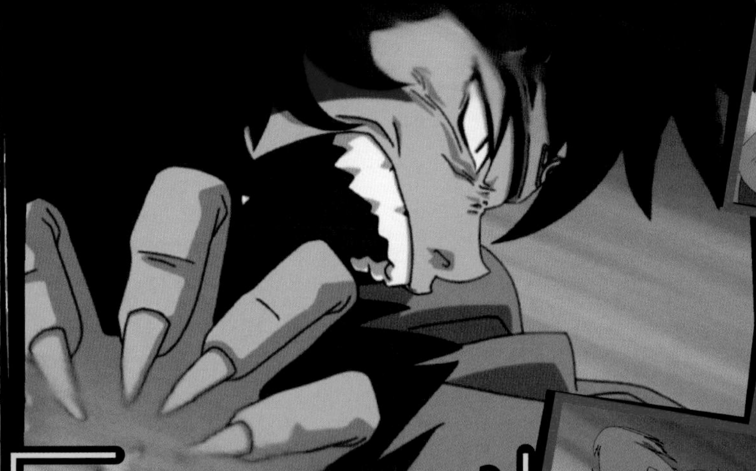

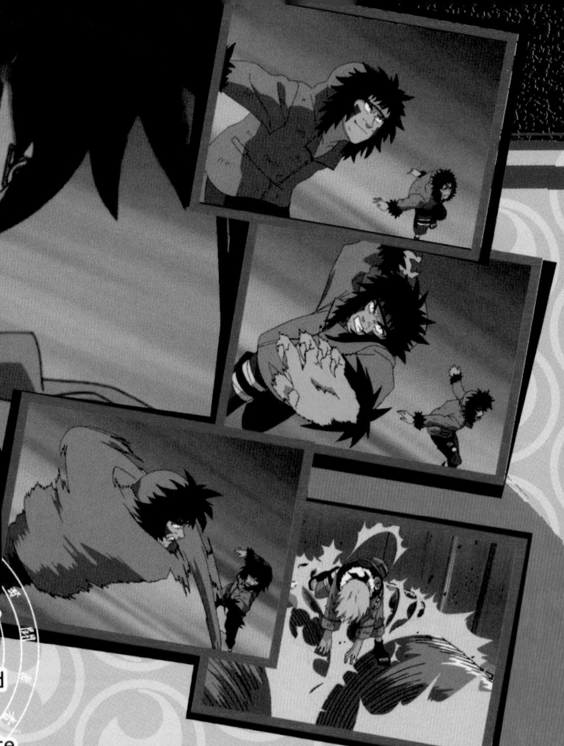

Fang Over Fang!

The fangs of a ferocious wild beast were inherited by Kiba via his close bond with his loving dog, Akamaru. Quick and continuous criss-crossing attacks, launched in perfect sync between man and beast, allow opponents no time to defend themselves and generate enough power to gouge a hole in the ground.

8 Trigrams 64 Palms!

The Byakugan's field of view spans all directions and is considered circular. Neji attacks opponents within its parameters with his 64 deadly blows. He has mastered this secret technique, which is exclusive to the Hyuga Clan Main Branch, by virtue of his natural talent alone.

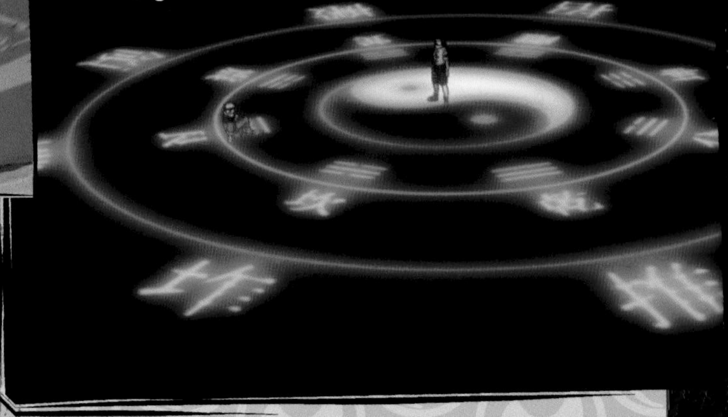

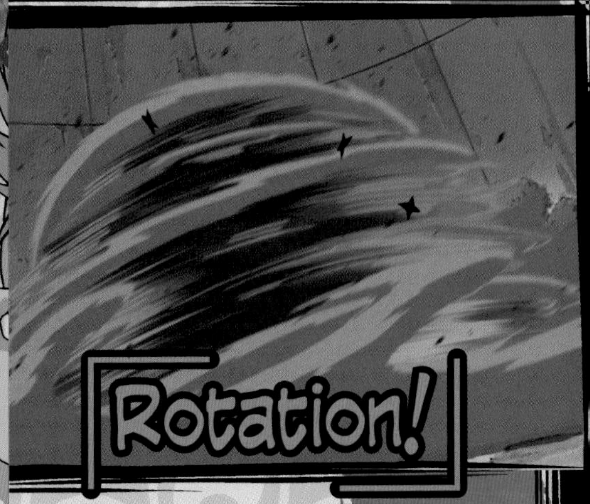

Rotation!

An ultimate defense that repels any attack through release of chakra while rotating at ultra high speed. It has virtually no blind spots.

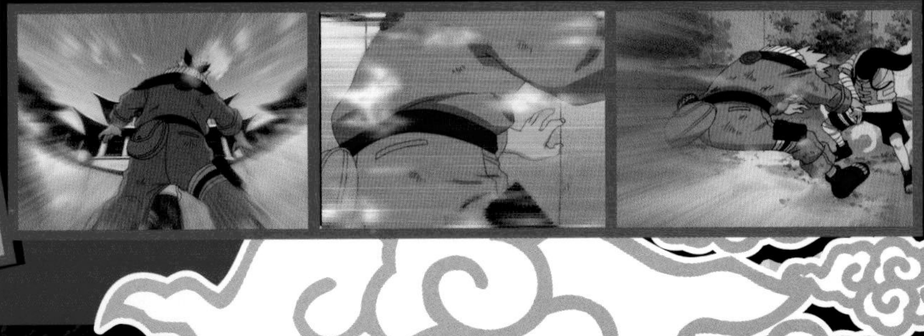

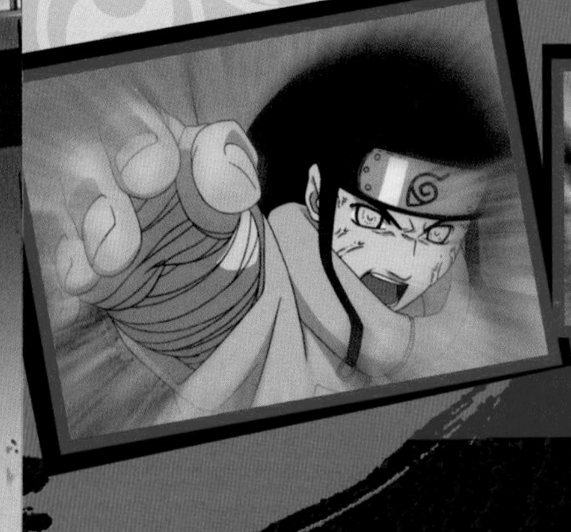

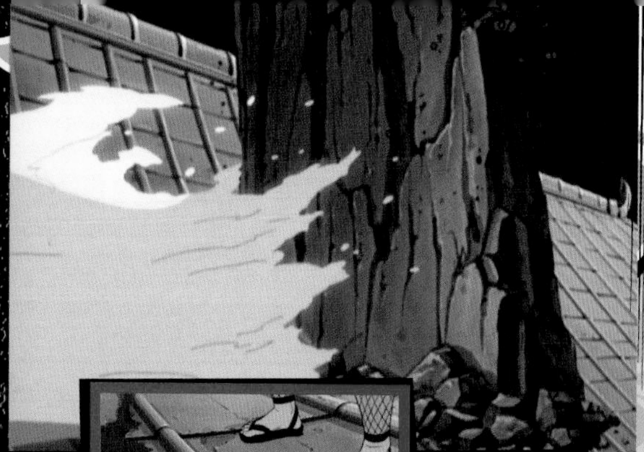

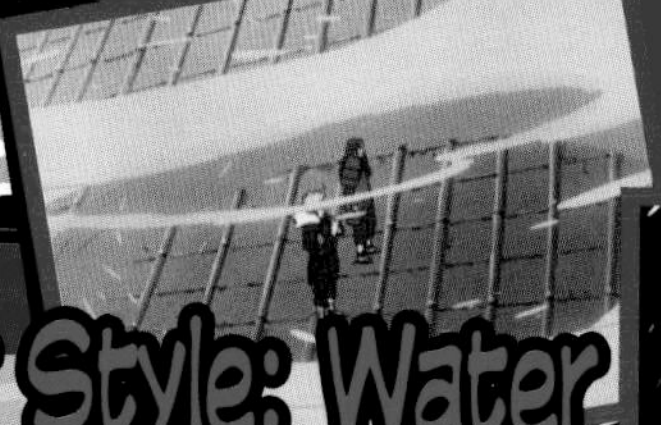

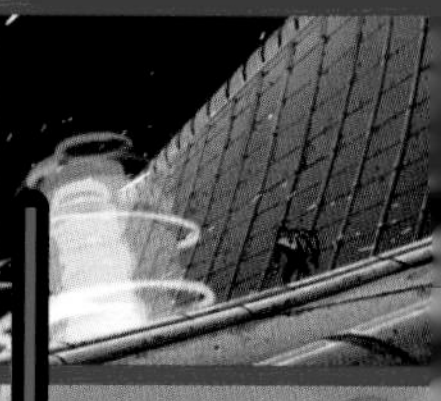

Water Style: Water Shock Wave!

Streams of water are gathered into a tornado and made to explode at full velocity! The impact is similar to a huge tsunami blanketing and swallowing everything!

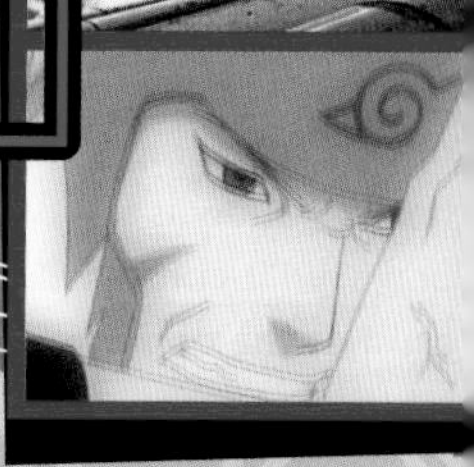

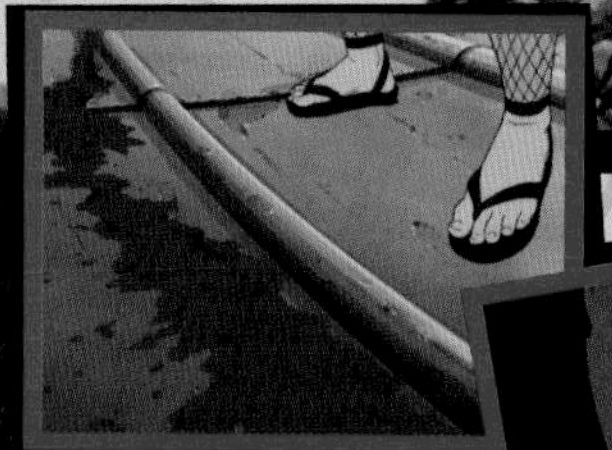

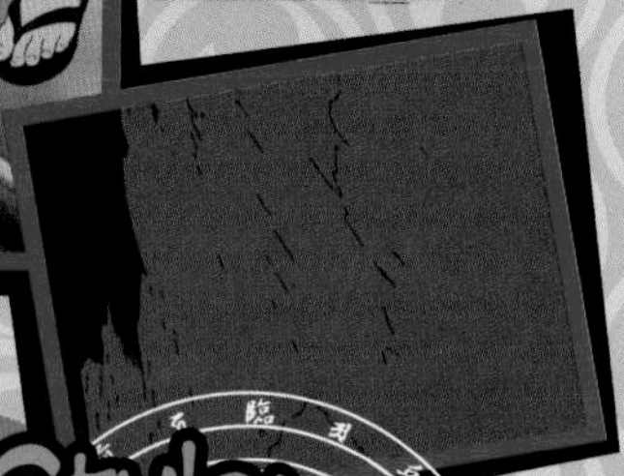

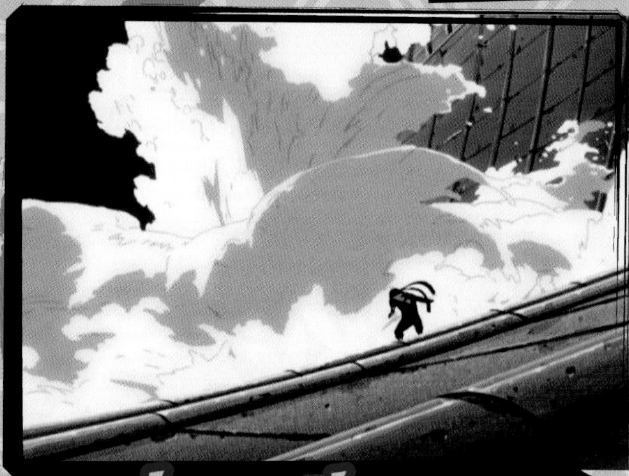

Earth Style: Mud Wall!

Sand and soil spew from the jutsu user's mouth to form a huge defensive wall! This jutsu is derived through absolute knowledge of soil characteristics.

Spitting blazing flame where there is no fire and summoning...

The Hokage's secret jutsu revealed!

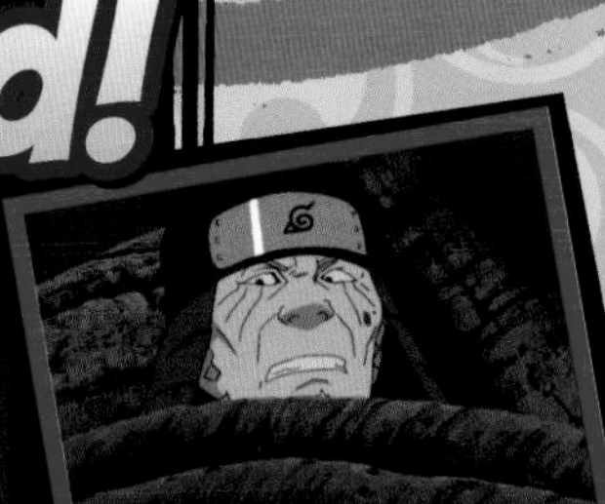

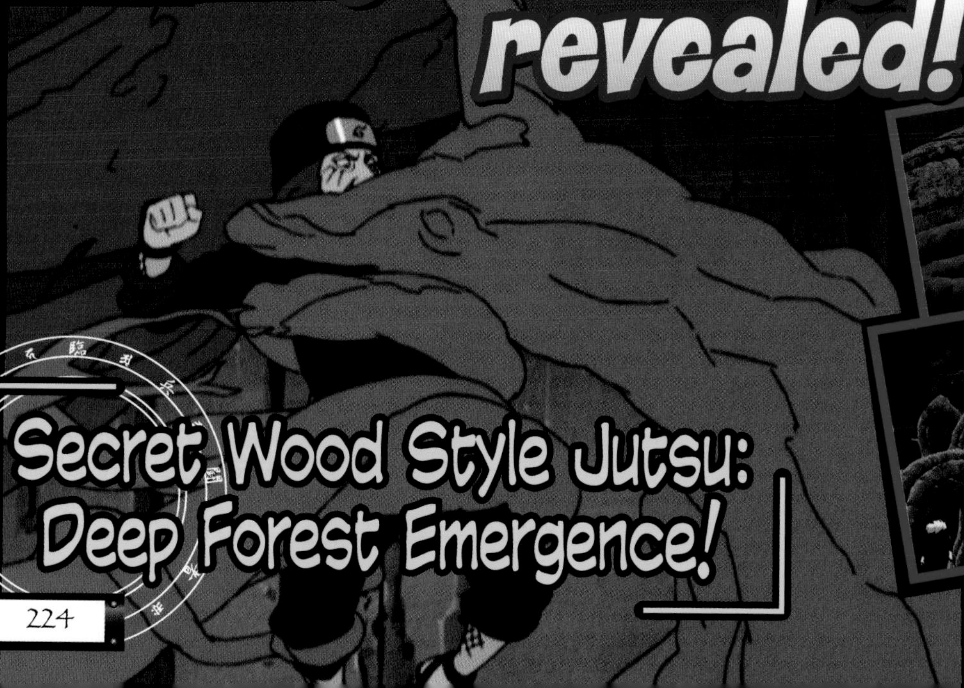

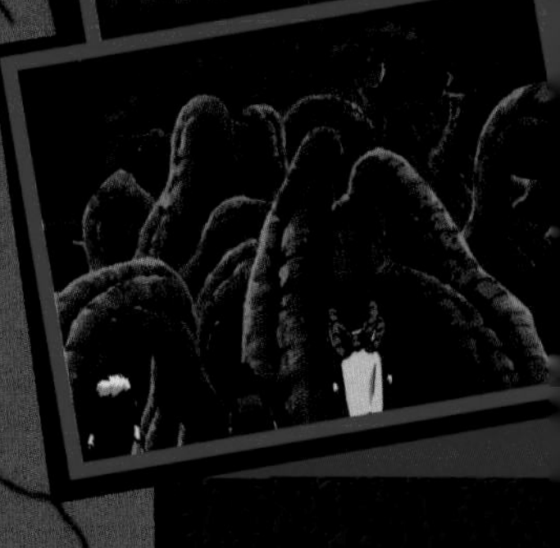

Secret Wood Style Jutsu: Deep Forest Emergence!

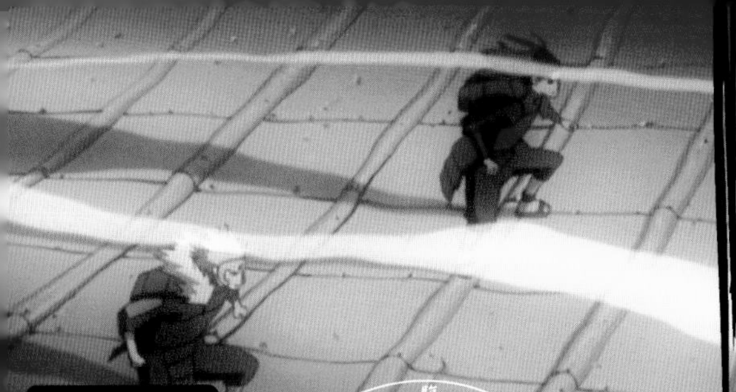

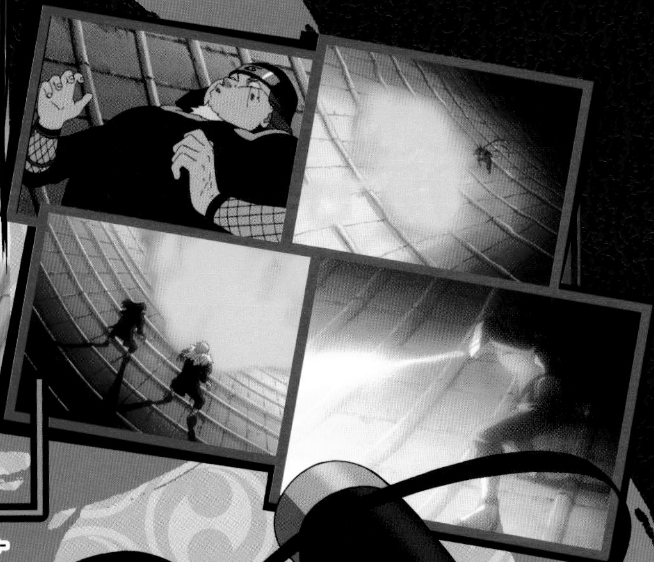

Fire Style: Dragon Flame Bombs!

Flame Bombs that hit the opponent with the overwhelming power of Dragon Flame! It is several times more intense and has an attack range far exceeding that of the Fire Ball Jutsu. This is the strongest of all fire-style ninjutsu!

A Hokage understands all natural phenomena and masters all variety of jutsu. By closely observing this battle, we can learn the true level of a Hokage!

...gushing streams of water where there is no water!

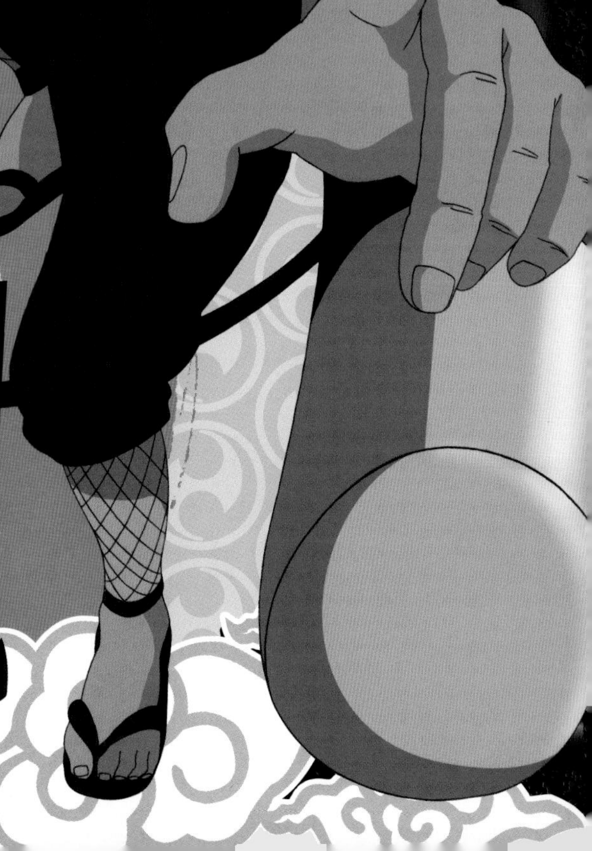

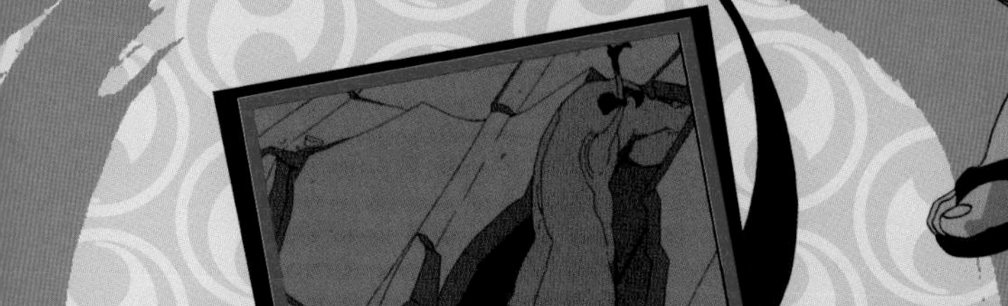

An astounding secret jutsu that uses chakra as bio-energy. Trees instantly grow into forests and forests into deep woods! Only the First Hokage, he who brought calm to chaotic times and founded the Hidden Leaf Village, could use this legendary jutsu. And now he brings it back!

TOP SECRET ARTS?! TOAD SAGE-STYLE SECRET TECHNIQUES DIVULGED!

Keep your eyes wide open and pay attention, squirts! The masterly techniques of Jiraiya, the Toad Sage, will be revealed!

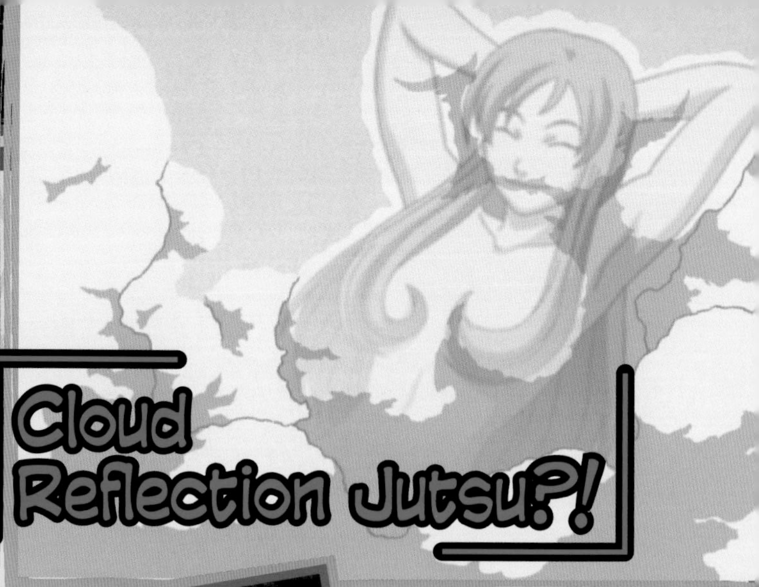

Cloud Reflection Jutsu?!

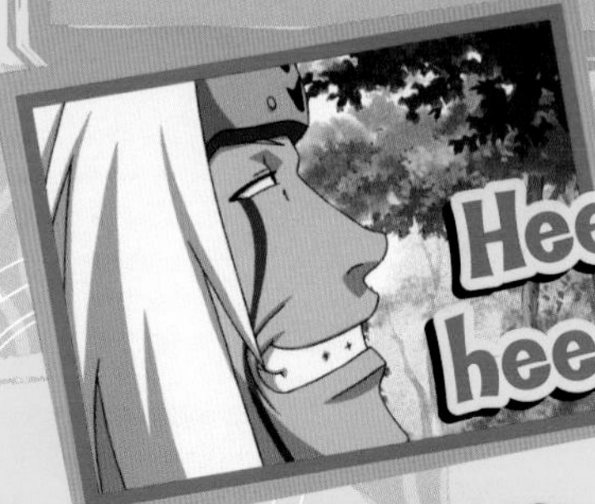
Hee hee...

Even simple white clouds drifting in the sky look sexy to Jiraiya's eyes! Mastering the ways of the pervy sage allows you to find beauties everywhere!

Raccoon & Toad Substitution Jutsu!

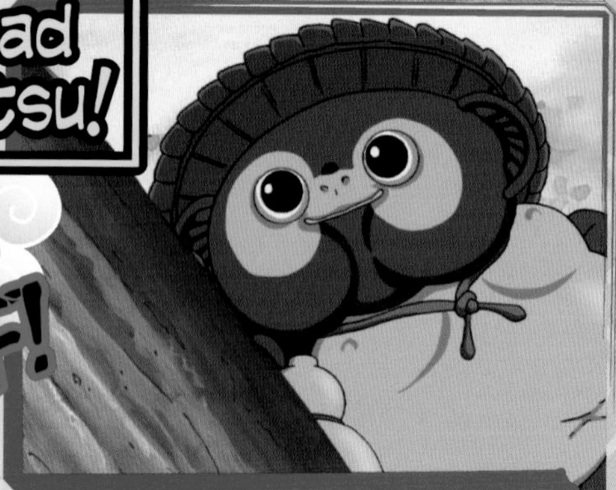
POOF!

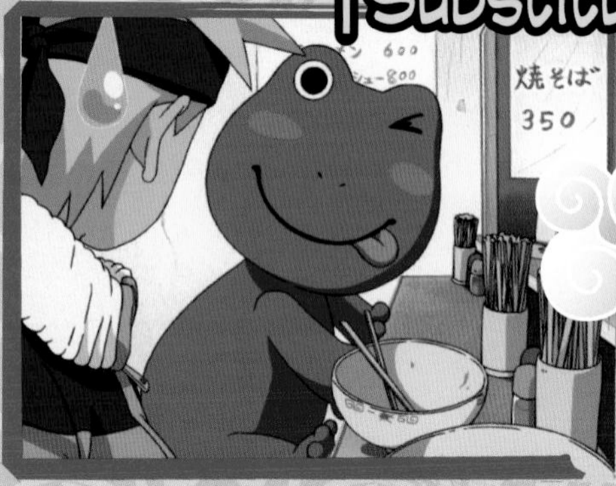
焼そば
350

Sometimes it's a dignified-looking raccoon and at other times a cute toad. A sage ought to maintain his class and charm even in a Substitution Jutsu.

Telescope...Jutsu?!

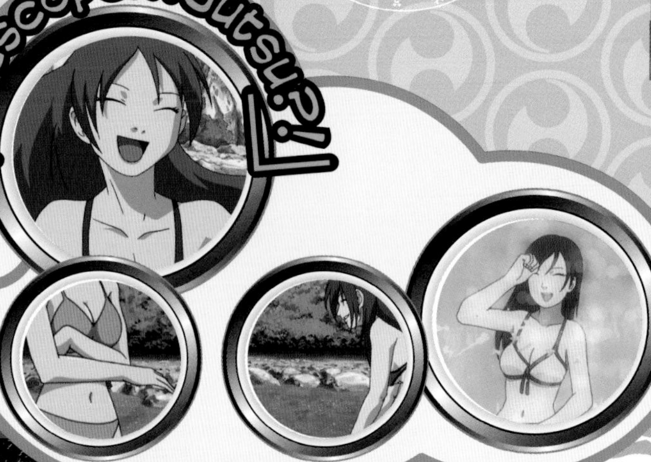

Hold in your excitement when you feel like exploding and maintain your ability to observe! That's the secret of sage-style research!

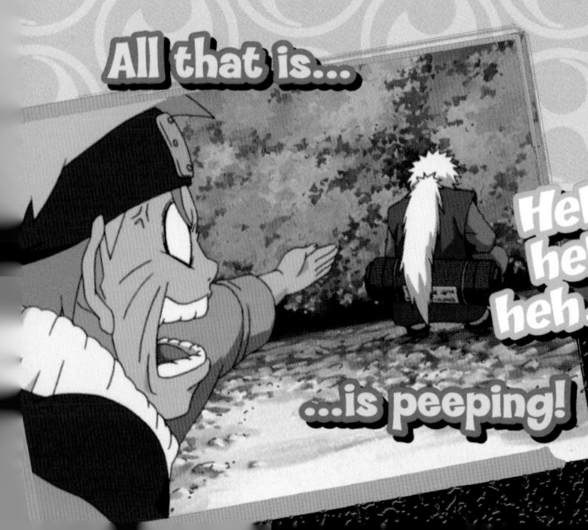
All that is...
Heh heh heh...
...is peeping!

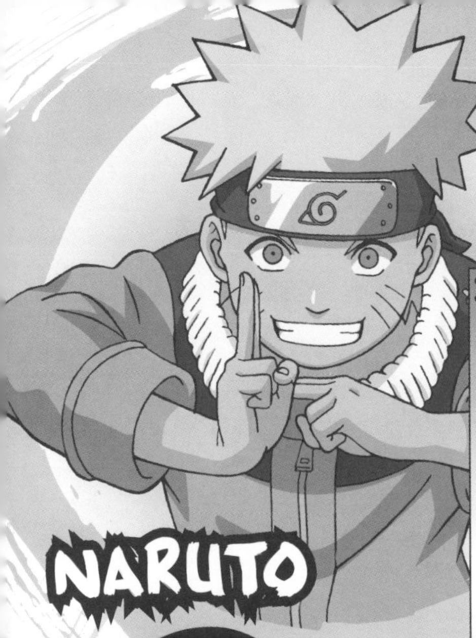
NARUTO

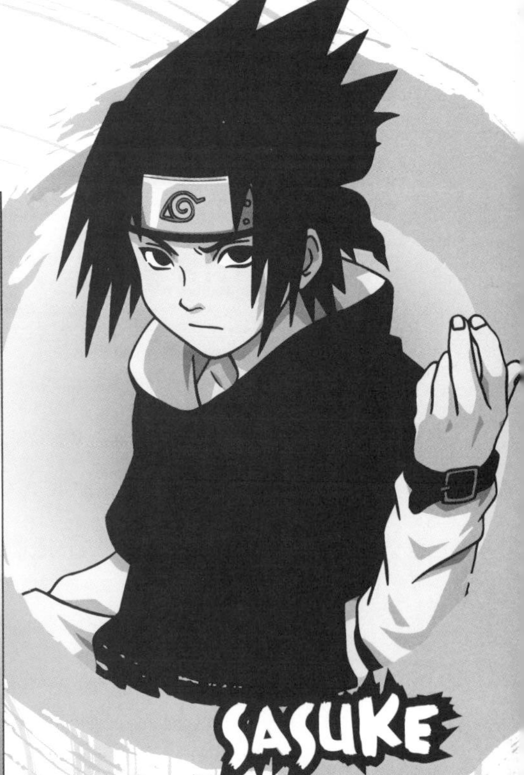
SASUKE

Naruto Voice Actors Revealed!

What's that Naruto's saying? Well, without voice-over actors, you'd never know! It takes talent to talk like a ninja. Turn the pages of this section to learn a little more about the people who bring *Naruto* to life every day.

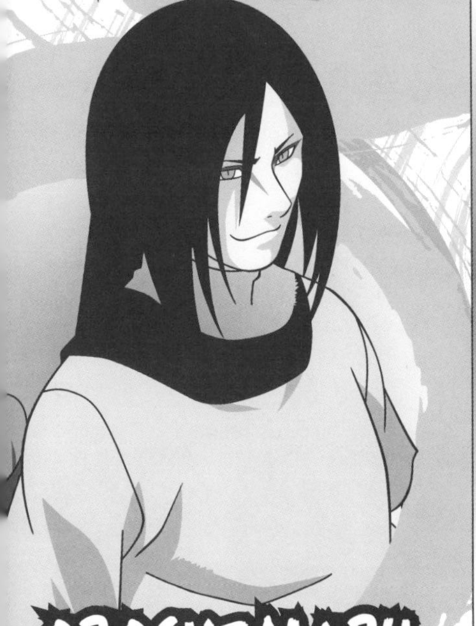
OROCHIMARU

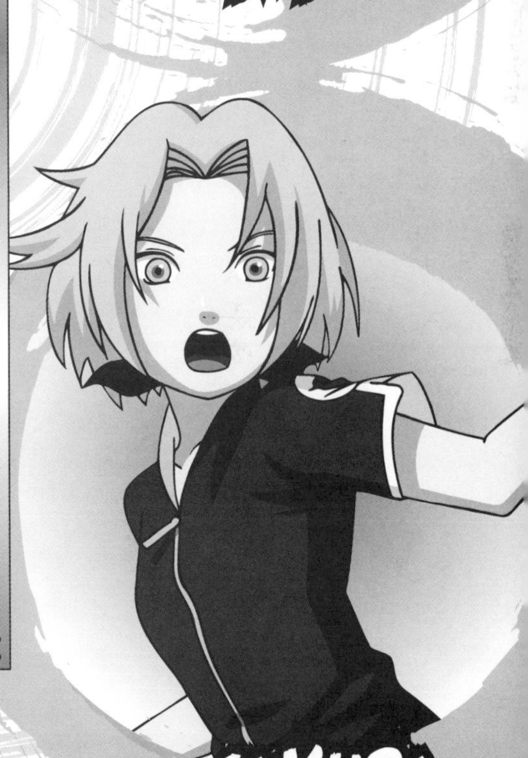
SAKURA

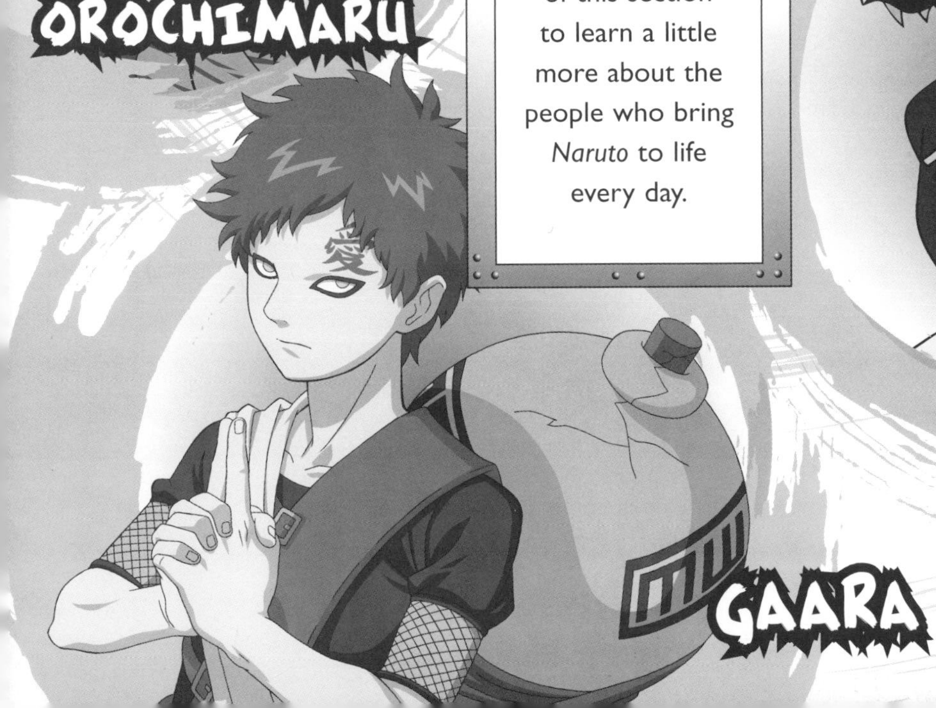
GAARA

Meet Maile Flanagan The Voice of Naruto!

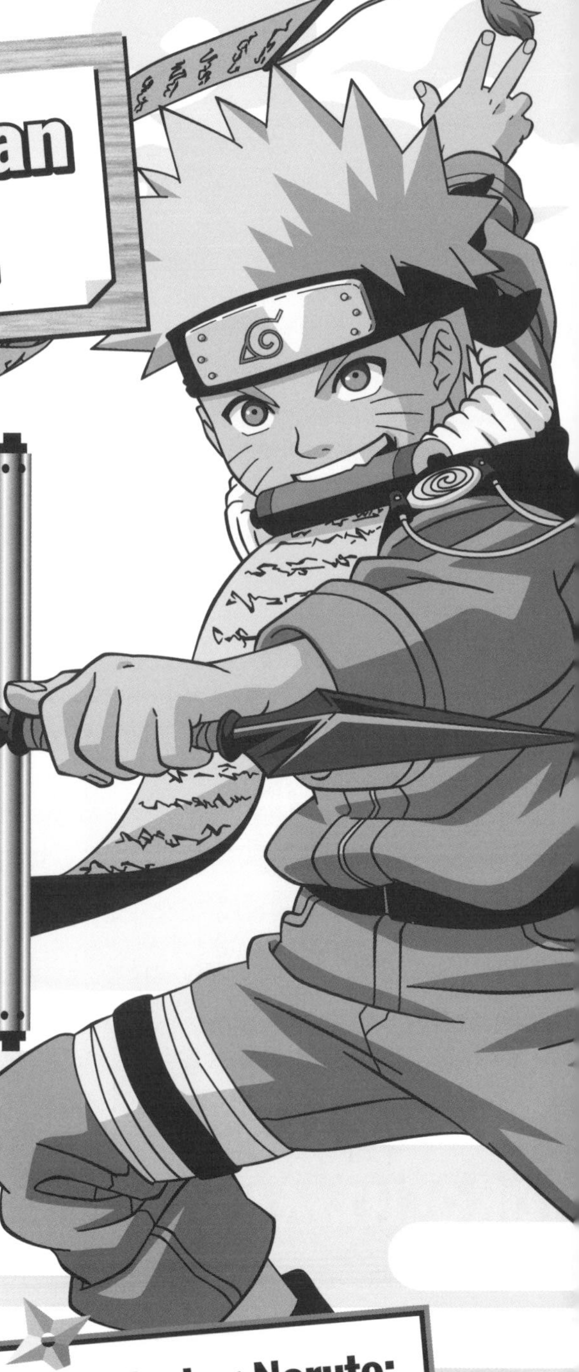

Naruto's played by a girl?! Yes, and not just in America. In Japan, Naruto is voiced by Junko Takeuchi, also a woman!! You've heard Maile's voice before Naruto though. She even won an Emmy in 2006 for *Jakers! The Adventures of Piggley Winks*. Maile's also voice acted in tons of cartoons, including *Men in Black* and *Jackie Chan* and the animated film *Tom and Jerry: The Magic Ring*. She's been on live-action TV in *ER*, *Desperate Housewives*, and *Grey's Anatomy* and in the major motion picture *Evan Almighty*.

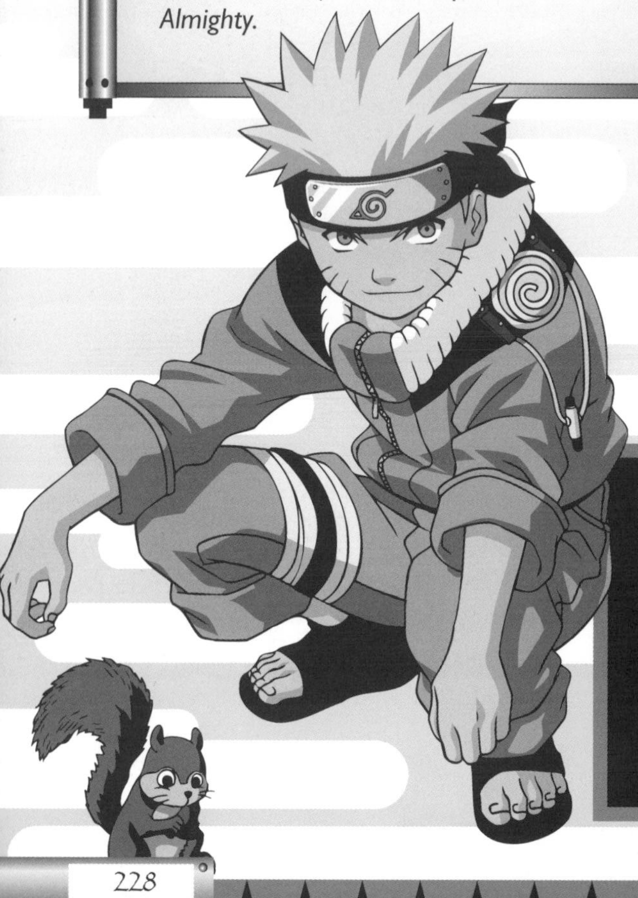

About Playing Naruto:

Maile says: Naruto is a blast to portray because he's complex, feisty, emotional, a self-starter, a true friend, a fighter and kind of wacky. He's a true original! Believe it!

Meet Yuri Lowenthal The Voice of Sasuke

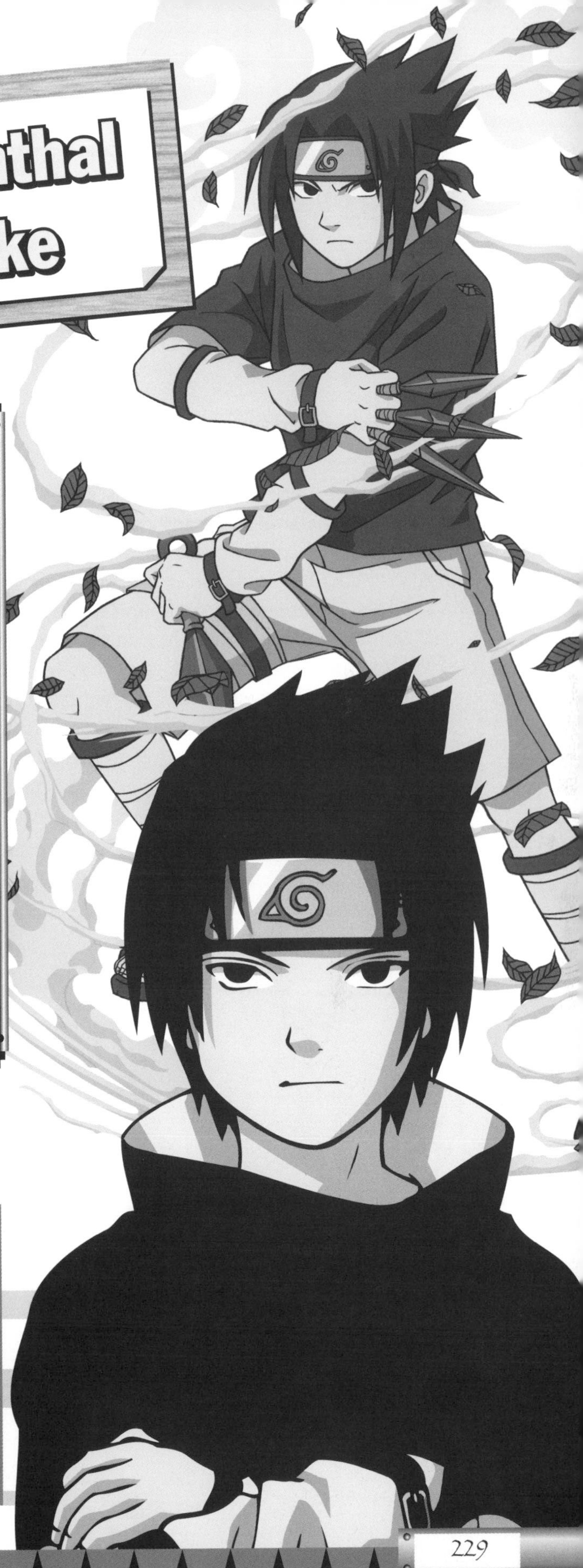

If you're a gamer, you might already know Yuri from the *Prince of Persia* video games. Or maybe you know of him as the voice of Keigo Asano on *Bleach*. But he's also voice acted in lots of other anime, playing feisty little Bakunetsumaru in *SD Gundam Force*, plus Haru Glory in *Ravemaster*, Leo Skorpus in *Scrapped Princess*, Mark in *Cybuster*, Tsujiai in *Ultramaniac*, Goku in *Saiyuki: Reload* and a whole bunch more! An impressive list for sure, but we think his best character is, of course, Sasuke!

About Playing Sasuke:

Yuri says: I love playing Sasuke because he's got all the darkness I don't have in real life. It's fun exploring that!

Meet Kate Higgins The Voice of Sakura

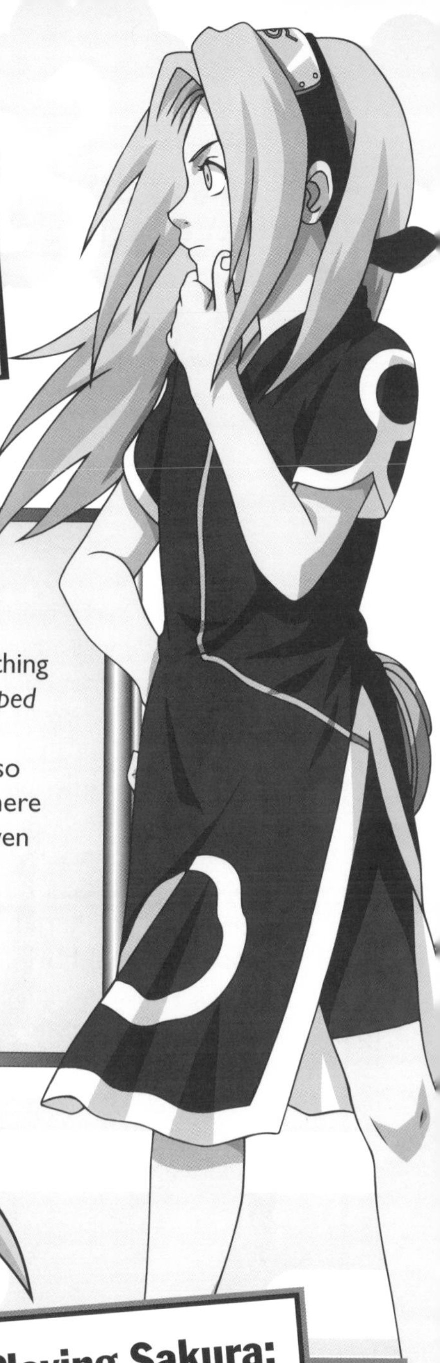

Kate shares more than just her voice with Sakura! She's also super-talented in many other areas, just like your favorite kunoichi. Not only has Kate voice acted in everything from *Zatch Bell* to *Animalia,* including *Rug Rats* and *Scrapped Princess,* in between, she's been the "voice of the Disney Channel," and has worked on many commercials. She also voices the infant learning line of toys by Fisher Price, where she gets to play a variety of characters and sing. She's even got an album out, *Bigger than Love,* which showcases her songwriting and piano playing.

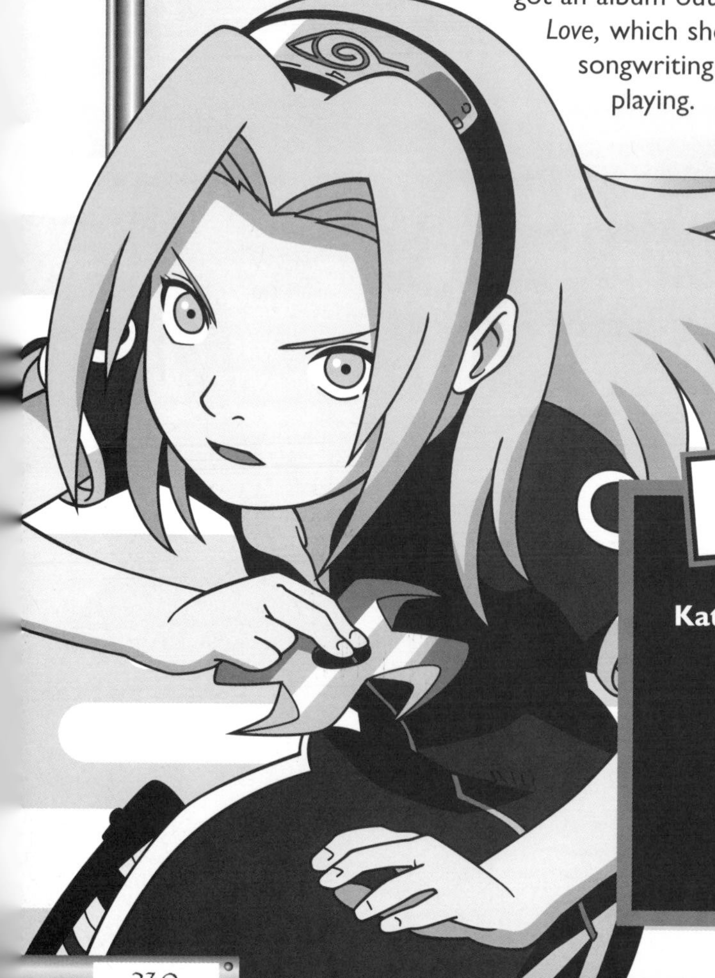

About Playing Sakura:

Kate says: Sakura is the coolest chick in anime!!!! She's my favorite character I've yet to play. She's a good role model for girls, even though she gives Sasuke far too much of her time. But she's learning to love herself, so she'll change.

Meet Liam O'Brien The Voice of Gaara

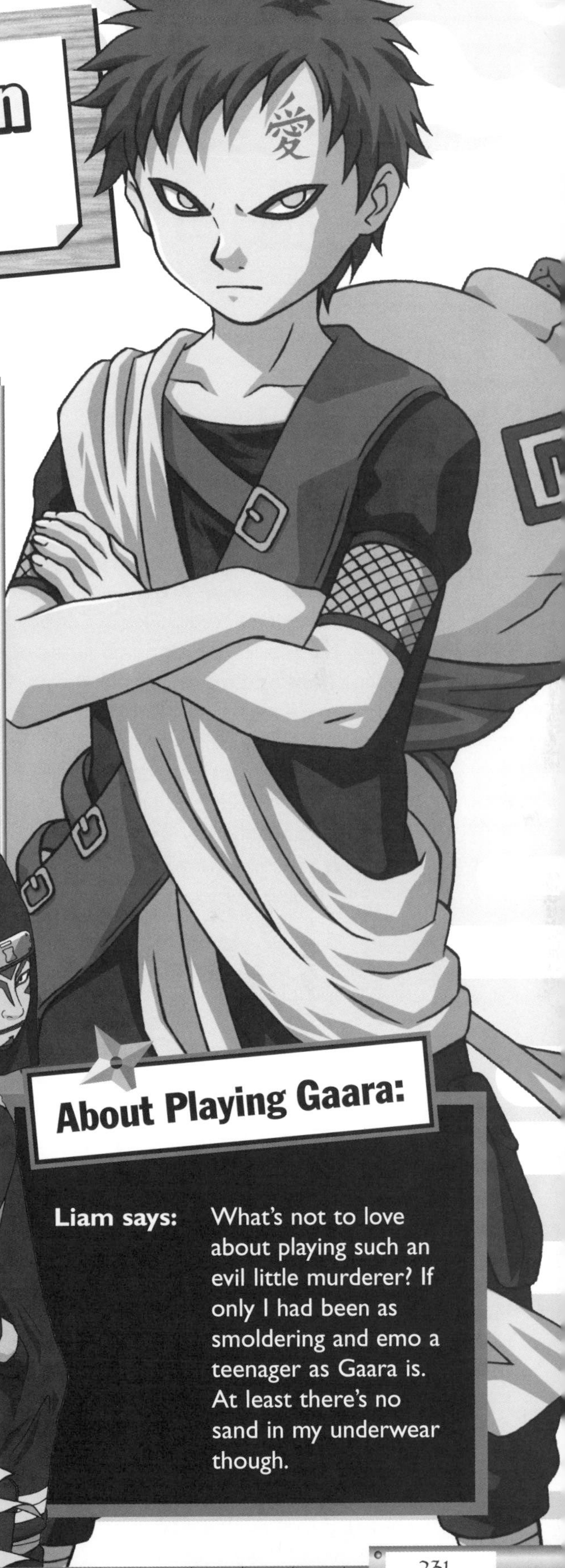

Another video game crossover actor (*World of Warcraft*), Liam has voice acted in all sorts of anime. You might recognize him from Shobu in *Duel Masters,* or maybe Vincent Law in *Ergo Agent.* He's also directed and written for *Koi Kaze* and *GunSword,* and even adapted scripts for the *Naruto* and *Bleach* anime! We bet he gave himself the best lines when he wrote for Gaara!

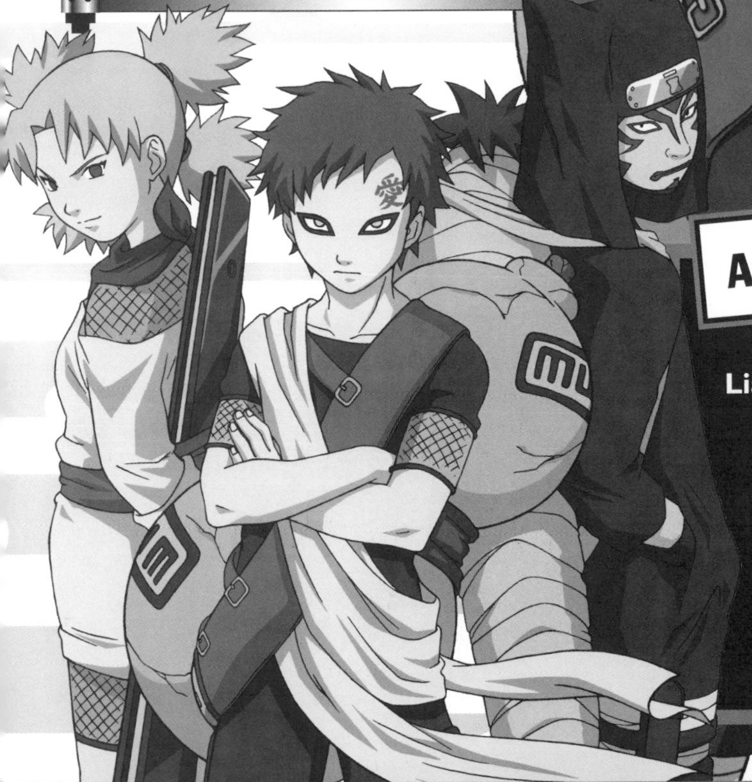

About Playing Gaara:

Liam says: What's not to love about playing such an evil little murderer? If only I had been as smoldering and emo a teenager as Gaara is. At least there's no sand in my underwear though.

Meet Steve Blum The Voice of Orochimaru & Zabuza

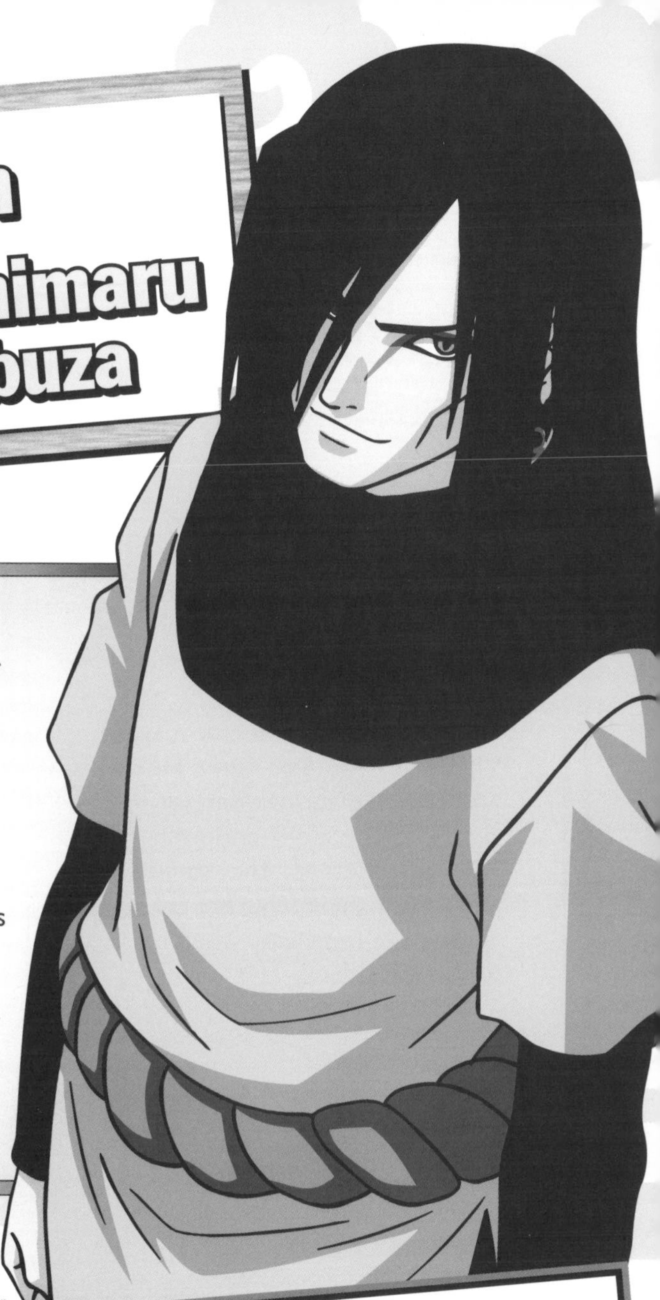

Steve Blum has done double-duty on *Naruto* with two very different sorts of nasty dudes! In season 1, he played Zabuza, and now he plays Orochimaru! He's also voice acted Spike in *Cowboy Bebop the Movie,* and done all kinds of voices (kids and monsters alike) for *Digimon*. He played Vincent Valentine in the *Final Fantasy* video games – and was even the video game voice of another truly evil guy: Jabba the Hutt! But don't think he can only play baddies. Another of his video game voices? Wolverine from the *X-Men*!

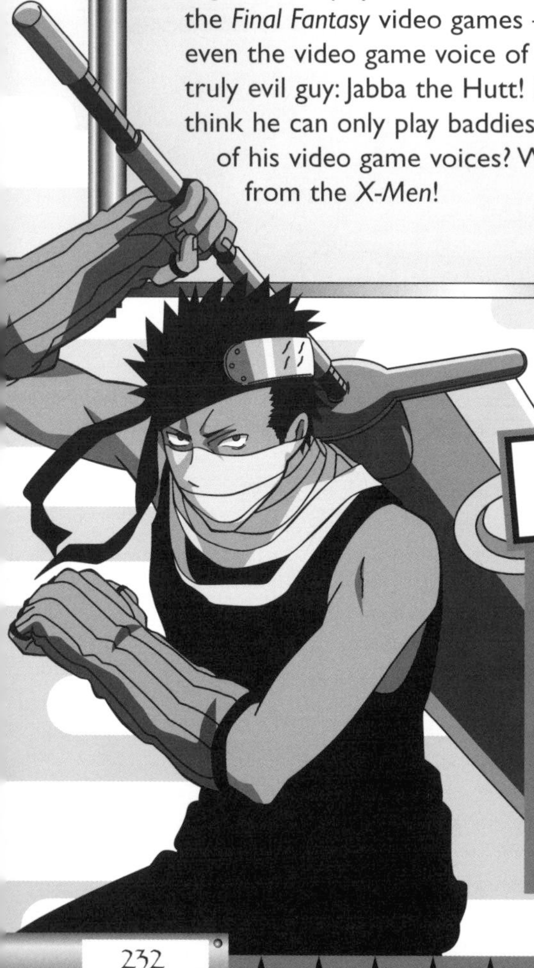

About Playing Orochimaru & Zabuza:

Steve says: Zabuza Momochi was my kinda guy: cool, tough, soft spoken, and carried a huge sword. Great death... like a stegosaurus on steroids. Sad to see him go. Now I'm playing Orochimaru. My favorite pastime? Throwing up sssssssssssnakes, of courssssse. What's your jutsu? Good... I'll take it.

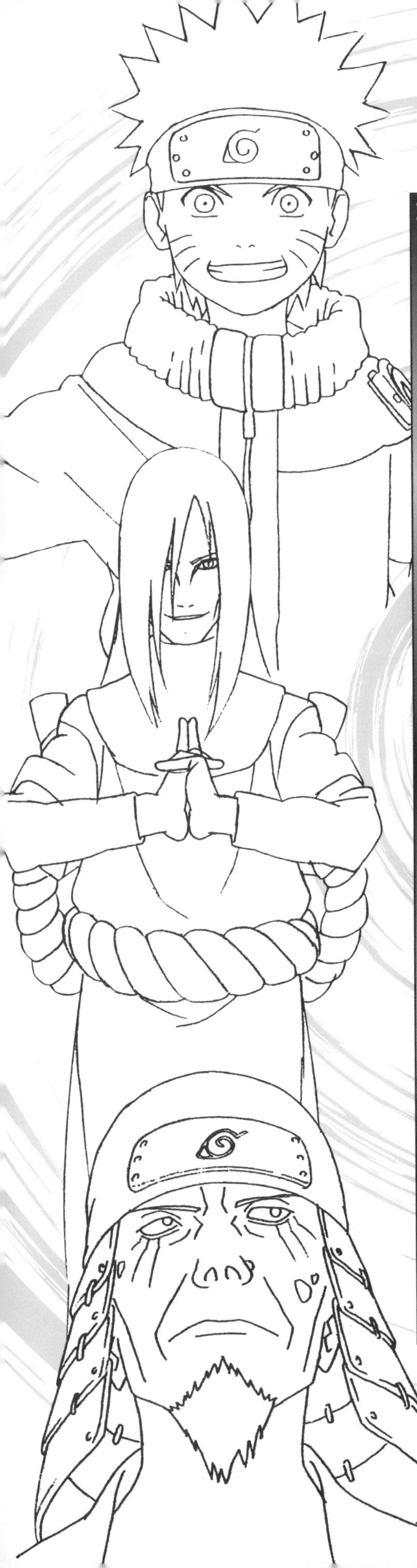

Design Illustrations Revealed to the Public for the First Time!

Character Designs by Tetsuya Nishio & Hirofumi Suzuki

From a massive collection of design illustrations, a select few have been chosen to be shared with the public! Examine them closely to see the subtle differences from the original manga and anime!

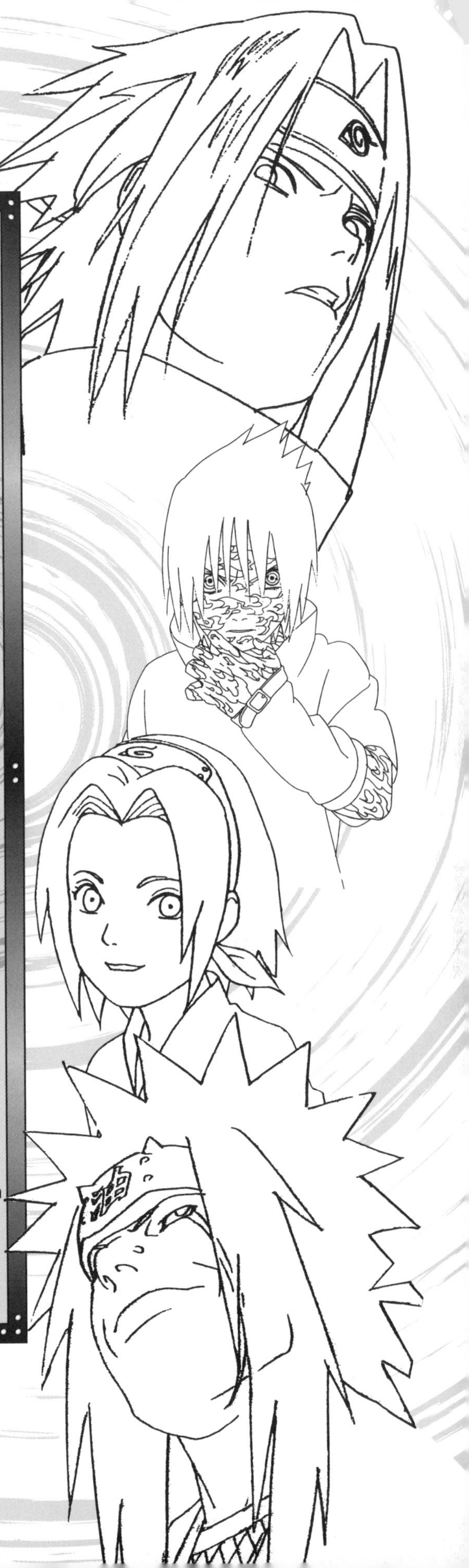

Naruto Uzumaki

Naruto follows the ninja way he believes in, with his sights always set on his dream of becoming Hokage!

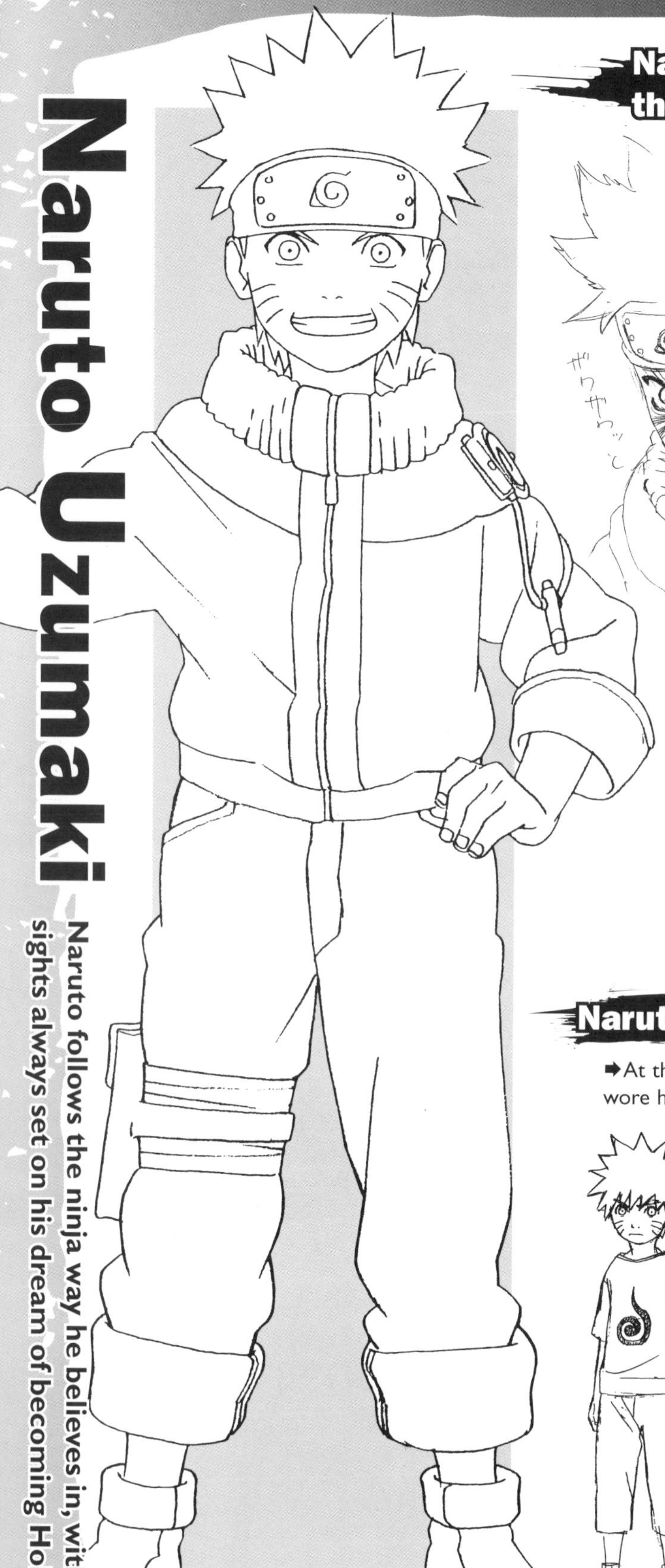

Naruto when the chakra of the Nine-Tailed Fox is activated

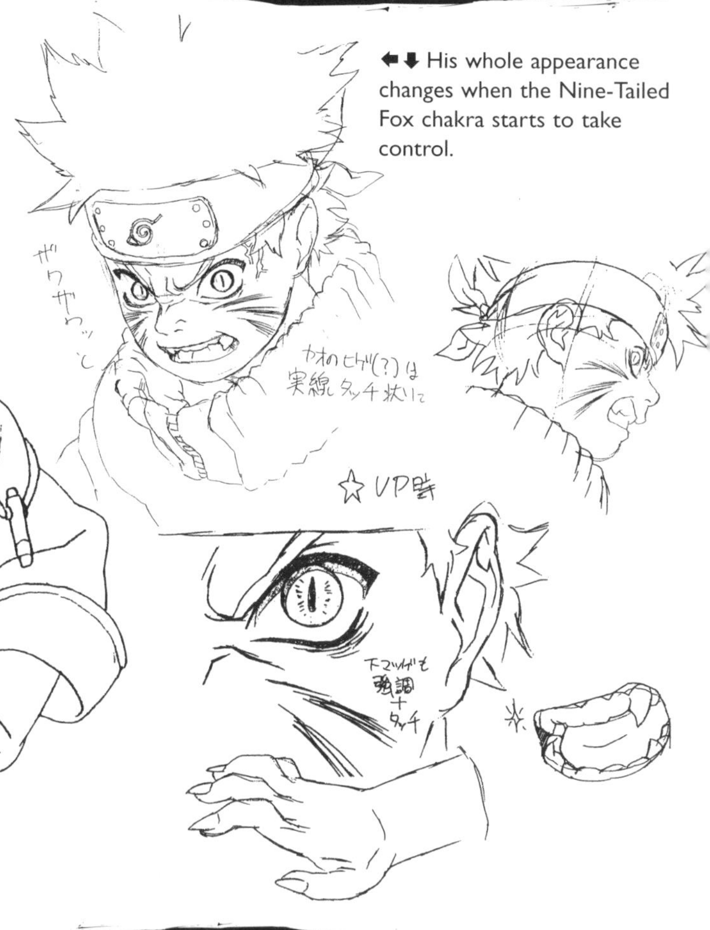

カオのヒゲ(?)は
実線タッチ状に
☆UP時
下マツゲも
強調
+
タッチ

⬅⬇ His whole appearance changes when the Nine-Tailed Fox chakra starts to take control.

Naruto at the funeral

➡At the Third Hokage's funeral he wore his headband around his neck.

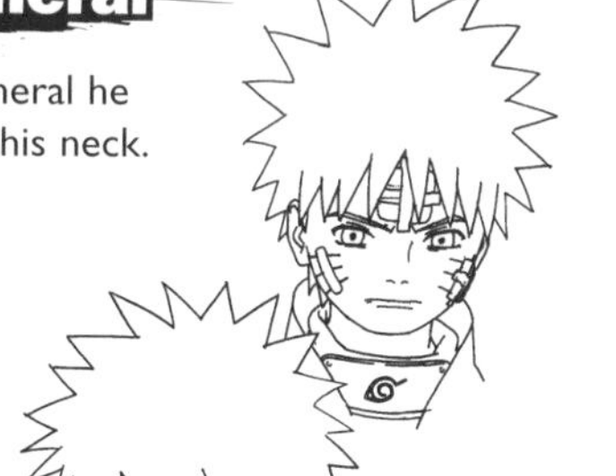

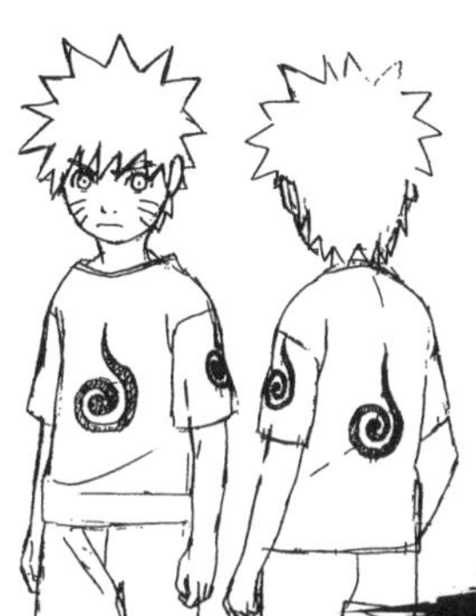

Pre-genin Naruto

⬅There is a swirl pattern on both sleeves and the back and front of his T-shirt.

The Nine-Tailed Fox

⬇ The legendary beast that attacked the Hidden Leaf Village 12 years ago. It's sealed within Naruto's body, but its chakra emerges in response to Naruto's feelings.

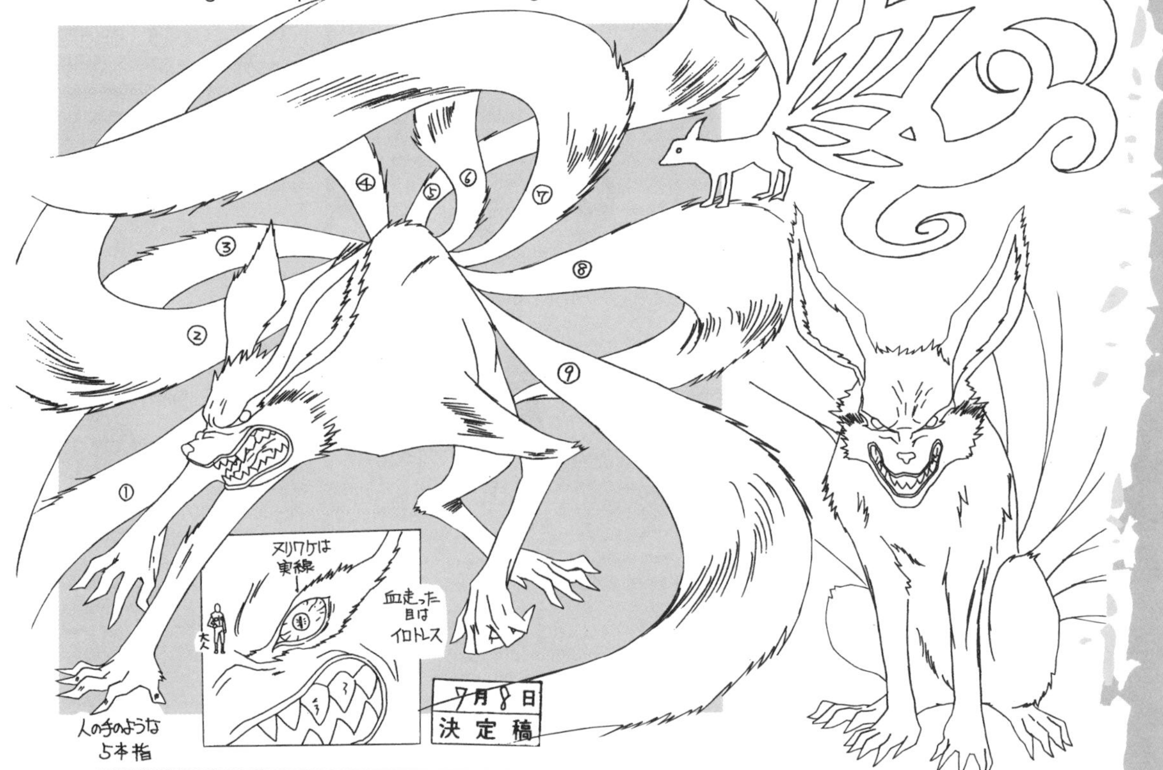
ヌリワケは
実線
血走った
目は
イロトレス
7月8日
決定稿
人の手のような
5本指

Pakkun

⬅ ⬇ Pakkun was also at the battle against Zabuza. He is one of Kakashi's eight ninja dogs. With his excellent sense of smell, he has amazing tracking abilities.

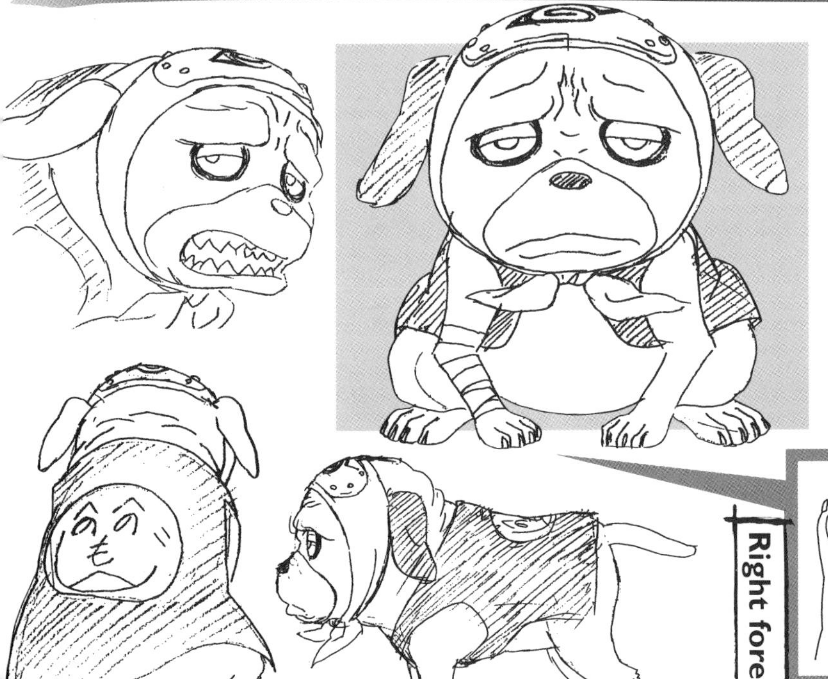

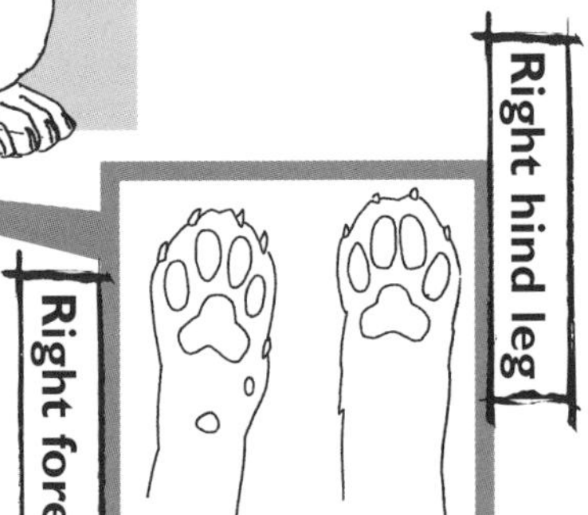
Right hind leg
Right foreleg

Sasuke Uchiha

Since training with Kakashi he's been wearing a streamlined bodysuit. Bandages and belts are wrapped around his left arm, the one that unleashes the Chidori.

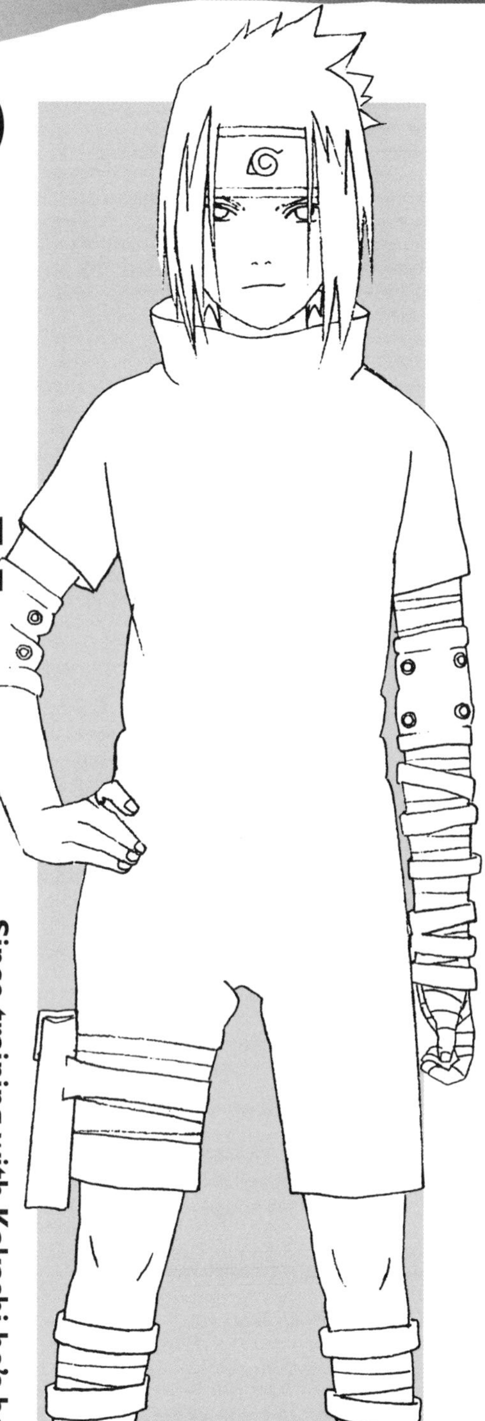

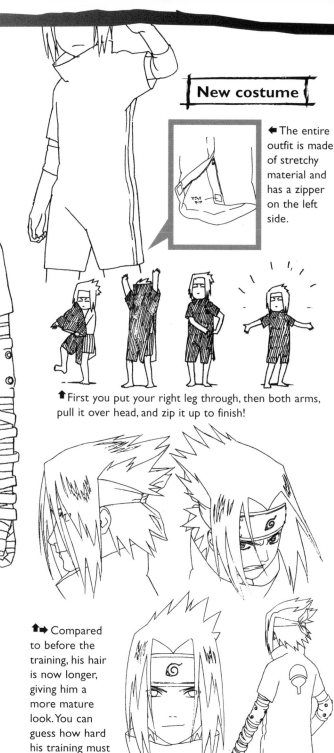

New costume

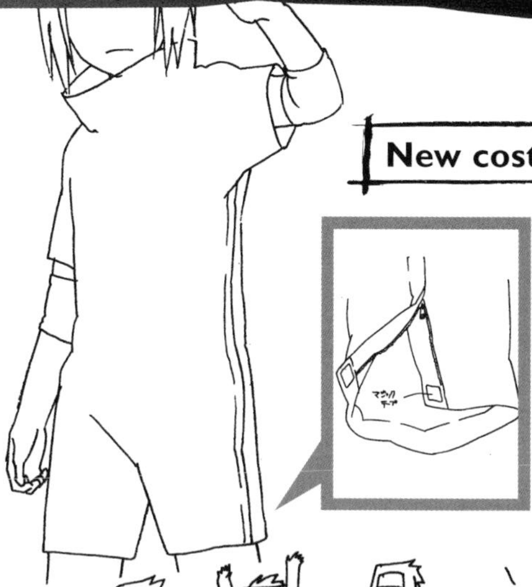

⬅The entire outfit is made of stretchy material and has a zipper on the left side.

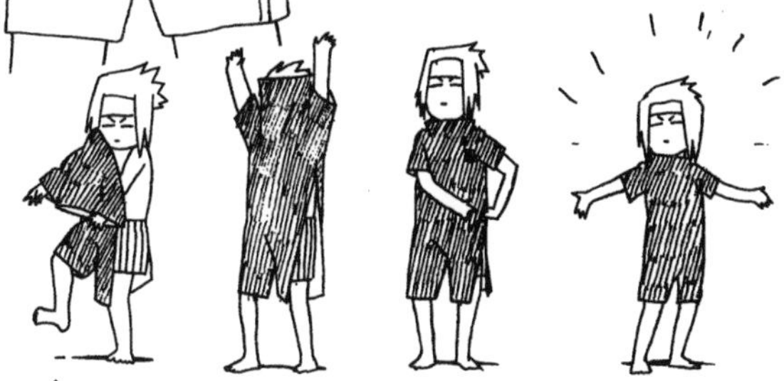

⬆First you put your right leg through, then both arms, pull it over head, and zip it up to finish!

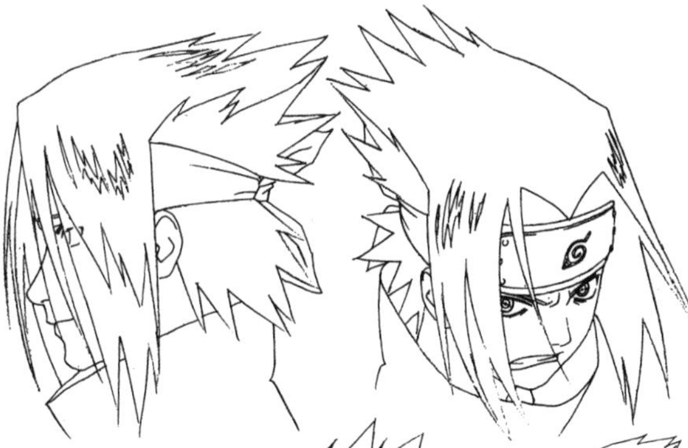

⬆➡ Compared to before the training, his hair is now longer, giving him a more mature look. You can guess how hard his training must have been from the drastic changes in his appearance.

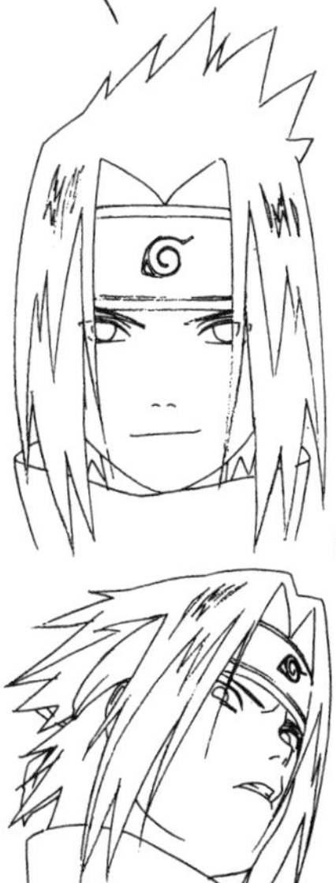

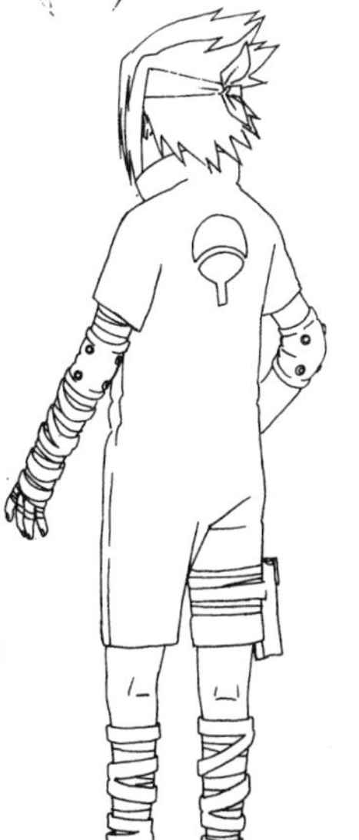

Curse Sealing

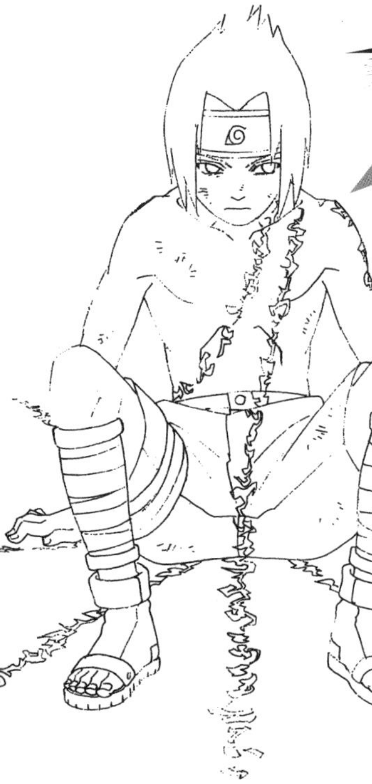

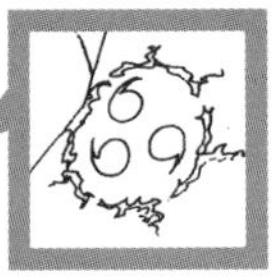

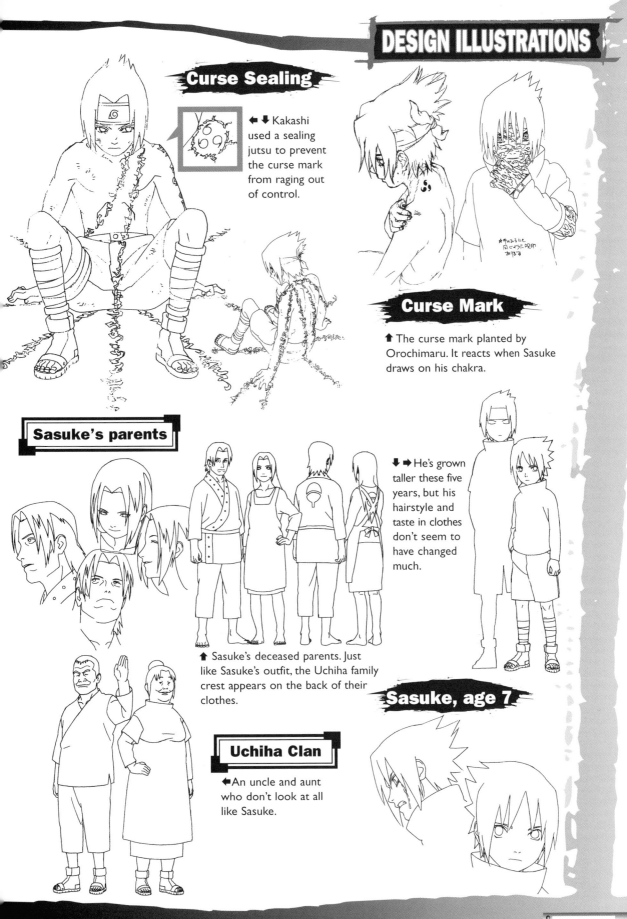

⬅ ⬇ Kakashi used a sealing jutsu to prevent the curse mark from raging out of control.

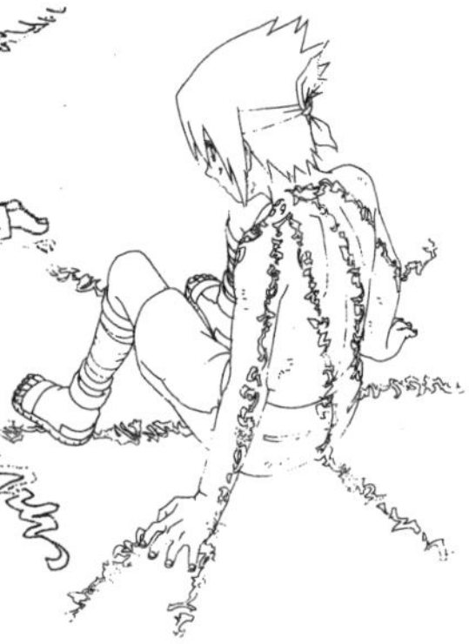

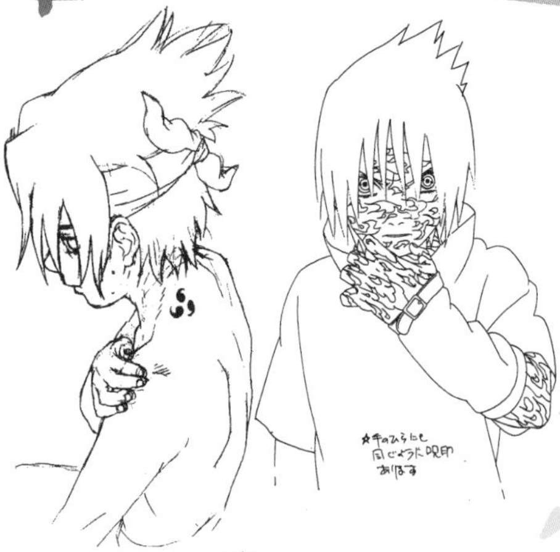

Curse Mark

⬆ The curse mark planted by Orochimaru. It reacts when Sasuke draws on his chakra.

Sasuke's parents

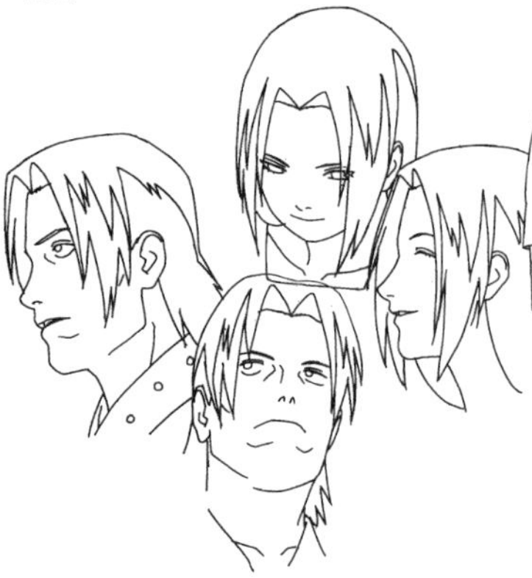

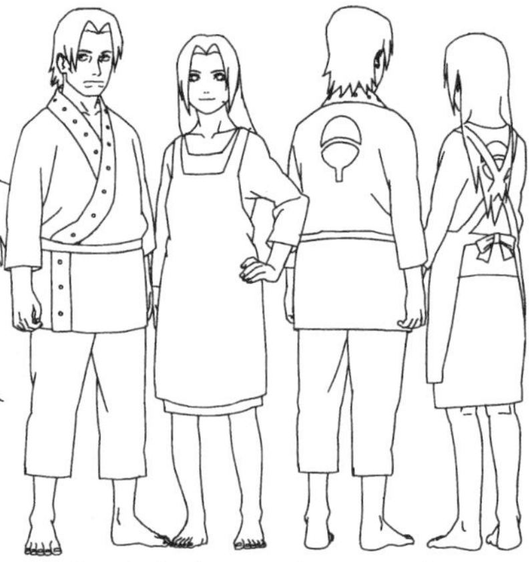

⬆ Sasuke's deceased parents. Just like Sasuke's outfit, the Uchiha family crest appears on the back of their clothes.

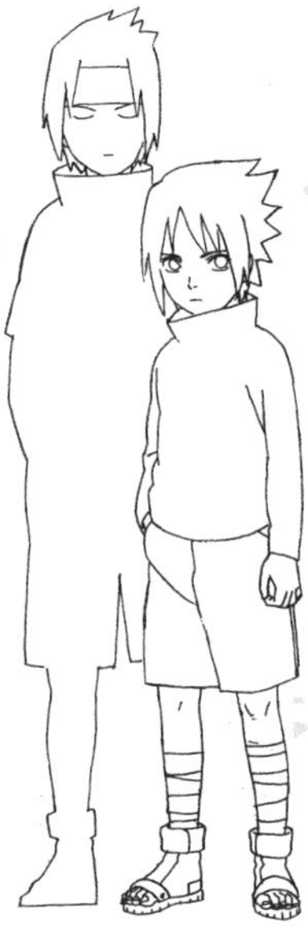

⬇ ➡ He's grown taller these five years, but his hairstyle and taste in clothes don't seem to have changed much.

Sasuke, age 7

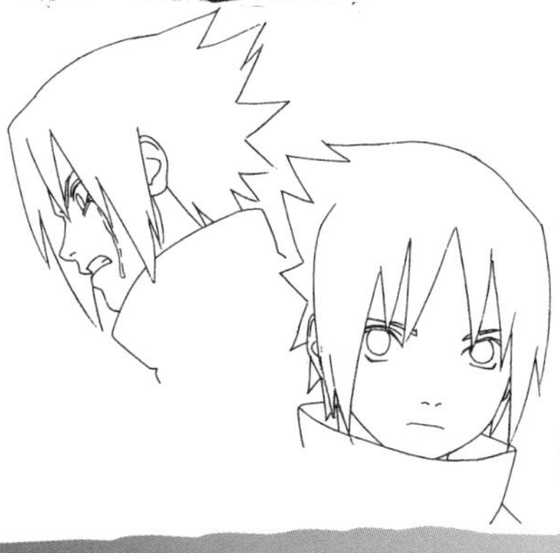

Uchiha Clan

⬅ An uncle and aunt who don't look at all like Sasuke.

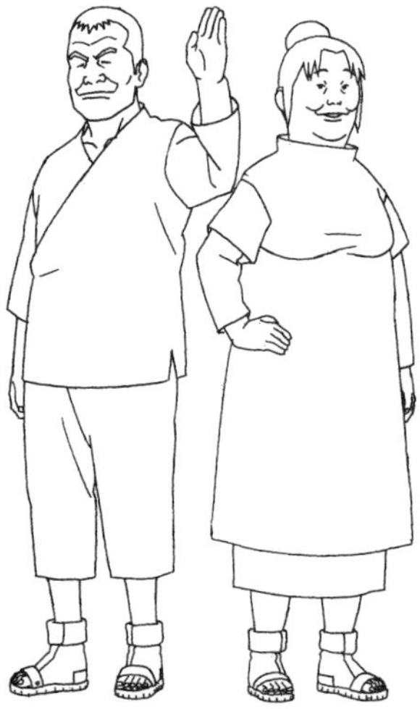

Sakura Haruno

During the battle against the Sound ninja in the Chunin Exam's second stage, Sakura cut her own hair to prove she is prepared to protect those precious to her.

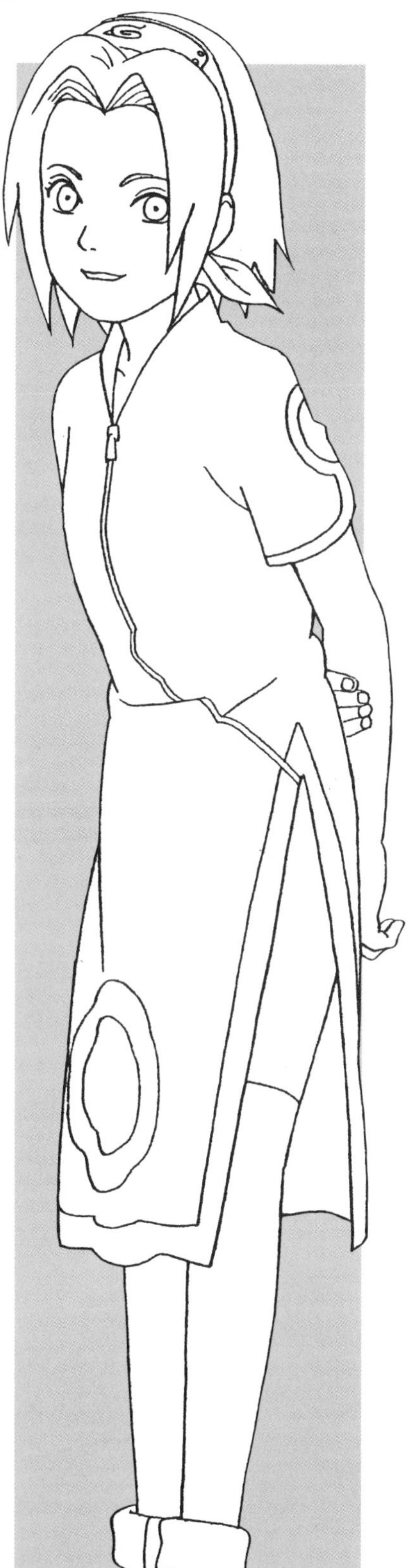

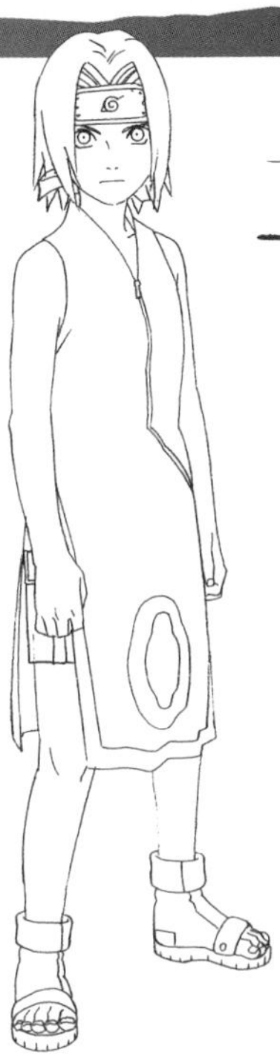

Wearing her headband

⬅⬇ Sakura usually wears it like a hair band, but she tied it around her forehead when she got serious in her fight with Ino.

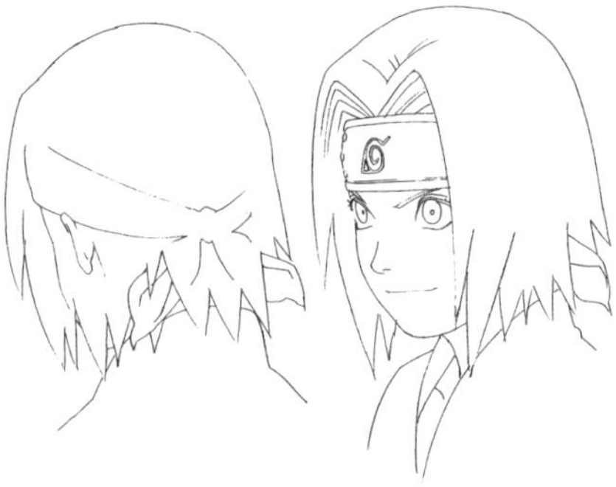

Sakura as a child

➡ Sakura wore bangs when she was a child because her broad forehead embarrassed her. The ribbon that Ino gave her not only changed Sakura's hair-style, but also her personality.

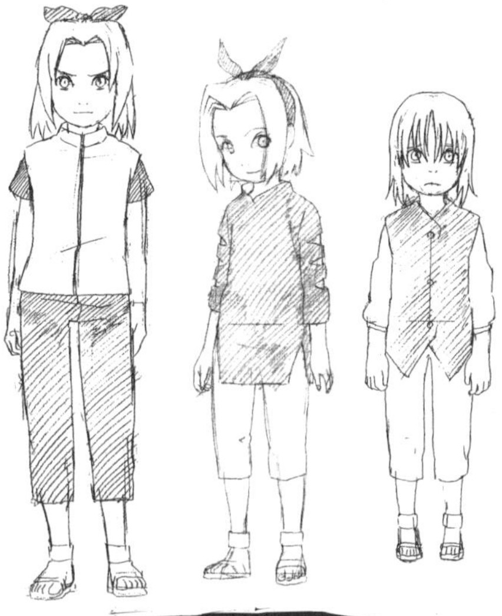

Ino as a child

➡ Ino has always been cheerful and stylish. She used to wear her hair short, but she's started growing it out, probably because she knows Sasuke likes long hair.

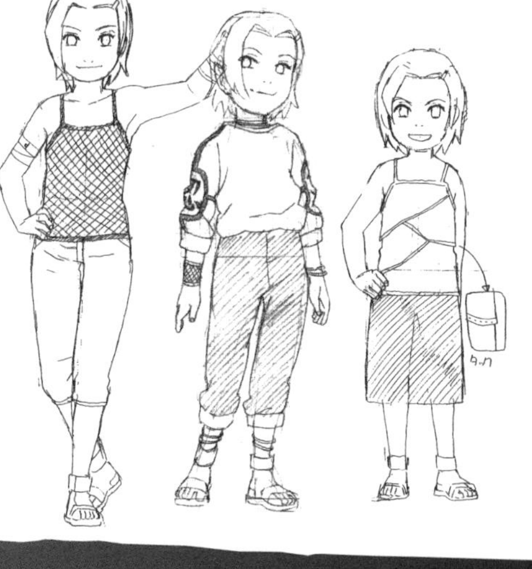

Ino Yamanaka

Ino's signature technique is the Mind Transfer Jutsu, which allows her to possess her opponent. She wears her headband around her waist to demonstrate her superb sense of style.

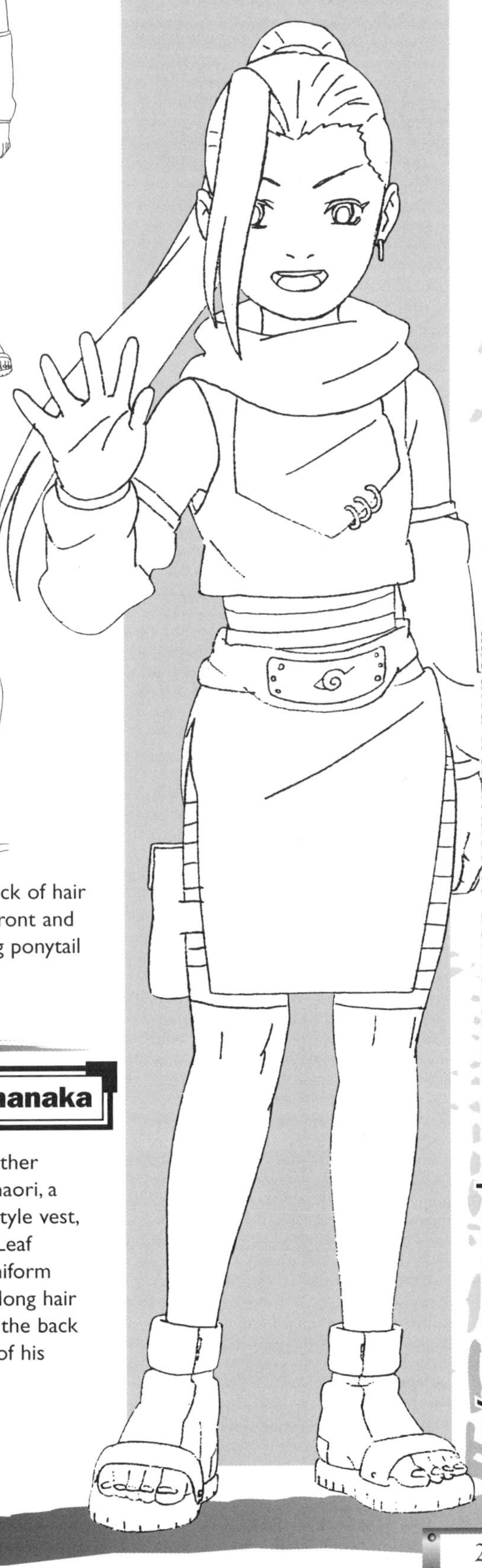

Wearing her headband

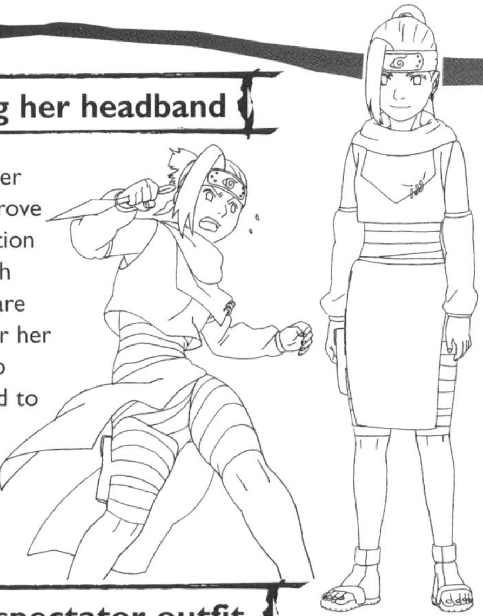

➡Ino put on her headband to prove her determination in the fight with Sakura. There are bandages under her skirt as well, so there's no need to worry if it flies up.

Ino's spectator outfit

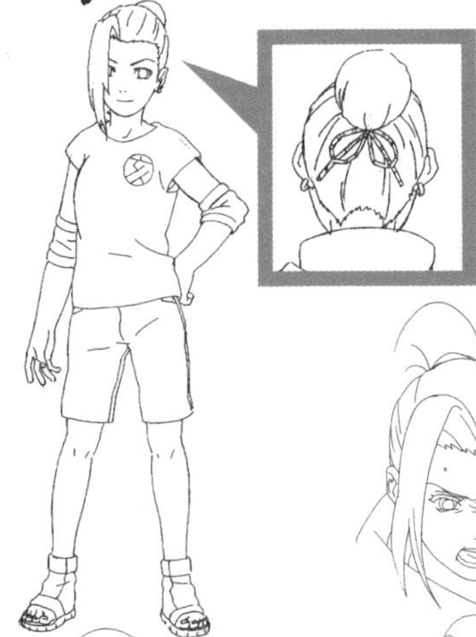

⬅This outfit looks cool and comfortable. Her hair, now shorter at the back, is bound with a cloth.

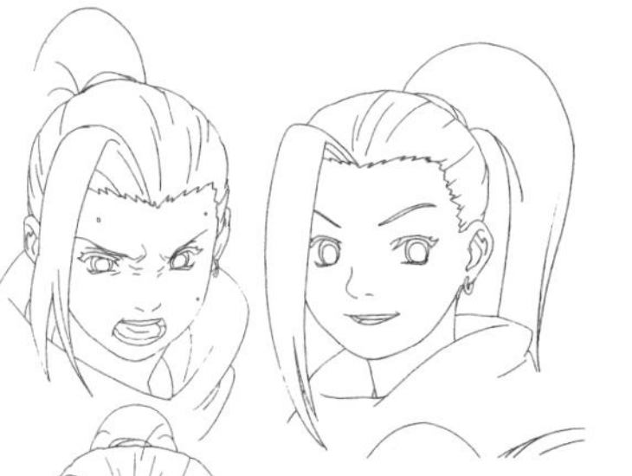

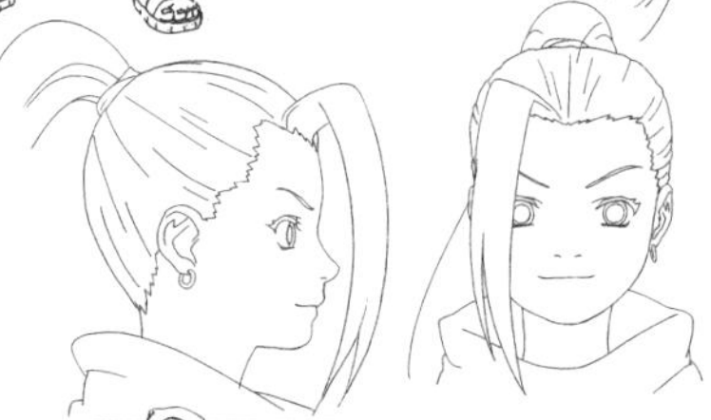

⬆⬅ The long lock of hair that dangles in front and her long swaying ponytail look cute.

Inoichi Yamanaka

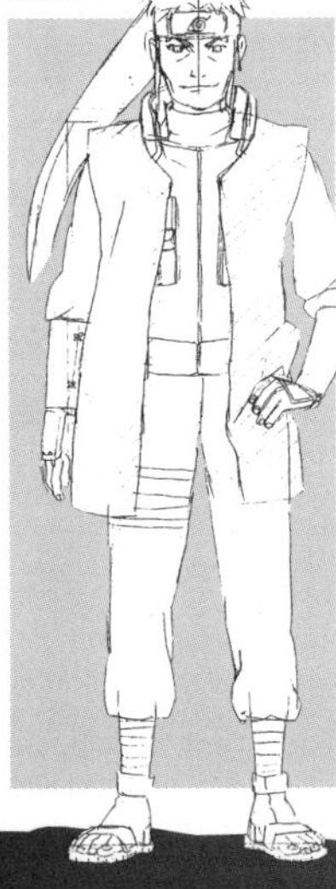

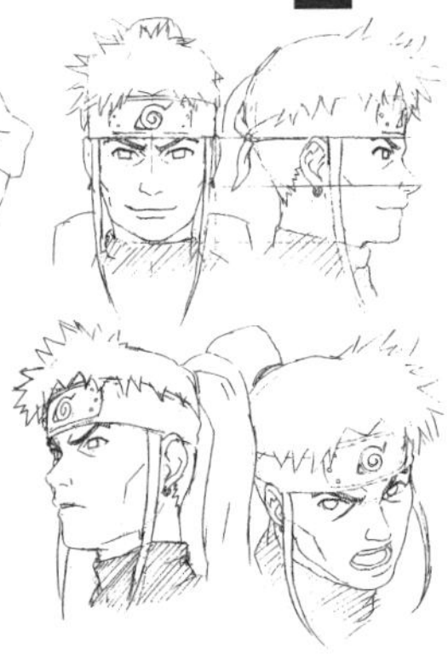

⬅Ino's father wears a haori, a kimono-style vest, over his Leaf Village uniform vest. His long hair is tied at the back like that of his daughter.

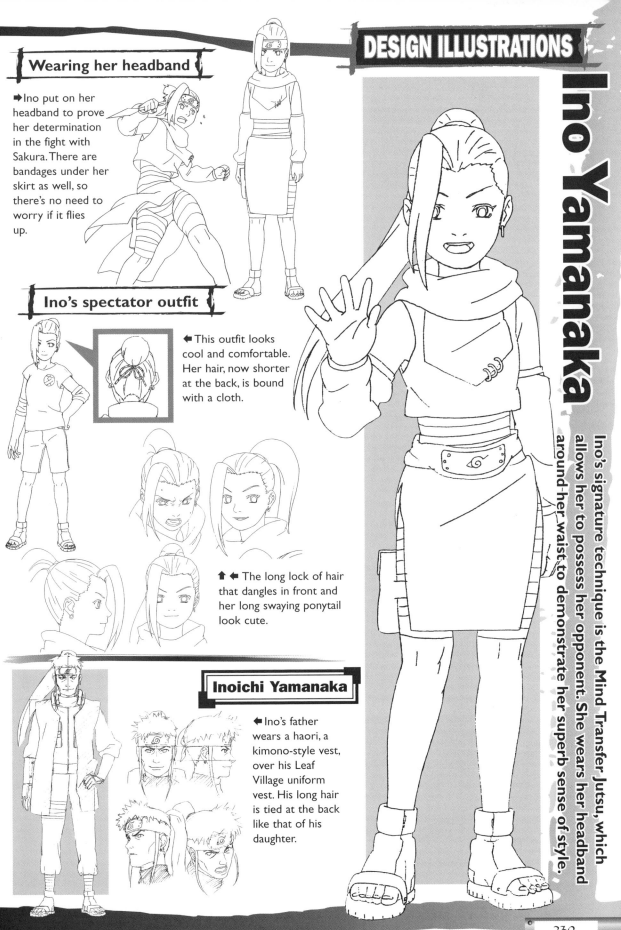

Shikamaru Nara

Shikamaru has zero motivation but, with an IQ over 200, is extremely intelligent. He wears a symbol like a family crest on his sleeves and back.

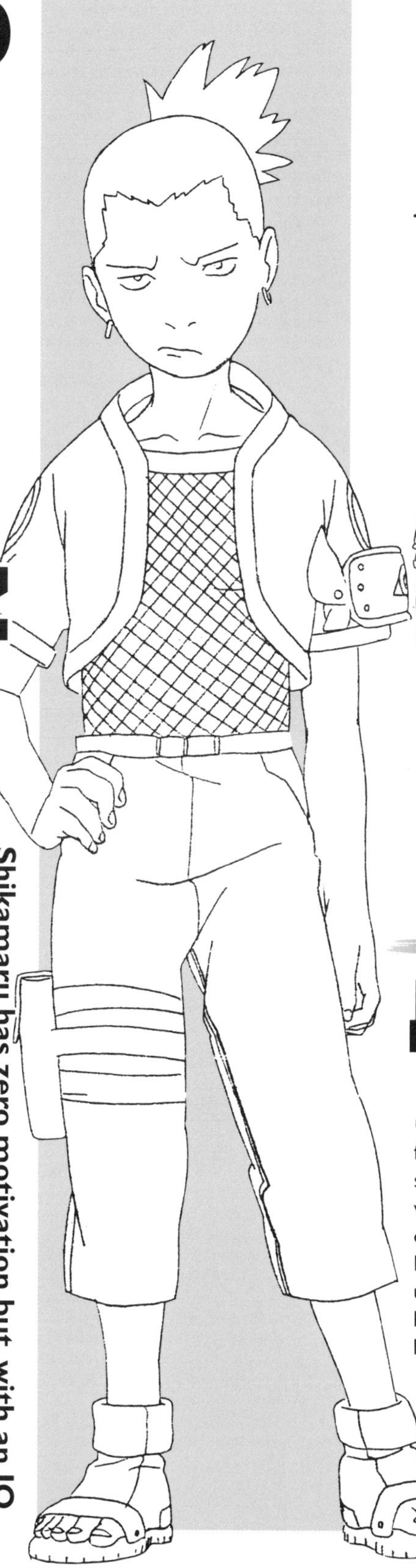

Earrings

➡All three members of Squad 10 wear these small silver hoop earrings.

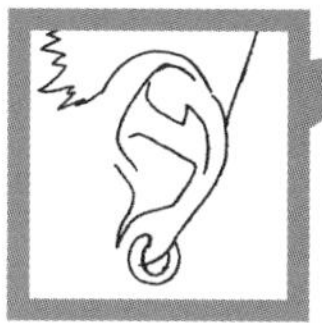

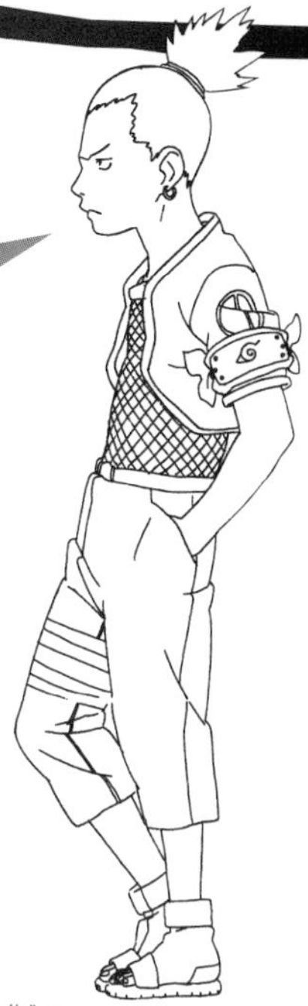

Headband

➡He wears his headband on his left arm, securing it with a button.

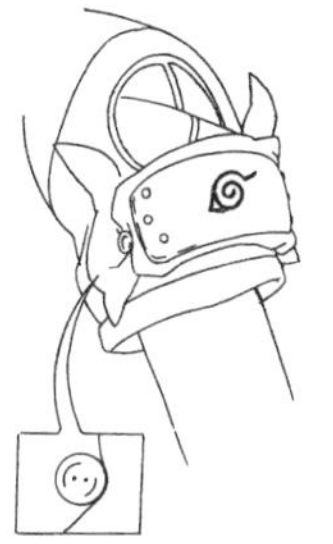

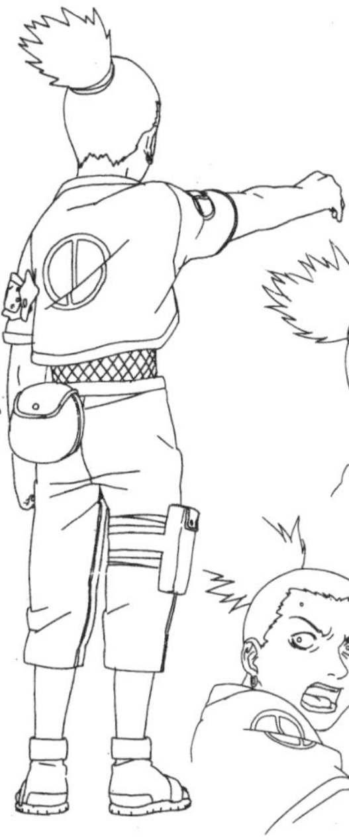

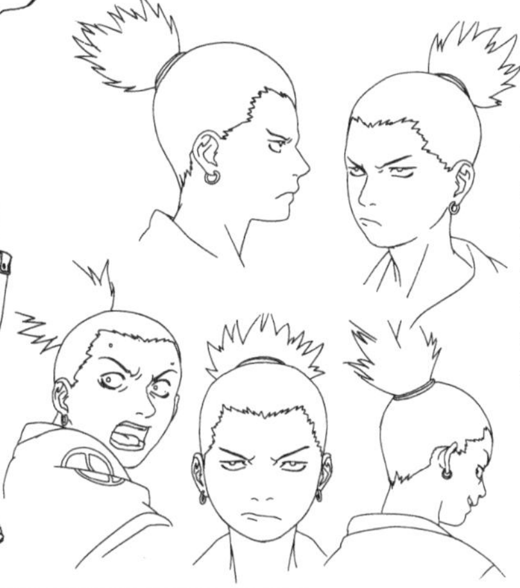

⬅Shikamaru usually looks disinterested, but he occasionally shows sharper expressions.

Shikaku Nara

➡Shikamaru's father wears some pretty wild threads over his Hidden Leaf Village uniform. He has large scars on his face.

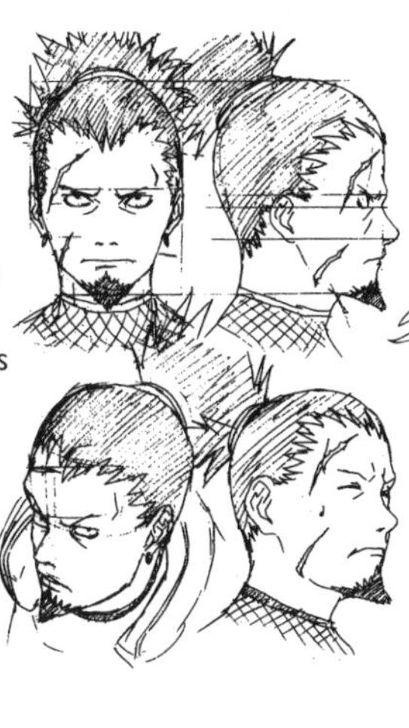

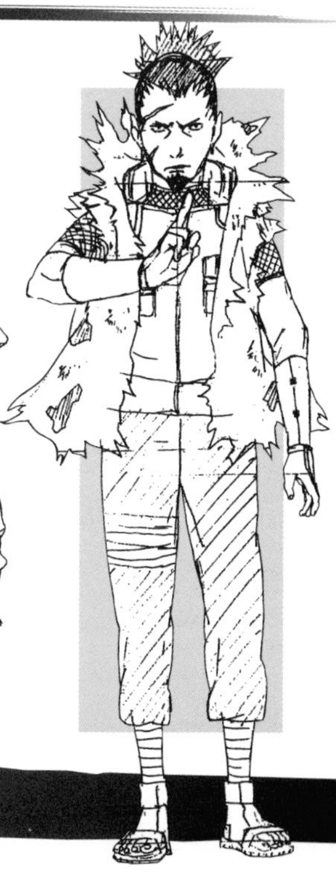

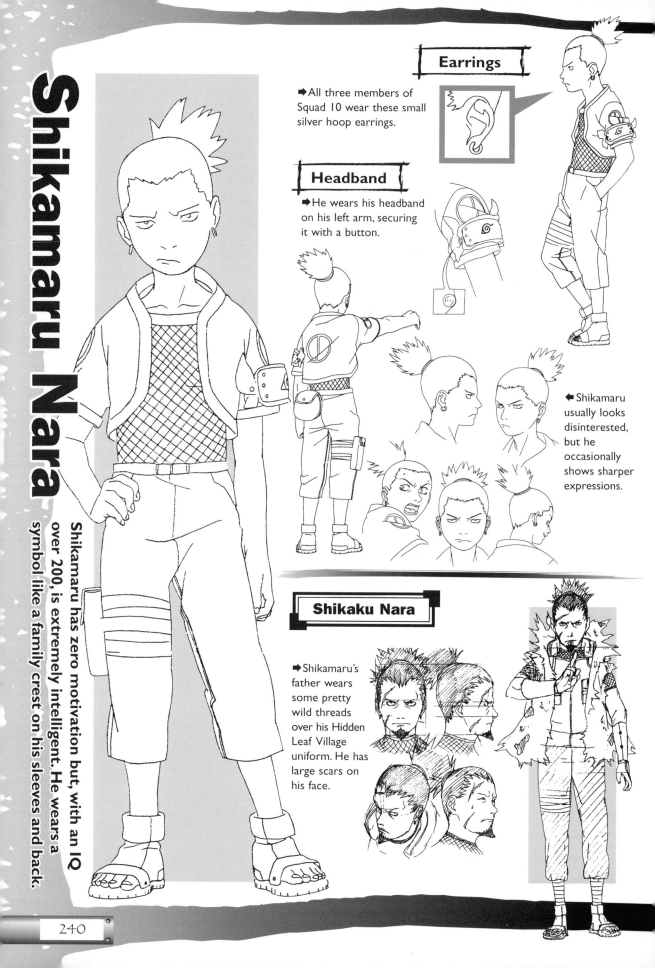

DESIGN ILLUSTRATIONS

Choji Akimichi

Choji loves to eat. The scarf he always wears must be one of his favorite things.

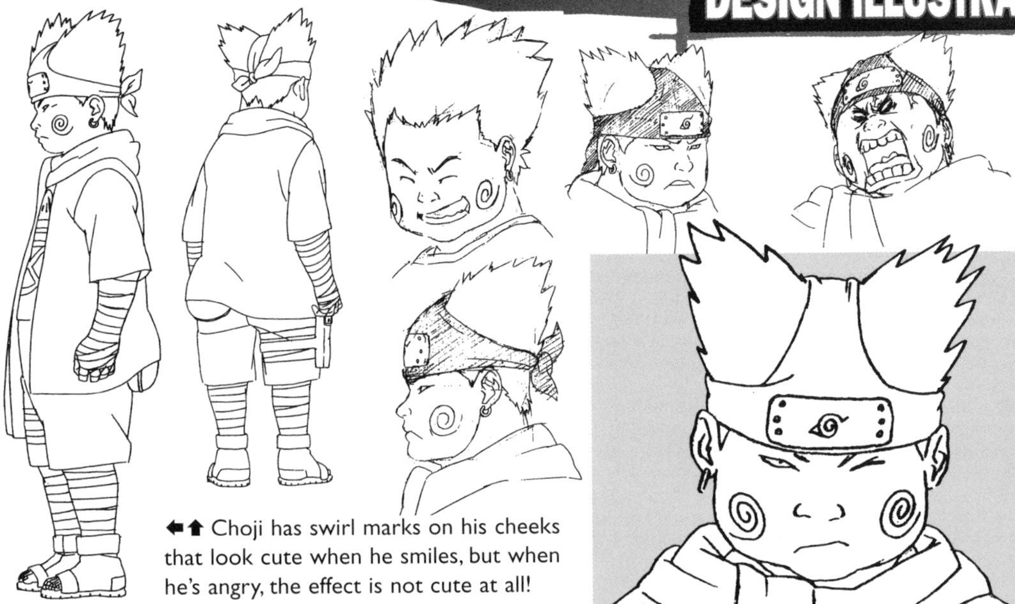

⬅⬆ Choji has swirl marks on his cheeks that look cute when he smiles, but when he's angry, the effect is not cute at all!

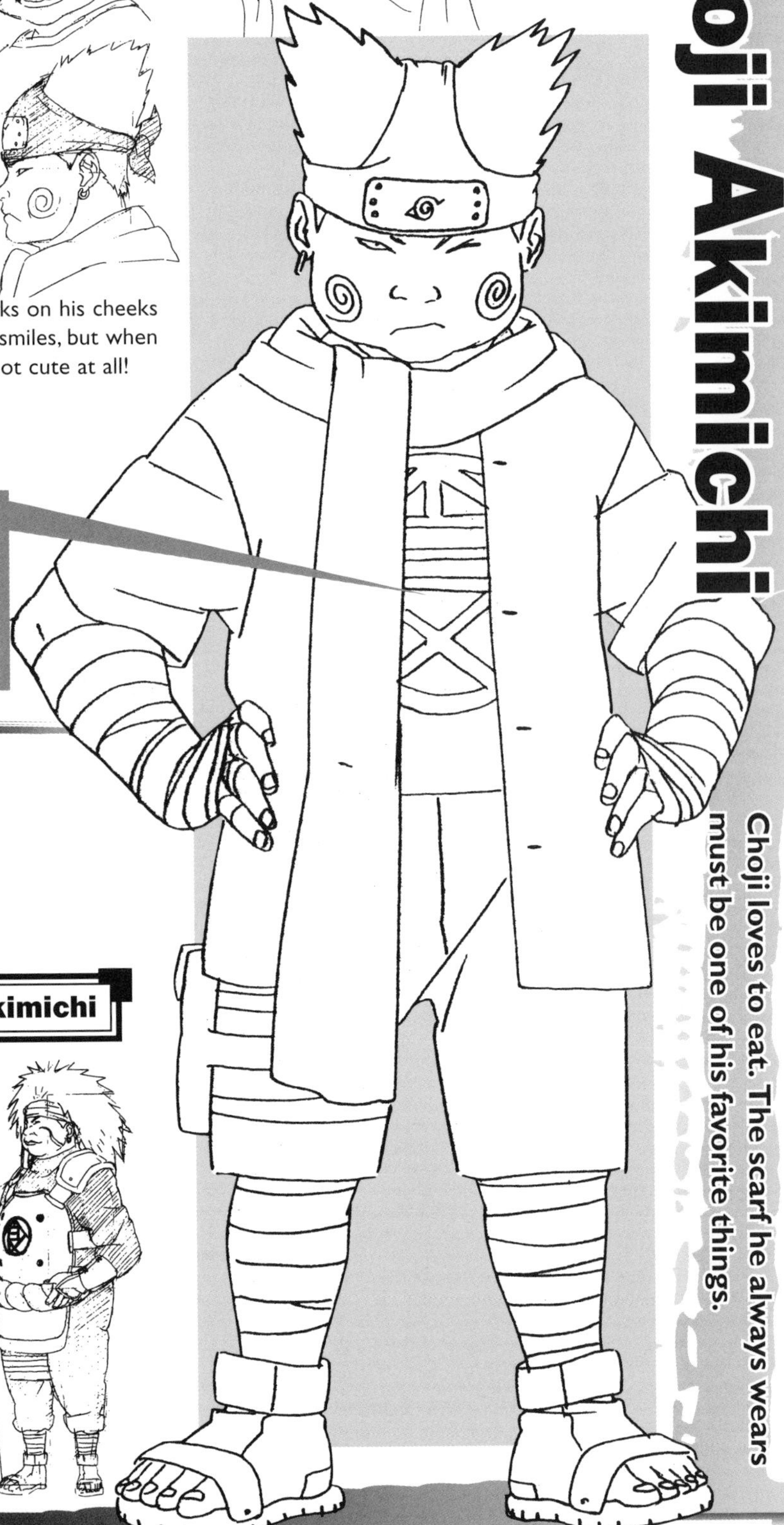

Mark

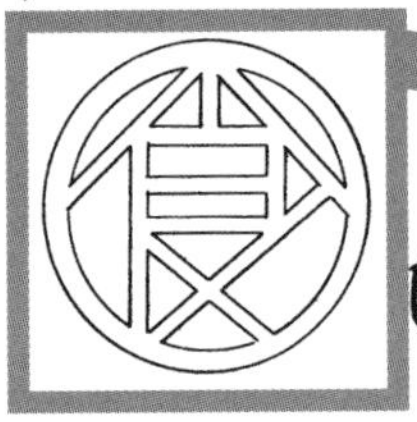

➡The symbol printed on his shirt, which appears to be a variation on the Chinese character for "food" or "eating." Could this be his family crest?

Choza Akimichi

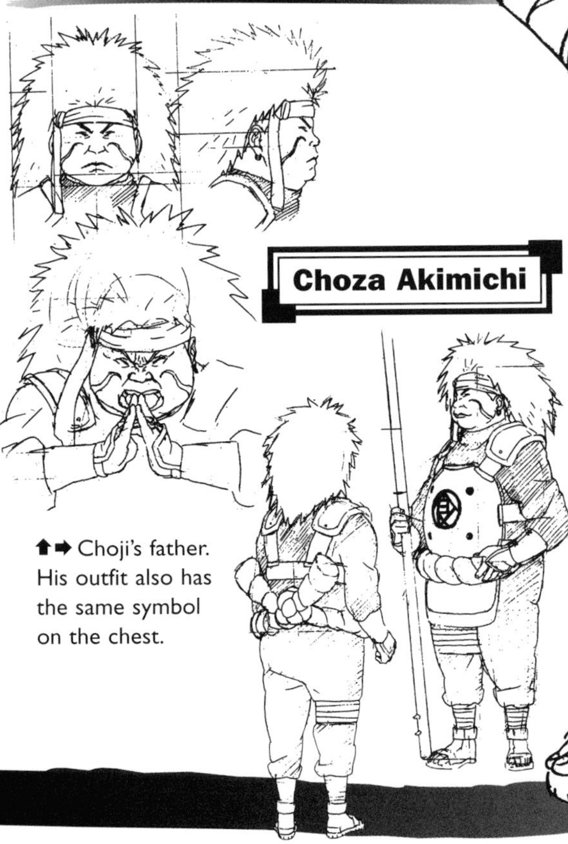

⬆➡ Choji's father. His outfit also has the same symbol on the chest.

Kiba Inuzuka

Kiba is a fiery-tempered user of the Ninja Art of Beast Mimicry. He always wears a coat with a flashy hood. Akamaru likes to stick his head out the front.

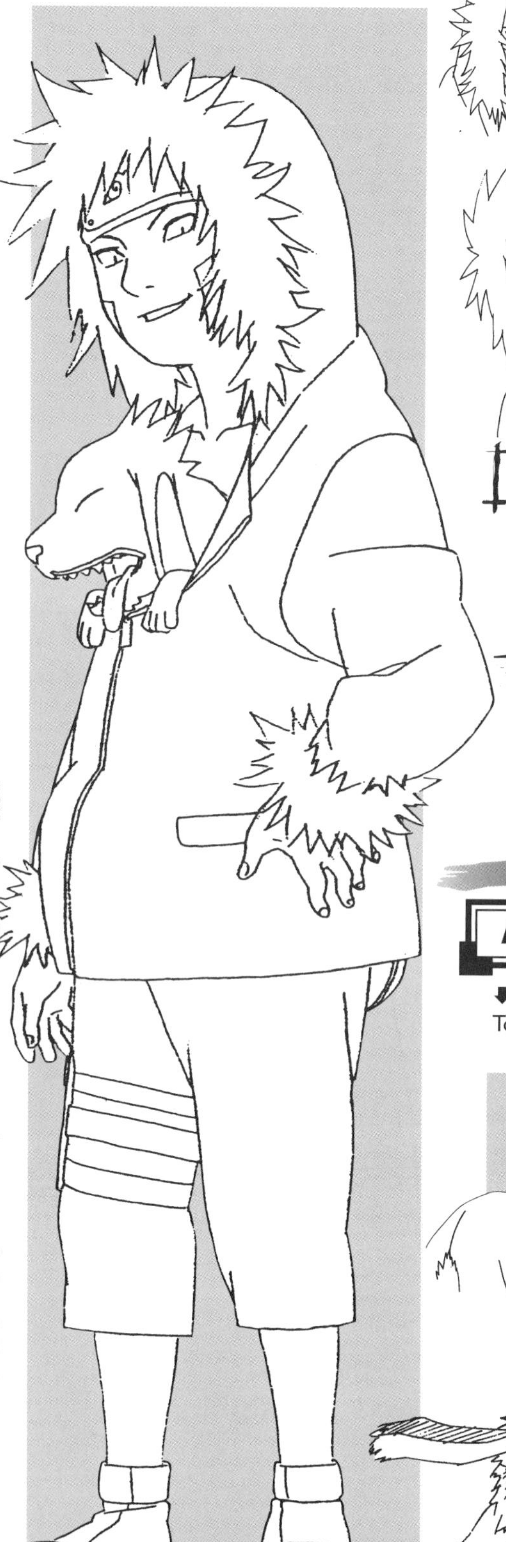

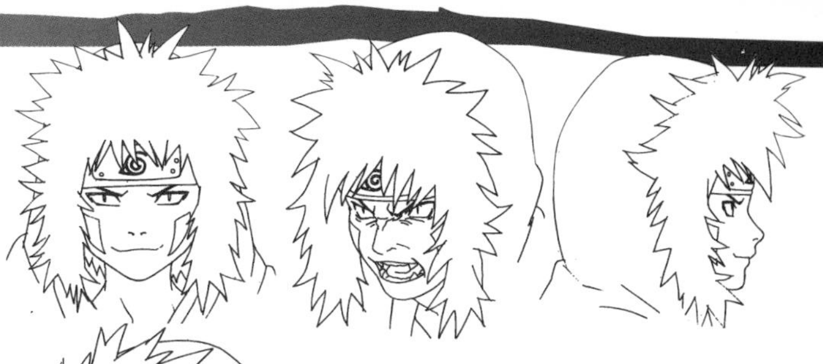

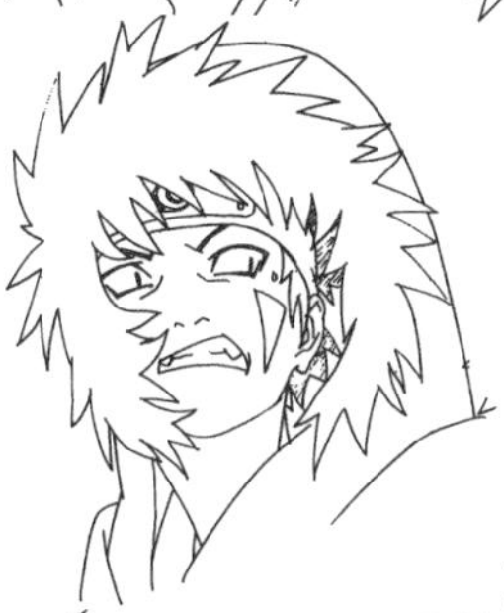

⬅⬆ Having such a quick temper, his facial expressions are often gruff. He always smiles at Akamaru, though.

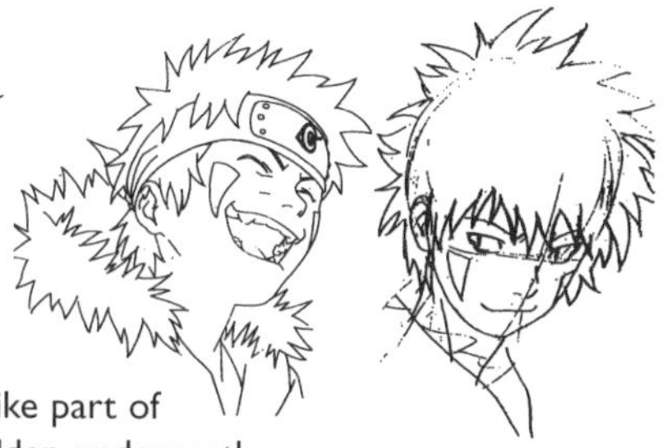

Hairstyle

➡ His hood looks like part of his hairstyle, but hidden underneath it his hair is short and clean-cut. .

Kiba, one year ago

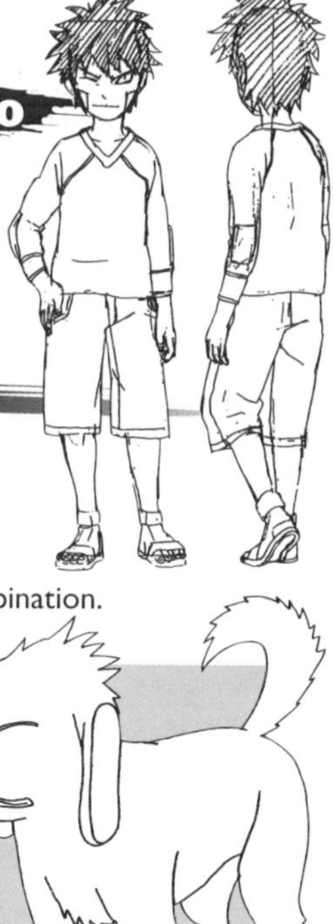

➡In his Ninja Academy days he was in the same class as Naruto. He used to wear outfits that were easy to move in, just like the other kids.

Akamaru

⬇ Kiba's companion and ideal partner. Together, they create the perfect combination.

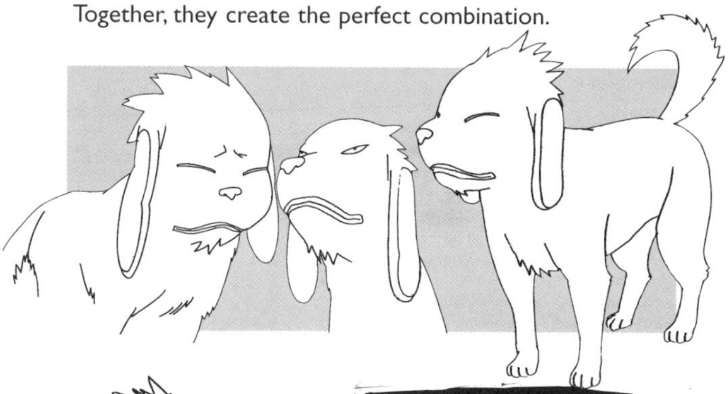

Akamaru on food pills

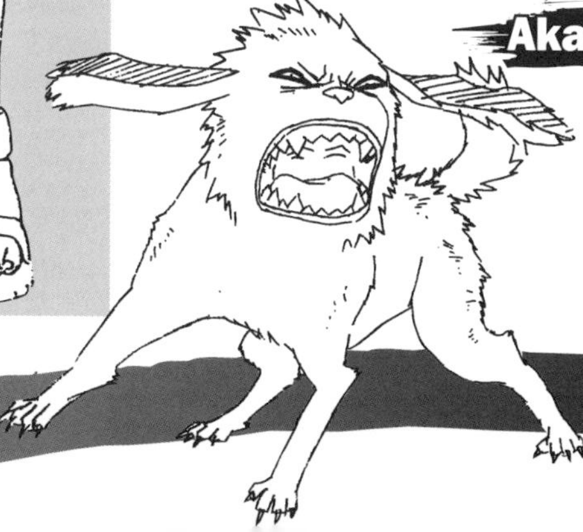

⬅ Food pills get him hyper. His chakra level doubles and his fur turns red.

Shino Aburame

Shino Aburame, a descendant of the Insect Tamer Clan of the Hidden Leaf Village. Wearing sunglasses and his collar up so it almost hides his face is his distinctive style.

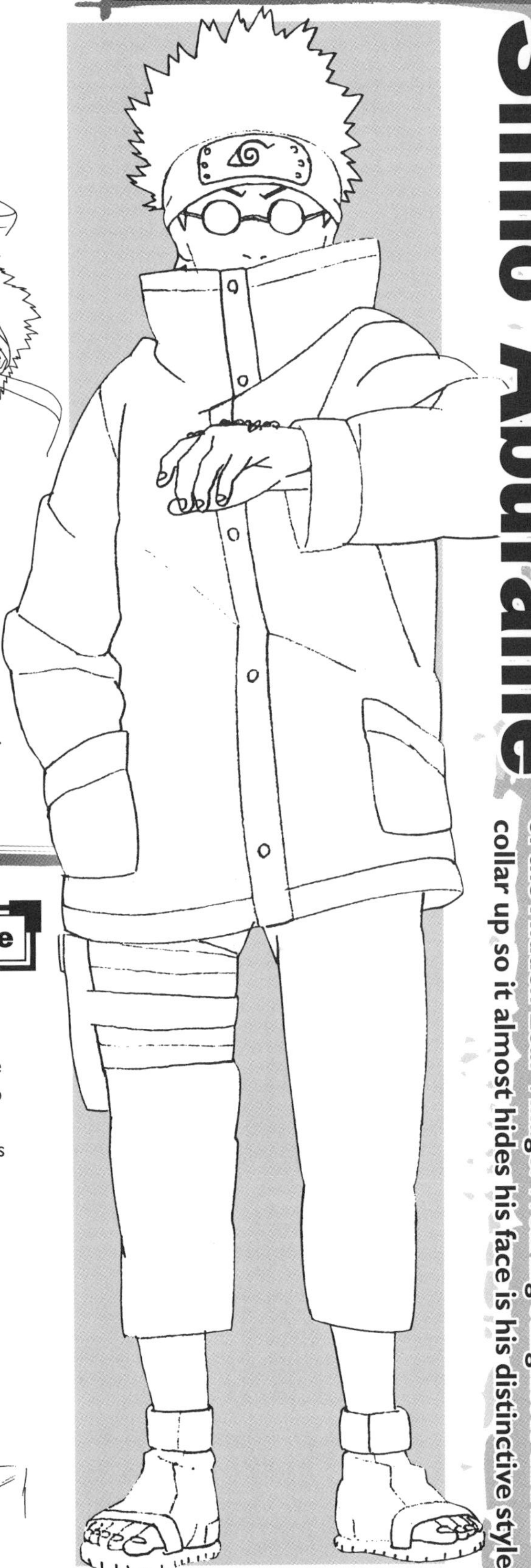

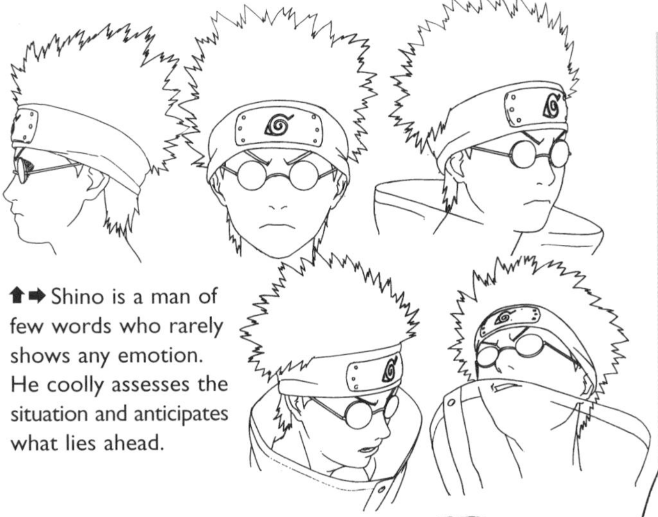

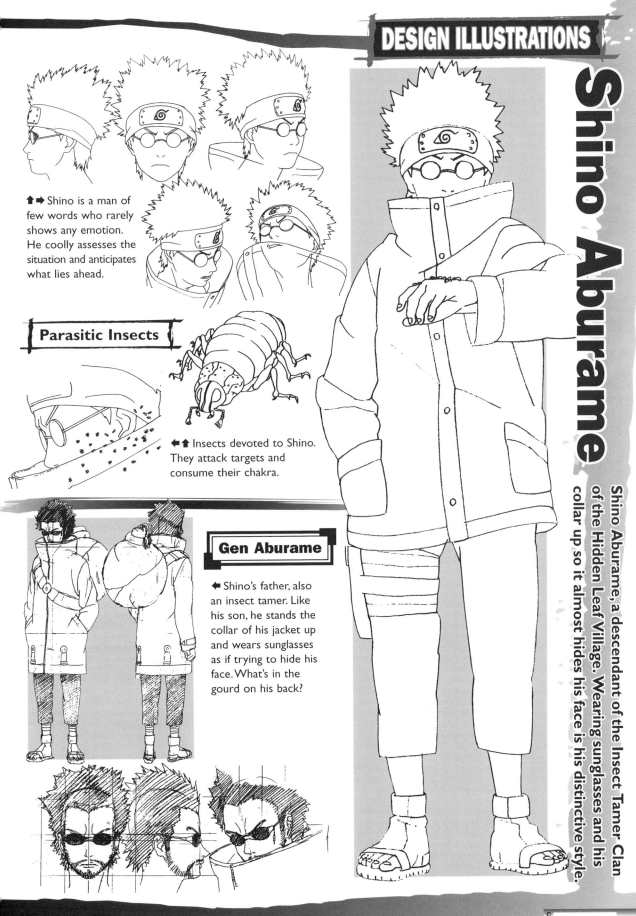

⬆➡ Shino is a man of few words who rarely shows any emotion. He coolly assesses the situation and anticipates what lies ahead.

Parasitic Insects

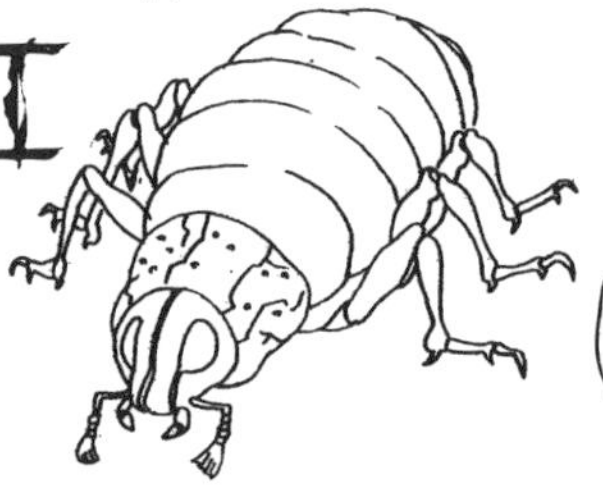

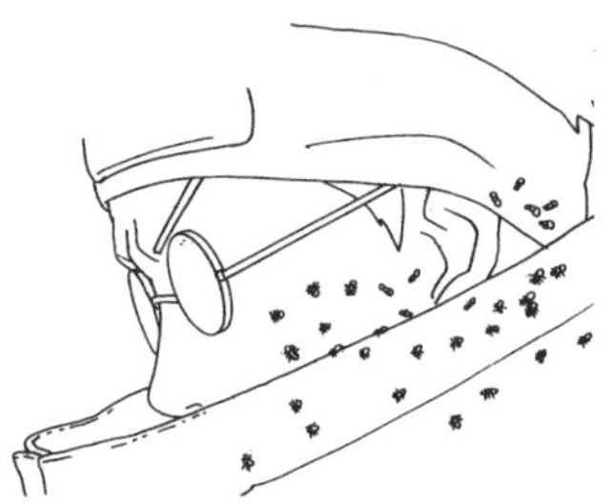

⬅⬆ Insects devoted to Shino. They attack targets and consume their chakra.

Gen Aburame

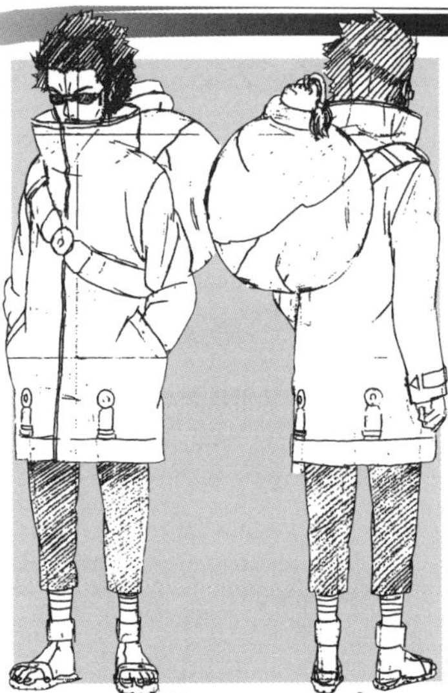

⬅ Shino's father, also an insect tamer. Like his son, he stands the collar of his jacket up and wears sunglasses as if trying to hide his face. What's in the gourd on his back?

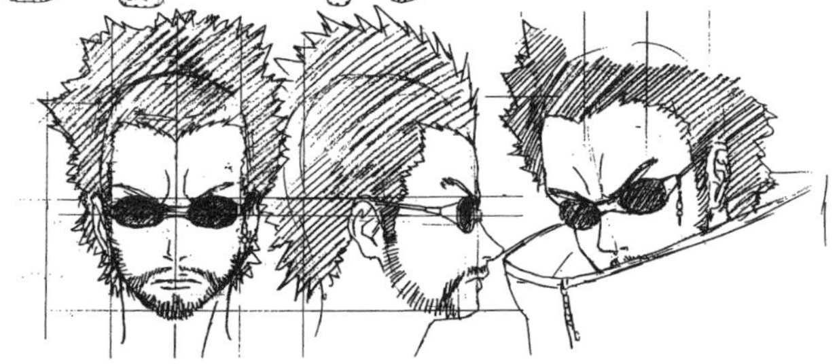

Hinata Hyuga

Hinata Hyuga belongs to the Main Branch of the Hidden Leaf Village's prestigious Hyuga Clan. However, her manners are mild, much like her style in clothes. She has special feelings for Naruto, but...

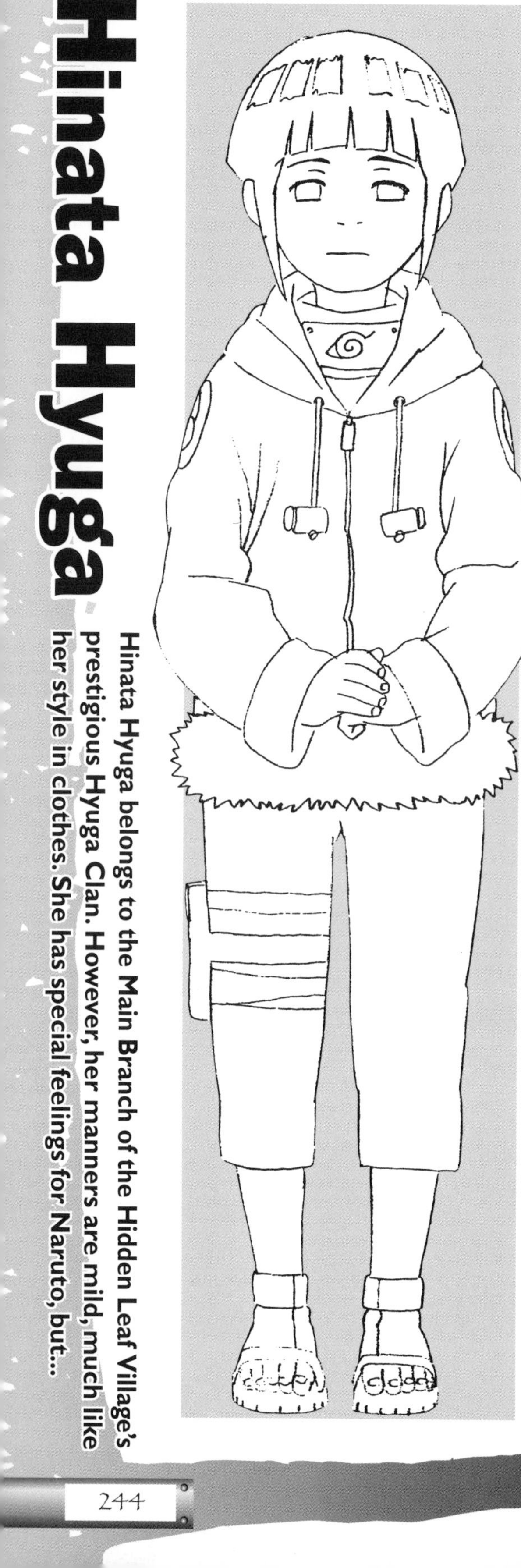

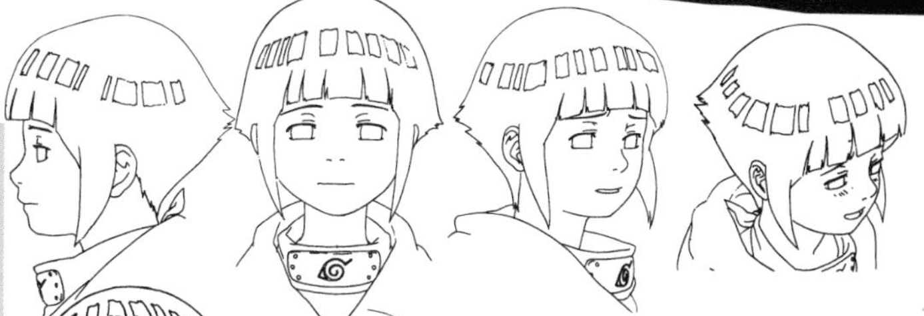

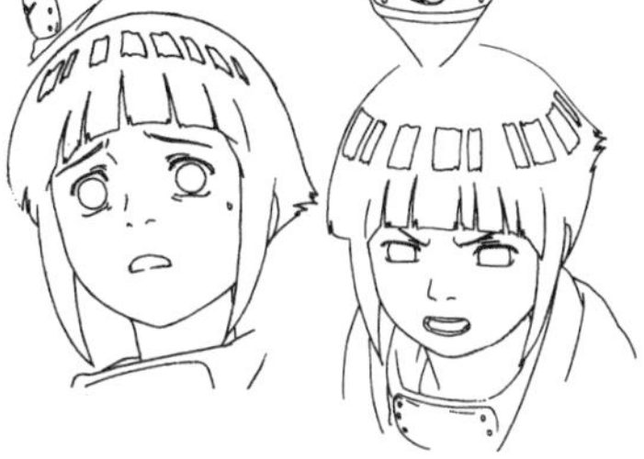

⬅⬆ Her genial personality and aversion to conflict is evident in her gentle expressions. She shyly looks at the ground whenever she notices Naruto glancing her way.

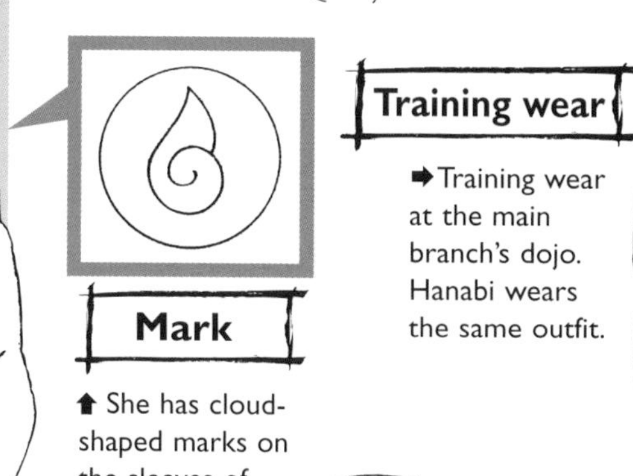

Mark

⬆ She has cloud-shaped marks on the sleeves of her jacket.

Training wear

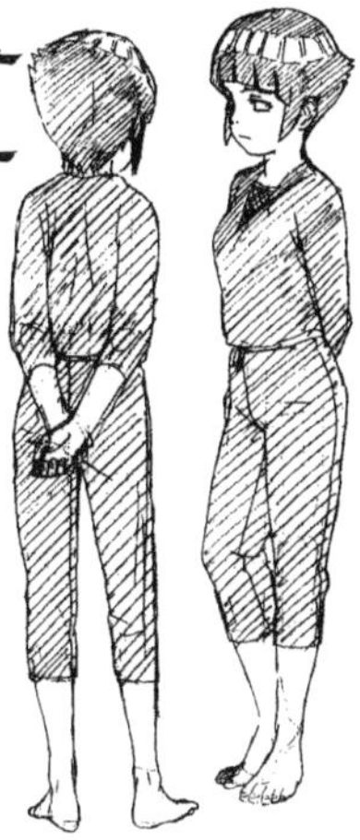

➡ Training wear at the main branch's dojo. Hanabi wears the same outfit.

Byakugan

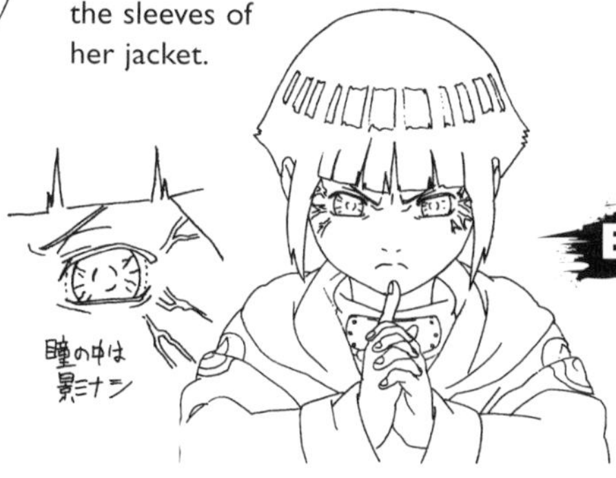
瞳の中は
影ナシ

⬅ When her Byakugan is unleashed, large blood vessels stand out around her eyes.

Hanabi Hyuga

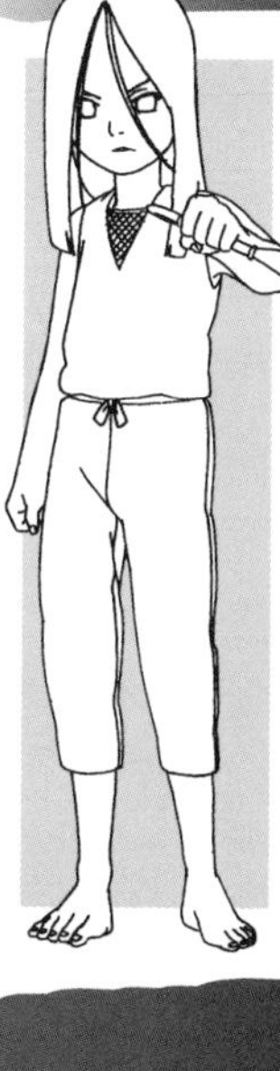

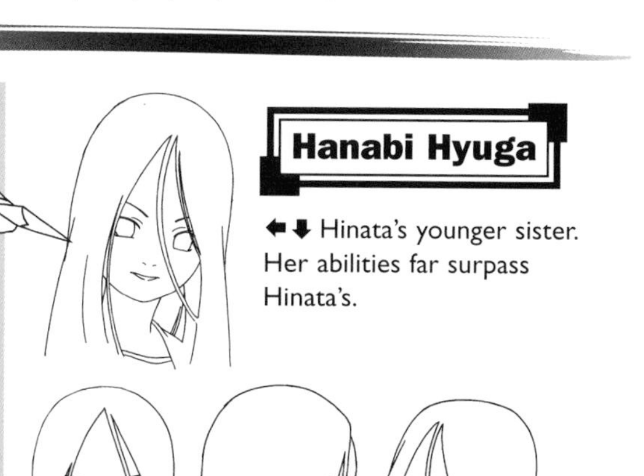

⬅⬇ Hinata's younger sister. Her abilities far surpass Hinata's.

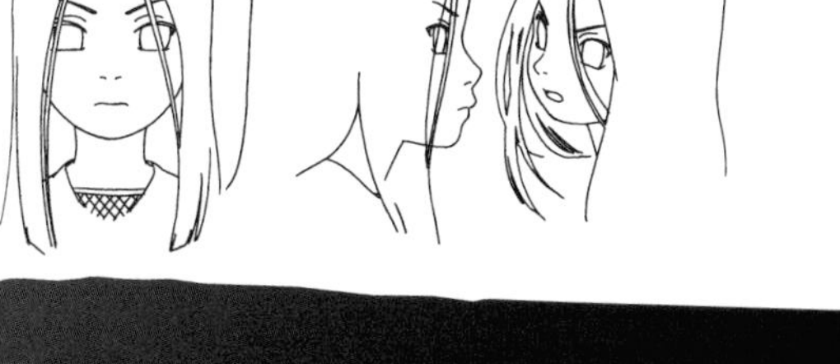

Neji Hyuga

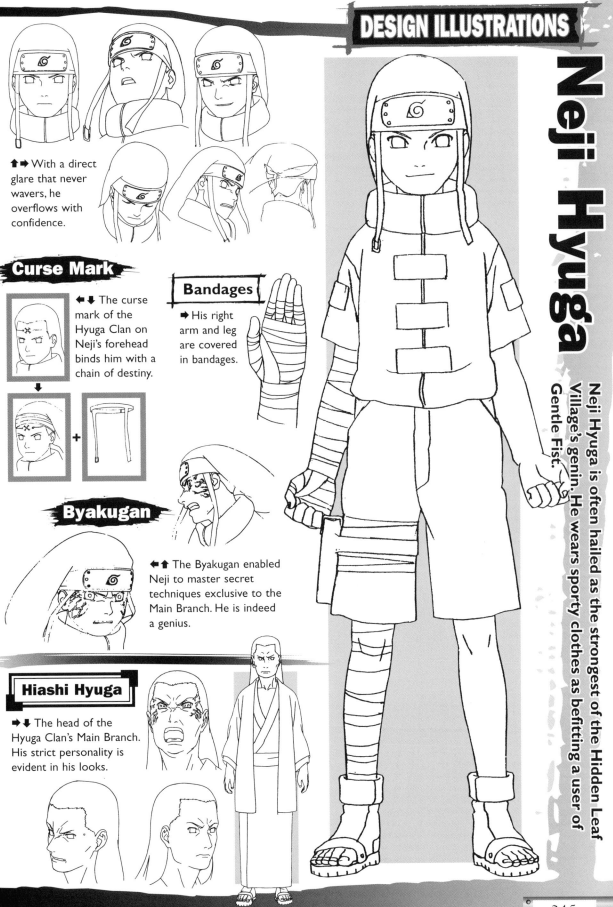

Neji Hyuga is often hailed as the strongest of the Hidden Leaf Village's genin. He wears sporty clothes as befitting a user of Gentle Fist.

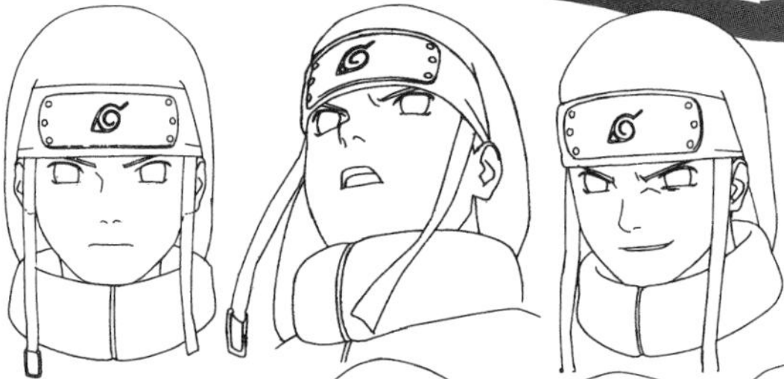

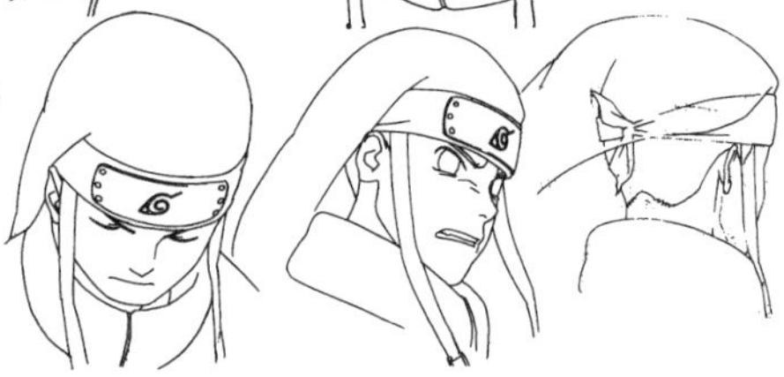

⬆➡ With a direct glare that never wavers, he overflows with confidence.

Curse Mark

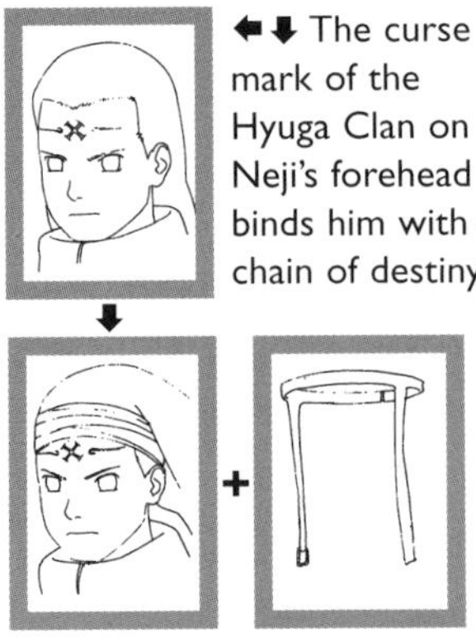

⬅⬇ The curse mark of the Hyuga Clan on Neji's forehead binds him with a chain of destiny.

Bandages

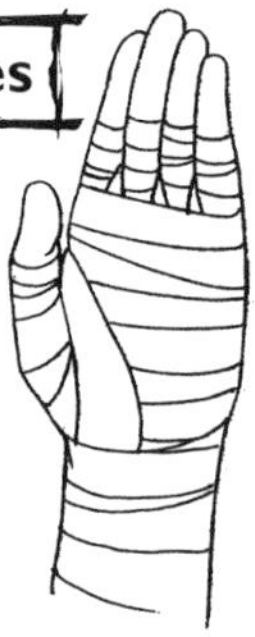

➡ His right arm and leg are covered in bandages.

Byakugan

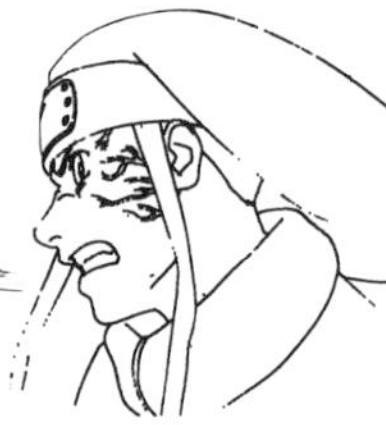

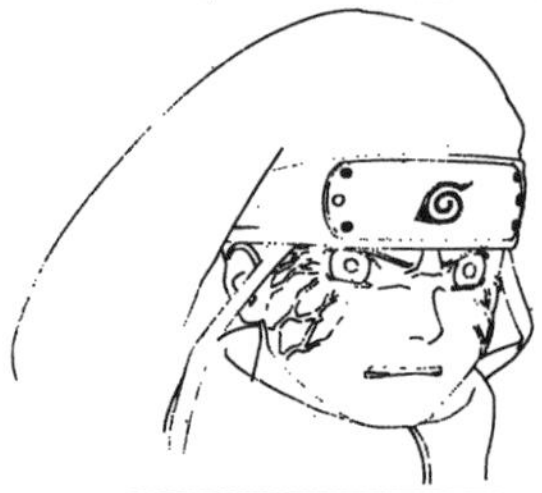

⬅⬆ The Byakugan enabled Neji to master secret techniques exclusive to the Main Branch. He is indeed a genius.

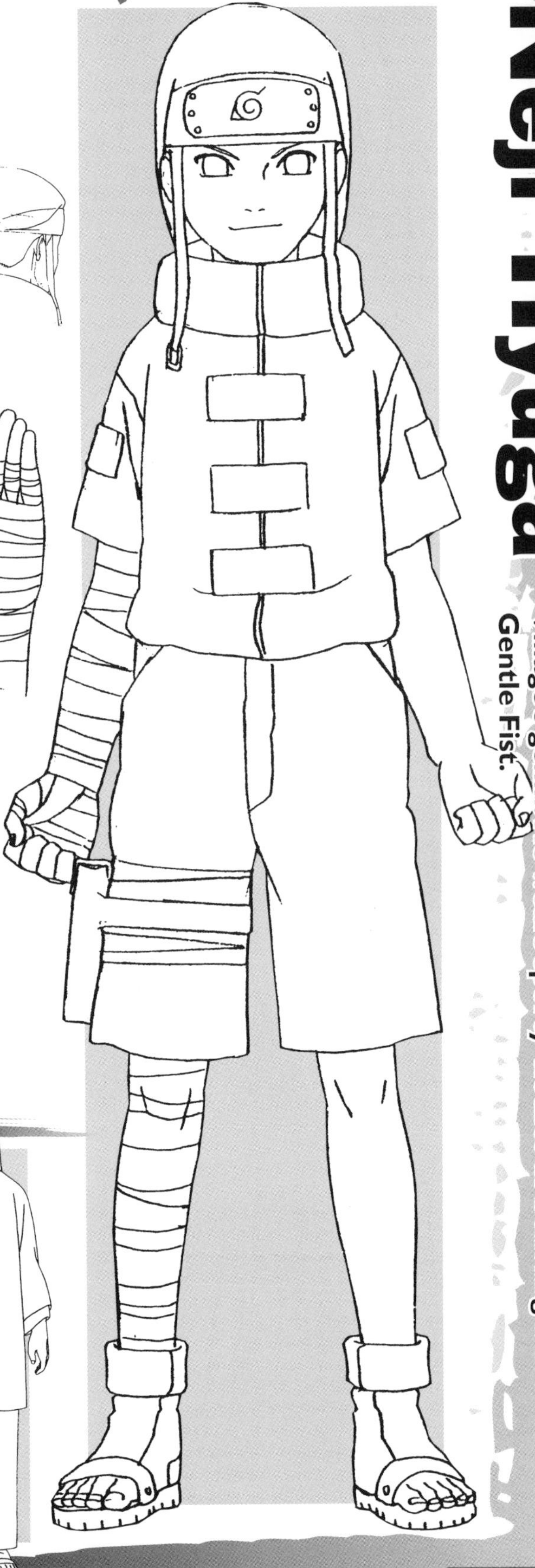

Hiashi Hyuga

➡⬇ The head of the Hyuga Clan's Main Branch. His strict personality is evident in his looks.

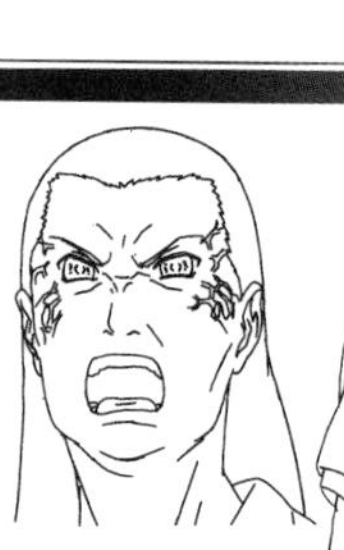

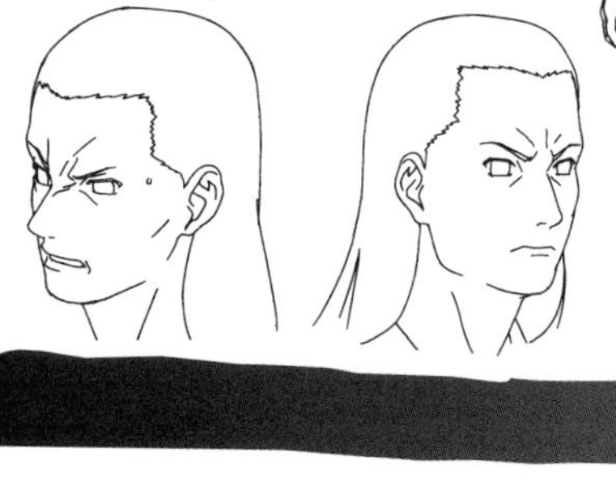

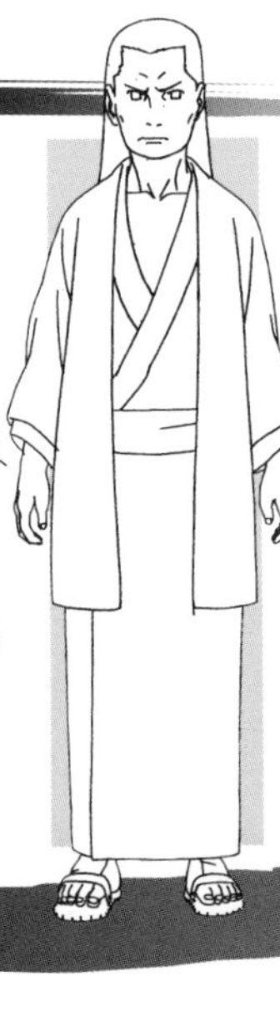

Rock Lee

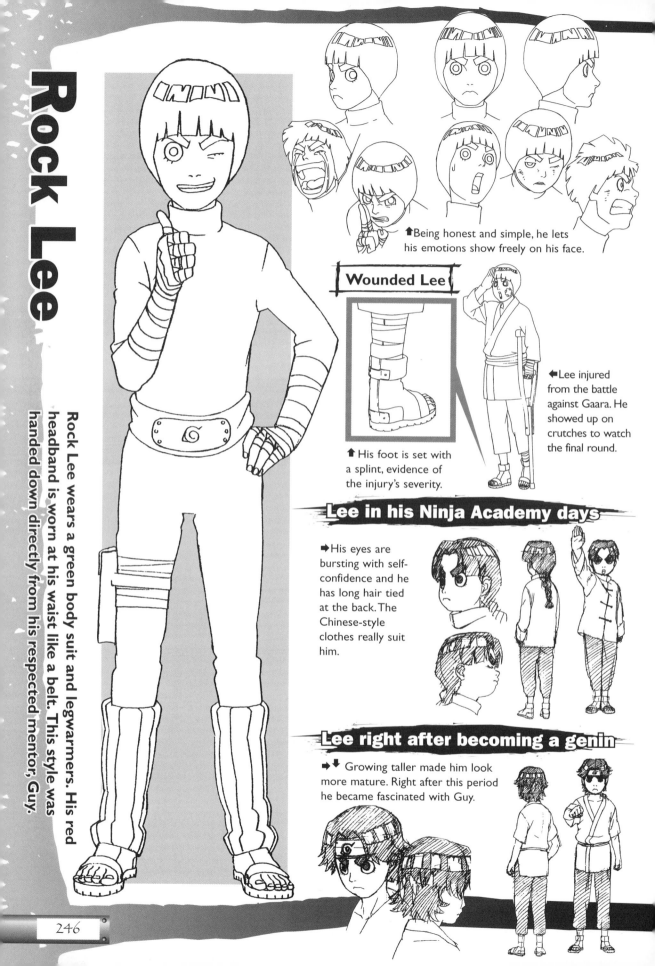

Rock Lee wears a green body suit and legwarmers. His red headband is worn at his waist like a belt. This style was handed down directly from his respected mentor, Guy.

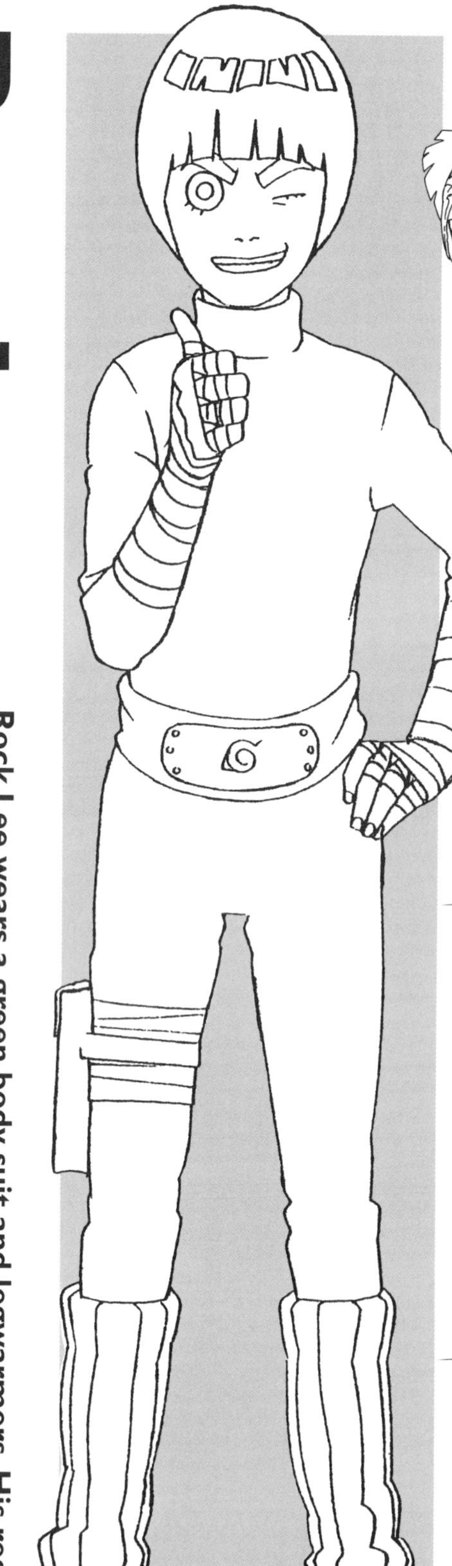

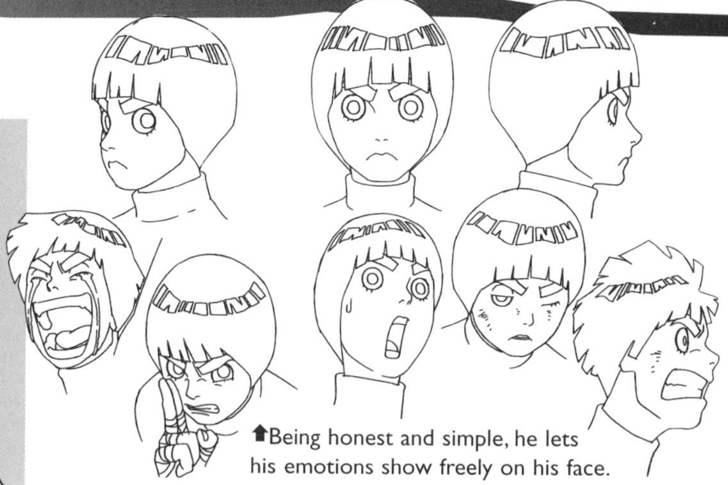

⬆Being honest and simple, he lets his emotions show freely on his face.

Wounded Lee

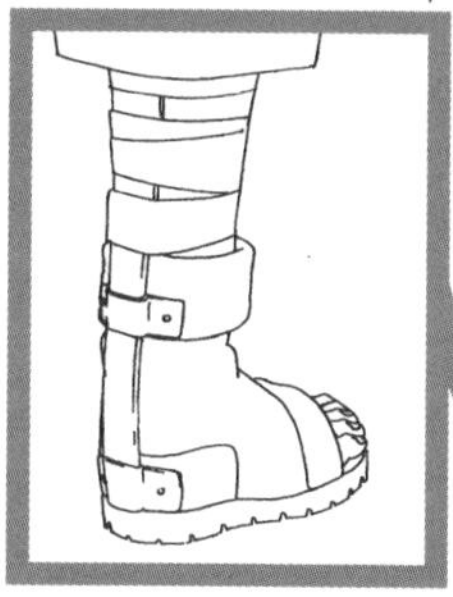

⬆ His foot is set with a splint, evidence of the injury's severity.

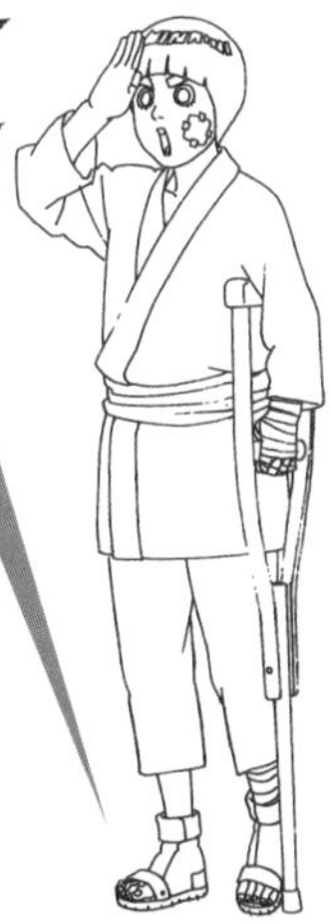

⬅Lee injured from the battle against Gaara. He showed up on crutches to watch the final round.

Lee in his Ninja Academy days

➡His eyes are bursting with self-confidence and he has long hair tied at the back. The Chinese-style clothes really suit him.

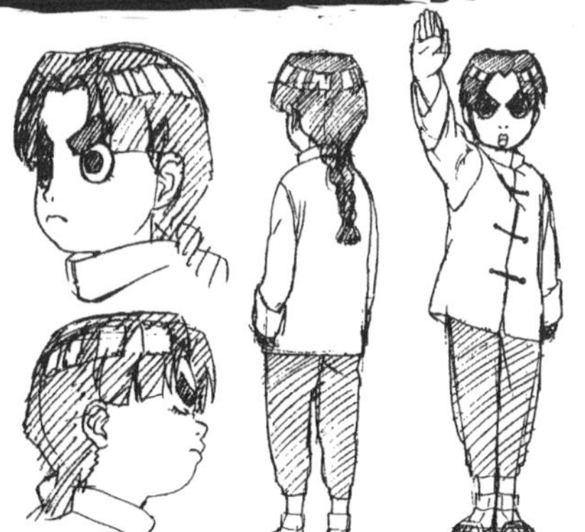

Lee right after becoming a genin

➡⬇ Growing taller made him look more mature. Right after this period he became fascinated with Guy.

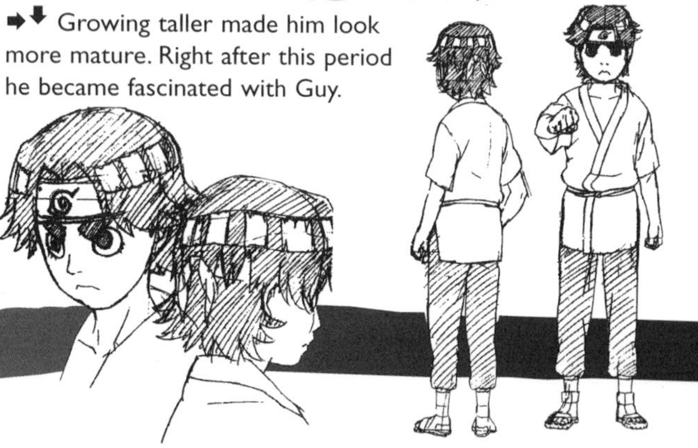

Tenten

Tenten, the only girl in Guy's squad, is an expert with weapons. Her sleeveless Chinese clothes look cute, but they're more for functionality than fashion since they allow her to move more freely.

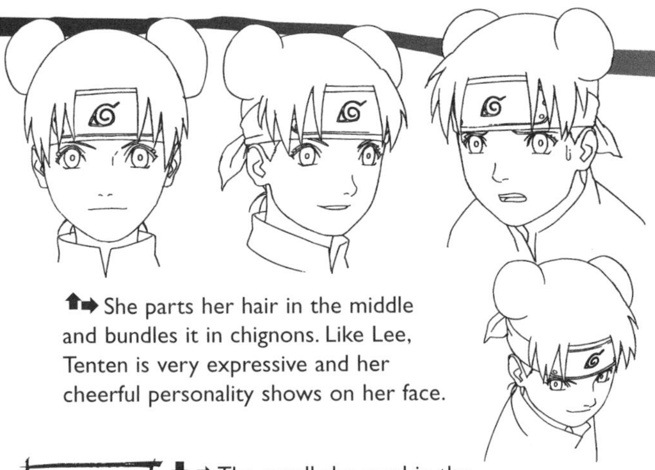

⬆➡ She parts her hair in the middle and bundles it in chignons. Like Lee, Tenten is very expressive and her cheerful personality shows on her face.

Scroll

⬇ ➡ The scroll she used in the battle against Temari. She used it to summon various weapons.

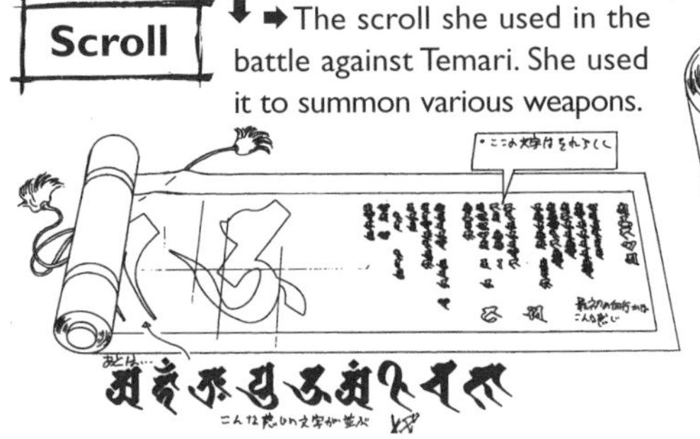

Rising Twin Dragons

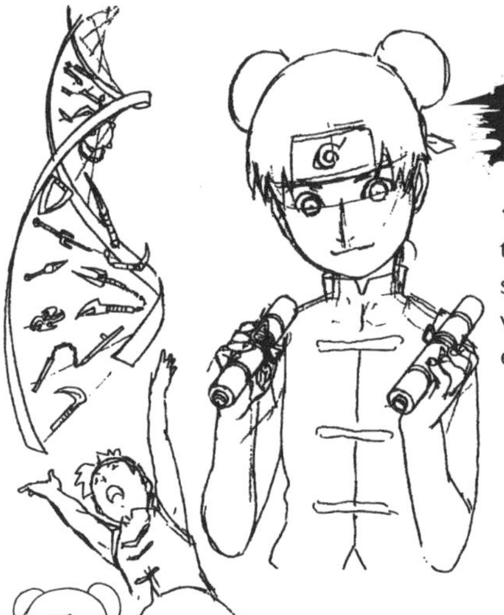

⬅ Tenten's deadly secret technique in which two scrolls fly into the air while twisting around each other like dragons.

Casual spectator clothes

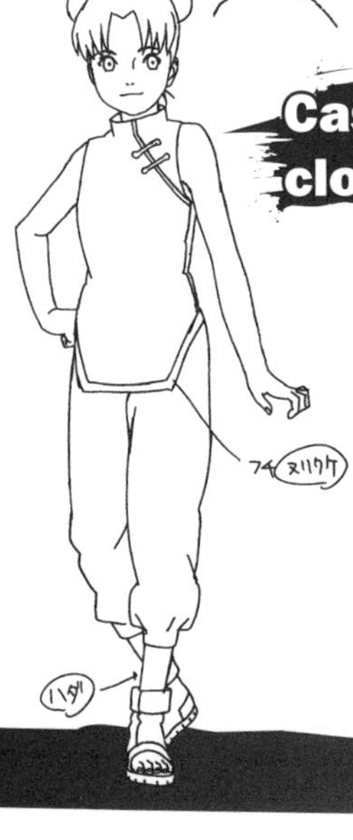

⬅ Tenten visited the arena to cheer on Neji in the final round of the Chunin Exam. This outfit has a very grown-up look—much different from the pink clothes she usually wears.

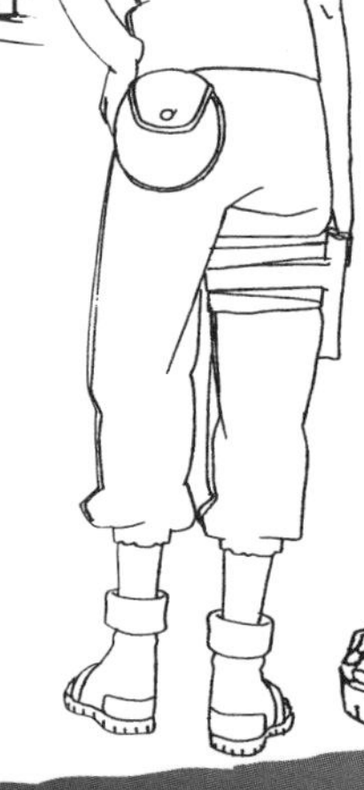

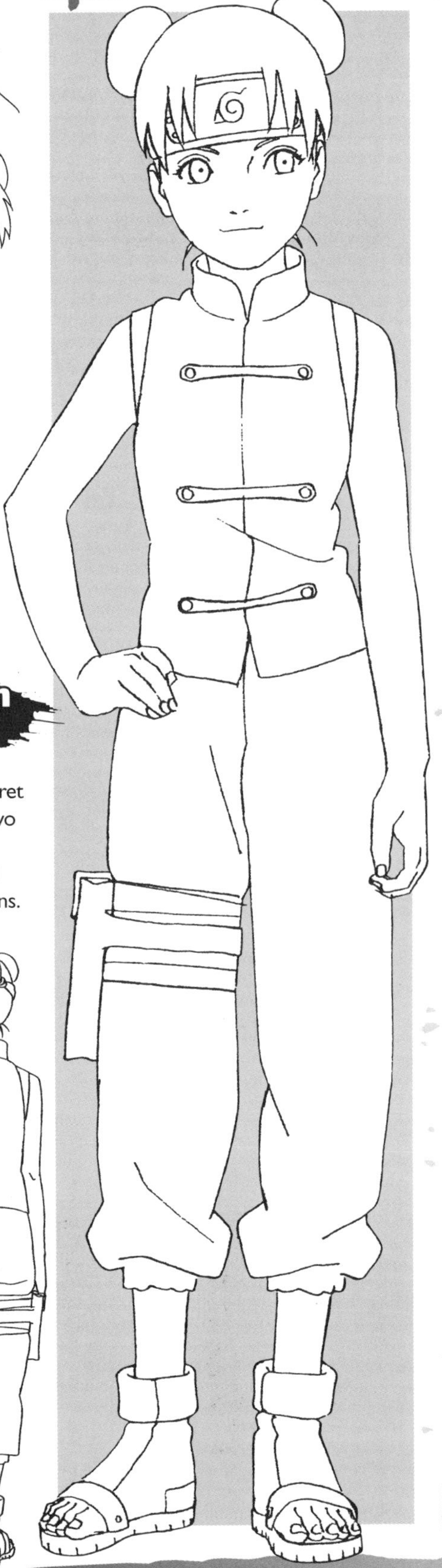

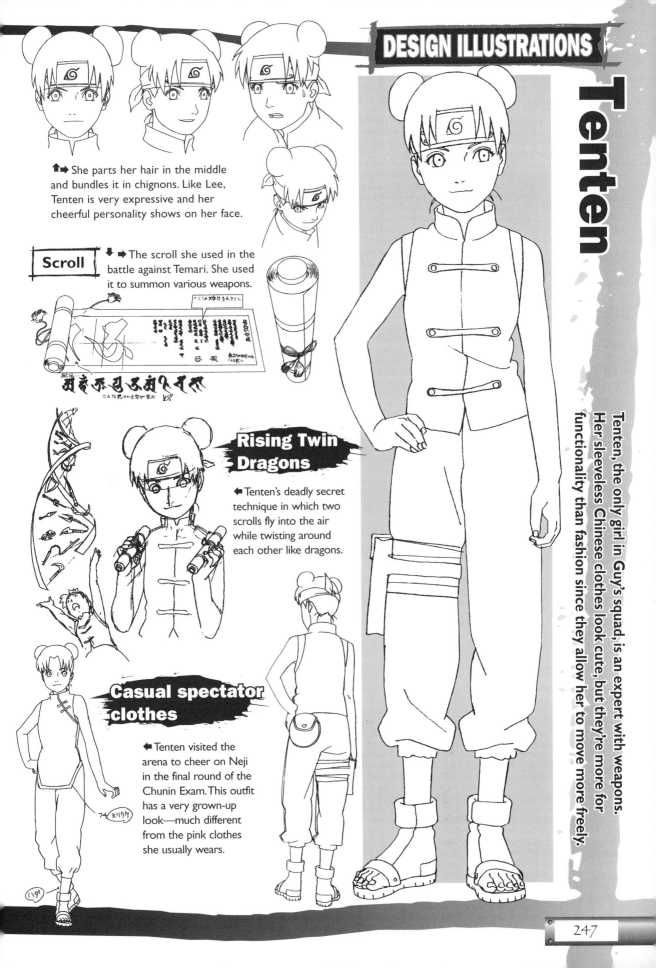

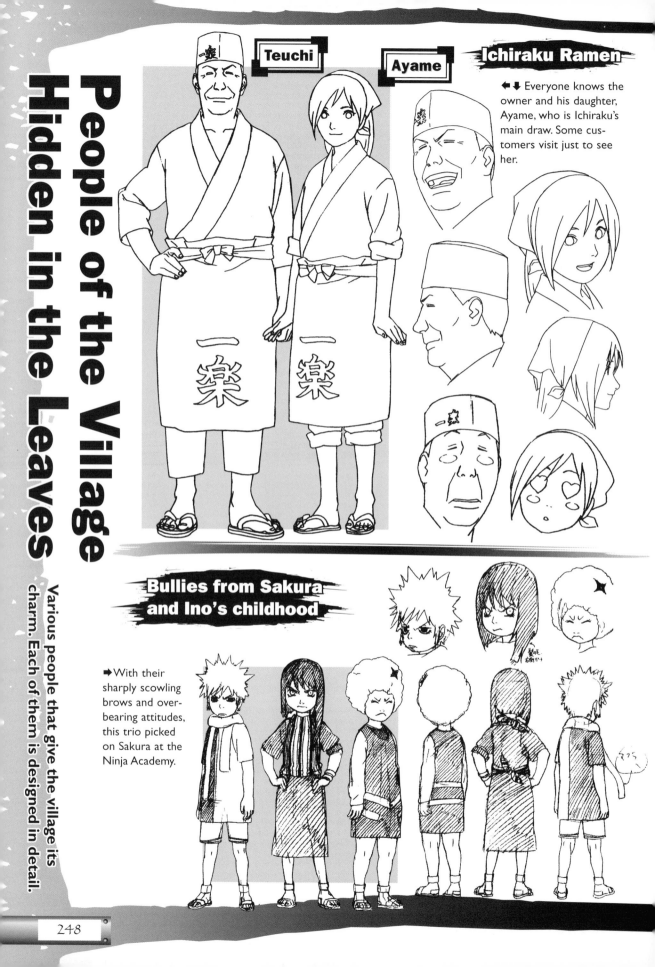

People of the Village Hidden in the Leaves

Various people that give the village its charm. Each of them is designed in detail.

Ichiraku Ramen

Teuchi **Ayame**

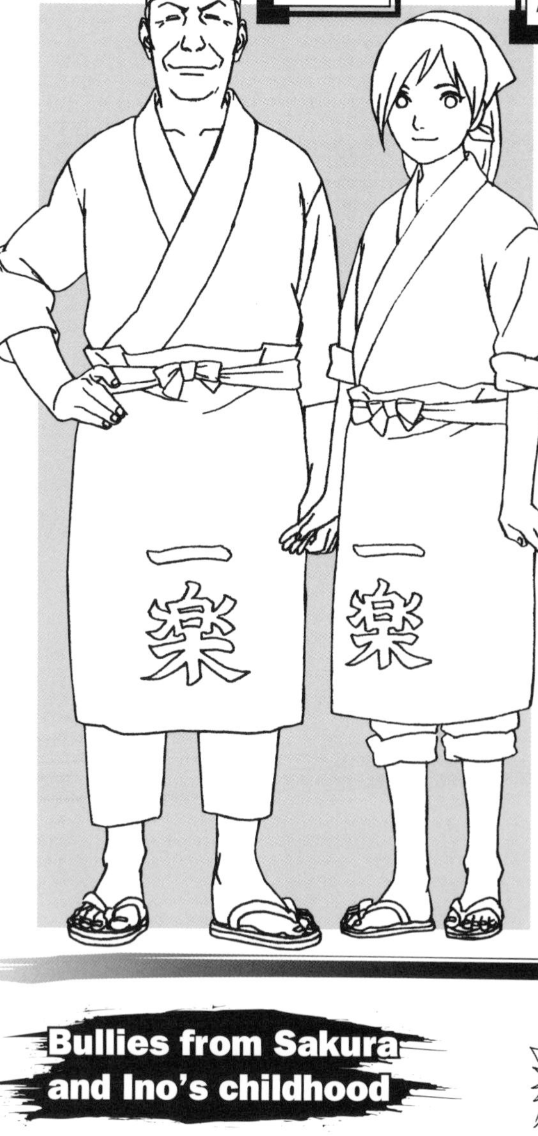

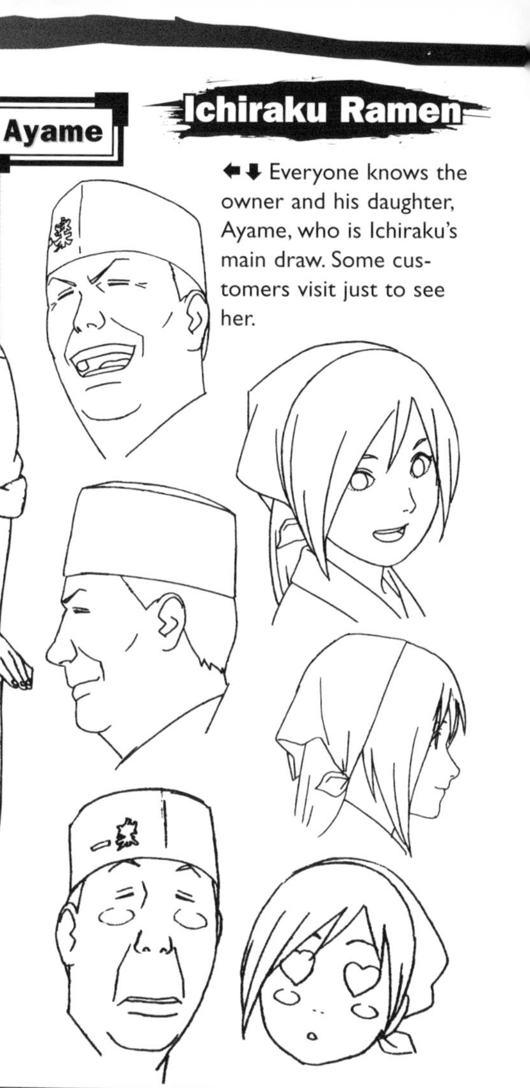

⬅⬇ Everyone knows the owner and his daughter, Ayame, who is Ichiraku's main draw. Some customers visit just to see her.

Bullies from Sakura and Ino's childhood

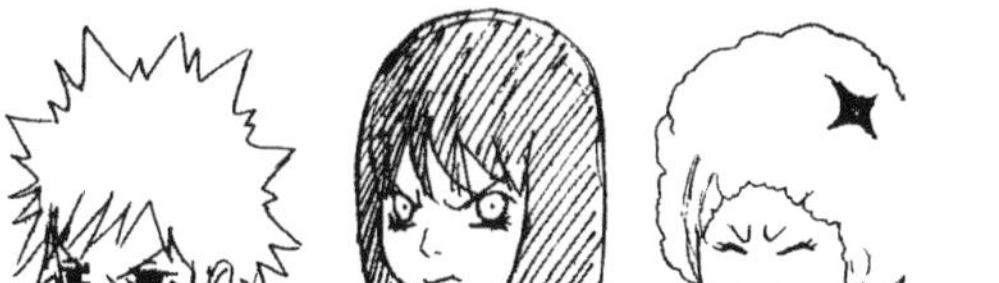

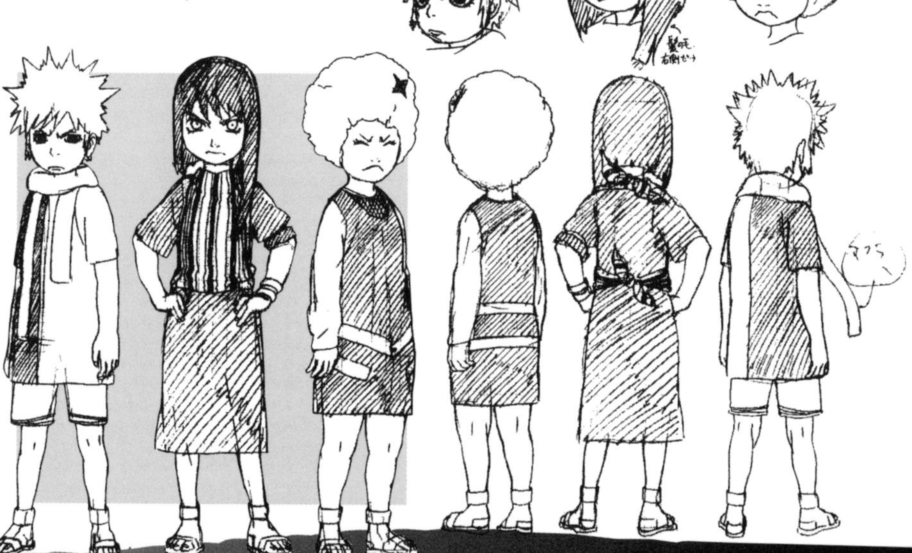

➡With their sharply scowling brows and overbearing attitudes, this trio picked on Sakura at the Ninja Academy.

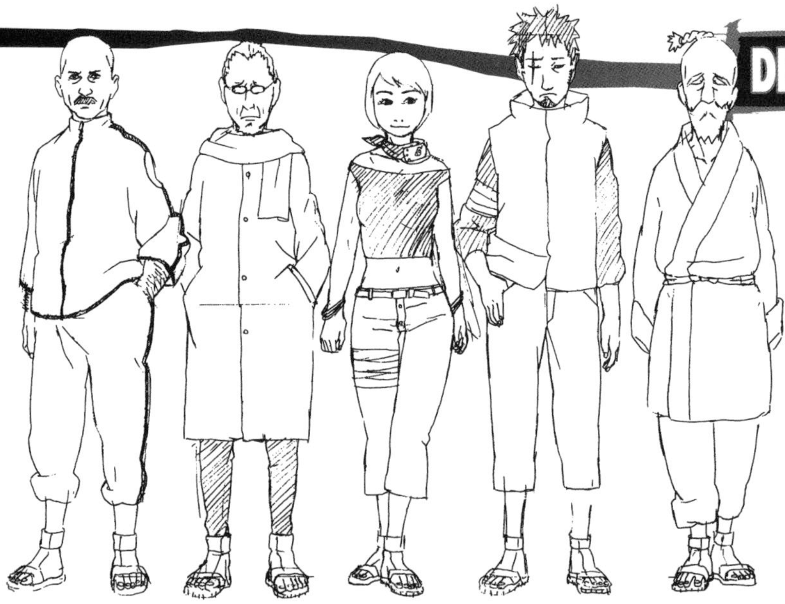

Local people

⬅People of the Hot Spring District. The woman with a headband around her neck could be a ninja. Although in different clothing, they all wear sandals.

Local women

➡These women are also from the Hot Spring District. They are all young and dress casually. Jiraiya probably already conducted his research on them!

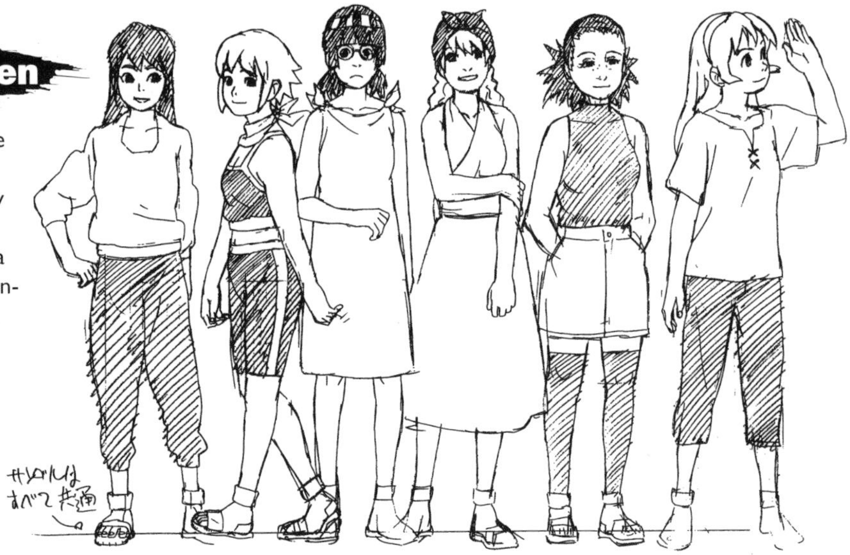

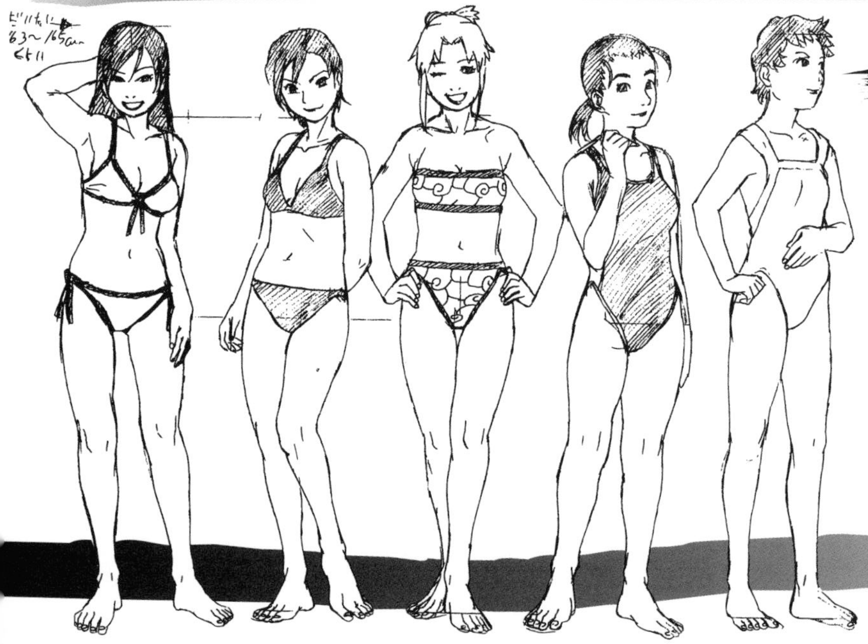

Swimsuit Girls

⬅A bevy of lovely ladies!! Jiraiya has definitely researched them!

The Third Hokage

As head of the village, he provides leadership and guidance and is the bond that unified the village. He is reputed to be the strongest Hokage ever. He is usually quiet and gentle, but in his ninja battle gear he looks brave and dignified.

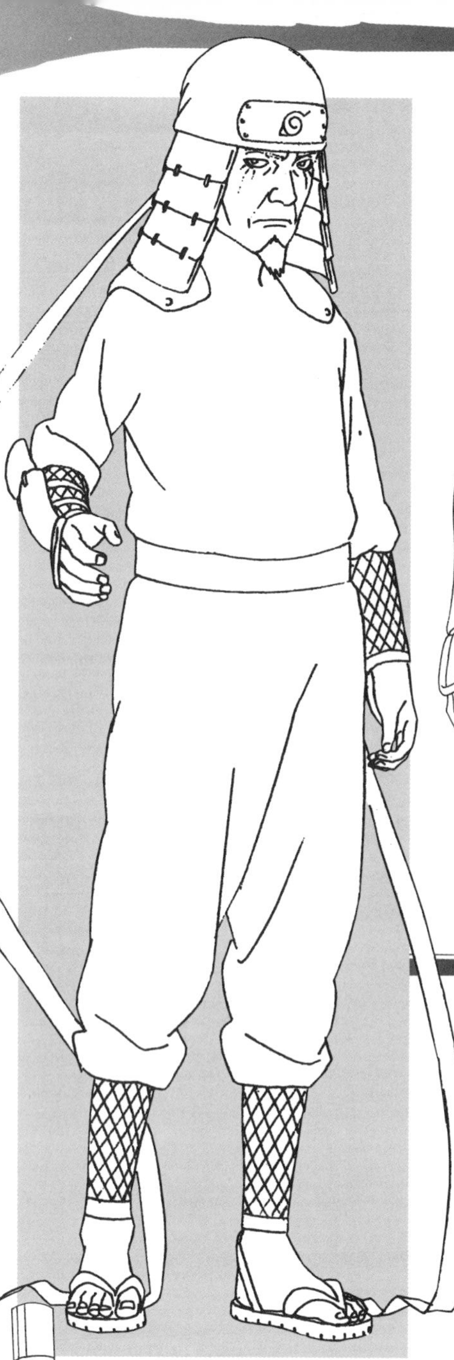

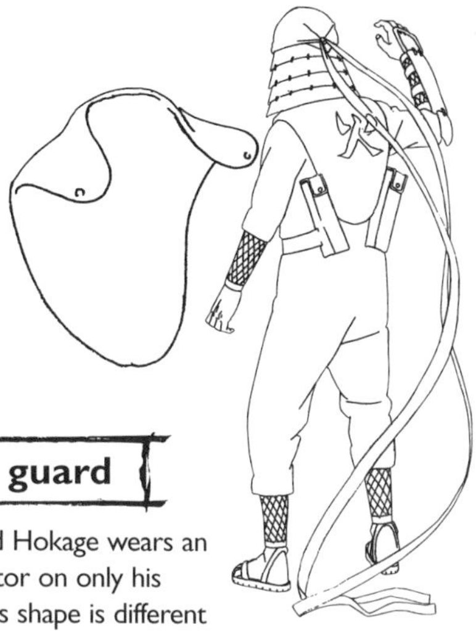

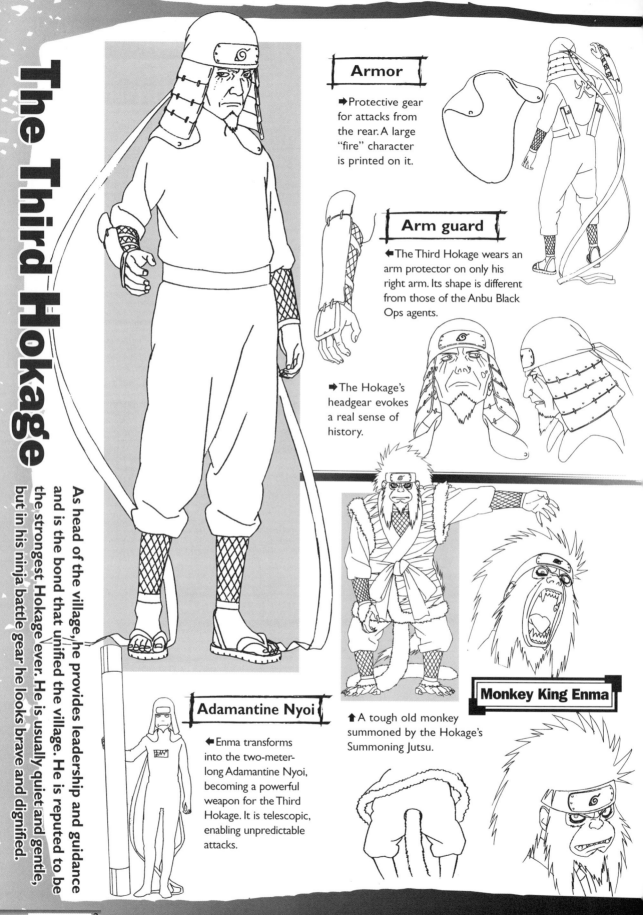

Armor

➡Protective gear for attacks from the rear. A large "fire" character is printed on it.

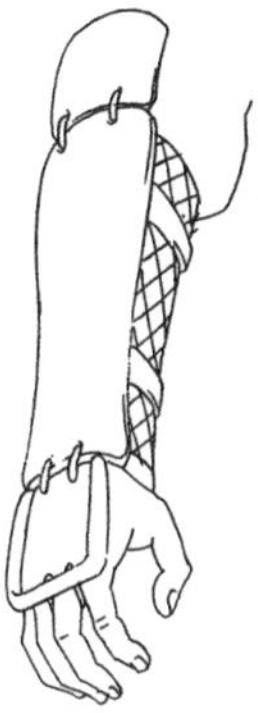

Arm guard

⬅The Third Hokage wears an arm protector on only his right arm. Its shape is different from those of the Anbu Black Ops agents.

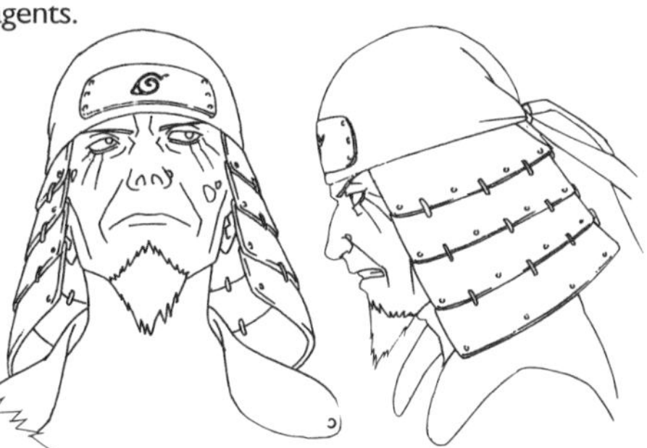

➡The Hokage's headgear evokes a real sense of history.

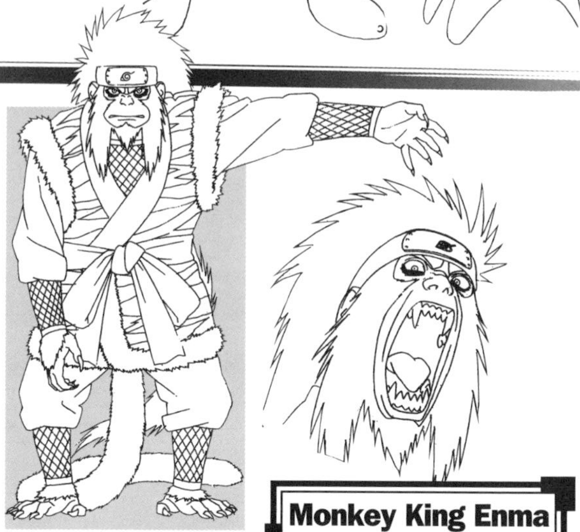

Monkey King Enma

⬆A tough old monkey summoned by the Hokage's Summoning Jutsu.

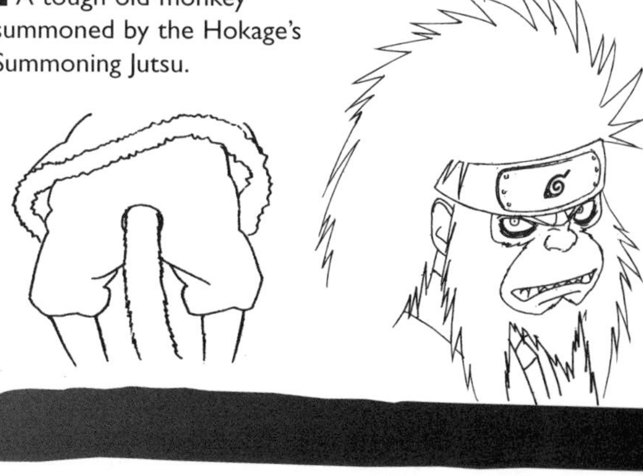

Adamantine Nyoi

⬅Enma transforms into the two-meter-long Adamantine Nyoi, becoming a powerful weapon for the Third Hokage. It is telescopic, enabling unpredictable attacks.

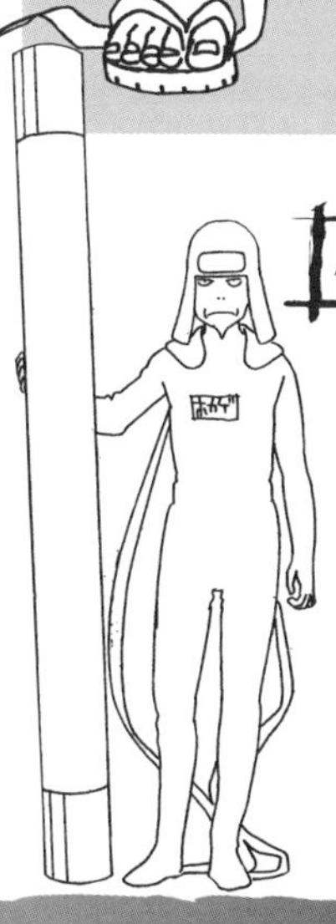

The Grim Reaper

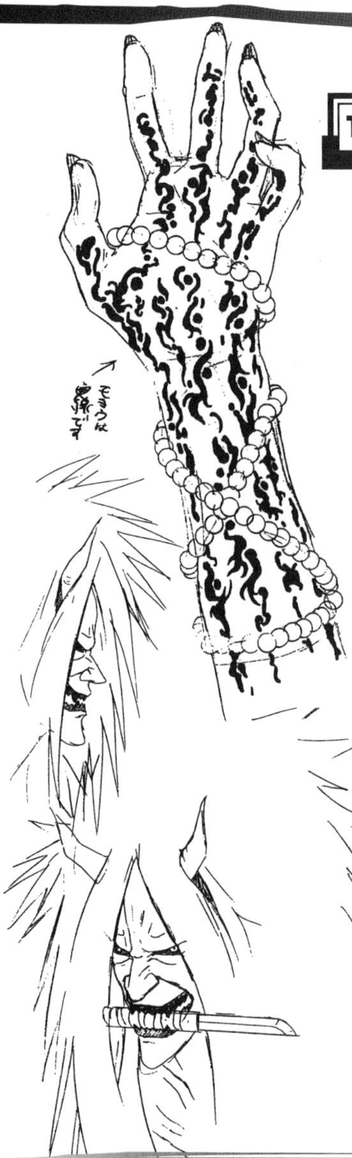

Sealing Jutsu: Reaper Death Seal

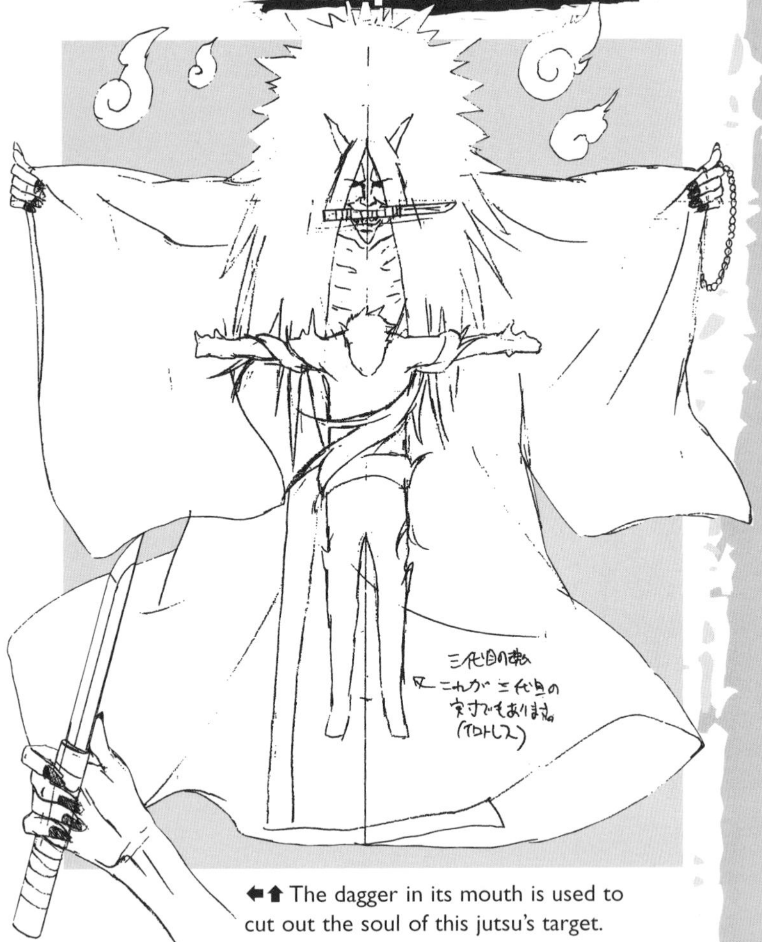

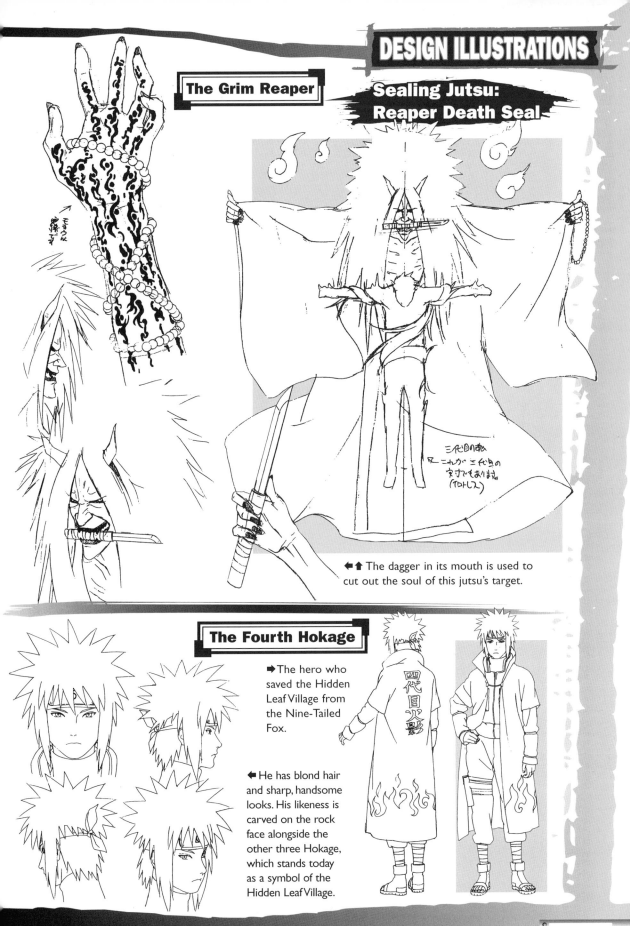

⬅⬆ The dagger in its mouth is used to cut out the soul of this jutsu's target.

The Fourth Hokage

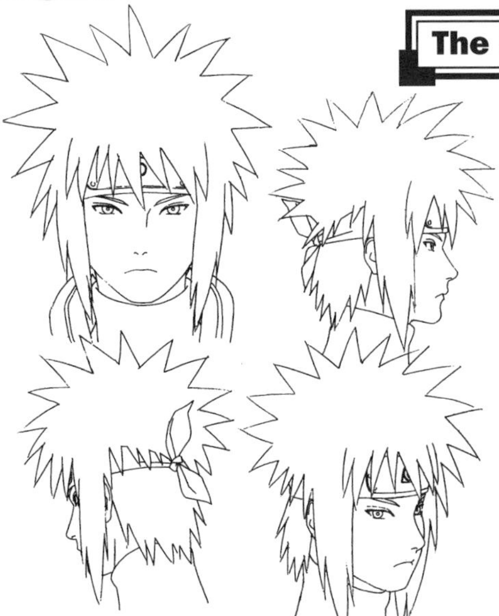

➡ The hero who saved the Hidden Leaf Village from the Nine-Tailed Fox.

⬅ He has blond hair and sharp, handsome looks. His likeness is carved on the rock face alongside the other three Hokage, which stands today as a symbol of the Hidden Leaf Village.

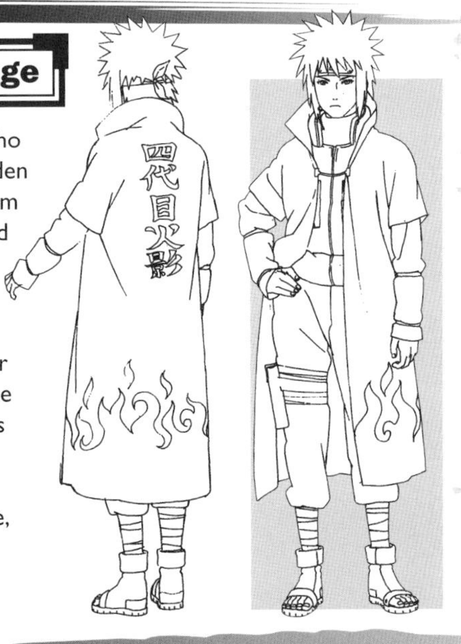
四代目火影

Jiraiya

His mentor is the Third Hokage, and the Fourth Hokage was his student. He has superb abilities worthy of his reputation as one of the legendary Sannin. His openhearted personality is apparent in the way he is dressed.

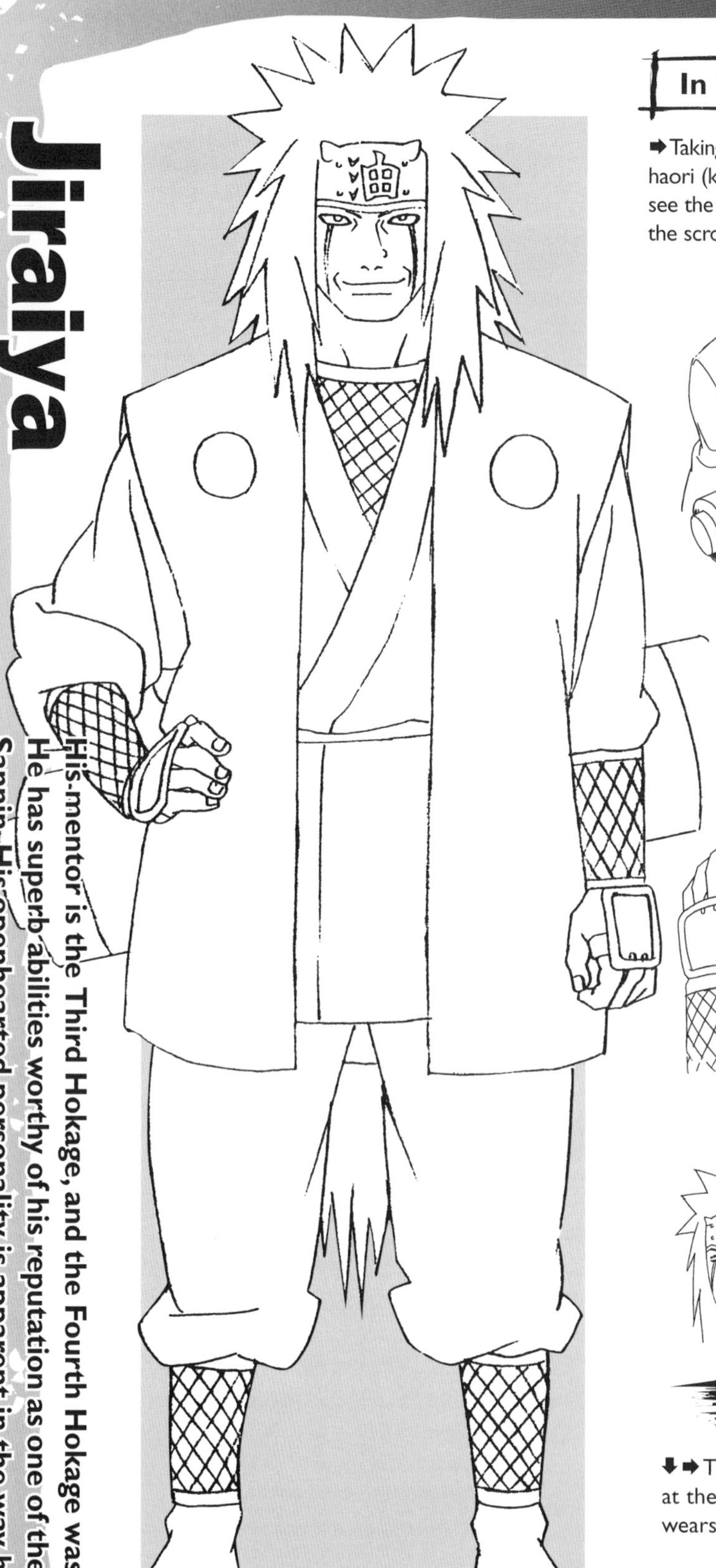

In his haori

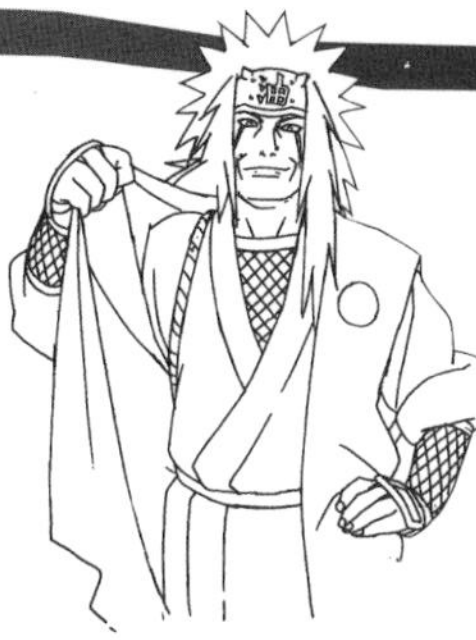

➡Taking a peek under his haori (kimono coat), we can see the rope that secures the scroll on his back.

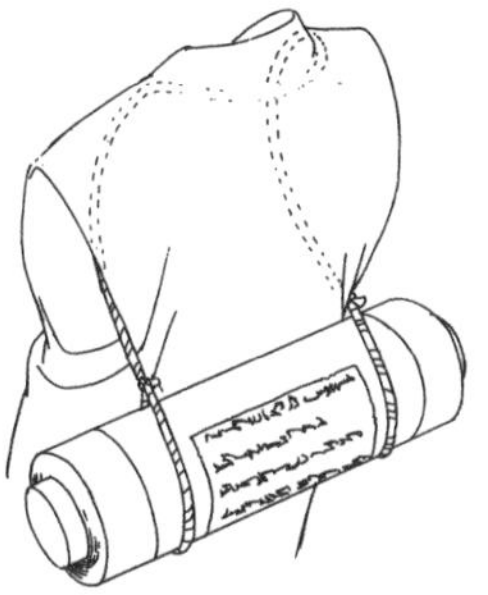

The scroll

⬅He always carries a large scroll on his back. Is it for jutsu or for research?!

Geta

➡His favorite geta (wooden clogs) are the same color as his haori. How can he manage to sneak around quietly when he's doing research in those?

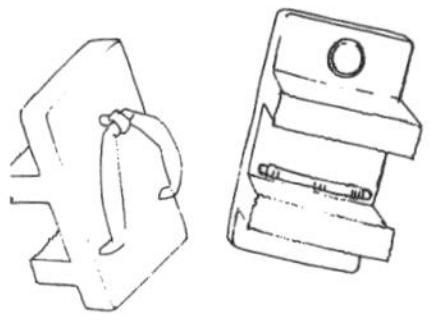

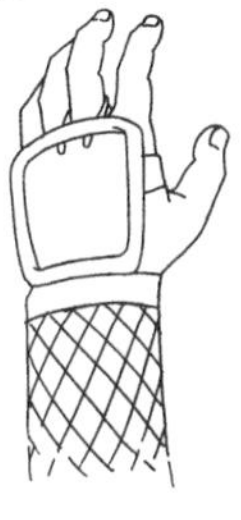

Arm guards

⬅He wears guards on both arms. Compared to Kakashi's, they look steeped in history.

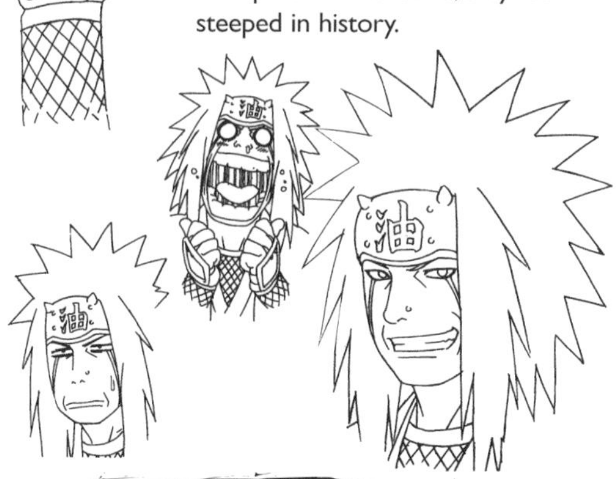

Summoned toad

⬇➡The toad Jiraiya summoned at the Hot Spring District. It wears a huge necklace.

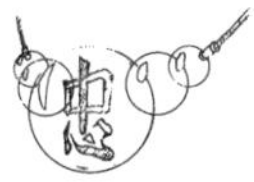

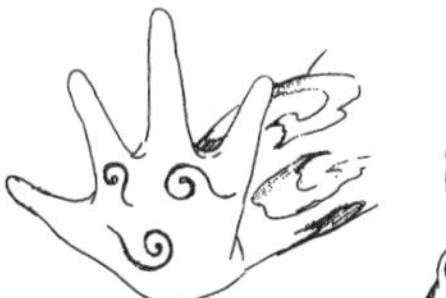

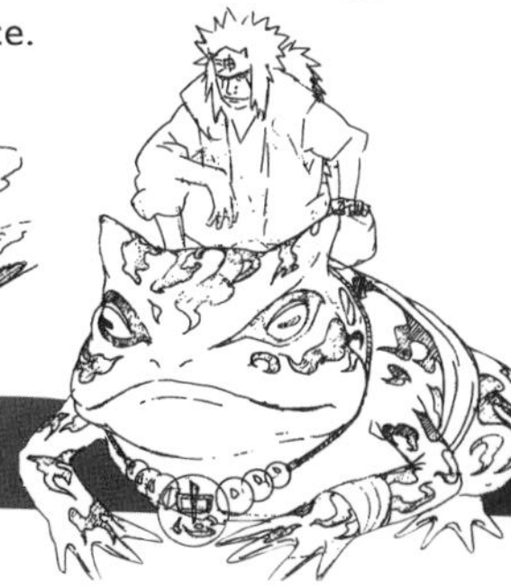

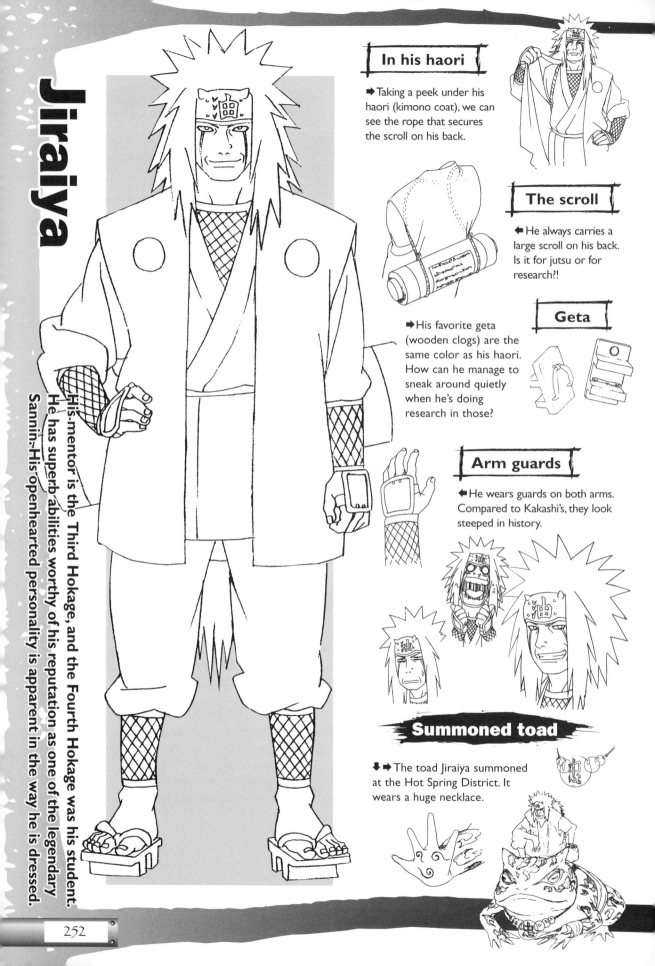

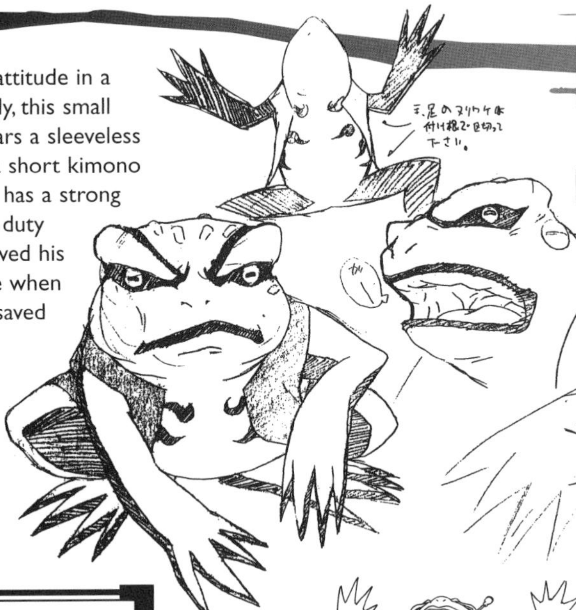
手、足のヌリワケは付け根で区切って下さい。

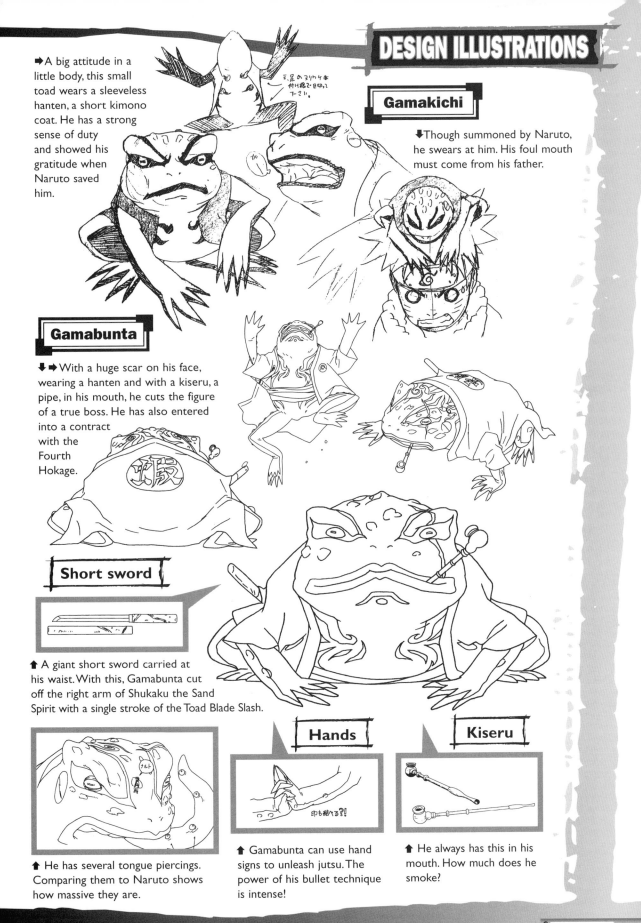

➡A big attitude in a little body, this small toad wears a sleeveless hanten, a short kimono coat. He has a strong sense of duty and showed his gratitude when Naruto saved him.

Gamakichi

⬇Though summoned by Naruto, he swears at him. His foul mouth must come from his father.

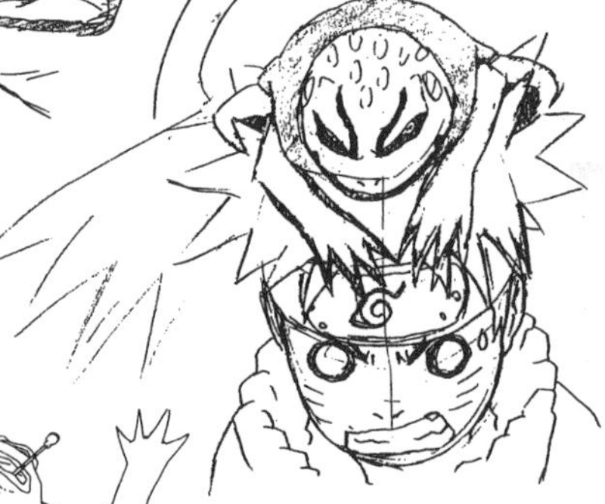

Gamabunta

⬇➡With a huge scar on his face, wearing a hanten and with a kiseru, a pipe, in his mouth, he cuts the figure of a true boss. He has also entered into a contract with the Fourth Hokage.

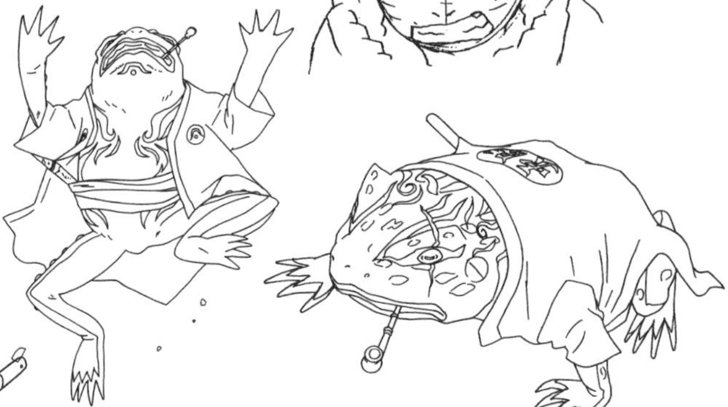

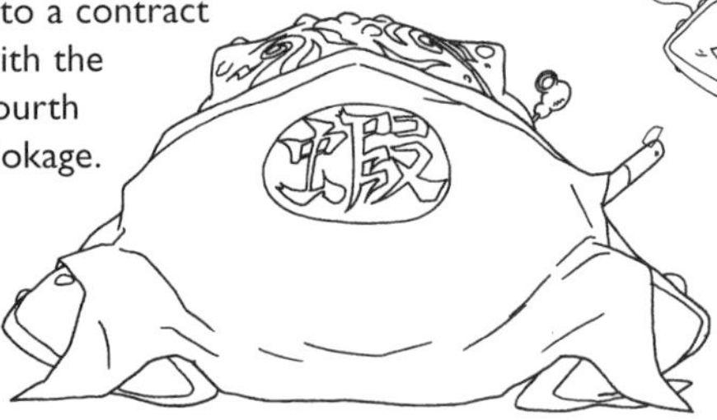

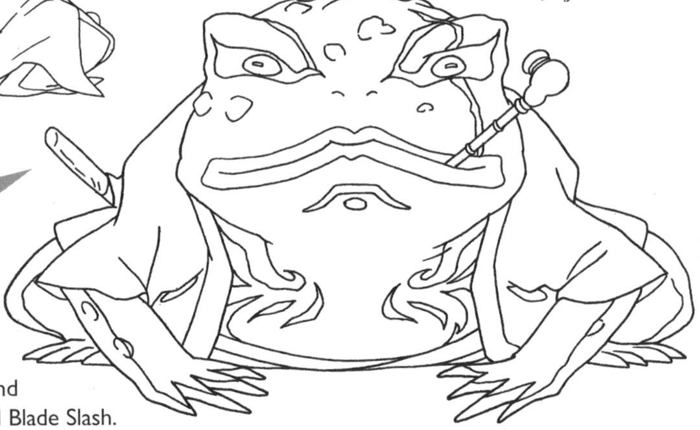

Short sword

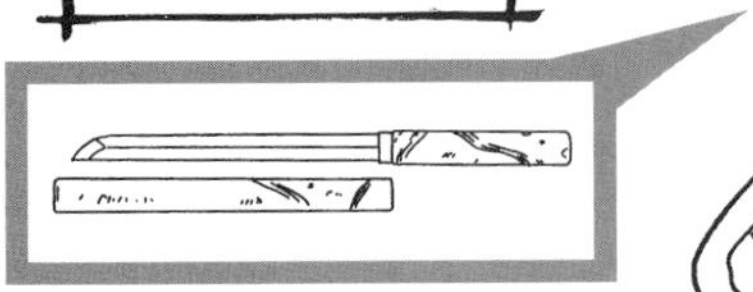

⬆ A giant short sword carried at his waist. With this, Gamabunta cut off the right arm of Shukaku the Sand Spirit with a single stroke of the Toad Blade Slash.

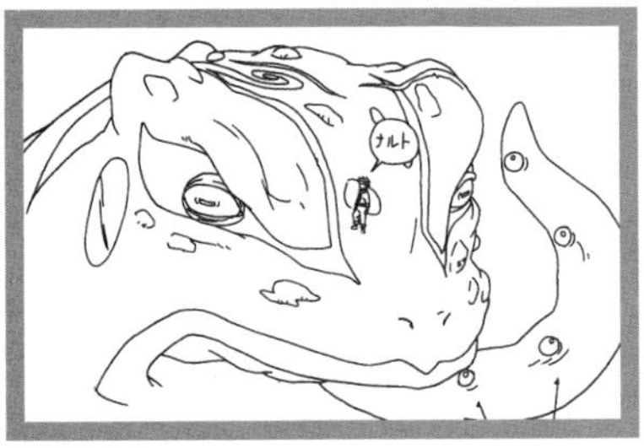
ナルト

⬆ He has several tongue piercings. Comparing them to Naruto shows how massive they are.

Hands

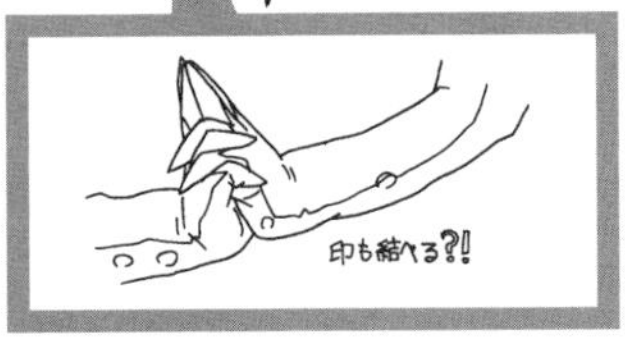
印も結べる?!

⬆ Gamabunta can use hand signs to unleash jutsu. The power of his bullet technique is intense!

Kiseru

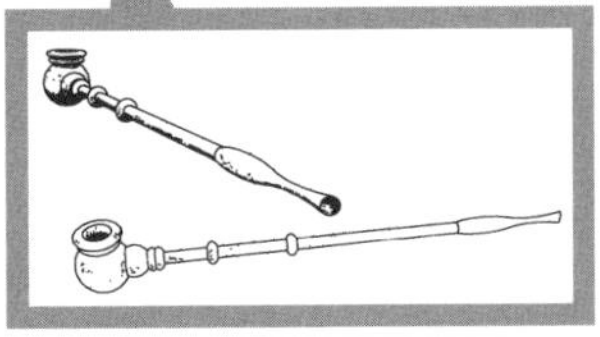

⬆ He always has this in his mouth. How much does he smoke?

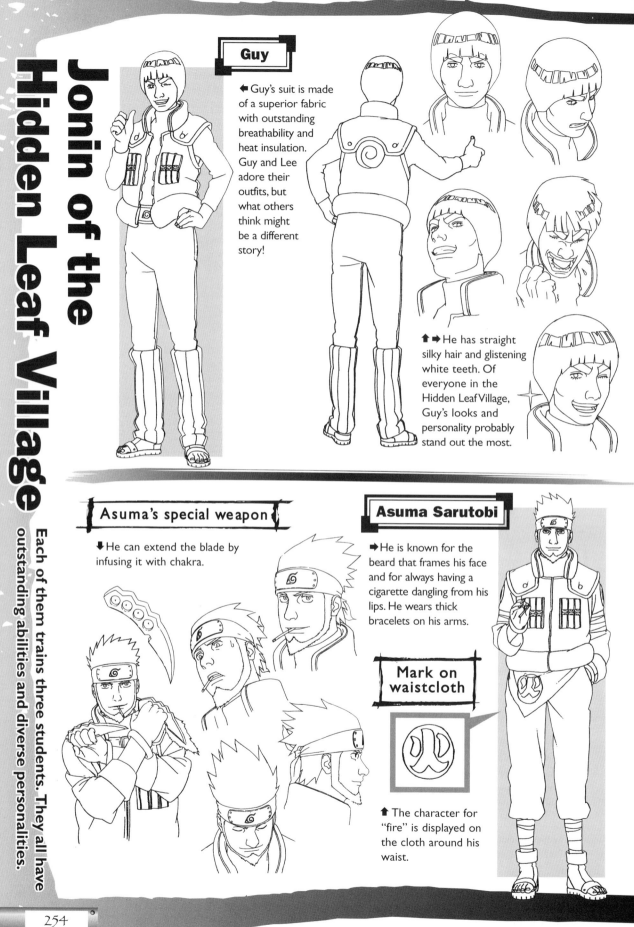

Jonin of the Hidden Leaf Village

Each of them trains three students. They all have outstanding abilities and diverse personalities.

Guy

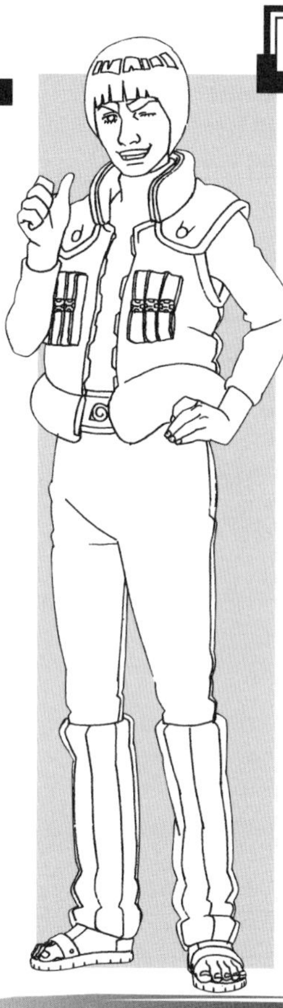

⬅Guy's suit is made of a superior fabric with outstanding breathability and heat insulation. Guy and Lee adore their outfits, but what others think might be a different story!

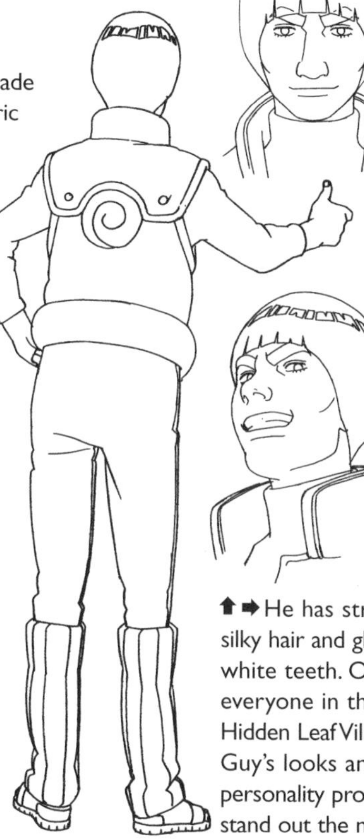

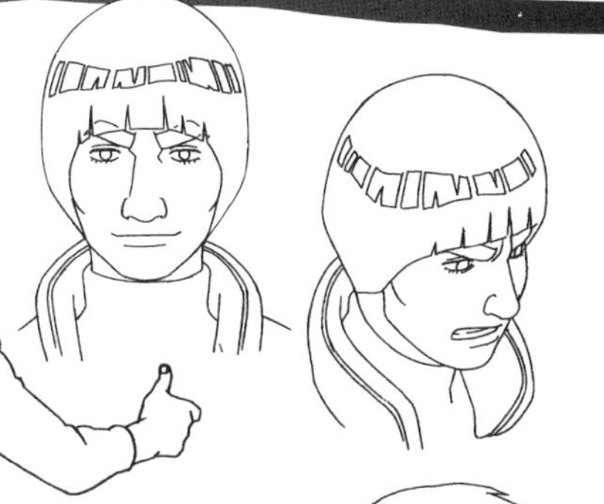

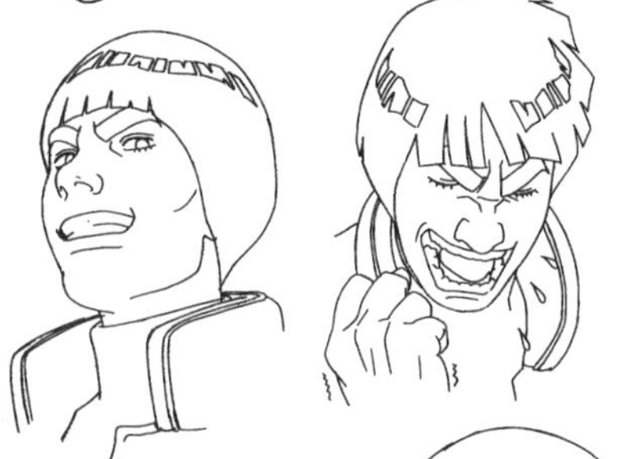

⬆➡He has straight silky hair and glistening white teeth. Of everyone in the Hidden Leaf Village, Guy's looks and personality probably stand out the most.

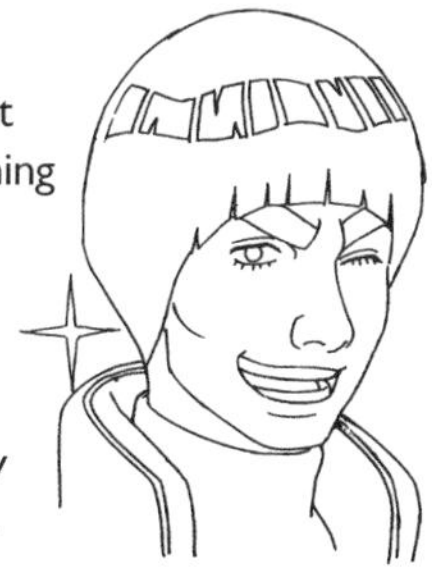

Asuma's special weapon

⬇He can extend the blade by infusing it with chakra.

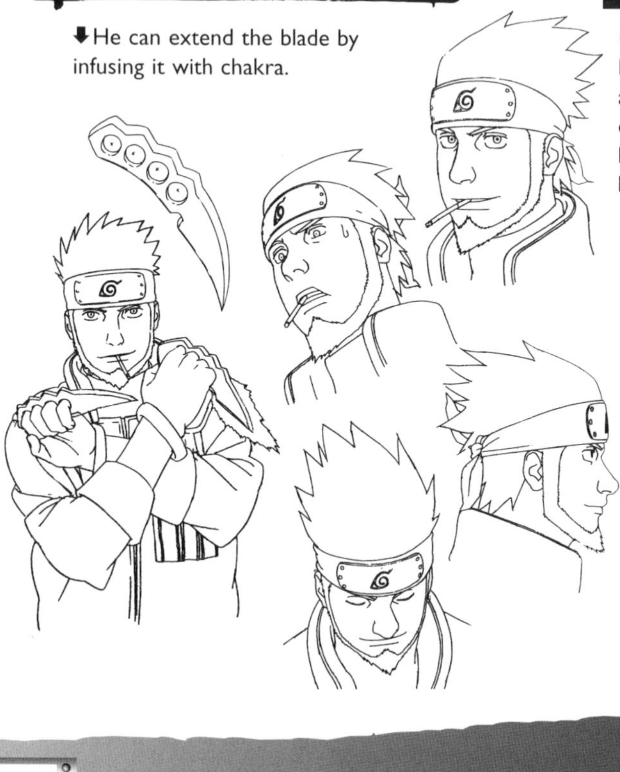

Asuma Sarutobi

➡He is known for the beard that frames his face and for always having a cigarette dangling from his lips. He wears thick bracelets on his arms.

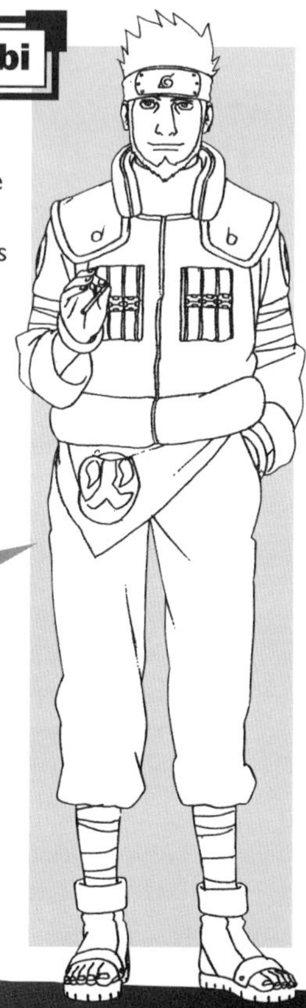

Mark on waistcloth

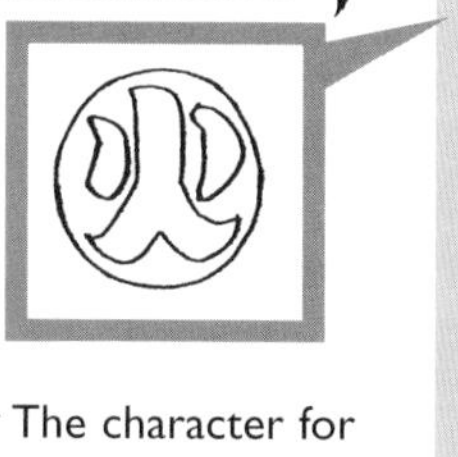

⬆The character for "fire" is displayed on the cloth around his waist.

Kurenai Yuhi

⬇➡Kurenai is the leader of Squad 8. Here she's wearing an outfit without a vest that looks like fabric wrapped around her body.

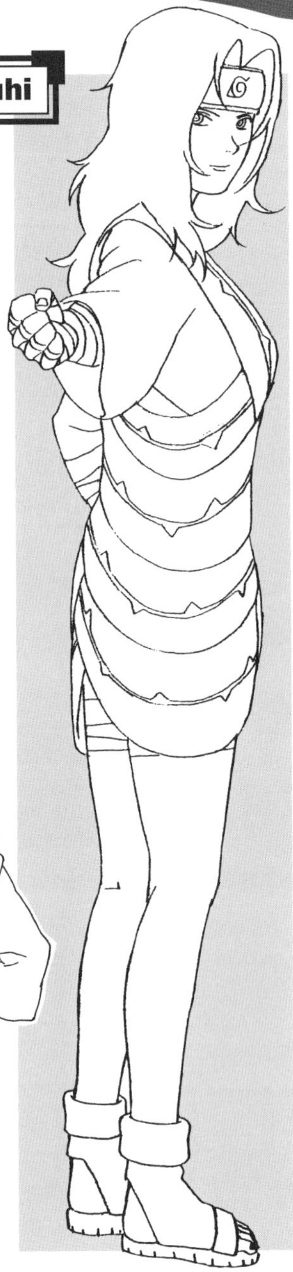

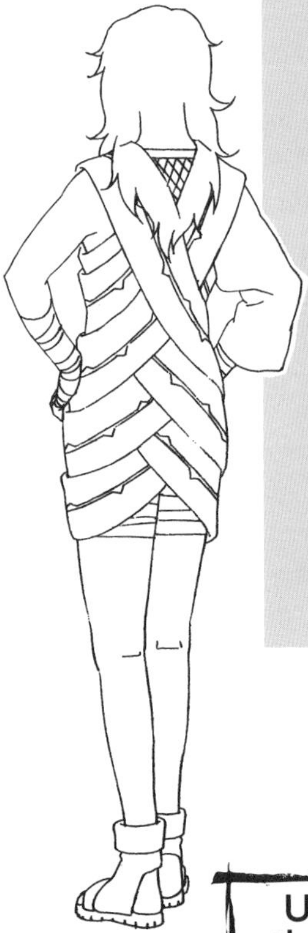

Pupils

⬅"Yuhi" means sunset in Japanese, and her pupils are as red as the setting sun. She watches over her students with a feminine touch.

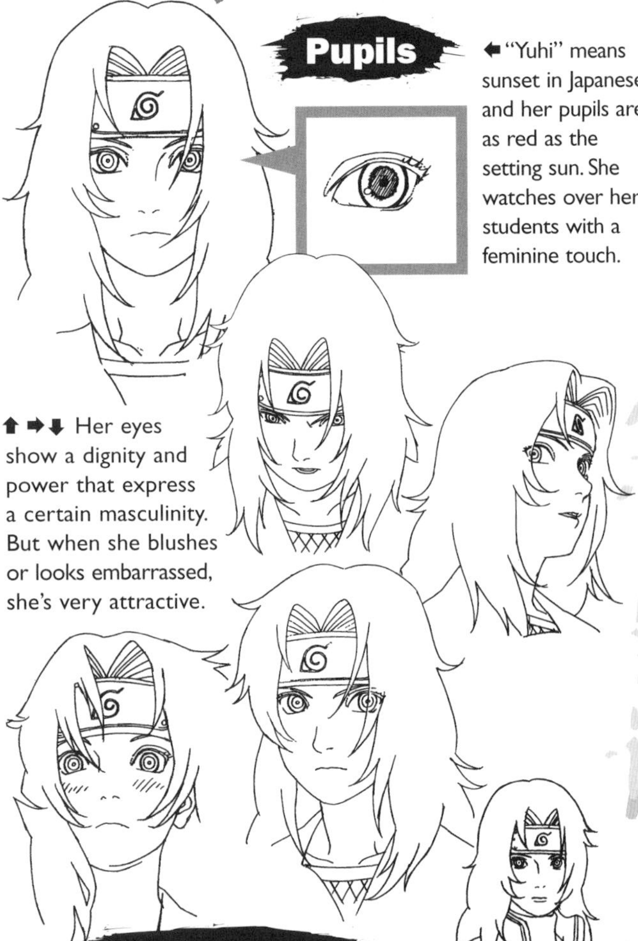

⬆➡⬇ Her eyes show a dignity and power that express a certain masculinity. But when she blushes or looks embarrassed, she's very attractive.

Wearing a vest

⬅ She visited the Hyuga Clan Main Branch's dojo wearing a vest. This is not something normally seen, making this a rare illustration.

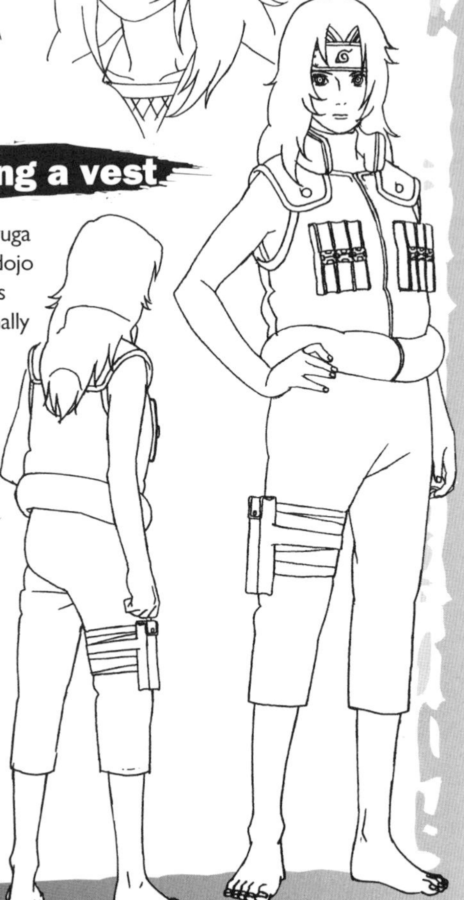

Under the vest

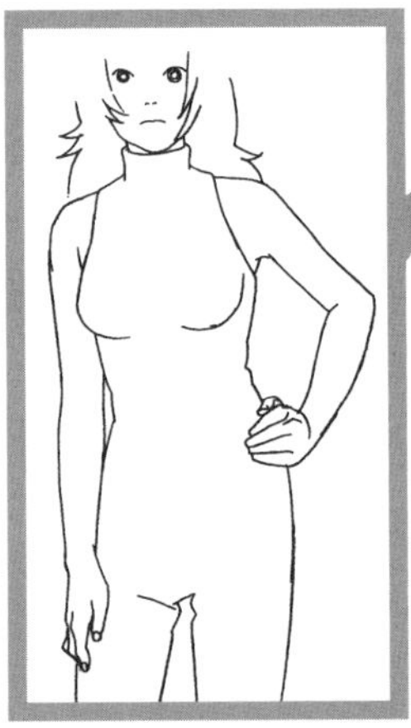

➡She wears a sleeveless jumpsuit under her vest.

Shinobi of the Hidden Leaf Village

The village is renowned for its profound power. These select shinobi make the village proud by supporting it with their outstanding abilities.

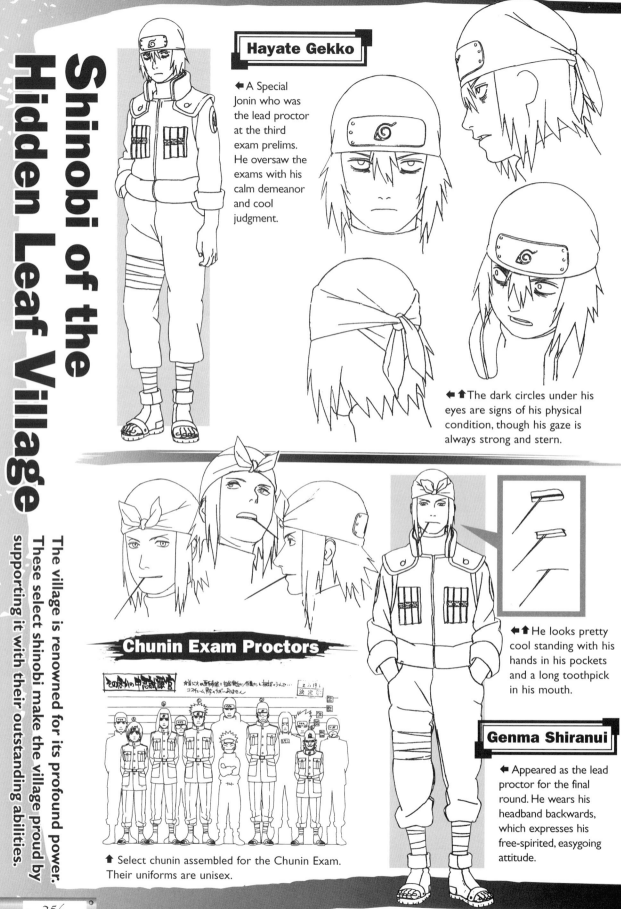

Hayate Gekko

← A Special Jonin who was the lead proctor at the third exam prelims. He oversaw the exams with his calm demeanor and cool judgment.

←↑ The dark circles under his eyes are signs of his physical condition, though his gaze is always strong and stern.

Chunin Exam Proctors

↑ Select chunin assembled for the Chunin Exam. Their uniforms are unisex.

←↑ He looks pretty cool standing with his hands in his pockets and a long toothpick in his mouth.

Genma Shiranui

← Appeared as the lead proctor for the final round. He wears his headband backwards, which expresses his free-spirited, easygoing attitude.

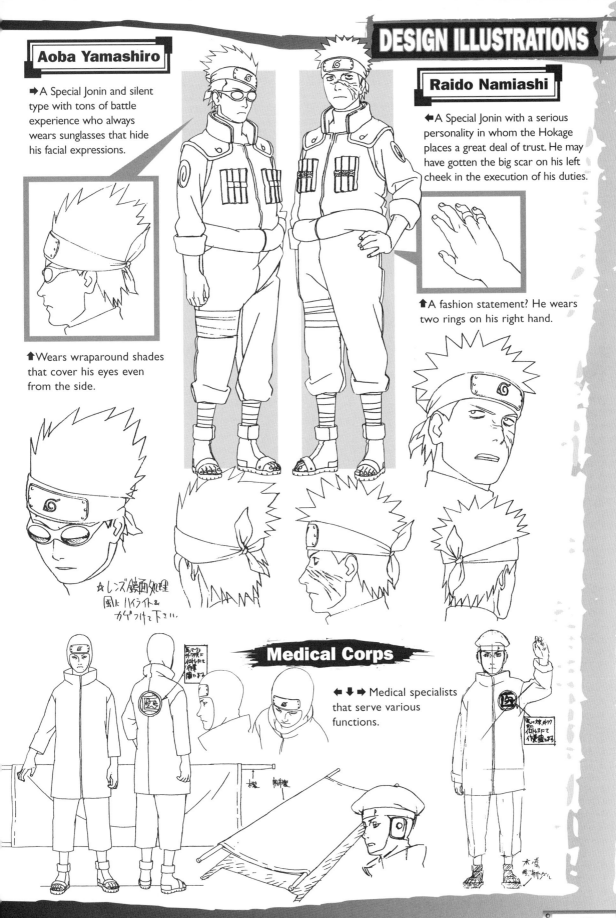

Aoba Yamashiro

➡A Special Jonin and silent type with tons of battle experience who always wears sunglasses that hide his facial expressions.

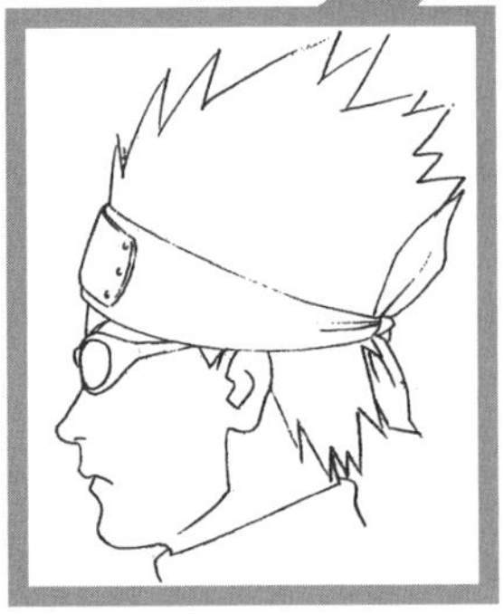

⬆Wears wraparound shades that cover his eyes even from the side.

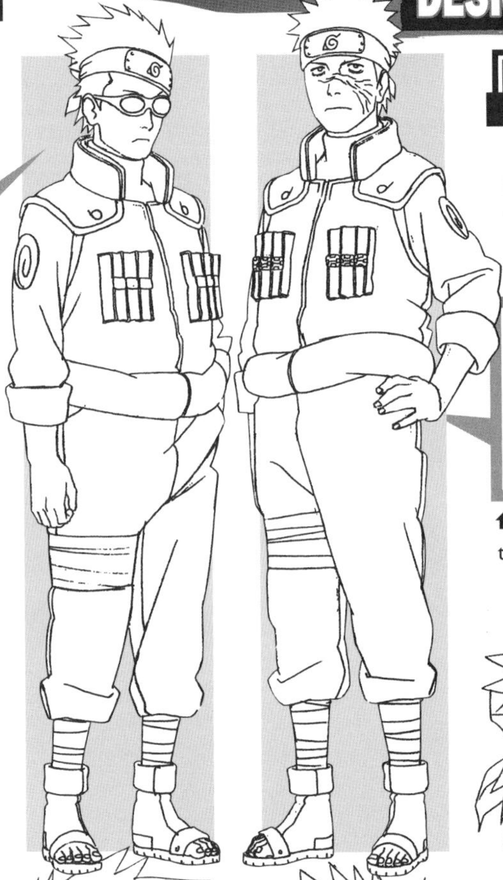

Raido Namiashi

⬅A Special Jonin with a serious personality in whom the Hokage places a great deal of trust. He may have gotten the big scar on his left cheek in the execution of his duties.

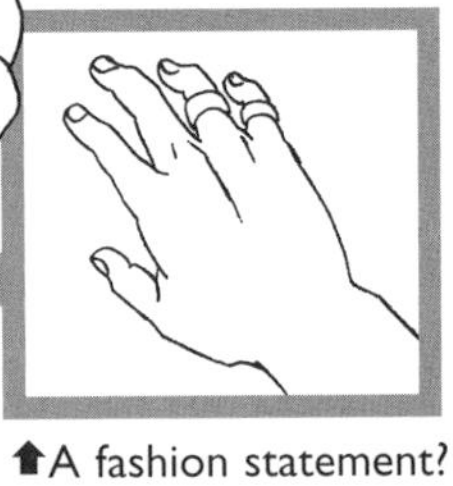

⬆A fashion statement? He wears two rings on his right hand.

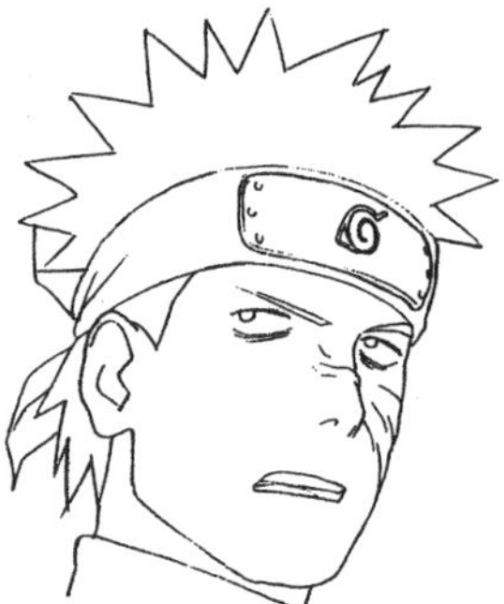

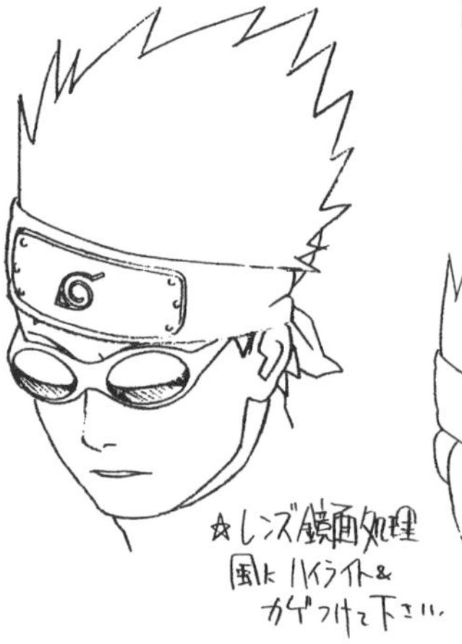
☆レンズ鏡面処理
風にハイライト＆
カゲつけて下さい

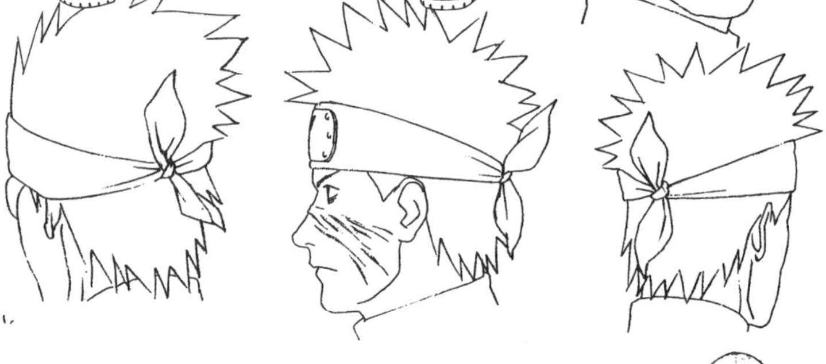

Medical Corps

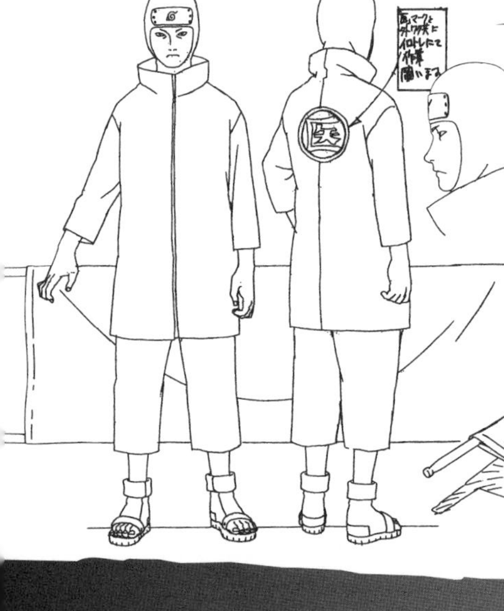

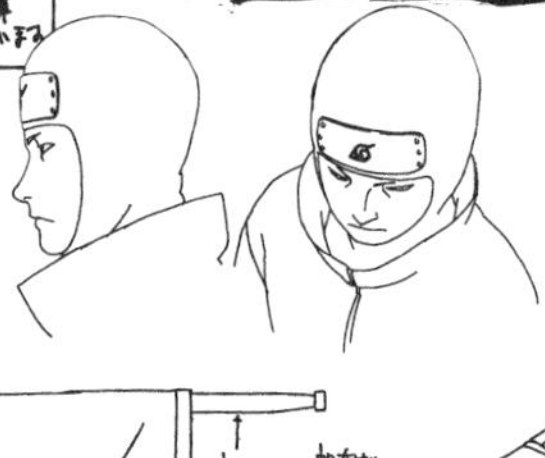

⬅⬇➡ Medical specialists that serve various functions.

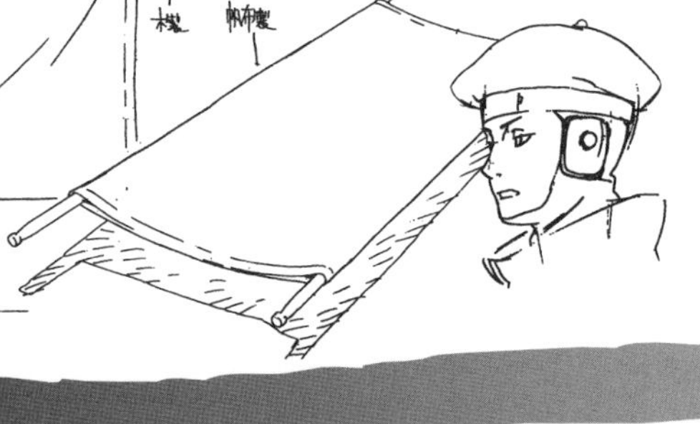

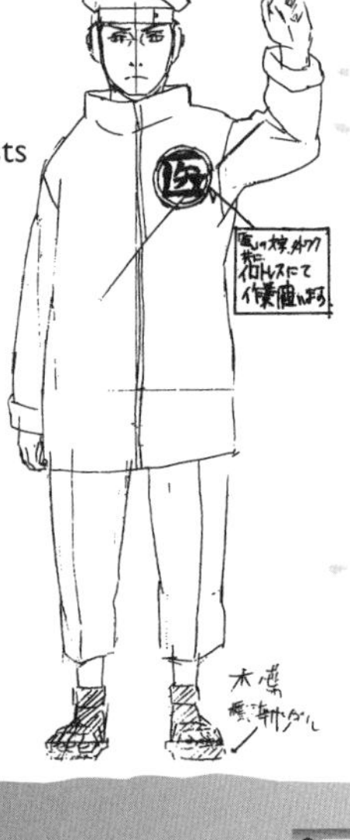

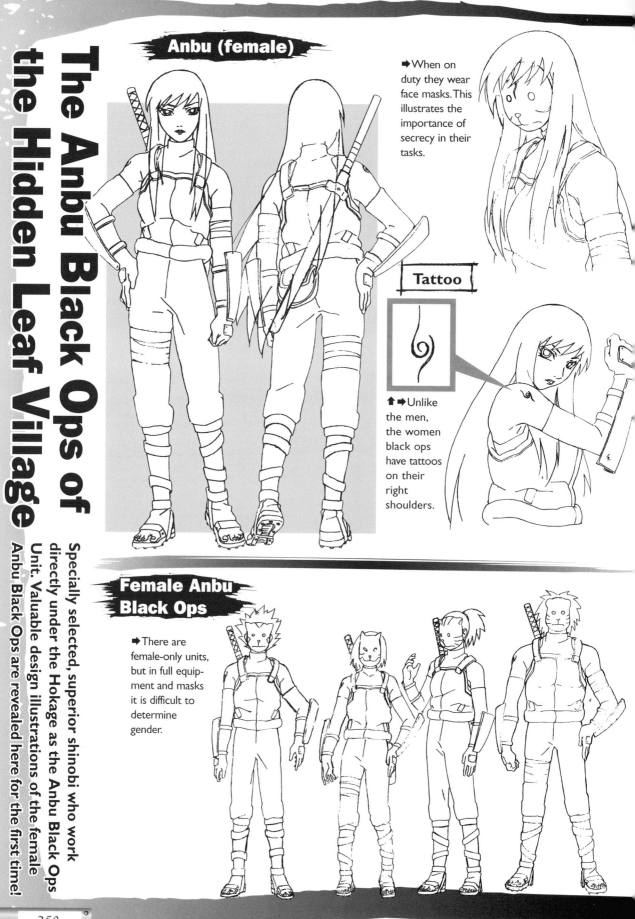

The Anbu Black Ops of the Hidden Leaf Village

Specially selected, superior shinobi who work directly under the Hokage as the Anbu Black Ops Unit. Valuable design illustrations of the female Anbu Black Ops are revealed here for the first time!

Anbu (female)

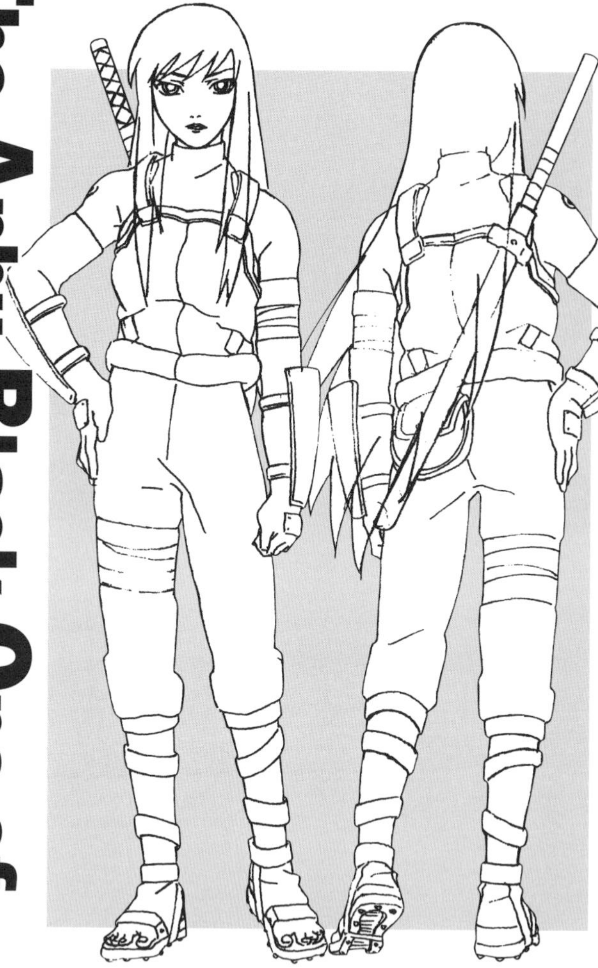

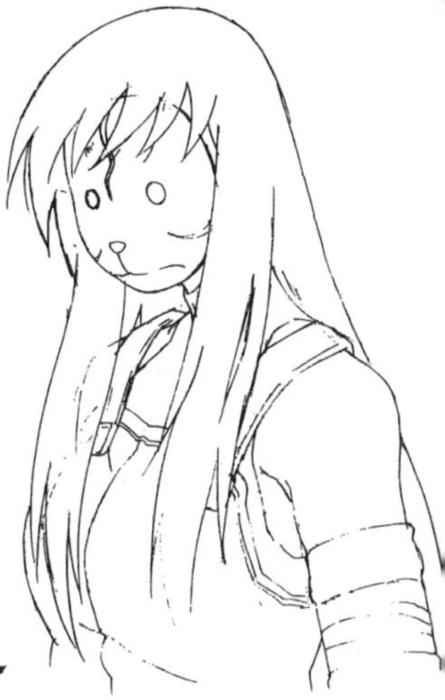

➡When on duty they wear face masks. This illustrates the importance of secrecy in their tasks.

Tattoo

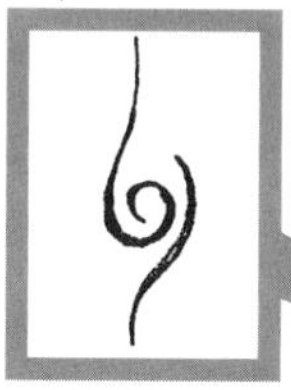

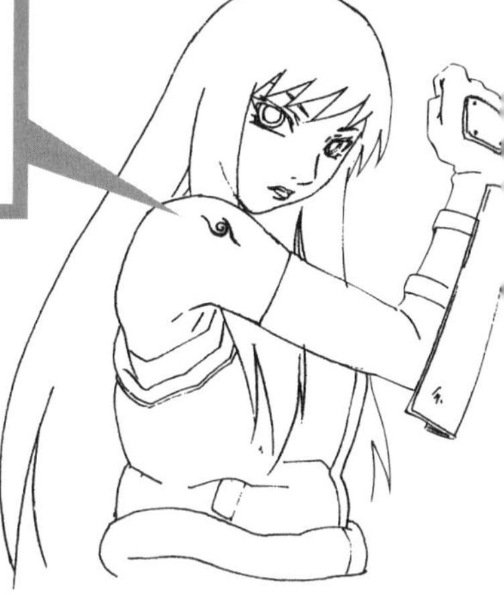

⬆➡Unlike the men, the women black ops have tattoos on their right shoulders.

Female Anbu Black Ops

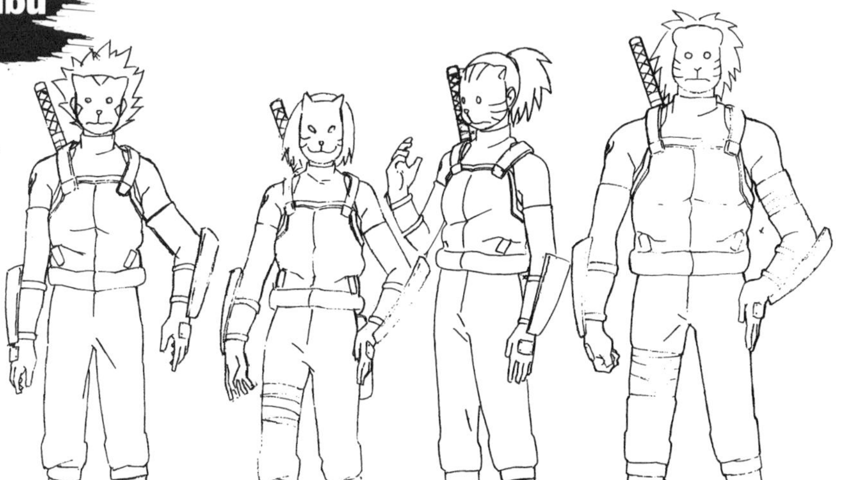

➡There are female-only units, but in full equipment and masks it is difficult to determine gender.

Shinobi of the Hidden Sand Village

Having gone through demilitarization, the Hidden Sand Village is now in the process of nurturing truly powerful shinobi. In collusion with the Sound Village, they plot the destruction of the Hidden Leaf Village.

Baki

⬇The jonin that leads Gaara and his team. White fabric hangs over his face and hides one eye.

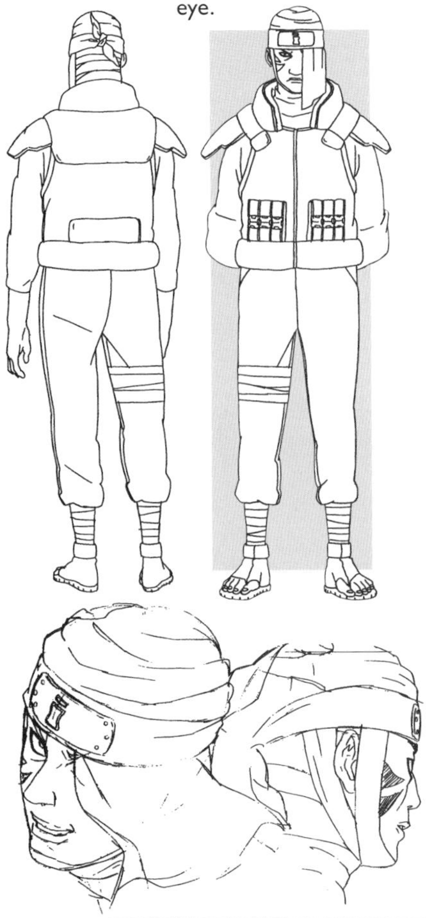

The Kazekage

⬅The leader of the Hidden Sand Village in his youth. He is Gaara's father.

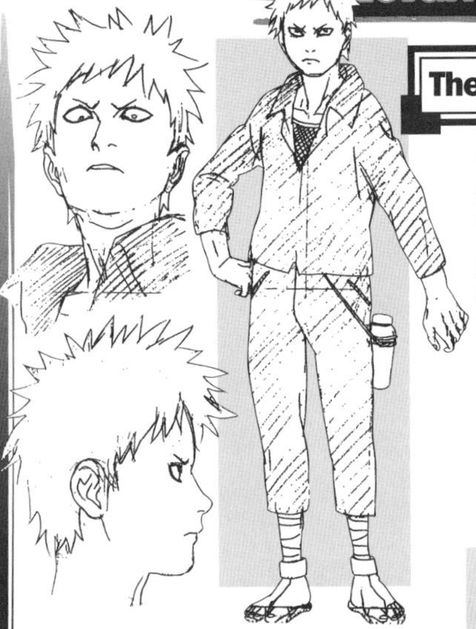

⬇➡He is basically on the same level as the Hokage. Incidentally, at this point the Kazekage is actually Orochimaru in disguise.

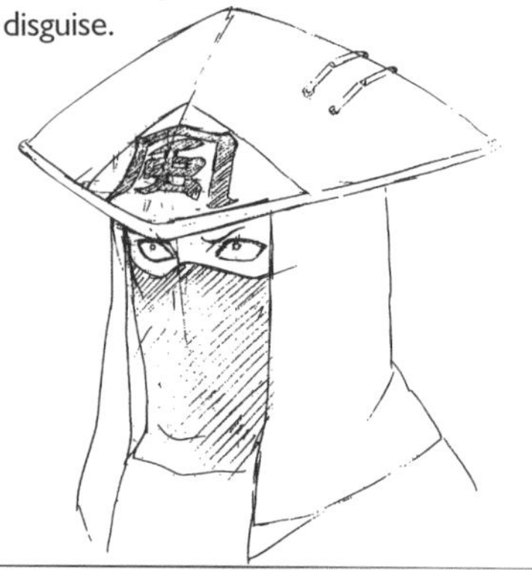

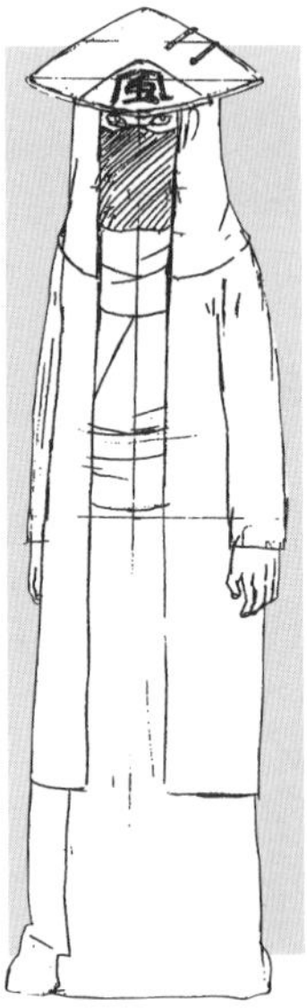

Bandages

⬇Rolling up the sleeves reveals bandages that cover the painful-looking wounds inflicted by Gaara's attack.

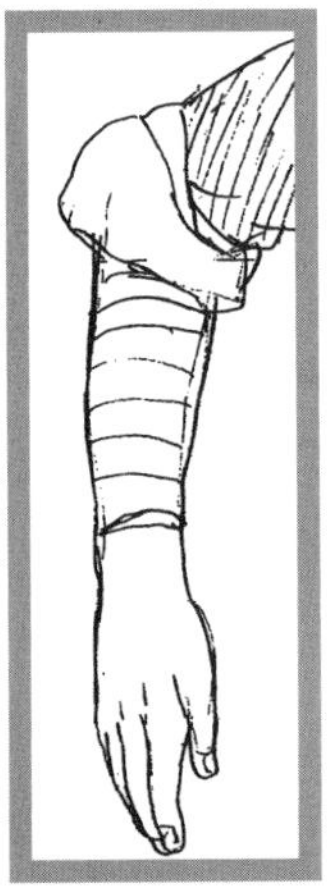

Yashamaru

⬇➡Caretaker of the infant Gaara, Yashamaru wears an apron.

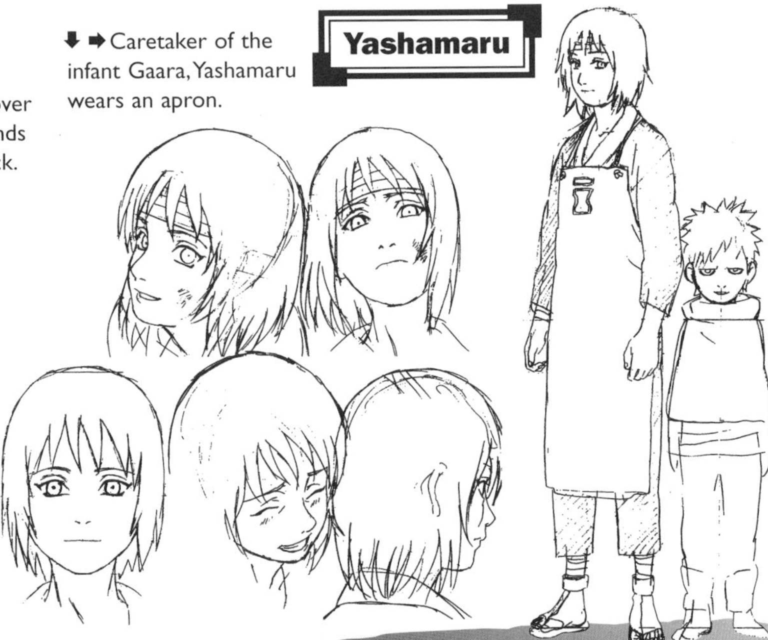

Gaara

When Gaara was born, his father, the Kazekage, used jutsu to implant Shukaku, the Sand Spirit, into his body. His headband, the symbol of shinobi status, is casually tied to the shoulder strap that holds his gourd.

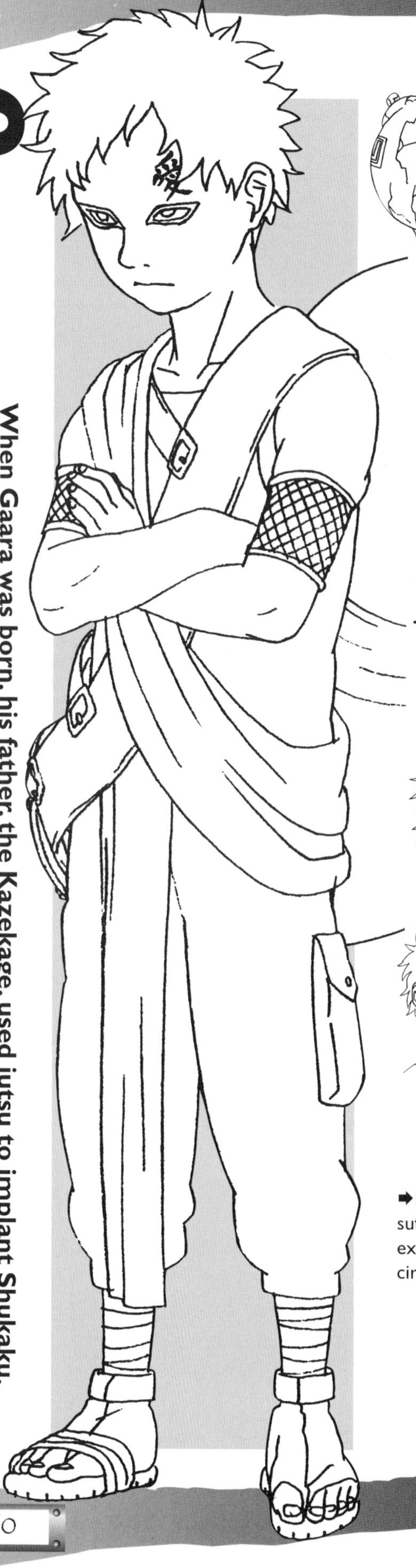

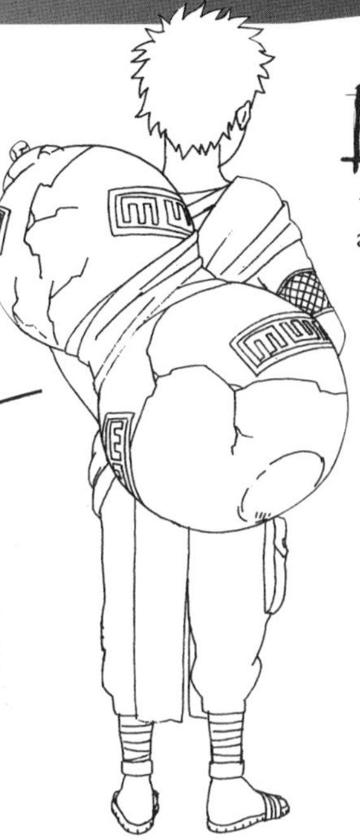

Gourd

⬅A container for sand and a powerful weapon.

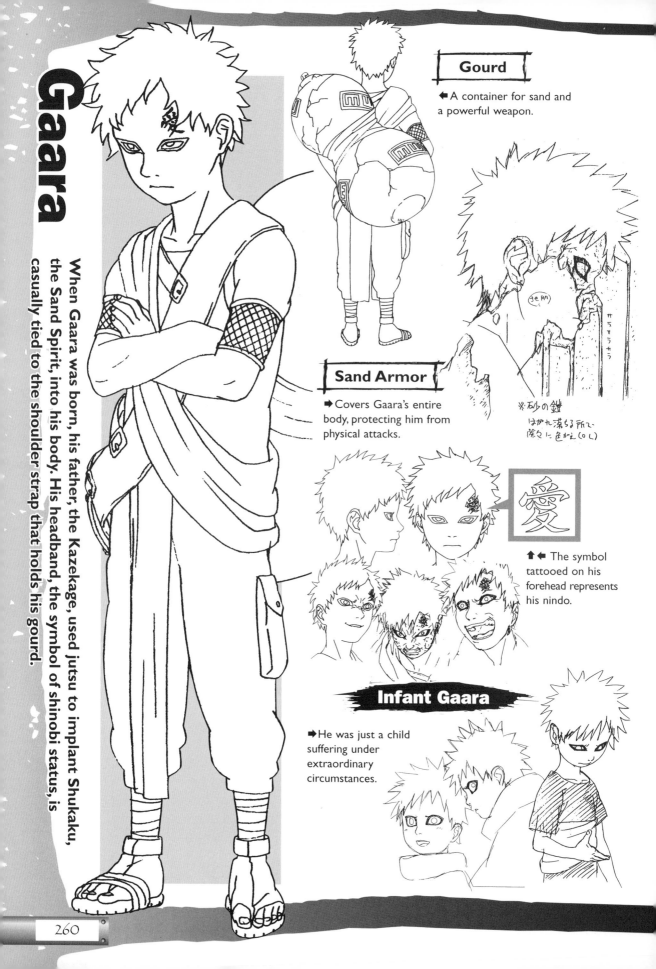

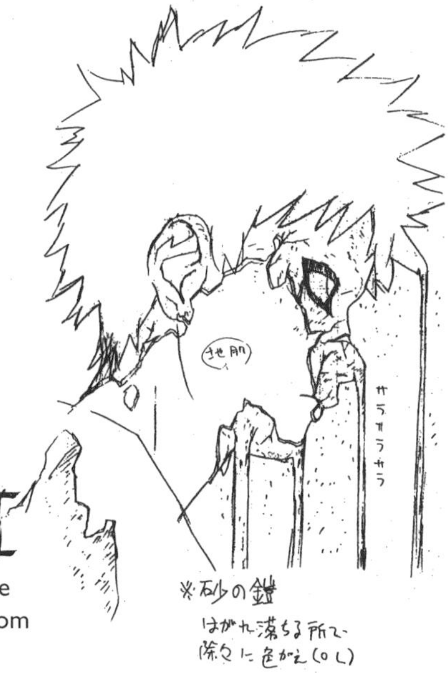
地肌
サラサラサラ
※砂の鎧
はがれ落ちる所で
除々に色がえ(OL)

Sand Armor

➡Covers Gaara's entire body, protecting him from physical attacks.

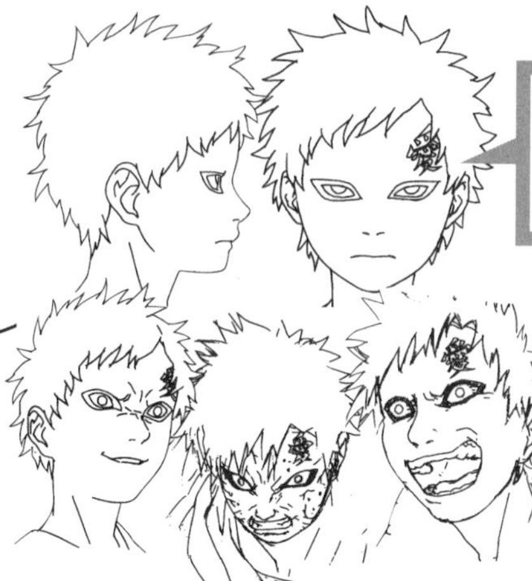

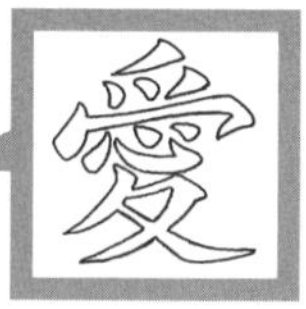
愛

⬆⬅ The symbol tattooed on his forehead represents his nindo.

Infant Gaara

➡He was just a child suffering under extraordinary circumstances.

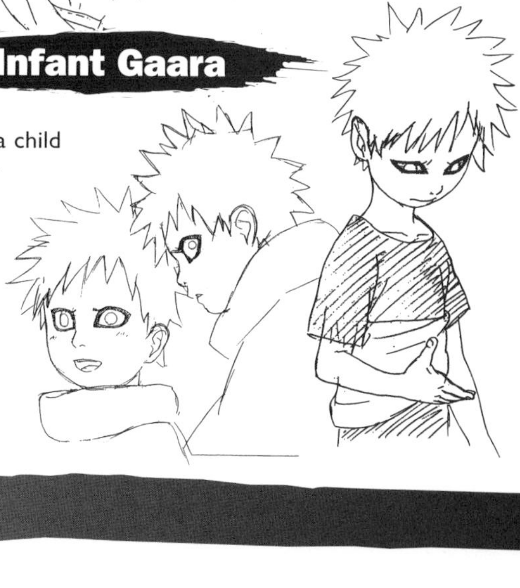

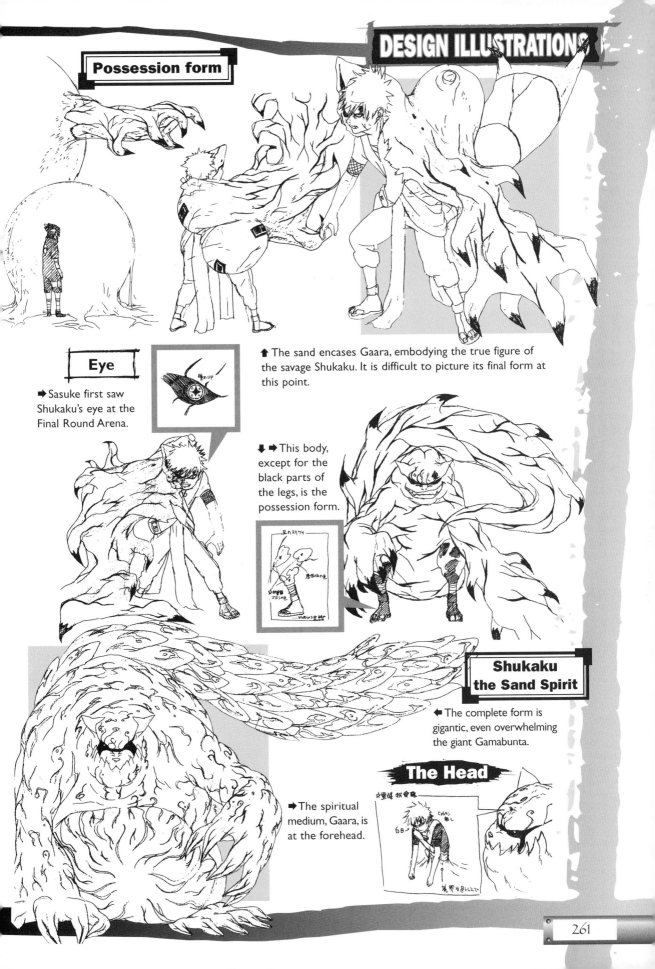

Possession form

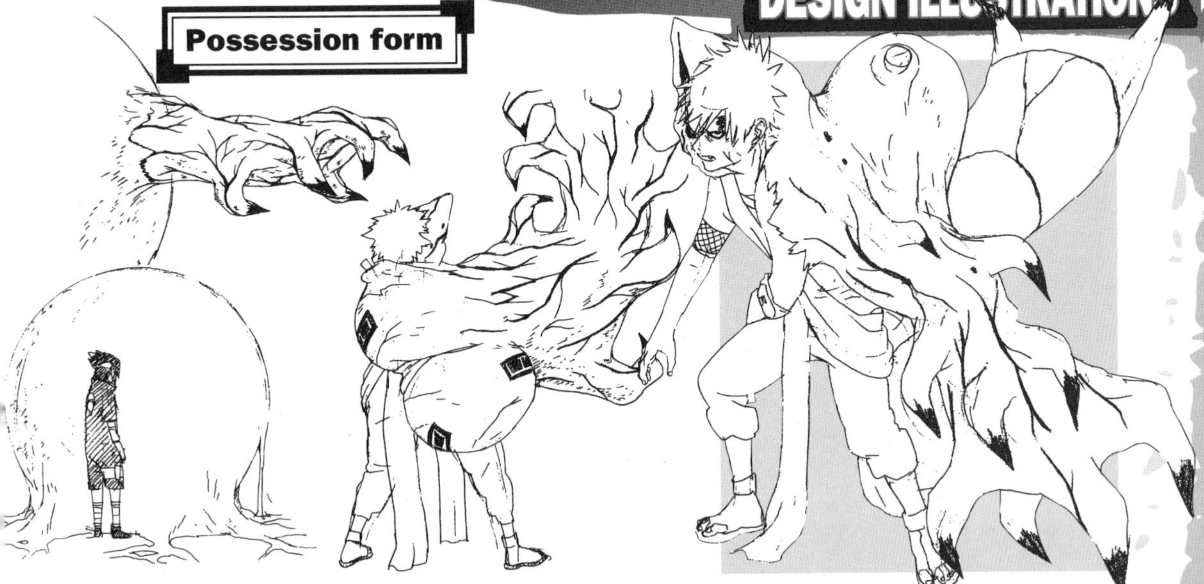

Eye

➡ Sasuke first saw Shukaku's eye at the Final Round Arena.

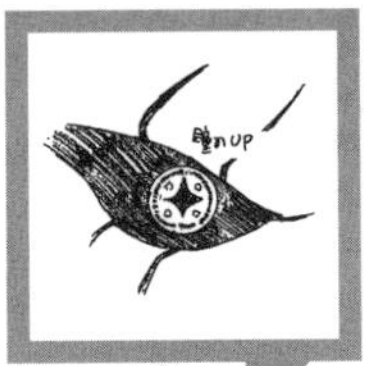

⬆ The sand encases Gaara, embodying the true figure of the savage Shukaku. It is difficult to picture its final form at this point.

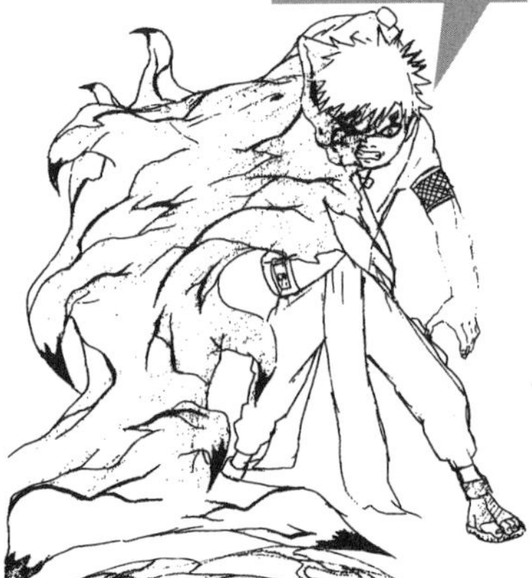

⬇ ➡ This body, except for the black parts of the legs, is the possession form.

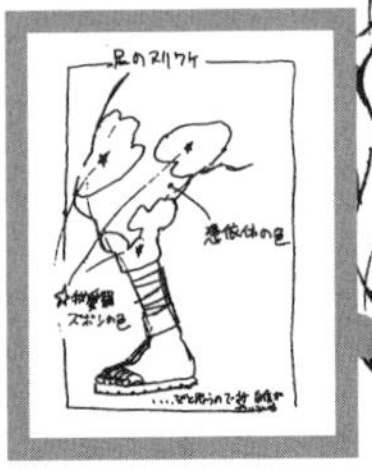

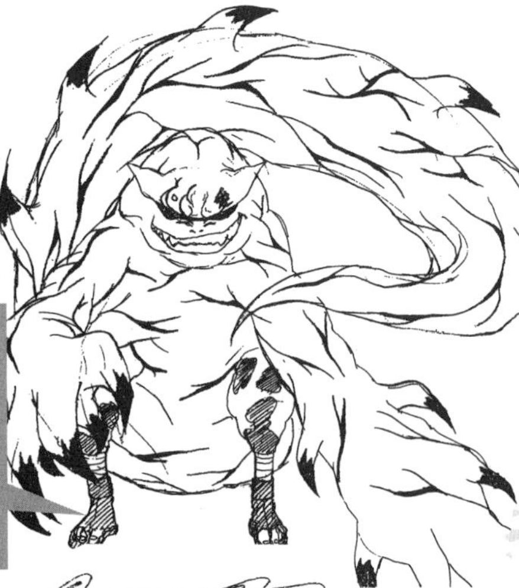

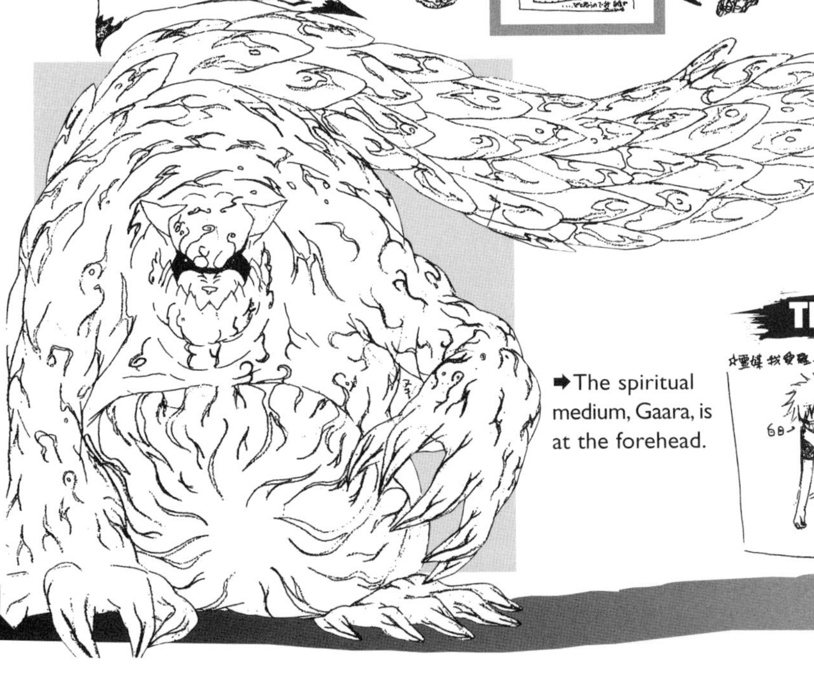

Shukaku the Sand Spirit

⬅ The complete form is gigantic, even overwhelming the giant Gamabunta.

The Head

➡ The spiritual medium, Gaara, is at the forehead.

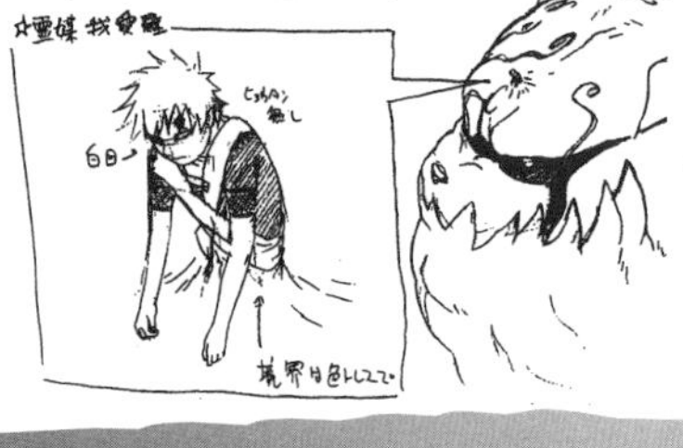

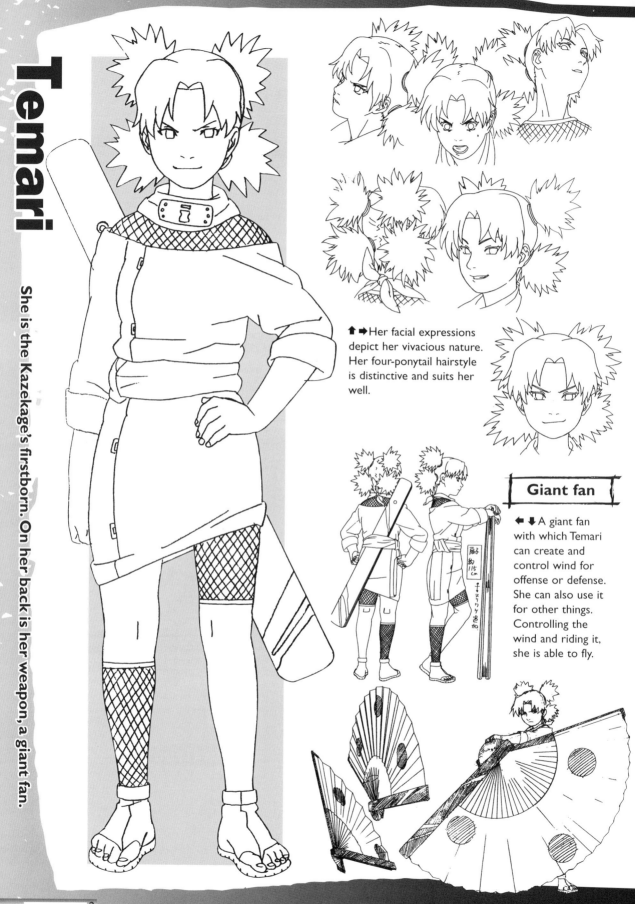

Temari

She is the Kazekage's firstborn. On her back is her weapon, a giant fan.

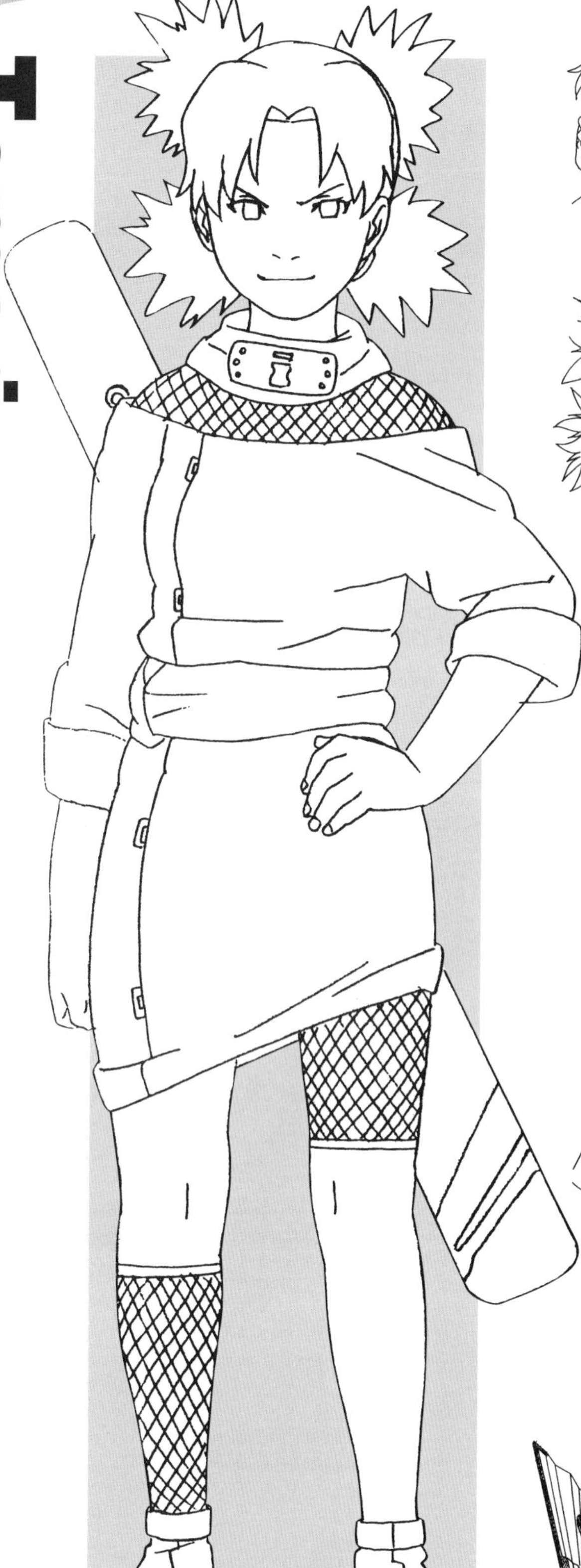

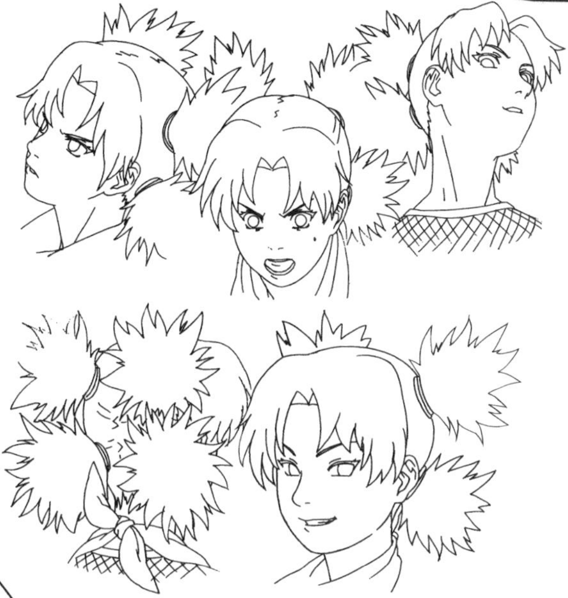

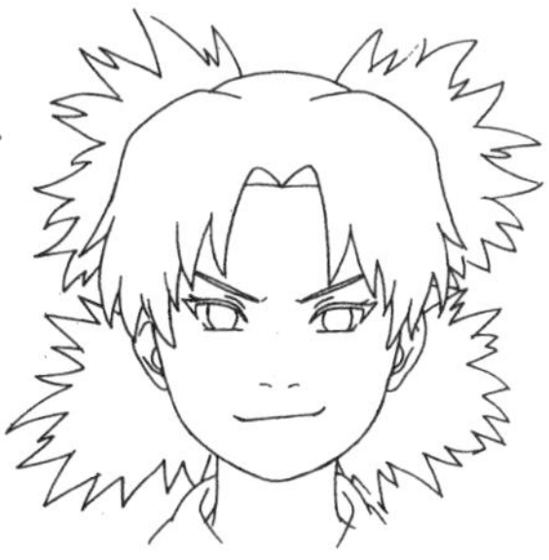

⬆➡Her facial expressions depict her vivacious nature. Her four-ponytail hairstyle is distinctive and suits her well.

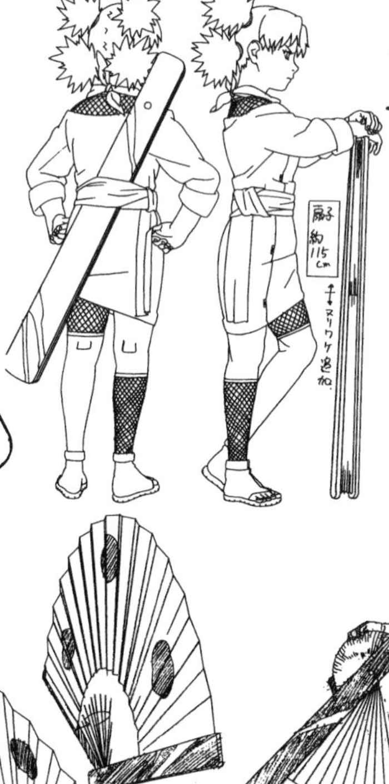

Giant fan

⬅⬇A giant fan with which Temari can create and control wind for offense or defense. She can also use it for other things. Controlling the wind and riding it, she is able to fly.

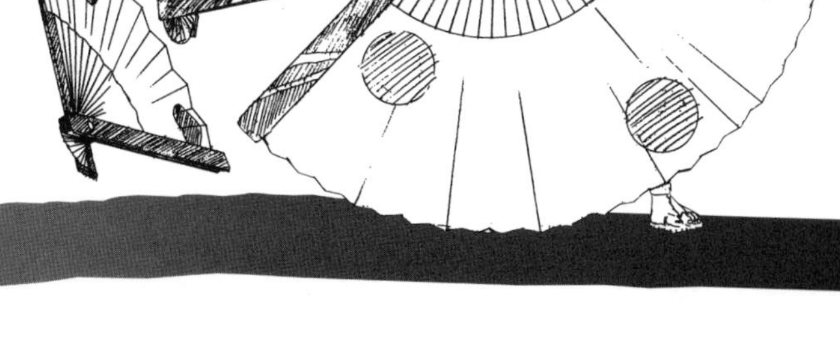

Kankuro

His puppet is the main player on the battlefield, and Kankuro is entirely covered in a black puppeteer's outfit. Like his siblings, he carries his weapon on his back.

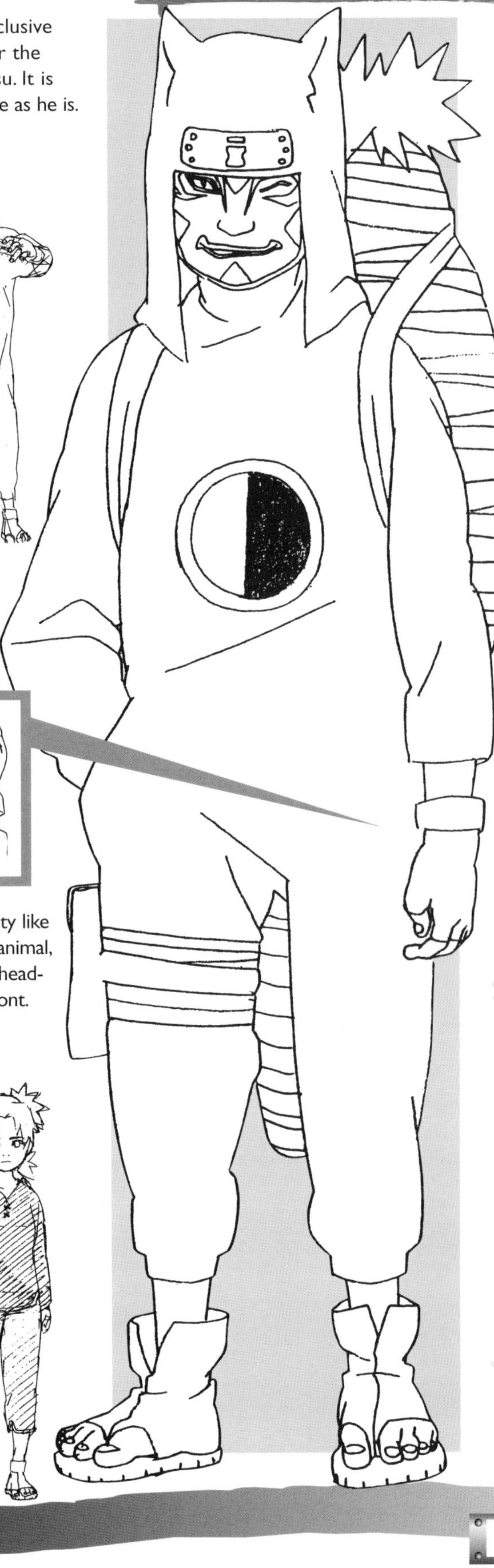

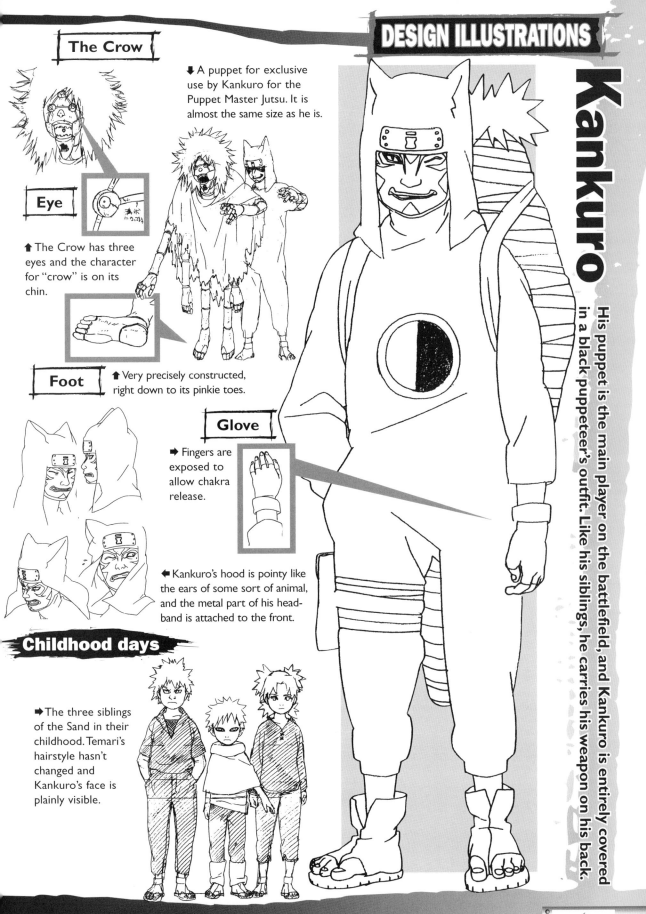

The Crow

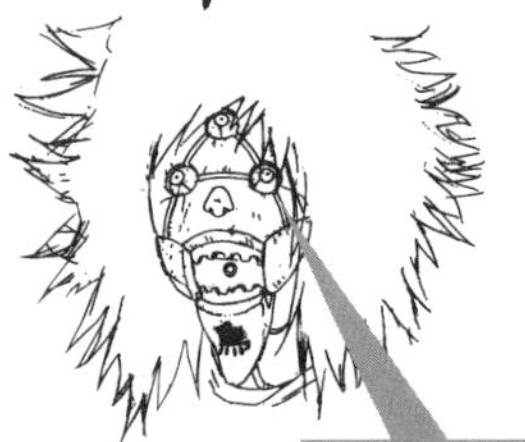

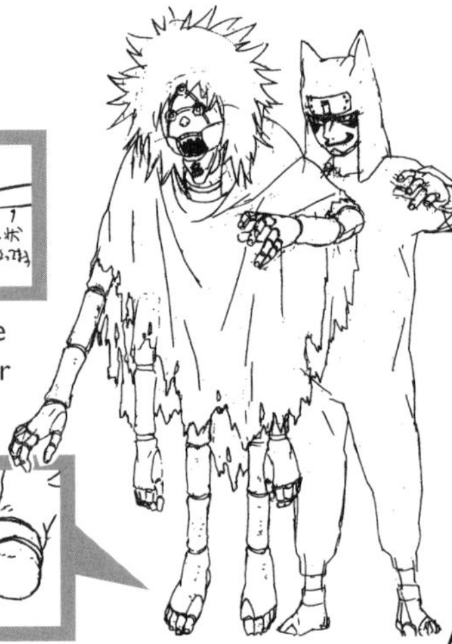

⬇ A puppet for exclusive use by Kankuro for the Puppet Master Jutsu. It is almost the same size as he is.

Eye

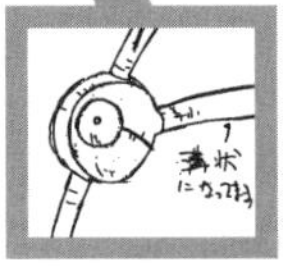

⬆ The Crow has three eyes and the character for "crow" is on its chin.

Foot

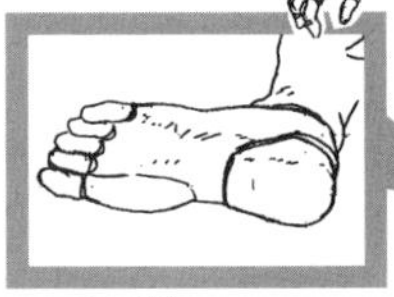

⬆ Very precisely constructed, right down to its pinkie toes.

Glove

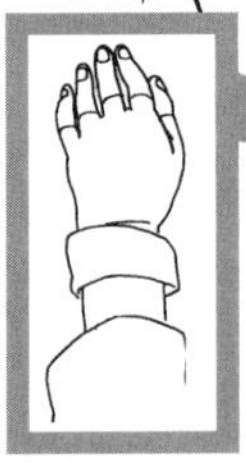

➡ Fingers are exposed to allow chakra release.

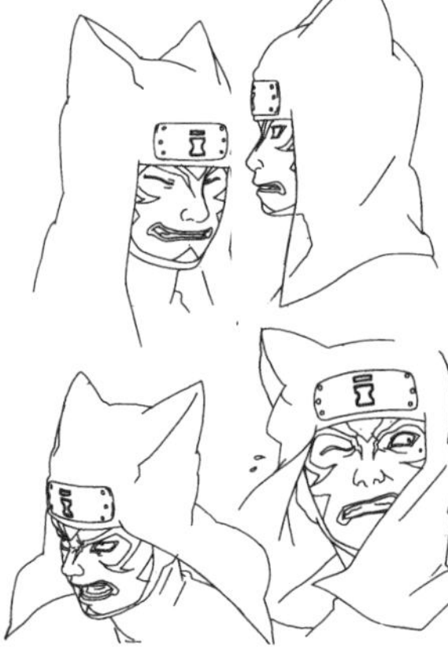

⬅ Kankuro's hood is pointy like the ears of some sort of animal, and the metal part of his headband is attached to the front.

Childhood days

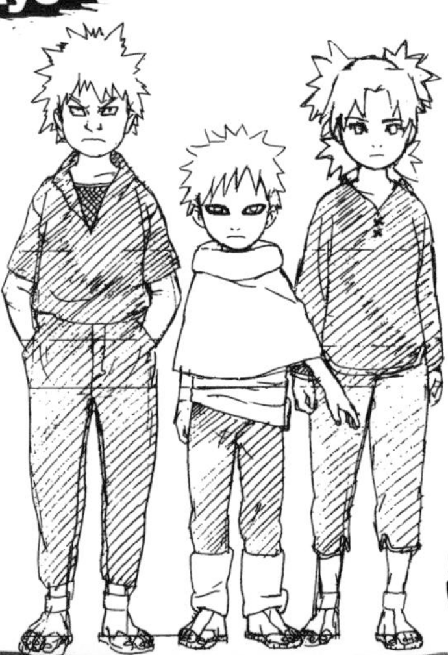

➡ The three siblings of the Sand in their childhood. Temari's hairstyle hasn't changed and Kankuro's face is plainly visible.

A full view of the Sand Village landscape

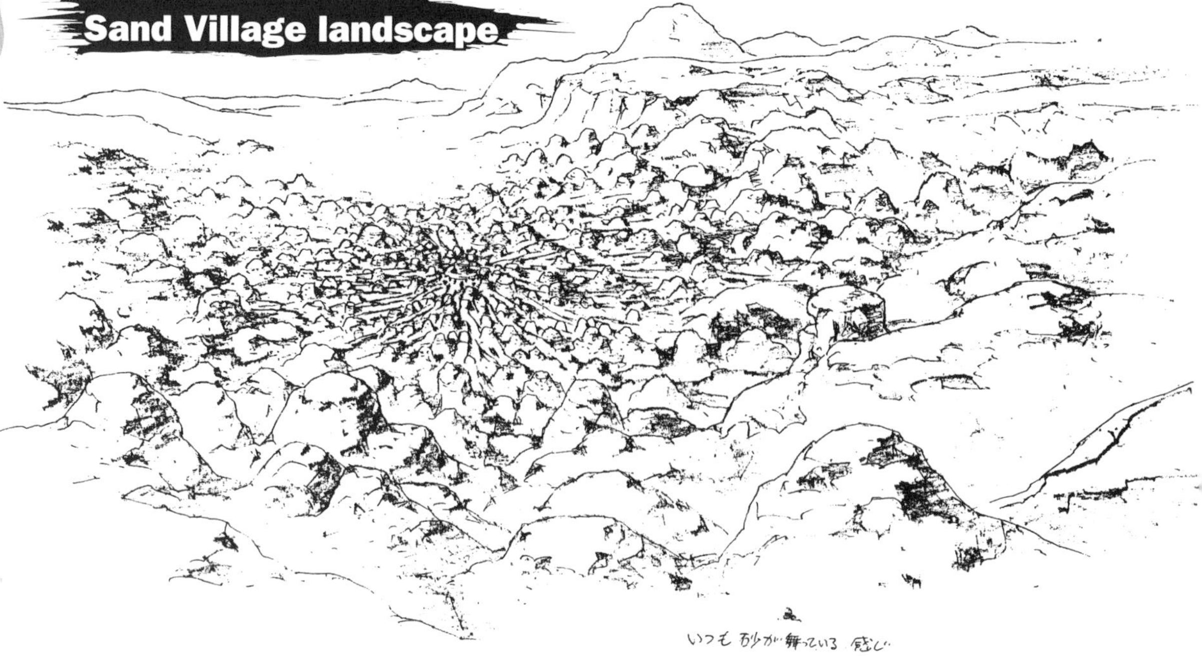
いつも砂が舞っている感じ

⬆ Most of the Land of Wind is barren, and rugged mountains and desert surround the Hidden Sand Village. This harsh, sandswept environment may be the reason this village produces so many expert ninja.

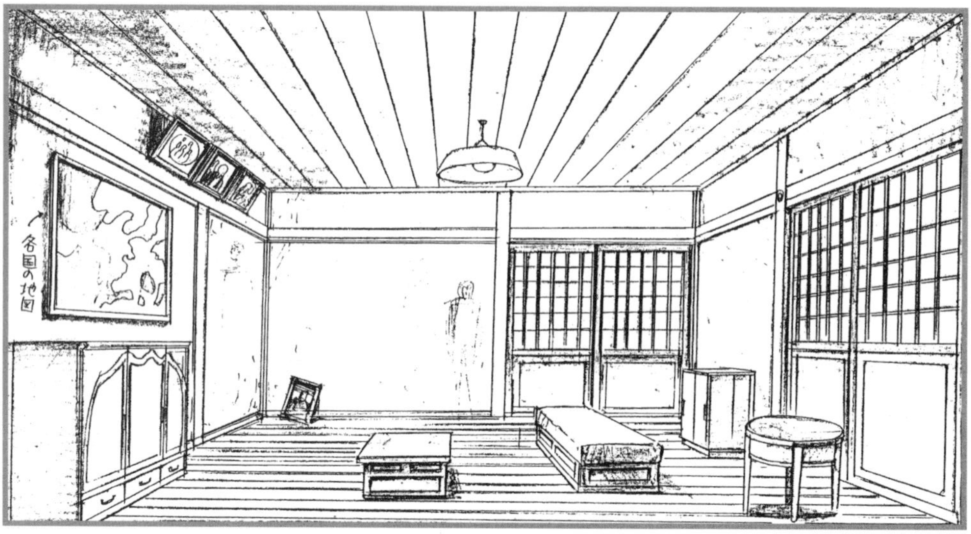
各国の地図

The room where Gaara and his team were assigned their mission

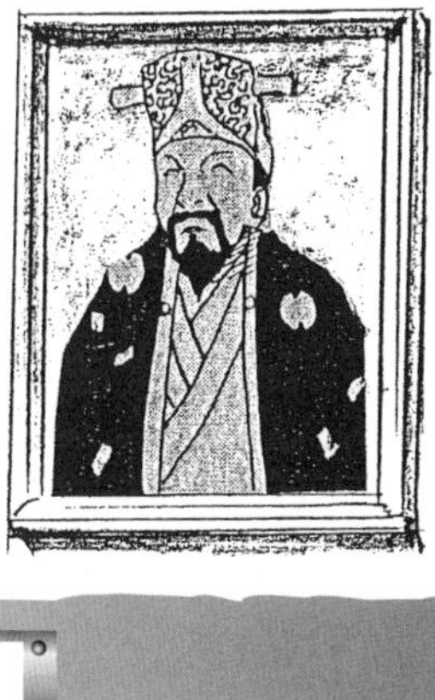

⬆ It was here that Baki assigned the three to the destruction of the Hidden Leaf Village. The empty atmosphere of this room seems to illustrate the decline of the Hidden Sand Village.

Portrait of the Lord of the Land of Wind

⬅ This lord has a very kind-looking face. He consistently promoted a demilitarization policy, causing the nation's military strength to drastically decline.

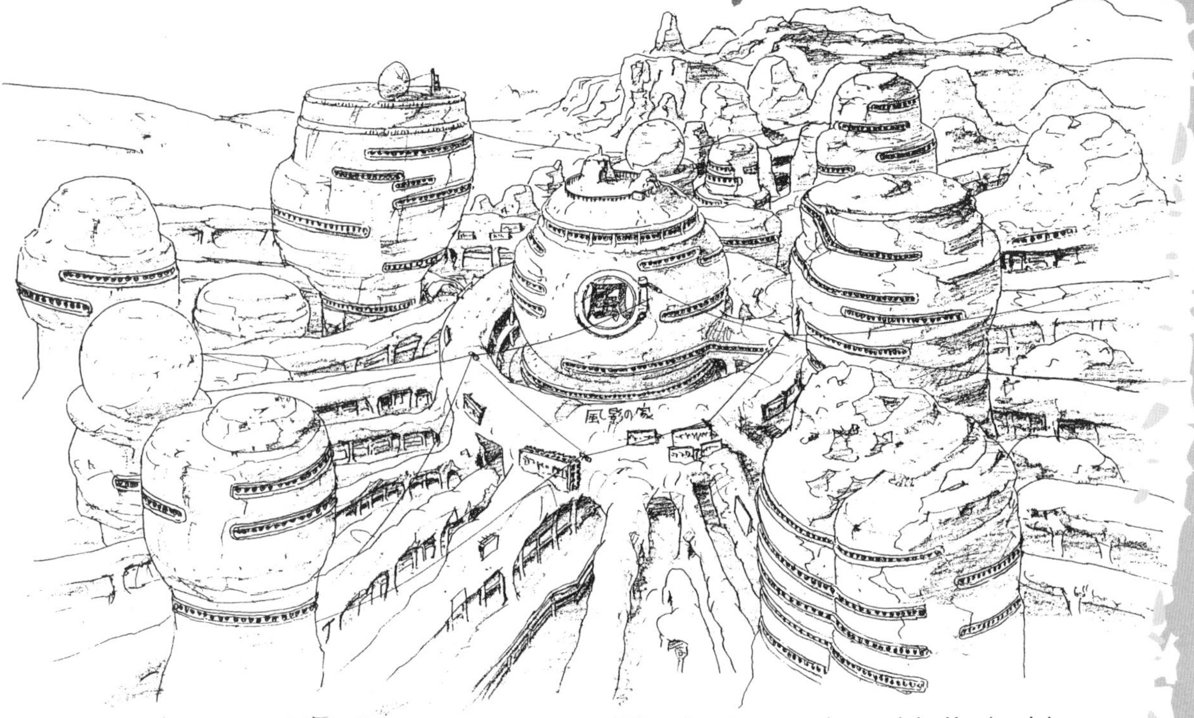
風影の家

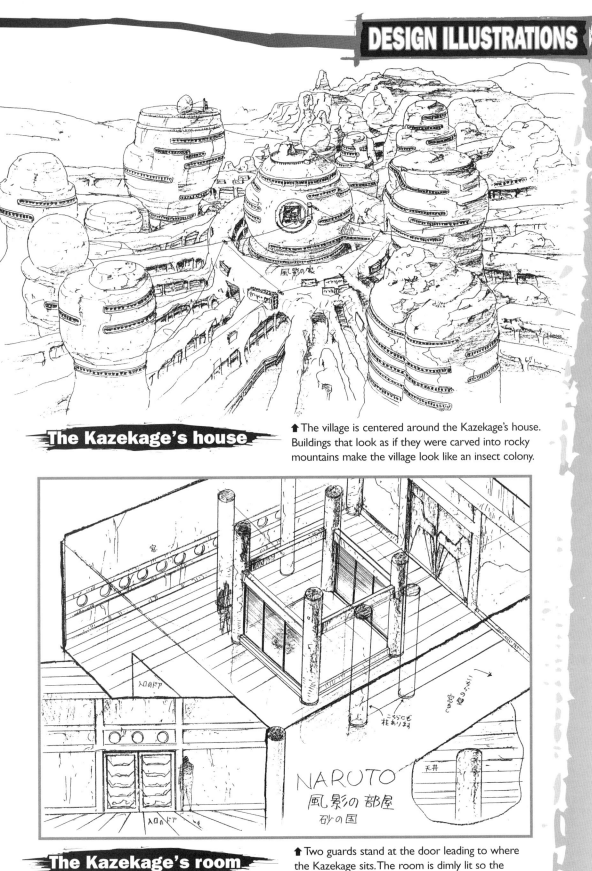

The Kazekage's house

⬆ The village is centered around the Kazekage's house. Buildings that look as if they were carved into rocky mountains make the village look like an insect colony.

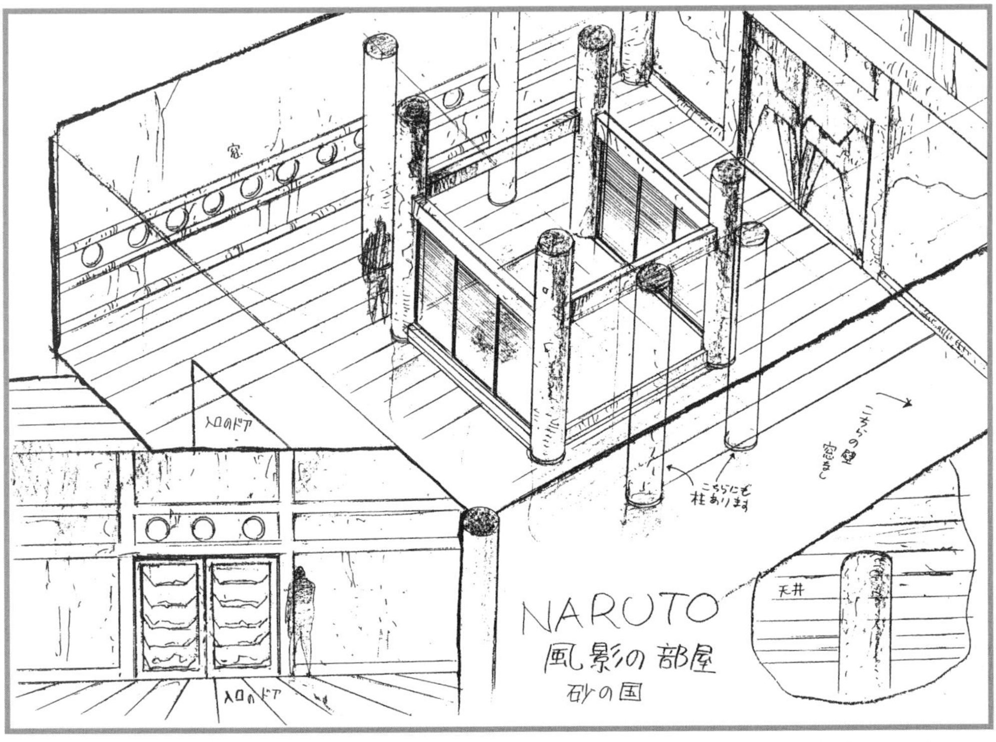
窓
入口のドア
こちらにも
柱あります
NARUTO
風影の部屋
砂の国
天井
入口のドア

The Kazekage's room

⬆ Two guards stand at the door leading to where the Kazekage sits. The room is dimly lit so the Kazekage's face cannot be seen clearly.

Shinobi of the Hidden Sound Village

Orochimaru established the Sound Village only recently. Although not very large, it consists of powerful, highly skilled ninja.

Kabuto Yakushi

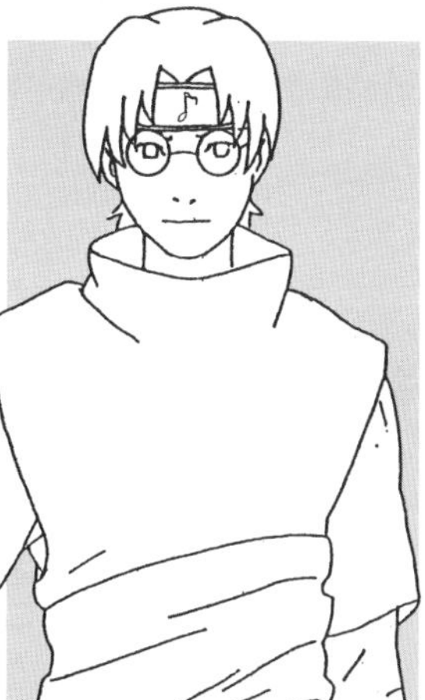

⬅⬇ Highly skilled and able, he is Orochimaru's right-hand man. He worked undercover for many years in the Hidden Leaf Village. His round glasses help conceal his true nature.

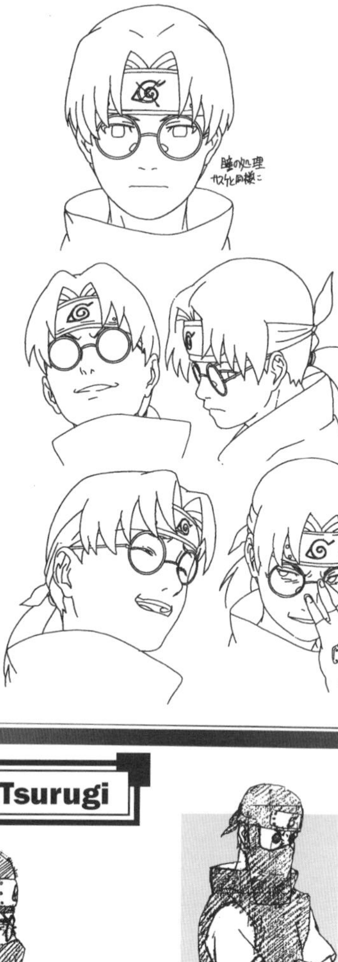

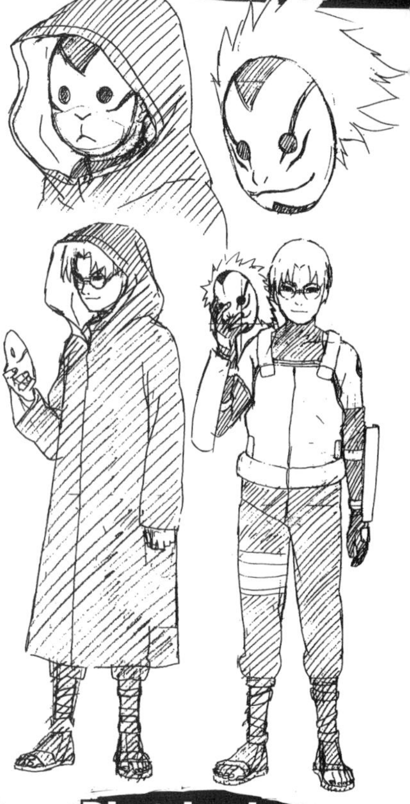

Disguised as Anbu Black Ops

⬆ Kabuto appeared in disguise twice during the Chunin Exams. Right: in the assault on Sasuke's hospital room. Left: in the Final Round Arena spectator area.

Misumi Tsurugi

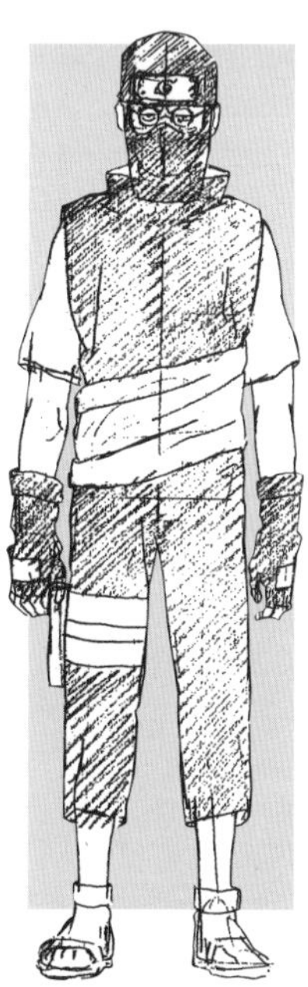

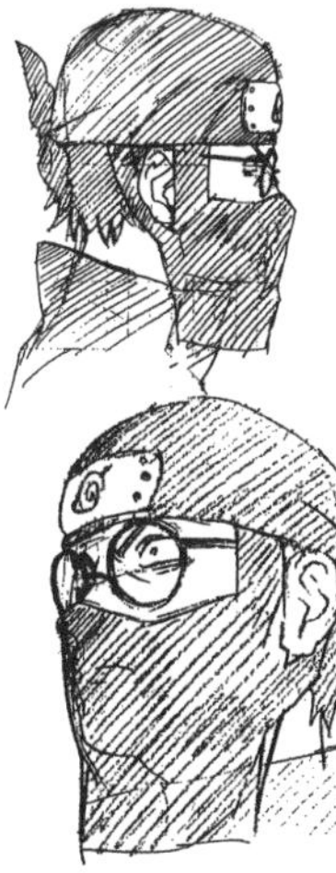

⬆ Covers his entire face, except for his eyes, with a mask. His body is extremely elastic.

Yoroi Akado

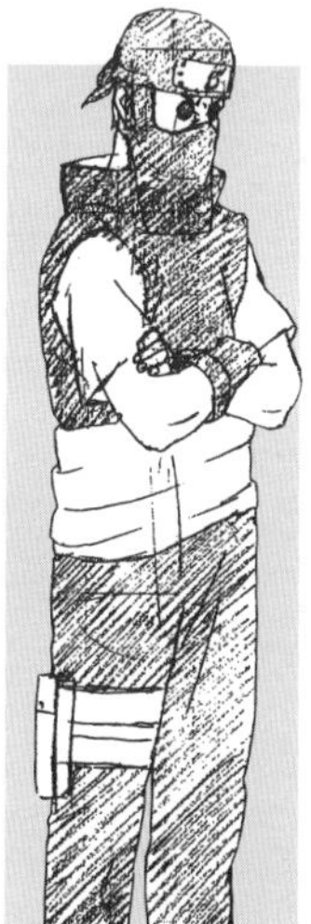

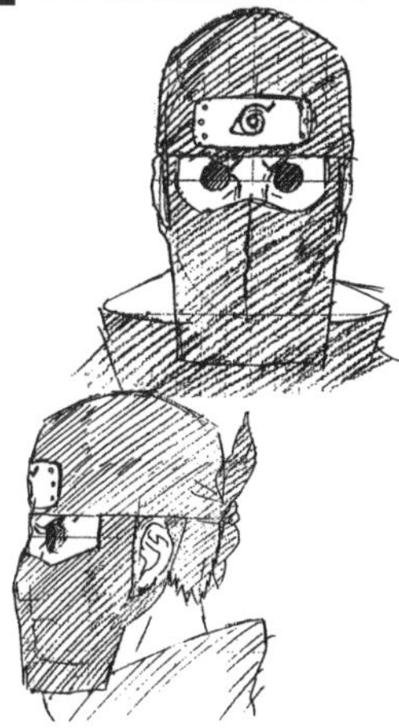

⬆ Like Misumi, he covers his head with a hood that has the metal part of his headband attached to it. He uses jutsu that absorbs his opponents' chakra.

The Sound Ninja Four

➡They snuck into the Leaf Village disguised as the Kazekage's attendants and deployed a Barrier Jutsu that even the Anbu Black Ops accents couldn't contend with. Their bizarre appearance concealed their true identity.

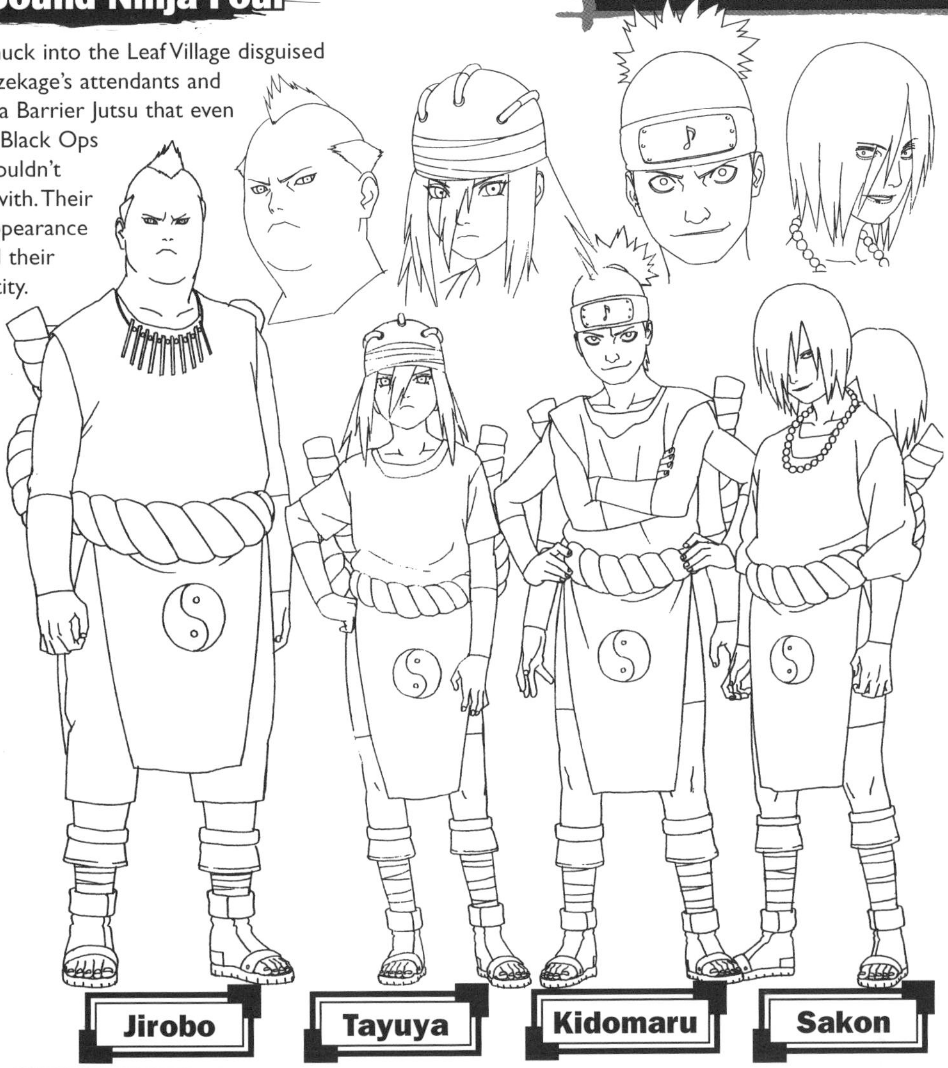
Jirobo
Tayuya
Kidomaru
Sakon

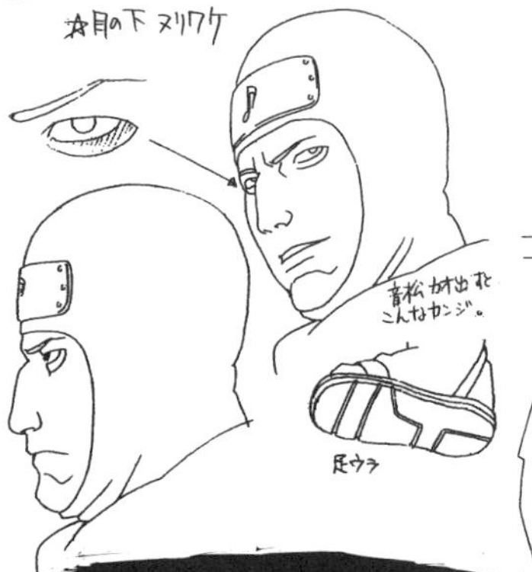
足ウラ

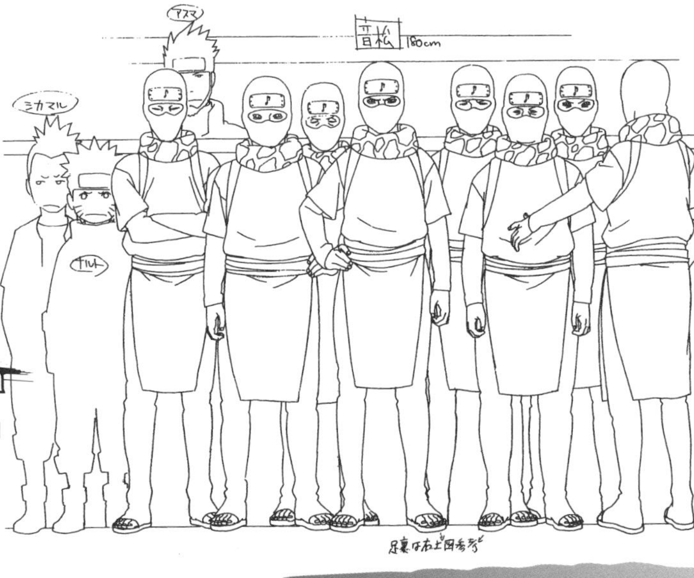
アスマ
180cm
シカマル
ナルト

Other Sound ninja

➡⬆ These Sound ninja participated in the attack on the Hidden Leaf Village. One distinctive feature they share is the snake-patterned cloth around their necks.

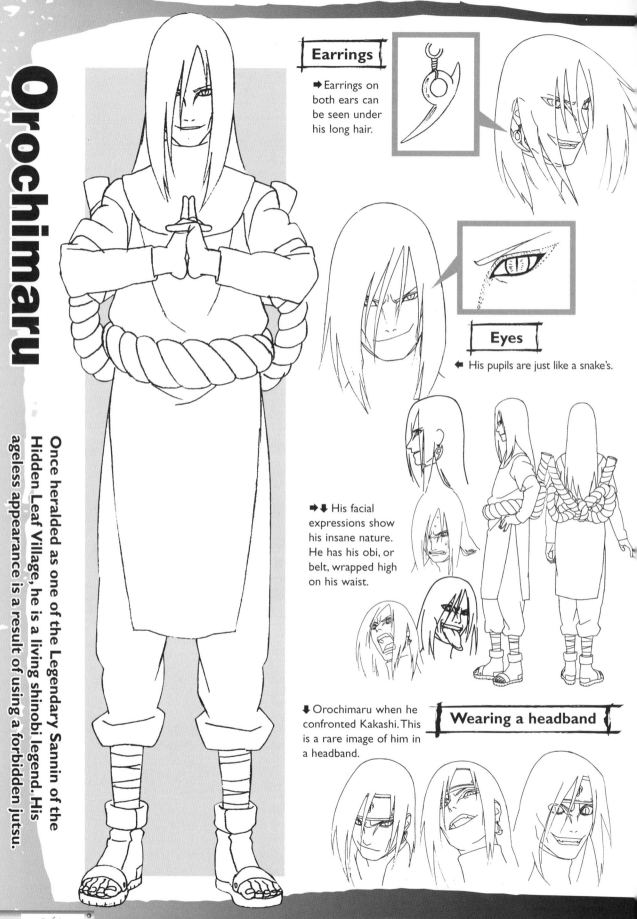

Orochimaru

Once heralded as one of the Legendary Sannin of the Hidden Leaf Village, he is a living shinobi legend. His ageless appearance is a result of using a forbidden jutsu.

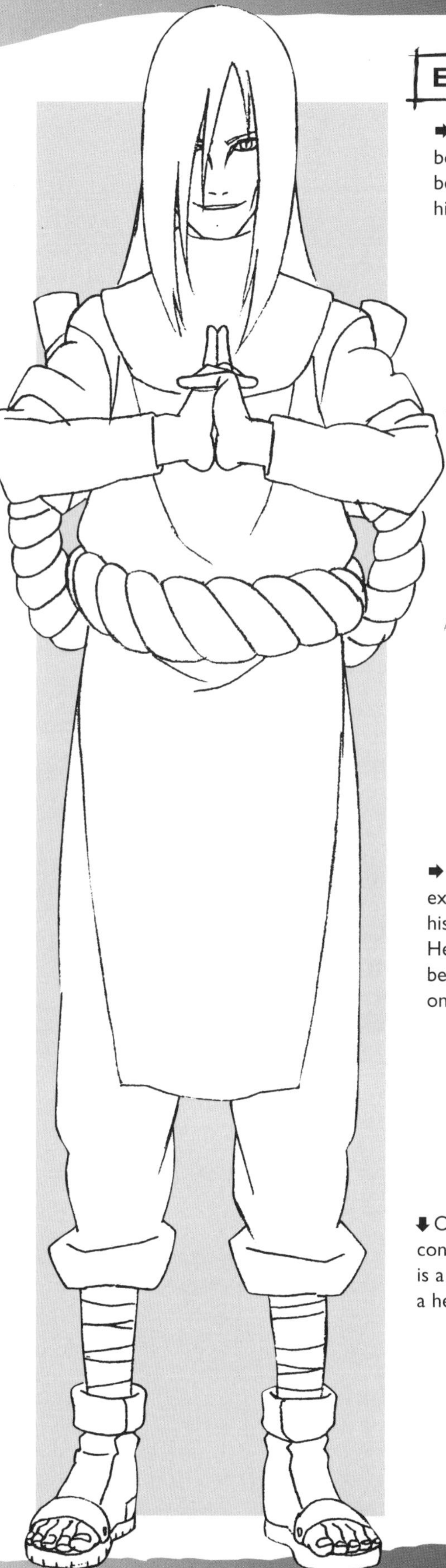

Earrings

➡Earrings on both ears can be seen under his long hair.

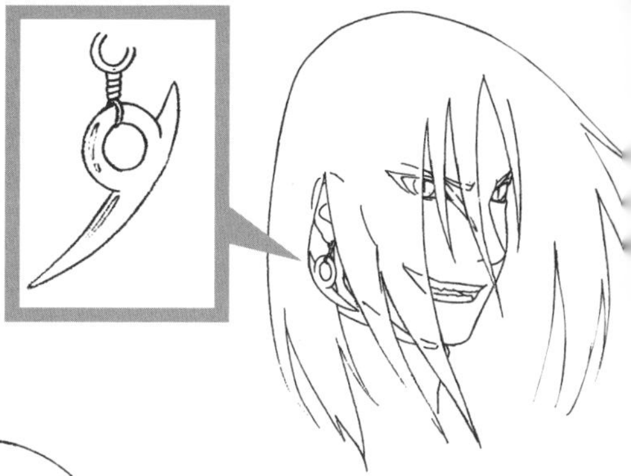

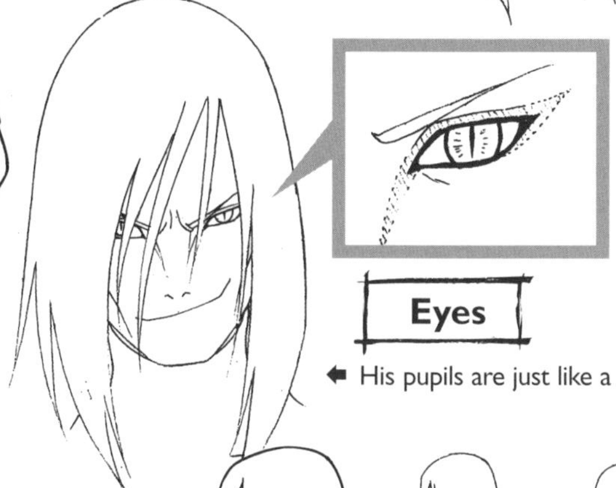

Eyes

⬅ His pupils are just like a snake's.

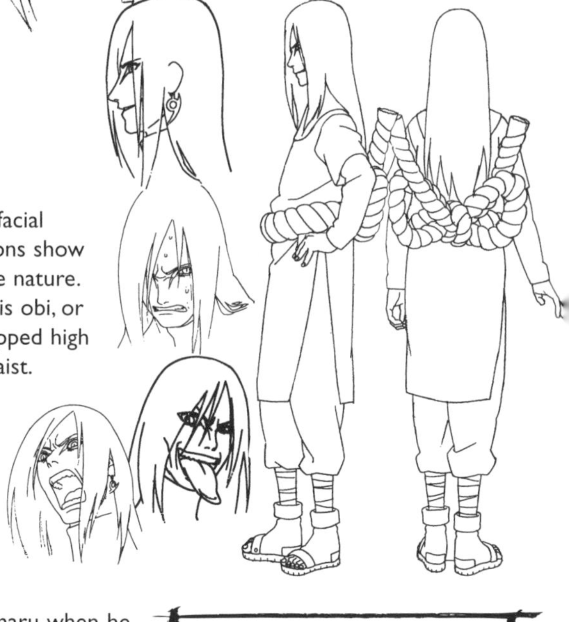

➡⬇ His facial expressions show his insane nature. He has his obi, or belt, wrapped high on his waist.

⬇Orochimaru when he confronted Kakashi. This is a rare image of him in a headband.

Wearing a headband

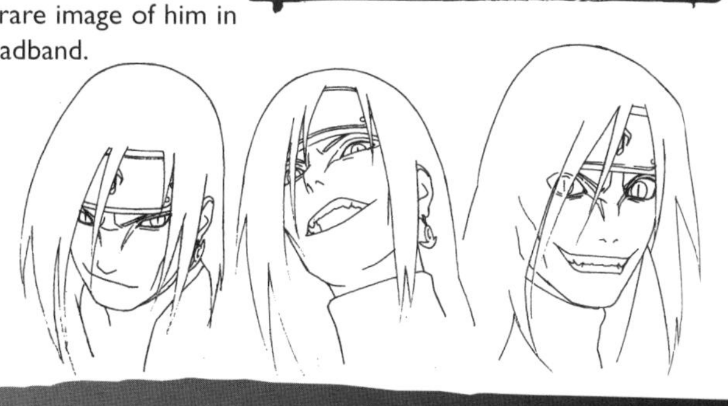

Snake Sword

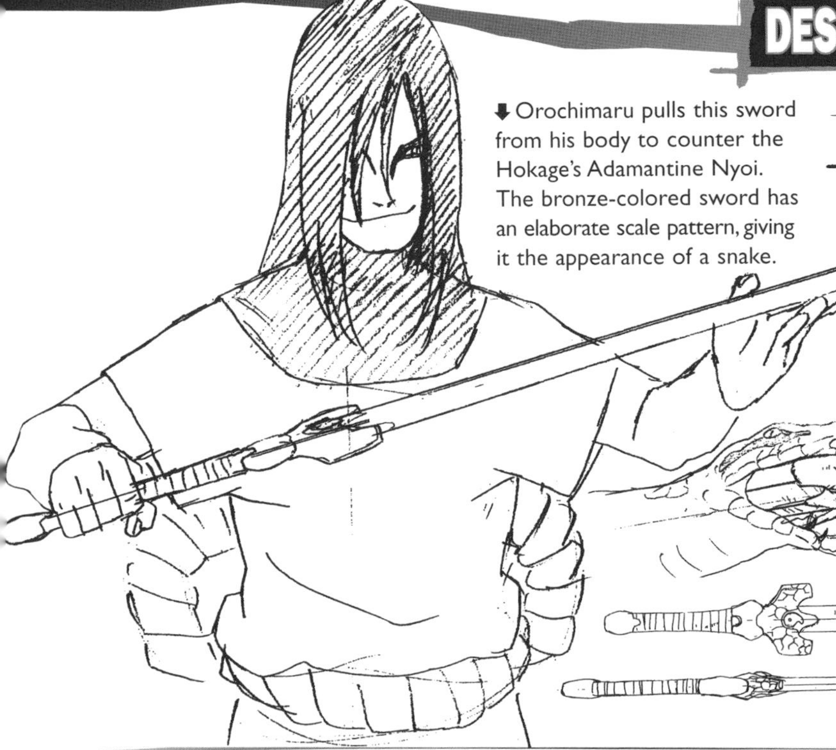

⬇ Orochimaru pulls this sword from his body to counter the Hokage's Adamantine Nyoi. The bronze-colored sword has an elaborate scale pattern, giving it the appearance of a snake.

⬇ Coated in snake slime.

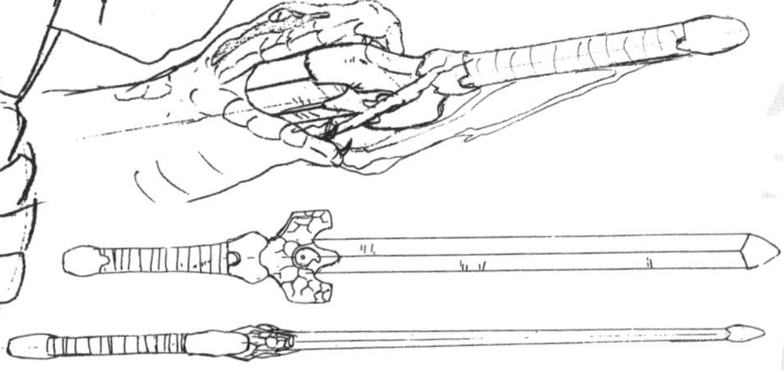

Disguised as a Sound ninja

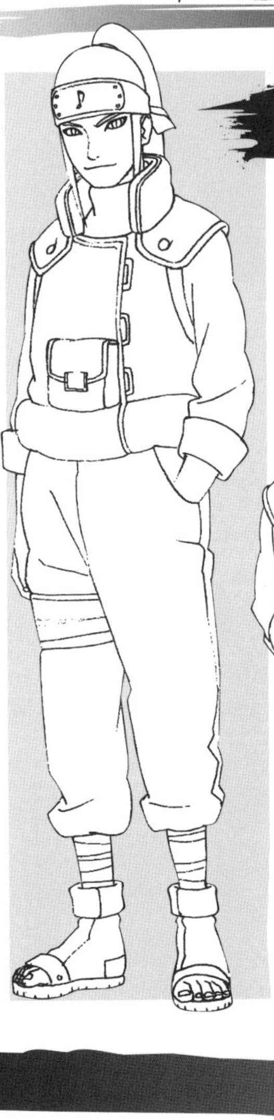

⬅⬇ He infiltrated the Leaf Village as a teacher for the Sound ninja participating in the exams. Black shading has been added all around his eyes.

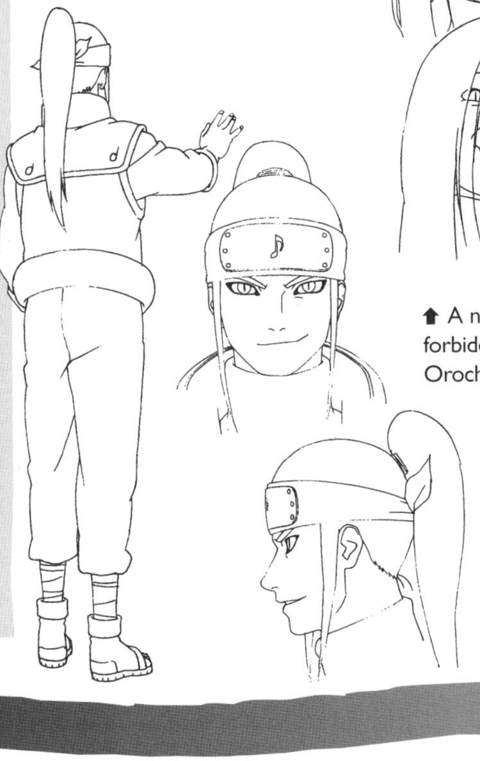

A new look

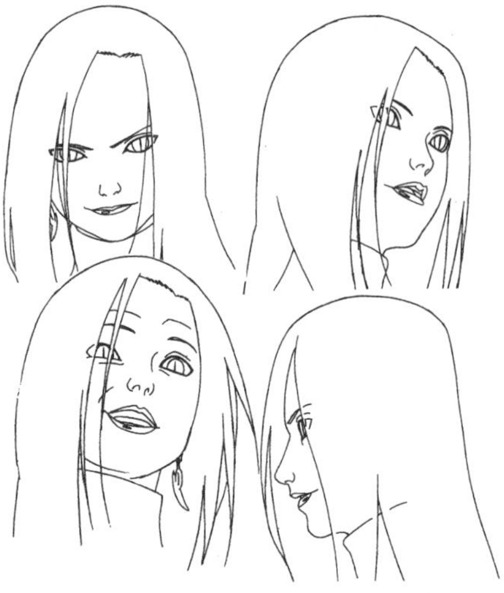

⬆ A new body, appropriated through a forbidden jutsu. The only trace left of Orochimaru is his ice-cold eyes.

Reanimation Jutsu

The First and Second Hokage were summoned by Orochimaru using the forbidden Reanimation Jutsu. With their souls having been wiped out, they were nothing more than murderous puppets unleashed upon the Third Hokage.

The First Hokage

⬇ ➡ He is the founder of the Hidden Leaf Village. His outfit is more like a suit of armor than contemporary ninja wear.

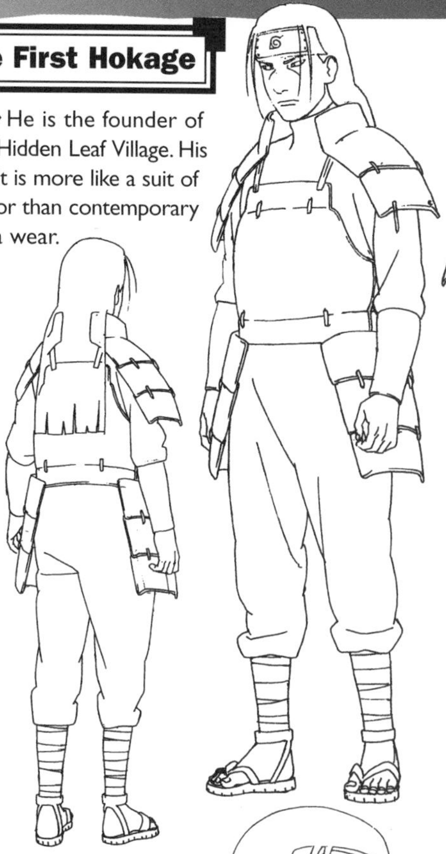

The Second Hokage

⬅⬇ The younger brother of the First Hokage and the founder of the Ninja Academy.

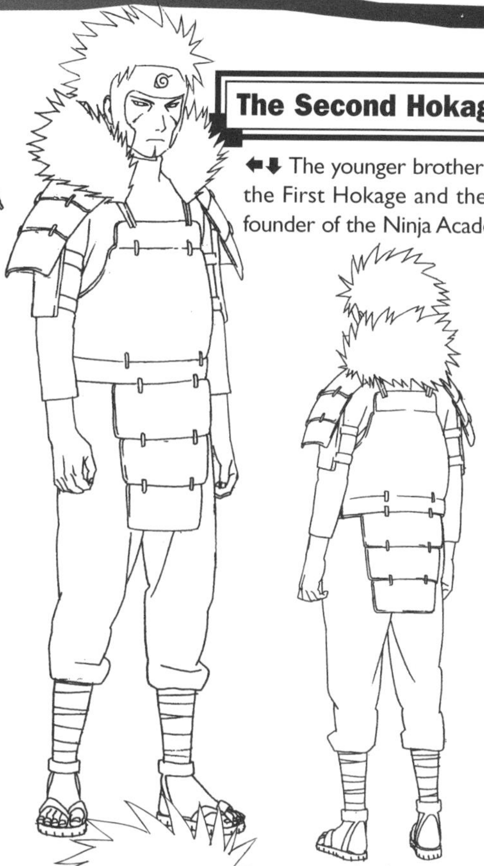

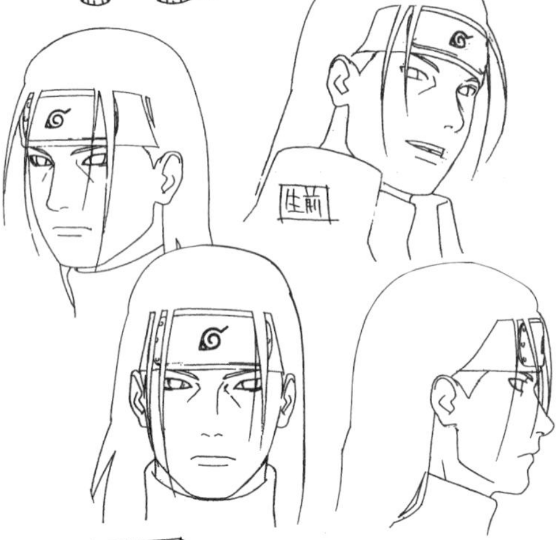
生前

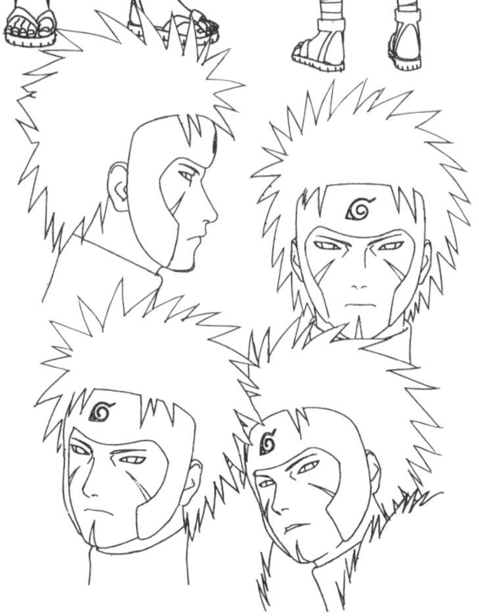

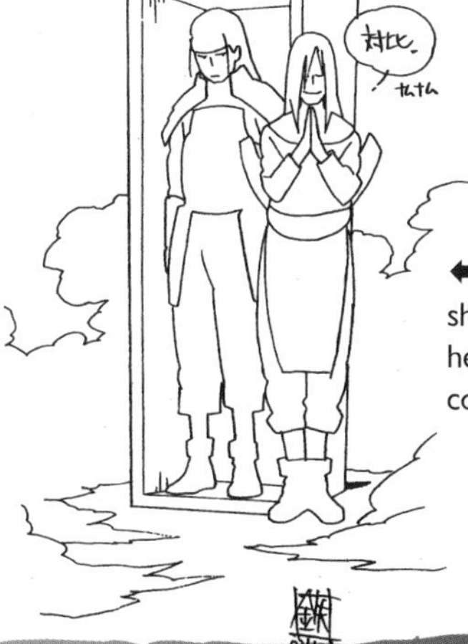

⬅ Its thickness shows how heavy-duty this coffin is.

Coffin

⬇ Coffins of the Hokage summoned by the reanimation jutsu. Characters for "first" and "second" are on each lid.

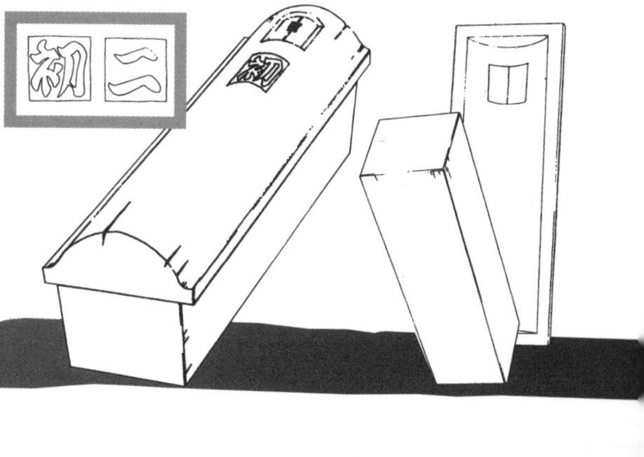
初
二

The slums

Countless desires cross paths in the slums. Houses are packed together, obstructing the sky and sunlight.

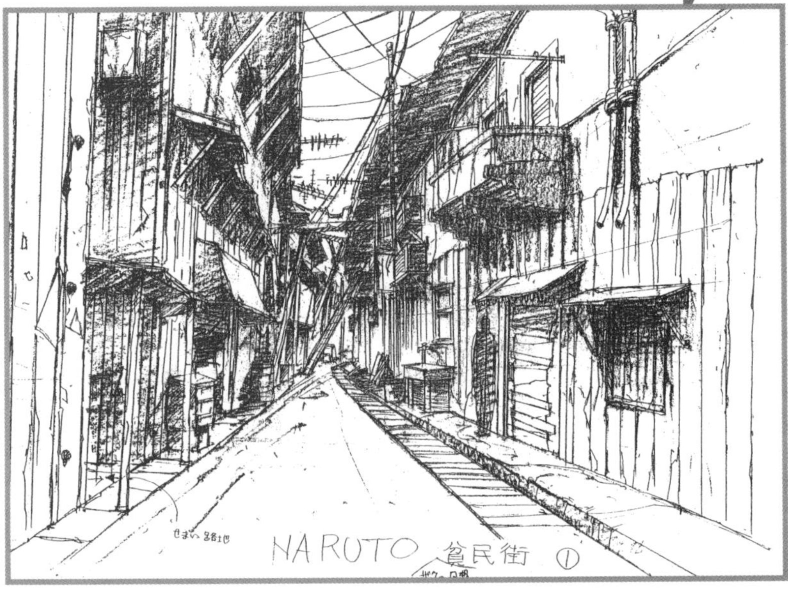
NARUTO 貧民街 ①

⬆ Pipes and electric wires run randomly all over this chaotic scene.

Zaku as a child

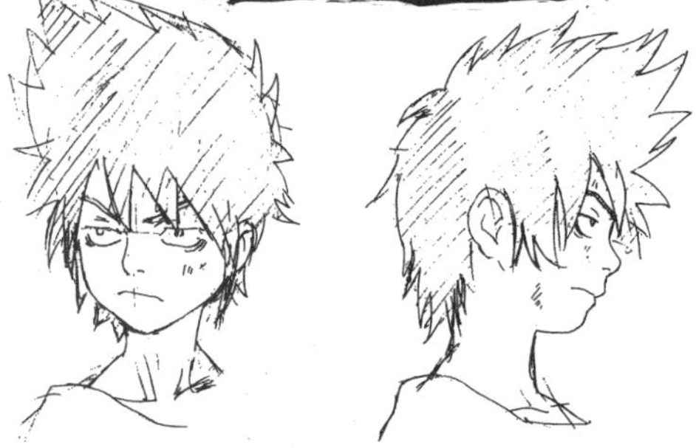

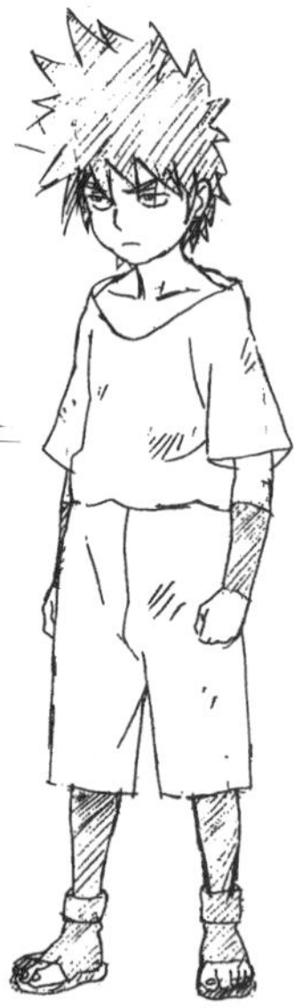

⬆ Clenched fists and a grim stare. Zaku was drawn to Orochimaru's power because he trusted no one.

Orochimaru in a kimono

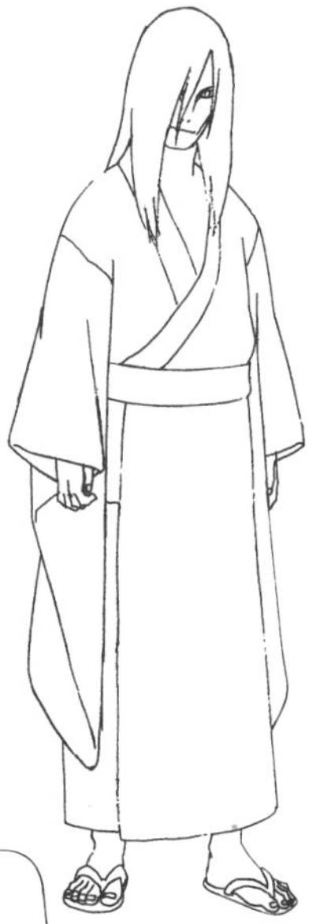

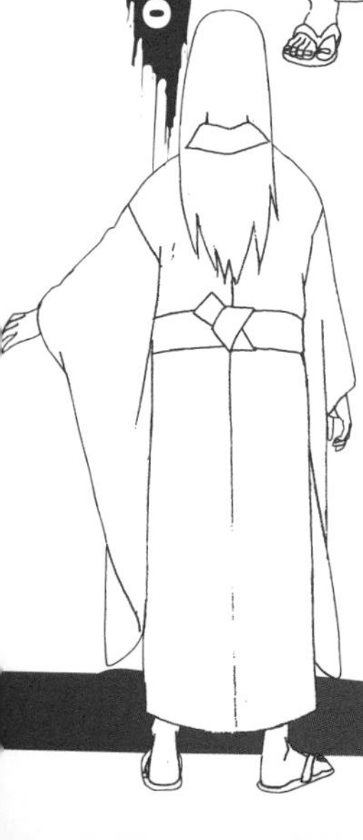

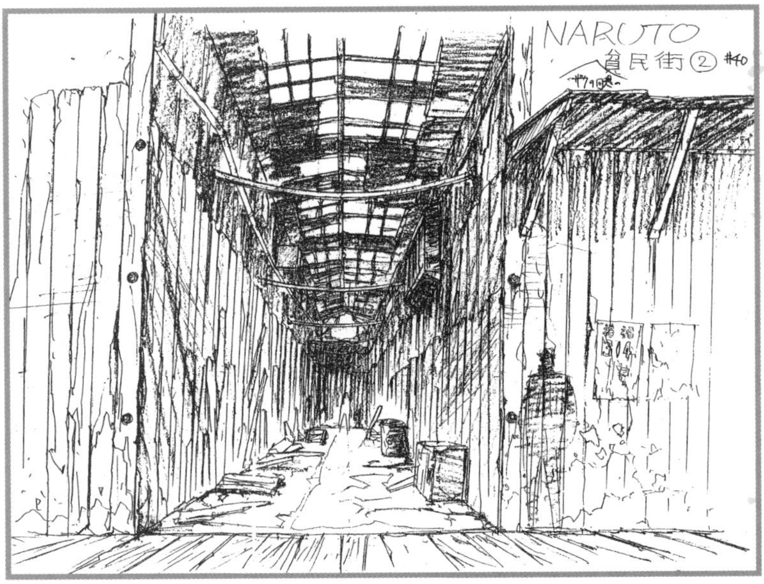
NARUTO
貧民街 ② #40

⬆ Zaku encounters Orochimaru after Zaku was beaten by the townspeople.

Naruto's Rapid-Fire Digest of Every Episode

Check out my exploits from the Third Exam preliminaries to the battle against Gaara!

Relive all my awesome performances! Believe it!

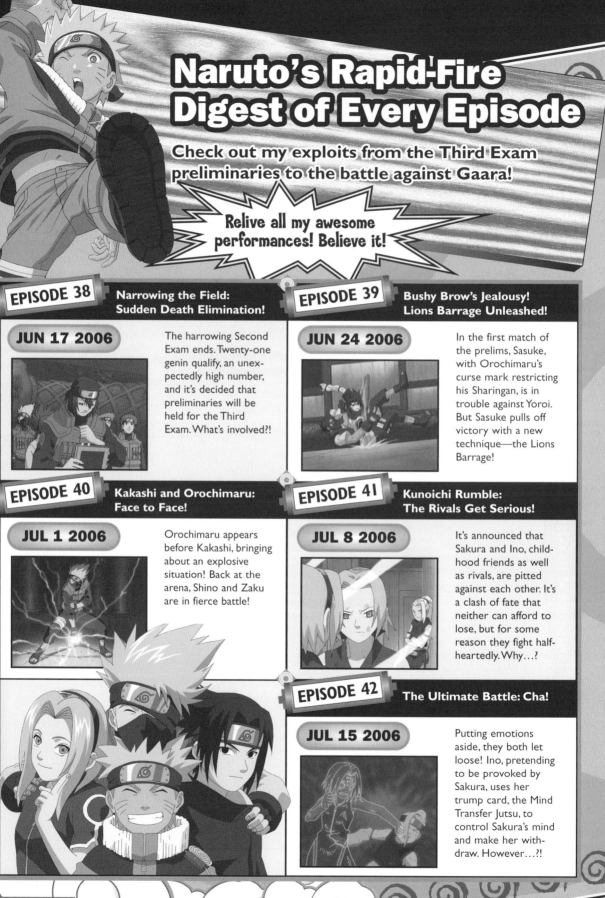

EPISODE 38 — Narrowing the Field: Sudden Death Elimination!

JUN 17 2006

The harrowing Second Exam ends. Twenty-one genin qualify, an unexpectedly high number, and it's decided that preliminaries will be held for the Third Exam. What's involved?!

EPISODE 39 — Bushy Brow's Jealousy! Lions Barrage Unleashed!

JUN 24 2006

In the first match of the prelims, Sasuke, with Orochimaru's curse mark restricting his Sharingan, is in trouble against Yoroi. But Sasuke pulls off victory with a new technique—the Lions Barrage!

EPISODE 40 — Kakashi and Orochimaru: Face to Face!

JUL 1 2006

Orochimaru appears before Kakashi, bringing about an explosive situation! Back at the arena, Shino and Zaku are in fierce battle!

EPISODE 41 — Kunoichi Rumble: The Rivals Get Serious!

JUL 8 2006

It's announced that Sakura and Ino, childhood friends as well as rivals, are pitted against each other. It's a clash of fate that neither can afford to lose, but for some reason they fight halfheartedly. Why…?

EPISODE 42 — The Ultimate Battle: Cha!

JUL 15 2006

Putting emotions aside, they both let loose! Ino, pretending to be provoked by Sakura, uses her trump card, the Mind Transfer Jutsu, to control Sakura's mind and make her withdraw. However…?!

EPISODE 43 — Killer Kunoichi and a Shaky Shikamaru

JUL 22 2006

Tenten takes on Temari with her multitude of ninja weapons, but all her attacks are stymied by Temari's giant fan. How does Tenten counter when all her weapons are stopped cold?

EPISODE 44 — Akamaru Unleashed! Who's Top Dog Now?

JUL 29 2006

At last Naruto Uzumaki's number comes up! His opponent is Kiba Inuzuka and his ninja dog partner Akamaru! Right from the start Naruto is baffled by their quick, synchronized attacks. But...?!

EPISODE 45 — Surprise Attack! Naruto's Secret Weapon!

AUG 5 2006

Kiba and Akamaru take food pills that instantly double their chakra and they go on the offensive! Naruto discovers their weak point and counters with a cunning plan! The result of this battle...?

EPISODE 46 — Byakugan Battle: Hinata Grows Bold!

AUG 5 2006

The eighth match, Neji vs. Hinata, is made personal by the feud between the main and side branches of the Hyuga Clan. Hinata is overwhelmed by Neji's power but faces up to him with some encouragement from Naruto, the person she admires most.

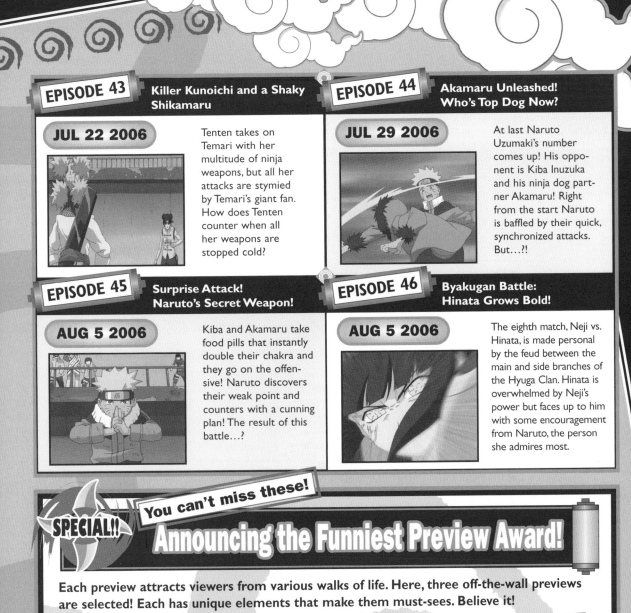

SPECIAL!! You can't miss these! Announcing the Funniest Preview Award!

Each preview attracts viewers from various walks of life. Here, three off-the-wall previews are selected! Each has unique elements that make them must-sees. Believe it!

Trash Talk Award

Naruto, constantly on the defensive against Kiba in this episode, pulls off an impressive counterattack in this preview that aired at the end of Episode 44. His provocation of Kiba makes viewers cheer! Give him a round of applause!

Hysterics Award

Sakura's enthusiasm to visit the hospitalized Sasuke is tightly condensed in this approximately 30-second preview that aired at the end of Episode 54. But isn't she getting a little too worked up?

Slapstick Award

This preview aired at the end of Episode 58. Naruto, on the brink of being late for his match, vents his frustration at Konohamaru. The amazing tempo of anger is impressive. And the punch line is perfect!

EPISODE 47 — A Failure Stands Tall!

AUG 12 2006

Hinata confronts Neji head-on! Hinata's chakra flow is cut off by Neji's strikes at her chakra points. What will the cornered Hinata try next…?!

EPISODE 48 — Gaara vs. Rock Lee! The Power of Youth Explodes!

AUG 19 2006

The ninth match is between Gaara, the elite ninja of the Sand Village, and Rock Lee, the taijutsu specialist. Making full use of his astounding speed, Lee pins down Gaara, who manipulates sand as if it were an extension of his body. But…!

EPISODE 49 — Lee's Hidden Strength: Forbidden Secret Jutsu!

AUG 26 2006

Lee attacks with the forbidden jutsu Primary Lotus, but it's futile against Gaara's Sand Armor defense. Even worse, Gaara, as if playing with a toy, continues to assault the exhausted Lee.

EPISODE 50 — The Fifth Gate: A Splendid Ninja Is Born!

SEP 2 2006

The Lotus of the Hidden Leaf Village blooms twice! To protect his ninja way, Lee forces his Inner Gates open and rains down super high-speed taijutsu attacks that even Gaara's sand can't keep up with!

EPISODE 51 — A Shadow in Darkness: Danger Approaches Sasuke

SEP 9 2006

After a series of intense battles, the prelims end and the lineup for the Final Rounds are announced! Orochimaru's subordinate, Kabuto, launches an assault on the unconscious Sasuke! Danger closes in!

EPISODE 52 — Ebisu Returns: Naruto's Toughest Training Yet

SEP 16 2006

In preparation for the Final Rounds, Kakashi introduces Naruto to the elite tutor Ebisu! Ebisu challenges the reluctant Naruto to a catch-me-if-you-can chase!

EPISODE 53 — Long Time No See: Jiraiya Returns!

SEP 30 2006

While training at the Hot Spring District, Naruto and Ebisu encounter a Peeping Tom. Ebisu tries to administer justice, but ends up knocked silly for his trouble! Who on earth is this man with the power to instantly K.O. Ebisu?

EPISODE 54 — The Summoning Jutsu: The Wisdom of the Toad Sage!

OCT 10 2006

The pervy sage turns out to be one of the legendary Sannin, Jiraiya. With his best technique, Sexy Jutsu, Naruto succeeds in getting Jiraiya to train him. What training lies ahead?

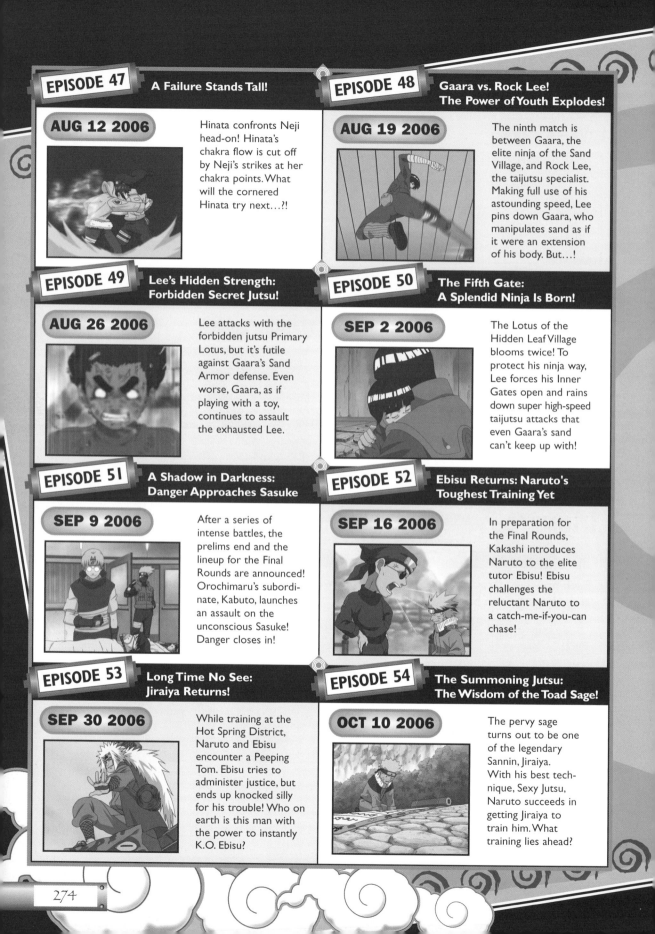

EPISODE 55 A Feeling of Yearning, A Flower Full of Hope

NOV 4 2006

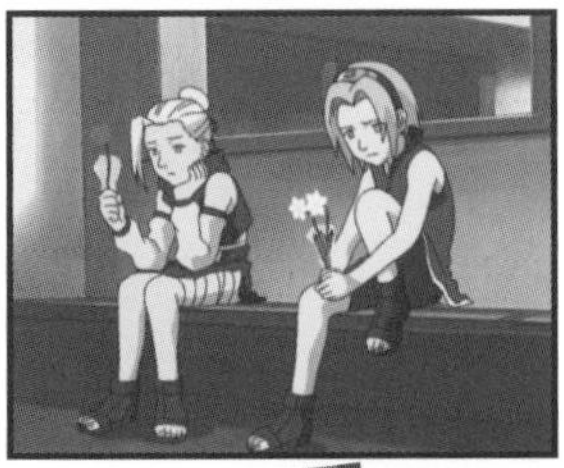

Worried about Sasuke's condition, Sakura decides to visit him in the hospital. On the way she drops by the flower shop and encounters Ino, who's in charge of the shop... Are they about to go for round two?!

EPISODE 56 Live or Die: Risk It All to Win It All!

NOV 4 2006

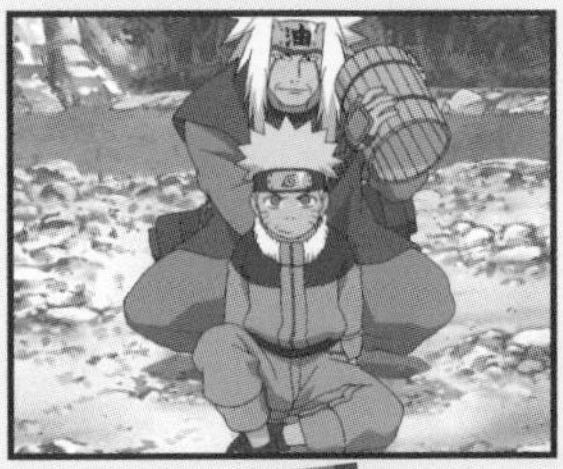

Seeing Naruto's lack of progress, Jiraiya makes up his mind to do something about it. He takes Naruto to eat ramen at Ichiraku and makes him confess his feelings to Sakura. What kind of training is this?

EPISODE 57 He Flies! He Jumps! He Lurks! Chief Toad Appears!

NOV 4 2006

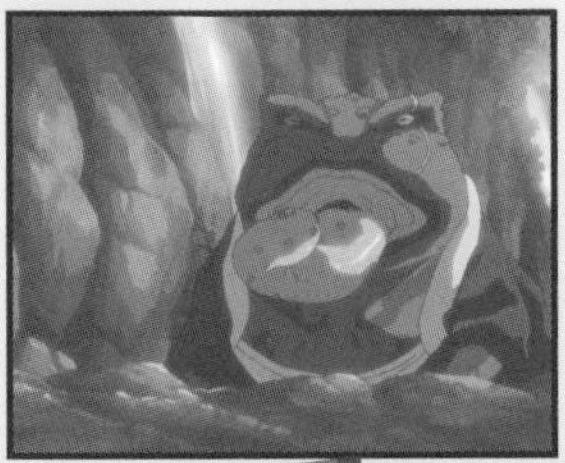

Finally Naruto succeeds in drawing out the chakra of the Nine-Tailed Fox and masters the Summoning Jutsu. But what he gets is a big toad with an even bigger attitude named Gamabunta that scares the pants off him…!

EPISODE 58 Hospital Besieged: The Evil Hand Revealed!

NOV 11 2006

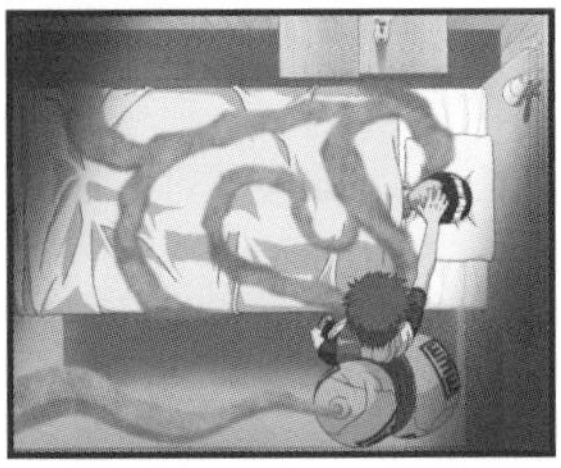

Gaara sneaks into Lee's hospital room to finish him off. Naruto and Shikamaru arrive in the nick of time to prevent the heinous act, but Gaara directs his murderous intent at the two of them…

EPISODE 59 The Final Rounds: Rush to the Battle Arena!

NOV 18 2006

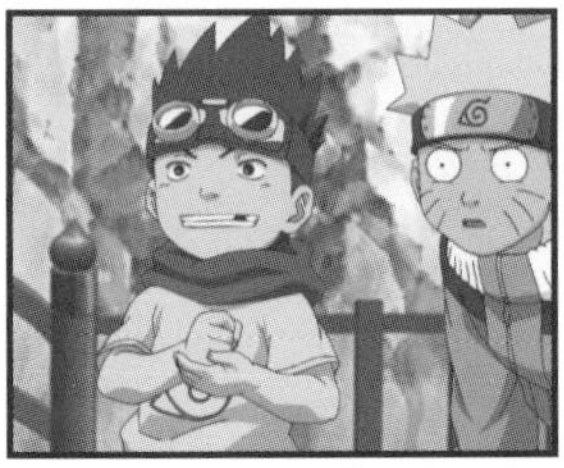

Dropping by the training field makes Naruto late for his match. While rushing to the arena he encounters Konohamaru, who tells Naruto he knows all the shortcuts and to leave it to him! But is this really a good idea?

EPISODE 60 Byakugan vs. Shadow Clone Jutsu!

NOV 18 2006

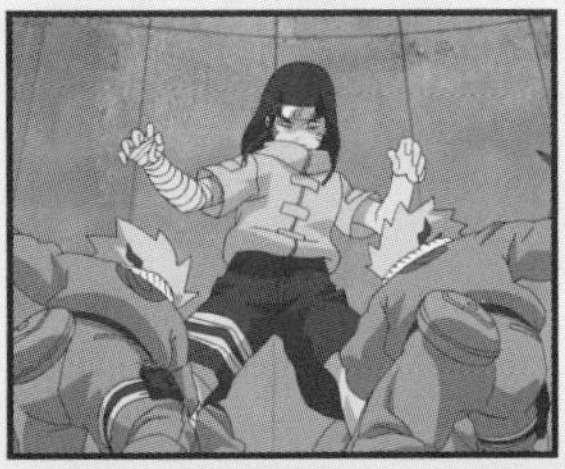

The Final Round starts with Sasuke still a no-show! Naruto can't stand Neji's insults! Tensions are high right from the first fight!

Anime Exclusive!

SPECIAL!!

Episodes from the eve of the Final Round!

How did the genin finalists spend their nervous night before the finals? Enjoy exclusive anime scenes you won't find in the manga!

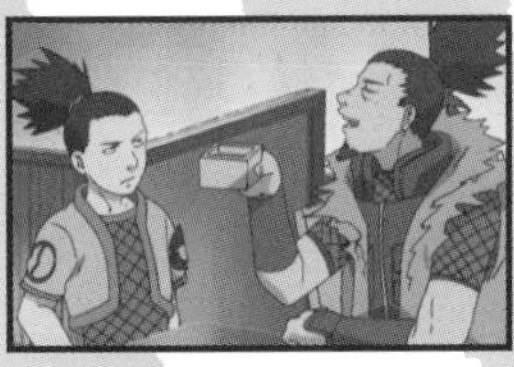

Shikamaru goes to pick up his father. Ino's and Choji's fathers also show up!

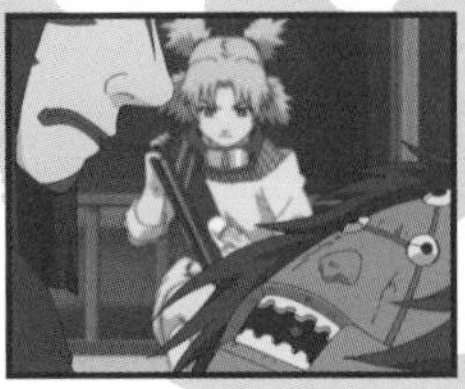

Temari and Kankuro are completely absorbed with ninja tool maintenance in their room.

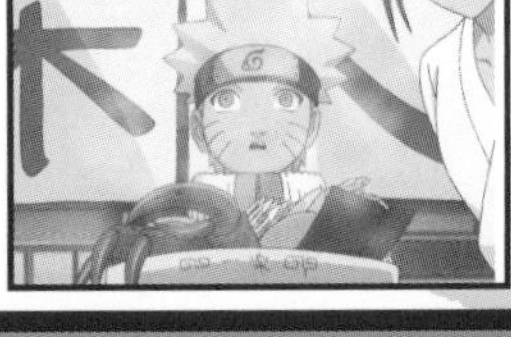

Naruto goes to Ichiraku Ramen alone. What does the owner offer the disheartened Naruto?!

EPISODE 61 Ultimate Defense: Zero Blind Spot!

NOV 18 2006

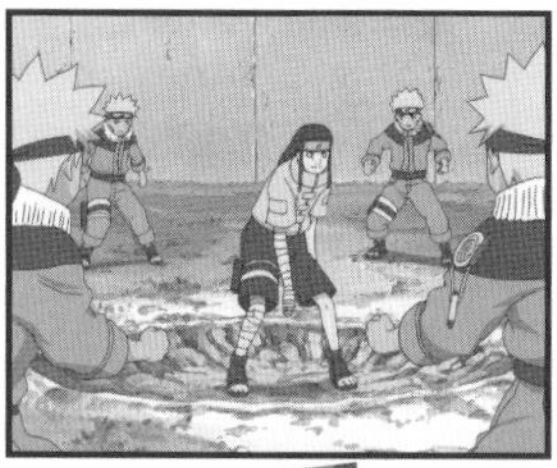

Neji's Byakugan is out of Naruto's league, and Naruto's best move, Shadow Clone Jutsu, isn't having much effect! But Naruto is relentless in his attacks, and Neji responds with a secret Hyuga Clan technique: Rotation! This really exhibits the skill gap between them.

EPISODE 62 A Failure's True Power!

NOV 25 2006

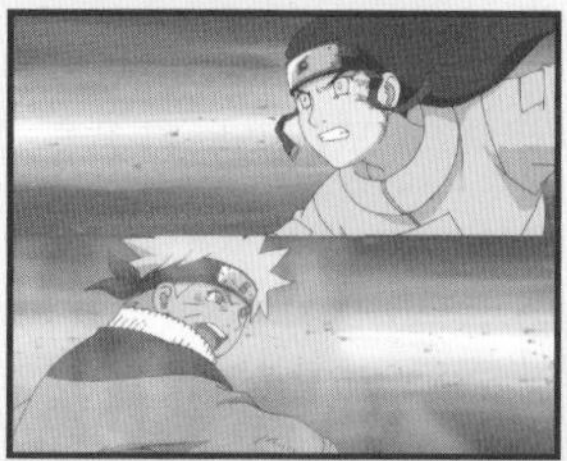

Naruto is unable to manipulate his chakra after Neji's strikes at his chakra points. The winner appears obvious, and Neji is confident in victory until Naruto releases the chakra of the Nine-Tailed Fox!

EPISODE 63 Hit It or Quit It: The Final Rounds Get Complicated!

NOV 25 2006

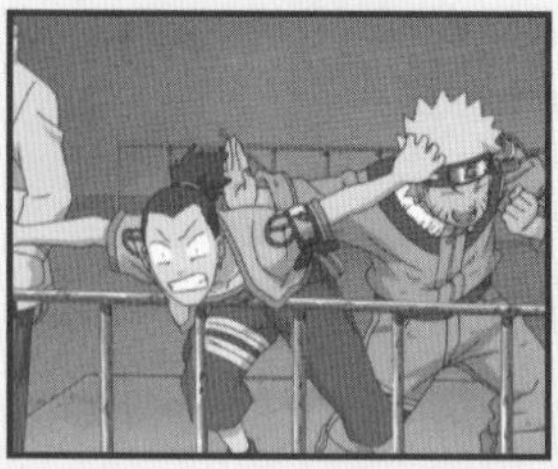

Kankuro withdraws, making the next match Shikamaru vs. Temari. Temari is on the battlefield and ready to rumble, but Shikamaru intends to forfeit—until Naruto pushes him onto the battlefield and…?!

EPISODE 64 Zero Motivation: The Guy with Cloud Envy!

DEC 2 2006

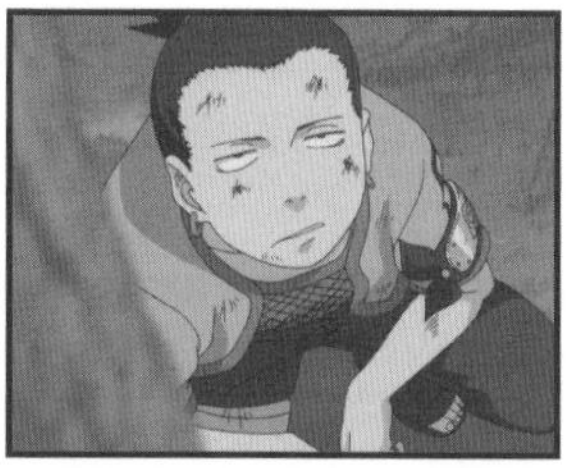

Temari persistently attacks Shikamaru, who looks up vacantly at the sky, showing no interest in the match at all. Shikamaru seems to be just running around avoiding the attacks, but he's got a plan!

SPECIAL!! Choji chows down!

Presenting must-have munchies for those with, ahem, big appetites!

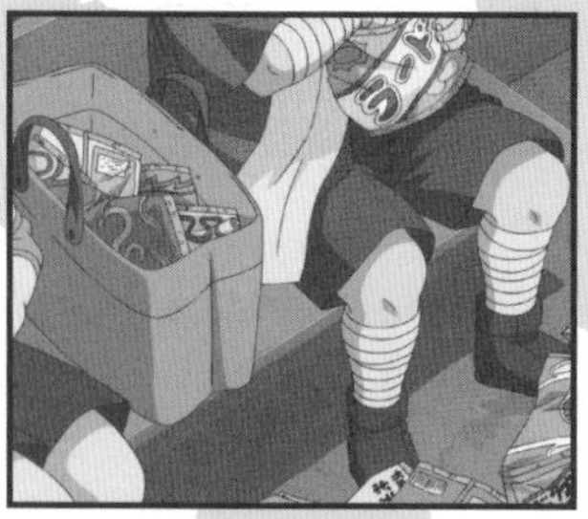

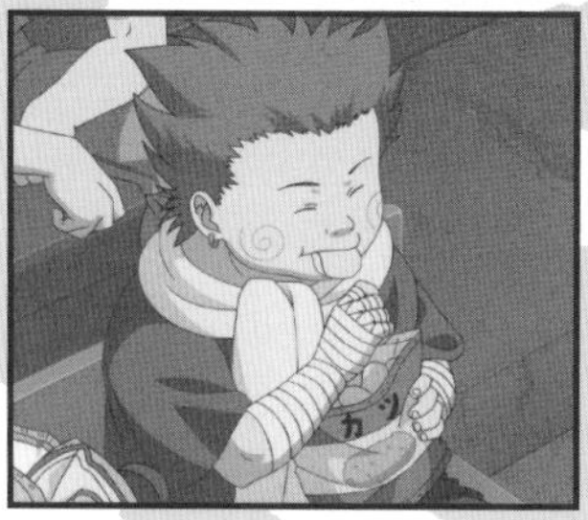

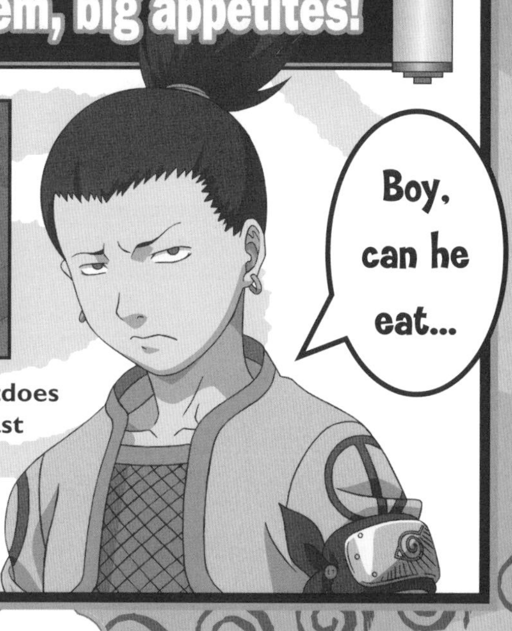
Boy, can he eat...

When it comes to a passion for eating, no one outdoes Choji Akimichi. Just a glance and we can see at least 10 bags of munchies he devoured while watching the Final Round. With flavors like lard, cutlet, fatty pork, ribs and consommé, they all sound pretty greasy. What a glutton!

EPISODE 65 — Dancing Leaf, Squirming Sand

DEC 9 2006

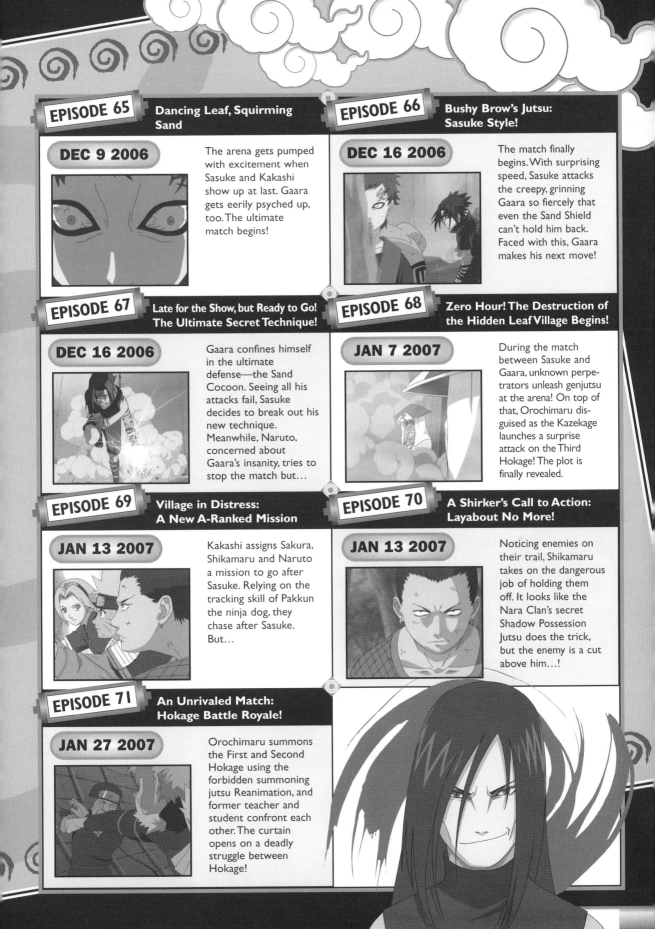

The arena gets pumped with excitement when Sasuke and Kakashi show up at last. Gaara gets eerily psyched up, too. The ultimate match begins!

EPISODE 66 — Bushy Brow's Jutsu: Sasuke Style!

DEC 16 2006

The match finally begins. With surprising speed, Sasuke attacks the creepy, grinning Gaara so fiercely that even the Sand Shield can't hold him back. Faced with this, Gaara makes his next move!

EPISODE 67 — Late for the Show, but Ready to Go! The Ultimate Secret Technique!

DEC 16 2006

Gaara confines himself in the ultimate defense—the Sand Cocoon. Seeing all his attacks fail, Sasuke decides to break out his new technique. Meanwhile, Naruto, concerned about Gaara's insanity, tries to stop the match but…

EPISODE 68 — Zero Hour! The Destruction of the Hidden Leaf Village Begins!

JAN 7 2007

During the match between Sasuke and Gaara, unknown perpetrators unleash genjutsu at the arena! On top of that, Orochimaru disguised as the Kazekage launches a surprise attack on the Third Hokage! The plot is finally revealed.

EPISODE 69 — Village in Distress: A New A-Ranked Mission

JAN 13 2007

Kakashi assigns Sakura, Shikamaru and Naruto a mission to go after Sasuke. Relying on the tracking skill of Pakkun the ninja dog, they chase after Sasuke. But…

EPISODE 70 — A Shirker's Call to Action: Layabout No More!

JAN 13 2007

Noticing enemies on their trail, Shikamaru takes on the dangerous job of holding them off. It looks like the Nara Clan's secret Shadow Possession Jutsu does the trick, but the enemy is a cut above him…!

EPISODE 71 — An Unrivaled Match: Hokage Battle Royale!

JAN 27 2007

Orochimaru summons the First and Second Hokage using the forbidden summoning jutsu Reanimation, and former teacher and student confront each other. The curtain opens on a deadly struggle between Hokage!

EPISODE 72 — A Mistake from the Past: A Face Revealed!

JAN 27 2007

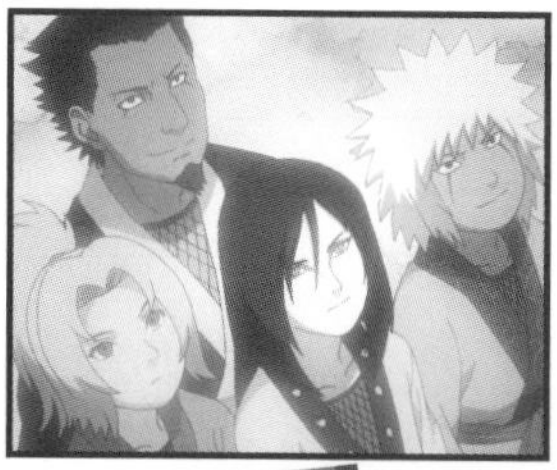

The Third Hokage suffers with remorse in seeing what Orochimaru has become. He recognized Orochimaru's dangerous potential long ago, but could do nothing about it. To atone and to end it once and for all, the Hokage makes a fateful decision!

EPISODE 73 — Forbidden Secret Technique: Reaper Death Seal!

FEB 3 2007

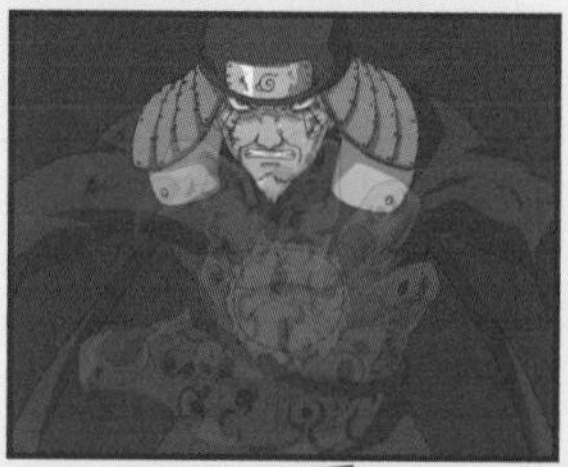

The Third Hokage unleashes the sealing jutsu Reaper Death Seal to thwart Orochimaru's ambition! It is, however, a forbidden jutsu requiring the sacrifice of the Hokage's life!

EPISODE 74 — Astonishing Truth: Gaara's Identity Emerges!

FEB 10 2007

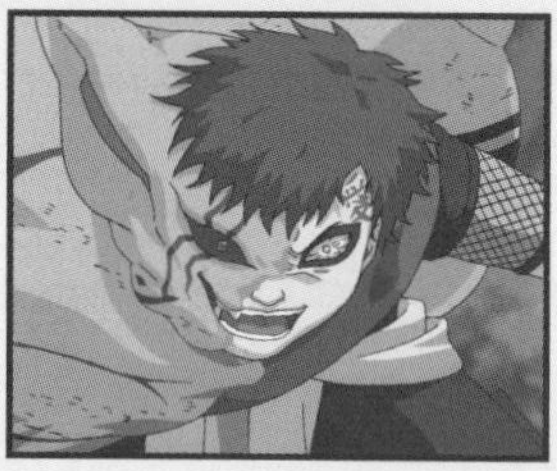

At last Sasuke catches Temari and Gaara! The moment the ensuing fight seems to have finally reached a conclusion, Gaara's body is subjected to a massive transformation!

EPISODE 75 — Sasuke's Decision: Pushed to the Edge!

FEB 17 2007

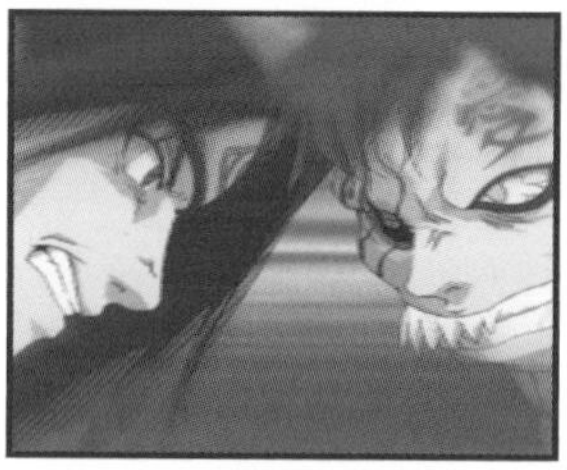

Sasuke is only able to dodge Gaara's overwhelming attacks and decides to gamble it all on one blow with the Chidori! But again, his curse mark is activated and eats away at him.

SPECIAL!!

It boggles Sakura too...

Pakkun's forbidden secrets!

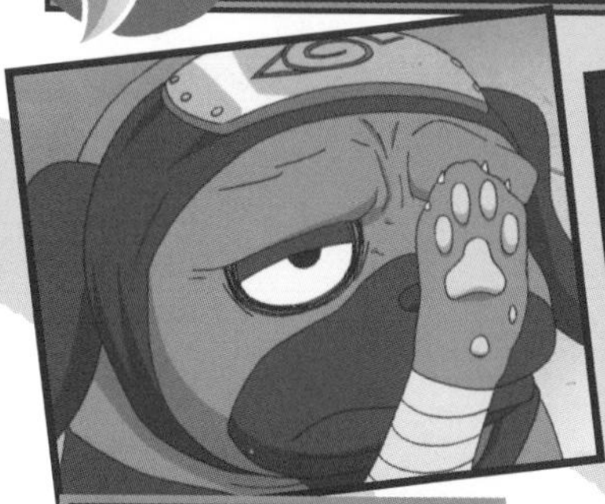

Episode 69

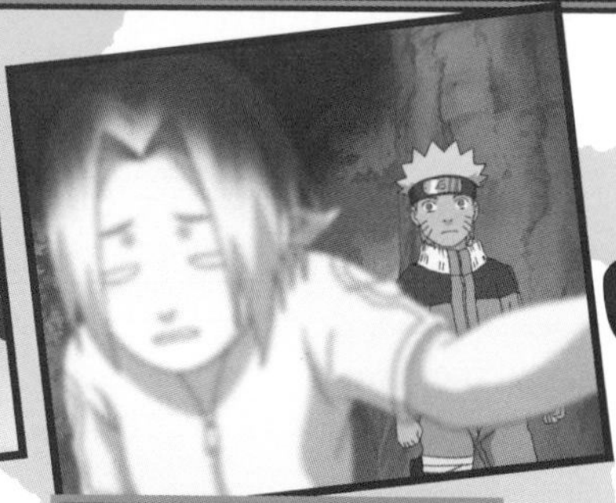

Episode 72

The Ninja dog Pakkun continues to fascinate fans with his old man's voice and contrasting cute appearance. His secrets are revealed in the TV series in original anime-only episodes. Check out the surprise revelations (?!) in Episodes 69 and 72!

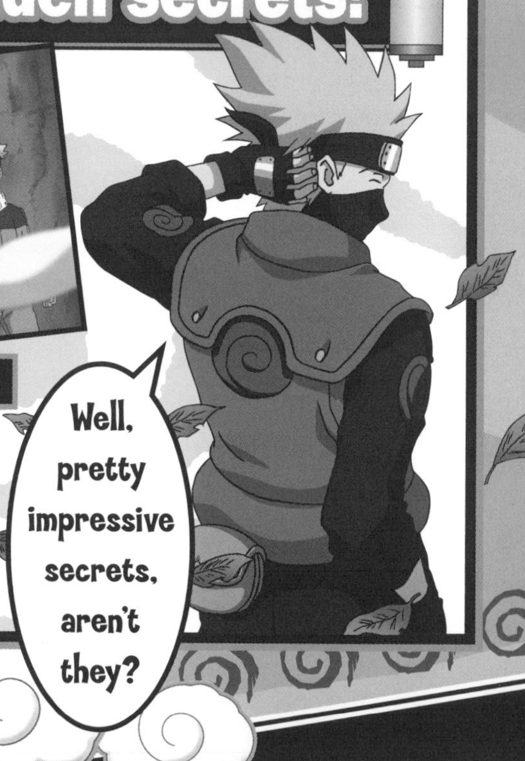
Well, pretty impressive secrets, aren't they?

EPISODE 76 — Assassin of the Moonlit Night

FEB 24 2007

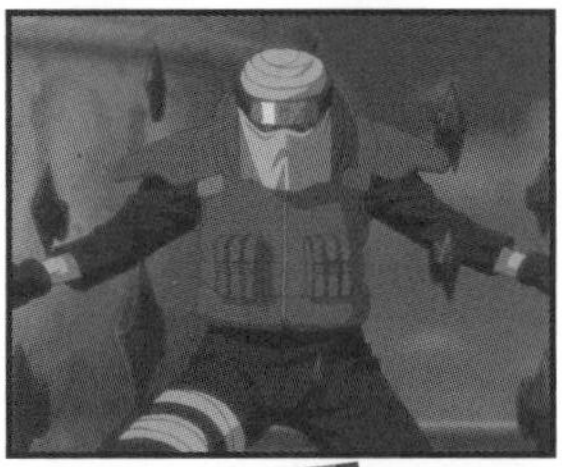

Sakura stands in Gaara's way as he goes to finish off Sasuke. It's a grim situation, but when Gaara sees Sakura shielding Sasuke, he begins reeling in pain.

EPISODE 77 — Light vs Dark: The Two Faces of Gaara

MAR 3 2007

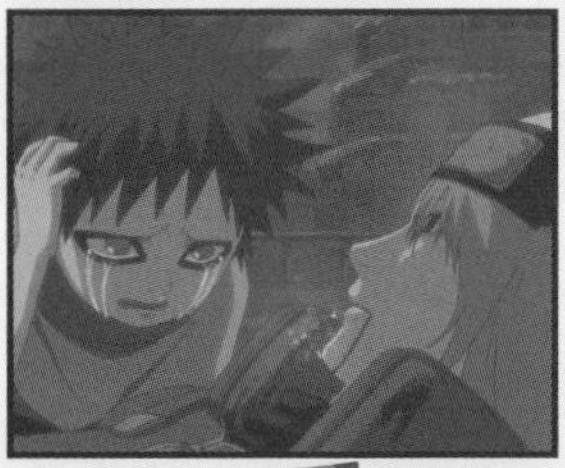

Naruto is no match for Gaara, who says he fights only for himself. But to save Sakura and Sasuke and stand firm in his ninja way, Naruto can't afford to lose!

EPISODE 78 — Naruto's Ninja Handbook

MAR 10 2007

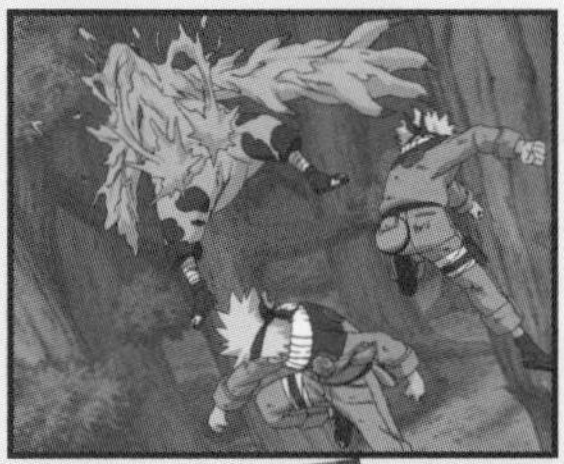

Naruto turns the tables through his determination to protect those he cares about. The battle seems to have reached its end, but then Gaara transforms into his giant, completely possessed form!

EPISODE 79 — Beyond the Limit of Darkness and Light

MAR 17 2007

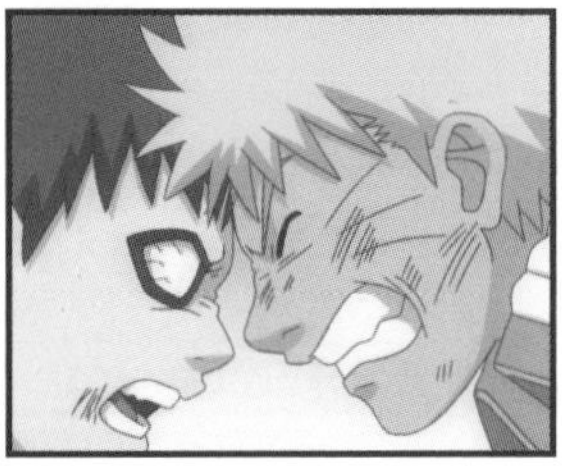

Through Gaara's Playing Possum Jutsu, Shukaku the Sand Spirit begins to display its inherent evil and immense power. To put an end to this, Naruto and Gamabunta take on Shukaku with a combo jutsu.

EPISODE 80 — The Third Hokage Forever...!

MAR 24 2007

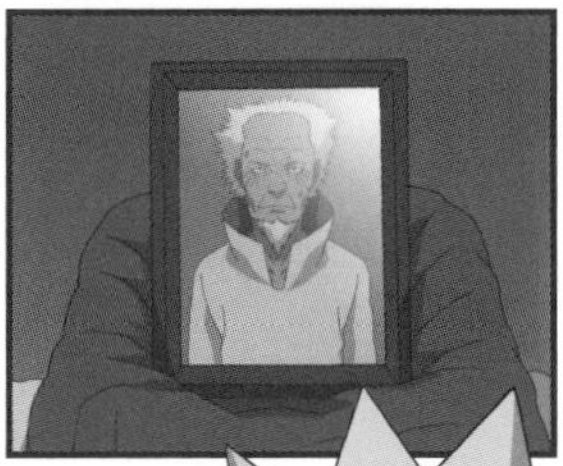

The destruction of the Hidden Leaf Village is thwarted! Orochimaru's ambition collapses in the battle on which the Hokage has staked his life. However, the scars left are deep and all the shinobi mourn…

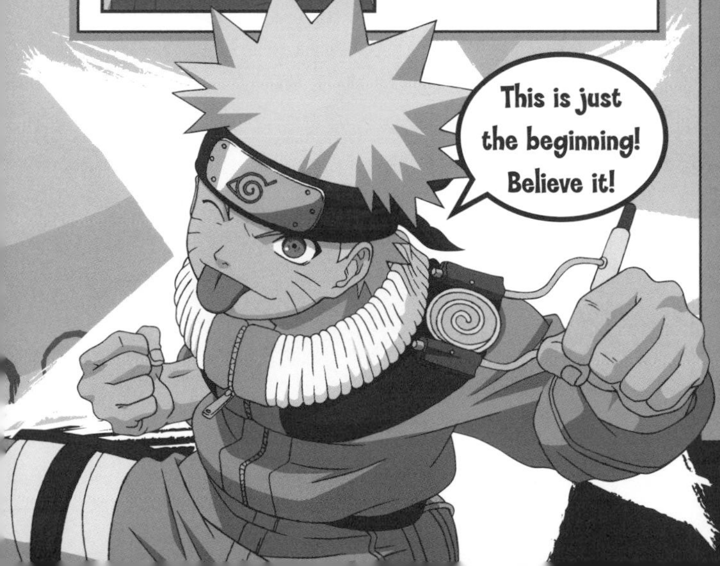
This is just the beginning! Believe it!

CREW

Original manga by Masashi Kishimoto
Published in Japan by *Weekly Shonen Jump*
Director: Hayato Date
Series Producer: Katsuyuki Sumisawa
Character Design: Tetsuya Nishio & Hirofumi Suzuki
Art Director: Shigenori Takada
Color Design: Takuya Kawami
Cinematography: Atsuho Matsumoto
Recording Production: Chiharu Kamio
Sound Production: Yasunori Ebina
Producer: Tomoko Gushima (TV Tokyo) & Ken Hagino
Music: Musashi Project, Toshiro Masuda
Animation Production: Studio Pierrot
Production: TV Tokyo & Studio Pierrot
North American Production: VIZ Media, LLC
North American Dubbing Studio: Studiopolis Inc.

Hidden Leaf Training Quiz Answers!

Now's the time to check your answers! I'm here in person to teach you the right ones!

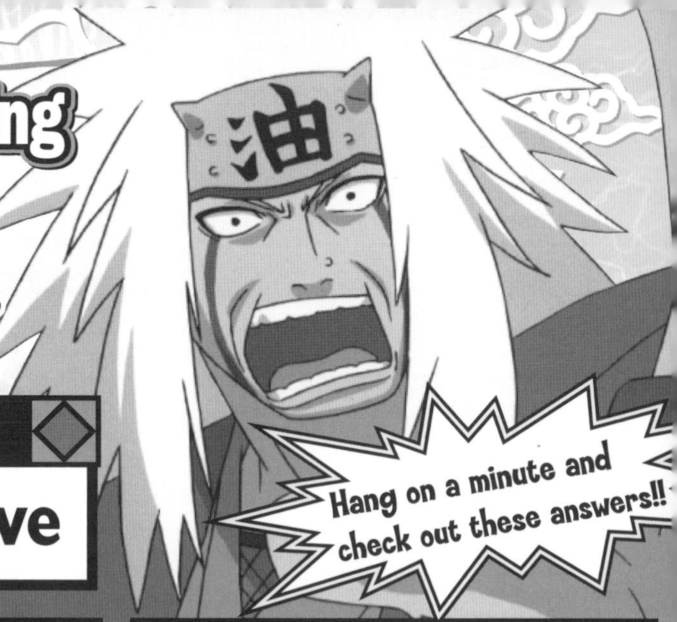
Hang on a minute and check out these answers!!

P.74 ◆ Part 1 ◆ See through the Multiple Shadow Clone Jutsu! ◆ Answers

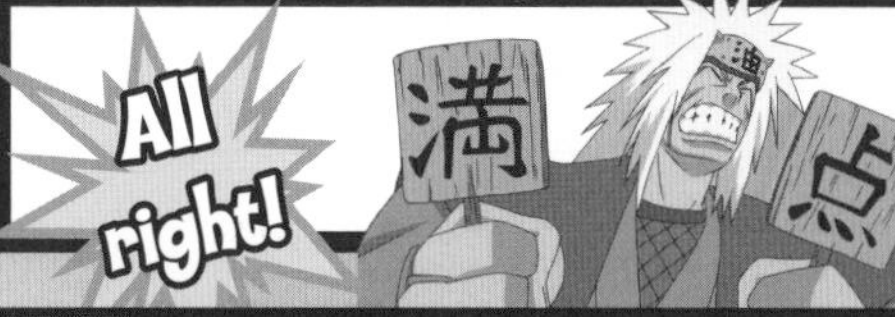
All right!
満
点

Five

P.114 ◆ Part 2 ◆ Jiraiya's Research at the Women's Spa! ◆ Answers

A1 Pakkun

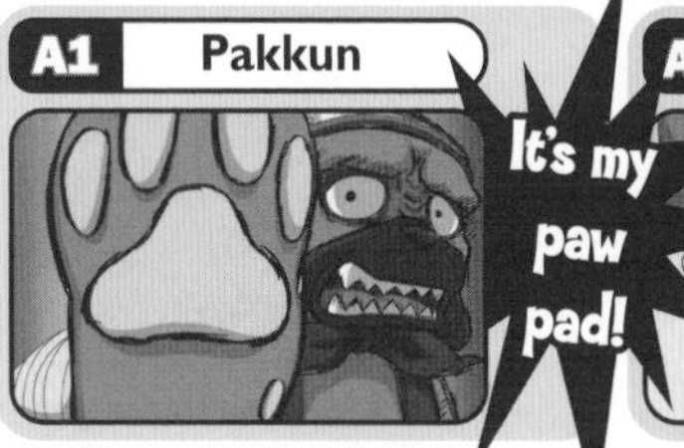
It's my paw pad!

A2 Choji Akimichi

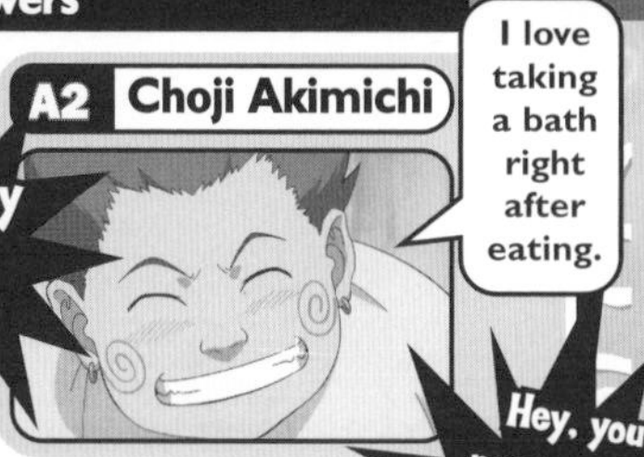
I love taking a bath right after eating.

A3 Giant Toad

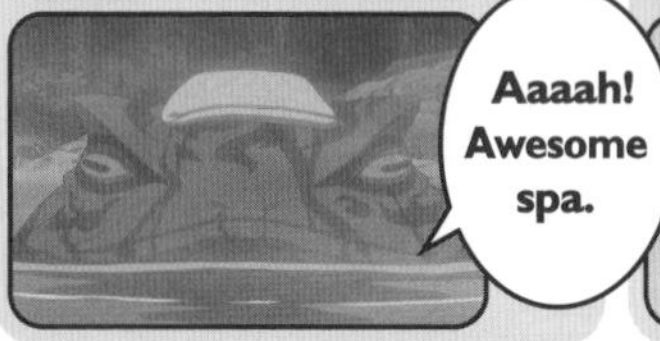
Aaaah! Awesome spa.

A4 Naruto

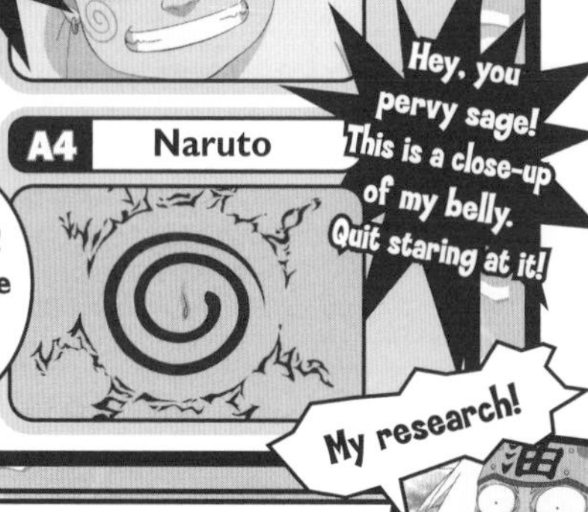
Hey, you pervy sage! This is a close-up of my belly. Quit staring at it!
My research!

P.154 ◆ Part 3 ◆ Find the similarities! ◆ Answers

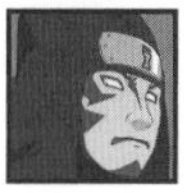

It's Kankuro!
They're the genin that participated in the Final Round.

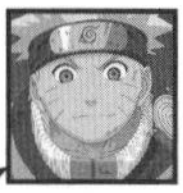

It's Naruto!
They're lined up in order of mentor jonin and student.

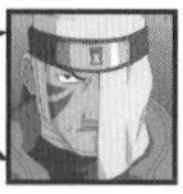

It's Baki!
They're ninja from villages other than the Hidden Leaf Village.

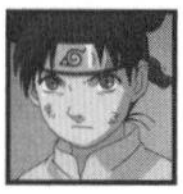

It's Tenten!
They're genin of the Hidden Leaf village.

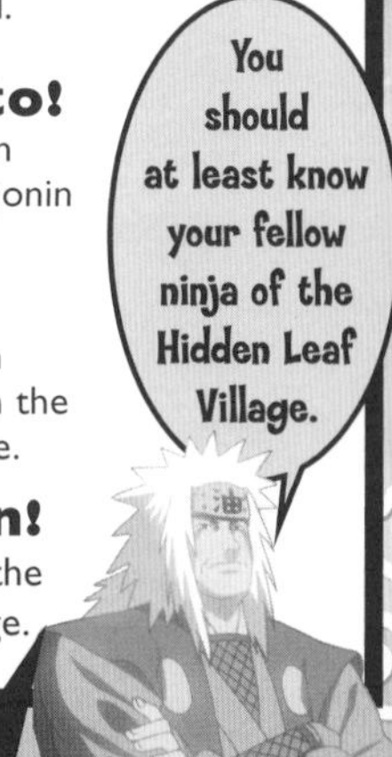
You should at least know your fellow ninja of the Hidden Leaf Village.

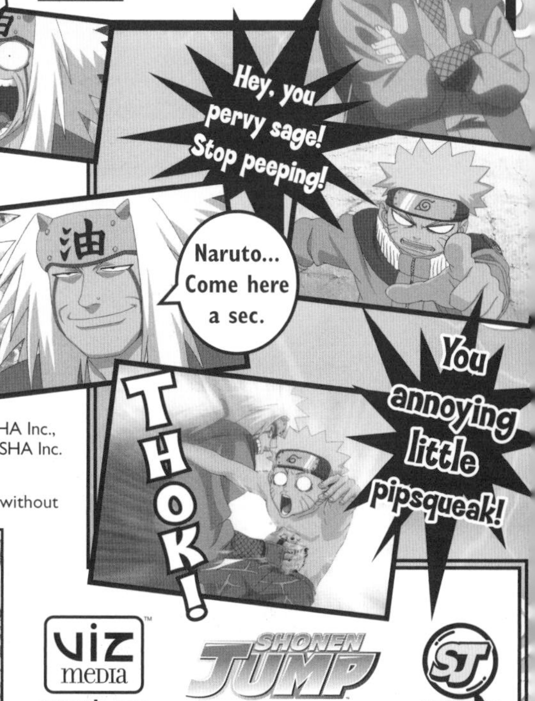
Hey, you pervy sage! Stop peeping!
Naruto... Come here a sec.
You annoying little pipsqueak!
THOK!

NARUTO ANIME PROFILES 2

Translation/Riyo Odate, HC Language Solutions, Inc.
English Adaptation/Ian Reid, HC Language Solutions, Inc.
Text Layout & Design/Sean Lee
Design Assistance/Casey Dillon, Izumi Hirayama, Melanie Lewis & Andrea Rice
Special Thanks/Jason Bergenfeld, Rebecca Downer & Carolina Ugalde
Editorial Directors/Frances E. Wall & Masumi Washington
Editor/Joel Enos

Editor in Chief, Books/Alvin Lu
Editor in Chief, Magazines/Marc Weidenbaum
VP of Publishing Licensing/Rika Inouye
VP of Sales/Gonzalo Ferreyra
Sr. VP of Marketing/Liza Coppola
Publisher/Hyoe Narita

NARUTO –HIDEN • SHIPPUEMAKI– OFFICIAL ANIMATION BOOK

Printed in China

Published by VIZ Media, LLC
P.O. Box 77010
San Francisco, CA 94107

SHONEN JUMP Profiles Edition
10 9 8 7 6 5 4 3 2 1
First printing, September 2007

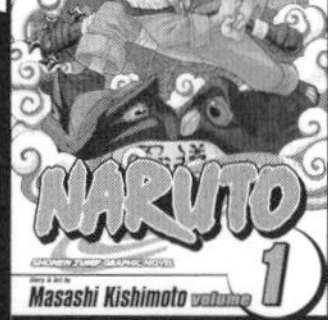
NARUTO
Masashi Kishimoto
1

www.viz.com

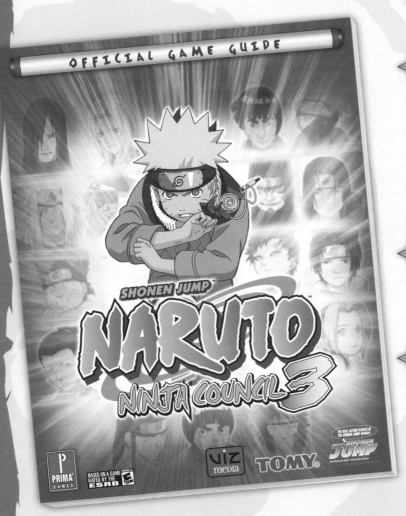